Criminalistics

Criminalistics
An Introduction
to Forensic Science

edition 10

Richard Saferstein, Ph.D.

Forensic Science Consultant, Mt. Laurel, New Jersey
Lecturer, Widener University School of Law

Pearson Education International

Boston Columbus Indianapolis New York San Francisco Upper Saddle River
Amsterdam Cape Town Dubai London Madrid Milan Munich Paris Montreal Toronto
Delhi Mexico City Sao Paulo Sydney Hong Kong Seoul Singapore Taipei Tokyo

Editor in Chief: Vernon R. Anthony
Acquisitions Editor: Eric Krassow
Editorial Assistant: Lynda Kramer
Senior Managing Editor: JoEllen Gohr
Project Manager: Steve Robb
AV Project Manager: Janet Portisch
Senior Operations Supervisor: Pat Tonneman
Operations Specialist: Matt Ottenweller
Art Director: Diane Ernsberger
Text Designer: Rokusek Design

Director of Marketing: David Gesell
Marketing Manager: Adam Kloza
Senior Marketing Coordinator: Alicia Wozniak

Marketing Assistant: Les Roberts
Manager, Rights and Permissions: Zina Arabia
Manager, Visual Research: Beth Brenzel
Manager, Cover Visual Research & Cover Permissions: Karen Sanatar
Image Interior Permission Coordinator: Annette Linder
Image Cover Permission Coordinator: Kathy Mazzucca
Media Editor: Michelle Churma
Media Project Manager: Karen Bretz
Full-Service Project Management: Linda Zuk, WordCraft LLC
Copy Editor: Amy Schneider
Composition: S4Carlisle Publishing Services
Printer/Binder: Quebecor Printing/Dubuque
Cover Printer: Coral Graphics
Text Font: Times Roman

Credits and acknowledgments borrowed from other sources and reproduced, with permission, in this textbook appear on the appropriate pages within the text.

Microsoft® and Windows® are registered trademarks of the Microsoft Corporation in the U.S.A. and other countries. Screen shots and icons reprinted with permission from the Microsoft Corporation. This book is not sponsored or endorsed by or affiliated with the Microsoft Corporation.

10 9 8 7 6 5 4 3 2 1

ISBN 10: 0-13-254579-9
ISBN 13: 978-0-13-254579-2

Prentice Hall
is an imprint of

To the memory of Fran and Michael

brief contents

preface xv
about the author xix

■ **chapter 1**
Introduction   3

■ **chapter 2**
The Crime Scene   27

■ **chapter 3**
Physical Evidence   59

■ **chapter 4**
Physical Properties: Glass
and Soil   93

■ **chapter 5**
Organic Analysis   119

■ **chapter 6**
Inorganic Analysis   145

■ **chapter 7**
The Microscope   165

■ **chapter 8**
Drugs   189

■ **chapter 9**
Forensic Toxicology   213

■ **chapter 10**
Forensic Serology   241

■ **chapter 11**
DNA: The Indispensable
Forensic Science Tool   265

■ **chapter 12**
Crime–Scene Reconstruction:
Bloodstain Pattern Analysis   297

■ **chapter 13**
Hairs, Fibers, and Paint   321

■ **chapter 14**
Forensic Aspects of Fire
Investigation   353

■ **chapter 15**
Forensic Investigation
of Explosions   373

■ **chapter 16**
Fingerprints   389

■ **chapter 17**
Firearms, Tool Marks, and
Other Impressions   417

■ **chapter 18**
Document Examination   451

■ **chapter 19**
Computer Forensics   471

■ **chapter 20**
The Future   501

Appendixes 507

Answers to Review Questions 533

Index 543

contents

preface xv

about the author xix

chapter 1

Introduction 3

Definition and Scope of Forensic
  Science 4
History and Development of
  Forensic Science 5
Important Contributors to
  Forensic Science 6
Crime Laboratories 8
Organization of a Crime Laboratory 10
Services of the Crime Laboratory 12
Functions of the Forensic Scientist 15

Case Study

Dr. Coppolino's Deadly House Calls 18
Other Forensic Science Services 20
Forensic Science on the Internet 22
  Chapter Summary 23
  Review Questions 24
  Application and Critical Thinking 25
  Further References 25

chapter 2

The Crime Scene 27

Processing the Crime Scene 28
Legal Considerations at the
  Crime Scene 46
  Chapter Summary 47
  Review Questions 48
  Application and Critical Thinking 49
  Further References 50
  Case Analysis 50

Case Study

The Enrique Camarena Case: A Forensic
Nightmare 51

chapter 3

Physical Evidence 59

Common Types of Physical Evidence 60
The Significance of Physical Evidence 61
Forensic Databases 68
The Murder Scene: Death Investigation 72

Case Study

Identifying a Serial Killer's Victims 77

Case Study

The Danielle Van Dam Murder Case 80
  Chapter Summary 81
  Review Questions 82
  Application and Critical Thinking 83
  Further References 83
  Case Analysis 84

Case Study

Fiber Evidence and the Wayne Williams Trial 85

chapter 4

Physical Properties: Glass and Soil 93

The Metric System 94
Physical Properties 96
Forensic Analysis of Glass 101
Glass Fractures 107
Collection and Preservation of
  Glass Evidence 110
Forensic Analysis of Soil 110
Collection and Preservation of
  Soil Evidence 112
  Chapter Summary 114
  Review Questions 115
  Application and Critical Thinking 116
  Further References 117

chapter 5

Organic Analysis   119

The Nature of Matter   120
Elements and Compounds   120
Selecting an Analytical Technique   123
Chromatography   123
Spectrophotometry   132
Mass Spectrometry   138

Chapter Summary   141
Review Questions   141
Application and Critical Thinking   143
Further References   143

chapter 6

Inorganic Analysis   145

Inorganics as Forensic Evidence   146
Evidence in the Assassination of President Kennedy   147
The Emission Spectrum of Elements   149
Atomic Absorption Spectrophotometry   152
The Origin of Emission and Absorption Spectra   153
Neutron Activation Analysis   155

Case Study

Death by Radiation Poisoning   156
X-Ray Diffraction   158

Chapter Summary   161
Review Questions   161
Application and Critical Thinking   162
Further References   162

chapter 7

The Microscope   165

Basics of the Microscope   166
The Compound Microscope   167
The Comparison Microscope   169
The Stereoscopic Microscope   171
The Polarizing Microscope   172
The Microspectrophotometer   173
The Scanning Electron Microscope (SEM)   175

Chapter Summary   180
Review Questions   181

Application and Critical Thinking   181
Further References   182
Case Analysis   182

Case Study

Microscopic Trace Evidence—The Overlooked Clue   183
Arthur Koehler—Wood Detective

chapter 8

Drugs   189

Drug Dependence   190
Types of Drugs   192
Drug-Control Laws   202
Drug Identification   204
Collection and Preservation of Drug Evidence   208

Chapter Summary   209
Review Questions   209
Application and Critical Thinking   210
Further References   211

chapter 9

Forensic Toxicology   213

The Fate of Alcohol in the Body   214
Testing for Intoxication   219
Collection and Preservation of Blood   224
Alcohol and the Law   225
The Role of the Toxicologist   227

Case Study

Joann Curley: Caught by a Hair   233
The Drug Recognition Expert   234

Chapter Summary   236
Review Questions   237
Application and Critical Thinking   238
Further References   239

chapter 10

Forensic Serology   241

The Nature of Blood   242
Immunoassay Techniques   245
Forensic Characterization of Bloodstains   247

Principles of Heredity   251
Forensic Characterization of Semen   254
Collection and Preservation of
    Rape Evidence   256
    Chapter Summary   261
    Review Questions   261
    Application and Critical Thinking   262
    Further References   263

chapter 11

DNA: The Indispensable Forensic Science Tool   265

What Is DNA?   266
DNA at Work   268
Polymerase Chain Reaction (PCR)   269
DNA Typing   270
The Combined DNA Index System
    (CODIS)   278
Mitochondrial DNA   278
Collection and Preservation of Biological
    Evidence for DNA Analysis   281
    Chapter Summary   290
    Review Questions   290
    Application and Critical Thinking   291
    Further References   292

Case Study

The Forensic Community's Response
to September 11   293

chapter 12

Crime–Scene Reconstruction: Bloodstain Pattern Analysis   297

Fundamentals of Crime-Scene
    Reconstruction   298
General Features of Bloodstain
    Formation   299
Impact Bloodstain Spatter Patterns   301
More Bloodstain Spatter Patterns   305
Other Bloodstain Patterns   309
Documenting Bloodstain Pattern
    Evidence   313
    Chapter Summary   316
    Review Questions   316
    Application and Critical Thinking   318
    Further References   319

chapter 13

Hairs, Fibers, and Paint   321

Morphology of Hair   322
Identification and Comparison of Hair   324

Case Study

The Central Park Jogger Case Revisited   328
    Collection and Preservation of
        Hair Evidence   329
    Types of Fibers   330
    Identification and Comparison of
        Manufactured Fibers   335
    Collection and Preservation of
        Fiber Evidence   342
    Forensic Examination of Paint   342
    Collection and Preservation of
        Paint Evidence   347
    Chapter Summary   349
    Review Questions   349
    Application and Critical Thinking   350
    Further References   351

chapter 14

Forensic Aspects of Fire Investigation   353

Forensic Investigation of Arson   354
The Chemistry of Fire   354
Searching the Fire Scene   361
Collection and Preservation of
    Arson Evidence   364
Analysis of Flammable Residues   365
    Chapter Summary   369
    Review Questions   369
    Application and Critical Thinking   370
    Further References   371

chapter 15

Forensic Investigation of Explosions   373

Explosions and Explosives   374
Collection and Analysis of Evidence
    of Explosives   380
    Chapter Summary   386
    Review Questions   386

Application and Critical Thinking   387

Further References   387

chapter 16

Fingerprints   389

History of Fingerprinting   390

Fundamental Principles of Fingerprints   391

Classification of Fingerprints   395

Automated Fingerprint Identification Systems   396

Methods of Detecting Fingerprints   400

Preservation of Developed Prints   409

Digital Imaging for Fingerprint Enhancement   410

Chapter Summary   412

Review Questions   413

Application and Critical Thinking   414

Further References   415

chapter 17

Firearms, Tool Marks, and Other Impressions   417

Bullet and Cartridge Comparisons   418

Case Study

Sacco and Vanzetti   424

Automated Firearms Search Systems   424

Gunpowder Residues   427

Primer Residues on the Hands   430

Serial Number Restoration   434

Collection and Preservation of Firearms Evidence   434

Tool Marks   435

Other Impressions   438

Case Study

The O. J. Simpson Trial—Who Left the Impressions at the Crime Scene?   446

Chapter Summary   447

Review Questions   447

Application and Critical Thinking   448

Further References   449

chapter 18

Document Examination   451

Document Examiner   452

Handwriting Comparisons   452

Typescript Comparisons   457

Alterations, Erasures, and Obliterations   459

Other Document Problems   462

Chapter Summary   467

Review Questions   468

Application and Critical Thinking   468

Further References   469

chapter 19

Computer Forensics   471
by Andrew W. Donofrio

From Input to Output: How Does the Computer Work?   472

Storing and Retrieving Data   476

Processing the Electronic Crime Scene   478

Analysis of Electronic Data   480

Forensic Analysis of Internet Data   486

Forensic Investigation of Internet Communications   487

Chapter Summary   492

Review Questions   492

Application and Critical Thinking   493

Case Analysis 1   494

Case Analysis 2   494

Further References   494

Case Reading 1

Computer Forensic Analysis Answers the Question "Arson or Accident?"   495

Case Reading 2

Counterfeiting and Fraud: A Forensic Computer Investigation   497

chapter 20

the future   501

Further References   505

appendixes

I   Guides to the Collection of Physical
     Evidence—FBI   507

II   Instructions for Collecting Gunshot
     Residue (GSR)   523

III Chemical Formulas for Latent
     Fingerprint Development   525

IV   Chemical Formulas for Development
     of Footwear Impressions in Blood   529

answers to review questions   533

index   543

chapter opener photo credits   551

preface

New to This Edition

- New! Chapter 12, Crime-Scene Reconstruction, emphasizes the science of blood spatter investigation at crime scenes.
- New! Coverage of the latest DNA forensic technology includes mini-STR and familial DNA databasing and introduces students to the latest DNA technologies and their capabilities and limitations.
- NEW! Critical Thinking questions are added to each chapter.
- Chapter 13, Hair, Fibers, and Paint, is reorganized.
- New! Chapter 15, Forensic Investigation of Explosions, emphasizes the importance of this post-9/11 topic to criminal investigations.
- Chapter 19, Computer Forensics, is reorganized and revised.
- New! Two lab manuals with experiments support this edition. The manuals help students with immediate application of techniques and give instructors flexibility in selecting assignments based on available equipment and supplies.
- New! MyCrimeKit is an online supplement that offers book-specific content such as Learning Objectives, Chapter Summaries, Flashcards, Practice Tests, Video Clips, Web Extras and Animations, and Activities.

Public Fascination with Forensic Science

Many readers of this book have been drawn to the subject of forensic science by the assortment of television shows about scientific crime investigation. Story lines depicting the crime-solving abilities of forensic scientists have greatly excited the imagination of the general public. Furthermore, a constant of forensic science is how frequently its applications become front-page news. Whether the story is the sudden death of pop music superstar Michael Jackson, sniper shootings, or the tragic consequences of the terrorist attacks of 9/11, forensic science is at the forefront of the public response.

During the highly publicized O. J. Simpson criminal and civil trials, forensic scientists systematically placed Simpson at the crime scene through DNA analyses, hair and fiber comparisons, and footwear impressions. As millions of Americans watched the case unfold, they, in a sense, became students of forensic science. Intense media coverage of the crime-scene search and investigation, as well as the ramifications of findings of physical evidence at the crime scene, became the subject of study, commentary, and conjecture.

For instructors who have taught forensic science in the classroom, it comes as no surprise that forensic science can grab and hold the attention of those who otherwise would have no interest in any area of science. The O. J. Simpson case, for example, amply demonstrates the extent to which forensic science has intertwined with criminal investigation.

Perhaps we can attribute our obsession with forensic science to the yearnings of a society bent on apprehending criminals but desirous of a system of justice that ensures the correctness of its verdicts. The level of sophistication that forensic science has brought to criminal investigations is formidable. But once one puts aside all the drama of a forensic science case, what remains is *an academic subject emphasizing logic and technology.*

Purpose of This Book

It is to this end—revealing that essence of forensic science—that the tenth edition of *Criminalistics* is dedicated. The basic aim of the book is still to make the subject of forensic science clear and comprehensible to a wide variety of readers who are or plan to be aligned with the forensic science profession, as well as to those who have a curiosity about the subject's underpinnings.

Criminalistics strives to make the technology of the modern crime laboratory clear and comprehensible to nonscientists in particular. The nature of physical evidence is defined, and the limitations that technology and current knowledge impose on its individualization and characterization are examined. By combining case stories with applicable technology, *Criminalistics* endeavors to capture the pulse and fervor of forensic science investigations.

For example, the book relates how DNA has played a critical role in identifying victims of horrific terrorist attacks and other mass disasters. DNA profiling has also altered the complexion of criminal investigation. DNA collected from saliva on a cup or from dandruff or sweat on a hat exemplifies the emergence of nontraditional forms of evidence collection at crime scenes. Currently, the criminal justice system is creating vast DNA data banks designed to snare criminals who are unaware of the consequences of leaving the minutest quantity of biological material behind at a crime scene.

Focus on Cutting-Edge Tools and Techniques

Through ten editions, *Criminalistics* has strived to depict the role of the forensic scientist in the criminal justice system. The current edition builds on the content of its predecessors and updates the reader on the latest technologies available to crime laboratory personnel.

The computer and the Internet have influenced all aspects of modern life, and forensic science is no exception. Chapter 19, "Computer Forensics," explores the retrieval of computerized information thought to be lost or erased during the course of a criminal investigation and delves into the investigation of hacking incidents. The Internet contains a wealth of information on forensic science. This book has purposely made the Internet an integral part of the reader's learning experience. Readers are directed to sites that contain updated articles reviewing various facets of the subjects covered in this text. My Crime Kit: Web Extras, found in the book's companion Web site, steer readers to specific web sites with animations and other graphics that amplify the textbook's coverage of topics and enhance the learning experience.

A major portion of the text centers on discussions of the common items of physical evidence encountered at crime scenes. Various chapters include descriptions of forensic analysis, as well as updated techniques for the proper collection and preservation of evidence at crime scenes. Particular attention is paid to the meaning and role of probability in interpreting the evidential significance of scientifically evaluated evidence.

The implications of DNA profiling are important enough to warrant their inclusion in a separate chapter in *Criminalistics*. Chapter 11 describes the topic of DNA in a manner that is comprehensible and relevant to readers who lack a scientific background. The discussion defines DNA and explains its central role in controlling the body's chemistry. Finally, Chapter 11 explains the process of DNA typing and illustrates its application to criminal investigations through the presentation of actual case histories.

A Grounded Approach

The content of *Criminalistics* reflects the author's experience as both an active forensic scientist and an instructor of forensic science at the college level. The author assumes that readers have no prior knowledge of scientific principles or techniques. The areas of chemistry and biology relating to the analysis of physical evidence are presented with a minimum of scientific terminology and equations. The discussion involving chemistry and biology is limited to a minimum core of facts and principles that make the subject matter understandable and meaningful to the nonscientist. Although it is not the intent of this book to turn readers into scientists or forensic experts, the author would certainly be gratified if the book motivates some students to seek further scientific knowledge and perhaps direct their education toward careers in forensic science.

Although *Criminalistics* is an outgrowth of a one-semester course offered as part of a criminal justice program at many New Jersey colleges, the value of the book is not limited to college students. Optimum utilization of crime laboratory services requires that criminal investigators have knowledge of the techniques and capabilities of the laboratory. That awareness extends beyond any summary that may be gleaned from departmental brochures dealing with the collection and packaging of physical evidence. Investigators must mesh knowledge of the principles and techniques of forensic science with logic and common sense to gain comprehensive insight into the meaning and significance of physical evidence and its role in criminal investigations. Forensic science begins at the crime scene. If the investigator cannot recognize, collect, and package evidence properly, no amount of equipment or expertise will salvage the situation.

Likewise, there is a dire need to bridge the "communication gap" that currently exists among lawyers, judges, and forensic scientists. An intelligent evaluation of the scientist's data and any subsequent testimony will again depend on familiarity with the underlying principles of forensic science. Too many practitioners of the law profess ignorance of the subject or attempt to gain a superficial understanding of its meaning and significance only minutes before meeting the expert witness. It is hoped that the book will provide a painless route to comprehending the nature of the science.

In order to merge theory with practice, actual forensic case histories are included in the text. The intent is for these illustrations to move forensic science from the domain of the abstract into the real world of criminal investigation.

Instructor Supplements

The following supplements are available for instructors using *Criminalistics: An Introduction to Forensic Science:*

Instructor's Manual (print version)
Online Instructor's Manual
Online TestGen
PowerPoint Presentation
PowerPoint Image Bank

To access supplementary materials online, instructors need to request an instructor access code. Go to www.pearsonhighered.com, click the Instructor Resource Center link, and then click Request IRC access for an instructor access code. Within 48 hours after registering, you will receive a confirming e-mail including an instructor access code. Once you have received your code, go the site and log on for full instructions on downloading the materials you wish to use.

Acknowledgments

I am most appreciative of the contribution that Detective Sergeant Andrew (Drew) Donofrio of New Jersey's Bergen County Prosecutor's Office made to this new edition of *Criminalistics*. I was fortunate to find in Drew a contributor who not only possesses extraordinary skill, knowledge, and hands-on experience with computer forensics, but was able to combine those attributes with sophisticated communication skills.

Sarah A. Skorupsky, MSFS, invested an extraordinary amount of time and effort in preparing an accompanying supplement to this edition: *Basic Laboratory Exercises for Forensic Science*. Her skills and tenacity in carrying out this task are acknowledged and greatly appreciated.

Many people provided assistance and advice in the preparation of this book. Many faculty members, colleagues, and friends have read and commented on various portions of the text. Particular thanks go to the following people for their critical reading and discussions of the manuscript: Norman Demeter, John Lintott, Charles Midkiff, Raymond Murray, and Richard Tidey. In addition, I would like to acknowledge the contributions of Jeffrey C. Kercheval, Robert Thompson, Roger Ely, Jose R. Almirall, Darlene Brezinski, Michael Malone, Anita Wonder, and Ray Feldherr.

The assistance and research efforts of Pamela Cook, Gonul Turhan, and Michelle Tetreault are an integral part of this text, and were invaluable to the book's success. I am also appreciative of the time and talent given by Peggy Cole and this book's production editor, Linda Zuk.

I am grateful to those law enforcement agencies, governmental agencies, private individuals, and equipment manufacturers cited in the text for contributing their photographs and illustrations. Finally, I particularly wish to express my appreciation to Major E. R. Leibe (retired) and Major V. P. O'Donoghue (retired) for their encouragement and support.

Any author of a textbook must be prepared to contribute countless hours to the task, often at the expense of family obligations. My efforts would have fallen well short of completion without the patience and encouragement of my wife, Gail. Her typing and critical readings of the manuscript, as well as her strength of character under circumstances that were less than ideal, will always be remembered.

Richard Saferstein, Ph.D.

about the author

Richard Saferstein, Ph.D., retired in 1991 after serving 21 years as the Chief Forensic Scientist of the New Jersey State Police Laboratory, one of the largest crime laboratories in the United States. He currently acts as a consultant for attorneys and the media in the area of forensic science. During the O. J. Simpson criminal trial, Dr. Saferstein provided extensive commentary on forensic aspects of the case for the *Rivera Live* show, the E! television network, ABC radio, and various radio talk shows. Dr. Saferstein holds degrees from the City College of New York and earned his doctorate degree in chemistry in 1970 from the City University of New York. From 1972 to 1991, he taught an introductory forensic science course in the criminal justice programs at the College of New Jersey and Ocean County College. These teaching experiences played an influential role in Dr. Saferstein's authorship in 1977 of the widely used introductory textbook *Criminalistics: An Introduction to Forensic Science,* currently in this tenth edition. Saferstein's basic philosophy in writing *Criminalistics* is to make forensic science understandable and meaningful to the nonscience reader, while giving the reader an appreciation for the scientific principles that underlie the subject.

Dr. Saferstein has authored or co-authored more than 45 technical papers and chapters covering a variety of forensic topics. Dr. Saferstein has co-authored *Lab Manual for Criminalistics* (Prentice Hall, 2011) to be used in conjunction with this text. He is also the author of *Forensic Science: An Introduction* (Prentice Hall, 2008 and 2011) and *Forensic Science: From the Crime Scene to the Crime Lab* (Prentice Hall, 2009). He has also edited the widely used professional reference books *Forensic Science Handbook,* Volumes I, II, and III, Second Edition (published in 2002, 2005, and 2010, respectively, by Prentice Hall).

Dr. Saferstein is a member of the American Chemical Society, the American Academy of Forensic Sciences, the Canadian Society of Forensic Scientists, the International Association for Identification, the Mid-Atlantic Association of Forensic Scientists, the Northeastern Association of Forensic Scientists, and the Society of Forensic Toxicologists. He is the recipient of the American Academy of Forensic Sciences 2006 Paul L. Kirk Award for distinguished service and contributions to the field of criminalistics.

Criminalistics

Ted Bundy, Serial Killer

The name Ted Bundy is synonymous with the term *serial killer*. This handsome, gregarious, and worldly onetime law student is believed to be responsible for forty murders between 1964 and 1978. His reign of terror stretched from the Pacific Northwest down into California and into Utah, Idaho, and Colorado, finally ending in Florida. His victims were typically young women, usually murdered with a blunt instrument or by strangulation and sexually assaulted before and after death. First convicted in Utah in 1976 on a charge of kidnapping, Bundy managed to escape after his extradition to Colorado on a murder charge. Ultimately, Bundy found his way to the Tallahassee area of Florida. There he unleashed mayhem, killing two women at a Florida State University sorority house and then murdering a 12-year-old girl three weeks later. Fortunately, future victims were spared when Bundy was arrested while driving a stolen vehicle. As police investigated the sorority murders, they noted that one victim, who had been beaten over the head with a log, raped, and strangled, also had bite marks on her left buttock and breast.

Supremely confident that he could beat the sorority murder charges, the arrogant Bundy insisted on acting as his own attorney. His unfounded optimism was shattered in the courtroom when a forensic odontologist matched the bite mark on the victim's buttock to Bundy's front teeth. Bundy was ultimately executed in 1989.

chapter 1

Introduction

Learning Objectives

After studying this chapter you should be able to:

- Define and distinguish forensic science and criminalistics

- Recognize the major contributors to the development of forensic science

- Account for the rapid growth of forensic laboratories in the past forty years

- Describe the services of a typical comprehensive crime laboratory in the criminal justice system

- Compare and contrast the *Frye* and *Daubert* decisions relating to the admissibility of scientific evidence in the courtroom

- Explain the role and responsibilities of the expert witness

- Understand what specialized forensic services, aside from the crime laboratory, are generally available to law enforcement personnel

Definition and Scope of Forensic Science

Forensic science, in its broadest definition, is the application of science to law. As our society has grown more complex, it has become more dependent on rules of law to regulate the activities of its members. Forensic science applies the knowledge and technology of science to the definition and enforcement of such laws.

Each year, as government finds it increasingly necessary to regulate the activities that most intimately influence our daily lives, science merges more closely with civil and criminal law. Consider, for example, the laws and agencies that regulate the quality of our food, the nature and potency of drugs, the extent of automobile emissions, the kind of fuel oil we burn, the purity of our drinking water, and the pesticides we use on our crops and plants. It would be difficult to conceive of any food and drug regulation or environmental protection act that could be effectively monitored and enforced without the assistance of scientific technology and the skill of the scientific community.

Laws are continually being broadened and revised to counter the alarming increase in crime rates. In response to public concern, law enforcement agencies have expanded their patrol and investigative functions, hoping to stem the rising tide of crime. At the same time they are looking more to the scientific community for advice and technical support for their efforts. Can the technology that put astronauts on the moon, split the atom, and eradicated most dreaded diseases be enlisted in this critical battle? Unfortunately, science cannot offer final and authoritative solutions to problems that stem from a maze of social and psychological factors. However, as the contents of this book will attest, science does occupy an important and unique role in the criminal justice system—a role that relates to the scientist's ability to supply accurate and objective information that reflects the events that have occurred at a crime. It will also become apparent to the reader that a good deal of work remains to be done if the full potential of science as applied to criminal investigations is to be realized.

Considering the vast array of civil and criminal laws that regulate society, forensic science, in its broadest sense, has become so comprehensive a subject as to make a meaningful introductory textbook treatment of its role and techniques most difficult, if not overwhelming. For this reason, we must find practical limits that narrow the scope of the subject. Fortunately, common usage provides us with such a limited definition: **Forensic science is the application of science to the criminal and civil laws that are enforced by police agencies in a criminal justice system.** *Forensic science* is an umbrella term encompassing a myriad of professions that use their skills to help law enforcement officials conduct their investigations.

The diversity of professions practicing forensic science is illustrated by the eleven sections of the American Academy of Forensic Science, the largest forensic science organization in the world:

1. Criminalistics
2. Digital and Multimedia Sciences
3. Engineering Sciences
4. General
5. Jurisprudence
6. Odontology
7. Pathology/Biology
8. Physical Anthropology
9. Psychiatry/Behavioral Sciences
10. Questioned Documents
11. Toxicology

Even within the limited definition just presented, we will restrict our discussion in this book to the areas of chemistry, biology, physics, geology, and computer technology, which are useful for determining the evidential value of crime-scene and related evidence, omitting any references to medicine and law. Forensic pathology, psychology, anthropology, and odontology encompass important and relevant areas of knowledge and practice in law enforcement, each being an integral part of the total forensic science service that is provided to any up-to-date criminal justice system. However, except for brief discussions, these subjects go beyond the intended range of this book, and the reader is referred elsewhere for discussions of their applications and techniques.[1] Instead, we will attempt to focus on the services of what has popularly become known as the crime laboratory, where the principles and techniques of the physical and natural sciences are practiced and applied to the analysis of crime-scene evidence.

For many, the term *criminalistics* seems more descriptive than *forensic science* for describing the services of a crime laboratory. The two terms will be used interchangeably in this text. Regardless of title—criminalist or forensic scientist—the trend of events has made the scientist in the crime laboratory an active participant in the criminal justice system.

Primetime television shows like *CSI: Crime Scene Investigation* have greatly increased the public's awareness of the use of science in criminal and civil investigations. However, by simplifying scientific procedures to fit into the available airtime, these shows have created unrealistic expectations of forensic science skills within both the public and the legal community. In these shows, members of the CSI team collect evidence at the crime scene, process all evidence, question witnesses, interrogate suspects, carry out search warrants, and testify in court. In the real world, these tasks are almost always delegated to different people in different parts of the criminal justice system. Procedures that could take days, weeks, months, or years in reality appear on these shows to take mere minutes. This false image is especially relevant to the public's high interest in and expectations for DNA evidence.

The dramatization of forensic science on television has led the public to believe that every crime scene will yield forensic evidence and produces unrealistic expectations that a prosecutor's case should always be bolstered and supported by forensic evidence. This phenomenon is known as the *CSI effect*. Some jurists have come to believe that this phenomenon ultimately detracts from the search for truth and justice in the courtroom.

History and Development of Forensic Science

Forensic science owes its origins first to the individuals who developed the principles and techniques needed to identify or compare physical evidence, and second to those who recognized the need to merge these principles into a coherent discipline that could be practically applied to a criminal justice system.

Literary Roots

Today many believe that Sir Arthur Conan Doyle had a considerable influence on popularizing scientific crime-detection methods through his fictional character Sherlock Holmes (see Figure 1–1), who first applied the newly developing principles of serology (see Chapter 10), fingerprinting, firearms identification, and questioned-document examination long before their value was first recognized and accepted by real-life criminal investigators. Holmes's feats excited the imagination of an emerging generation of forensic scientists and criminal investigators. Even in the first Sherlock Holmes novel, *A Study in Scarlet*, published in 1887, we find examples of Doyle's uncanny ability to describe scientific methods of detection years before they were actually discovered and implemented. For instance, here Holmes probes and recognizes the potential usefulness of forensic serology to criminal investigation:

> "I've found it. I've found it," he shouted to my companion, running towards us with a test tube in his hand. "I have found a reagent which is precipitated by hemoglobin and by nothing else. . . . Why, man, it is the most practical medico-legal discovery for years. Don't you see that it gives us an infallible test for blood stains? . . . The old guaiacum test was very clumsy and uncertain.

FIGURE 1–1

Sir Arthur Conan Doyle's legendary detective Sherlock Holmes applied many of the principles of modern forensic science long before they were adopted widely by police.
© Paul C. Chauncey/CORBIS. All rights reserved.

[1] Two excellent references are André A. Moenssens, Fred E. Inbau, James Starrs, and Carol E. Henderson, *Scientific Evidence in Civil and Criminal Cases*, 4th ed. (Mineola, N.Y.: Foundation Press, 1995); and Werner U. Spitz, ed., *Medicolegal Investigation of Death*, 4th ed. (Springfield, Ill.: Charles C. Thomas, 2006).

So is the microscopic examination for blood corpuscles. The latter is valueless if the stains are a few hours old. Now, this appears to act as well whether the blood is old or new. Had this test been invented, there are hundreds of men now walking the earth who would long ago have paid the penalty of their crimes. . . . Criminal cases are continually hinging upon that one point. A man is suspected of a crime months perhaps after it has been committed. His linen or clothes are examined and brownish stains discovered upon them. Are they blood stains, or rust stains, or fruit stains, or what are they? That is a question which has puzzled many an expert, and why? Because there was no reliable test. Now we have the Sherlock Holmes test, and there will no longer be any difficulty."

Important Contributors to Forensic Science

Many people can be cited for their specific contributions to the field of forensic science. The following is just a brief list of those who made the earliest contributions to formulating the disciplines that now constitute forensic science.

MATHIEU ORFILA (1787–1853)   Orfila is considered the father of forensic toxicology. A native of Spain, he ultimately became a renowned teacher of medicine in France. In 1814, Orfila published the first scientific treatise on the detection of poisons and their effects on animals. This treatise established forensic toxicology as a legitimate scientific endeavor.

ALPHONSE BERTILLON (1853–1914)   Bertillon devised the first scientific system of personal identification. In 1879, Bertillon began to develop the science of *anthropometry* (see Chapter 16), a systematic procedure of taking a series of body measurements as a means of distinguishing one individual from another. (See Figure 1–2.) For nearly two decades, this system was considered the most accurate method of personal identification. Although anthropometry was eventually replaced by fingerprinting in the early 1900s, Bertillon's early efforts have earned him the distinction of being known as the father of criminal identification.

FRANCIS GALTON (1822–1911)   Galton undertook the first definitive study of fingerprints and developed a methodology of classifying them for filing. In 1892, he published a book titled *Finger Prints*, which contained the first statistical proof supporting the uniqueness of his method of personal identification. His work went on to describe the basic principles that form the present system of identification by fingerprints.

LEONE LATTES (1887–1954)   In 1901, Dr. Karl Landsteiner discovered that blood can be grouped into different categories. These blood groups or types are now recognized as A, B, AB, and O. The possibility that blood grouping could be a useful characteristic for the identification of an individual intrigued Dr. Lattes, a professor at the Institute of Forensic Medicine at the University of Turin in Italy. In 1915, he devised a relatively simple procedure for determining the blood group of a dried bloodstain, a technique that he immediately applied to criminal investigations.

CALVIN GODDARD (1891–1955)   To determine whether a particular gun has fired a bullet requires a comparison of the bullet with one that has been test-fired from the suspect's weapon. Goddard, a U.S. Army colonel, refined the techniques of such an examination by using the comparison microscope. Goddard's expertise established the comparison microscope as the indispensable tool of the modern firearms examiner.

ALBERT S. OSBORN (1858–1946)   Osborn's development of the fundamental principles of document examination was responsible for the acceptance of documents as scientific evidence by the courts. In 1910, Osborn authored the first significant text in this field, *Questioned Documents*. This book is still considered a primary reference for document examiners.

WALTER C. McCRONE (1916–2002)   Dr. McCrone's career paralleled startling advances in sophisticated analytical technology. Nevertheless, during his lifetime McCrone became the world's preeminent microscopist. Through his books, journal publications, and research institute, McCrone was a tireless advocate for applying microscopy to analytical problems, particularly

FIGURE 1–2

Bertillon's system of bodily measurements as used for the identification of an individual.
Courtesy Sirchie Finger Print Laboratories, Inc., Youngsville, N.C., www.sirchie.com

forensic science cases. McCrone's exceptional communication skills made him a much-sought-after instructor, and he was responsible for educating thousands of forensic scientists throughout the world in the application of microscopic techniques. Dr. McCrone used microscopy, often in conjunction with other analytical methodologies, to examine evidence in thousands of criminal and civil cases throughout a long and illustrious career.

HANS GROSS (1847–1915)   Gross wrote the first treatise describing the application of scientific disciplines to the field of criminal investigation in 1893. A public prosecutor and judge in Graz, Austria, Gross spent many years studying and developing principles of criminal investigation. In his classic book *Handbuch für Untersuchungsrichter als System der Kriminalistik* (later published in English under the title *Criminal Investigation*), he detailed the assistance that investigators could expect from the fields of microscopy, chemistry, physics, mineralogy, zoology, botany, anthropometry, and fingerprinting. He later introduced the forensic journal *Archiv für Kriminal Anthropologie und Kriminalistik*, which still serves as a medium for reporting improved methods of scientific crime detection.

EDMOND LOCARD (1877–1966)   Although Gross was a strong advocate of the use of the scientific method in criminal investigation, he did not make any specific technical contributions to this philosophy. Locard, a Frenchman, demonstrated how the principles enunciated by Gross could be incorporated within a workable crime laboratory. Locard's formal education was in both medicine and law. In 1910, he persuaded the Lyons police department to give him two attic rooms and two assistants to start a police laboratory.

During Locard's first years of work, the only available instruments were a microscope and a rudimentary spectrometer. However, his enthusiasm quickly overcame the technical and monetary deficiencies he encountered. From these modest beginnings, Locard's research and accomplishments became known throughout the world by forensic scientists and criminal investigators. Eventually he became the founder and director of the Institute of Criminalistics at the University of Lyons; this quickly developed into a leading international center for study and research in forensic science.

Locard believed that when a person comes in contact with an object or person, a cross-transfer of materials occurs (**Locard's exchange principle**). Locard maintained that every criminal can be connected to a crime by dust particles carried from the crime scene. This concept was reinforced by a series of successful and well-publicized investigations. In one case, presented with counterfeit coins and the names of three suspects, Locard urged the police to bring the suspects' clothing to his laboratory. On careful examination, he located small metallic particles in all the garments. Chemical analysis revealed that the particles and coins were composed of exactly the same metallic elements. Confronted with this evidence, the suspects were arrested and soon confessed to the crime. After World War I, Locard's successes served as an impetus for the formation of police laboratories in Vienna, Berlin, Sweden, Finland, and Holland.

Locard's exchange principle
Whenever two objects come into contact with one another, there is exchange of materials between them

Crime Laboratories

The most ambitious commitment to forensic science occurred in the United States with the systematic development of national and state crime laboratories. This development greatly hastened the progress of forensic science.

Crime Labs in the United States

In 1932, the Federal Bureau of Investigation (FBI), under the directorship of J. Edgar Hoover, organized a national laboratory that offered forensic services to all law enforcement agencies in the country. During its formative stages, agents consulted extensively with business executives, manufacturers, and scientists whose knowledge and experience were useful in guiding the new facility through its infancy. The FBI Laboratory is now the world's largest forensic laboratory, performing more than one million examinations every year. Its accomplishments have earned it worldwide recognition, and its structure and organization have served as a model for forensic laboratories formed at the state and local levels in the United States as well as in other countries. Furthermore, the opening of the FBI's Forensic Science Research and Training Center in 1981 gave the United States, for the first time, a facility dedicated to conducting research to develop new and reliable scientific methods that can be applied to forensic science. This facility is also used to train crime laboratory personnel in the latest forensic science techniques and methods.

The oldest forensic laboratory in the United States is that of the Los Angeles Police Department, created in 1923 by August Vollmer, a police chief from Berkeley, California. In the 1930s, Vollmer headed the first U.S. university institute for criminology and criminalistics at the University of California at Berkeley. However, this institute lacked any official status in the university until 1948, when a school of criminology was formed. The famous criminalist Paul Kirk (see Figure 1–3) was selected to head its criminalistics department. Many graduates of this school have gone on to help develop forensic laboratories in other parts of the state and country.

California has numerous federal, state, county, and city crime laboratories, many of which operate independently. However, in 1972 the California Department of Justice embarked on an ambitious plan to create a network of state-operated crime laboratories. As a result, California has created a model system of integrated forensic laboratories consisting of regional and satellite facilities. An informal exchange of information and expertise is facilitated among California's criminalist community through a regional professional society, the California Association of Criminalists. This organization was the forerunner of a number of regional organizations that have developed throughout the United States to foster cooperation among the nation's growing community of criminalists.

International Crime Labs

In contrast to the American system of independent local laboratories, Great Britain has developed a national system of regional laboratories under the direction of the government's Home Office. England and Wales are serviced by six regional laboratories, including the Metropolitan Police Laboratory (established in 1935), which services London. In the early 1990s, the British Home Office reorganized the country's forensic laboratories into the Forensic Science Service and instituted a system in which police agencies are charged a fee for services rendered by the laboratory. The fees are based on "products," or a set of examinations that are packaged together and designed to be suitable for particular types of physical evidence. The fee-for-service concept has encouraged the creation of a number of private laboratories that provide services to both police and criminal defense attorneys. One such organization, LGC in the United Kingdom, employs more than one thousand forensic scientists.

In Canada, forensic services are provided by three government-funded institutes: (1) six Royal Canadian Mounted Police regional laboratories, (2) the Centre of Forensic Sciences in Toronto, and (3) the Institute of Legal Medicine and Police Science in Montreal. Altogether, more than a hundred countries throughout the world have at least one laboratory facility offering services in the field of forensic science.

FIGURE 1–3
Paul Leland Kirk, 1902–1970.
Courtesy Blackstone-Shelburne, N.Y.

Organization of a Crime Laboratory

The development of crime laboratories in the United States has been characterized by rapid growth accompanied by a lack of national and regional planning and coordination. At present, nearly four hundred public crime laboratories operate at various levels of government (federal, state, county, and municipal)—more than three times the number of crime laboratories operating in 1966.

The size and diversity of crime laboratories make it impossible to select any one model that best describes a typical crime laboratory. Although most of these facilities function as part of a police department, others operate under the direction of the prosecutor's or district attorney's office; some work with the laboratories of the medical examiner or coroner. Far fewer are affiliated with universities or exist as independent agencies in government. Laboratory staff sizes range from one person to more than a hundred, and their services may be diverse or specialized, depending on the responsibilities of the agency that houses the laboratory.

The Growth of Crime Laboratories

Crime laboratories have mostly been organized by agencies that either foresaw their potential application to criminal investigation or were pressed by the increasing demands of casework. Several reasons explain the unparalleled growth of crime laboratories during the past thirty-five years. Supreme Court decisions in the 1960s were responsible for greater police emphasis on securing scientifically evaluated evidence. The requirement to advise criminal suspects of their constitutional rights and their right of immediate access to counsel has all but eliminated confessions as a routine investigative tool. Successful prosecution of criminal cases requires a thorough and professional police investigation, frequently incorporating the skills of forensic science experts. Modern technology has provided forensic scientists with many new skills and techniques to meet the challenges accompanying their increased participation in the criminal justice system.

Coinciding with changing judicial requirements has been the staggering increase in crime rates in the United States over the past forty years. This factor alone would probably have accounted for the increased use of crime laboratory services by police agencies, but only a small percentage of police investigations generate evidence requiring scientific examination. There is, however, one important exception to this observation: drug-related arrests. All illicit-drug seizures must be sent to a forensic laboratory for confirmatory chemical analysis before the case can be adjudicated. Since the mid-1960s, drug abuse has accelerated to nearly uncontrollable levels and has resulted in crime laboratories being inundated with drug specimens. Current estimates indicate that nearly half of all requests for examination of forensic evidence deal with abused drugs.

Future Challenges

A more recent impetus leading to the growth and maturation of crime laboratories has been the advent of DNA profiling. Since the early 1990s, this technology has progressed to the point at which traces of blood, semen stains, hair, and saliva residues left behind on stamps and cups, as well as bite marks, have made possible the individualization or near-individualization of biological evidence. To meet the demands of DNA technology, crime labs have expanded staff and in many cases modernized their physical plants. The labor-intensive demands and sophisticated requirements of the technology have affected the structure of the forensic laboratory as has no other technology in the past fifty years. Likewise, DNA profiling has become the dominant factor in explaining how the general public perceives the workings and capabilities of the modern crime laboratory.

In coming years thousands of forensic scientists will be added to the rolls of both public and private forensic laboratories to process crime-scene evidence for DNA and to acquire DNA profiles, as mandated by state laws, from the hundreds of thousands of individuals convicted of crimes. This endeavor has already added many new scientists to the field and will eventually more than double the number of scientists employed by forensic laboratories in the United States.

A major problem facing the forensic DNA community is the substantial backlog of unanalyzed DNA samples from crime scenes. The number of unanalyzed casework DNA samples reported by state and national agencies is more than 57,000. The estimated number of untested convicted offender samples is over 500,000. In an attempt to eliminate the backlog of convicted offender or arrestee samples to be analyzed and entered into the Combined DNA Index System (CODIS), the federal government has initiated funding for in-house analysis of samples at the crime laboratory or outsourcing samples to private laboratories for analysis.

Beginning in 2008, California began collecting DNA samples from all people arrested on suspicion of a felony, not waiting until a person is convicted. The state's database, with approximately one million DNA profiles, is already the third largest in the world, behind those maintained by the United Kingdom and the FBI. The federal government plans to begin doing the same.

Types of Crime Laboratories

Historically, a federal system of government, combined with a desire to retain local control, has produced a variety of independent laboratories in the United States, precluding the creation of a national system. Crime laboratories to a large extent mirror the fragmented law enforcement structure that exists on the national, state, and local levels.

FEDERAL CRIME LABORATORIES   The federal government has no single law enforcement or investigative agency with unlimited jurisdiction. Four major federal crime laboratories have been created to help investigate and enforce criminal laws that extend beyond the jurisdictional boundaries of state and local forces.

The FBI (Department of Justice) maintains the largest crime laboratory in the world. An ultramodern facility housing the FBI's forensic science services is located in Quantico, Virginia (see Figure 1–4). Its expertise and technology support its broad investigative powers. The Drug Enforcement Administration laboratories (Department of Justice) analyze drugs seized in violation of federal laws regulating the production, sale, and transportation of drugs. The laboratories of the Bureau of Alcohol, Tobacco, Firearms and Explosives (Department of Justice) analyze alcoholic beverages and documents relating to alcohol and firearm excise tax law enforcement and examine weapons, explosive devices, and related evidence to enforce the Gun Control Act of 1968 and the Organized Crime Control Act of 1970. The U.S. Postal Inspection Service maintains laboratories concerned with criminal investigations relating to the postal service. Each of these federal facilities will offer its expertise to any local agency that requests assistance in relevant investigative matters.

STATE AND LOCAL CRIME LABORATORIES   Most state governments maintain a crime laboratory to service state and local law enforcement agencies that do not have ready access to a laboratory. Some states, such as Alabama, California, Illinois, Michigan, New Jersey, Texas, Washington, Oregon, Virginia, and Florida, have developed a comprehensive statewide system of regional or satellite laboratories. These operate under the direction of a central facility and provide forensic services to most areas of the state. The concept of a regional laboratory operating as part of a statewide system has increased the accessibility of many local law enforcement agencies to a crime laboratory, while minimizing duplication of services and ensuring maximum interlaboratory cooperation through the sharing of expertise and equipment.

(a)

(b)

FIGURE 1–4

(a) Exterior and (b) interior views of the FBI crime laboratory in Quantico, Virginia.
Courtesy AP Wide World Photos

Local laboratories provide services to county and municipal agencies. Generally, these facilities operate independently of the state crime laboratory and are financed directly by local government. However, as costs have risen, some counties have combined resources and created multicounty laboratories to service their jurisdictions. Many of the larger cities in the United States maintain their own crime laboratories, usually under the direction of the local police department. Frequently, high population and high crime rates combine to make a municipal facility, such as that of New York City, the largest crime laboratory in the state.

Services of the Crime Laboratory

Bearing in mind the independent development of crime laboratories in the United States, the wide variation in total services offered in different communities is not surprising. There are many reasons for this, including (1) variations in local laws, (2) the different capabilities and functions of the organization to which a laboratory is attached, and (3) budgetary and staffing limitations.

In recent years, many local crime laboratories have been created solely to process drug specimens. Often these facilities were staffed with few personnel and operated under limited budgets. Although many have expanded their forensic services, some still primarily perform drug analyses. However, even among crime laboratories providing services beyond drug identification, the diversity and quality of services rendered varies significantly. For the purposes of this text, I have taken the liberty of arbitrarily designating the following units as those that should constitute a "full-service" crime laboratory.

Basic Services Provided by Full-Service Crime Laboratories

PHYSICAL SCIENCE UNIT   The physical science unit applies principles and techniques of chemistry, physics, and geology to the identification and comparison of crime-scene evidence. It is staffed by criminalists who have the expertise to use chemical tests and modern analytical instrumentation to examine items as diverse as drugs, glass, paint, explosives, and soil. In a laboratory that has a staff large enough to permit specialization, the responsibilities of this unit may be further subdivided into drug identification, soil and mineral analysis, and examination of a variety of trace physical evidence.

BIOLOGY UNIT   The biology unit is staffed with biologists and biochemists who identify and perform DNA profiling on dried bloodstains and other body fluids, compare hairs and fibers, and identify and compare botanical materials such as wood and plants (see Figure 1–5).

FIREARMS UNIT   The firearms unit examines firearms, discharged bullets, cartridge cases, shotgun shells, and ammunition of all types. Garments and other objects are also examined to detect firearms discharge residues and to approximate the distance from a target at which a weapon was fired. The basic principles of firearms examination are also applied here to the comparison of marks made by tools (see Figure 1–6).

DOCUMENT EXAMINATION UNIT   The document examination unit studies the handwriting and typewriting on questioned documents to ascertain authenticity and/or source. Related responsibilities include analyzing paper and ink and examining indented writings (the term usually applied to the partially visible depressions appearing on a sheet of paper underneath the one on which the visible writing appears), obliterations, erasures, and burned or charred documents (see Figure 1–7).

PHOTOGRAPHY UNIT   A complete photographic laboratory examines and records physical evidence. Its procedures may require the use of highly specialized photographic techniques, such as digital imaging, infrared, ultraviolet, and X-ray photography, to make invisible information visible to the naked eye. This unit also prepares photographic exhibits for courtroom presentation.

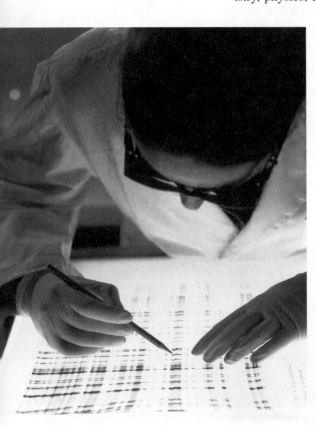

FIGURE 1–5

A forensic scientist performing DNA analysis.
Courtesy Mauro Fermariello, Photo Researchers, Inc.

FIGURE 1–6

A forensic analyst examining a firearm.
Courtesy Mediacolors, Alamy Images

Optional Services Provided by Full-Service Crime Laboratories

TOXICOLOGY UNIT   The toxicology group examines body fluids and organs to determine the presence or absence of drugs and poisons. Frequently, such functions are shared with or may be the sole responsibility of a separate laboratory facility placed under the direction of the medical examiner's or coroner's office.

In most jurisdictions, field instruments such as the Intoxilyzer are used to determine the alcoholic consumption of individuals. Often the toxicology section also trains operators and maintains and services these instruments.

LATENT FINGERPRINT UNIT   The latent fingerprint unit processes and examines evidence for latent fingerprints when they are submitted in conjunction with other laboratory examinations.

POLYGRAPH UNIT   The polygraph, or lie detector, has come to be recognized as an essential tool of the criminal investigator rather than the forensic scientist. However, during the formative years of polygraph technology, many police agencies incorporated this unit into the laboratory's administrative structure, where it sometimes remains today. In any case, its functions are handled by people trained in the techniques of criminal investigation and interrogation.

VOICEPRINT ANALYSIS UNIT   In cases involving telephoned threats or tape-recorded messages, investigators may require the skills of the voiceprint analysis unit to tie the voice to a particular suspect. To this end, a good deal of casework has been performed with the sound spectrograph, an instrument that transforms speech into a visual display called a *voiceprint*. The validity of this technique as a means of personal identification rests on the premise that the sound patterns produced in speech are unique to the individual and that the voiceprint displays this uniqueness.

CRIME-SCENE INVESTIGATION UNIT   The concept of incorporating crime-scene evidence collection into the total forensic science service is slowly gaining recognition in the United States. This unit dispatches specially trained personnel (civilian and/or police) to the crime scene to collect and preserve physical evidence that will later be processed at the crime laboratory.

Whatever the organizational structure of a forensic science laboratory may be, specialization must not impede the overall coordination of services demanded by today's criminal investigator.

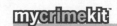

WEBEXTRA 1.1
Take a Tour of a Forensic
Laboratory
www.mycrimekit.com

Fingerprints may be detectable on paper using a variety of chemical developing techniques (pp. 403–404).

Paper examination may identify a manufacturer. General appearance, watermarks, fiber analysis, and chemical analysis of pigments, additives, and fillers may reveal a paper's origin (p. 468).

DNA may be recovered from saliva residues on the back of a stamp (pp. 284–286). However, in this case, the stamp is printed onto the envelope.

Ink analysis may reveal a pen's manufacturer (pp. 463–464).

Trace evidence, such as hairs and fibers, may be present within the contents of the envelope.

Photocopier toner may reveal its manufacturer through chemical and physical properties (pp. 457–458).

Indented writing may be deposited on paper left underneath a sheet of paper being written upon. Electrostatic imaging is used to visualize indented impressions on paper (p. 462).

Handwriting examination reveals that block lettering is consistent with a single writer who wrote three other anthrax letters (pp. 452–457).

DNA may be recovered from saliva used to seal an envelope (pp. 284–286)

Cellophane tape was used to seal four envelopes containing the anthrax letters. The fitting together of the serrated ends of the tape strips confirmed that they were torn in succession from the same roll of tape (pp. 62–63)

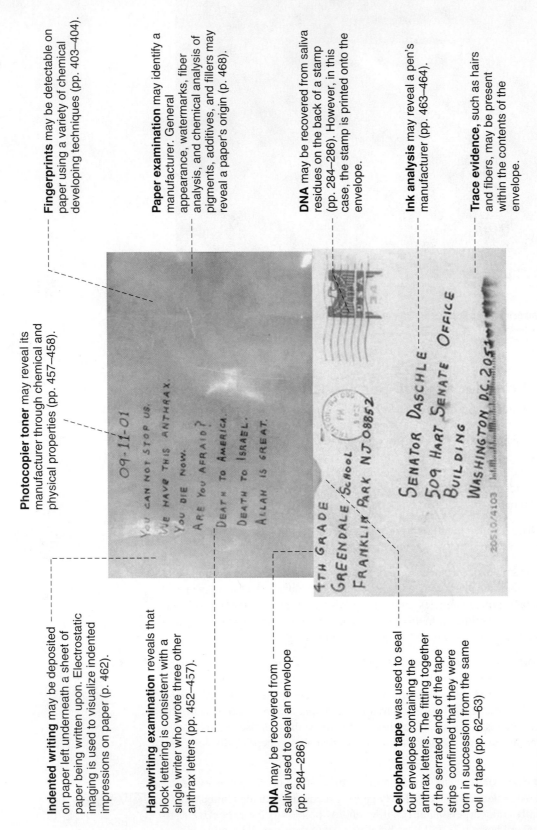

09-11-01

You can not stop us.
We have this anthrax.
You die now.
Are you afraid?

Death to America.
Death to Israel.
Allah is great.

4th Grade
Greendale School
Franklin Park NJ 08852

Senator Daschle
509 Hart Senate Office
Building
Washington D.C. 20510

20510/4103

FIGURE 1–7

An envelope containing anthrax spores along with an anonymous letter was sent to the office of Senator Tom Daschle shortly after the terrorist attacks of September 11, 2001. A variety of forensic skills were used to examine the envelope and letter. Also, bar codes placed on the front and back of the envelope by mail-sorting machines contain address information and information about where the envelope was first processed.

Laboratory administrators need to keep open the lines of communication among analysts (civilian and uniform), crime-scene investigators, and police personnel. Inevitably, forensic investigations require the skills of many individuals. One notoriously high-profile investigation illustrates this process—the search to uncover the source of the anthrax letters mailed shortly after September 11, 2001. Figure 1–7 shows one of the letters and illustrates the multitude of skills required in the investigation—skills possessed by forensic chemists and biologists, fingerprint examiners, and forensic document examiners.

Functions of the Forensic Scientist

Although a forensic scientist relies primarily on scientific knowledge and skill in performing analyses in the laboratory, a good deal of the forensic scientists's time is spent in the courtroom, where the ultimate significance of the evidence is determined. The forensic scientist must not only analyze physical evidence but also persuade a jury to accept the conclusions derived from that analysis.

Analysis of Physical Evidence

First and foremost, the forensic scientist must be skilled in applying the principles and techniques of the physical and natural sciences to analyze the many types of physical evidence that may be recovered during a criminal investigation. Of the three major avenues available to police investigators for assistance in solving a crime—confessions, eyewitness accounts by victims or witnesses, and the evaluation of physical evidence retrieved from the crime scene—only physical evidence is free of inherent error or bias.

THE IMPORTANCE OF PHYSICAL EVIDENCE   Criminal cases are replete with examples of individuals who were incorrectly charged with and convicted of committing a crime because of faulty memories or lapses in judgment. For example, investigators may be led astray during their preliminary evaluation of the events and circumstances surrounding the commission of a crime. These errors may be compounded by misleading eyewitness statements and inappropriate confessions. These same concerns don't apply to physical evidence.

What about physical evidence allows investigators to sort out facts as they are and not what one wishes they were? The hallmark of physical evidence is that it must undergo scientific inquiry. Science derives its integrity from adherence to strict guidelines that ensure the careful and systematic collection, organization, and analysis of information—a process known as the **scientific method**. The underlying principles of the scientific method provide a safety net to ensure that the outcome of an investigation is not tainted by human emotion or compromised by distorting, belittling, or ignoring contrary evidence.

scientific method
A process that uses strict guidelines to ensure careful and systematic collection, organization, and analysis of information

The scientific method begins by formulating a question worthy of investigation, such as who committed a particular crime. The investigator next formulates a hypothesis, a reasonable explanation proposed to answer the question. What follows is the basic foundation of scientific inquiry—the testing of the hypothesis through experimentation. The testing process must be thorough and recognized by other scientists as valid. Scientists and investigators must accept the experimental findings even when they wish they were different. Finally, when the hypothesis is validated by experimentation, it becomes suitable as scientific evidence, appropriate for use in a criminal investigation and ultimately available for admission in a court of law.

DETERMINING ADMISSIBILITY OF EVIDENCE   In rejecting the scientific validity of the lie detector (polygraph), the District of Columbia Circuit Court in 1923 set forth what has since become a standard guideline for determining the judicial admissibility of scientific examinations. In *Frye* v. *United States*,[2] the court stated the following:

> Just when a scientific principle or discovery crosses the line between the experimental and demonstrable stages is difficult to define. Somewhere in this twilight zone the evidential force of the principle must be recognized, and while the courts will go a long way in admitting expert testimony deduced from a well-recognized scientific principle or discovery, the

---

[2] 293 Fed. 1013 (D.C. Cir. 1923).

thing from which the deduction is made must be sufficiently established to have gained general acceptance in the particular field in which it belongs.

To meet the *Frye* standard, the court must decide whether the questioned procedure, technique, or principle is "generally accepted" by a meaningful segment of the relevant scientific community. In practice, this approach required the proponent of a scientific test to present to the court a collection of experts who could testify that the scientific issue before the court is generally accepted by the relevant members of the scientific community. Furthermore, in determining whether a novel technique meets criteria associated with "general acceptance," courts have frequently taken note of books and papers written on the subject, as well as prior judicial decisions relating to the reliability and general acceptance of the technique. In recent years this approach has engendered a great deal of debate as to whether it is sufficiently flexible to deal with new and novel scientific issues that may not have gained widespread support within the scientific community.

OTHER STANDARDS OF ADMISSIBILITY   As an alternative to the *Frye* standard, some courts came to believe that the Federal Rules of Evidence espoused a more flexible standard that did not rely on general acceptance as an absolute prerequisite for admitting scientific evidence. Part of the Federal Rules of Evidence governs the admissibility of all evidence, including expert testimony, in federal courts, and many states have adopted codes similar to those of the Federal Rules. Specifically, Rule 702 of the Federal Rules of Evidence deals with the admissibility of expert testimony:

> If scientific, technical, or other specialized knowledge will assist the trier of fact to understand the evidence or to determine a fact in issue, a witness qualified as an expert by knowledge, skill, experience, training, or education, may testify thereto in the form of an opinion or otherwise, if (1) the testimony is based upon sufficient facts or data, (2) the testimony is the product of reliable principles and methods, and (3) the witness has applied the principles and methods reliably to the facts of the case.

In a landmark ruling in the 1993 case of *Daubert* v. *Merrell Dow Pharmaceuticals, Inc.*,[3] the U.S. Supreme Court asserted that "general acceptance," or the *Frye* standard, is not an absolute prerequisite to the admissibility of scientific evidence under the Federal Rules of Evidence. According to the Court, the Rules of Evidence—especially Rule 702—assign to the trial judge the task of ensuring that an expert's testimony rests on a reliable foundation and is relevant to the case. Although this ruling applies only to federal courts, many state courts are expected to use this decision as a guideline in setting standards for the admissibility of scientific evidence.

JUDGING SCIENTIFIC EVIDENCE   What the Court advocates in *Daubert* is that trial judges assume the ultimate responsibility for acting as a "gatekeeper" in judging the admissibility and reliability of scientific evidence presented in their courts (see Figure 1–8). The Court offered some guidelines as to how a judge can gauge the veracity of scientific evidence, emphasizing that the inquiry should be flexible. Suggested areas of inquiry include the following:

1. Whether the scientific technique or theory can be (and has been) tested
2. Whether the technique or theory has been subject to peer review and publication
3. The technique's potential rate of error
4. Existence and maintenance of standards controlling the technique's operation
5. Whether the scientific theory or method has attracted widespread acceptance within a relevant scientific community

Some legal practitioners have expressed concern that abandoning *Frye*'s general-acceptance test will result in the introduction of absurd and irrational pseudoscientific claims in the courtroom. The Supreme Court rejected these concerns:

> In this regard the respondent seems to us to be overly pessimistic about the capabilities of the jury and of the adversary system generally. Vigorous cross-examination, presentation of contrary evidence, and careful instruction on the burden of proof are the traditional and appropriate means of attacking shaky but admissible evidence.

[3] 509 U.S. 579 (1993).

FIGURE 1–8

Sketch of a U.S. Supreme Court hearing.
© Art Lien, Court Artist

In a 1999 decision, *Kumho Tire Co., Ltd.* v. *Carmichael*,[4] the Court unanimously ruled that the "gatekeeping" role of the trial judge applied not only to scientific testimony, but to all expert testimony:

> We conclude that *Daubert*'s general holding—setting forth the trial judge's general "gate-keeping" obligation—applies not only to testimony based on "scientific" knowledge, but also to testimony based on "technical" and "other specialized" knowledge. . . . We also conclude that a trial court may consider one or more of the more specific factors that *Daubert* mentioned when doing so will help determine that testimony's reliability. But, as the Court stated in *Daubert*, the test of reliability is "flexible," and *Daubert*'s list of specific factors neither necessarily nor exclusively applies to all experts in every case.

A leading case that exemplifies the type of flexibility and wide discretion that the *Daubert* ruling apparently gives trial judges in matters of scientific inquiry is *Coppolino* v. *State*.[5] Here a medical examiner testified to his finding that the victim had died of an overdose of a drug known as succinylcholine chloride. This drug had never before been detected in the human body. The medical examiner's findings were dependent on a toxicological report that identified an abnormally high concentration of succinic acid, a breakdown product of the drug, in the victim's body. The defense argued that this test for the presence of succinylcholine chloride was new and the absence of corroborative experimental data by other scientists meant that it had not yet gained general acceptance in the toxicology profession. The court, in rejecting this argument, recognized the necessity for devising new scientific tests to solve the special problems that are continually arising in the forensic laboratory. It emphasized, however, that although these tests may be new and unique, they are admissible only if they are based on scientifically valid principles and techniques: "The tests by which the medical examiner sought to determine whether death was caused by succinylcholine chloride were novel and devised specifically for this case. This does not render the evidence inadmissible. Society need not tolerate homicide until there develops a body of medical literature about some particular lethal agent."

---

[4] 526 U.S. 137 (1999).
[5] 223 So. 2d 68 (Fla. Dist. Ct. App. 1968), *app. dismissed*, 234 So. 2d 120 (Fla. 1969), *cert. denied*, 399 U.S. 927 (1970).

> >

Dr. Coppolino's Deadly House Calls

A frantic late-night telephone call to Dr. Juliette Karow brought her to the Longport Key, Florida, home of Drs. Carl and Carmela Coppolino. Carl had called for Dr. Karow's help because he believed Carmela was dying. He said she had complained of chest pains earlier in the evening and he was certain she had suffered a heart attack. Dr. Karow arrived to find Carmela beyond help.

Although Dr. Karow felt that the scene in the room appeared staged, and her own observations of Carmela's body did not support Carl's claim of heart trouble, she agreed to sign 32-year-old Carmela's death certificate. Dr. Karow cited "coronary occlusion" as the cause of death but reported the death to the local police department. The investigating officer was satisfied that Dr. Karow had correctly listed the cause of death, so he did not apply the law that required that an autopsy be performed. The medical examiner could not order an autopsy without a request from the police or the district attorney, which was not forthcoming. Thus, Carmela Coppolino's body, unexamined by anyone, was buried in her family's plot in her home state of New Jersey.

A little more than a month later, Carl married a moneyed socialite, Mary Gibson. News of Carl's marriage infuriated Marjorie Farber, a former New Jersey neighbor of Dr. Coppolino who had been having an affair with the good doctor. Soon Marjorie had an interesting story to recount to investigators. Her husband's death two years before, although ruled to be from natural causes, had actually been murder! Carl, an anesthesiologist, had given Marjorie a syringe containing some medication and told her to inject her husband, William, while he was sleeping. Ultimately, Marjorie claimed, she was unable to inject the full dose and called Carl, who finished the job by suffocating William with a pillow.

In a cruel and ironic twist, Carl called his wife, Carmela, to sign William Farber's death certificate. She listed the cause of death, at Carl's insistence, as coronary artery disease. This type of death is common, especially in men in their fifties. Such deaths are rarely questioned, and the Department of Health accepted the certificate without any inquiry.

Marjorie Farber's astonishing story was supported in part by Carl's recent increase in his wife's life insurance. Carmela's $65,000 policy, along with his new wife's fortune, would keep Dr. Coppolino in high society for the rest of his life. Based on this information, authorities in New Jersey and Florida now obtained exhumation orders for both William Farber and Carmela Coppolino. After examination of both bodies, Dr. Coppolino was charged with the murders of William and Carmela.

Officials decided to try Dr. Coppolino first in New Jersey for the murder of William Farber. Coppolino was represented by the famous defense attorney F. Lee Bailey. The Farber autopsy did not reveal any evidence of poisoning, but seemed to show strong evidence of strangulation. The absence of toxicological findings left the jury to deliberate the conflicting medical expert testimony versus the sensational story told by a scorned and embittered woman. In the end, Bailey secured an acquittal for his client.

The Florida trial presented another chance to bring Carl Coppolino to justice. Florida officials called on the experienced New York City medical examiner Dr. Milton Halpern and his colleague, toxicologist Dr. Charles Umberger, to determine how Carl Coppolino had killed his wife. Recalling Dr. Coppolino's career as an anesthesiologist, Halpern theorized that Coppolino had exploited his access to the many potent drugs used during surgery to commit these murders, specifically an injectable paralytic agent called succinylcholine chloride.

After having Carmela's body exhumed, Halpern examined her body with a magnifying glass in search of an injection site. He found that Carmela had been injected in her left buttock shortly before her death. Dr. Umberger's mission as the toxicologist in this case was to prove the administration of succinylcholine chloride by chemical analysis of Carmela's tissues.

This presented a serious problem because succinylcholine was purported to be untraceable in human tissue. The drug breaks down in the body to succinic acid and choline, both of which are naturally occurring chemicals in the human body. The chemical method necessary to make this determination did not exist at the time of the murder.

Ultimately, Dr. Umberger developed a completely novel procedure for detecting succinylcholine chloride. He isolated elevated levels of succinic acid in Carmela's brain, which proved that she had received a large dose of the paralytic drug shortly before her death. This evidence, along with the finding of the same drug residues in the injection site on her buttock, was presented in the Florida murder trial of Carl Coppolino, who was convicted of second-degree murder.

On appeal, the defense raised an interesting point of law. Can a defendant be convicted of murder based on a series of tests that were specifically devised for this case? Tests that indirectly showed that Carmela had been injected with succinylcholine chloride had never before been used in a criminal trial. The court ruled that the novelty of a scientific method does not preclude its significance to a criminal prosecution. Just because an otherwise valid method was developed specifically for this trial and had not yet been proven in court did not mean that the murderer should be allowed to get away with the perfect crime. The conviction of Dr. Coppolino was upheld.

Provision of Expert Testimony

expert witness
An individual whom the court determines to possess knowledge relevant to the trial that is not expected of the average layperson

Because their work product may ultimately be a factor in determining a person's guilt or innocence, forensic scientists may be required to testify with respect to their methods and conclusions at a trial or hearing. Trial courts have broad discretion in accepting an individual as an **expert witness** on any particular subject. Generally, if a witness can establish to the satisfaction of a trial judge that he or she possesses a particular skill or has knowledge in a trade or profession that will aid the court in determining the truth of the matter at issue, that individual will be accepted as an expert witness. Depending on the subject area in question, the court will usually consider knowledge acquired through experience, training, education, or a combination sufficient grounds for qualification as an expert witness.

DETERMINING COMPETENCE   In court, the qualifying questions that counsel asks the expert are often directed toward demonstrating the witness's ability and competence pertaining to the matter at hand. Competency may be established by having him or her cite educational degrees, participation in special courses, membership in professional societies, and any professional articles or books published. Also important is the number of years of occupational experience the witness has in areas related to the matter before the court.

Unfortunately, few schools confer degrees in forensic science. Most chemists, biologists, geologists, and physicists prepare themselves for careers in forensic science by combining training under an experienced examiner with independent study. Of course, formal education provides the scientist with a firm foundation for learning and understanding the principles and techniques of forensic science. Nevertheless, for the most part, courts must rely on training and years of experience as a measurement of the knowledge and ability of the expert.

Before the judge rules on the witness's qualifications, the opposing attorney is given the opportunity to cross-examine the witness and to point out weaknesses in his or her background and knowledge. Most courts are reluctant to disqualify an individual as an expert even when presented with someone whose background is only remotely associated with the issue at hand. The question of what credentials are suitable for qualification as an expert is ambiguous and highly subjective and one that the courts wisely try to avoid. However, the weight that a judge or jury assigns to "expert" testimony in subsequent deliberations is quite another matter. Undoubtedly, education and experience have considerable bearing on the value assigned to the expert's opinions. Just as important may be the witness's demeanor and ability to explain scientific data and conclusions clearly, concisely, and logically to a judge and jury composed of nonscientists. The problem of sorting out the strengths and weaknesses of expert testimony falls to prosecution and defense counsel, who must endeavor to prepare themselves adequately for this undertaking.

EXPERT TESTIMONY   The ordinary or lay witness must give testimony on events or observations that arise from personal knowledge. This testimony must be factual and, with few exceptions, cannot contain the personal opinions of the witness. On the other hand, the expert witness is called on to evaluate evidence when the court lacks the expertise to do so. This expert then expresses an opinion as to the significance of the findings. The views expressed are accepted only as representing the expert's opinion and may later be accepted or ignored in jury deliberations (see Figure 1–9).

It must be recognized that the expert cannot render any view with absolute certainty. At best, he or she may only be able to offer an opinion that is based on a reasonable scientific certainty derived from training and experience. Obviously, the expert is expected to defend vigorously the techniques and conclusions of the analysis, but at the same time must not be reluctant to discuss impartially any findings that could minimize the significance of the analysis. The forensic scientist should not be an advocate of one party's cause, but only an advocate of truth. An adversary system of justice must give the prosecutor and defense ample opportunity to offer expert opinions and to argue the merits of such testimony. Ultimately, the duty of the judge or jury is to weigh the pros and cons of all the information presented in deciding guilt or innocence.

Furnishing Training in the Proper Recognition, Collection, and Preservation of Physical Evidence

The competence of a laboratory staff and the sophistication of its analytical equipment have little or no value if relevant evidence cannot be properly recognized, collected, and preserved at the site of a crime. For this reason, the forensic staff must have responsibilities that will influence the conduct of the crime-scene investigation.

The most direct and effective response to this problem has been to dispatch specially trained evidence-collection technicians to the crime scene. A growing number of crime laboratories and the police agencies they service keep trained "evidence technicians" on 24-hour call to help criminal investigators retrieve evidence. These technicians are trained by the laboratory staff to recognize and gather pertinent physical evidence at the crime scene. They are administratively assigned

mycrimekit

WEBEXTRA 1.2
Watch a Forensic Expert Witness
Testify—I
www.mycrimekit.com

mycrimekit

WEB EXTRA 1.3
Watch a Forensic Expert Witness
Testify—II
www.mycrimekit.com

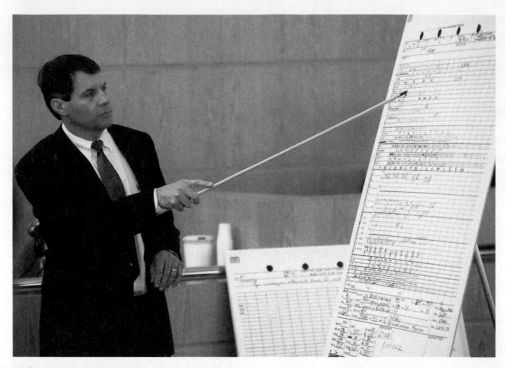

FIGURE 1–9

An expert witness testifying in court.
Courtesy Jeff Siner, Corbis/Sygma

to the laboratory to facilitate their continued exposure to forensic techniques and procedures. They have at their disposal all the proper tools and supplies for proper collection and packaging of evidence for future scientific examination.

Unfortunately, many police forces have still not adopted this approach. Often a patrol officer or detective is charged with collecting the evidence. His or her effectiveness in this role depends on the extent of his or her training and working relationship with the laboratory. For maximum use of the skills of the crime laboratory, training of the crime-scene investigator must go beyond superficial classroom lectures to involve extensive personal contact with the forensic scientist. Each must become aware of the other's problems, techniques, and limitations.

The training of police officers in evidence collection and their familiarization with the capabilities of a crime laboratory should not be restricted to a select group of personnel on the force. Every officer engaged in fieldwork, whether it be traffic, patrol, investigation, or juvenile control, often must process evidence for laboratory examination. Obviously, it would be a difficult and time-consuming operation to give everyone the in-depth training and attention that a qualified criminal investigator requires. However, familiarity with crime laboratory services and capabilities can be facilitated through periodic lectures, laboratory tours, and dissemination of manuals prepared by the laboratory staff that outline proper methods for collecting and submitting physical evidence to the laboratory. Examples of such manuals are shown in Figure 1–10.

A brief outline describing the proper collection and packaging of common types of physical evidence is found in Appendix I. The procedures and information summarized in this appendix are discussed in greater detail in forthcoming chapters.

Other Forensic Science Services

Even though this textbook is devoted to describing the services normally provided by a crime laboratory, the field of forensic science is by no means limited to the areas covered in this book. A number of specialized forensic science services outside the crime laboratory are routinely available to law enforcement personnel. These services are important aids to a criminal investigation and require the involvement of individuals who have highly specialized skills.

FIGURE 1–10

Representative evidence-collection guides prepared by various police agencies.

Forensic Psychiatry

Forensic psychiatry is a specialized area in which the relationship between human behavior and legal proceedings is examined. Forensic psychiatrists are retained for both civil and criminal litigations. For civil cases, forensic psychiatrists normally determine whether people are competent to make decisions about preparing wills, settling property, or refusing medical treatment. For criminal cases, they evaluate behavioral disorders and determine whether people are competent to stand trial. Forensic psychiatrists also examine behavioral patterns of criminals as an aid in developing a suspect's behavioral profile.

Forensic Odontology

Practitioners of forensic odontology help identify victims when the body is left in an unrecognizable state. Teeth are composed of enamel, the hardest substance in the body. Because of enamel's resilience, the teeth outlast tissues and organs as decomposition begins. The characteristics of teeth, their alignment, and the overall structure of the mouth provide individual evidence for identifying a specific person. With the use of dental records such as X-rays and dental casts or even a photograph of the person's smile, a set of dental remains can be compared to a suspected victim. Another application of forensic odontology to criminal investigations is bite mark analysis. At times in assault cases, bite marks are left on the victim. A forensic odontologist can compare the marks left on a victim and the tooth structure of the suspect. See Figure 1–11.

Forensic Engineering

Forensic engineers are concerned with failure analysis, accident reconstruction, and causes and origins of fires or explosions. Forensic engineers answer questions such as these: How did an accident or structural failure occur? Were the parties involved responsible? If so, how were they responsible? Accident scenes are examined, photographs are reviewed, and any mechanical objects involved are inspected.

Forensic Computer and Digital Analysis

Forensic computer science is a new and fast-growing field that involves the identification, collection, preservation, and examination of information derived from computers and other digital devices, such as cell phones. Law enforcement aspects of this work normally involve the recovery of deleted or

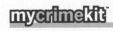

WEBEXTRA 1.4
Explore Forensic Dentistry
www.mycrimekit.com

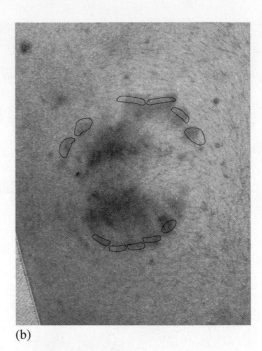

(a)   (b)

FIGURE 1–11

(a) Bite mark on victim's body. (b) Comparison to suspect's teeth.
Courtesy David Sweet, DMD, Ph.D., DABFP BOLD Forensic Laboratory, Vancouver, BC Canada

overwritten data from a computer's hard drive and the tracking of hacking activities within a compromised system. The field of forensic computer analysis will be addressed in detail in Chapter 19.

Forensic Science on the Internet

There are no limits to the amount or type of information that can be found on the Internet. The fields of law enforcement and forensic science have not been left behind by advancing computer technology. Extensive information about forensic science is available on the Internet. The types of Web pages range from simple explanations of the various fields of forensics to intricate details of crime-scene reconstruction. People can also find information on which colleges offer degree programs in forensics or pages posted by law enforcement agencies that detail their activities, as well as possible employment opportunities.

General Forensics Sites

Reddy's Forensic Home Page (www.forensicpage.com) is a valuable starting point. This site is a collection of forensic Web pages listed under categories such as new links in forensics; general forensic information sources; associations, colleges, and societies; literature and journals; forensic laboratories; general Web pages; forensic-related mailing lists and newsgroups; universities; conferences; and various forensic fields of expertise.

Another Web site offering a multitude of information related to forensic science is Zeno's Forensic Site (forensic.to/forensic.html). Here users can find links to forensic education and expert consultation, as well as a wealth of information concerning specific fields of forensic science.

A comprehensive and useful Web site for those interested in law enforcement is Officer.com (www.officer.com). This comprehensive collection of criminal justice resources is organized into easy-to-read subdirectories that relate to topics such as law enforcement agencies, police association and organization sites, criminal justice organizations, law research pages, and police mailing-list directories.

Web Sites on Specific Topics

AN INTRODUCTION TO FORENSIC FIREARM IDENTIFICATION   This Web site contains an extensive collection of information relating to the identification of firearms. An individual can explore in detail how to examine bullets, cartridge cases, and clothing for gunshot residues and suspect shooters' hands for primer residues. Information on the latest technology involving the automated firearms search system IBIS can also be found on this site.

CARPENTER'S FORENSIC SCIENCE RESOURCES   This site provides a bibliography with hypertext references pertaining to various aspects of criminal investigations involving forensic evidence. For example, the user can find references about DNA, fingerprints, hairs, fibers, and questioned documents as they relate to crime scenes and assist investigations. This Web site is an excellent place to start a research project in forensic science.

CRIME SCENE INVESTIGATOR NETWORK   For those who are interested in learning the process of crime-scene investigation, this site provides detailed guidelines and information regarding crime-scene response and the collection and preservation of evidence. For example, information concerning the packaging and analysis of bloodstains, seminal fluids, hairs, fibers, paint, glass, firearms, documents, and fingerprints can be found through this Web site. It explains the importance of inspecting the crime scene and the impact forensic evidence has on the investigation.

CRIME AND CLUES   Users interested in learning about the forensic aspects of fingerprinting will find this a useful and informative Web site. The site covers the history of fingerprints as well as subjects pertaining to the development of latent fingerprints. The user will also find links to other Web sites covering a variety of subjects pertaining to crime-scene investigation, documentation of the crime scene, and expert testimony.

INTERACTIVE INVESTIGATOR—DÉTECTIVE INTERACTIF   At this outstanding site, visitors can obtain general information and an introduction to the main aspects of forensic science from a database on the subject. They can also explore actual evidence gathered from notorious crime scenes. Users will be able to employ deductive skills and forensic knowledge while playing an interactive game in which they must help Detective Wilson and Detective Marlow solve a gruesome murder.

THE CHEMICAL DETECTIVE   This site offers descriptions of relevant forensic science disciplines. Topics such as fingerprints, fire and arson, and DNA analysis are described in informative layperson's terms. Case histories describe the application of forensic evidence to criminal investigations. Emphasis is placed on securing and documenting the crime scene. The site directs the reader to other important forensic links.

QUESTIONED-DOCUMENT EXAMINATION   This basic, informative Web page answers frequently asked questions concerning document examination, explains the application of typical document examinations, and details the basic facts and theory of handwriting and signatures. There are also links to noted document examination cases that present the user with real-life applications of forensic document examination.

mycrimekit

WEBEXTRA 1.7
Crime-Scene Investigation
www.mycrimekit.com

mycrimekit

WEBEXTRA 1.8
Crime and Clues
www.mycrimekit.com

mycrimekit

WEBEXTRA 1.9
Interactive Investigator—Détective Interactif
www.mycrimekit.com

mycrimekit

WEBEXTRA 1.10
The Chemical Detective
www.mycrimekit.com

mycrimekit

WEBEXTRA 1.11
Questioned-Document Examination
www.mycrimekit.com

chapter summary   > > > > > > > > > > >

In its broadest definition, forensic science is the application of science to criminal and civil laws. This book emphasizes the application of science to the criminal and civil laws that are enforced by police agencies in a criminal justice system. Forensic science owes its origins to individuals such as Bertillon, Galton, Lattes, Goddard, Osborn, and Locard, who developed the principles and techniques needed to identify or compare physical evidence.

The development of crime laboratories in the United States has been characterized by rapid growth accompanied by a lack of national and regional planning and coordination. At present, approximately four hundred public crime laboratories

operate at various levels of government—federal, state, county, and municipal.

The technical support provided by crime laboratories can be assigned to five basic services. The physical science unit uses the principles of chemistry, physics, and geology to identify and compare physical evidence. The biology unit uses knowledge of biological sciences to investigate blood samples, body fluids, hair, and fiber samples. The firearms unit investigates discharged bullets, cartridge cases, shotgun shells, and ammunition. The document examination unit performs handwriting analysis and other questioned-document examination. Finally, the photography unit uses specialized photographic techniques to record and examine physical evidence. Some crime laboratories offer the optional services of toxicology, fingerprint analysis, polygraph administration, voiceprint analysis, and crime-scene investigation and evidence collection.

A forensic scientist must be skilled in applying the principles and techniques of the physical and natural sciences to the analysis of the many types of evidence that may be recovered during a criminal investigation. A forensic scientist may also provide expert court testimony. An expert witness is called on to evaluate evidence based on specialized training and experience and to express an opinion as to the significance of the findings. Also, forensic scientists participate in training law enforcement personnel in proper recognition, collection, and preservation of physical evidence.

The *Frye* v. *United States* decision set guidelines for determining the admissibility of scientific evidence into the courtroom. To meet the *Frye* standard, the evidence in question must be "generally accepted" by the scientific community. However, in the 1993 case of *Daubert* v. *Merrell Dow Pharmaceuticals, Inc.*, the U.S. Supreme Court asserted that the *Frye* standard is not an absolute prerequisite to the admissibility of scientific evidence. Trial judges were said to be ultimately responsible as "gatekeepers" for the admissibility and validity of scientific evidence presented in their courts.

A number of special forensic science services are available to the law enforcement community to augment the services of the crime laboratory. These services include forensic psychiatry, forensic odontology, forensic engineering, and forensic computer and digital analysis.

review questions

1. The application of science to law describes _____.

2. The fictional exploits of _____ excited the imagination of an emerging generation of forensic scientists and criminal investigators.

3. A system of personal identification using a series of body measurements was first devised by _____.

4. _____ is responsible for developing the first statistical study proving the uniqueness of fingerprints.

5. The Italian scientist _____ devised the first workable procedure for typing dried bloodstains.

6. The comparison microscope became an indispensable tool of firearms examination through the efforts of _____.

7. Early efforts at applying scientific principles to document examination are associated with _____.

8. The application of science to criminal investigation was advocated by the Austrian magistrate _____.

9. One of the first functional crime laboratories was formed in Lyons, France, under the direction of _____.

10. The transfer of evidence that occurs when two objects come in contact with one another was a concept first advocated by the forensic scientist _____.

11. The first forensic laboratory in the United States was created in 1923 by the _____ Police Department.

12. The state of _____ is an excellent example of a geographical area in the United States that has created a system of integrated regional and satellite laboratories.

13. In contrast to the United States, Britain's crime laboratory system is characterized by a national system of _____ laboratories.

14. The increasing demand for _____ analyses has been the single most important factor in the recent expansion of crime laboratory services in the United States.

15. Four important federal agencies offering forensic services are _____, _____, _____, and _____.

16. A decentralized system of crime laboratories currently exists in the United States under the auspices of various governmental agencies at the _____, _____, _____, and _____ levels of government.

17. The application of chemistry, physics, and geology to the identification and comparison of crime-scene evidence is the function of the _____ unit of a crime laboratory.

18. The examination of blood, hairs, fibers, and botanical materials is conducted in the _____ unit of a crime laboratory.

19. The examination of bullets, cartridge cases, shotgun shells, and ammunition of all types is the responsibility of the _____ unit.

20. The examination of body fluids and organs for drugs and poisons is a function of the _____ unit.

21. The _____ unit dispatches trained personnel to the scene of a crime to retrieve evidence for laboratory examination.

22. The "general acceptance" principle, which serves as a criterion for the judicial admissibility of scientific evidence, was set forth in the case of _____.

23. In the case of _____, the Supreme Court ruled that, in assessing the admissibility of new and unique scientific tests, the trial judge did not have to rely solely on the concept of "general acceptance."

24. True or False: The U.S. Supreme Court decision in *Kumho Tire Co., Ltd.* v. *Carmichael* restricted the "gate-keeping" role of a trial judge only to scientific testimony. _____

25. A Florida case that exemplifies the flexibility and wide discretion that the trial judge has in matters of scientific inquiry is _____.

26. A(n) _____ is a person who can demonstrate a particular skill or has knowledge in a trade or profession that will help the court determine the truth of the matter at issue.

27. True or False: The expert witness's courtroom demeanor may play an important role in deciding what weight the court will assign to his or her testimony. _____

28. True or False: The testimony of an expert witness incorporates his or her personal opinion relating to a matter he or she has either studied or examined. _____

29. The ability of the investigator to recognize and collect crime-scene evidence properly depends on the amount of _____ received from the crime laboratory.

application and critical thinking

1. Most crime labs in the United States are funded and operated by the government and provide services free to police and prosecutors. Great Britain, however, uses a quasi-governmental agency that charges fees for its services and keeps any profits it makes. Suggest potential strengths and weaknesses of each system.

2. Police investigating an apparent suicide collect the following items at the scene: a note purportedly written by the victim, a revolver bearing very faint fingerprints, and traces of skin and blood under the victim's fingernails. What units of the crime laboratory will examine each piece of evidence?

3. List at least three advantages of having an evidence-collection unit process a crime scene instead of a patrol officer or detective.

4. What legal issue was raised on appeal by the defense in Carl Coppolino's Florida murder trial? What court ruling is most relevant to the decision to reject the appeal? Explain your answer.

further references

Berg, Stanton O., "Sherlock Holmes: Father of Scientific Crime Detection," *Journal of Criminal Law, Criminology and Police Science* 61, no. 3 (1970): 446–52.

Cohen, Stanley A., "The Role of the Forensic Expert in a Criminal Trial," *Canadian Society of Forensic Science Journal* 12 (1979): 75.

Doyle, Sir Arthur Conan, *The Complete Sherlock Holmes*, vol. 1. New York: Doubleday, 1956.

Gallop, A. M. C., "Forensic Science Coming of Age," *Science & Justice*, 43 (2003): 55.

James, S. H., and Nordby, J. J., eds., *Forensic Science—An Introduction to Scientific and Investigative Techniques*, 3rd ed. Boca Raton, Fla.: CRC Press, 2009.

Kagan, J. D., "On Being a Good Expert Witness in a Criminal Case," *Journal of Forensic Sciences* 23 (1978): 190.

Lucas, D. M., "North of 49—The Development of Forensic Science in Canada," *Science & Justice*, 37 (1997): 47.

Midkiff, C. R., "More Mountebanks," in R. Saferstein, ed., *Forensic Science Handbook*, vol. 2, 2nd ed. Upper Saddle River, N.J.: Prentice Hall, 2005.

National Research Council, *Strengthening Forensic Science in the United States: A Path Forward,* Washington, D.C.: The National Academies Press, 2009, http://books.nap.edu/openbook.php?record_id=12589&page=R1

Sapir, Gil I., "Legal Aspects of Forensic Science," in R. Saferstein, ed., *Forensic Science Handbook*, vol. 1, 2nd ed. Upper Saddle River, N.J.: Prentice Hall, 2002.

Starrs, James E., "Mountebanks among Forensic Scientists," in R. Saferstein, ed., *Forensic Science Handbook*, vol. 2, 2nd ed. Upper Saddle River, N.J.: Prentice Hall, 2005.

Waggoner, Kim. "The FBI Laboratory: 75 Years of Forensic Science Service," *Forensic Science Communications*, 9, no. 4 (2007). www.fbi.gov/hq/lab/fsc/backissu/oct2007/research/2007_10_research01_test1.htm

JonBenet Ramsey: Who Did It?

Patsy Ramsey awoke just after five A.M. on December 26, 1996, and walked downstairs to her kitchen. At the foot of the staircase, she found a two-and-a-half-page note saying that her 6-year-old daughter, JonBenet, had been kidnapped. The note contained a ransom demand of $118,000. Patsy and John Ramsey were in the upper crust of Boulder, Colorado, society. In the span of five short years, John had built his computer company into a billion-dollar corporation. When the police arrived to investigate, it was quite apparent to all that JonBenet was missing. In retrospect, some serious mistakes were made in securing the crime scene—the Ramsey household. Initially, the police conducted a cursory search of the house, but failed to find JonBenet. The house was not sealed off; in fact, four friends along with the Ramsey pastor were let into the home and allowed to move about at will. John was permitted to leave the premises unattended for one and a half hours. One hour after his return, John and two of his friends searched the house again. This time John went down into the basement, where he discovered JonBenet's body. He removed a white blanket from JonBenet and carried her upstairs, placing the body on the living room floor.

The murder of JonBenet Ramsey remains as baffling a mystery today as it was on its first day. Ample physical evidence exists to support the theory that the crime was committed by an outsider, and also that JonBenet was murdered by someone who resided in the Ramsey household. Twelve years after the commission of the crime, Boulder district attorney Mary T. Lacy issued a statement exonerating members of the Ramsey family on the basis of DNA evidence. Perhaps better care in securing and processing the crime scene could have resolved some of the crime's outstanding questions. A more detailed analysis of this crime can be found on pages 288–291.

the crime scene

KEY TERMS

buccal swab
chain of custody
finished sketch
physical evidence
rough sketch
standard/reference
  sample
substrate control

Learning Objectives

After studying this chapter you should be able to:

- Define physical evidence

- Discuss the responsibilities of the first police officer who arrives at a crime scene

- Explain the steps to be taken to thoroughly record the crime scene

- Describe proper procedures for conducting a systematic search of a crime scene for physical evidence

- Describe proper techniques for packaging common types of physical evidence

- Define and understand the concept of chain of custody

- Relate what steps are typically required to maintain appropriate health and safety standards at the crime scene

- Understand the implications of the *Mincey* and *Tyler* cases

Processing the Crime Scene

As automobiles run on gasoline, crime laboratories "run" on **physical evidence**. Physical evidence encompasses any and all objects that can establish that a crime has or has not been committed or can link a crime and its victim or its perpetrator. But if physical evidence is to be used effectively to aid the investigator, its presence first must be recognized at the crime scene. If all the natural and commercial objects within a reasonable distance of a crime were gathered so that the scientist could uncover significant clues from them, the deluge of material would quickly immobilize the laboratory facility. Physical evidence can achieve its optimum value in criminal investigations only when its collection is performed with a selectivity governed by the collector's thorough knowledge of the crime laboratory's techniques, capabilities, and limitations.

Forthcoming chapters will be devoted to discussions of methods and techniques available to forensic scientists to evaluate physical evidence. Although current technology has given the crime laboratory capabilities far exceeding those of past decades, these advances are no excuse for complacency on the part of criminal investigators. Crime laboratories do not solve crimes; only a thorough and competent investigation conducted by professional police officers will enhance the chances for a successful criminal investigation. Forensic science is, and will continue to be, an important element of the total investigative process, but it is only one aspect of an endeavor that must be a team effort. The investigator who believes the crime laboratory to be a panacea for laxity or ineptness is in for a rude awakening.

Forensic science begins at the crime scene. If the investigator cannot recognize physical evidence or cannot properly preserve it for laboratory examination, no amount of sophisticated laboratory instrumentation or technical expertise can salvage the situation. The know-how for conducting a proper crime-scene search for physical evidence is within the grasp of any police department, regardless of its size. With proper training, police agencies can ensure competent performance at crime scenes. In many jurisdictions, police agencies have delegated this task to a specialized team of technicians. However, the techniques of crime-scene investigation are not difficult to master and certainly lie within the bounds of comprehension of the average police officer.

Not all crime scenes require retrieval of physical evidence, and limited resources and personnel have forced many police agencies to restrict their efforts in this area to crimes of a more serious nature. Once the commitment is made to completely process a crime site for physical evidence, however, certain fundamental practices must be followed.

Securing and Isolating the Crime Scene

The first officer arriving on the scene of a crime is responsible for preserving and protecting the area as much as possible. The officer should not let his or her guard down and must rely on his or her training to deal with any violent or hazardous circumstances. Special note should be taken of any vehicles or people leaving the scene.

Of course, first priority should be given to obtaining medical assistance for individuals in need of it and to arresting the perpetrator. However, as soon as possible, extensive efforts must be made to exclude all unauthorized personnel from the scene. If medical assistance is needed, the officer should direct medical workers to approach the body by an indirect route to minimize the possibility of disturbing evidence. The first responding officer must evaluate the victim's condition and record any statements made by the victim. This information should later be included in notes.

As additional officers arrive, measures are immediately initiated to isolate the area. See Figure 2–1. The boundaries should encompass the center of the scene where the crime occurred, any paths of entry or exit, and any areas where evidence may have been discarded or moved. Ropes or barricades along with strategic positioning of guards will prevent unauthorized access to the area. Efforts must be taken to identify all individuals at the scene and detain all potential suspects or witnesses still at the scene. At the same time, officers should exclude all unauthorized personnel from the scene. This includes family and friends of the victim, who should be shown as much compassion as possible. Only investigative personnel assigned to the scene should be admitted. The responding officers must keep an accurate log of who enters and exits the scene and the time at which they do so.

Sometimes the exclusion of unauthorized personnel proves more difficult than expected. Violent crimes are especially susceptible to attention from higher-level police officials and members

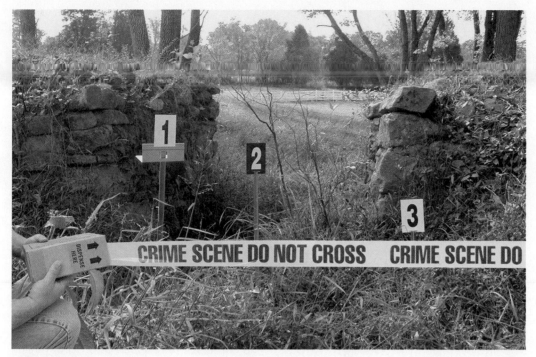

FIGURE 2–1

The first investigators to arrive must secure the crime scene and establish the crime-scene perimeter.

Courtesy Sirchie Finger Print Laboratories, Inc., Youngsville, N.C., www.sirchie.com

of the press, as well as by emotionally charged neighbors and curiosity seekers. Every individual who enters the scene is a potential destroyer of physical evidence, even if it is by unintentional carelessness. To exercise proper control over the crime scene, the officer responsible for protecting it must have the authority to exclude everyone, including fellow police officers not directly involved in processing the site or in conducting the investigation. Seasoned criminal investigators are always prepared to relate horror stories about crime scenes where physical evidence was rendered totally valueless by hordes of people who, for one reason or another, trampled through the site. Securing and isolating the crime scene are critical steps in an investigation, the accomplishment of which is the mark of a trained and professional crime-scene investigative team.

Once the scene has been secured, a lead investigator starts evaluating the area. First, he or she determines the boundaries of the scene and then establishes the perpetrator's path of entry and exit. Logic dictates that obvious items of crime-scene evidence will first come to the attention of the crime-scene investigator. These items must be documented and photographed. The investigator then proceeds with an initial walk-through of the scene to gain an overview of the situation and develop a strategy for systematically examining and documenting the entire crime scene.

Personnel should *never* do anything while at the crime scene—including smoking, eating, drinking, and littering—that may alter the scene. No aspects of the scene, including a body at a death scene, should be moved or disturbed unless they pose a serious threat to investigating officers or bystanders. This means that no one should open or close faucets or flush toilets at the scene. Also, officers should avoid altering temperature conditions at the scene by adjusting windows, doors, or the heating or air conditioning.

Recording the Crime Scene

Investigators have only a limited amount of time to work a crime site in its untouched state. The opportunity to permanently record the scene in its original state must not be lost. Such records not only will prove useful during the subsequent investigation but are also required for presentation at a trial in order to document the condition of the crime site and to delineate the location of physical evidence. Notes, photography, and sketches are the three methods for crime-scene recording (see Figure 2–2). Ideally all three should be employed; however, personnel and

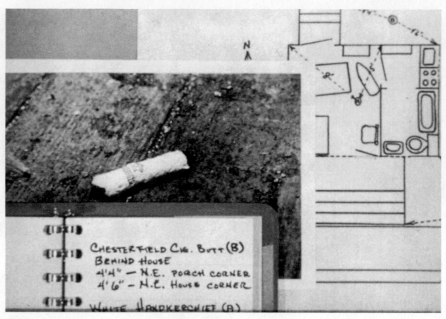

FIGURE 2–2

The finding of an evidential cigarette butt at the crime scene requires photographing it, making a sketch showing its relation to the crime scene, and recording the find in field notes.
Courtesy Police Science Services, Niles, Ill.

monetary limitations often prohibit the use of photography at every crime site. Under these circumstances, departmental guidelines will establish priorities for deploying photographic resources. However, there is no reason not to make sketches and notes at the crime scene.

NOTES   The note-taking process begins with the call to a crime-scene investigator to report to a scene. The notes should start by identifying the person who contacted the investigator, the time of the contact, and any preliminary information disclosed, including the case number. When the lead investigator arrives, the note taker should record the date and time of arrival, who is present, and the identities of any other personnel who are being contacted. If additional personnel are contacted, their names, titles, and time of arrival should be recorded. Investigators must keep a precise record of personnel movements in and out of the scene, beginning with an interview of the first responding officer in order to record his or her movements. It is also important to record the tasks assigned to each member of a team, as well as the beginning and ending times for the processing of the scene.

Before the scene is sketched, photographed, or searched, the lead investigator carries out the initial walk-through. During this walk-through, the investigator should take notes on many aspects of the crime scene in its original condition. These notes should be uniform in layout for all cases. The notes should be in ink (preferably black or blue) and written in a bound notebook. Most important, notes should be written at the time of the crime-scene investigation, not left to memory to record later.

Once a search for evidence has taken place, the team members mark the location of all evidence and fully describe each item in their notes. If a victim is present at a homicide scene, the investigator should observe and record the state of the body before the medical examiner or coroner moves it. Any preliminary identification of a victim or suspect should be recorded.

Tape-recording notes at a scene can be advantageous—detailed notes can be taped much faster than they can be written. This may also leave hands free to carry out other tasks while recording the notes. Audiotapes have the added security feature of preventing erasure or taping over if the security tab on the tape is removed. However, care must be taken to avoid embarrassing conversation on tapes that will be used as evidence in a trial. Some investigators may use digital voice recorders to record their notes. These recordings are easily uploaded to a computer, but they must be copied to a disk to produce a hard copy. Another method of recording notes is by narrating a videotape of the crime scene. This has the advantage of combining note-taking with photography. However, at some point the tape must be transcribed into a written document.

PHOTOGRAPHY The most important prerequisite for photographing a crime scene is for it to be unaltered. Unless injured people are involved, objects must not be moved until they have been photographed from all necessary angles. If objects are removed, positions changed, or items added, the photographs may not be admissible as evidence at a trial, and their intended value will be lost. If evidence has been moved or removed before photography, the fact should be noted in the report, but the evidence should not be reintroduced into the scene in order to take photographs.

Crime-scene photographs have great value in their ability to show the layout of the scene, the position of evidence to be collected, and the relation of objects at the scene to one another. Photographs taken from many angles can show possible lines of sight of victims, suspects, or witnesses. An accurate description of the scene must be available to investigators for future analysis. Photography is also important for documenting biological evidence in its original condition, as this kind of evidence is often altered during testing. Photographs cannot stand alone, however, and they are complementary to notes and sketches.

FIGURE 2–3

An example of a digital single lens reflex (DSLR) camera.
Courtesy Sony Electronics Inc.

Currently there are two approaches to crime-scene photography: film and digital photography. Obvious differences exist between the ways film and digital imaging technology record scenes, notably the methods by which each type of photography converts light into an image. Photographic film consists of a sheet of light-reactive silver halide grains and comes in several varieties. A digital photograph is made when a light-sensitive microchip inside the camera is exposed to light coming from the object or scene to be captured. The light is recorded on millions of tiny picture elements, or *pixels*, as a specific electric charge. The camera reads this charge number as image information, then stores the image as a file on a memory card. Most modern crime-scene investigators use a digital camera, such as the digital single-lens reflex camera in Figure 2–3, to document crime scenes, and digital photography is rapidly becoming the method of choice in the field of forensic science.

The nature of digital images, however, opens digital photography to important criticisms within forensic science casework. Because the photographs are digital, they can be easily manipulated by using computer software. This manipulation goes beyond traditional photograph enhancement such as adjusting brightness and contrast or color balancing. Because the main function of crime-scene photography is to provide an accurate depiction, this is a major concern. To ensure that their digital images are admissible, many jurisdictions set guidelines for determining the circumstances under which digital photography may be used and establish and enforce strict protocols for image security and chain of custody.

Photographic Procedures Each crime scene should be photographed as completely as possible. This means that the crime scene should include the area in which the crime took place and all adjacent areas where important acts occurred immediately before or after the commission of the crime. Overview photographs of the entire scene and surrounding area, including points of exit and entry, must be taken from various angles. If the crime took place indoors, the entire room should be photographed to show each wall area. Rooms adjacent to the actual crime site must be similarly photographed. If the crime scene includes a body, photographs must be taken to show the body's position and location relative to the entire scene. Close-up photos depicting injuries and weapons lying near the body are also necessary (see Figure 2–4). After the body is removed from the scene, the surface beneath the body should be photographed.

As items of physical evidence are discovered, they are photographed to show their position and location relative to the entire scene. After these overviews are taken, close-ups should be taken to record the details of the object itself. When the size of an item is of significance, a ruler or other measuring scale may be inserted near the object and included in the photograph as a point of reference. The digital revolution promises to bring enhanced photographic capabilities to the crime scene. For example, individual images of the crime scene captured with a digital camera can be stitched together electronically to reveal a near three-dimensional panoramic view of the crime scene (see Figure 2–5).

mycrimekit

WEBEXTRA 2.1
Making a Photographic Record of the Crime Scene
www.mycrimekit.com

(a)

(b)

(c)

FIGURE 2–4

This sequence of crime-scene photographs shows the proper progression of photographing the scene. (a) The sequence begins with an overview photograph of the entry to the victim's bedroom showing evidence markers in place. (b) The medium-range photograph shows the evidence marker next to the door denoting a cartridge case. (c) The close-up photograph shows the cartridge in detail with a scale in the photograph.

FIGURE 2–5

Individual images (top) are shown before being electronically stitched together into a single panoramic image (bottom). Individual photographs should be taken with about a 30 percent overlap.

Courtesy Imaging Forensics, Fountain Valley, Calif., www.imagingforensics.com

FIGURE 2–6

A computer-controlled scanner has both a high-resolution, professional digital camera and a long-range laser rangefinder. The tripod-mounted device rotates a full 360 degrees, taking dozens of photographs and measuring millions of individual points. Photographic and laser data from multiple scan locations are combined to produce 3D models of the scene.

Courtesy 3rd Tech, Inc., Durham, N.C. 27713, www.deltasphere.com

The digital era promises new and elegant approaches to document the crime scene. Cameras such as that shown in Figure 2–6 are capable of taking dozens of digital images while scanning the crime scene. Photographic and laser data from multiple scan locations are combined to produce 3-D models of the scene in full color that can be viewed from any vantage point, measured, and used for analysis and courtroom presentations.

Video Recording   The use of videotape or digital video at crime scenes is becoming increasingly popular because the cost of this equipment is decreasing. The same principles used in crime-scene photographs apply to videotaping or digital video. As with conventional photography, videotaping or digital video should include the entire scene and the immediate surrounding area. Long shots as well as close-ups should be taken in a slow and systematic manner. Furthermore, it is desirable to have one crime-scene investigator narrate the events and scenes being recorded while another does the shooting.

Videotaping or digital video can have advantages over still photography in certain situations. For example, modern video cameras allow the user to play back recordings of a scene and check it for completeness. In addition, many video cameras can also take still photographs, or stills can be created from the tape on a computer. Video essentially combines notes and photography. Some cameras even have a "night vision" feature, which is similar to infrared photography.

There are also disadvantages to video recording crime scenes. The camera will always shake, zooming and panning can be sloppy, and extra noise can obscure narration or may be inappropriate and damaging. Still images taken from video recordings are usually of much poorer quality than those taken by film or digital camera. Videotape, if used, also deteriorates because the tape is sensitive, and it can be affected by high temperatures, humidity, and magnetic fields.

Although video recording can capture the sounds and scenes of the crime site with relative ease, the technique cannot at this time be used in place of still photography. The still photograph remains unsurpassed in the definition of detail it provides to the human eye.

SKETCHES   Once photographs have been taken, the crime-scene investigator sketches the scene. The sketch serves many important functions in the legal investigation of a crime. If done correctly, a sketch can clearly show the layout of an indoor or outdoor crime scene and the relationship in space of all the items and features significant to the investigation. Sketches are especially important to illustrate the location of collected evidence. Possible paths of entry, exit, and movement through the scene may be speculated from a good sketch.

The investigator may have neither the skill nor the time to make a polished sketch of the scene. However, this is not required during the early phase of the investigation. What is necessary is a **rough sketch** containing an accurate depiction of the dimensions of the scene and showing

mycrimekit

WEBEXTRA 2.2
Three-Dimensional Crime-Scene Imaging
www.mycrimekit.com

rough sketch
A draft representation of all essential information and measurements at a crime scene; this sketch is drawn at the crime scene

FIGURE 2–7

A basic kit for sketching the crime scene.
Courtesy Sirchie Finger Print Laboratories, Youngsville, N.C., www.sirchie.com

the location of all objects having a bearing on the case. This may be achieved through the use of a sketching kit like the one shown in Figure 2–7.

A rough sketch is illustrated in Figure 2–8. It shows all recovered items of physical evidence as well as other important features of the crime scene. Objects are located in the sketch by distance measurements from two fixed points, such as the walls of a room. Distances shown on the sketch must be accurate and not the result of a guess or estimate. For this reason, all measurements are made with a tape measure. The simplest way to designate an item in a sketch is to assign it a number or letter. A legend or list placed below the sketch then correlates the letter to the item's description. The sketch should also show a compass heading designating north as well as a title block designating the location of the crime scene and any case information.

finished sketch
A precise rendering of the crime scene, usually drawn to scale

Unlike the rough sketch, the **finished sketch** in Figure 2–9 is constructed with care and concern for aesthetic appearance. When the finished sketch is completed, it must reflect information contained within the rough sketch in order to be admissible evidence in a courtroom. Computer-aided drafting (CAD) has become the norm to reconstruct crime scenes from rough sketches. The software, ranging from simple, low-cost programs to complex, expensive programs, contains predrawn intersections and roadways or buildings and rooms onto which information can be entered (see Figure 2–10). A generous symbol library provides the operator with a variety of images that can be used to add intricate details such as blood spatters to a crime-scene sketch. Equipped with a zoom function, computerized sketching can focus on a specific area for a more detailed picture. CAD programs allow the operator to select scale size so that the ultimate product can be produced in a size suitable for courtroom presentation.

Conducting a Systematic Search for Evidence

The search for physical evidence at a crime scene must be thorough and systematic. For a factual, unbiased reconstruction of the crime, the investigator, relying on his or her training and experience, must not overlook any pertinent evidence. Even when suspects are immediately seized and the motives and circumstances of the crime are readily apparent, a thorough search for physical evidence must be conducted at once. Failure in this, even though it may seem unnecessary, can lead to accusations of negligence or charges that the investigative agency knowingly "covered up" evidence that would be detrimental to its case.

CASE: 10-789-96
301 N. CENTRE ST.
OCT. 6, 1996   11:40 PM
HOMICIDE

VICTIM: LESTER W. BROWN
INVESTIGATOR: SGT. L.A. DUTTY
ASS'T BY: PTLM. R.W. HICKS

BOOK CASE
F
8'-1"
4'-3"
4'-10"
4'-6"
7'-7"
1'-18"
9'-4"
4'-2"
5-7"
5'-1"
C
E
E
E
26'-0
COUCH
TABLE
A
FIRE PLACE
5'-9"
DESK
B
7'-4"
2'-2"
4'-0
LAMP
TABLE
CHAIR
3'-3"
2'-0
BOOK CASE
D
6'-5"   1'-10½"
1-9'-10"

LEGEND
A = COCKTAIL GLASS
B = TELEPHONE
C = VICTIM
D = BULLET HOLE
E = BLOOD STAINS
F = SHELL CASING
▲ = CAMERA LOCATIONS

* D 3'-4¾" FROM FLOOR

¼" = 1 FOOT

FIGURE 2–8

Rough-sketch diagram of a crime scene.
Courtesy Sirchie Finger Print Laboratories, Youngsville, N.C., www.sirchie.com

FIGURE 2–9

Finished-sketch diagram of a crime scene.
Courtesy Sirchie Finger Print Laboratories, Youngsville, N.C., www.sirchie.com

Assigning those responsible for searching a crime scene is a function of the investigator in charge. Except in major crimes, or when the evidence is complex, the assistance of a forensic scientist at the crime scene is usually not necessary; his or her role appropriately begins when evidence is submitted to the crime laboratory. As has already been observed, some police agencies have trained field evidence technicians to search for physical evidence at the crime scene. They have the equipment and skill to photograph the scene and examine it for the presence of fingerprints, footprints, tool marks, or any other type of evidence that may be relevant to the crime.

SEARCH PATTERNS   How one conducts a crime-scene search will depend on the locale and size of the area, as well as on the actions of the suspect(s) and victim(s) at the scene. When possible, one person should supervise and coordinate the collection of evidence. Without proper control, the search may be conducted in an atmosphere of confusion with needless duplication of effort. The various search patterns that may be used can be observed in Figure 2–11.

FIGURE 2–10

Construction of a crime-scene diagram with the aid of a computer-aided drafting program.
Courtesy Sirchie Finger Print Laboratories, Youngsville, N.C., www.sirchie.com

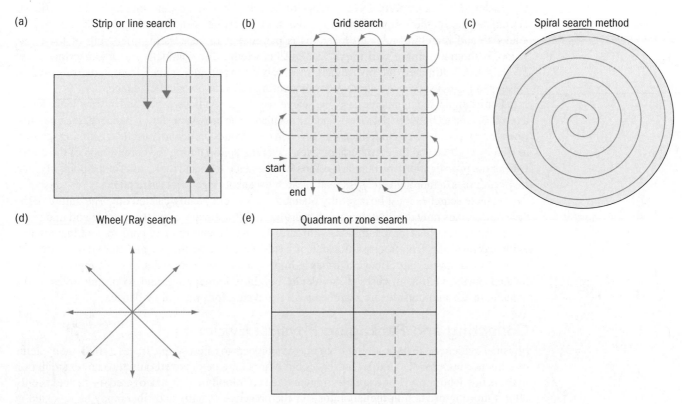

FIGURE 2–11

(a) Strip or line search pattern. (b) Grid search pattern. (c) Spiral search pattern.
(d) Wheel or ray search pattern. (e) Quadrant or zone search pattern.

Strip or Line Search Pattern   In the line or strip method, one or two investigators start at the boundary at one end of the scene and walk straight across to the other side. They then move a little farther along the border and walk straight back to the other side. This method is best used in scenes where the boundaries are well established because the boundaries dictate the beginning and end of the search lines. If the boundary is incorrectly chosen, important evidence may remain undiscovered outside the search area.

Grid Search Pattern   The grid method employs two people performing line searches that originate from adjacent corners and form perpendicular lines. This method is very thorough, but the boundaries must be well established in order to use this method as well.

Spiral Search Pattern   The spiral search pattern usually employs one person. The investigator moves either in an inward spiral from the boundary to the center of the scene or in an outward spiral from the center to the boundary. The inward spiral method is helpful because the searcher is moving from an area light with evidence to an area where more evidence will most likely be found. With either spiral approach the searcher can easily locate footprints leading away from the scene in any direction. However, completing a perfect spiral is often difficult, and evidence could be missed.

Wheel or Ray Search Pattern   The wheel or ray method employs several people moving from the boundary straight toward the center of the scene (inward) or from the center straight to the boundary (outward). This method is not preferred because the areas between the "rays" are not searched.

Quadrant or Zone Search Pattern   The quadrant or zone method divides the scene into zones or quadrants, and team members are assigned to search each section. Each of these sections can be subdivided into smaller sections for smaller teams to search thoroughly. This method is best suited for scenes that cover a large area. The areas searched must include all probable points of entry and exit used by the criminals.

LOCATING PHYSICAL EVIDENCE   What to search for will be determined by the particular circumstances of the crime. Obviously, the skill of crime-scene investigators at recognizing evidence and searching relevant locations is paramount to successful processing of the crime scene. Although training will impart general knowledge for conducting a proper crime-scene investigation, ultimately the investigator must rely on experience gained from numerous investigations to form a successful strategy for recovering relevant physical evidence.

For example, in a homicide case, the search will center on the weapon and any evidence left as a result of contact between the victim and the assailant. The cross-transfer of evidence, such as hairs, fibers, and blood, between individuals involved in the crime is particularly useful for linking suspects to the crime scene and for corroborating events that transpired during the commission of the crime. During the investigation of a burglary, efforts will be made to locate tool marks at the point of entry. In most crimes, a thorough and systematic search for latent fingerprints is required.

Vehicle searches must be carefully planned and systematically carried out. The nature of the case determines how detailed the search must be. In hit-and-run cases, the outside and undercarriage of the car must be examined with care. Particular attention is paid to looking for any evidence resulting from a cross-transfer of evidence between the car and the victim—this includes blood, tissue, hair, fibers, and fabric impressions. Traces of paint or broken glass may be located on the victim. In cases of homicide, burglary, kidnapping, and so on, all areas of the vehicle, inside and outside, are searched with equal care for physical evidence.

Collecting and Packaging Physical Evidence

Physical evidence can be anything from massive objects to microscopic traces. Often, many items of evidence are obvious in their presence, but others may be detected only through examination in the crime laboratory. For example, minute traces of blood may be discovered on garments only after a thorough search in the laboratory, or the presence of hairs and fibers may be revealed in vacuum sweepings or on garments only after close laboratory scrutiny. For this reason, it is important to collect possible carriers of trace evidence in addition to more discernible items. Hence, it may be necessary to take custody of all clothing worn by the participants in a crime.

COLLECTING PHYSICAL EVIDENCE   Each clothing item should be handled carefully and wrapped separately to avoid loss of trace materials. Critical areas of the crime scene should be

(a)   (b)

FIGURE 2–12

Vacuum sweeper attachment, constructed of clear plastic in two pieces that are joined by a threaded joint. A metal screen is mounted in one half to support a filter paper to collect debris. The unit attaches to the hose of the vacuum sweeper. After a designated area of the crime scene is vacuumed, the filter paper is removed and retained for laboratory examination.

Courtesy Sirchie Finger Print Laboratories, Youngsville, N.C., www.sirchie.com

vacuumed and the sweepings submitted to the laboratory for analysis. The sweepings from different areas must be collected and packaged separately. A portable vacuum cleaner equipped with a special filter attachment is suitable for this purpose (see Figure 2–12). Additionally, fingernail scrapings from individuals who were in contact with other individuals may contain minute fragments of evidence capable of linking the assailant and victim. The undersurface of each nail is best scraped with a dull object such as a toothpick to avoid cutting the skin. These scrapings will be subjected to microscopic examination in the laboratory.

The search for physical evidence must extend beyond the crime scene to the autopsy room of a deceased victim. Here, the medical examiner or coroner carefully examines the victim to establish a cause and manner of death. Tissues and organs are routinely retained for pathological and toxicological examination. At the same time, arrangements must be made between the examiner and investigator to secure a variety of items that may be obtainable from the body for laboratory examination. The following are to be collected and sent to the forensic laboratory:

1. Victim's clothing
2. Fingernail scrapings
3. Head and pubic hairs
4. Blood (for DNA typing purposes)
5. Vaginal, anal, and oral swabs (in sex-related crimes)
6. Recovered bullets from the body
7. Hand swabs from shooting victims (for gunshot residue analysis)

Once the body is buried, efforts at obtaining these items may prove difficult or futile. Furthermore, a lengthy time delay in obtaining many of these items will diminish or destroy their forensic value.

In recent years, many police departments have gone to the expense of purchasing and equipping "mobile crime laboratories" (see Figure 2–13) for their evidence technicians. However, the term *mobile crime laboratory* is a misnomer. These vehicles carry the necessary supplies to protect the crime scene; photograph, collect, and package physical evidence; and perform latent print development. They are not designed to carry out the functions of a chemical laboratory. *Crime-scene search vehicle* would be a more appropriate but perhaps less dramatic name for such a vehicle.

HANDLING EVIDENCE Investigators must handle and process physical evidence in a way that prevents any change from taking place between the time the evidence is removed from the crime scene and the time it is received by the crime laboratory. Changes can arise through contamination, breakage, evaporation, accidental scratching or bending, or improper or careless packaging.

(a)

(b)

FIGURE 2–13

Inside view of a mobile crime-scene van: (a) driver's side and (b) passenger's side.
Courtesy Sirchie Finger Print Laboratories, Inc., Youngsville, N.C., www.sirchie.com

The use of latex gloves or disposable forceps when touching evidence often can prevent such problems. Any equipment that is not disposable should be cleaned and/or sanitized between collecting each piece of evidence. Evidence should remain unmoved until investigators have documented its location and appearance in notes, sketches, and photographs.

Evidence best maintains its integrity when kept in its original condition as found at the crime site. Whenever possible, one should submit evidence to the laboratory intact. The investigator normally should not remove blood, hairs, fibers, soil particles, and other types of trace evidence from garments, weapons, or other articles that bear them. Instead, he or she should send the entire object to the laboratory for processing.

Of course, if evidence is adhering to an object in a precarious manner, good judgment dictates removing and packaging the item. Use common sense when handling evidence adhering to a large structure, such as a door, wall, or floor; remove the specimen with a forceps or other appropriate tool. In the case of a bloodstain, one may either scrape the stain off the surface, transfer the stain to a moistened swab, or cut out the area of the object bearing the stain.

PACKAGING EVIDENCE   The well-prepared evidence collector arrives at a crime scene with a large assortment of packaging materials and tools, ready to encounter any type of situation. Forceps and similar tools may be used to pick up small items. Unbreakable plastic pill bottles with pressure lids are excellent containers for hairs, glass, fibers, and various other kinds of small or trace evidence. Alternatively, manila envelopes, screw-cap glass vials, sealable plastic bags, or metal pillboxes are adequate containers for most trace evidence encountered at crime sites (see Figure 2–14). Charred debris recovered from the scene of a suspicious fire must be sealed in an

(a)

(b)

(c)

FIGURE 2–14

(a) Manila evidence envelope. (b) Metal pillboxes. (c) Sealable plastic evidence bag.
Courtesy Sirchie Finger Print Laboratories, Youngsville, N.C., www.sirchie.com

FIGURE 2–15

Airtight metal cans used to package arson evidence.
Courtesy Sirchie Finger Print Laboratories, Youngsville, N.C., www.sirchie.com

airtight container to prevent the evaporation of volatile petroleum residues. New paint cans or tightly sealed jars are recommended in such situations (see Figure 2–15).

One should not use ordinary mailing envelopes as evidence containers because powders and fine particles will leak out of their corners. Instead, small amounts of trace evidence can be conveniently packaged in a carefully folded paper, using what is known as a "druggist fold" (see Figure 2–16). This consists of folding one end of the paper over by one-third, then folding the other end (one-third) over that, and repeating the process from the other two sides. After folding the paper in this manner, tuck the outside two edges into each other to produce a closed container that keeps the specimen from falling out.

Place each different item or similar items collected at different locations in separate containers. Packaging evidence separately prevents damage through contact and prevents cross-contamination.

Biological Materials Use only disposable tools to collect biological materials for packaging. If biological materials are stored in airtight containers, the accumulation of moisture may

FIGURE 2–16

A druggist fold is used to package paint transfer evidence.

Courtesy Sirchie Finger Print Laboratories, Youngsville, N.C., www.sirchie.com

FIGURE 2–17

Paper bags are recommended evidence containers for objects suspected of containing blood and semen stains. Each object should be packaged in a separate bag.

Courtesy Sirchie Finger Print Laboratories, Youngsville, N.C., www.sirchie.com

encourage the growth of mold, which can destroy the evidential value of blood. In these instances, wrapping paper, manila envelopes, or paper bags are recommended packaging materials (see Figure 2–17). As a matter of routine, air-dry all items possibly containing biological fluid evidence and place them individually in separate paper bags to ensure a constant circulation of air through them. This will prevent the formation of mold and mildew. Paper packaging is easily written on, but seals may not be sturdy.

The evidence collector must handle all body fluids and biologically stained materials with a minimum of personal contact. All body fluids must be assumed to be infectious, so investigators must wear disposable latex gloves while handling the evidence. Latex gloves also significantly reduce the possibility that the evidence collector will contaminate the evidence. Investigators should change gloves frequently while collecting evidence. Safety considerations and avoidance of contamination also dictate that evidence collectors wear face masks and shoe covers.

DNA Evidence   The advent of DNA analysis is one of the most significant recent advances in crime-scene investigation. This technique is valuable in its ability to identify suspects by detecting and analyzing minute quantities of DNA deposited on evidence as a result of contact with saliva, sweat, or skin cells. The search for evidence should include all objects with which the suspect or victim may have come into bodily contact because DNA evidence may be present on the object. Likely sources of DNA evidence include stamps and envelopes licked with saliva, a cup or can that has touched a person's lips, chewing gum, the sweatband of a hat, and a bedsheet containing dead skin cells.

One key concern during the collection of a DNA-containing specimen is contamination. Contamination can occur by introducing foreign DNA through coughing or sneezing onto evidence during the collection process. Transfer of DNA can also occur when items of evidence are incorrectly placed in contact with each other during packaging. The evidence collector must take extraordinary care to avoid potential contamination from transferring DNA onto objects of evidential value. To prevent contamination, the evidence collector must wear a face mask and use disposable latex gloves and disposable forceps. The evidence collector may also consider wearing coveralls and shoe covers as an extra precaution to avoid contaminating DNA evidence.

Blood has great evidential value when the investigator can demonstrate a transfer between a victim and a suspect. For this reason, all clothing from both the victim and suspect should be collected and sent to the laboratory for examination, even when the presence of blood on a garment does not appear obvious to the investigator. Laboratory search procedures are far more revealing and sensitive than any that can be conducted at the crime scene.

Proper collection and packaging of various types of physical evidence will be discussed in detail in forthcoming chapters; additionally, most of this information is summarized in the evidence guide found in Appendix I.

Maintaining the Chain of Custody

Continuity of possession, or the **chain of custody**, must be established whenever evidence is presented in court as an exhibit. Adherence to standard procedures in recording the location of evidence, marking it for identification, and properly completing evidence submission forms for laboratory analysis is the best guarantee that the evidence will withstand inquiries of what happened to it from the time of its finding to its presentation in court. This means that every person who handled or examined the evidence must be accounted for. Failure to substantiate the evidence's chain of custody may lead to serious questions regarding the authenticity and integrity of the evidence and examinations of it.

All items of physical evidence should be carefully packaged and marked upon their retrieval at crime sites. This should be done with the utmost care to avoid destroying their evidential value or restricting the number and kind of examinations to which the criminalist may subject them. If possible, the evidence itself should be marked for identification. Normally, the collector's initials and the date of collection are inscribed directly on the article. However, if the evidence collector is unsure of the necessity of marking the item itself or of where to mark it, it is best to omit this step. Once an evidence container is selected for the evidence, whether a box, bag, vial, or can, it also must be marked for identification. Evidence containers often have a preprinted identification form that the evidence collector fills out. Otherwise, the collector must attach an evidence tag to the container. The investigator who packaged the evidence must write his or her initials and the date on the evidence tape seal. Anyone who removes the evidence for further testing or observation at a later time should try to avoid breaking the original seal if possible so that the information on the seal will not be lost. The person who reseals the packaging should record his or her initials and the date on the new seal.

A minimum chain-of-custody record would show the collector's initials, location of the evidence, and date of collection. If the evidence is turned over to another individual for care or delivery to the laboratory, this transfer must be recorded in notes and other appropriate forms. In fact, every individual who possesses the evidence must maintain a written record of its acquisition and disposition. Frequently, all of the individuals involved in the collection and transportation of the evidence may be requested to testify in court. Thus, to avoid confusion and to retain complete control of the evidence at all times, the chain of custody should be kept to a minimum.

Obtaining Standard/Reference Samples

The examination of evidence, whether soil, blood, glass, hair, fibers, and so on, often requires comparison with a known **standard/reference sample**. Although most investigators have little difficulty recognizing and collecting relevant crime-scene evidence, few seem aware of the necessity and importance of providing the crime lab with a thorough sampling of standard/reference materials. Such materials may be obtained from the victim, a suspect, or other known sources. For instance, investigation of a hit-and-run incident may require the removal of standard/reference paint from a suspect vehicle. This will permit its comparison to paint recovered at the scene. Similarly, hair found at the crime scene will be of optimum value only when compared to standard/reference

chain of custody
A list of all people who came into possession of an item of evidence

standard/reference sample
Physical evidence whose origin is known, such as blood or hair from a suspect, that can be compared to crime-scene evidence

buccal swab
A swab of the inner portion of the cheek; cheek cells are usually collected to determine the DNA profile of an individual

substrate control
Uncontaminated surface material close to an area where physical evidence has been deposited; this sample is to be used to ensure that the surface on which a sample has been deposited does not interfere with laboratory tests

hairs removed from the suspect and victim. Likewise, bloodstained evidence must be accompanied by a whole-blood or **buccal swab** standard/reference sample obtained from all relevant crime-scene participants. The quality and quantity of standard/reference specimens often determine the evidential value of crime-scene evidence, and these standard/reference specimens must be treated with equal care.

Some types of evidence must also be accompanied by the collection of **substrate controls**. These are materials adjacent or close to areas where physical evidence has been deposited. For example, substrate controls are normally collected at arson scenes. If an investigator suspects that a particular surface has been exposed to gasoline or some other accelerant, the investigator should also collect a piece of the same surface material that is believed *not* to have been exposed to the accelerant. At the laboratory, the substrate control is tested to ensure that the surface on which the accelerant was deposited does not interfere with testing procedures. Another common example of a substrate control is a material on which a bloodstain has been deposited. Unstained areas close to the stain may be sampled for the purpose of determining whether this material will have an impact on the interpretation of laboratory results.

Thorough collection and proper packaging of standard/reference specimens and substrate controls are the mark of a skilled investigator.

Submitting Evidence to the Laboratory

Evidence is usually submitted to the laboratory either by personal delivery or by mail shipment. The method of transmittal is determined by the distance the submitting agency must travel to the laboratory and the urgency of the case. If the evidence is delivered personally, the deliverer should be familiar with the case, to facilitate any discussions between laboratory personnel and the deliverer concerning specific aspects of the case.

If desired, most evidence can be conveniently shipped by mail. However, postal regulations restrict the shipment of certain chemicals and live ammunition and prohibit the mailing of explosives. In such situations, the laboratory must be consulted to determine the disposition of these substances. Care must also be exercised in the packaging of evidence in order to prevent breakage or other accidental destruction while it is in transit to the laboratory.

Most laboratories require that an evidence submission form accompany all evidence submitted. One such form is shown in Figure 2–18. This form must be properly completed. Its information will enable the laboratory analyst to make an intelligent and complete examination of the evidence. Particular attention should be paid to providing the laboratory with a brief description of the case history. This information will allow the examiner to analyze the specimens in a logical sequence and make the proper comparisons, and it will also facilitate the search for trace quantities of evidence.

The particular kind of examination requested for each type of evidence is to be delineated. However, the analyst will not be bound to adhere strictly to the specific tests requested by the investigator. As the examination proceeds, new evidence may be uncovered, and as a result the complexity of the case may change. Furthermore, the analyst may find the initial requests incomplete or not totally relevant to the case. Finally, a list of items submitted for examination must be included on the evidence submission form. Each item is to be packaged separately and assigned a number or letter, which should be listed in an orderly and logical sequence on the form.

Ensuring Crime-Scene Safety

The increasing spread of AIDS and hepatitis B has sensitized the law enforcement community to the potential health hazards at crime scenes. Law enforcement officers have an extremely small chance of contracting AIDS or hepatitis at the crime scene. Both diseases are normally transmitted by the exchange of body fluids, such as blood, semen, and vaginal and cervical secretions; intravenous drug needles and syringes; and transfusion of infected blood products. However, the presence of blood and semen at crime scenes presents the investigator with biological specimens of unknown origin; the investigator has no way of gauging what health hazards they may contain. Therefore, caution and protection must be used at all times.

Fortunately, inoculation can easily prevent hepatitis B infection in most people. Furthermore, the federal Occupational Safety and Health Administration (OSHA) requires that law enforcement agencies offer hepatitis B vaccinations to all officers who may have contact with body fluids while on the job, at no expense to the officer.

| CRIME: | | | | | COUNTY OF: | | | |
| Homicide; Aggravated Sexual Assault | | | | | Mercer | | | |

VICTIM:	Age	Sex	Race	SUSPECT:		Age	Sex	Race
Jane Doe (v)	25	F	C	John Doe(s)		30	M	C

SUBMITTING AGENCY: (Address)
Trenton P.D. Central Evidence 225 N. Clinton Avenue, Trenton, N.J. 08609

FORWARD REPLIES TO:	(Name)	(Address)	Telephone Number:
Capt. John Smith, Chief of Detectives	Same as above		609 555-5555

INVESTIGATED BY:	DELIVERED BY: (Signature of Person Delivering Evidence)
Detective John Jones	

BRIEF HISTORY OF CASE: (Include Date and Location, if Applicable)
On March 1st, 2001 the victim was found dead in her bedroom. Victim was partially clothed and autopsy revealed that victim was stabbed numerous times and medical examiner stated that there was evidence of sexual assault. Victim was last seen drinking with suspect at a local tavern. Suspect was arrested and item # 23, a folding knife, was found in his pocket.

* Note* Suspect is HIV+

EXAMINATION REQUESTED ON SPECIMENS LISTED BELOW:

Examine items 2, 5, 8-11, 13-15, 18 and 19 for seminal material and compare to controls #'s 12 and 26. Examine #1, 2, 4, 7, 13, 14, 15, 18, 20, 21, 22 and 23 for trace evidence transfer. Examine #3 for saliva from suspect. Examine #6 for skin, blood and trace evidence. Examine #'s 20-23 for transfer blood evidence and compare to control #'s 12 and 26.

(Right margin checkboxes: DRUG ☐ TRACE ☐ BIO/CHEM ☐ TOX ☐ ABC ☐ EQUINE ☐ BALLISTICS ☐   (LABORATORY USE ONLY))

Item #	* Code	LIST OF SPECIMENS *SOURCE OF EVIDENCE CODE (V-Victim, S-Suspect, SC-Scene)
1	V	Debris collection
2	V	Clothing, white panties
3	V	Dried Secretions/bite marks
4	V	Head Hair Combings
5	V	Oral Specimens
6	V	Fingernail Specimens
7	V	Pubic Hair Combings
8	V	External Genital Specimen
9	V	Vaginal Specimens
10	V	Cervical Specimens

FOR ADDITIONAL INFORMATION USE FORM 631A AND ATTACH   Page 1 of 2 pages

FIGURE 2–18

An example of a properly completed evidence submission form.

The International Association for Identification Safety Committee has proposed the following guidelines to protect investigators at crime scenes containing potentially infectious materials:

1. Forensic and crime-scene personnel may encounter potentially infectious materials, such as in the case of a homicide, in which blood or body fluids may be localized to the area of the body or dispersed throughout the crime scene. At such scenes, it is recommended that personnel wear a minimum of latex gloves (double gloved) and protective (Tyvek-type) shoe covers. In cases of large contamination areas, liquid repellent coveralls (Tyvek or Kleengard suits) are recommended along with the gloves and shoe covers.
2. The use of a particle mask/respirator, goggles, or face shield is recommended in addition to the protective items listed in item 1 when potentially infectious dust or mist may be encountered at the crime scene. This includes collection of dried bloodstains by scraping; collection,

folding, and preservation of garments that may be contaminated with blood or body fluids, especially if they are in a dried state; and application of aerosol chemicals to bloodstains or prints for their detection and/or enhancement.

3. When processing and collecting evidence at a crime scene, personnel should be alert to sharp objects, knives, hypodermic syringes, razor blades, and similar items. If such sharp objects are encountered and must be recovered as evidence, the items should be placed in an appropriate container and properly labeled. When conventional latent-print powder techniques are used in or around areas contaminated with blood, a specific brush should be designated so that it can be subsequently decontaminated or appropriately disposed of after processing is complete. If latents are developed in or around blood-contaminated areas, they should be photographed, or lifted and placed in a sealed plastic bag. The sealed bag then should be affixed with an appropriate biohazard label.

    Evidence collected for transport should be packaged to maintain its integrity and to prevent contamination of personnel or personal items. Evidence contaminated with wet blood should first be placed in a paper bag and then temporarily stored in a red biohazard plastic bag for immediate transport to an appropriate drying facility.

4. When potentially infectious materials are present at a crime scene, personnel should maintain a red biohazard plastic bag for the disposal of contaminated gloves, clothing, masks, pencils, wrapping paper, and so on. On departure from the scene, the biohazard bag must be taped shut and transported to an approved biohazardous waste pickup site.

5. Note taking should be done while wearing uncontaminated gloves to avoid contamination of pens, pencils, notebook, paper, and so on. Pens or markers used to mark and package contaminated evidence should be designated for proper disposal in a red biohazard bag before investigators leave the crime scene.

6. If individual protective equipment becomes soiled or torn, it must be removed immediately. Personnel must then disinfect/decontaminate the potentially contaminated body areas using a recommended solution, such as a 10 percent bleach solution, or an antimicrobial soap or towelette. After cleansing, the area must be covered with clean, replacement protective equipment. On departure from the scene, this procedure should be repeated on any body area where contamination could have occurred.

7. Eating, drinking, smoking, and application of makeup are prohibited at the immediate crime scene.

8. All nondisposable items, such as lab coats, towels, and personal clothing, that may be contaminated with potentially infectious material should be placed in a yellow plastic bag labeled "Infectious Linen" and laundered, at the expense of the employer, by a qualified laundry service. Personal clothing that may have been contaminated should never be taken home for cleaning.

Legal Considerations at the Crime Scene

In police work, perhaps no experience is more exasperating or demoralizing than to see valuable evidence excluded from use against the accused because of legal considerations. This situation most often arises from what is deemed an "unreasonable" search and seizure of evidence. Therefore, removal of any evidence from a person or from the scene of a crime must be done in conformity with Fourth Amendment privileges: "The right of the people to be secure in their persons, houses, papers, and effects, against unreasonable searches and seizure, shall not be violated, and no warrants shall issue, but upon probable cause, supported by oath or affirmation, and particularly describing the place to be searched, and the persons or things to be seized."

Since the 1960s, the Supreme Court has been particularly concerned with defining the circumstances under which the police can search for evidence in the absence of a court-approved search warrant. A number of allowances have been made to justify a warrantless search: (1) the existence of emergency circumstances, (2) the need to prevent the immediate loss or destruction of evidence, (3) a search of a person and property within the immediate control of the person provided it is made incident to a lawful arrest, and (4) a search made by consent of the parties involved. In cases other than these, police must be particularly cautious about processing a crime scene without a search warrant. In 1978, the Supreme Court addressed this very issue and in so doing set forth guidelines for investigators to follow in determining the propriety of conducting a warrantless search at a crime scene. Significantly, the two cases decided on this issue related to homicide and arson crime scenes, both of which are normally subjected to the most intensive forms of physical evidence searches by police.

In the case of *Mincey* v. *Arizona*,[1] the Court dealt with the legality of a four-day search at a homicide scene. The case involved a police raid on the home of Rufus Mincey, who had been suspected of dealing drugs. Under the pretext of buying drugs, an undercover police officer forced entry into Mincey's apartment and was killed in a scuffle that ensued. Without a search warrant, the police spent four days searching the apartment, recovering, among other things, bullets, drugs, and drug paraphernalia. These items were subsequently introduced as evidence at the trial. Mincey was convicted and on appeal contended that the evidence gathered from his apartment, without a warrant and without his consent, was illegally seized. The Court unanimously upheld Mincey's position, stating:

> We do not question the right of the police to respond to emergency situations. Numerous state and federal cases have recognized that the Fourth Amendment does not bar police officers from making warrantless entries and searches when they reasonably believe that a person within is in need of immediate aid. Similarly, when the police come upon the scene of a homicide they may make a prompt warrantless search of the area to see if there are other victims or if a killer is still on the premises. . . . Except for the fact that the offense under investigation was a homicide, there were no exigent circumstances in this case. . . . There was no indication that evidence would be lost, destroyed or removed during the time required to obtain a search warrant. Indeed, the police guard at the apartment minimized that possibility. And there is no suggestion that a search warrant could not easily and conveniently have been obtained. We decline to hold that the seriousness of the offense under investigation itself creates exigent circumstances of the kind that under the Fourth Amendment justify a warrantless search.

In *Michigan* v. *Tyler*,[2] a business establishment leased by Loren Tyler and a business partner was destroyed by fire. The fire was finally extinguished in the early hours of the morning; however, hampered by smoke, steam, and darkness, fire officials and police were prevented from thoroughly examining the scene for evidence of arson. The building was then left unattended until eight A.M. of that day, when officials returned and began an inspection of the burned premises. During the morning search, assorted items of evidence were recovered and removed from the building. On three other occasions—four days, seven days, and twenty-five days after the fire—investigators reentered the premises and removed additional items of evidence. Each of these searches was made without a warrant or without consent, and the evidence seized was used to convict Tyler and his partner of conspiracy to burn real property and related offenses. The Supreme Court upheld the reversal of the conviction, holding the initial morning search to be proper but contending that evidence obtained from subsequent reentries to the scene was inadmissible: "We hold that an entry to fight a fire requires no warrant, and that once in the building, officials may remain there for a reasonable time to investigate the cause of a blaze. Thereafter, additional entries to investigate the cause of the fire must be made pursuant to the warrant procedures."

The message from the Supreme Court is clear: when time and circumstances permit, obtain a search warrant before investigating and retrieving physical evidence at the crime scene.

chapter summary > > > > > > > > >

Physical evidence includes all objects that can establish or disprove that a crime has been committed or can link a crime and its victim or its perpetrator. Forensic science begins at the crime scene. Here, investigators must recognize and properly preserve evidence for laboratory examination. The first officer to arrive is responsible for securing the crime scene. Once the scene is secured, relevant investigators record the crime scene by using photographs, sketches, and notes. Before processing the crime scene for physical evidence, the investigator should make a preliminary examination of the scene as it was left by

[1]437 U.S. 385 (1978).
[2]436 U.S. 499 (1978).

the perpetrator. The search for physical evidence at a crime scene must be thorough and systematic. The search pattern selected normally depends on the size and locale of the scene and the number of collectors participating in the search.

Physical evidence can be anything from massive objects to microscopic traces. Often, many items of evidence are clearly visible, but others may be detected only through examination at the crime laboratory. For this reason, it is important to collect possible carriers of trace evidence, such as clothing, vacuum sweepings, and fingernail scrapings, in addition to more discernible items. Each different item or similar items collected at different locations must be placed in a separate container. Packaging evidence separately prevents damage through contact and prevents cross-contamination.

During the collection of evidence, the chain of custody, a record for denoting the location of the evidence, must be maintained. In addition, proper standard/reference samples, such as hairs, blood, and fibers, must be collected at the crime scene and from appropriate subjects for comparison in the laboratory. The removal of any evidence from a person or from the scene of a crime must be done in accordance with appropriate search and seizure protocols.

review questions

1. The term _____ encompasses all objects that can establish or disprove whether a crime has been committed or can link a crime and its victim or its perpetrator.

2. True or False: Scientific evaluation of crime-scene evidence can usually overcome the results of a poorly conducted criminal investigation. _____

3. True or False: The techniques of physical evidence collection require a highly skilled individual who must specialize in this area of investigation. _____

4. All unauthorized personnel must be _____ from crime scenes.

5. True or False: Failure to protect a crime scene properly may result in the destruction or altering of evidence. _____

6. The _____ arriving on the scene of a crime is responsible for taking steps to preserve and protect the area to the greatest extent possible, and this person must rely on his or her training to deal with any violent or hazardous circumstances.

7. At a crime scene, first priority should be given to obtaining _____ for individuals in need of it and attempting to minimize disturbance of evidence.

8. True or False: The boundaries of the crime scene, denoted by crime-scene tape, rope, or traffic cones, should encompass only the center of the scene where the crime occurred. _____

9. Even though no unauthorized personnel are admitted to the scene, an accurate _____ must be kept of those who do enter and exit the scene and the time they do so.

10. True or False: The lead investigator will immediately proceed to gain an overview of the situation and develop a strategy for the systematic examination of the crime scene during the final survey. _____

11. Three methods for recording the crime scene are _____, _____, and _____.

12. True or False: The note-taking process begins with the call to a crime-scene investigator to report to a scene. _____

13. The crime-scene notes should include a precise record of personnel movements in and out of the scene starting with the _____.

14. True or False: Crime-scene notes should be written from memory back at the laboratory. _____

15. Before located evidence is collected, it must be fully described in the investigator's _____.

16. True or False: When an injured or deceased victim is present at the scene, the state of the body before being moved should be observed but not recorded. _____

17. The most important prerequisite for photographing a crime scene is to have it in a(n) _____ condition.

18. Photographs of physical evidence must include overviews as well as _____ to record the details of objects.

19. True or False: The value of crime-scene photographs lies in their ability to show the layout of the scene, position of witnesses, and relation of people to one another in the scene. _____

20. The most commonly used camera for crime-scene photography is the _____ camera, which can be film or digital.

21. A digital camera captures light on a light-sensitive _____.

22. True or False: Each crime scene should be photographed as completely as possible in a logical succession and the photographs should include the area in which the crime actually took place and all adjacent areas where important acts occurred. _____

23. The succession of photographs taken at a crime scene is _____ photographs first and _____ photographs last.

24. True or False: Overview photographs should include only points of entry and points of exit. _____

25. To ensure that their digital images will be admissible, many jurisdictions have developed or are developing _____ for the use of digital photography to avoid the possibility of enhancement or doctoring of crime-scene photographs.

26. The process of _____ the crime scene essentially combines notes and photography.

27. Unlike the rough sketch, the _____ is constructed with care and concern for aesthetic appearance and must be drawn to scale.

28. _____ programs provide an extensive symbol library and may create a three-dimensional sketch.

29. An investigator need only draw a(n) _____ sketch at the crime scene to show its dimensions and pertinent objects.

30. A detailed search of the crime scene for physical evidence must be conducted in a(n) _____ manner.

31. The crime-scene search is undertaken to locate _____.

32. True or False: The search patterns that may be used to search a crime scene for evidence include the line pattern, grid pattern, polar coordinate pattern, and spiral pattern. _____

33. True or False: If the investigator does not recognize physical evidence or does not properly preserve it for laboratory examination, sophisticated laboratory instrumentation or technical expertise can salvage the situation and attain the desired results. _____

34. Besides the more obvious items of physical evidence, possible _____ of trace evidence must be collected for detailed examination in the laboratory.

35. Whenever possible, trace evidence (is, is not) to be removed from the object that bears it.

36. Each item collected at the crime scene must be placed in a(n) _____ container.

37. True or False: An ordinary mailing envelope is considered a good general-purpose evidence container. _____

38. An airtight container (is, is not) recommended packaging material for bloodstained garments.

39. As a matter of routine, all items of clothing are to be _____ before packaging.

40. True or False: Charred debris recovered from the scene of an arson is best placed in a porous container. _____

41. The possibility of future legal proceedings requires that a(n) _____ be established with respect to the possession and location of physical evidence.

42. Most physical evidence collected at the crime scene will require the accompanying submission of _____ material for comparison purposes.

43. In the case of *Mincey* v. *Arizona*, the Supreme Court restricted the practice of conducting a(n) _____ search at a homicide scene.

44. In the case of *Michigan* v. *Tyler*, the Supreme Court dealt with search and seizure procedures at a(n) _____ scene.

application and critical thinking

1. You are the first officer at the scene of an outdoor assault. You find the victim bleeding but conscious, with two of the victim's friends and several onlookers standing nearby. You call for backup and quickly glance around but see no one fleeing the scene. Describe the steps you would take while you wait for backup to arrive.

2. What kind of search pattern(s) would investigators be most likely to employ in each of the following situations:
   a. Two people searching a small area with well-defined boundaries
   b. Several people searching a large area
   c. A single person searching a large area

3. Officer Bill Walter arrives at the scene of an apparent murder: a body bearing several gunshot wounds lies on the floor of a small, unair-conditioned house in late July. A pungent odor almost overwhelms him when he enters the house, so he opens a window to allow him to breathe so he can investigate the scene. While airing out the house, he secures the scene and interviews bystanders. When he inspects the scene, he discovers very little blood in the room and little evidence of a struggle. What mistake did Officer Walter make in his investigation? What conclusion did he draw about the scene from his observations?

4. Officer Martin Guajardo is the first responder at an apparent homicide scene. After securing the area, interviewing the sole witness, and calling for backup, he begins to search for evidence. He makes note of a bloody knife lying next to the body, with a small scrap of bloody cloth clinging precariously to the knife. Because it is a very windy day, Officer Guajardo removes the scrap of fabric and seals it in a plastic bag. A few moments later, a crime-scene team, including a photographer, arrives to take over the investigation. What mistakes, if any, did Officer Guajardo make before the crime-scene team arrived?

5. During his search of a homicide scene, investigator David Gurney collects evidence that includes a bloody shirt. After the crime-scene team has completely processed the scene, Investigator Gurney packages the shirt in a paper bag, seals the bag, and labels it to indicate the contents. He then delivers the shirt to the laboratory

with an evidence submission form. There, a forensic scientist breaks the seal, removes the shirt, and performs a series of tests on it. He replaces the shirt, discards the old seal, and places a new seal on the package containing his initials and the date on which it was resealed. What mistakes, if any, were made in handling the shirt?

6. What important elements are missing from the following crime-scene sketch?

further references

Geberth, Vernon J., *Practical Homicide Investigation: Tactics, Procedures, and Forensic Techniques*, 4th ed. Boca Raton, Fla.: Taylor & Francis, 2006.

Nickell, J., and J. F. Fischer, *Crime Scene: Methods of Forensic Detection*. Lexington: University Press of Kentucky, 1999.

Ogle, R. R., Jr., *Crime Scene Investigation and Reconstruction,* 2nd ed. Upper Saddle River, N.J.: Prentice Hall, 2007.

Osterburg, James W., and Richard H. Ward, *Criminal Investigation—A Method for Reconstructing the Past,* 5th ed. Cincinnati, Ohio: Anderson, 2007.

case analysis

Investigators looking into the kidnapping and murder of DEA special agent Enrique Camarena and DEA source Alfredo Zavala faced several hurdles that threatened to derail their efforts to collect evidence in the case. These hurdles almost prevented forensics experts from determining the facts of the case and threatened to undermine the investigation of the crime. However, despite these obstacles, use of standard forensic techniques eventually enabled investigators to solve the case.

1. What were the main challenges facing investigators who were collecting evidence in the case? Give specific examples of these challenges.

2. Explain how investigators used reference samples to determine that the victims had been held at the residence located at 881 Lope De Vega.

3. Explain how investigators used reference samples to determine that the victims' bodies had been buried and later moved to the site where they were discovered. Also explain how they used such evidence to determine the original burial place.

The Enrique Camarena Case: A Forensic Nightmare

On February 7, 1985, U.S. Drug Enforcement Agency (DEA) Special Agent (SA) Enrique Camarena was abducted near the U.S. Consulate in Guadalajara, Mexico. A short time later, Capt. Alfredo Zavala, a DEA source, was also abducted from a car near the Guadalajara Airport. These two abductions would trigger a series of events leading to one of the largest investigations ever conducted by the DEA and would result in one of the most extensive cases ever received by the FBI Laboratory.

Michael P. Malone
Special Agent, Laboratory Division
Federal Bureau of Investigation,
Washington, D.C.

Throughout this lengthy investigation, unusual forensic problems arose that required unusual solutions. Eventually, numerous suspects were arrested, both in the United States and Mexico, which culminated in an 8-week trial held in U.S. District Court in Los Angeles, CA.

The Abduction

On February 7, 1985, SA Camarena left the DEA Resident Office to meet his wife for lunch. On this day, a witness observed a man being forced into the rear seat of a light-colored compact car in front of the Camelot Restaurant and provided descriptions of several of the assailants. After some initial reluctance, Primer Comandante Pavon-Reyes of the Mexican Federal Judicial Police (MFJP) was put in charge of the investigation, and Mexican investigators were assigned to the case. Two known drug traffickers, Rafael Caro-Quintero and Ernesto Fonseca, were quickly developed as suspects. A short time later at the Guadalajara Airport, as Caro-Quintero and his men attempted to flee by private jet, a confrontation developed between Caro-Quintero's men, the MFJP, and DEA agents. After some discussion, Caro-Quintero and his men were permitted to board and leave. It was later learned that a 6-figure bribe had been paid to Pavon-Reyes to allow this departure.

The Investigation

During February 1985, searches of several residences and ranches throughout Mexico proved fruitless, despite the efforts of the DEA task force assigned to investigate this matter and the tremendous pressure being applied by the U.S. government to accelerate the investigation. High-level U.S. government officials, as well as their Mexican counterparts, were becoming directly involved in the case. It is believed that because of this "heat," the Mexican drug traffickers and certain Mexican law enforcement officials fabricated a plan. According to the plan, the MFJP would receive an anonymous letter indicating that SA Camarena and Captain Zavala were being held at the Bravo drug gang's ranch in La Angostura, Michoacan, approximately 60 miles southeast of Guadalajara. The MFJP was supposed to raid the ranch, eliminate the drug gang, and eventually discover the bodies of SA Camarena and Captain Zavala buried on the ranch. The DEA would then be notified and the case would be closed. Thus, the Bravo gang would provide an easy scapegoat.

Undated photo of Enrique Camarena.
Courtesy AP Wide World Photos

During early March, MFJP officers raided the Bravo ranch before the DEA agents arrived. In the resulting shootout, all of the gang members, as well as one MFJP officer, were killed. However, due to a mix-up, the bodies of SA Camarena and Captain Zavala were not buried on the Bravo ranch in time to be discovered as planned. The individuals paid to do this job simply left them by the side of a road near the ranch. It was later learned that certain Mexican law enforcement officials were paid a large sum of money to formulate and carry out this plan in order to obstruct and prematurely conclude the investigation.

Shortly after this shootout, a passerby found two partially decomposed bodies, wrapped in plastic bags, along a road near the Bravo ranch. The bodies were removed and transported to a local morgue where they were autopsied. The DEA was then advised of the discovery of the bodies and their subsequent removal to another morgue in Guadalajara, where a second autopsy was performed.

Reprinted from *FBI Law Enforcement Bulletin*, September 1989.

On March 7, 1985, the FBI dispatched a forensic team to Guadalajara. They immediately proceeded to the morgue to identify the bodies and to process any evidence which might be present. After much bureaucratic delay from the local officials, they were finally allowed to proceed. The bodies were identified only as cadavers number 1 and number 2. It was apparent that each body had been autopsied and that both were in an advanced state of decomposition. Cadaver number 1 was quickly identified by the fingerprint expert as that of SA Camarena. Mexican officials would not allow the second body to be identified at this time; however, it was later identified through dental records as Captain Zavala.

The FBI forensic team requested permission to process the clothing, cordage, and burial sheet found with the bodies but the request was denied. However, they were allowed to cut small, "known" samples from these items and obtain hair samples from both bodies. Soil samples were also removed from the bodies and the clothing items.

A forensic pathologist from the Armed Forces Institute of Pathology was allowed to examine the body of SA Camarena. He concluded that SA Camarena's death was caused by blunt-force injuries. In addition, SA Camarena had a hole in his skull caused by a rod-like instrument. SA Camarena's body was then released to the American officials and immediately flown to the United States.

The next day, both FBI and DEA personnel proceeded to the Bravo ranch where the bodies were initially found. Because this site had been a completely uncontrolled crime scene, contaminated by both police personnel and onlookers, only a limited crime-scene search was conducted. It was immediately noted that there was no grave site in the area and that the color of the soil where the bodies had been deposited differed from the soil that had been removed from the bodies. Therefore, "known" soil samples from the drop site were taken to compare with soil removed from the victims. It was also noted that there were no significant body fluids at the "burial" site. This led the forensic team to conclude that the bodies had been buried elsewhere, exhumed, and transported to this site.

The MFJP officials were later confronted with the evidence that the bodies had been relocated to the Michoacan area. This was one of the factors which led to a new, unilateral MFJP investigation. As a result, several suspects, including State Judicial Police Officers, were arrested and interrogated concerning the kidnapping of SA Camarena. Primer Comandante Pavon-Reyes was fired, and arrest warrants were issued for a number of international drug traffickers, including Rafael Caro-Quintero and Ernesto Fonseca.

In late March 1985, DEA agents located a black Mercury Gran Marquis which they believed was used in the kidnapping or transportation of SA Camarena. The vehicle had been stored in a garage in Guadalajara, and a brick wall had been constructed at the entrance to conceal it. The vehicle was traced to a Ford dealership owned by Caro-Quintero. Under the watchful eye of the MFJP at the Guadalajara Airport, the FBI forensic team processed the vehicle for any hair, fiber, blood, and/or fingerprint evidence it might contain.

During April 1985, the MFJP informed the DEA that they believed they had located the residence where SA Camarena and Captain Zavala had been held. The FBI forensic team was immediately dispatched to Guadalajara; however, they were not allowed to proceed to the residence, located at 881 Lope De Vega, until an MFJP forensic team had processed the residence and had removed all of the obvious evidence. The DEA was also informed that since the abduction of SA Camarena, all of the interior walls had been painted, the entire residence had recently been cleaned, and that a group of MFJP officers were presently occupying, and thereby contaminating, the residence.

On the first day after the arrival of the FBI forensic team, they surveyed and began a crime scene search of the residence and surrounding grounds. The residence consists of a large, two-story structure with a swimming pool, covered patio, aviary, and tennis court surrounded by a common wall. The most logical place to hold a prisoner at this location would be in the small outbuilding located to the rear of the main residence. This outbuilding, designated as the "guest house," consisted of a small room, carpeted by a beige rug, with an adjoining bathroom. The entire room and bathroom were processed for hairs, fibers, and latent fingerprints. The single door into this room was made of steel and reinforced by iron bars. It was ultimately determined by means of testimony and forensic evidence that several individuals interrogated and tortured SA Camarena in this room. In addition, a locked bedroom, located on the second floor of the main house, was also processed, and the bed linens were removed from a single bed. Known carpet samples were taken from every room in the residence.

A beige VW Atlantic, which fit the general description of the smaller vehicle noted by the person who witnessed SA Camarena's abduction, was parked under a carport at the rear of the residence. The VW Atlantic was also processed for hairs, fibers, and fingerprints.

On the second day, a thorough grounds search was conducted. As FBI forensic team members were walking around the tennis court, they caught a glimpse of something blue in one of the drains. Upon closer inspection, it appeared to be a folded license plate, at the bottom of the drain. However, a heavy iron grate covered the drain and prevented the plate's immediate retrieval.

When one of the FBI agents returned to the main house to ask the MFJP officers for a crowbar, they became extremely curious and followed the agent as he returned, empty handed, to the tennis court. By this time, a second agent had managed to remove the grate by using a heavy-wire coat hanger. The license plate was retrieved, unfolded, and photographed. The MFJP officers, all of whom were now at the tennis court, became upset at this discovery, and one of them immediately contacted his superior at MFJP headquarters, who ordered them to secure the license plate until the Assistant Primer Comandante arrived on the scene. After his arrival approximately 20 minutes later, he seized the license plate and would not allow the Americans to conduct any further searches.

However, by this time, five very large plastic bags of evidence had been recovered and were placed in the rear of a DEA truck. The evidence was quickly transported to the DEA vault in the U.S. Consulate.

After negotiations between the United States and Mexico, the MFJP did allow a second, final search of the residence. On June 24, 1985, a forensic team returned and processed the four remaining rooms on the first floor of the main house.

By this point in the investigation, an associate of Rafael Caro-Quintero had been arrested and interrogated by the MFJP. He stated that the bodies of two Americans, Albert Radelat and John Walker, who had been abducted and killed by Mexican drug traffickers, were buried on the south side of La Primavera Park, a large, primitive park west of Guadalajara. The bodies of Radelat and Walker were located and recovered. Soil samples taken from the surface of an area near their graves were similar in most respects to the soil recovered earlier from the bodies of SA Camarena and Captain Zavala.

In September 1985, DEA personnel went to La Primavera Park and sampled an area approximately 2 feet below the surface near the same site. This sample matched the soil samples from SA Camarena and Captain Zavala almost grain for grain, indicating that this site was almost certainly their burial site before they were relocated to the Bravo ranch.

Later that fall, after further negotiations between the U.S. and the Mexican governments, permission was finally granted for an FBI forensic team to process the evidence seized by the MFJP forensic team from 881 Lope De Vega the previous April. The evidence consisted of small samples the MFJP had taken of SA Camarena's burial sheet, a piece of rope used to bind SA Camarena, a portion of a pillowcase removed from bedroom number 3, a piece of unsoiled rope removed from the covered patio, and a laboratory report prepared by the MFJP Crime Laboratory. The remainder of the evidence had been destroyed for "health reasons."

In January 1986, a drug trafficker named Rene Verdugo, who was considered to be a high-ranking member of the Caro-Quintero gang, was apprehended and taken to San Diego, where he was arrested by the DEA. He was then transported to Washington, D.C., where hair samples were taken. He refused to testify before a federal grand jury investigating the Camarena case. Later that year, DEA personnel obtained hair samples in Mexico City from Sergio Espino-Verdin, a former federal comandante, who is believed to have been SA Camarena's primary interrogator during his ordeal at 881 Lope De Vega.

The Trial

In July 1988, the main trial of the murder, interrogation, and abduction of SA Camarena began in U.S. District Court in Los Angeles, CA. The forensic evidence presented in this trial identified 881 Lope De Vega as the site where SA Camarena had been held. [See Figure 1.] The evidence also strongly associated two Mexican citizens, Rene Verdugo and Sergio Espino-Verdin, with the "guest house" at 881 Lope De Vega. Several types of forensic evidence were used to associate SA Camarena with 881 Lope De Vega: forcibly removed head hairs, found in the "guest house" and bedroom number 4, in the VW Atlantic and in the Mercury Gran Marquis, and two types of polyester rug fibers, a dark, rose-colored fiber and a light-colored fiber. [See Figures 2 and 3.] Fabric evidence was also presented, which demonstrated the similarities of color, composition, construction, and design between SA Camarena's burial sheet and the two pillowcases recovered from bedrooms number 3 and 5.

Based on this evidence associating SA Camarena and 881 Lope De Vega, the FBI Laboratory examiner was able to testify that SA Camarena was at this residence, as well as in the VW Atlantic and the Mercury Gran Marquis, and that he had been in a position such that his head hairs were forcibly removed. Captain Alfredo Zavala was also found to be associated with the "guest house" at 881 Lope De Vega. Light-colored nylon rug fibers, found on samples of his clothing taken at the second autopsy, matched the fibers from the "guest house" carpet.

A detailed model of the residence at 881 Lope De Vega was prepared by the Special Projects Section of the FBI Laboratory for the trial. [See Figure 4.] Over 20 trial charts were also prepared to explain the various types of forensic evidence. These charts proved invaluable in clarifying the complicated techniques and characteristics used in the examination of the hair, fiber, fabric, and cordage evidence. [See Figure 5.]

FIGURE 1

Diagram of the 881 Lope De Vega grounds. Camarena was held prisoner in the guest house.

FIGURE 2

Trial chart showing hair comparisons between known Camarena hairs and hairs recovered from 881 Lope De Vega.

FIGURE 3

Trial chart showing hair comparisons between known Camarena hairs and hairs recovered from the Mercury Gran Marquis.

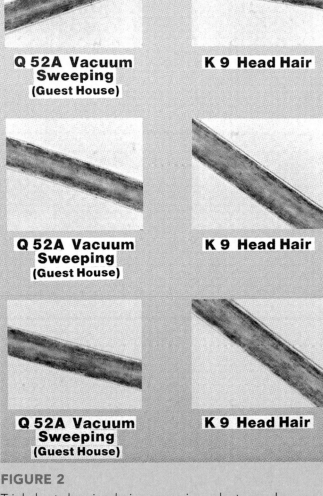

FIGURE 4

A model of 881 Lope De Vega prepared as a trial exhibit.

CATEGORIES OF FORENSIC EVIDENCE IN CAMARENA CASE						
TYPE OF EVIDENCE						
LOCATION	*Hair*	*Carpet Fibers*	*Fabric Match*	*Cordage Match*	*Tape Match*	*Misc.*
Mercury	**Camarena Head Hair**					Blood on Floor Mat
VW Atlantic	**Camarena Head Hair**					Blood on Tissue
Guest House	**Camarena Head Hair**	Zavala Clothes Nylon				
Bedroom #3		Camarena Blindfold Polyester	Pillow Case Camarena Burial Sheet			
Bedroom #4	**Camarena Head Hair**	Camarena Blindfold & Burial Sheet Polyester				
Bedroom #5			Pillow Case Camarena Burial Sheet			
Tennis Court						License Plate VW/Merc.
Camarena Burial Sheet	**Camarena Head Hair**	Bedroom #4 Polyester	Pillow Case Bedrooms #3 and #5			Soil La Primavera
Source – Blindfold/ Rope	**Camarena Head Hair**	Bedrooms #3 and #4 Polyester			Camarena Blindfold Tape	
Camarena Burial Cordage				Burial Rope from Covered Patio		
Zavala Clothing	**Zavala Head Hair**	Guest House Nylon				Soil La Primavera

FIGURE 5

Trial chart used to show the association of Camarena and Zavala with various locations.

Conclusion

The forensic pitfalls and problems in this case (i.e., destruction of evidence, contamination of crime scenes) were eventually resolved. In some cases, certain routine procedures had to be ignored or unconventional methods employed. However, in many instances, detailed trial testimony overcame the limitations of certain evidence, and eventually, almost all of the evidence introduced at the trial made a tremendous impact on the outcome of this proceeding. After an 8-week trial, conducted under tight security and involving hundreds of witnesses, all of the defendants were found guilty, convicted on all counts, and are currently serving lengthy sentences.

Scott Peterson: A Case of Circumstantial Evidence

Modesto Police Department Handout\AP Wide World Photos

On the surface, Scott Peterson and his wife, Laci, appeared to live a happy and contented lifestyle in Modesto, California. The 30-year-old Peterson and his 27-year-old former college sweetheart, a substitute teacher, were expecting their first child in about one month when Laci suddenly disappeared. Scott Peterson told investigators that he had last seen his wife on December 24, 2002, at 9:30 A.M. when he left home for a fishing trip off San Francisco Bay. In April 2003, Laci's decomposed remains washed ashore not far from where Scott said he had gone fishing on the day she vanished. Peterson claimed that Laci was dressed in a white top and black pants when he last saw her, but when her body was found she was wearing khaki pants. Scott's sister recalled that Laci was wearing khaki pants the night before her disappearance.

When questioned, Peterson claimed that he had gone fishing for sturgeon or striped bass. However, the police investigation revealed that he failed to bring the appropriate fishing rod and lines to catch such fish. Further revelations surfaced when it became known that Scott was having an affair with another woman. A search of Scott's warehouse led to the recovery of a black hair on a pair of pliers resting in Scott's boat. A mitochondrial DNA profile of the hair was consistent with Laci's DNA. Scott Peterson was charged with murder and convicted and currently awaits his fate on death row.

Visit MyCrimeKit 3.1 to view the evidence that prosecutors presented to convict Scott Peterson.

physical evidence

Learning Objectives

After studying this chapter you should be able to:

- Review the common types of physical evidence encountered at crime scenes

- Explain the difference between the identification and comparison of physical evidence

- Define and contrast individual and class characteristics of physical evidence

- Appreciate the value of class evidence as it relates to a criminal investigation

- List and explain the function of national databases available to forensic scientists

- Understand the contributions the forensic pathologist, forensic anthropologist, and forensic entomologist can make to a death investigation

KEY TERMS

algor mortis
autopsy
class characteristics
comparison
identification
individual
   characteristics
livor mortis
product rule
rigor mortis

mycrimekit

WEBEXTRA 3.1
The Scott Peterson Case
www.mycrimekit.com

It would be impossible to list all the objects that could conceivably be of importance to a crime; every crime scene obviously has to be treated on an individual basis, having its own peculiar history, circumstances, and problems. It is practical, however, to list items whose scientific examination is likely to yield significant results in ascertaining the nature and circumstances of a crime. The investigator who is thoroughly familiar with the recognition, collection, and analysis of these items, as well as with laboratory procedures and capabilities, can make logical decisions when the uncommon and unexpected are encountered at the crime scene. Just as important, a qualified evidence collector cannot rely on collection procedures memorized from a pamphlet but must be able to make innovative, on-the-spot decisions at the crime scene.

Common Types of Physical Evidence

1. *Blood, semen, and saliva.* All suspected blood, semen, or saliva—liquid or dried, animal or human—present in a form to suggest a relation to the offense or the people involved in a crime. This category includes blood or semen dried onto fabrics or other objects, as well as cigarette butts that may contain saliva residues. These substances are subjected to serological and biochemical analysis to determine their identity and possible origin.
2. *Documents.* Any handwriting and typewriting submitted so that authenticity or source can be determined. Related items include paper, ink, indented writings, obliterations, and burned or charred documents.
3. *Drugs.* Any substance seized in violation of laws regulating the sale, manufacture, distribution, and use of drugs.
4. *Explosives.* Any device containing an explosive charge, as well as all objects removed from the scene of an explosion that are suspected to contain the residues of an explosive.
5. *Fibers.* Any natural or synthetic fiber whose transfer may be useful in establishing a relationship between objects and/or people.
6. *Fingerprints.* All prints of this nature, latent and visible.
7. *Firearms and ammunition.* Any firearm, as well as discharged or intact ammunition, suspected of being involved in a criminal offense.
8. *Glass.* Any glass particle or fragment that may have been transferred to a person or object involved in a crime. Windowpanes containing holes made by a bullet or other projectile are included in this category.
9. *Hair.* Any animal or human hair present that could link a person with a crime.
10. *Impressions.* Tire markings, shoe prints, depressions in soft soils, and all other forms of tracks. Glove and other fabric impressions, as well as bite marks in skin or foodstuffs, are also included.
11. *Organs and physiological fluids.* Body organs and fluids are submitted for toxicology to detect possible existence of drugs and poisons. This category includes blood to be analyzed for the presence of alcohol and other drugs.
12. *Paint.* Any paint, liquid or dried, that may have been transferred from the surface of one object to another during the commission of a crime. A common example is the transfer of paint from one vehicle to another during an automobile collision.
13. *Petroleum products.* Any petroleum product removed from a suspect or recovered from a crime scene. The most common examples are gasoline residues removed from the scene of an arson, or grease and oil stains whose presence may suggest involvement in a crime.
14. *Plastic bags.* A disposable polyethylene bag such as a garbage bag may be evidential in a homicide or drug case. Examinations are conducted to associate a bag with a similar bag in the possession of a suspect.
15. *Plastic, rubber, and other polymers.* Remnants of these manufactured materials recovered at crime scenes may be linked to objects recovered in the possession of a suspect perpetrator.
16. *Powder residues.* Any item suspected of containing firearm discharge residues (see Figure 3–1).
17. *Serial numbers.* This category includes all stolen property submitted to the laboratory for the restoration of erased identification numbers.
18. *Soil and minerals.* All items containing soil or minerals that could link a person or object to a particular location. Common examples are soil embedded in shoes and safe insulation found on garments.

19. *Tool marks.* This category includes any object suspected of containing the impression of another object that served as a tool in a crime. For example, a screwdriver or crowbar could produce tool marks by being impressed into or scraped along a surface of a wall.

20. *Vehicle lights.* Examination of vehicle headlights and taillights is normally conducted to determine whether a light was on or off at the time of impact.

21. *Wood and other vegetative matter.* Any fragments of wood, sawdust, shavings, or vegetative matter discovered on clothing, shoes, or tools that could link a person or object to a crime location.

The Significance of Physical Evidence

The examination of physical evidence by a forensic scientist is usually undertaken for identification or comparison.

Identification

Identification has as its purpose the determination of the physical or chemical identity of a substance with as near absolute certainty as existing analytical techniques will permit. For example, the crime laboratory is frequently asked to identify the chemical composition of an illicit-drug preparation that may contain heroin, cocaine, barbiturates, and so on. It may be asked to identify gasoline in residues recovered from the debris of a fire, or it may have to identify the nature of explosive residues—for example, dynamite or TNT. Also, the identification of blood, semen, hair, or wood would, as a matter of routine, include a determination of species origin. For example, did an evidential bloodstain originate from a human as opposed to a dog or cat? Each of these requests requires the analysis and ultimate identification of a specific physical or chemical substance to the exclusion of all other possible substances.

The process of identification first requires the adoption of testing procedures that give characteristic results for specific standard materials. Once these test results have been established, they may be permanently recorded and used repeatedly to prove the identity of suspect materials. For example, to ascertain that a particular suspect powder is heroin, the test results on the powder must be identical to those that have been previously obtained from a known heroin sample. Second, identification requires that the number and type of tests needed to identify a substance be sufficient to exclude all other substances. This means that the examiner must devise a specific analytical scheme that will eliminate all but one substance from consideration. Hence, if the examiner concludes that a white powder contains heroin, the test results must have been comprehensive enough to have excluded all other drugs—or, for that matter, all other substances—from consideration.

Simple rules cannot be devised for defining what constitutes a thorough and foolproof analytical scheme. Each type of evidence obviously requires different tests, and each test has a different degree of specificity. Thus, one substance could conceivably be identified by one test, whereas another may require a combination of five or six different tests to arrive at an identification. In a science in which the practitioner has little or no control over the quality and quantity of the specimens received, a standard series of tests cannot encompass all possible problems and pitfalls. So the forensic scientist must determine at what point the analysis can be concluded and the criteria for positive identification satisfied; for this, he or she must rely on knowledge gained through education and experience. Ultimately, the conclusion will have to be substantiated beyond any reasonable doubt in a court of law.

Comparison

A comparison analysis subjects a suspect specimen and a standard/reference specimen to the same tests and examinations for the ultimate purpose of determining whether they have a common origin. For example, the forensic scientist may place a suspect at a particular location by noting the similarities of a hair found at the crime scene to hairs removed from a suspect's head (see Figure 3–2). Or a paint chip found on a hit-and-run victim's garment may be compared with paint removed from a vehicle suspected of being involved in the incident. The forensic comparison is

FIGURE 3–1

The gun is fired at a set distance from the target and the gunpowder left on the target is compared to powder stains found on a victim's clothing. The density and shape of the powder stains vary with the distance the gun was fired.
Courtesy Mikael Karlsson, Arresting Images

identification
The process of determining a substance's physical or chemical identity; drug analysis, species determination, and explosive residue analysis are typical examples of this undertaking in a forensic setting

comparison
The process of ascertaining whether two or more objects have a common origin

FIGURE 3–2

Side-by-side comparison of hairs.

Courtesy Chris Palenik, Microtrace, Elgin, Ill., www.microtracescientific.com

actually a two-step procedure. First, combinations of select properties are chosen from the suspect and the standard/reference specimen for comparison. The question of which and how many properties are selected obviously depends on the type of materials being examined. (This subject will receive a good deal of discussion in forthcoming chapters.) The overriding consideration must be the ultimate evidential value of the conclusion. This brings us to the second objective. Once the examination has been completed, the forensic scientist must draw a conclusion about the origins of the specimens. Do they or do they not come from the same source? Certainly if one or more of the properties selected for comparison do not agree, the analyst will conclude that the specimens are not the same and hence could not have originated from the same source. Suppose, on the other hand, that all the properties do compare and the specimens, as far as the examiner can determine, are indistinguishable. Does it logically follow that they come from the same source? Not necessarily so.

To comprehend the evidential value of a comparison, one must appreciate the role that probability has in ascertaining the origins of two or more specimens. Simply defined, *probability* is the frequency of occurrence of an event. If a coin is flipped one hundred times, in theory we can expect heads to come up fifty times. Hence, the probability of the event (heads) occurring is 50 in 100. In other words, probability defines the odds at which a certain event will occur.

INDIVIDUAL CHARACTERISTICS   Evidence that can be associated with a common source with an extremely high degree of probability is said to possess **individual characteristics**. Examples of this are the ridge characteristics of fingerprints, random striation markings on bullets or tool marks, irregular and random wear patterns in tire or footwear impressions, handwriting characteristics, irregular edges of broken objects that can be fitted together like a jigsaw puzzle (see Figure 3–3), or sequentially made plastic bags that can be matched by striation marks running across the bags (see Figure 3–4). In all of these cases, it is not possible to state with mathematical exactness the probability that the specimens are of common origin; it can only be concluded that this probability is so high as to defy mathematical calculations or human comprehension. Furthermore, the conclusion of common origin must be substantiated

individual characteristics
Properties of evidence that can be attributed to a common source with an extremely high degree of certainty

FIGURE 3–3

The body of a woman was found with evidence of beating about the head and a stablike wound in the neck. Her husband was charged with the murder. The pathologist found a knife blade tip in the wound in the neck. The knife blade tip was compared with the broken blade of a penknife found in the trousers pocket of the accused. Note that in addition to the fit of the indentations on the edges, the scratch marks running across the blade tip correspond in detail to those on the broken blade.
Courtesy Centre of Forensic Sciences, Ministry of Community Safety and Correctional Services, Toronto, ON, Canada.

FIGURE 3–4

The bound body of a young woman was recovered from a river. Her head was covered with a black polyethylene trash bag (shown on the right). Among the items recovered from one of several suspects was a black polyethylene trash bag (shown on the left). A side-by-side comparison of the two bags' extrusion marks and pigment bands showed them to be consecutively manufactured. This information allowed investigators to focus their attention on one suspect, who ultimately was convicted of the homicide.
Courtesy George W. Neighbor, New Jersey State Police.

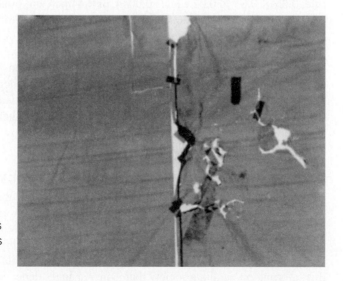

by the practical experience of the examiner. For example, the French scientist Victor Balthazard has mathematically determined that the probability of two individuals having the same fingerprints is one out of 1×10^{60}, or 1 followed by sixty zeros. This probability is so small as to exclude the possibility of any two individuals having the same fingerprints. This contention is also supported by the experience of fingerprint examiners who, after classifying millions of prints over the past hundred years, have never found any two to be exactly alike.

CLASS CHARACTERISTICS   One disappointment awaiting the investigator unfamiliar with the limitations of forensic science is the frequent inability of the laboratory to relate physical evidence to a common origin with a high degree of certainty. Evidence is said to possess **class characteristics** when it can be associated only with a group and never with a single source. Here again, probability is a determining factor. For example, if we compare two one-layer automobile paint chips of a similar color, their chance of originating from the same car is not nearly as great as when we compare two paint chips having seven similar layers of paint, not all of which were part of the car's original color. The former will have class characteristics and could only be associated at best with one car model (which may number in the thousands), whereas the latter may be judged to have individual characteristics and to have a high probability of originating from one specific car.

Blood offers another good example of evidence that can have class characteristics. For example, suppose that two blood specimens are compared and both are found to be of human origin, type A. The frequency of occurrence in the population of type A blood is 26 percent—hardly offering a basis for establishing the common origin of the stains. However, if other blood factors are also determined and are found to compare, the probability that the two blood samples originated from a common source increases. Thus, if one uses a series of blood factors that occur independently of each other, one can apply the **product rule** to calculate the overall frequency of occurrence of the blood in a population.

For example, in the O. J. Simpson case, a bloodstain located at the crime scene was found to contain a number of factors that compared to O. J.'s blood:

Blood Factors	Frequency
A	26%
EsD	85%
PGM 2+ 2−	2%

The product of all the frequencies shown in the table determines the probability that any one individual possesses such a combination of blood factors. In this instance, applying the product rule, $0.25 \times 0.85 \times 0.02$ equals 0.0044, or 0.44 percent, or about 1 in 200 people who would be expected to have this particular combination of blood factors. These bloodstain factors did not match either of the two victims, Nicole Brown Simpson or Ronald Goldman, thus eliminating them as possible sources of the blood. Although the forensic scientist has still not individualized the bloodstains to one person—in this case, O. J. Simpson—data have been provided that will permit investigators and the courts to better assess the evidential value of the crime-scene stain. As we will learn in Chapter 11, the product rule is used to determine the frequency of occurrence of DNA profiles typically determined from blood and other biological materials. Importantly, modern DNA technology provides enough factors to allow an analyst to individualize blood, semen, and other biological materials to a single person.

Assessing the Significance of Physical Evidence

One of the current weaknesses of forensic science is the inability of the examiner to assign exact or even approximate probability values to the comparison of most class physical evidence. For example, what is the probability that a nylon fiber originated from a particular sweater, or that a hair came from a particular person's head, or that a paint chip came from a car suspected to have been involved in a hit-and-run accident? Few statistical data are available from which to derive this information, and in a society that is increasingly dependent on mass-produced products, the gathering of such data is becoming an increasingly elusive goal.

One of the primary endeavors of forensic scientists must be to create and update statistical databases for evaluating the significance of class physical evidence. Of course, when such information—for example, the population frequency of blood factors—is available, it is used; but for the most part, the forensic scientist must rely on personal experience when called on to interpret the significance of class physical evidence.

People who are unfamiliar with the realities of modern criminalistics are often disappointed to learn that most items of physical evidence retrieved at crime scenes cannot be linked definitively to a single person or object. Although investigators always try to uncover physical evidence with individual characteristics—such as fingerprints, tool marks, and bullets—the chances of finding class physical evidence are far greater. To deny or belittle the value of such evidence is to reject the potential role that criminalistics can play in a criminal investigation. In practice, criminal cases are fashioned for the courtroom around a collection of diverse elements, each pointing to the guilt or involvement of a party in a criminal act. Often, most of the evidence gathered is subjective in nature, prone to human error and bias. The believability of eyewitness accounts, confessions, and informant testimony can all be disputed, maligned, and subjected to severe attack and skepticism in the courtroom. Under these circumstances, errors in human judgment are often magnified to detract from the credibility of the witness.

Assessing the Value of Physical Evidence

The value of class physical evidence lies in its ability to corroborate events with data in a manner that is, as nearly as possible, free of human error and bias. It is the thread that binds together other investigative findings that are more dependent on human judgments and, therefore, more prone to human failings. The fact that scientists have not yet learned to individualize many kinds of physical evidence means that criminal investigators should not abdicate or falter in their pursuit of all investigative leads. However, the ability of scientists to achieve a high degree of success in evaluating class physical evidence means that criminal investigators can pursue their work with a much greater chance of success.

Admittedly, in most situations, trying to define the significance of an item of class evidence in exact mathematical terms is a difficult if not impossible goal. Although class evidence is by its nature not unique, our common experience tells us that meaningful items of physical evidence, such as those listed on pages 60–61, are extremely diverse in our environment. Select, for example, a colored fiber from an article of clothing and try to locate the exact same color on the clothing of random individuals you meet, or select a car color and try to match it to other automobiles you see on local streets. Furthermore, keep in mind that a forensic comparison actually goes beyond a mere color comparison and involves examining and comparing a variety of chemical and/or physical properties (see Figure 3–5). The point is that the chances are low of encountering two

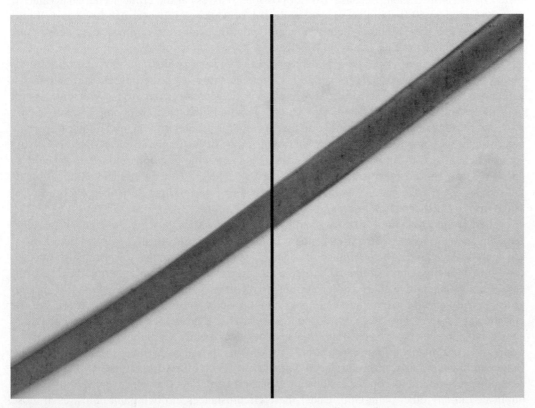

FIGURE 3–5
Side-by-side comparison of fibers.
Courtesy of Chris Palenik, Ph.D., Microtrace LLC, Elgin, IL.

indistinguishable items of physical evidence at a crime scene that actually originated from differ-ent sources. Obviously, given these circumstances, only objects that exhibit a significant amount of diversity in our environment are deemed appropriate for classification as physical evidence.

In the same way, when one is dealing with more than one type of class evidence, their col-lective presence may lead to an extremely high certainty that they originated from the same source. As the number of different objects linking an individual to a crime increases, the proba-bility of involvement increases dramatically. A classic example of this situation can be found in the evidence presented at the trial of Wayne Williams (see the case reading at the end of this chapter). Wayne Williams was charged with the murders of two individuals in the Atlanta, Georgia, metropolitan area; he was also linked to the murders of ten other boys or young men. An essential element of the state's case involved the association of Williams with the victims through a variety of fiber evidence. Twenty-eight different types of fibers linked Williams to the murder victims, evidence that the forensic examiner characterized as "overwhelming."

Cautions and Limitations in Dealing with Physical Evidence

In further evaluating the contribution of physical evidence, one cannot overlook one important re-ality in the courtroom: the weight or significance accorded physical evidence is a determination left entirely to the trier of fact, usually a jury of laypeople. Given the high esteem in which scien-tists are generally held by society and the infallible image created for forensic science by books and television, it is not hard to understand why scientifically evaluated evidence often takes on an aura of special reliability and trustworthiness in the courtroom. Often physical evidence, whether individual or class, is accorded great weight during jury deliberations and becomes a primary fac-tor in reinforcing or overcoming lingering doubts about guilt or innocence. In fact, a number of jurists have already cautioned against giving carte blanche approval to admitting scientific testi-mony without first considering its relevance in a case. Given the potential weight of scientific evidence, failure to take proper safeguards may unfairly prejudice a case against the accused.

Physical evidence may also exclude or exonerate a person from suspicion. For instance, if type A blood is linked to the suspect, all individuals who have type B, AB, or O blood can be elim-inated from consideration. Because it is not possible to assess at the crime scene what value, if any, the scientist will find in the evidence collected, or what significance such findings will ulti-mately have to a jury, a thorough collection and scientific evaluation of physical evidence must become a routine part of all criminal investigations.

Just when an item of physical evidence crosses the line that distinguishes class from indi-vidual is a difficult question to answer and is often the source of heated debate and honest dis-agreement among forensic scientists. How many striations are necessary to individualize a mark to a single tool and no other? How many color layers individualize a paint chip to a single car? How many ridge characteristics individualize a fingerprint, and how many handwriting char-acteristics tie a person to a signature? These questions defy simple answers. The task of the forensic scientist is to find as many characteristics as possible to compare one substance with another. The significance attached to the findings is decided by the quality and composition of the evidence, the case history, and the examiner's experience. Ultimately, the conclusion can range from mere speculation to near certainty.

There are practical limits to the properties and characteristics the forensic scientist can select for comparison. Carried to the extreme, no two things in this world are alike in every detail. Mod-ern analytical techniques have become so sophisticated and sensitive that the criminalist must be careful to define the limits of natural variation among materials when interpreting the data gath-ered from a comparative analysis. For example, we will learn in the next chapter that two prop-erties, density and refractive index, are best suited for comparing two pieces of glass. But the latest techniques that have been developed to measure these properties are so sensitive that they can even distinguish glass originating from a single pane of glass. Certainly this goes beyond the desires of a criminalist trying to determine only whether two glass particles originated from the same window. Similarly, if the surface of a paint chip is magnified 1,600 times with a powerful scanning electron microscope, it is apparent that the fine details that are revealed could not be duplicated in any other paint chip. Under these circumstances, no two paint chips, even those coming from the same surface, could ever compare in the true sense of the word. Therefore, practicality dictates that such examinations be conducted at a less revealing, but more meaningful, magnification (see Figure 3–6).

(a)

(b)

FIGURE 3–6

(a) Two-layer paint chip magnified 244× with a scanning electron microscope. (b) The same paint chip viewed at a magnification of 1,600×.

Distinguishing evidential variations from natural variations is not always an easy task. Learning how to use the microscope and all the other modern instruments in a crime laboratory properly is one thing; gaining the proficiency needed to interpret the observations and data is another. As new crime laboratories are created and others expand to meet the requirements of the law enforcement community, many individuals are starting new careers in forensic science. They must be cautioned that merely reading relevant textbooks and journals is no substitute for experience in this most practical of sciences.

Forensic Databases

In a criminal investigation, the ultimate contribution a criminalist can make is to link a suspect to a crime through comparative analyses. This comparison defines the unique role of the criminalist in a criminal investigation. Of course, a one-on-one comparison requires a suspect. Little or nothing of evidential value can be accomplished if crime-scene investigators acquire fingerprints, hairs, fibers, paint, blood, and semen without the ability to link these items to a suspect. In this respect, computer technology has dramatically altered the role of the crime laboratory in the investigative process. No longer is the crime laboratory a passive bystander waiting for investigators to uncover clues about who may have committed a crime. Today, the crime laboratory is on the forefront of the investigation seeking to identify perpetrators. This dramatic reversal of the role of forensic science in criminal investigation has come about through the creation of computerized databases that not only link all 50 states, but tie together police agencies throughout the world.

Fingerprint Databases

The premier model of all forensic database systems is the *Integrated Automated Fingerprint Identification System* (IAFIS), a national fingerprint and criminal history system maintained by the FBI. IAFIS, which first became operational in 1999, contains fingerprints and access to corresponding criminal history information for nearly 50 million subjects (or 500 million fingerprint images), which are submitted voluntarily to the FBI by state, local, and federal law enforcement agencies. In the United States each state has its own *Automated Fingerprint Identification System* (AFIS), which is linked to the FBI's IAFIS. A crime-scene fingerprint or latent fingerprint is a dramatic find for the criminal investigator. Once the quality of the print has been deemed suitable for the IAFIS search, the latent-print examiner creates a digital image of the print with either a digital camera or a scanner. Next, the examiner, with the aid of a coder, marks points on the print to guide the computerized search. The print is then electronically submitted to IAFIS and within

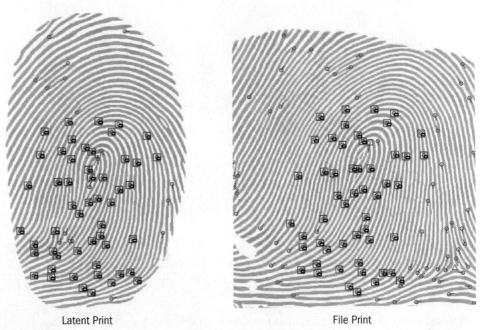

Latent Print   File Print

FIGURE 3–7

The computerized search of a fingerprint database first requires that selected ridge characteristics be designated by a coder. The positions of these ridge characteristics serve as a basis for comparing the latent print against file fingerprints.
Courtesy Sirchie Finger Print Laboratories, Youngsville, N.C., www.sirchie.com

minutes the search is completed against all fingerprint images in IAFIS; the examiner may receive a list of potential candidates and their corresponding fingerprints for comparison and verification (see Figure 3–7).

Many countries throughout the world have created national automated fingerprint identification systems that are comparable to the FBI's model. For example, a computerized fingerprint database containing nearly nine million ten-print records connects the Home Office and 43 police forces throughout England and Wales.

DNA Databases

In 1998, the FBI's *Combined DNA Index System* (CODIS) became fully operational. CODIS enables federal, state, and local crime laboratories to electronically exchange and compare DNA profiles, thereby linking crimes to each other and to convicted offenders. All 50 states have enacted legislation to establish a data bank containing DNA profiles of individuals convicted of felony sexual offenses (and other crimes, depending on each state's statute). CODIS creates investigative leads from two indexes: the *forensic* and *offender* indexes. The forensic index currently contains about 110,000 DNA profiles from unsolved crime-scene evidence. Based on a match, police in multiple jurisdictions can identify serial crimes, allowing coordination of investigations and sharing of leads developed independently. The offender index contains the profiles of nearly seven million convicted or arrested individuals. The FBI has joined 15 states that collect DNA samples from those awaiting trail and will collect DNA from detained immigrants. This information will be entered into an arrestee index database. Unfortunately, hundreds of thousands of samples are backlogged, still awaiting DNA analysis and entry into the offender index. Law enforcement agencies search this index against DNA profiles recovered from biological evidence found at unsolved crime scenes. This approach has proven to be tremendously successful in identifying perpetrators because most crimes involving biological evidence are committed by repeat offenders.

Several countries throughout the world have initiated national DNA data banks. The United Kingdom's *National DNA Database*, established in 1995, was the world's first national database. Currently it holds more than four million profiles, and DNA can be taken for entry into the database from anyone arrested for an offense likely to involve a prison term. In a typical month, matches are found linking suspects to 26 murders; 57 rapes and other sexual offenses; and 3,000 motor vehicle, property, and drug crimes.

Other Databases

The *National Integrated Ballistics Information Network* (NIBIN), maintained by the Bureau of Alcohol, Tobacco, Firearms and Explosives, allows firearms analysts to acquire, digitize, and compare markings made by a firearm on bullets and cartridge casings recovered from crime

forensic brief

In 1975, police found Gerald Wallace's body on his living room couch. He had been savagely beaten, his hands bound with an electric cord. Detectives searched his ransacked house, cataloging every piece of evidence they could find. None of it led to the murderer. They had no witnesses. Sixteen years after the fact, a lone fingerprint, lifted from a cigarette pack found in Wallace's house and kept for sixteen years in the police files, was entered into the Pennsylvania State Police AFIS database. Within minutes, it hit a match. That print, police say, gave investigators the identity of a man who had been at the house the night of the murder. Police talked to him. He led them to other witnesses, who led them to the man police ultimately charged with the murder of Gerald Wallace.

scenes. The NIBIN program currently has 236 sites that are electronically joined to 16 multistate regions. The heart of NIBIN is the *Integrated Ballistic Identification System* (IBIS), comprising a microscope and a computer unit that can capture an image of a bullet or cartridge casing. The images are then forwarded to a regional server, where they are stored and correlated against other images in the regional database. IBIS does not positively match bullets or casings fired from the same weapon; this must be done by a firearms examiner. IBIS does, however, facilitate the work of the firearms examiner by producing a short list of candidates for the examiner to manually compare. Nearly 900,000 pieces of crime-scene evidence have been entered in NIBIN and more than 10,000 "hits" have been recorded, many of them yielding investigative information not obtainable by other means.

forensic brief

Fort Collins, Colorado, and Philadelphia, Pennsylvania, are separated by nearly 1,800 miles, but in 2001 they were tragically linked through DNA. Troy Graves left the Philadelphia area in 1999, joined the Air Force, and settled down with his wife in Colorado. A frenzied string of eight sexual assaults around the Colorado University campus set off a manhunt that ultimately resulted in the arrest of Graves. However, his DNA profile inextricably identified him as Philadelphia's notorious "Center City rapist." This assailant attacked four women in 1997 and brutally murdered Shannon Schieber, a Wharton School graduate student, in 1998. His last known attack in Philadelphia was the rape of an 18-year-old student in August 1999, shortly before he left the city. In 2002 Graves was returned to Philadelphia, where he was sentenced to life in prison without parole.

forensic brief

After a series of armed robberies in which suspects fired shots, the sheriff's office of Broward County, Florida, entered the cartridge casings from the crime scenes into NIBIN. Through NIBIN, four of the armed robberies were linked to the same 40-caliber handgun. A short time later, sheriff's deputies noticed suspicious activity around a local business. When they attempted to interview the suspects, the suspects fled in a vehicle. During the chase, the suspects attempted to dispose of a handgun; deputies recovered the gun after making the arrests. The gun was test-fired and the resulting evidence entered into NIBIN, which indicated a possible link between this handgun and the four previous armed robberies. Firearms examiners confirmed the link through examination of the original evidence. The suspects were arrested and charged with four prior armed robbery offenses.

> >

forensic brief

A 53 year-old man was walking his dog in the early morning hours. He was struck and killed by an unknown vehicle and later found lying in the roadway. No witnesses were present, and the police had no leads regarding the suspect vehicle. A gold metallic painted plastic fragment recovered from the scene and the victim's clothing were submitted to the Virginia Department of Forensic Science for analysis.

The victim's clothing was scraped, and several minute gold metallic paint particles were recovered. Most of these particles contained only topcoats, whereas one minute particle contained two primer layers and a limited amount of colorcoat. The color of the primer surface layer was similar to that typically associated with some Fords. Subsequent spectral searches in the Paint Data Query (PDQ) database indicated that the paint most likely originated from a 1990 or newer Ford.

The most discriminating aspect of this paint was the unusual-looking gold metallic topcoat color. A search of automotive repaint books yielded only one color that closely matched the paint recovered

in the case. The color, Aztec Gold Metallic, was determined to have been used only on 1997 Ford Mustangs.

The results of the examination were relayed via telephone to the investigating detective. The investigating detective quickly determined that only 11,000 1997 Ford Mustangs were produced in Aztec Gold Metallic. Only two of these vehicles were registered, and had been previously stopped, in the jurisdiction of the offense. Ninety minutes after the make, model, and year information was relayed to the investigator, he called back to say he had located a suspect vehicle. Molding from the vehicle and known paint samples were submitted for comparison. Subsequent laboratory comparisons showed that the painted plastic piece recovered from the scene could be physically fitted together with the molding, and paint recovered from the victim's clothing was consistent with paint samples taken from the suspect vehicle.

Source: Brenda Christy, Virginia Department of Forensic Science

---

The *International Forensic Automotive Paint Data Query* (PDQ) database contains chemical and color information pertaining to original automotive paints. This database, developed and maintained by the Forensic Laboratory Services of the Royal Canadian Mounted Police (RCMP), contains information about make, model, year, and assembly plant on more than 13,000 vehicles with a library of more than 50,000 layers of paint. Contributors to the PDQ include the RCMP and forensic laboratories in Ontario and Quebec, as well as 40 U.S. forensic laboratories and police agencies in 21 other countries. Accredited users of PDQ are required to submit 60 new automotive paint samples per year for addition to the database. The PDQ database has found its greatest utility in the investigation of hit-and-runs by providing police with possible make, model, and year information to aid in the search for the unknown vehicle.

The previously described databases are maintained and controlled by government agencies. There is one exception: a commercially available computer retrieval system for comparing and identifying crime-scene shoe prints known as *SICAR* (shoeprint image capture and retrieval).[1] SICAR's pattern-coding system enables an analyst to create a simple description of a shoe print by assigning codes to individual pattern features (see Figure 3–8). Shoe print images can be entered into SICAR by either a scanner or a digital camera. This product has a comprehensive shoe sole database (Solemate™) that includes more than 17,000 footwear entries, representing over 700 shoe brands, providing investigators with a means for linking a crime-scene footwear impression to a particular shoe manufacturer.

---

[1] Foster & Freeman Limited, http://www.fosterfreeman.co.uk.

FIGURE 3–8

The crime-scene footwear print on the right is being searched against eight thousand sole patterns to determine its make and model.

Courtesy Foster & Freeman Limited, Worcestershire, U.K., www.fosterfreeman.co.uk

The Murder Scene: Death Investigation

Unfortunately, the most important piece of evidence at many crime scenes is the dead body of a victim. When foul play is suspected, a victim's corpse is subjected to the same kind of intense physical analysis as any other piece of evidence. This task falls primarily to a **forensic pathologist**, often aided by the skills of specialists including forensic anthropologists and forensic entomologists. In its broadest sense, forensic pathology involves the study of medicine as it relates to the application of the law, particularly criminal law. In practice, this most often involves the investigation of sudden, unnatural, unexplained, or violent deaths.

Role of the Forensic Pathologist

Forensic pathology involves the investigation of sudden, unnatural, unexplained, or violent deaths. Typically, forensic pathologists, in their role as medical examiners or coroners, must answer several basic questions: Who is the victim? What injuries are present? When did the injuries occur? Why and how were the injuries produced? The primary role of the medical examiner is to determine the cause of death. If a cause cannot be found through observation, an **autopsy** is normally performed to establish the cause of death. The manner in which death occurred is classified into five categories: natural, homicide, suicide, accident, or undetermined, based on the circumstances surrounding the incident.

ESTIMATING TIME OF DEATH   After a human body expires, it goes through several stages of decomposition. A medical examiner participating in a criminal investigation can often estimate the time of death by evaluating the stage of decomposition in which the victim was found. Immediately following death, the muscles relax and then become rigid. This condition, **rigor mortis**, manifests itself within the first 24 hours and disappears within 36 hours. Another condition occurring in the early stages of decomposition is **livor mortis**. When the human heart stops pumping, the blood begins to settle in the parts of the body closest to the ground. The skin will appear dark blue or purple in these areas. The onset of this condition begins immediately and continues for up to 12 hours after death. The skin will not appear discolored in areas where the body is

---

forensic pathologist
An individual who investigates sudden, unnatural, unexplained, or violent deaths.

autopsy
The medical dissection and examination of a body in order to determine the cause of death

rigor mortis
A medical condition that occurs after death and results in the stiffening of muscle mass. The rigidity of the body gradually disappears 24 hours after death and disappears within 36 hours

livor mortis
A medical condition that occurs after death and results in the settling of blood in areas of the body closest to the ground

restricted by either clothing or an object pressing against the body. This information can be useful in determining whether the victim's position was changed after death occurred.

Other physical and chemical changes within the body are also helpful in approximating the time of death. **Algor mortis** is the process by which the body temperature continually cools after death until it reaches the ambient or room temperature. The rate of heat loss is influenced by factors such as the location and size of the body, the victim's clothing, and weather conditions. Because of such factors, this method can only estimate the approximate time period since death. As a general rule, beginning about an hour after death, the body will lose heat at a rate of approximately 1–1.5°F per hour until the body reaches the environmental temperature.

Another approach helpful for estimating the time of death is determining potassium levels in the ocular fluid (vitreous humor). After death, cells within the inner surface of the eyeball release potassium into the ocular fluid. By analyzing the amount of potassium present at various intervals after death, the forensic pathologist can determine the rate at which potassium is released into the vitreous humor and use it to approximate the time of death. During the autopsy, other factors may indicate the time period in which death occurred. For example, the amount of food in the stomach can help estimate when a person's last meal was eaten. This information can be valuable when investigating a death.

Frequently, medical examiners must perform autopsies if a death is deemed suspicious or unexplained. The cause of death may not always be what it seems at first glance. For example, a decedent with a gunshot wound and a gun in his hand may appear to have committed suicide. However, an autopsy may reveal that the victim actually died of suffocation and the gunshot wound occurred after death to cover up the commission of a crime.

Role of the Forensic Anthropologist

Forensic anthropology is concerned primarily with the identification and examination of human skeletal remains. Skeletal bones are remarkably durable and undergo an extremely slow breakdown process that lasts decades or centuries. Because of their resistance to rapid decomposition, skeletal remains can provide a multitude of individual characteristics. An examination of bones may reveal their sex, approximate age, race, and skeletal injury.

RECOVERING AND PROCESSING REMAINS   Thorough documentation is required throughout the processes of recovery and examination of human remains. The sites where human remains are found must be treated as a crime scene (see Figure 3–9). These sites are usually located by

algor mortis
Postmortem changes that cause a body to lose heat

mycrimekit™

WEBEXTRA 3.2
See How an Autopsy Is Done
www.mycrimekit.com

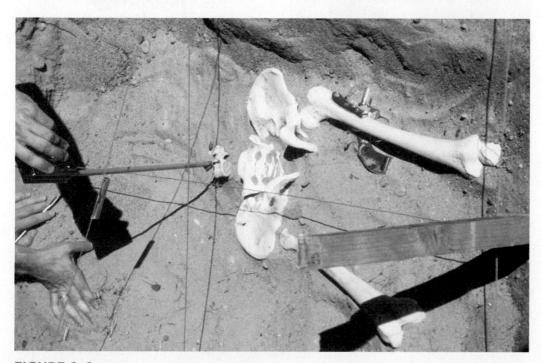

FIGURE 3–9
Crime-scene site showing a pelvis partly buried in sand and a femur lying across a revolver.
Courtesy Paul Sledzik, National Transportation Safety Board

civilians who then contact law enforcement personnel. The scene should be secured as soon as possible to prevent any further alteration of the scene. The scene should then be searched to locate all bones if they are scattered or other aspects of evidence such as footwear impressions or discarded items. Some tools can be useful in the search for evidence at a "tomb" site, including aerial photography, metal detectors, ground-penetrating radar, infrared photography, apparatuses that detect the gases produced by biological decomposition, and so-called cadaver dogs that detect the odors caused by biological decomposition. All items that are found must be tagged, photographed, sketched, and documented in notes. Once all bones and other evidence are found, a scene sketch should be made to show the exact location of each item (preferably using Global Positioning System [GPS] coordinates) and the spatial relationship of all evidence. Once the skeletal remains have been recovered, they can be examined to deduce information about the identity of the decedent.

DETERMINING VICTIM CHARACTERISTICS   The gender of the decedent can be determined by the size and shape of various skeletal features, especially those in the pelvis and skull or cranium. Female pelvic bones tend to show a wider, more circular opening than that of a male pelvis because of a woman's childbearing capabilities. The female sacrum (flat bone above the tailbone) is wider and shorter (see Figure 3–10 [a]); the length and width of the male sacrum are roughly equal (see Figure 3–11 [b]). In general, male craniums are larger in overall size than those of females. A male cranium tends to have a more pronounced brow bone and mastoid process (a bony protrusion behind the jaw) than a female cranium (see Figure 3–10).

(a)

(b)

FIGURE 3–10

(a) Frontal shot of female pelvis and hips. This view shows the wide, circular nature of the pelvic opening and the short, wide nature of the sacrum. (b) Human male pelvis. This view shows the narrow pelvic opening and long, narrow sacrum.

(a) Geoff Brightling/ESPL-modelmaker © ESPL/Dorling Kindersley; (b) Giuliano Fornari © Dorling Kindersley

FIGURE 3–11

Male (left) and female (right) human skulls showing male skull's larger size and more pronounced brow bone.

Courtesy Corbis RF

The method for determining the age of a decedent varies depending on the victim's growth stage. For infants and toddlers, age can be estimated by the length of the long bones (femur and humerus) when compared to a known growth curve. Different sections of the skull also fuse together at different stages during early development, and the appearance of fused or divided sections can be used to estimate age of bones still in early developmental stages (see Figure 3–12). If the skeletal remains belong to a child, the age of the decedent may be determined by observing the fusion or lack of fusion of epiphyseal regions of bones such as those of the mandible (lower jaw), fingers, wrist, long bones, and clavicle (see Figure 3–13). The average age at which each of these regions fuses is known and can be compared against the state of the remains to provide a range of possible ages for the decedent. A child's cranium may also be identified by the smaller size and the presence of developing teeth (see Figure 3–14). After age 21, age is estimated by the level of change experienced by the surfaces of the bones, especially in area of common wear such as the pubic symphysis. The pubic symphyseal face shown in Figure 3–15 is a raised platform that slowly changes over the years from a rough, rugged surface to a smooth, well-defined area.

Although the categorization of "race" has come under scrutiny and is hard to define, forensic anthropologists use broad classes to characterize the likely (but not definite) ancestry of skeletal remains. The possible racial ancestry of the decedent can be assessed by the appearance of various cranial features on the skeletal remains. For example, eye orbits tend to be circular in Mongoloid skeletons (Asian descent), oval in Caucasoid skeletons (European descent), and square in Negroid skeletons (African descent). The nasal cavity tends to be small and rounded in Mongoloids, long

FIGURE 3–12

A lateral view of a fetal skull showing the separated bones of the skull before they have had a chance to fuse.
Courtesy Ralph T. Hutchings

FIGURE 3–13

Colored X-rays of healthy human hands at 3 years (left) and 20 years. Bones are red with blue flesh. The child's hand has areas of cartilage in the joints between the finger bones (epiphyseal areas), where bone growth and fusion will occur. In the adult hand, all the bones are present and the joints have closed.
Courtesy SPL, Photo Researchers, Inc.

FIGURE 3–14

The skull of a young child, with part of the jaw cut away to show the developing teeth.
Courtesy Ralph T. Hutchings

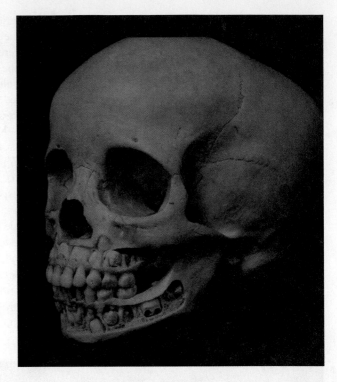

FIGURE 3–15

The pubic symphysis shown magnified beneath human pelvic bones.
Courtesy Pearson Education Custom Publishing

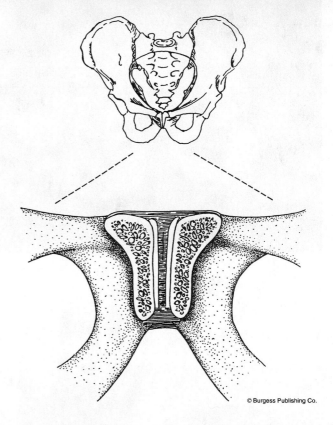

© Burgess Publishing Co.

and narrow in Caucasoids, and wide in Negroids. Skeletal remains of Asian ancestry, including those of Native American descent, also tend to have "scooped-out" or shovel-shaped incisor teeth.

The height of the victim when alive can be estimated by measuring the long bones of the skeleton, especially in the lower limbs. Even partial bones can yield useful results. However, meaningful stature calculations from known equations must be based on the determined sex and race of the remains.

> >

Identifying a Serial Killer's Victims

The worst serial killer in America calmly admitted his guilt as he led investigators to a crawl space under his house. There, John Wayne Gacy had buried 28 young men after brutally raping and murdering them in cold blood. Because no identification was found with the bodies, the police were forced to examine missing-person reports for leads. However, these boys and men were so alike in age, race, and stature that police were unable to make individual identifications for most of the victims. Clyde Snow, the world-renowned forensic anthropologist from Oklahoma, was asked to help the investigators make these difficult identifications.

Snow began by making a 35-point examination of each skull for comparison to known individuals. By examining each skeleton, he made sure each bone was correctly attributed to an individual. This was crucial to later efforts because some of the victims had been buried on top of older graves, mingling their remains. Once Snow was sure all the bones were sorted properly, he began his in-depth study. Long bones such as the femur (thigh bone) were used to estimate

each individual's height. This helped narrow the search when attempting to match the victims with the descriptions of missing people.

After narrowing the possibilities to missing people fitting the general description, investigators consulted potential victims' hospital and dental records. Evidence of injury, illness, surgery, or other unique skeletal defects was used to make identifications. Snow also pointed out features that gave clues to the victim's behavior and medical history. For example, he discovered that one of Gacy's victims had an old fracture of his left arm, and that his left scapula (shoulder blade) and arm bore the telltale signs of a left-handed individual. These details were matched to a missing-person report, and another young victim was identified.

For the most difficult cases, Snow called in the help of forensic sculptor and facial reconstructionist Betty Pat Gatliff. She used clay and depth markers to put the flesh back on the faces of these forgotten boys in the hopes that someone would recognize them after their photographs were released to the media. Her efforts were successful, but investigators found some families unwilling to accept the idea that their loved ones were among Gacy's victims. Even with Gatliff's help, nine of Gacy's victims remain unidentified.

OTHER CONTRIBUTIONS OF FORENSIC ANTHROPOLOGY   A forensic anthropologist may also create facial reconstructions to help identify skeletal remains. Facial reconstruction uses the victim's actual cranium and takes into account the estimated age, ancestry, and gender (see Figure 3–16). With the help of this technique, a composite of the victim can be drawn and advertised in an attempt to identify the victim.

Forensic anthropologists are also helpful in identifying victims of a mass disaster such as a plane crash. When such a tragedy occurs, forensic anthropologists can help identify victims through the collection of bone fragments. Definite identification of remains can be made only by analyzing the decedent's DNA profile, fingerprints, or medical records. Recovered remains may still contain some soft tissue material, which may yield a DNA profile for identification purposes. Sometimes the tissue of the hand is still present, though dried out. It may be possible to rehydrate the tissue to recover fingerprints. However, usually the identification of the remains will depend on medical records, especially dental records of the individual.

Role of the Forensic Entomologist

The study of insects and their relation to a criminal investigation is known as forensic entomology. Such a practice is commonly used to estimate the time of death when the circumstances surrounding the crime are unknown. This determination can be carried out by studying the stage of development of maggots or insect sequence of arrival.

DETERMINING TIME OF DEATH   After decomposition begins, *necrophilious insects*, or insects that feed on dead tissue, are the first to infest the body, usually within 24 hours. The most common and important of these is the blowfly, recognized by its green or blue color. Blowfly eggs are laid in the human remains and ultimately hatch into maggots, or fly larvae, which consume human organs and tissues (see Figure 3–17). Typically, a single blowfly can lay thousands of eggs during its lifetime (see Figure 3–18). The resulting larvae gather and feed as a "maggot mass" on the decomposing remains. Forensic entomologists can approximate how long a body has been left exposed by examining the stage of development of the fly larvae. This kind of determination is

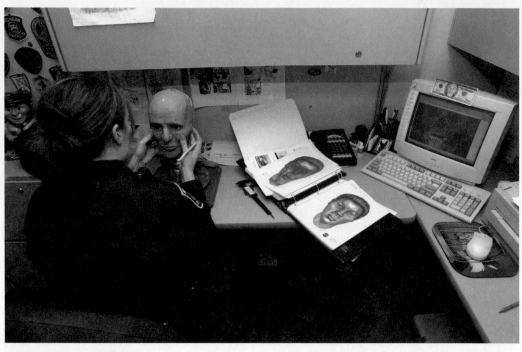

FIGURE 3–16

Trooper Sarah Foster, a Michigan State Police forensic artist, works on a three-dimensional facial reconstruction from an unidentified human skull at the Richmond post in Richmond, Michigan.
Courtesy Paul Sancya, AP Wide World Photos

FIGURE 3–17

A scanning electron micrograph of 2-hour-old blowfly maggots.
Courtesy Dr. Jeremy Burgess, Photo Researchers, Inc.

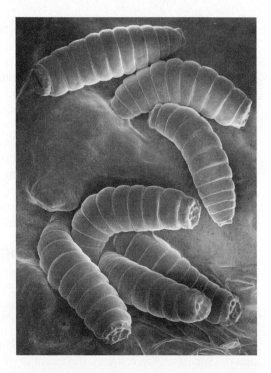

best for a timeline of hours to approximately 1 month, because the blowfly goes through the stages of its life cycle at known time intervals and in an identifiable sequence. By determining the most developed stage of fly found on the body, entomologists can approximate the post-mortem interval (PMI), or the time that has elapsed since death (see Figure 3–19). Newly emerged flies are of important forensic interest, as they indicate that an entire blowfly cycle has

FIGURE 3–18

A blowfly depositing a mass of eggs.

Courtesy Volker Steger, Photo Researchers, Inc.

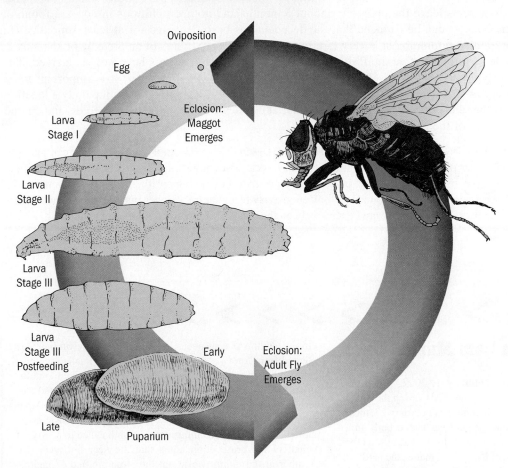

FIGURE 3–19

Typical blowfly life cycle from egg deposition to adult fly emergence. This cycle is representative of any one of the nearly ninety species of blowflies in North America.

Courtesy E. P. Catts, Ph.D., deceased, and Neal H. Haskell, Ph.D., forensic entomology consultant, www.forensic-entomology.com

been completed on the decomposing body. Likewise, empty pupal cases indicate that a fly has completed its entire life cycle on the body.

These determinations are not always straightforward, however. The time required for stage development is affected by environmental influences such as geographical location, climate, weather conditions, and the presence of drugs. For example, cold temperatures hinder the development of fly eggs into adult flies. The forensic entomologist must consider these conditions when estimating the PMI.

Information about the arrival of other species of insects may also aid in determining the PMI. The sequence of arrival of these groups is dependent primarily on the body's natural decomposition process. Predator insects generally arrive to prey on the necrophagous insects. Several kinds of beetles may be found, either feeding directly on the corpse tissues or as predators feeding on blowfly eggs and maggots present on the corpse. Next, omnivore insects arrive at the body. These insects feed on the body, on other insects, and on surrounding vegetation. Ants and wasps are an example of omnivore insects. Finally, indigenous insects, such as spiders, arrive; their presence on or near the body is coincidental as they move about their environment.

The known sequence of arrival of different insect groups can help determine the PMI. This method is usually used when months have elapsed between the time when the decedent died and when the body was found. In order to make an accurate estimate, the forensic entomologist must compare the species found on the body to experimental data from that geographical area. The entomologist then looks first for what earlier groups are missing. This sets a minimum PMI. For example, if experiments in that area have shown that all necrophilious insects leave the body after about 3 months and no necrophilious insects are found on the body, it can be deduced that the decedent has been deceased for at least 3 months. If a particular entomologist is very familiar with the insect patterns of an area, he or she may be able to further define the PMI range by looking for what groups have not yet arrived. This method may also be useful to determine season of death. However, it is important to remember that the diversity of insects found on a body is also affected by the body's location, weather and temperature conditions, habitat characteristics, indigenous species, and characteristics of the body.

OTHER CONTRIBUTIONS OF FORENSIC ENTOMOLOGY   Entomological evidence can also provide other pertinent information. In general, insects first colonize the body's natural moist orifices. However, if open wounds are present, they prefer to colonize there first. Because decomposition processes may conceal wounds, colonization away from natural orifices may help locate wounds on the body. If maggots are found extensively on the hands and forearms, for example, this suggests the

case study

The Danielle Van Dam Murder Case

Sometime during the night of February 1, 2002, 7-year-old Danielle Van Dam disappeared from her bedroom in the Sabre Springs suburb of San Diego, California. On February 27, three and a half weeks later, searchers found her naked body in a trash-covered lot about 25 miles from her home. Because of the high degree of decomposition of the girl's remains, the medical examiner could not pinpoint the exact time of the girl's death. Her neighbor, 50-year-old engineer David Westerfield, was accused of kidnapping Danielle, killing her, and dumping her body in the desert. During the subsequent investigation, Danielle's blood was found on Westerfield's clothes, her fingerprints and blood were found in his RV, and child pornography was found on his home computer.

The actual time of the 7-year-old's death became a central issue during the murder trial. Westerfield had been under constant police surveillance since February 4. Any suggestion that Danielle was placed at the dump site after that date would have eliminated him as a suspect. Conflicting expert testimony was elicited from forensic entomologists who were called upon to estimate when the body was dumped. The forensic entomologist who went to the dump site, witnessed the autopsy, and collected and analyzed insects from both locations estimated that Danielle died between February 16 and 18. A forensic entomologist and a forensic anthropologist both called to testify on behalf of the prosecution noted that the very hot, very dry weather at the dump site might have mummified Danielle's body almost immediately, thus causing a delay in the flies colonizing the body.

The jurors convicted Westerfield of the kidnapping and murder of Danielle Van Dam, and a San Diego judge sentenced David Westerfield to death. Danielle Van Dam's parents filed and settled a wrongful death suit against Westerfield requiring his automotive and homeowners' insurance carriers to pay the Van Dams an undisclosed amount, reported to be between $400,000 and $1 million.

presence of defensive wounds on the victim. Insects that have fed on the body may also have accumulated any drugs present in the flesh, and these insects can yield the identity of these drugs.

If resources allow, all insect evidence should be carefully collected by a forensic entomology expert. When this is not possible, collection should be carried out by an investigator with experience in death investigation. The entire body and the area where insect evidence was found must be photographed and documented before collection. Specimen samples should be taken from each area on the body where they are found and labeled to show where they were collected from.

chapter summary

< < < < < < < < < < < <

Physical evidence is usually examined by a forensic scientist for identification or comparison purposes. The object of identification is to determine the physical or chemical identity with as near absolute certainty as existing analytical techniques will permit. Identification first requires the adoption of testing procedures that give characteristic results for specific standard materials. Once this is done, the examiner uses an appropriate number of tests to identify a substance and exclude all other substances from consideration. The identification process is normally used in crime laboratories to identify drugs, explosives, and petroleum products. Also, evidence such as blood, semen, or hair is routinely identified in a crime laboratory. Normally, these identifications would include a determination for species origin (such as human blood or rabbit hair).

A comparative analysis has the important role of determining whether a suspect specimen and a standard/reference specimen have a common origin. Both the standard/reference specimen and the suspect specimen are subject to the same tests. Evidence that can be associated with a common source with an extremely high degree of probability is said to possess individual characteristics. Evidence associated only with a group is said to have class characteristics. Nevertheless, the high diversity of class evidence in our environment makes their comparison significant in the context of a criminal investigation. As the number of different objects linking an individual to a crime scene increases, so does the likelihood of that individual's involvement with the crime. Importantly, a person may be exonerated or excluded from suspicion if physical evidence collected at a crime scene is found to be different from standard/reference samples collected from that subject.

A dramatic enhancement of the role of forensic science in criminal investigation has come about through the creation of computerized databases. The Integrated Automated Fingerprint Identification System (IAFIS), a national fingerprint and criminal history system, is maintained by the FBI. The FBI's Combined DNA Index System (CODIS) enables federal, state, and local crime laboratories to electronically exchange and compare DNA profiles, thereby linking crimes to each other and to convicted offenders. The National Integrated Ballistics Information Network (NIBIN), maintained by the Bureau of Alcohol, Tobacco, Firearms and Explosives, allows firearms analysts to acquire, digitize, and compare markings made by a firearm on bullets and cartridge casings recovered from crime scenes. The International Forensic Automotive Paint Data Query (PDQ) database contains chemical and color information pertaining to original automotive paints. SICAR (shoeprint image capture and retrieval) has a comprehensive shoe sole database.

Physical evidence left behind at a crime scene, properly handled and preserved, plays a crucial role in reconstructing the events that took place surrounding the crime. Crime-scene reconstruction relies on the combined efforts of medical examiners, criminalists, and law enforcement personnel to recover physical evidence and to sort out the events surrounding the occurrence of a crime.

Several special forensic science services are available to the law enforcement community to augment the services of the crime laboratory in a death investigation. The services of a forensic pathologist, forensic anthropologist, and forensic entomologist may be required in the investigation of a sudden, unnatural, unexplained, or violent death. Forensic pathologists examine the body of a decedent to estimate cause of death and time since death or postmortem interval (PMI). Forensic anthropologists seek to identify human remains by examining characteristics of skeletal remains and creating an estimated profile of the victim. Forensic entomologists examine the insect evidence from a crime scene or associated with a body. They can then use this information to estimate PMI.

review questions

1. The process of _____ determines a substance's physical or chemical identity with as near absolute certainty as existing analytical techniques will permit.

2. The number and type of tests needed to identify a substance must be sufficient to _____ all other substances from consideration.

3. A(n) _____ analysis subjects a suspect specimen and a standard/reference specimen to the same tests and examination in order to determine whether they have a common origin.

4. _____ is the frequency of occurrence of an event.

5. Evidence that can be traced to a common source with an extremely high degree of probability is said to possess _____ characteristics.

6. Evidence associated with a group and not with a single source is said to possess _____ characteristics.

7. True or False: One of the major deficiencies of forensic science is the inability of the examiner to assign exact or approximate probability values to the comparison of most class physical evidence. _____

8. The value of class physical evidence lies in its ability to _____ events with data in a manner that is, as nearly as possible, free of human error and bias.

9. The _____ accorded physical evidence during a trial is left entirely to the trier of fact.

10. True or False: Physical evidence cannot be used to exclude or exonerate a person from suspicion of committing a crime. _____

11. True or False: The distinction between individual and class evidence is always easy to make. _____

12. Modern analytical techniques have become so sensitive that the forensic examiner must be aware of the _____ among materials when interpreting the significance of comparative data.

13. True or False: A fingerprint can be positively identified through the IAFIS database. _____

14. A database applicable to DNA profiling is _____.

15. When _____ sets in after death, the skin appears dark blue or purple in the areas closest to the ground.

16. True or False: One method for approximating the time of death is to determine body temperature. _____

17. _____ involves the study of medicine as it relates to the application of the law, most often pertaining to the investigation of sudden, unnatural, unexplained, or violent deaths.

18. The cause of death, whether natural, homicide, suicide, accident, or undetermined, is normally determined by performing a(n) _____ and investigating the circumstances surrounding the death.

19. In determining time of death, _____ occurs after death and results in the stiffening of body parts in the position they are in when death occurs, _____ occurs after death and results in the settling of blood in areas of the body closest to the ground, and _____ refers to postmortem changes that cause a body to lose heat.

20. Another approach for estimating the time of death is to determine potassium levels in the _____ fluid.

21. The field of _____ takes advantage of the durable nature of bones over long periods of time to examine and identify human skeletal remains through a multitude of individual characteristics.

22. Female bone structure differs from male bone structure within the _____ area because of a woman's childbearing capabilities.

23. A forensic anthropologist may also help create a(n) _____ of the decedent from which a composite drawing of the victim can be drawn and advertised in an attempt to identify the victim.

24. True or False: Definite identification of remains cannot be made through the analysis of the decedent's DNA profile, fingerprints, or medical records. _____

25. True or False: Sites where human remains are found must be treated as a crime scene, and the site and surrounding area should be secured, searched, and carefully processed. _____

26. Once all bones and other evidence are found at a "tomb" site, a(n) _____ should be made to show the exact location of each item.

27. The study of insects and their relation to a criminal investigation, known as _____, is commonly used to estimate the time of death when the circumstances surrounding the crime are unknown.

28. By determining the oldest stage of fly found on the body and taking environmental factors into consideration, entomologists can approximate the _____ interval.

29. Entomological evidence collected at a scene should include samples from every area where insects are found and _____ measurements.

30. True or False: Another method to determine PMI is by observing the schedule of arrival of different insect species on the body. _____

application and critical thinking

1. Arrange the following tasks in order from the one that would require the least extensive testing procedure to the one that would require the most extensive. Explain your answer.

   a. Determining whether an unknown substance contains an illicit drug

   b. Determining the composition of an unknown substance

   c. Determining whether an unknown substance contains heroin

2. The following are three possible combinations of DNA characteristics that may be found in an individual's genetic profile. Using the product rule, rank each of these combinations of DNA characteristics from most common to least common. The number after each characteristic indicates its percentage distribution in the population.

   a. FGA 24,24 (3.6%), TH01 6,8 (8.1%), and D16S539 11, 12 (8.9%)

   b. vWA 14,19 (6.2%), D21S11 30,30 (3.9%), and D13S317 12,12 (8.5%)

   c. CSF1PO 9,10 (11.2%), D18S51 14,17 (2.8%), and D8S1179 17,18 (6.7%)

3. For each of the following pieces of evidence, indicate whether the item is more likely to possess class or individual characteristics and explain your answers.

   a. An impression from a new automobile tire

   b. A fingerprint

   c. A spent bullet cartridge

   d. A mass-produced synthetic fiber

   e. Pieces of a shredded document

   f. Commercial potting soil

   g. Skin and hair scrapings

   h. Fragments of a multilayer custom automobile paint

4. Which of the forensic databases described in the text contain information that relates primarily to evidence exhibiting class characteristics? Which ones contain information that relates primarily to evidence exhibiting individual characteristics? Explain your answers.

5. Which of the discussed conditions examined during autopsy could help the forensic pathologist determine time since death if the victim expired within 1 or 2 hours of being discovered? Which would be of little or no assistance in this determination?

6. A highly weathered skeleton is recovered from a remote wooded site. Only the upper torso and cranium were recovered. The clavicle is found to be unfused and the cranium features a very prominent brow bone and sharp, protruding mastoid process. What can be surmised about the victim's identity from this information?

further references

Houck, M. M., "Statistics and Trace Evidence: The Tyranny of Numbers," *Forensic Science Communications,* 1, no. 3 (1999) www.fbi.gov/hq/lab/fsc/backissu/oct1999/houck.htm

Houck, M. M., and J. A. Siegel, *Fundamentals of Forensic Science.* Burlington, MA: Elsevier Academic Press, 2006.

Osterburg, James W., "The Evaluation of Physical Evidence in Criminalistics: Subjective or Objective Process?" *Journal of Criminal Law, Criminology and Police Science* 60 (1969): 97.

Thornton, John I., *Paul L. Kirk's Crime Investigation*, 2nd ed. New York: Wiley, 1974.

case analysis

In 1982, the state of Georgia convicted Wayne Williams of murdering several boys and young men in the Atlanta area. The case featured unique uses of fiber evidence that proved crucial to establishing Williams's guilt. The case also highlighted the effectiveness of statistical probability for establishing links between evidence found at multiple crime scenes.

1. In what respects did the use of fiber evidence in the Williams case differ significantly from its use in previous cases?

2. What did investigators hope to learn from their initial examination of fibers found on the bodies of several murder victims found in the Atlanta area from July 1979 to May 1981? What steps did they take to gather this information? What did they learn from their investigations? What was the significance of this information?

3. How could information on the source of the fibers be helpful to investigators? Explain how investigators may use information about the source of a fiber to help them locate the perpetrator.

4. What pieces of information did investigators collect from the West Point Pepperell Corporation that led them to conclude that the fibers found on Nathaniel Cater's body came from the carpeting in Wayne Williams's house? Explain the importance of each of these pieces of information for connecting Williams to Cater's murder.

5. Describe how investigators used the concepts of statistical probability to tie Williams to Nathaniel Cater as well as to his other victims.

Fiber Evidence and the Wayne Williams Trial

On February 26, 1982, a Fulton County, Ga., Superior Court jury returned a verdict of "guilty as charged" on two counts of murder brought against Wayne Bertram Williams by a Fulton County grand jury in July 1981. Williams had been on trial since December 28, 1981, for the asphyxial murders of Nathaniel Cater and Jimmy Payne in April and May of 1981. During the 8-week trial, evidence linking Williams to those murders and to the murders of 10 other boys or young men was introduced.

An essential part of this case, presented by the Fulton County District Attorney's Office, involved the association of fibrous debris removed from the bodies of 12 murder victims with objects from the everyday environment of Williams.

Fiber evidence has often been an important part of criminal cases, but the Williams trial differed from other cases in several respects. Fiber evidence has not played a significant role in any case involving a large number of murder victims. The victims whose deaths were charged to Williams were 2 of 30 black children and black young men who were reported missing or who had died under suspicious circumstances in the Atlanta area over a 22-month period beginning in July 1979. During the trial, fiber evidence was used to associate Williams with 12 of those victims.

Fiber evidence is often used to corroborate other evidence in a case—it is used to support other testimony presented at a trial. This was not the situation in the Williams trial. Other evidence and other aspects of the trial were important but were used to support and complement the fiber evidence, not the usual order of things. The "hair and fiber matches" between Williams's environment and 11 of the 12 murder victims discussed at the trial were so significant that, in the author's opinion, these victims were positively linked to both the residence and automobiles that were a major part of the world of Wayne Williams.

Another difference between this case and most other cases was the extremely large amount of publicity surrounding both the investigation of the missing and murdered children and the arrest and subsequent trial of Williams. Few other murder trials have received the attention that the Williams case received. . . .

It is often difficult to get an accurate picture from press reports of the physical evidence introduced at a trial and the significance of that evidence. This article will also set forth in some detail the fiber evidence that linked Williams to the murder victims.

By discussing only the fiber evidence introduced at the trial, many other aspects of the case against Williams are being neglected. Additional evidence dealing with Williams's motivations—his character and behavior, his association with several of the victims by eyewitness accounts, and his link to a victim recovered from a river in Atlanta—[were] also essential to the case. . . .

Harold A. Deadman
Special Agent, Microscopic Analysis Unit, Laboratory Division
Federal Bureau of Investigation, Washington, D.C.

Development of Williams as a Murder Suspect

Before Wayne Williams became a suspect in the Nathaniel Cater murder case, the Georgia State Crime Laboratory located a number of yellowish-green nylon fibers and some violet acetate fibers on the bodies and clothing of the murder victims whose bodies had been recovered during the period of July 1979 to May 1981. The names of those victims were included on the list of missing and murdered children that was compiled by the Atlanta Task Force (a large group of investigators from law enforcement agencies in the Atlanta area). The yellowish-green nylon fibers were generally similar to each other in appearance and properties and were considered to have originated from a single source. This was also true of the violet acetate fibers. Although there were many other similarities that would link these

Wayne Williams is shown talking to police outside his home.
Courtesy CORBIS-NY

Reprinted in part from *FBI Law Enforcement Bulletin*, March and May 1984.

murders together, the fiber linkage was notable since the possibility existed that a source of these fibers might be located in the future.

Initially, the major concern with these yellowish-green nylon fibers was determining what type of object could have been their source. This information could provide avenues of investigative activity. The fibers were very coarse and had a lobed cross-sectional appearance, tending to indicate that they originated from a carpet or a rug. The lobed cross-sectional shape of these fibers, however, was unique, and initially, the manufacturer of these fibers could not be determined. Photomicrographs of the fibers were prepared for display to contacts within the textile industry. On one occasion, these photomicrographs were distributed among several chemists attending a meeting at the research facilities of a large fiber producer. The chemists concurred that the yellowish-green nylon fiber was very unusual in cross-sectional shape and was consistent with being a carpet fiber, but again, the manufacturer of this fiber could not be determined. Contacts with other textile producers and textile chemists likewise did not result in an identification of the manufacturer.

In February 1981, an Atlanta newspaper article publicized that several different fiber types had been found on two murder victims. Following the publication of this article, bodies recovered from rivers in the Atlanta metropolitan area were either nude or clothed only in undershorts. It appeared possible that the victims were being disposed of in this undressed state and in rivers in order to eliminate fibers from being found on their bodies.[1]

On May 22, 1981, a four-man surveillance team of personnel from the Atlanta Police Department and the Atlanta Office of the FBI was situated under and at both ends of the James Jackson Parkway Bridge over the Chattahoochee River in northwest Atlanta. Around 2 A.M., a loud splash alerted the surveillance team to the presence of an automobile being driven slowly off the bridge. The driver was stopped and identified as Wayne Bertram Williams.

Two days after Williams's presence on the bridge, the nude body of Nathaniel Cater was pulled from the Chattahoochee River, approximately 1 mile downstream from the James Jackson Parkway Bridge. A yellowish-green nylon carpet-type fiber, similar to the nylon fibers discussed above, was recovered from the head hair of Nathaniel Cater. When details of Williams's reason for being on the bridge at 2 A.M. could not be confirmed, search warrants for Williams's home and automobile were obtained and were served on the afternoon of June 3, 1981. During the late evening hours of the same day, the initial associations of fibers from Cater and other murder victims were made with a green carpet in the home of Williams. Associations with a bedspread from Williams's bed and with [Williams's] family dog were also made at that time.

An apparent source of the yellowish-green nylon fibers had been found. It now became important to completely characterize these fibers in order to verify the associations and determine the strength of the associations resulting from the fiber matches. Because of the unusual cross-sectional appearance of the nylon fiber and the difficulty in determining the manufacturer, it was believed

[1]Prior to the publication of the February 11, 1981, newspaper article, one victim from the task force list, who was fully clothed, had been recovered from a river in the Atlanta area. In the 2½-month period after publication, the nude or nearly nude bodies of 7 of the 9 victims added to the task force list were recovered from rivers in the Atlanta area.

that this was a relatively rare fiber type, and therefore, would not be present in large amounts (or in a large number of carpets).

[Williams's] Carpet

Shortly after Williams was developed as a suspect, it was determined the yellowish-green nylon fibers were manufactured by the Wellman Corporation. The next step was to ascertain, if possible, how much carpet like Williams's bedroom carpet had been sold in the Atlanta area—carpet composed of the Wellman fiber and dyed with the same dye formulation as [Williams's] carpet. Names of Wellman Corporation customers who had purchased this fiber type, technical information about the fiber, and data concerning when and how much of this fiber type had been manufactured were obtained.

It was confirmed that the Wellman Corporation had, in fact, manufactured the fiber in Williams's carpet and that no other fiber manufacturer was known to have made a fiber with a similar cross section. It was also determined that fibers having this cross-sectional shape were manufactured and sold during the years 1967 through 1974. Prior to 1967, this company manufactured only a round cross section; after 1974, the unusual trilobal cross section seen in Williams's carpet was modified to a more regular trilobal cross-sectional shape. A list of sales of that fiber type during the period 1967 through 1974 was compiled. . . .

Through numerous contacts with yarn spinners and carpet manufacturers, it was determined that the West Point Pepperell Corporation of Dalton, Ga., had manufactured a line of carpet called "Luxaire," which was constructed in the same manner as [Williams's] carpet. One of the colors offered in the "Luxaire" line was called "English Olive," and this color was the same as that of [Williams's] carpet (both visually and by the use of discriminating chemical and instrumental tests).

It was learned that the West Point Pepperell Corporation had manufactured the "Luxaire" line for a five-year period from December 1970 through 1975; however, it had only purchased Wellman 181B fiber for this line during 1970 and 1971. In December 1971, the West Point Pepperell Corporation changed the fiber composition of the "Luxaire" line to a different nylon fiber, one that was dissimilar to the Wellman 181B fiber in appearance. Accordingly, "Luxaire" carpet, like [Williams's] carpet, was only manufactured for a 1-year period. This change of carpet fiber after only 1 year in production was yet another factor that made [Williams's] carpet unusual.

It is interesting to speculate on the course the investigation would have taken if the James Jackson Parkway Bridge had not been covered by the surveillance team. The identification of the manufacturer of the nylon fibers showing up on the bodies could still have occurred and the same list of purchasers of the Wellman fiber could have been obtained. The same contacts with the yarn and carpet manufacturers could have been made; however, there would not have been an actual carpet sample to display. It is believed that eventually the carpet manufacturer could have been determined. With a sample of carpet supplied by West Point Pepperell—which they had retained in their files for over 10 years—it would have been possible to conduct a house-by-house search of the Atlanta area in an attempt to find a similar carpet. Whether this very difficult task would have been attempted, of course, will never be known. A search of that type, however, would have accurately answered an important question that was discussed at the trial—the question of how many other homes in the Atlanta area had a carpet like [Williams's] carpet. An estimation, to be discussed later, based on sales records provided by the West Point Pepperell Corporation indicated that there was a very low chance (1/7,792) of finding a carpet like Williams's carpet by randomly selecting occupied residences in the Atlanta area.

Only the West Point Pepperell Corporation was found to have manufactured a carpet exactly like [Williams's] carpet. Even though several manufacturers had gone out of business and could not be located, it was believed that, considering the many variables that exist in the manufacture of carpet and the probable uniqueness of each carpet manufacturer's dye formulations, it would be extremely unlikely for two unrelated companies to construct a carpet or dye the carpet fibers in exactly the same way. A large number of other green fibers, visually similar in color to Williams's carpet, were examined. None was found to be consistent with fibers from [Williams's] carpet.

Probability Determinations

To convey the unusual nature of [Williams's] residential carpet, an attempt was made to develop a numerical probability—something never before done in connection with textile materials used as evidence in a criminal trial.[2] The following information was gathered from the West Point Pepperell Corporation:

1. West Point Pepperell reported purchases of Wellman 181B fiber for the "Luxaire" line during a 1-year period. The Wellman 181B fiber was used to manufacture "Luxaire" carpet from December 1970 until December 1971, at which time a new fiber type replaced that Wellman fiber.
2. In 1971, West Point Pepperell sold 5,710 square yards of English Olive "Luxaire" and "Dreamer" carpet to Region C (10 southeastern states which include Georgia). "Dreamer" was a line of carpet similar to "Luxaire" but contained a less dense pile. In order to account for the carpet manufactured during 1971, but sold after that time, all of the "Luxaire" English Olive carpet sold during 1972 to Region C (10,687 square yards) was added to the 1971 sales. Therefore, it was estimated that a total of 16,397 square yards of carpet containing the Wellman 181B fiber and dyed English Olive in color was sold by the West Point Pepperell Corporation to retailers in 10 southeastern states during 1971 and 1972. (In 1979, existing residential carpeted floor space in the United States was estimated at 6.7 billion square yards.)[3]
3. By assuming that this carpet was installed in one room, averaging 12 feet by 15 feet in size, per house, and also assuming that the total sales of carpet were divided equally among the 10 southeastern states, then approximately 82 rooms with this carpet could be found in the state of Georgia.

4. Information from the Atlanta Regional Commission showed that there were 638,995 occupied housing units in the Atlanta metropolitan area in November 1981.[4] Using this figure, the chance of randomly selecting an occupied housing unit in metropolitan Atlanta and finding a house with a room having carpet like Williams's carpet was determined to be 1 chance in 7,792—a very low chance.

To the degree that the assumptions used in calculating the above probability number are reasonable, we can be confident in arriving at a valid probability number. . . .

The probability figures illustrate clearly that [Williams's] carpet is, in fact, very uncommon. To enhance the figures even further, it is important to emphasize that these figures are based on the assumption that none of the carpet of concern had been discarded during the past 11 years. In fact, carpet of this type, often used in commercial settings, such as apartment houses, would probably have had a normal life span of only 4 or 5 years. . . .[5]

The Williams Trial

To any experienced forensic fiber examiner, the fiber evidence linking Williams to the murder victims was overwhelming. But regardless of the apparent validity of the fiber findings, it was during the trial that its true weight would be determined. Unless it could be conveyed meaningfully to a jury, its effect would be lost. Because of this, considerable time was spent determining what should be done to convey the full significance of the fiber evidence. Juries are not usually composed of individuals with a scientific background, and therefore, it was necessary to "educate" the jury in what procedures were followed and the significance of the fiber results. In the Williams case, over 40 charts with over 350 photographs were prepared to illustrate exactly what the crime laboratory examiners had observed. . . .

Representatives of the textile fiber industry, including technical representatives from the Wellman and West Point Pepperell Corporations, were involved in educating the jury regarding textile fibers in general and helped lay the foundation for the conclusions of the forensic fiber examiners. The jury also was told about fiber analysis in the crime laboratory.

The trial, as it developed, can be divided into two parts. Initially, testimony was given concerning the murders of Nathaniel Cater and Jimmy Ray Payne, the two victims included in the indictment drawn against Williams in July 1981. Testimony was then given concerning Williams's association with 10 other murder victims.

The fiber matches made between fibers in Williams's environment and fibers from victims Payne and Cater were discussed. The items from Williams's environment that were linked to either

[2] J. Mitchell and D. Holland, "An Unusual Case of Identification of Transferred Fibers," *Journal of the Forensic Science Society*, vol. 19, 1979, p. 23. This article describes a case in which carpet fibers transferred to a murder victim's body in England were traced back to the carpet manufacturer and finally to an automobile owned by the person who eventually confessed to the murder.

[3] This information was taken from a study by E. I. du Pont de Nemours & Co. concerned with the existing residential floor space with carpet in the United States. This study was reported in a marketing survey conducted by the Marketing Corporation of America, Westport, Conn.

[4] Information regarding the number of housing units in the Atlanta metropolitan area was obtained from a report provided by the Atlanta Regional Commission. The report, dated November 11, 1981, contained population and housing counts for counties, super districts, and census tracts in the Atlanta metropolitan area.

[5] Information about carpet similar to Williams's carpet was developed through contacts with carpet manufacturers and carpet salesmen in Georgia. It was determined that this type of carpet was often installed in commercial settings, such as apartments, and in those settings, had an average life span of 4 to 5 years.

**ITEMS FROM RESIDENCE AND
STATION WAGON OF WAYNE WILLIAMS**

STATION WAGON: CARPET
THROW RUG
BLUE RAYON FIBERS

JIMMY RAY PAYNE

Black male (21) 5'7", 135 lbs.
Body recovered Chattahoochee
River near I-85, 4/27/81
Death by Asphyxiation

BEDROOM: BEDSPREAD
BEDROOM CARPET
BLANKET FROM UNDER BED
WILLIAMS FAMILY DOG

NATHANIEL CATER

Black male (28) 5'11", 146 lbs.
Body recovered Chattahoochee
River near I-85, 5/24/81
Death by Asphyxiation

BACKROOM: CARPET SQUARE
YELLOW-GREEN SYNTHETIC FIBERS

FIGURE 1

Items from residence and station wagon of Wayne Williams that were found on Jimmy Ray Payne and Nathaniel Cater.

or both of the victims are shown in the center of the chart. (See Figure 1.) Not only is Payne linked to Williams's environment by seven items and Cater linked by six items, but both of the victims are linked strongly to each other based on the fiber matches and circumstances surrounding their deaths.

In discussing the significance or strength of an association based on textile fibers, it was emphasized that the more uncommon the fibers, the stronger the association. None of the fiber types from the items in Williams's environment shown in the center of Figure 1 is by definition a "common" fiber type. Several of the fiber types would be termed "uncommon."

One of the fibers linking the body of Jimmy Ray Payne to the carpet in the 1970 station wagon driven by Williams was a small rayon fiber fragment recovered from Payne's shorts. Data were obtained from the station wagon's manufacturer concerning which automobile models produced prior to 1973 contained carpet made of this fiber type. These data were coupled with additional information from Georgia concerning the number of these models registered in the Atlanta metropolitan area during 1981. This allowed a calculation to be made relating to the probability of randomly selecting an automobile having carpet like that in the 1970 Chevrolet station wagon from the 2,373,512 cars registered in the Atlanta metropolitan area. This probability is 1 chance in 3,828, a very low probability representing a significant association.

Another factor to consider when assessing the significance of fiber evidence is the increased strength of the association when multiple fiber matches become the basis of the association. This is true if different fiber types from more than one object are found and each fiber type either links two people together or links an individual with a particular environment. As the number of different objects increases, the strength of an association increases dramatically. That is, the chance of randomly finding several particular fiber types in a certain location is much smaller than the chance of finding one particular fiber type.

The following example can be used to illustrate the significance of multiple fiber matches linking two items together. If one were to throw a single die one time, the chance or probability of throwing a particular number would be one chance in six. The probability of throwing a second die and getting that same number also would be one chance in six. However, the probability of getting 2 of the same numbers on 2 dice thrown simultaneously is only 1 in every 36 double throws—a much smaller chance than with either of the single throws. This number is a result of the product rule of probability theory. That is, the probability of the joint occurrence of a number of mutually independent events equals the product of the individual probabilities of each of the events (in this example—$\frac{1}{6} \times \frac{1}{6} = \frac{1}{36}$). Since numerous fiber types are in existence, the chance of finding one particular fiber type, other than a common type, in a specific randomly selected location is small. The chance then of finding several fiber types together in a specific location is the product of several small probabilities, resulting in an extremely small chance. . . .

However, no attempt was made to use the product rule and multiply the individual probability numbers together to get an approximation of the probability of finding carpets like Williams's residential carpet and Williams's automobile carpet in the same household. The probability numbers were used only to show that the individual fiber types involved in these associations were very uncommon. . . .[6]

In addition to the two probability numbers already discussed (bedroom and station wagon carpets), each of the other fiber types linking Williams to both Cater and Payne has a probability of being found in a particular location. The chance of finding all of the fiber types indicated on the chart [Figure 1] in one location (seven types on Payne's body and six types on Cater's body) would be extremely small. Although an actual probability number for those findings could not be determined, it is believed that the multiple

[6] Joseph L. Peterson, ed., *Forensic Science* (New York: AMS Press, 1975), pp. 181–225. This collection of articles, dealing with various aspects of forensic science, contains five papers concerned with using statistics to interpret the meaning of physical evidence. It is a good discussion of probability theory and reviews cases where probability theory has been used in trial situations.

fiber associations shown on this chart are proof that Williams is linked to the bodies of these two victims, even though each fiber match by itself does not show a positive association with Williams's environment.

Studies have been conducted in England that show that transferred fibers are usually lost rapidly as people go about their daily routine.[7] Therefore, the foreign fibers present on a person are most often from recent surroundings. The fibrous debris found on a murder victim reflects the body's more recent surroundings, especially important if the body was moved after the killing. Accordingly, the victims' bodies in this particular case are not only associated with Williams but are apparently associated with Williams shortly before or after their deaths. It was also pointed out during the trial that the locations of the fibers—on Payne's shorts and in Cater's head hairs and pubic hairs—were not those where one would expect to find fibrous debris transferred from an automobile or a house to victims who had been fully clothed.

Although from these findings it would appear that the victims were in the residence of Williams, there was one other location that contained many of the same fibers as those in the composition of various objects in his residence—Williams's station wagon. The environment of a family automobile might be expected to reflect, to some extent, fibers from objects located within the residence. This was true of the 1970 station wagon. With one exception, all of the fiber types removed from Payne and Cater, consistent with originating from items shown in the center of Figure 1, were present in debris removed by vacuuming the station wagon. The automobile would be the most logical source of the foreign fibers found on both Payne and Cater if they were associated with Williams shortly before or after their deaths. It should also be pointed out that two objects, the bedspread and the blanket, were portable and could have at one time been present inside the station wagon.

Both Payne and Cater were recovered from the Chattahoochee River. Their bodies had been in the water for several days. Some of the fibers found on these victims were like fibers in the compositions of the bedroom carpet and bedspread except for color intensity. They appeared to have been bleached. By subjecting various known fibers to small amounts of Chattahoochee River water for different periods of time, it was found that bleaching did occur. This was especially true with the carpet and bedspread fibers from Williams's bedroom.

Two crime laboratory examiners testified during the closing stages of the first part of the trial about Williams's association with Payne and Cater. They concluded that it was highly unlikely that any environment other than that present in Wayne Williams's house and car could have resulted in the combination of fibers and hairs found on the victims and that it would be virtually impossible to have matched so many fibers found on Cater and Payne to items in Williams's house and car unless the victims were in contact with or in some way associated with the environment of Wayne Williams.

After testimony was presented concerning the Payne and Cater cases, the Fulton County District Attorney's Office asked the court to be allowed to introduce evidence in the cases of 10 other victims whose murders were similar in many respects. Georgia law allows evidence of another crime to be introduced ". . . if some logical connection can be shown between the two from which it can be said that proof of the one tends to establish the other as relevant to some fact other than general bad character."[8] There need be no conviction for the other crime in order for details about that crime to be admissible.

It was ruled that evidence concerning other murders could be introduced in an attempt to prove a "pattern or scheme" of killing that included the two murders with which Williams was charged. The additional evidence in these cases was to be used to help the jury ". . . decide whether Williams had committed the two murders with which he is charged."[9]

There were similarities between these additional victims and Payne and Cater. (See Figure 2.) Although some differences can also be seen on this chart, the prosecution considered these differences to fit within the "pattern of killing" of which Payne and Cater were a part. The most important similarities between these additional victims were the fiber matches that linked 9 of the 10 victims to Williams's environment. The fiber findings discussed during the trial and used to associate Williams to the 12 victims were illustrated during the trial. (See Figure 3.)

The 12 victims were listed in chronological order based on the dates their bodies were recovered. The time period covered by this chart, approximately 22 months, is from July 1979 until May 1981. During that time period, the Williams family had access to a large number of automobiles, including a number of rental cars. Three of these automobiles are listed at the top of Figure 3. If one or more of the cars was in the possession of the Williams family at the time a victim was found to be missing, the space under that car(s) and after the particular victim's name is shaded.

Four objects (including the dog) from Williams's residence are listed horizontally across the top of Figure 3, along with objects from three of his automobiles. An "X" on the chart indicates an apparent transfer of textile fibers from the listed object to a victim. Other objects from Williams's environment which were linked to various victims by an apparent fiber transfer are listed on the right side of the chart. Fiber types from objects (never actually located) that were matched to fiber types from one or more victims are also listed either at the top or on the right side of the chart. Fourteen specific objects and five fiber types (probably from five other objects) listed on this chart are linked to one or more of the victims. More than 28 different fiber types, along with the dog hairs, were used to link up to 19 objects from Williams's environment to 1 or more of the victims. Of the more than 28 fiber types from Williams's environment, 14 of these originated from a rug or carpet.

The combination of more than 28 different fiber types would not be considered so significant if they were primarily common fiber types. In fact, there is only 1 light green cotton fiber of the 28 that might be considered common. This cotton fiber was blended with acetate fibers in Williams's bedspread. Light green cotton fibers removed from many victims were not considered or compared unless they were physically intermingled with violet acetate fibers which were consistent with originating from the

[7] C. A. Pounds and K. W. Smalldon, "The Transfer of Fibers between Clothing Materials during Simulated Contacts and Their Persistence during Wear," *Journal of the Forensic Science Society*, vol. 15, 1975, pp. 29–37.

[8] *Encyclopedia of Georgia Law*, vol. 11A (The Harrison Company, 1979), p. 70.
[9] *The Atlanta Constitution*, "Williams Jury Told of Other Slayings," Sec. 1-A, 1/26/82, p. 25.

VICTIM'S NAME	DATE VICTIM MISSING	DAYS MISSING	BODY RECOVERY AREA	CAUSE OF DEATH	AGE	WEIGHT	HEIGHT
EVANS	7/25/79	3	WOODED AREA S.W. ATLANTA	PROBABLE ASPHYXIATION/ STRANGULATION	13	87 LBS.	5'4"
MIDDLEBROOKS	5/18/80	1	NEAR STREET S.E. ATLANTA	BLUNT TRAUMA TO HEAD	14	88 LBS.	4'10"
STEPHENS	10/9/80	1	NEAR STREET S.E. ATLANTA	ASPHYXIATION	10	120 LBS.	5'0"
GETER	1/3/81	33	WOODED AREA FULTON COUNTY	MANUAL STRANGULATION	14	130 LBS.	5'4"
PUE	1/22/81	1	NEAR HIGHWAY ROCKDALE CO.	LIGATURE STRANGULATION	15	105 LBS.	5'5"
BALTAZAR	2/6/81	7	NEAR HIGHWAY DEKALB CO.	LIGATURE STRANGULATION	12	125 LBS.	5'4"
BELL	3/2/81	31	SOUTH RIVER DEKALB CO.	ASPHYXIATION	16	100 LBS.	5'2"
ROGERS	3/30/81	10	NEAR STREET N.W. ATLANTA	ASPHYXIATION/ STRANGULATION	20	110 LBS.	5'3"
PORTER	4/10/81	1	NEAR STREET S.W. ATLANTA	STABBING	28	123 LBS.	5'7"
PAYNE	4/22/81	5	CHATTAHOOCHEE RIVER FULTON COUNTY	ASPHYXIATION	21	135 LBS.	5'7"
BARRETT	5/11/81	1	NEAR STREET DEKALB CO.	LIGATURE STRANGULATION (3 PUNCTURE WOUNDS)	17	125 LBS.	5'4"
CATER	5/21/81	3	CHATTAHOOCHEE RIVER FULTON COUNTY	ASPHYXIATION/ STRANGULATION	28	146 LBS.	5'11"

FIGURE 2

Chart used during the trial to show similarities between Payne and Cater and 10 other murder victims.

bedspread. It should be noted that a combination of cotton and acetate fibers blended together in a single textile material, as in the bedspread, is in itself uncommon. . . .

The previous discussion concerning the significance of multiple fiber matches can be applied to the associations made in the cases of all the victims except Bell, but especially to the association of Patrick Baltazar to Williams's environment. Fibers and animal hairs consistent with having originated from 10 sources were removed from Baltazar's body. These 10 sources include the uncommon bedroom carpet and station wagon carpet. In addition to the fiber (and animal hair) linkage, two head hairs of Negroid origin were removed from Baltazar's body that were consistent with originating from the scalp area of Williams. Head hair matches were also very significant in linking Williams to Baltazar's body. In the opinion of the author, the association based upon the hair and fiber analyses is a positive association.

Another important aspect of the fiber linkage between Williams and these victims is the correspondence between the fiber findings and the time periods during which Williams had access to the three automobiles listed on the chart. Nine victims are linked to automobiles used by the Williams family. When Williams did not have access to a particular car, no fibers were recovered that were consistent with having originated from that automobile. Trunk liner fibers of the type used in the trunks of many late-model Ford Motor Company automobiles were also recovered from the bodies of two victims.

One final point should be made concerning Williams's bedroom and station wagon carpets where probability numbers had been determined. Fibers consistent with having originated from both of these "unusual" carpets were recovered from Payne's body. Of the 9 victims who were killed during the time period when Williams had access to the 1970 station wagon, fibers consistent with having originated from both the station wagon carpet and the bedroom carpet were recovered from 6 of these victims.

The apparent bleaching of several fibers removed from the bodies of Payne and Cater was consistent with having been caused by river water. Several fibers similar to those from Payne and Cater were removed from many of the victims whose bodies were recovered on land. Consistent with the bleaching argument, none of the fibers from the victims found on land showed any apparent bleaching. The finding of many of the same fiber types on the remaining victims, who were recovered from many different locations, refutes the possibility that Payne's and Cater's bodies picked up foreign fibers from the river.

NAME OF VICTIM	VIOLET-GREEN BEDSPREAD WILLIAMS' BEDROOM	GREEN CARPET WILLIAMS' BEDROOM	DOG HAIRS WILLIAMS' DOG	YELLOW BLANKET WILLIAMS' BEDROOM	BLUE RAYON FIBERS, DEBRIS FROM WILLIAMS' HOME	TRUNK LINER 1978 PLYMOUTH	CARPET 1979 FORD	CARPET 1970 CHEVROLET	ADDITIONAL ITEMS FROM WILLIAMS' HOME, AUTOMOBILES OR PERSON
Alfred Evans	X	X	X			X			
Eric Middlebrooks	X		X				X		YELLOW NYLON — FORD TRUNK LINER
Charles Stephens	X	X	X	X					YELLOW NYLON, WHITE POLYESTER — BACKROOM CARPET, FORD TRUNK LINER
Lubie Geter	X	X	X					X	KITCHEN CARPET
Terry Pue	X	X	X						WHITE POLYESTER — BACKROOM CARPET
Patrick Baltazar	X	X	X	X				X	YELLOW NYLON, WHITE POLYESTER, HEAD HAIR — GLOVE, JACKET, PIGMENTED POLYPROPYLENE
Joseph Bell	X			X					
Larry Rogers	X	X	X	X				X	YELLOW NYLON — PORCH BEDSPREAD
John Porter	X	X	X	X	X			X	PORCH BEDSPREAD
Jimmy Payne	X	X	X	X	X			X	BLUE THROW RUG
William Barrett	X	X	X	X	X			X	GLOVE
Nathaniel Cater	X	X	X	X					BACKROOM CARPET — YELLOW-GREEN SYNTHETIC

FIGURE 3

Fiber findings discussed during the trial and used to associate Williams with the 12 victims.

The fact that many of the victims were involved with so many of the same fiber types, all of which linked the victims to Williams's environment, is the basis for arguing conclusively against these fibers originating from a source other than Williams's environment.

It is hoped that this article has provided valuable insight concerning the use of fiber evidence in a criminal trial, has provided answers to questions from those in the law enforcement community about textile fiber evidence in general, and has presented convincing arguments to establish Wayne Williams's association with the bodies of the murder victims.

Murder and the Horse Chestnut Tree

Roger Severs was the son of a wealthy English couple, Eileen and Derek Severs. The elder Severses were reported missing in 1983. Police investigators were greeted at the Severs home by Roger, who at first explained that his parents had decided to spend some time in London. Suspicion of foul play quickly arose when investigators located traces of blood in the residence. More blood was found in Derek's car, and signs of blood spatter were on the garage door. Curiously, a number of green fibers were located throughout the house, as well as in the trunk of Derek's car. A thorough geological examination of soil and vegetation caked onto Severs's car wheel rims seemed to indicate that the car had been in a location at the edge of a wooded area. Closer examination of the debris also revealed the presence of horse chestnut pollen. Horse chestnut is an exceptionally rare tree in the region of the Severs residence. Using land maps, a geologist located possible areas where horse chestnut pollen might be found. In one of the locations, investigators found a shallow grave that contained the bludgeoned bodies of the elder Severses. Not surprisingly, they were wrapped in a green blanket. A jury rejected Roger's defense of diminished capacity and found him guilty of murder.

physical properties: glass and soil

Learning Objectives

After studying this chapter you should be able to:

- Define and distinguish the physical and chemical properties of matter

- Understand how to use the basic units of the metric system

- Define and understand the properties of density and refractive index

- Understand and explain the dispersion of light through a prism

- List and explain forensic methods for comparing glass fragments

- Understand how to examine glass fractures to determine the direction of impact for a projectile

- List the important forensic properties of soil

- Describe the proper collection of glass and soil evidence

KEY TERMS

amorphous solid
atom
Becke line
birefringence
Celsius scale
chemical property
concentric fracture
crystalline solid
density
dispersion
Fahrenheit scale
intensive property
laminated glass
mass
mineral
physical property
radial fracture
refraction
refractive index
tempered glass
weight

The forensic scientist must constantly determine the properties that impart distinguishing characteristics to matter, giving it a unique identity. The continuing search for distinctive properties ends only when the scientist has completely individualized a substance to one correct source. Properties are the identifying characteristics of substances. In this and succeeding chapters, we will examine properties that are most useful for characterizing soil, glass, and other physical evidence. However, before we begin, we can simplify our understanding of the nature of properties by classifying them into two broad categories: physical and chemical.

physical property
The behavior of a substance without alteration of the substance's composition through a chemical reaction

chemical property
The behavior of a substance when it reacts or combines with another substance

Physical properties describe a substance without reference to any other substance. For example, weight, volume, color, boiling point, and melting point are typical physical properties that can be measured for a particular substance without altering the material's composition through a chemical reaction; they are associated only with the physical existence of that substance. **A chemical property describes the behavior of a substance when it reacts or combines with another substance.** For example, when wood burns, it chemically combines with oxygen in the air to form new substances; this transformation describes a chemical property of wood. In the crime laboratory, a routine procedure for determining the presence of heroin in a suspect specimen is to react it with a chemical reagent known as the Marquis reagent, which turns purple in the presence of heroin. This color transformation becomes a chemical property of heroin and provides a convenient test for its identification.

Which physical and chemical properties the forensic scientist ultimately chooses to observe and measure depends on the type of material that is being examined. Logic requires, however, that if the property can be assigned a numerical value, it must relate to a standard system of measurement accepted throughout the scientific community.

The Metric System

Although scientists, including forensic scientists, throughout the world have been using the metric system of measurement for more than a century, the United States still uses the cumbersome "English system" to express length in inches, feet, or yards; weight in ounces or pounds; and volume in pints or quarts. The inherent difficulty of this system is that no simple numerical relationship exists between the various units of measurement. For example, to convert inches to feet one must know that 1 foot equals 12 inches; conversion of ounces to pounds requires the knowledge that 16 ounces equals 1 pound. In 1791, the French Academy of Science devised the simple system of measurement known as the metric system. This system uses a simple decimal relationship so that a unit of length, volume, or mass can be converted into a subunit by simply multiplying or dividing by a multiple of 10—for example, 10, 100, or 1,000.

Even though the United States has not yet adopted the metric system, its system of currency is decimal and, hence, is analogous to the metric system. The basic unit of currency is the dollar. A dollar is divided into 10 equal units called dimes, and each dime is further divided into 10 equal units of cents.

Basic Units of Measurement

The metric system has basic units of measurement for length, mass, and volume: the meter, gram, and liter, respectively. These three basic units can be converted into subunits that are decimal multiples of the basic unit by simply attaching a prefix to the unit name. The following are common prefixes and their equivalent decimal value:

Prefix	Equivalent Value
deci-	1/10 or 0.1
centi-	1/100 or 0.01
milli-	1/1000 or 0.001
micro-	1/100,000 or 0.000001
nano-	1/1,000,000,000 or 0.000000001
kilo-	1,000
mega-	1,000,000

Hence, 1/10 or 0.1 gram (g) is the same as a decigram (dg), 1/100 or 0.01 meter is equal to a centimeter (cm), and 1/1,000 liter is a milliliter (mL). A metric conversion is carried out simply by moving the decimal point to the right or left and inserting the proper prefix to show the direction and number of places that the decimal point has been moved. For example, if the weight of a powder is 0.0165 gram, it may be more convenient to multiply this value by 100 and express it as 1.65 centigrams or by 1,000 to show it as its equivalent value of 16.5 milligrams. Similarly, an object that weighs 264,450 grams may be expressed as 264.45 kilograms simply by dividing it by 1,000. It is important to remember that in any of these conversions, the value of the measurement has not changed; 0.0165 gram is still equivalent to 1.65 centigrams, just as one dollar is still equal to 100 cents. We have simply adjusted the position of the decimal and shown the extent of the adjustment with a prefix.

One interesting aspect of the metric system is that volume can be defined in terms of length. A liter by definition is the volume of a cube with sides of length 10 centimeters. One liter is therefore equivalent to a volume of 10 cm $\times$ 10 cm $\times$ 10 cm, or 1,000 cubic centimeters (cc). Thus, 1/1,000 liter or 1 milliliter (mL) is equal to 1 cubic centimeter (cc) (see Figure 4–1). Scientists commonly use the subunits mL and cc interchangeably to express volume.

Metric Conversion

At times, it may be necessary to convert units from the metric system into the English system, or vice versa (see Figure 4–2). To accomplish this, we must consult references that list English units and their metric equivalents. Some of the more useful equivalents follow:

1 inch = 2.54 centimeters
1 meter = 39.37 inches
1 pound = 453.6 grams
1 liter = 1.06 quarts
1 kilogram = 2.2 pounds

The general mathematical procedures for converting from one system to another can be illustrated by converting 12 inches into centimeters. To change inches into centimeters, we need to know that there are 2.54 centimeters per inch. Hence, if we multiply 12 inches by 2.54 centimeters per inch (12 in. $\times$ 2.54 cm/in.), the unit of inches will cancel out, leaving the product

FIGURE 4–1

Volume equivalencies in the metric system.

FIGURE 4–2

Comparison of the metric and English systems of length measurement; 2.54 centimeters = 1 inch.

Fahrenheit scale
The temperature scale using the melting point of ice as 32° and the boiling point of water as 212°, with 180 equal divisions or degrees between

Celsius scale
The temperature scale using the melting point of ice as 0° and the boiling point of water as 100°, with 100 equal divisions or degrees between

weight
A property of matter that depends on both the mass of a substance and the effects of gravity on that mass

mass
A constant property of matter that reflects the amount of material present

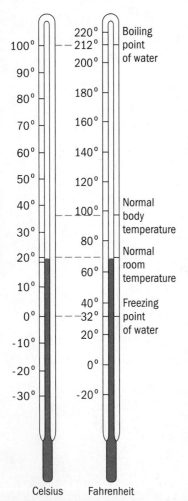

FIGURE 4–3

Comparison of the Celsius and Fahrenheit temperature scales.

30.48 cm. Similarly, applying the conversion of grams to pounds, 227 grams is equivalent to 227 g × 1 lb/453.6 g or 0.5 lb.

Physical Properties

All materials possess a range of physical properties whose measurement is critical to the work of the forensic scientist. Several of the most important of these are temperature, weight, mass, density, and refractive index.

Temperature

Determining the physical properties of any material often requires measuring its temperature. For instance, the temperatures at which a substance melts or boils are readily determinable characteristics that will help identify it. Temperature is a measure of heat intensity, or the amount of heat in a substance.

Temperature is usually measured by causing a thermometer to come into contact with a substance. The familiar mercury-in-glass thermometer functions because mercury expands more than glass when heated and contracts more than glass when cooled. Thus, the length of the mercury column in the glass tube provides a measure of the surrounding environment's temperature.

The construction of a temperature scale requires two reference points and a choice of units. The reference points most conveniently chosen are the freezing point and boiling point of water. The two most common temperature scales used are the **Fahrenheit** and **Celsius** (formerly called *centigrade*) **scales.**

The Fahrenheit scale is based on assigning a value of 32°F to the freezing point of water and a value of 212°F to its boiling point. The difference between the two points is evenly divided into 180 units. Thus, a degree Fahrenheit is 1/180 of the temperature change between the freezing point and boiling point of water. The Celsius scale is derived by assigning the freezing point of water a value of 0°C and its boiling point a value of 100°C. A degree Celsius is thus 1/100 of the temperature change between the two reference points. Scientists in most countries use the Celsius scale to measure temperature. A comparison of the two scales is shown in Figure 4–3.

Weight and Mass

The force with which gravity attracts a body is called **weight.** If your weight is 180 pounds, this means that the earth's gravity is pulling you down with a force of 180 pounds; on the moon, where the force of gravity is one-sixth that of the earth, your weight would be 30 pounds.

Mass differs from weight because it refers to the amount of matter an object contains and is independent of its location on earth or any other place in the universe. The mathematical relationship between weight (*w*) and mass (*m*) is shown in Equation (4–1), where *g* is the acceleration imparted to a body by the force of gravity.

$$W = mg \tag{4–1}$$

The weight of a body is directly proportional to its mass; hence, a large mass weighs more than a small mass.

In the metric system, the mass of an object is always specified, rather than its weight. The basic unit of mass is the gram. An object that has a mass of 40 grams on earth will have a mass of 40 grams anywhere else in this universe. Normally, however, the terms *mass* and *weight* are used interchangeably, and we often speak of the weight of an object when we really mean its mass.

The mass of an object is determined by comparing it against the known mass of standard objects. The comparison is confusingly called *weighing*, and the standard objects are called *weights* (*masses* would be a more correct term). The comparison is performed on a balance. The simplest type of balance for weighing is the equal-arm balance shown in Figure 4–4. The object to be weighed is placed on the left pan, and the standard weights are placed on the right pan; when the pointer between the two pans is at the center mark, the total mass on the right pan is equal to the mass of the object on the left pan.

The modern laboratory has progressed beyond the simple equal-arm balance, and either the top-loading balance or the single-pan analytical balance (see Figure 4–5) is now likely to be used. The choice depends on the accuracy required and the amount of material being weighed. Each

FIGURE 4-4

The measurement of mass.

(a)

(b)

FIGURE 4-5

(a) Top-loading balance. (b) Single-pan analytical balance.

(a) Scientech, Inc., Boulder, Colo., www.scientech-inc.com, Superior Scale, Deptford, NJ, www.superiorscale.com (b) Courtesy Sirchie Fingerprint Laboratories, Youngsville, N.C., www.sirchie.com

works on the same counterbalancing principle as the simple equal-arm balance. Earlier versions of the single-pan balance had a second pan, the one on which the standard weights were placed. This pan was hidden from view within the balance's housing. Once the object whose weight was to be determined was placed on the visible pan, the operator selected the proper standard weights (also contained within the housing) by manually turning a set of knobs located on the front side of the balance. At the point of balance, the weights selected were automatically recorded on optical readout scales. Modern single-pan balances rely on an electromagnetic field to generate a current to balance the force pressing down on the pan from the sample being weighed. When the scale is properly calibrated, the amount of current needed to keep the pan balanced is used to determine the weight of the sample. The strength of the current is converted to a digitized signal for a readout. The top-loading balance can accurately weigh an object to the nearest 1 milligram or 0.001 gram; the analytical balance is even more accurate, weighing to the nearest tenth of a milligram or 0.0001 gram.

Density

density
A physical property of matter that is equivalent to the mass per unit volume of a substance

intensive property
A property that is not dependent on the size of an object

An important physical property of matter with respect to the analysis of certain kinds of physical evidence is **density. Density is defined as mass per unit volume** [see Equation (4–2)].

$$\text{Density} = \frac{\text{mass}}{\text{volume}} \qquad\qquad \textbf{(4–2)}$$

Density is an **intensive property** of matter—that is, it is the same regardless of the size of a substance; thus, it is a characteristic property of a substance and can be used as an aid in identification. Solids tend to be more dense than liquids, and liquids more dense than gases. The densities of some common substances are shown in Table 4–1.

A simple procedure for determining the density of a solid is illustrated in Figure 4–6. First, the solid is weighed on a balance against known standard gram weights to determine its mass.

TABLE 4–1

Densities of Select Materials (at 20°C unless otherwise stated)

Substance	Density (g/mL)
Solids	
Silver	10.5
Lead	11.5
Iron	7.8
Aluminum	2.7
Window glass	2.47–2.54
Ice (0°C)	0.92
Liquids	
Mercury	13.6
Benzene	0.88
Ethyl alcohol	0.79
Gasoline	0.69
Water at 4°C	1.00
Water	0.998
Gases	
Air (0°C)	0.0013
Chlorine (0°C)	0.0032
Oxygen (0°C)	0.0014
Carbon dioxide (0°C)	0.0020

FIGURE 4–6

A simple procedure for determining the density of a solid is to first weigh it and then measure its volume by noting the volume of water it displaces.

Mass

Volume

The solid's volume is then determined from the volume of water it displaces. This is easily measured by filling a cylinder with a known volume of water ($V1$), adding the object, and measuring the new water level ($V2$). The difference $V2 - V1$ in milliliters is equal to the volume of the solid. Density can now be calculated from Equation (4–2) in grams per milliliter.

The volumes of gases and liquids vary considerably with temperature; hence, when determining density, it is important to control and record the temperature at which the measurements are made. For example, 1 gram of water occupies a volume of 1 milliliter at 4°C and thus has a density of 1.0 g/mL. However, as the temperature of water increases, its volume expands. Therefore, at 20°C (room temperature) 1 gram of water occupies a volume of 1.002 mL and has a density of 0.998 g/mL.

The observation that a solid object either sinks, floats, or remains suspended when immersed in a liquid can be accounted for by the property of density. For instance, if the density of a solid is greater than that of the liquid in which it is immersed, the object sinks; if the solid's density is less than that of the liquid, it floats; and when the solid and liquid have equal densities, the solid remains suspended in the liquid. As we will shortly see, these observations provide a convenient technique for comparing the densities of solid objects.

Refractive Index

Light, as we will learn in the next chapter, can have the property of a wave. Light waves travel in air at a constant velocity of nearly 300 million meters per second until they penetrate another medium, such as glass or water, at which point they are suddenly slowed, causing the rays to bend. The bending of a light wave because of a change in velocity is called **refraction**.

The phenomenon of refraction is apparent when we view an object that is immersed in a transparent medium; because we are accustomed to thinking that light travels in a straight line, we often forget to take refraction into account. For instance, suppose a ball is observed at the bottom of a pool of water; the light rays reflected from the ball travel through the water and into the air to reach the eye. As the rays leave the water and enter the air, their velocity suddenly increases, causing them to be refracted. However, because of our assumption that light travels in a straight line, our eyes deceive us and make us think we see an object lying at a higher point than is actually the case. This phenomenon is illustrated in Figure 4–7.

The ratio of the velocity of light in a vacuum to that in any medium determines the **refractive index** of that medium and is expressed as follows:

$$\text{Refractive index} = \frac{\text{velocity of light in vacuum}}{\text{velocity of light in medium}}$$

For example, at 25°C the refractive index of water is 1.333. This means that light travels 1.333 times as fast in a vacuum as it does in water at this temperature.

Like density, the refractive index is an intensive physical property of matter and characterizes a substance. However, any procedure used to determine a substance's refractive index must be performed under carefully controlled temperature and lighting conditions because the refractive index of a substance varies with its temperature and the wavelength of light passing through it. Nearly all tabulated refractive indices are determined at a standard wavelength,

refraction
The bending of a light wave as it passes from one medium to another

refractive index
The ratio of the speed of light in a vacuum to its speed in a given substance

FIGURE 4–7

Light is refracted when it travels obliquely from one medium to another.

usually 589.3 nanometers; this is the predominant wavelength emitted by sodium light and is commonly known as the sodium D light.

COMPARING REFRACTIVE INDICES   When a transparent solid is immersed in a liquid with a similar refractive index, light is not refracted as it passes from the liquid into the solid. For this reason, the eye cannot distinguish the liquid–solid boundary, and the solid seems to disappear from view. This observation, as we will see, offers the forensic scientist a simple method for comparing the refractive indices of transparent solids.

Normally, we expect a solid or a liquid to exhibit only one refractive index value for each wavelength of light; however, many crystalline solids have two refractive indices whose values depend in part on the direction in which the light enters the crystal with respect to the crystal axis. **Crystalline solids have definite geometric forms because of the orderly arrangement of the fundamental particle of a solid, the atom.** In any type of crystal, the relative locations and distances between its atoms are repetitive throughout the solid. Figure 4–8 shows the crystalline structure of sodium chloride, or ordinary table salt. Sodium chloride is an example of a cubic crystal in which each sodium atom is surrounded by six chloride atoms and each chloride atom by six sodium atoms, except at the crystal surface. Not all solids are crystalline in nature; some, such as glass, have their atoms arranged randomly throughout the solid; these materials are known as **amorphous solids.**

Most crystals, excluding those that have cubic configurations, refract a beam of light into two different light-ray components. This phenomenon, known as *double refraction*, can be observed by studying the behavior of the crystal calcite. When the calcite is laid on a printed page, the observer sees not one but two images of each word covered. The two light rays that give rise to the double image are refracted at different angles, and each has a different refractive index value. The indices of refraction for calcite are 1.486 and 1.658, and subtracting the two values yields a difference of 0.172; this difference is known as **birefringence.** Thus, the optical properties of crystals provide points of identification that help characterize them.

DISPERSION   Many of us have held a glass prism up toward the sunlight and watched it transform light into the colors of the rainbow. This observation demonstrates that visible "white light" is not homogeneous but is actually composed of many different colors. The process of separating light into its component colors is called **dispersion.** The ability of a prism to disperse light into its component colors is explained by the property of refraction. Each color component of light, on passing through the glass, is slowed to a speed slightly different from those of the others, causing each component to bend at a different angle as it emerges from the prism. As shown in Figure 4–9, the component colors of visible light extend from red to violet. We will learn in Chapter 5 that each color corresponds to a different range of wavelengths of light. Dispersion thus separates light into its component wavelengths and demonstrates that glass has a slightly different index of refraction for each wavelength of light passing through it.

Now that we have investigated various physical properties of objects, we are ready to apply such properties to the characterization of two substances—glass and soil—that commonly must be examined by the criminalist.

crystalline solid
A solid in which the constituent atoms have a regular arrangement

atom
The smallest unit of an element, which is not divisible by ordinary chemical means; atoms are made up of electrons, protons, and neutrons plus other subatomic particles

amorphous solid
A solid in which the constituent atoms or molecules are arranged in random or disordered positions; there is no regular order in amorphous solids

birefringence
A difference in the two indices of refraction exhibited by most crystalline materials

dispersion
The separation of light into its component wavelengths

FIGURE 4–8

Diagram of a sodium chloride crystal. Sodium is represented by the darker spheres, chlorine by the lighter spheres.

FIGURE 4–9
Representation of the dispersion of light by a glass prism.

Forensic Analysis of Glass

Glass that is broken and shattered into fragments and minute particles during the commission of a crime can be used to place a suspect at the crime scene. For example, chips of broken glass from a window may lodge in a suspect's shoes or garments during a burglary, or particles of headlight glass found at the scene of a hit-and-run accident may offer clues that can confirm the identity of a suspect vehicle. All of these possibilities require the comparison of glass fragments found on the suspect, whether a person or vehicle, with the shattered glass remaining at the crime scene.

Composition of Glass

Glass is a hard, brittle, amorphous substance composed of sand (silicon oxides) mixed with various metal oxides. When sand is mixed with other metal oxides, melted at high temperatures, and then cooled to a rigid condition without crystallization, the product is glass. Soda (sodium carbonate) is normally added to the sand to lower its melting point and make it easier to work with. Another necessary ingredient is lime (calcium oxide), needed to prevent the "soda-lime" glass from dissolving in water. The forensic scientist is often asked to analyze soda-lime glass, which is used for manufacturing most window and bottle glass. Usually the molten glass is cooled on a bed of molten tin. This manufacturing process produces flat glass typically used for windows. This type of glass is called *float glass*.

In addition, a wide variety of special glasses can be made by substituting in whole or in part other metal oxides for the silica, sodium, and calcium oxides. For example, automobile headlights and heat-resistant glass, such as Pyrex, are manufactured by adding boron oxide to the oxide mix. These glasses are therefore known as *borosilicates*.

Another type of glass that the reader may be familiar with is **tempered glass.** This glass is made stronger than ordinary window glass by introducing stress through rapid heating and cooling of the glass surfaces. When tempered glass breaks, it does not shatter but rather fragments or "dices" into small squares with little splintering (see Figure 4–10). Because of this safety feature, tempered glass is used in the side and rear windows of automobiles made in the United States, as well as in the windshields of some foreign-made cars. The windshields of all cars manufactured in the United States are constructed from **laminated glass.** This glass derives its strength by sandwiching one layer of plastic between two pieces of ordinary window glass.

Comparing Glass Fragments

For the forensic scientist, comparing glass consists of finding and measuring the properties that will associate one glass fragment with another while minimizing or eliminating the possible existence of other sources. Considering the prevalence of glass in our society, it is easy to appreciate the magnitude of this analytical problem. Obviously, glass possesses its greatest evidential value when it can be individualized to one source. Such a determination, however, can be made only when the suspect and crime-scene fragments are assembled and physically fitted together. Comparisons of this type require piecing together irregular edges of broken glass as well as matching all irregularities and striations on the broken surfaces (see Figure 4–11). The possibility that two pieces of glass originating from different sources will fit together exactly is so unlikely as to exclude all other sources from practical consideration.

tempered glass
Glass that is strengthened by introducing stress through rapid heating and cooling of the glass surfaces

laminated glass
Two sheets of ordinary glass bonded together with a plastic film

FIGURE 4–10

When tempered glass breaks, it usually holds together without splintering.
Courtesy Robert Llewellyn, Alamy Images

FIGURE 4–11

Match of broken glass. Note the physical fit of the edges.
Courtesy Sirchie Finger Print Laboratories, Youngsville, N.C., www.sirchie.com

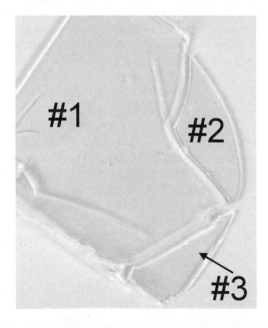

Unfortunately, most glass evidence is either too fragmentary or too minute to permit a comparison of this type. In such instances, the search for individual properties has proven fruitless. For example, the general chemical composition of various window glasses within the capability of current analytical methods has so far been found relatively uniform among various manufacturers and thus offers no basis for individualization. However, trace elements present in glass have been shown to be useful for narrowing the origin of a glass specimen. **The physical properties of density and refractive index are most widely used for characterizing glass particles.** However, these properties are class characteristics, which cannot provide the sole criteria for individualizing glass to a common source. They do, however, give the analyst sufficient data to evaluate the significance of a glass comparison, and the absence of comparable density and refractive index values will certainly exclude glass fragments that originate from different sources.

Measuring and Comparing Density

Recall that a solid particle will either float, sink, or remain suspended in a liquid, depending on its density relative to the liquid. This knowledge gives the criminalist a rather precise and rapid method for comparing densities of glass. In a method known as *flotation*, a standard/reference glass particle is immersed in a liquid; a mixture of bromoform and bromobenzene may be used. The composition of the liquid is carefully adjusted by the addition of small amounts of bromoform or bromobenzene until the glass chip remains suspended in the liquid medium. At this point, the standard/reference glass and liquid each have the same density. Glass chips of approximately the same size and shape as the standard/reference are now added to the liquid for comparison. If both the unknown and the standard/reference particles remain suspended in the liquid, their densities are equal to each other and to that of the liquid.[1] Particles of different densities either sink or float, depending on whether they are more or less dense than the liquid.

The density of a single sheet of window glass is not completely homogeneous throughout. It has a range of values that can differ by as much as 0.0003 g/mL. Therefore, in order to distinguish between the normal internal density variations of a single sheet of glass and those of glasses of different origins, it is advisable to let the comparative density approach but not exceed a sensitivity value of 0.0003 g/mL. The flotation method meets this requirement and can adequately distinguish glass particles that differ in density by 0.001 g/mL.

Determining and Comparing Refractive Index

Once glass has been distinguished by a density determination, different origins are immediately concluded. Comparable density results, however, require the added comparison of refractive indices. This determination is best accomplished by the *immersion method*. For this, glass particles are immersed in a liquid medium whose refractive index is adjusted until it equals that of the glass particles. At this point, known as the *match point*, the observer notes the disappearance of the **Becke line** and minimum contrast between the glass and liquid medium. The Becke line is a bright halo that is observed near the border of a particle that is immersed in a liquid of a different refractive index. This halo disappears when the medium and fragment have similar refractive indices.

The refractive index of an immersion fluid is best adjusted by changing the temperature of the liquid. Temperature control is, of course, critical to the success of the procedure. One approach to this procedure is to heat the liquid in a special apparatus known as a *hot stage*. The glass is immersed in a boiling liquid, usually a silicone oil, and heated at the rate of 0.2°C per minute until the match point is reached. Increasing the temperature of the liquid has a negligible effect on the refractive index of glass, whereas the liquid's index decreases at the rate of approximately 0.0004 per degree Celsius. The hot stage, as shown in Figure 4–12, is designed to be used

Becke line

A bright halo that is observed near the border of a particle immersed in a liquid of a different refractive index

FIGURE 4–12

Hot-stage microscope.
Courtesy of Chris Palenik, Ph.D.,
Microtrace LLC, Elgin, IL.

[1] As an added step, the analyst can determine the exact numerical density value of the particles of glass by transferring the liquid to a density meter, which will electrically measure and calculate the liquid's density. See A. P. Beveridge and C. Semen, "Glass Density Measurement Using a Calculating Digital Density Meter," *Canadian Society of Forensic Science Journal* 12 (1979): 113.

FIGURE 4–13

Determination of the refractive index of glass. (a) Glass particles are immersed in a liquid of a much higher refractive index at a temperature of 77°C. (b) At 87°C the liquid still has a higher refractive index than the glass. (c) The refractive index of the liquid is closest to that of the glass at 97°C, as shown by the disappearance of the glass and the Becke lines. (d) At the higher temperature of 117°C, the liquid has a much lower index than the glass, and the glass is plainly visible.

Courtesy Walter C. McCrone

(a)

(b)

(c)

(d)

in conjunction with a microscope, through which the examiner can observe the disappearance of the Becke line on minute glass particles that are illuminated with sodium D light or other wavelengths of light. If all the glass fragments examined have similar match points, it can be concluded that they have comparable refractive indices (see Figure 4–13). Furthermore, the examiner can determine the refractive index value of the immersion fluid as it changes with temperature. With this information, the exact numerical value of the glass refractive index can be calculated at the match point temperature.[2]

An automated approach for measuring the refractive index of glass fragments by temperature control using the immersion method with a hot stage is with the instrument known as GRIM 3 (glass refractive index measurement) (see Figure 4–14). The GRIM 3 is a personal computer/video system designed to automate the measurements of the match temperature and refractive index for glass fragments. This instrument uses a video camera to view the glass fragments as they are being heated. As the immersion oil is heated or cooled, the contrast of the video image is measured continually until a minimum, the match point, is detected (see Figure 4–15). The match point temperature is then converted to a refractive index using stored calibration data.

As with density, glass fragments removed from a single sheet of plate glass may not have a uniform refractive index value; instead, their values may vary by as much as 0.0002. Hence, for

[2] A. R. Cassista and P. M. L. Sandercock, "Precision of Glass Refractive Index Measurements: Temperature Variation and Double Variation Methods, and the Value of Dispersion," *Canadian Society of Forensic Science Journal* 27 (1994): 203.

FIGURE 4–14

An automated system for glass fragment identification.

Courtesy Foster & Freeman Limited, Worcestershire, U.K., www.fosterfreeman.co.uk

FIGURE 4–15

GRIM 3 identifies the refraction match point by monitoring a video image of four different areas of the glass fragment immersed in an oil. As the immersion oil is heated or cooled, the contrast of the image is measured continuously until a minimum, the match point, is detected.

Courtesy Foster & Freeman Limited, Worcestershire, U.K., www.fosterfreeman.co.uk

comparison purposes, the difference in refractive index between a standard/reference and questioned glass must exceed this value. This allows the examiner to differentiate between the normal internal variations present in a sheet of glass and those present in glasses that originated from completely different sources.

Classification of Glass Samples

A significant difference in either density or refractive index proves that the glasses examined do not have a common origin. But what if two pieces of glass exhibit comparable densities and comparable refractive indices? How certain can one be that they did, indeed, come from the same source? After all, there are untold millions of windows and other glass objects in this world. To provide a reasonable answer to this question, the FBI Laboratory has collected density and refractive index values from glass submitted to it for examination. What has emerged is a data bank correlating these values to their frequency of occurrence in the glass population of the United States. This collection is available to all forensic laboratories in the United States.

Once a criminalist has completed a comparison of glass fragments, he or she can correlate their density and refractive index values to their frequency of occurrence and assess probability that the fragments came from the same source. Figure 4–16 shows the distribution of refractive index values (measured with sodium D light) for approximately two thousand glasses analyzed by the FBI. The wide distribution of values clearly demonstrates that the refractive index is a highly distinctive property of glass and is thus useful for defining its frequency of occurrence and hence its evidential value. For example, a glass fragment with a refractive index value of 1.5290 is found in approximately only 1 out of 2,000 specimens, whereas glass with a value of 1.5180 occurs approximately in 22 glasses out of 2,000.

Although refractive index and density have been routinely used for the comparison of glass for some time, forensic scientists have long desired to extract additional information from glass

FIGURE 4–16

Frequency of occurrence of refractive index values (measured with sodium D light) for approximately two thousand flat glass specimens received by the FBI Laboratory.
Courtesy FBI Laboratory, Washington, D.C.

FIGURE 4–17

The elemental profile of a glass fragment is obtained by aiming a high-energy laser beam at a glass particle, inducing the emission of light wavelengths corresponding to the identity of the elements present in the glass.

Courtesy Foster & Freeman Limited, Worcestershire, U.K., www.fosterfreeman.co.uk

fragments that would make their comparison more meaningful. The trace elemental composition of glass held a longtime attraction to forensic scientists for this purpose. However, until recently, the analytical instrumentation sensitive enough to develop a trace elemental profile from a glass fragment was too costly for most crime laboratories. This handicap has been overcome with the introduction of a technique that aims a high-energy laser pulse to vaporize a microscopic amount of glass, raising its temperature by thousands of degrees. As a result, the elements present in the glass are induced to emit light whose wavelengths correspond to the identity of the elements present (see Figure 4–17).

The distinction between tempered and nontempered glass particles can be made by slowly heating and then cooling the glass (a process known as *annealing*). The change in the refractive index value for tempered glass upon annealing is significantly greater when compared to nontempered glass and thus serves as a point of distinction.[3]

Glass Fractures

Glass bends in response to any force exerted on any one of its surfaces; when the limit of its elasticity is reached, the glass fractures. Frequently, fractured window glass reveals information that can be related to the force and direction of an impact; such knowledge may be useful for reconstructing events at a crime-scene investigation.

The penetration of ordinary window glass by a projectile, whether a bullet or a stone, produces a familiar fracture pattern in which cracks both radiate outward and encircle the hole, as shown in Figure 4–18. The radiating lines are appropriately known as **radial fractures,** and the circular lines are termed **concentric fractures.**

Often it is difficult to determine just from the size and shape of a hole in glass whether it was made by a bullet or by some other projectile. For instance, a small stone thrown at a comparatively

radial fracture

A crack in a glass that extends outward like the spoke of a wheel from the point at which the glass was struck

concentric fracture

A crack in a glass that forms a rough circle around the point of impact

[3] G. Edmondstone, "The Identification of Heat Strengthened Glass in Windshields," *Canadian Society of Forensic Science Journal* 30 (1997): 181.

FIGURE 4–18

Radial and concentric fracture lines in a sheet of glass.
Courtesy Sirchie Finger Print Laboratories, Youngsville, N.C., www.sirchie.com

FIGURE 4–19

Crater-shaped hole made by a bullet passing through glass. The upper surface is the exit side of the projectile.
Courtesy Don Farrall, Getty Images, Inc. Photodisc/Royalty Free

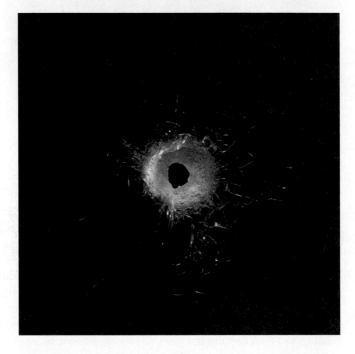

high speed against a pane of glass often produces a hole similar to that produced by a bullet. On the other hand, a large stone can completely shatter a pane of glass in a manner closely resembling the result of a close-range shot. However, in the latter instance, the presence of gunpowder deposits on the shattered glass fragments points to damage caused by a firearm.

When it penetrates glass, a high-velocity projectile such as a bullet often leaves a round, crater-shaped hole surrounded by a nearly symmetrical pattern of radial and concentric cracks. The hole is inevitably wider on the exit side (see Figure 4–19), and hence examining it is an important step in determining the direction of impact. However, as the velocity of the penetrating projectile decreases, the irregularity of the shape of the hole and of its surrounding cracks increases, so that at some point the hole shape will not help determine the direction of impact. At this time, examining the radial and concentric fracture lines may help determine the direction of impact.

When a force pushes on one side of a pane of glass, the elasticity of the glass permits it to bend in the direction of the force applied. Once the elastic limit is exceeded, the glass begins to crack. As shown in Figure 4–20, the first fractures form on the surface opposite that of the penetrating force and develop into radial lines. The continued motion of the force places tension on the front surface of the glass, resulting in the formation of concentric cracks. An examination of the edges of the radial and concentric cracks frequently reveals stress markings (*Wallner lines*) whose shape can be related to the side on which the window first cracked.

FIGURE 4–20

Production of radial and concentric fractures in glass. (a) Radial cracks are formed first, commencing on the side of the glass opposite to the destructive force. (b) Concentric cracks occur afterward, starting on the same side as the force.

FIGURE 4–21

Stress marks on the edge of a radial glass fracture. Arrow indicates direction of force.

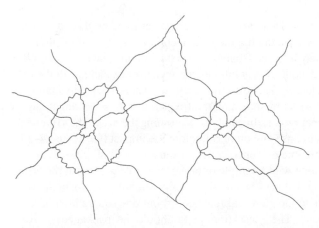

FIGURE 4–22

Two bullet holes in a piece of glass. The left hole preceded the right hole.

Stress marks, shown in Figure 4–21, are shaped like arches that are perpendicular to one glass surface and curved nearly parallel to the opposite surface. The importance of stress marks stems from the observation that the perpendicular edge always faces the surface on which the crack originated. Thus, in examining the stress marks on the edge of a radial crack near the point of impact, the perpendicular end is always found opposite the side from which the force of impact was applied. For a concentric fracture, the perpendicular end always faces the surface on which the force originated. A convenient way for remembering these observations is the 3R rule—**Radial cracks form a *R*ight angle on the *R*everse side of the force.** These facts enable the examiner to determine the side on which a window was broken. Unfortunately, the absence of radial or concentric fracture lines prevents these observations from being applied to broken tempered glass.

When there have been successive penetrations of glass, it is frequently possible to determine the sequence of impact by observing the existing fracture lines and their points of termination. **A fracture always terminates at an existing line of fracture.** In Figure 4–22, the fracture on the left preceded that on the right; we know this because the latter's radial fracture lines terminate at the cracks of the former.

FIGURE 4–23

Presence of black tungsten oxide on the upper filament indicates that the filament was on when it was exposed to air. The lower filament was off, but its surface was coated with a yellow/white tungsten oxide, which was vaporized from the upper ("on") filament and condensed onto the lower filament.
Courtesy New Jersey State Police.

Collection and Preservation of Glass Evidence

The gathering of glass evidence at the crime scene and from the suspect must be thorough if the examiner is to have any chance to individualize the fragments to a common source. If even the remotest possibility exists that fragments may be pieced together, every effort must be made to collect all the glass found. For example, evidence collection at hit-and-run scenes must include all the broken parts of the headlight and reflector lenses. This evidence may ultimately prove invaluable in placing a suspect vehicle at the accident scene by matching the fragments with glass remaining in the headlight or reflector shell of the suspect vehicle. In addition, examining the headlight's filaments may reveal whether an automobile's headlights were on or off before the impact (see Figure 4–23).

When an individual fit is improbable, the evidence collector must submit all glass evidence found in the possession of the suspect along with a sample of broken glass remaining at the crime scene. This standard/reference glass should always be taken from any remaining glass in the window or door frames, as close as possible to the point of breakage. About one square inch of sample is usually adequate for this purpose. The glass fragments should be packaged in solid containers to avoid further breakage. If the suspect's shoes and/or clothing are to be examined for the presence of glass fragments, they should be individually wrapped in paper and transmitted to the laboratory. The field investigator should avoid removing such evidence from garments unless absolutely necessary for its preservation.

When a determination of the direction of impact is desired, all broken glass must be recovered and submitted for analysis. Wherever possible, the exterior and interior surfaces of the glass must be indicated. When this is not immediately apparent, the presence of dirt, paint, grease, or putty may indicate the exterior surface of the glass.

Forensic Analysis of Soil

The term *soil* has many definitions; however, for forensic purposes, soil may be thought of as any disintegrated surface material, natural or artificial, that lies on or near the earth's surface. Therefore, forensic examination of soil not only is concerned with analysis of naturally occurring rocks, minerals, vegetation, and animal matter; it also encompasses detection of such manufactured objects as glass, paint chips, asphalt, brick fragments, and cinders, whose presence may impart soil with characteristics that make it unique to a particular location. When this material is collected accidentally or deliberately in a manner that associates it with a crime under investigation, it becomes valuable physical evidence.[4]

The Significance of Soil Evidence

The value of soil as evidence rests with its prevalence at crime scenes and its transferability between the scene and the criminal. Thus, soil or dried mud found adhering to a suspect's clothing or shoes or to an automobile, when compared to soil samples collected at the crime site, may link a suspect or object to the crime scene. As with most types of physical evidence, forensic soil analysis is comparative in nature; soil found in the possession of the suspect must be carefully collected to be compared to soil samplings from the crime scene and its vicinity.

However, one should not rule out the value of soil even if the site of the crime has not been ascertained. For instance, small amounts of soil may be found on a person or object far from the actual site of a crime. A geologist who knows the local geology may be able to use geological maps to direct police to the general vicinity where the soil was originally picked up and the crime committed.

Forensic Examination of Soil

Most soils can be differentiated by their gross appearance. A side-by-side visual comparison of the color and texture of soil specimens is easy to perform and provides a sensitive property for distinguishing soils that originate from different locations. Soil is darker when it is wet; therefore, color comparisons must always be made when all the samples are dried under identical laboratory conditions. It is estimated that there are nearly 1,100 distinguishable soil colors; hence, color offers a logical first step in a forensic soil comparison.

Low-power microscopic examination of soil reveals the presence of plant and animal materials as well as of artificial debris. Further high-power microscopic examination helps characterize minerals and rocks in earth materials. Although this approach to forensic soil identification requires the expertise of an investigator trained in geology, it can provide the most varied and significant points of comparison between soil samples. Only by carefully examining and comparing the minerals and rocks naturally present in soil can one take advantage of the large number of variations between soils and thus add to the evidential value of a positive comparison.[5]

A **mineral** is a naturally occurring crystal, and like any other crystal, its physical properties—for example, color, geometric shape, density, and refractive index or birefringence—are useful for identification. More than 2,200 minerals exist; however, most are so rare that forensic geologists usually encounter only about 20 of the more common ones. Rocks are composed of a combination of minerals and therefore exist in thousands of varieties on the earth's surface. They are usually identified by characterizing their mineral content and grain size (see Figure 4–24).

mineral
A naturally occurring crystalline solid

Considering the vast variety of minerals and rocks and the possible presence of artificial debris in soil, the forensic geologist is presented with many points of comparison between two or more specimens. The number of comparative points and their frequency of occurrence must be considered before concluding similarity between specimens and judging the probability of common origin.

Rocks and minerals not only are present in earth materials but also are used to manufacture a wide variety of industrial and commercial products. For example, the tools and garments of an individual suspected of breaking into a safe often contain traces of safe insulation. Safe insulation may be made from a wide combination of mineral mixtures that provide significant points of identification. Similarly, building materials such as brick, plaster, and concrete blocks are combinations of minerals and rocks that can easily be recognized and compared microscopically to similar minerals found on the breaking-and-entering suspect.

[4] E. P. Junger, "Assessing the Unique Characteristics of Close-Proximity Soil Samples: Just How Useful Is Soil Evidence?" *Journal of Forensic Sciences* 41 (1996): 27.
[5] W. J. Graves, "A Mineralogical Soil Classification Technique for the Forensic Scientist," *Journal of Forensic Sciences* 24 (1979): 323; M. J. McVicar and W. J. Graves, "The Forensic Comparison of Soil by Automated Scanning Electron Microscopy," *Canadian Society of Forensic Science Journal* 30 (1997): 241.

FIGURE 4–24

A mineral viewed under a microscope.
Courtesy of Chris Palenik, Ph.D., Microtrace LLC, Elgin, IL.

Variations in Soil

The ultimate forensic value of soil evidence depends on its variation at the crime scene. If, for example, soil is indistinguishable for miles surrounding the location of a crime, it will have limited value in associating soil found on the suspect with that particular site. Significant conclusions relating a suspect to a particular location through a soil comparison may be made when variations in soil composition occur every 10–100 yards from the crime site. However, even when such variations do exist, the forensic geologist usually cannot individualize soil to any one location unless an unusual combination of rare minerals, rocks, or artificial debris can be located.

No statistically valid forensic studies have examined the variability of soil evidence. A study conducted in southern Ontario, Canada, seems to indicate that soil in that part of Canada shows extensive diversity. It estimated a probability of less than 1 in 50 of finding two soils that are indistinguishable in both color and mineral properties but originate in two different locations separated by a distance of 1,000 feet. Based on these preliminary results, similar diversity may be expected in the northern United States, Canada, northern Europe, and eastern Europe. However, such probability values can only generally indicate the variation of soil within these geographical areas. Each crime scene must be evaluated separately to establish its own soil variation probabilities.

Collection and Preservation of Soil Evidence

When gathering soil specimens, the evidence collector must give primary consideration to establishing the variation of soil at the crime-scene area. For this reason, standard/reference soils should be collected at various intervals within a 100-yard radius of the crime scene, as well as at the site of the crime, for comparison to the questioned soil. Soil specimens also should be collected at all possible alibi locations that the suspect may claim.

All specimens gathered should be representative of the soil that was removed by the suspect. In most cases, only the top layer of soil is picked up during the commission of a crime. Thus, standard/reference specimens must be removed from the surface without digging too deeply into the unrepresentative subsurface layers. Approximately a tablespoon or two of soil is all the laboratory needs for a thorough comparative analysis. All specimens collected should be packaged in individual containers, such as plastic vials. Each vial should be marked to indicate the location at which the sampling was made.

Soil found on a suspect must be carefully preserved for analysis. If it is found adhering to an object, as in the case of soil on a shoe, the investigator must not remove it. Instead, each object should be individually wrapped in paper, with the soil intact, and transmitted to the laboratory. Similarly, loose soil adhering to garments should not be removed; these items should be carefully and individually wrapped in paper bags and sent to the laboratory for analysis. Care must be taken that particles that may accidentally fall off the garment during transportation will remain in the paper bag.

forensic brief

Soil: The Silent Witness

Alice Redmond was reported missing by her husband on a Monday night in 1983. Police learned that she had been seen with a co-worker, Mark Miller, after work that evening. When police questioned Miller, he stated that the two just "drove around" after work and then she dropped him off at home. Despite his statement, Miller was the prime suspect because he had a criminal record for burglary and theft.

Alice's car was recovered in town the following morning. The wheel wells were thickly coated in mud, which investigators hoped might provide a good lead. These hopes were dampened when police learned that Alice and her husband had attended a motorcycle race on Sunday, where her car was driven through deep mud.

After careful scrutiny, analysts found two colors of soil on the undercarriage of Alice's car. The thickest soil was brown; on top of the brown layer was a reddish soil that looked unlike anything in the county. Investigators hoped the reddish soil, which had to have been deposited sometime after the Sunday night motorcycle event and before the vehicle was discovered on Tuesday morning, could link the vehicle to the location of Alice Redmond.

An interview with Mark Miller's sister provided a break in the case. She told police that Mark had visited her on Monday evening. During that visit, he confessed that he had driven Alice in her car across the Alabama state line into Georgia, killed her, and buried her in a remote location. Now that investigators had a better idea where to look for Alice, forensic analysts took soil samples that would prove or disprove Miller's sister's story.

Each field sample was dried and compared for color and texture by eye and stereomicroscopy to the reddish-colored soil gathered from the car. Next, soils that compared to the car were passed through a series of mesh filters, each of a finer gauge than the last. In this way, the components of the soil samples were physically separated by size. Finally, each fraction was analyzed and compared for mineral composition with the aid of a polarizing light microscope.

Only samples collected from areas across the Alabama state line near the suspected dump site were consistent with the topmost reddish soil recovered from Alice's car. This finding supported Miller's sister's story and was instrumental in Mark Miller's being charged with murder and kidnapping. After pleading guilty, the defendant led the authorities to where he had buried the body. The burial site was within a half mile of the location where forensic analysts had collected a soil sample consistent with the soil removed from Alice's vehicle.

Source: T. J. Hopen, "The Value of Soil Evidence," in M. M. Houck, ed., *Trace Evidence Analysis: More Cases in Mute Witnesses* (Burlington, Mass.: Elsevier Academic Press, 2004), pp. 105–22.

When a lump of soil is found, it should be collected and preserved intact. For example, an automobile tends to collect and build up layers of soil under the fenders, body, and so on. The impact of an automobile with another object may jar some of this soil loose. Once the suspect car has been apprehended, a comparison of the soil left at the scene with soil remaining on the automobile may help establish that the car was present at the accident scene. In these situations, separate samples are collected from under all the fender and frame areas of the vehicle; care is taken to remove the soil in lump form in order to preserve the order in which the soil adhered to the car. Undoubtedly, during the normal use of an automobile, soil will be picked up from numerous locations over a period of months and years. This layering effect may impart soil with greater variation, and hence greater evidential value, than that normally associated with loose soil.

The prevalence of glass and soil in our environment makes them common types of physical evidence at crime scenes. Their proper collection and preservation by the criminal investigator will help ensure that a proper scientific examination can support investigative conclusions placing a suspect or object at the crime scene. Equally important is that glass and soil, like other types of physical evidence, when properly collected and examined, may exonerate the innocent from involvement in a crime.

Virtual Forensics Lab

Forensic Glass Analysis:
To perform a virtual forensic glass analysis, go to www.pearsoncustom.com/us/vlm/

chapter summary

The forensic scientist must constantly determine the properties that impart distinguishing characteristics to matter, giving it a unique identity. Physical properties such as weight, volume, color, boiling point, and melting point describe a substance without reference to any other substance. A chemical property describes the behavior of a substance when it reacts or combines with another substance. Scientists throughout the world use the metric system of measurement. The metric system has basic units of measurement for length, mass, and volume: the meter, gram, and liter, respectively. Temperature is a measure of heat intensity, or the amount of heat in a substance. In science, the most commonly used temperature scale is the Celsius scale. This scale is derived by assigning the freezing point of water a value of 0°C and its boiling point a value of 100°C.

To compare glass fragments, a forensic scientist evaluates two important physical properties: density and refractive index. Density is defined as the mass per unit volume. Refractive index is the ratio of the velocity of light in a vacuum to that in the medium under examination. Crystalline solids have definite geometric forms because of the orderly arrangement of their atoms. These solids refract a beam of light in two different light-ray components. This results in double refraction. Birefringence is the numerical difference between these two refractive indices. Not all solids are crystalline in nature. For example, glass has a random arrangement of atoms to form an amorphous or noncrystalline solid.

The flotation and immersion methods are best used to determine a glass fragment's density and refractive index, respectively. In the flotation method, a glass particle is immersed in a liquid. The density of the liquid is carefully adjusted by the addition of small amounts of an appropriate liquid until the glass chip remains suspended in the liquid medium. At this point, the glass will have the same density as the liquid medium and can be compared to other relevant pieces of glass. The immersion method involves immersing a glass particle in a liquid medium whose refractive index is varied until it is equal to that of the glass particle. At this point, known as the match point, minimum contrast between liquid and particle is observed.

By analyzing the radial and concentric fracture patterns in glass, the forensic scientist can determine the direction of impact. This can be accomplished by applying the 3R rule: *R*adial cracks form a *R*ight angle on the *R*everse side of the force.

The value of soil as evidence rests with its prevalence at crime scenes and its transferability between the scene and the criminal. Most soils can be differentiated by their gross appearance. A side-by-side visual comparison of the color and texture of soil specimens is easy to perform and provides a sensitive property for distinguishing soils that originate from different locations. In many forensic laboratories, forensic geologists characterize and compare the mineral content of soils.

review questions

1. A(n) _____ property describes the behavior of a substance without reference to any other substance.

2. A(n) _____ property describes the behavior of a substance when it reacts or combines with another substance.

3. The _____ system of measurement was devised by the French Academy of Science in 1791.

4. The basic units of measurement for length, mass, and volume in the metric system are the _____, _____, and _____, respectively.

5. A centigram is equivalent to _____ gram(s).

6. A milliliter is equivalent to _____ liter(s).

7. 0.2 gram is equivalent to _____ milligram(s).

8. One cubic centimeter (cc) is equivalent to one _____.

9. True or False: One meter is slightly longer than a yard. _____

10. The equivalent of 1 pound in grams is _____.

11. True or False: A liter is slightly larger than a quart. _____

12. _____ is a measure of a substance's heat intensity.

13. There are _____ degrees Fahrenheit between the freezing and boiling points of water.

14. There are _____ degrees Celsius between the freezing and boiling points of water.

15. The amount of matter an object contains determines its _____.

16. The simplest type of balance for weighing is the _____.

17. Mass per unit volume defines the property of _____.

18. If an object is immersed in a liquid of greater density, it will (sink, float).

19. The bending of a light wave because of a change in velocity is called _____.

20. The physical property of _____ is determined by the ratio of the velocity of light in a vacuum to light's velocity in a substance.

21. True or False: Solids having an orderly arrangement of their constituent atoms are crystalline. _____

22. Solids that have their atoms randomly arranged are said to be _____.

23. The crystal calcite has two indices of refraction. The difference between these two values is known as _____.

24. The process of separating light into its component colors or frequencies is known as _____.

25. A hard, brittle, amorphous substance composed mainly of silicon oxides is _____.

26. Glass that can be physically pieced together has _____ characteristics.

27. The two most useful physical properties of glass for forensic comparisons are _____ and _____.

28. Comparing the relative densities of glass fragments is readily accomplished by a method known as _____.

29. When glass is immersed in a liquid of similar refractive index, its _____ disappears and minimum contrast between the glass and liquid is observed.

30. The exact numerical density and refractive indices of glass can be correlated to _____ in order to assess the evidential value of the comparison.

31. The fracture lines radiating outward from a crack in glass are known as _____ fractures.

32. A crater-shaped hole in glass is (narrower, wider) on the side where the projectile entered the glass.

33. True or False: It is easy to determine from the size and shape of a hole in glass whether it was made by a bullet or some other projectile. _____

34. True or False: Stress marks on the edge of a radial crack are always perpendicular to the edge of the surface on which the impact force originated. _____

35. A fracture line (will, will not) terminate at an existing line fracture.

36. True or False: Most soils have indistinguishable color and texture. _____

37. Naturally occurring crystals commonly found in soils are _____.

38. True or False: The ultimate value of soil as evidence depends on its variation at the crime scene. _____

39. To develop an idea of the soil variation within the crime-scene area, standard/reference soils should be collected at various intervals within a(n) _____-yard radius of the crime scene.

40. True or False: Each object collected at the crime scene that contains soil evidence must be individually wrapped in plastic, with the soil intact, and transmitted to the laboratory. _____

application and critical thinking

1. An accident investigator arrives at the scene of a hit-and-run collision. The driver who remained at the scene reports that the windshield or a side window of the car that struck him shattered on impact. The investigator searches the accident site and collects a large number of fragments of tempered glass. This is the only type of glass recovered from the scene. How can the glass evidence help the investigator locate the vehicle that fled the scene?

2. Indicate the order in which the bullet holes were made in the glass depicted in the accompanying figure. Explain the reason for your answer.

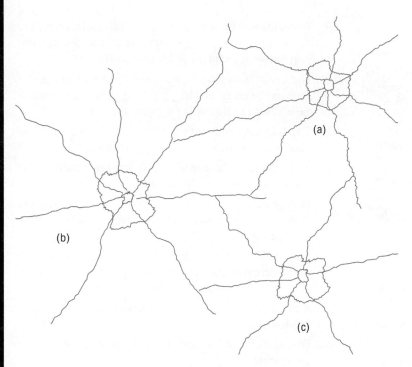

3. The accompanying figure depicts stress marks on the edge of a glass fracture caused by the application of force. If this is a radial fracture, from which side of the glass (left or right) was the force applied? From which

side was force applied if it is a concentric fracture? Explain the reason for your answers.

4. Criminalist Jared Heath responds to the scene of an assault on an unpaved lane in a rural neighborhood. Rain had fallen steadily the night before, making the area quite muddy. A suspect with very muddy shoes was apprehended nearby but claimed to have picked up the mud either from his garden or from the unpaved parking lot of a local restaurant. Jared uses a spade to remove several samples of soil, each about 2 inches deep, from the immediate crime scene and places each in a separate plastic vial. He collects the muddy shoes and wraps them in plastic as well. At the laboratory, he unpackages the soil samples and examines them carefully, one at a time. He then analyzes the soil on the shoes to see if it matches the soil from the crime scene. What mistakes, if any, did Jared make in his investigation?

further references

Caddy, B., ed., *Forensic Examination of Glass and Paint* New York: Taylor & Francis, 2001.

Bottrell, M.C., "Forensic Glass Comparison: Background Information Used in Data Interpretation," *Forensic Science Communications* 11, no. 2 (2009), www.fbi.gov/hq/lab/fsc/backissu/april2009/review/2009_04_review01.htm

Demmelmeyer, H., and J. Adam, "Forensic Investigation of Soil and Vegetable Materials," *Forensic Science Review* 7 (1995): 119–42.

Koons, R. D., J. Buscaglia, M. Bottrell, and E. T. Miller, "Forensic Glass Comparisons," in R. Saferstein, ed., *Forensic Science Handbook*, vol. 1, 2nd ed. Upper Saddle River, N.J.: Prentice Hall, 2002.

Murray, R. C., *Evidence from the Earth: Forensic Geology and Criminal Investigation*. Missoula, Mont.: Mountain Press, 2004.

Murray, R. C., and L. P. Solebello, "Forensic Examination of Soil," in R. Saferstein, ed., *Forensic Science Handbook*, vol. 1, 2nd ed. Upper Saddle River, N.J.: Prentice Hall, 2002.

Thornton, J. I., "Interpretation of Physical Aspects of Glass Evidence," in B. Caddy, ed., *Forensic Examination of Glass and Paint*. New York: Taylor & Francis, 2001.

headline news

Death by Tylenol

In 1982, two firefighters from a Chicago suburb were casually discussing four bizarre deaths that had recently taken place in a neighboring area. As they discussed the circumstances of the deaths, they realized that each of the victims had taken Tylenol. Their suspicions were immediately reported to police investigators. Tragically, before the general public could be alerted, three more victims died after taking poison-laced Tylenol capsules. Seven individuals, all in the Chicago area, were the first victims to die from what has become known as *product tampering*. A forensic chemical analysis of Tylenol capsules recovered from the victims' residences showed that the capsules were filled with potassium cyanide in a quantity ten thousand times what was needed to kill an average person. It was quickly determined that the cyanide was not introduced into the bottles at the factory. Instead, the perpetrator methodically emptied each of twenty to thirty capsules and then refilled them with potassium cyanide. The tampered capsules were rebottled, carefully repackaged, and placed on the shelves of six different stores. The case of the Tylenol murders remains unsolved, and the $100,000 reward offered by Tylenol's manufacturer remains unclaimed.

organic analysis

Learning Objectives

After studying this chapter you should be able to:

- Define and distinguish elements and compounds
- Contrast the differences among a solid, liquid, and gas
- Define and distinguish organic and inorganic compounds
- Understand the difference between qualitative and quantitative analysis
- Describe and explain the process of chromatography
- List and describe the parts of a gas chromatograph
- Explain the differences among thin-layer chromatography, gas chromatography, and electrophoresis
- Understand the differences between the wave and particle theories of light
- Describe the electromagnetic spectrum
- Name the parts of a simple absorption spectrophotometer
- Describe the utility of ultraviolet and infrared spectroscopy for the identification of organic compounds
- Describe the concept and utility of mass spectrometry for identification analysis

KEY TERMS

chromatography
compound
electromagnetic
  spectrum
electrophoresis
element
fluoresce
frequency
gas (vapor)
infrared
inorganic
ion
laser
liquid
matter
monochromatic light
monochromator
organic
periodic table
phase
photon
physical state
pyrolysis
solid
spectrophotometry
sublimation
ultraviolet
visible light
wavelength
X-ray

The Nature of Matter

In the previous chapter, some physical properties were described and used to characterize glass and soil evidence. Before we can apply other physical properties, as well as chemical properties, to the identification and comparison of evidence, we need to gain an insight into the composition of matter. Beginning with knowledge of the fundamental building block of all substances—the element—it will be convenient for us to classify all evidence as either organic or inorganic. The procedures used to measure the properties associated with each class are distinctly different and merit separate chapters for their description. In later chapters, we will continually return to these procedures as we discuss the examination of the various kinds of physical evidence. This chapter will be devoted, in large part, to reviewing a variety of techniques and instruments that have become the indispensable tools of the forensic scientist for examining organic evidence.

Elements and Compounds

matter
All things of substance; matter is composed of atoms or molecules

Matter is anything that has mass and occupies space. As we examine the world that surrounds us and consider the countless variety of materials that we encounter, we must consider one of humankind's most remarkable accomplishments: the discovery of the concept of the atom to explain the composition of all matter. This search had its earliest contribution from the ancient Greek philosophers, who suggested air, water, fire, and earth as matter's fundamental building blocks. It culminated with the development of the atomic theory and the discovery of matter's simplest identity, the **element**.

element
A fundamental particle of matter; an element cannot be broken down into simpler substances by chemical means

An element is the simplest substance known and provides the building block from which all matter is composed. At present, 118 elements have been identified (see Table 5–1); of these, 89 occur naturally on the earth, and the remainder have been created in the laboratory. In Figure 5–1, all of the elements are listed by name and symbol in a form that has become known as the **periodic table**. This table is most useful to chemists because it systematically arranges elements with similar chemical properties in the same vertical row or group.

periodic table
A chart of elements arranged in a systematic fashion; vertical rows are called groups or families, and horizontal rows are called series; elements in a given row have similar properties

For convenience, chemists have chosen letter symbols to represent the elements. Many of these symbols come from the first letter of the element's English name—for example, carbon (C), hydrogen (H), and oxygen (O). Others are two-letter abbreviations of the English name—for example, calcium (Ca) and zinc (Zn). Some symbols are derived from the first letters of Latin or Greek names. Thus, the symbol for silver, Ag, comes from the Latin name *argentum*; copper, Cu, from the Latin *cuprum*; and helium, He, from the Greek name *helios*.

compound
A pure substance composed of two or more elements

The smallest particle of an element that can exist and still retain its identity as that element is the atom. When we write the symbol C we mean one atom of carbon; the chemical symbol for carbon dioxide, CO_2, signifies one atom of carbon combined with two atoms of oxygen. When two or more elements are combined to form a substance, as with carbon dioxide, a new substance is created, different in its physical and chemical properties from its elemental components. This new material is called a **compound**. Compounds contain at least two elements. Considering that there are eighty-nine natural elements, it is easy to imagine the large number of possible elemental combinations that may form compounds. Not surprisingly, more than 16 million known compounds have already been identified.

physical state
A condition or stage in the form of matter; a solid, liquid, or gas

Just as the atom is the basic particle of an element, the molecule is the smallest unit of a compound. Thus, a molecule of carbon dioxide is represented by the symbol CO_2, and a molecule of table salt is symbolized by NaCl, representing the combination of one atom of the element sodium (Na) with one atom of the element chlorine (Cl).

solid
A state of matter in which the molecules are held closely together in a rigid state

States of Matter

liquid
A state of matter in which molecules are in contact with one another but are not rigidly held in place

As we look around us and view the materials that make up the earth, it becomes an awesome task even to attempt to estimate the number of different kinds of matter that exist. A much more logical approach is to classify matter according to the physical form it takes. These forms are called **physical states**. There are three such states: **solid**, **liquid**, and **gas (vapor)**. A solid is rigid and therefore has a definite shape and volume. A liquid also occupies a specific volume, but its fluidity causes it to take the shape of the container in which it is residing. A gas has neither a definite shape nor volume, and it will completely fill any container into which it is placed.

gas (vapor)
A state of matter in which the attractive forces between molecules are small enough to permit them to move with complete freedom

TABLE 5–1
List of Elements with Their Symbols and Atomic Masses

Element	Symbol	Atomic Mass[a] (amu)	Element	Symbol	Atomic Mass[a] (amu)
Actinum	Ac	(227)	Lead	Pb	207.2
Aluminum	Al	26.9815	Lithium	Li	6.941
Americium	Am	(243)	Lutetium	Lu	174.97
Antimony	Sb	121.75	Magnesium	Mg	24.305
Argon	Ar	39.948	Manganese	Mn	54.9380
Arsenic	As	74.9216	Meitnerium	Mt	(266)
Astatine	At	(210)	Mendelevium	Md	(256)
Barium	Ba	137.34	Mercury	Hg	200.59
Berkelium	Bk	(247)	Molybdenum	Mo	95.94
Beryllium	Be	9.01218	Neodymium	Nd	144.24
Bismuth	Bi	208.9806	Neon	Ne	20.179
Bohrium	Bh	(262)	Neptunium	Np	237.0482
Boron	B	10.81	Nickel	Ni	58.71
Bromine	Br	79.904	Niobium	Nb	92.9064
Cadmium	Cd	112.40	Nitrogen	N	14.0067
Calcium	Ca	40.08	Nobelium	No	(254)
Californium	Cf	(251)	Osmium	Os	190.2
Carbon	C	12.011	Oxygen	O	15.9994
Cerium	Ce	140.12	Palladium	Pd	106.4
Cesium	Cs	132.9055	Phosphorus	P	30.9738
Chlorine	Cl	35.453	Platinum	Pt	195.09
Chromium	Cr	51.996	Plutonium	Pu	(244)
Cobalt	Co	58.9332	Polonium	Po	(209)
Copernicium	Cp	(285)	Potassium	K	39.102
Copper	Cu	63.546	Praseodymium	Pr	140.9077
Curium	Cm	(247)	Promethium	Pm	(145)
Darmstadtium	Ds	(271)	Protactinium	Pa	231.0359
Dubnium	Db	(260)	Radium	Ra	226.0254
Dysprosium	Dy	162.50	Radon	Rn	(222)
Einsteinium	Es	(254)	Rhenium	Re	186.2
Erbium	Er	167.26	Rhodium	Rh	102.9055
Europium	Eu	151.96	Roentgenium	Rg	(272)
Fermium	Fm	(253)	Rubidium	Rb	85.4678
Fluorine	F	18.9984	Ruthenium	Ru	101.07
Francium	Fr	(223)	Rutherfordium	Rf	(257)
Gadolinium	Gd	157.25	Samarium	Sm	105.4
Gallium	Ga	69.72	Scandium	Sc	44.9559
Germanium	Ge	72.59	Seaborgium	Sg	(263)
Gold	Au	196.9665	Selenium	Se	78.96
Hafnium	Hf	178.49	Silicon	Si	28.086
Hassium	Hs	(265)	Silver	Ag	107.868
Helium	He	4.00260	Sodium	Na	22.9898
Holmium	Ho	164.9303	Strontium	Sr	87.62
Hydrogen	H	1.0080	Sulfur	S	32.06
Indium	In	114.82	Tantalum	Ta	180.9479
Iodine	I	126.9045	Technetium	Tc	98.9062
Iridium	Ir	192.22	Tellurium	Te	127.60
Iron	Fe	55.847	Terbium	Tb	158.9254
Krypton	Kr	83.80	Thallium	Tl	204.37
Lanthanum	La	138.9055	Thorium	Th	232.0381
Lawrencium	Lr	(257)	Thulium	Tm	168.9342

Continued

TABLE 5–1 Continued

Element	Symbol	Atomic Mass[a] (amu)	Element	Symbol	Atomic Mass[a] (amu)
Tin	Sn	118.69	Ununtrium	Uut	(284)
Titanium	Ti	47.90	Uranium	U	238.029
Tungsten	W	183.85	Vanadium	V	50.9414
Copernicium	Cp	(292)	Xenon	Xe	131.3
Ununoctium	Uuo	(294)	Ytterbium	Yb	173.04
Ununpentium	Uup	(288)	Yttrium	Y	88.9059
Ununquadium	Uuq	(289)	Zinc	Zn	65.57
Ununseptium	Uus	(?)	Zirconium	Zr	91.22

[a]Based on the assigned relative atomic mass of C = exactly 12; parentheses denote the mass number of the isotope with the longest half-life.

FIGURE 5–1

The periodic table.

CHANGES OF STATE   Substances can change from one state to another. For example, as water is heated, it is converted from a liquid form into a vapor. At a high enough temperature (100°C), water boils and rapidly changes into steam. Similarly, at 0°C, water solidifies or freezes into ice. Under certain conditions, some solids can be converted directly into a gaseous state. For instance, a piece of dry ice (solid carbon dioxide) left standing at room temperature quickly forms carbon dioxide vapor and disappears. This change of state from a solid to a gas is called **sublimation**.

In each of these examples, no new chemical species are formed; matter is simply being changed from one physical state to another. Water, whether in the form of liquid, ice, or steam, remains chemically H_2O. Simply, what has been altered are the attractive forces between the water molecules. In a solid, these forces are very strong, and the molecules are held closely together in a rigid state. In a liquid, the attractive forces are not as strong, and the molecules have more mobility. Finally, in the vapor state, appreciable attractive forces no longer exist among the molecules; thus, they may move in any direction at will.

sublimation

A physical change from the solid state directly into the gaseous state

PHASES Chemists are forever combining different substances, no matter whether they are in the solid, liquid, or gaseous states, hoping to create new and useful products. Our everyday observations should make it apparent that not all attempts at mixing matter can be productive. For instance, oil spills demonstrate that oil and water do not mix. **Whenever substances can be distinguished by a visible boundary, different phases are said to exist.** Thus, oil floating on water is an example of a two-phase system. The oil and water each constitute a separate liquid phase, clearly distinct from each other. Similarly, when sugar is first added to water, it does not dissolve, and two distinctly different phases exist: the solid sugar and the liquid water. However, after stirring, all the sugar dissolves, leaving just one liquid phase.

phase
A uniform body of matter; different phases are separated by definite visible boundaries

Selecting an Analytical Technique

Now that the basic components of matter have been defined, proper selection of analytical techniques that enable the forensic scientist to identify or compare matter can best be understood by categorizing all substances into one of two broad groups: **organics** and **inorganics**.

Organic vs. Inorganic Substances

Organic substances contain carbon, commonly in combination with hydrogen, oxygen, nitrogen, chlorine, phosphorus, or other elements. Inorganic substances encompass all other known chemical substances. Each of these two broad groups has distinctive and characteristic properties. Thus, once the analyst has determined whether a material is organic or inorganic, the properties to be measured and the choice of analytical techniques to be used are generally the same for all materials in each group.

organic
Describes a substance composed of carbon and often smaller amounts of hydrogen, oxygen, nitrogen, chlorine, phosphorus, or other elements

inorganic
Describes a chemical compound not based on carbon

Most evidence received by crime laboratories requires identification of organic compounds. These compounds may include substances such as commonly abused drugs (such as alcohol, marijuana, heroin, amphetamines, and barbiturates), synthetic fibers, petroleum products, paint binders, and high-order explosives. As we have already observed, organic compounds are composed of a combination of a relatively small number of elements that must include carbon; fortunately, the nature of the forces or bonds between these elements is such that the resultant compounds can readily be characterized by their absorption of light.

The study of the absorption of light by chemical substances, known as **spectrophotometry**, is a basic tool for the characterization and identification of organic materials. Although spectrophotometry is most applicable to organic analysis, its optimal use requires that a material be in a relatively pure state. Because the purity of physical evidence is almost always beyond the control of the criminalist, this criterion often is not met. For this reason, the analytical technique of **chromatography** is widely applied for the analysis of physical evidence. Chromatography is a means of separating and tentatively identifying the components of a mixture. We will discuss both techniques in this chapter.

spectrophotometry
An analytical method for identifying a substance by its selective absorption of different wavelengths of light

chromatography
Any of several analytical techniques for separating organic mixtures into their components by attraction to a stationary phase while being propelled by a moving phase

Qualitative vs. Quantitative Measurement

Another consideration in selecting an analytical technique is the need for either a *qualitative* or a *quantitative* determination. The former relates just to the identity of the material, whereas the latter refers to the percentage combination of the components of a mixture. Hence, a qualitative identification of a powder may reveal the presence of heroin and quinine, whereas a quantitative analysis may conclude the presence of 10 percent heroin and 90 percent quinine. Obviously, a qualitative identification must precede any attempt at quantitation, for little value is served by attempting to quantitate a material without first determining its identity. Essentially, a qualitative analysis of a material requires the determination of numerous properties using a variety of analytical techniques. On the other hand, a quantitative measurement is usually accomplished by the precise measurement of a single property of the material.

Chromatography

Chromatography as a technique for separating the components of a mixture is particularly useful for analyzing the multicomponent specimens that are frequently received in the crime laboratory. For example, illicit drugs sold on the street are not manufactured to meet government labeling standards; instead, they may be diluted with practically any material at the disposal of the drug

FIGURE 5-2

Evaporation of a liquid.

FIGURE 5-3

At equilibrium, there are more gas A molecules (green balls) than gas B molecules (blue balls) in the liquid phase.

dealer to increase the quantity of product available to prospective customers. Hence, the task of identifying an illicit-drug preparation would be arduous without the aid of chromatographic methods to first separate the mixture into its components.

Theory of Chromatography

The theory of chromatography is based on the observation that chemical substances tend to partially escape into the surrounding environment when dissolved in a liquid or when absorbed on a solid surface. This is best illustrated by a gas dissolved in a beaker of water kept at a constant temperature. It will be convenient for us to characterize the water in the beaker as the liquid phase and the air above it as the gas phase. If the beaker is covered with a bell jar, as shown in Figure 5–2, some of the gas molecules (represented by the green balls) escape from the water into the surrounding enclosed air. The molecules that remain are said to be in the liquid phase; the molecules that have escaped into the air are said to be in the gas phase. As the gas molecules escape into the surrounding air, they accumulate above the water; here, random motion carries some of them back into the water. Eventually, a point is reached at which the number of molecules leaving the water is equal to the number returning. At this time, the liquid and gas phases are in *equilibrium*. If the temperature of the water is increased, the equilibrium state readjusts itself to a point at which more gas molecules move into the gas phase.

This behavior was first observed in 1803 by a British chemist, William Henry. His explanation of this phenomenon, known appropriately as Henry's law, may be stated as follows: *When a volatile chemical compound is dissolved in a liquid and is brought to equilibrium with air, there is a fixed ratio between the concentration of the volatile compound in air and its concentration in the liquid, and this ratio remains constant for a given temperature.*

The distribution or partitioning of a gas between the liquid and gas phases is determined by the solubility of the gas in the liquid. The higher its solubility, the greater the tendency of the gas molecules to remain in the liquid phase. If two different gases are simultaneously dissolved in the same liquid, each will reach a state of equilibrium with the surrounding air independently of the other. For example, as shown in Figure 5–3, gas A (green balls) and gas B (blue balls) are both dissolved in water. At equilibrium, gas A has a greater number of molecules dissolved in the water than does gas B. This is so because gas A is more soluble in water than gas B.

Basic Chromatographic Process

Now return to the concept of chromatography. In Figures 5–2 and 5–3, both phases—liquid and gas—were kept stationary; that is, they were not moving. During a chromatographic process, this is not the case; instead, one phase is always made to move continuously in one direction over a stationary or fixed phase. For example, in Figure 5–3, showing the two gases represented by blue and green balls dissolved in water, chromatography will occur only when the air is forced to move continuously in one direction over the water. Because gas B has a greater percentage of its molecules in the moving gas phase than does gas A, its molecules will travel over the liquid at a faster pace than those of gas A. Eventually, when the moving phase has advanced a reasonable distance, gas B will become entirely separated from gas A and the chromatographic process will be complete. This process is illustrated in Figure 5–4.

Simply, we can think of chromatography as being analogous to a race between chemical compounds. At the starting line, all the participating substances are mixed together; however, as the race progresses, materials that prefer the moving phase slowly pull ahead of those that prefer to remain in the stationary phase. Finally, at the end of the race, all the participants are separated, each crossing the finish line at different times.

The different types of chromatographic systems are as varied as the number of stationary and moving-phase combinations that can be devised. However, three chromatographic processes—gas chromatography, high-performance liquid chromatography, and thin-layer chromatography—are most applicable for solving many analytical problems in the crime laboratory.

Gas Chromatography (GC)

Gas chromatography (GC) separates mixtures on the basis of their distribution between a stationary liquid phase and a moving gas phase. This technique is widely used because of its ability to resolve a highly complex mixture into its components, usually within minutes.

(a)
(b)
(c)

FIGURE 5–4

In this illustration of chromatography, the molecules represented by the blue balls have a greater affinity for the upper phase and hence will be pushed along at a faster rate by the moving air. Eventually, the two sets of molecules will separate from each other, completing the chromatographic process.

BASIC THEORY OF GC   In gas chromatography, the moving phase is actually a gas called the *carrier gas*, which flows through a column constructed of stainless steel or glass. The stationary phase is a thin film of liquid within the column. Two types of columns are used: the *packed column* and the *capillary column*. With the packed column, the stationary phase is a thin film of liquid that is fixed onto small granular particles packed into the column. This column is usually constructed of stainless steel or glass and is 2 to 6 meters long and about 3 millimeters in diameter. Capillary columns are composed of glass and are much longer than packed columns—15 to 60 meters long. These types of columns are very narrow, ranging from 0.25 to 0.75 millimeter in diameter. Capillary columns can be made narrower than packed columns because their stationary liquid phase is actually coated as a very thin film directly onto the column's inner wall. In any case, as the carrier gas flows through the packed or capillary column, it carries with it the components of a mixture that have been injected into the column. Components with a greater affinity for the moving gas phase travel through the column more quickly than those with a greater affinity for the stationary liquid phase. Eventually, after the mixture has traversed the length of the column, it emerges separated into its components.

THE GC PROCESS   A simplified scheme of the gas chromatograph is shown in Figure 5–5. The operation of the instrument can be summed up briefly as follows: A gas stream, the so-called carrier gas, is fed into the column at a constant rate. The carrier gas is chemically inert and is generally nitrogen or helium. The sample under investigation is injected as a liquid into a heated injection port with a syringe, where it is immediately vaporized and swept into the column by the carrier gas. The column itself is heated in an oven in order to keep the sample in a vapor state as it travels through the column. In the column, the components of the sample travel in the direction of the carrier gas flow at speeds that are determined by their distribution between the stationary and moving phases. If the analyst has selected the proper liquid phase and has made the column long enough, the components of the sample will be completely separated as they emerge from the column.

FIGURE 5–5

Basic gas chromatography. Gas chromatography permits rapid separation of complex mixtures into individual compounds and allows identification and quantitative determination of each compound. As shown, a sample is introduced by a syringe (1) into a heated injection chamber (2). A constant stream of nitrogen gas (3) flows through the injector, carrying the sample into the column (4), which contains a thin film of liquid. The sample is separated in the column, and the carrier gas and separated components emerge from the column and enter the detector (5). Signals developed by the detector activate the recorder (7), which makes a permanent record of the separation by tracing a series of peaks on the chromatograph (8). The time of elution identifies the component present, and the peak area identifies the concentration.

Courtesy Varian Inc., Palo Alto, Calif.

1. **Sample**
2. **Injector**
3. **Carrier gas**
4. **Column**
5. **Detector**
6. **Power supply**
7. **Recorder**
8. **Chromatogram**

As each component emerges from the column, it enters a detector. One type of detector uses a flame to ionize the emerging chemical substance, thus generating an electrical signal. The signal is recorded onto a strip-chart recorder as a function of time. This written record of the separation is called a *chromatogram*. A gas chromatogram is a plot of the recorder response (vertical axis) versus time (horizontal axis). A typical chromatogram shows a series of peaks, each peak corresponding to one component of the mixture. The time required for a component to emerge from the column from the time of its injection into the column is known as the *retention time*, which is a useful identifying characteristic of a material. Figure 5–6(a) shows the chromatogram of two barbiturates; each barbiturate has tentatively been identified by comparing its retention time to those of known barbiturates, shown in Figure 5–6(b). (See Appendix III for chromatographic conditions.) However, because other substances may have comparable retention times under similar chromatographic conditions, gas chromatography cannot be considered an absolute means of identification. Conclusions derived from this technique must be confirmed by other testing procedures.

An added advantage of gas chromatography is that it is extremely sensitive and can yield quantitative results. The amount of substance passing through the GC detector is proportional to the peak area recorded; therefore, by chromatographing a known concentration of a material and comparing it to the unknown, the amount of the sample may be determined by proportion. Gas chromatography has sufficient sensitivity to detect and quantitate materials at the nanogram (0.000000001 gram or 1×10^{-9} gram) level.[1]

PYROLYSIS GC   An important extension of the application of gas chromatography to forensic science is the technique of **pyrolysis** *gas chromatography*. Many solid materials commonly encountered as physical evidence—for example, paint chips, fibers, and plastics—cannot be readily dissolved in a solvent for injection into the gas chromatograph. Thus, under normal conditions these substances cannot be subjected to gas chromatographic analysis. However, materials such as these can be heated or pyrolyzed to high temperatures (500–1000°C) so that they will decompose into numerous gaseous products. Pyrolyzers permit these gaseous products to enter the carrier gas stream, where they flow into and through the GC column. The pyrolyzed material can then be characterized by the pattern produced by its chromatogram or *pyrogram*. Figure 5–7 illustrates the pyrogram of a paint chip. The complexity of the paint pyrogram serves as a "fingerprint" of the material and gives the examiner many points to compare with other paints that are analyzed in a similar fashion.

my crime kit

WEBEXTRA 5.1
Watch the Gas Chromatograph at Work
http://www.mycrimekit.com

pyrolysis
The decomposition of organic matter by heat

[1] Powers of 10 are quite useful and simple for handling large or small numbers. The exponent expresses the number of places the decimal point must be moved. If the exponent is positive, the decimal point is moved to the right; if it is negative, the decimal point is moved to the left. Thus, to express 1×10^{-9} as a number, the decimal point is simply moved nine places to the left of 1.

FIGURE 5–6

(a) An unknown mixture of barbiturates is identified by comparing its retention times to (b), a known mixture of barbiturates.

Courtesy Varian Inc., Palo Alto, Calif.

High-Performance Liquid Chromatography (HPLC)

Recall that a chromatographic system requires a moving phase and a stationary phase in contact with each other. The previous section described gas chromatography, in which the stationary phase is a thin film and the moving phase is a gas. However, by changing the nature of these phases, one can create different forms of chromatography. One form finding increasing utility in crime laboratories is high-performance liquid chromatography (HPLC). Its moving phase is a liquid that is pumped through a column filled with fine solid particles. In one form of HPLC, the

FIGURE 5–7

Pyrogram of a GM automobile paint.
Courtesy Varian Inc., Palo Alto, Calif.

surfaces of these solid particles are chemically treated and act as the stationary phase. As the liquid moving phase is pumped through the column, a sample is injected into the column. As the liquid carries the sample through the column, different components are retarded to different degrees, depending on their interaction with the stationary phase. This leads to a separation of the different components making up the sample mixture.

The major advantage of HPLC is that the entire process takes place at room temperature. With GC, the sample must first be vaporized and made to travel through a heated column. Hence, any materials sensitive to high temperatures may not survive their passage through the column. In such situations, the analyst may turn to HPLC as the method of choice. Organic explosives are generally heat sensitive and therefore more readily separated by HPLC. Likewise, heat-sensitive drugs, such as LSD, lend themselves to analysis by HPLC.

Thin-Layer Chromatography (TLC)

The technique of thin-layer chromatography (TLC) uses a solid stationary phase and a moving liquid phase to separate the constituents of a mixture.

THE TLC PROCESS   A thin-layer plate is prepared by coating a glass plate with a thin film of a granular material, usually silica gel or aluminum oxide. This granular material serves as the solid stationary phase and is usually held in place on the plate with a binding agent such as plaster of Paris. If the sample to be analyzed is a solid, it must first be dissolved in a suitable solvent and a few microliters of the solution spotted with a capillary tube onto the granular surface near the lower edge of the plate. A liquid sample may be applied directly to the plate in the same manner. The plate is then placed upright into a closed chamber that contains a selected liquid, with care that the liquid does not touch the sample spot.

The liquid slowly rises up the plate by capillary action. This rising liquid is the moving phase in thin-layer chromatography. As the liquid moves past the sample spot, the components of the sample become distributed between the stationary solid phase and the moving liquid phase. The components with the greatest affinity for the moving phase travel up the plate faster than

(a)   (b)

FIGURE 5-8

(a) In thin-layer chromatography, a liquid sample is spotted onto the granular surface of a gel-coated plate. (b) The plate is placed into a closed chamber that contains a liquid. As the liquid rises up the plate, the components of the sample distribute themselves between the coating and the moving liquid. The mixture is separated, with substances with a greater affinity for the moving liquid traveling up the plate at a faster speed.

(a)   (b)   (c)

FIGURE 5-9

(a) The liquid phase begins to move up the stationary phase. (b) Liquid moves past the ink spot carrying the ink components up the stationary phase. (c) The moving liquid has separated the ink into its several components.

Courtesy Richard Megna, Fundamental Photographs, NYC

those that have greater affinity for the stationary phase. When the liquid front has moved a sufficient distance (usually 10 cm), the development is complete, and the plate is removed from the chamber and dried (see Figure 5–8). An example of the chromatographic separation of ink is shown in Figure 5–9.

VISUALIZING SUBSTANCES   Because most compounds are colorless, no separation will be noticed after development unless the materials are *visualized*. To accomplish this, the plates are placed under ultraviolet light, revealing select materials that **fluoresce** as bright spots on a dark background. When a fluorescent dye has been incorporated into the solid phase, nonfluorescent substances appear as dark spots against a fluorescent background when exposed to the ultraviolet light. In a second method of visualization, the plate is sprayed with a chemical reagent that reacts with the separated substances and causes them to form colored spots. Figure 5–10 shows the chromatogram of a marijuana extract that has been separated into its components by TLC and visualized by having been sprayed with a chemical reagent.

fluoresce

To emit visible light when exposed to light of a shorter wavelength—that is, ultraviolet light

IDENTIFYING SUBSTANCES   Once the components of a sample have been separated, their identification must follow. For this, the questioned sample must be developed alongside an authentic or standard sample on the same TLC plate. If both the standard and the unknown travel the same distance up the plate from their origins, they can tentatively be identified as being the same. For example, suppose a sample suspected of containing heroin and quinine is chromatographed alongside known heroin and quinine standards, as shown in Figure 5–11. The identity of the suspect material is confirmed by comparing the migration distances of the heroin and quinine standards against those of the components of the unknown material. If the distances are the same, a tentative identification can be made. However, such an identification cannot be considered definitive because numerous other substances can migrate the same distance up the plate when chromatographed under similar conditions. Thus, thin-layer chromatography alone cannot provide an absolute identification; it must be used in conjunction with other testing procedures to prove absolute identity.

The distance a spot has traveled up a thin-layer plate can be assigned a numerical value known as the *Rf* value. This value is defined as the distance traveled by the component divided by the distance traveled by the moving liquid phase. For example, in Figure 5–11 the moving phase traveled 10 centimeters up the plate before the plate was removed from the tank. After visualization, the heroin spot moved 8 centimeters, which has an *Rf* value of 0.8; the quinine migrated 4 centimeters, for an *Rf* value of 0.4.

FIGURE 5–10

Thin-layer chromatogram of a marijuana extract.

Courtesy Sirchie Finger Print Laboratories, Youngsville, N.C., www.sirchie.com

FIGURE 5–11

Chromatograms of known heroin (1) and quinine (2) standards alongside suspect sample (3).

Thousands of possible combinations of liquid and solid phases can be chosen in thin-layer chromatography. Fortunately, years of research have produced much published data relating to the proper selection of TLC conditions for separating and identifying specific classes of substances — for example, drugs, dyes, and petroleum products. These references, along with the experience of the analyst, will aid in the proper selection of TLC conditions for specific problems.

Thin-layer chromatography is a powerful tool for solving many of the analytical problems presented to the forensic scientist. The method is both rapid and sensitive; moreover, less than 100 micrograms of suspect material are required for the analysis. In addition, the equipment necessary for TLC work has minimal cost and space requirements. Importantly, numerous samples can be analyzed simultaneously on one thin-layer plate. The principal application of this technique is in the detection and identification of components in complex mixtures.

Electrophoresis

Electrophoresis is somewhat related to thin-layer chromatography in that it separates materials according to their migration rates on a stationary solid phase. However, it does not use a moving liquid phase to move the material; instead, an electrical potential is placed across the stationary medium. The nature of this medium can vary; most forensic applications call for a starch or agar gel coated onto a glass plate. Under these conditions, only substances that possess an electrical charge migrate across the stationary phase (see Figure 5–12). The technique is particularly useful for separating and identifying complex biochemical mixtures. In forensic science, electrophoresis finds its most successful application in the characterization of DNA in dried blood (see Figure 5–13).

Because many substances in blood carry an electrical charge, they can be separated and identified by electrophoresis. As shown in Figure 5–12, mixtures of DNA fragments can be separated by gel electrophoresis by taking advantage of the fact that the rate of movement of DNA across a gel-coated plate depends on the molecule's size. Smaller DNA fragments move at a faster rate along the plate than larger DNA fragments. This technique will be discussed in further detail in Chapters 10 and 11.

electrophoresis
A technique for separating molecules through migration on a support medium while under the influence of an electrical potential

(a)

(b)

(c)

FIGURE 5–12

FIGURE 5–13
DNA fragments separated by gel electrophoresis are visualized under a UV light.
Courtesy Cytographics, Visuals Unlimited

visible light
Colored light ranging from red to violet in the electromagnetic spectrum

wavelength
The distance between crests of adjacent waves

frequency
The number of waves that pass a given point per second

electromagnetic spectrum
The entire range of radiation energy from the most energetic cosmic rays to the least energetic radio waves

X-ray
A high-energy, short-wavelength form of electromagnetic radiation

Spectrophotometry

We have already seen that when white light passes through a glass prism, it is dispersed into a continuous spectrum of colors. This phenomenon demonstrates that white light is not homogeneous but is actually composed of a range of colors that extends from red through violet. Similarly, the observation that a substance has a color is also consistent with this description of white light. For example, when light passes through a red glass, the glass absorbs all the component colors of light except red, which passes through or is transmitted by the glass. Likewise, one can determine the color of an opaque object by observing its ability to absorb some of the component colors of light while reflecting others back to the eye. Color is thus a visual indication that objects absorb certain portions of **visible light** and transmit or reflect others. Scientists have long recognized this phenomenon and have learned to characterize different chemical substances by the type and quantity of light they absorb.

Theory of Light

To understand why materials absorb light, one must first comprehend the nature of light. Two simple models explain light's behavior. The first model describes light as a continuous wave; the second depicts it as a stream of discrete energy particles. Together, these two very different descriptions explain all of the observed properties of light, but by itself, no one model can explain all the facets of the behavior of light.

LIGHT AS A WAVE   The wave concept depicts light as having an up-and-down motion of a continuous wave, as shown in Figure 5–14. Several terms are used to describe such a wave. The distance between two consecutive crests (or one trough to the next trough) is called the **wavelength**; the Greek letter *lambda* (λ) is used as its symbol, and the unit of nanometers is frequently used to express its value. The number of crests (or troughs) passing any one given point in a unit of time is defined as the **frequency** of the wave. Frequency is normally designated by the letter f and is expressed in cycles per second (cps). The speed of light in a vacuum is a universal constant at 300 million meters per second and is designated by the symbol c. Frequency and wavelength are inversely proportional to one another, as shown by the relationship expressed in Equation (5–1):

$$F = c/\lambda \tag{5–1}$$

THE ELECTROMAGNETIC SPECTRUM   Actually, visible light is only a small part of a large family of radiation waves known as the **electromagnetic spectrum**. All electromagnetic waves travel at the speed of light (c) and are distinguishable from one another only by their different wavelengths or frequencies. (Figure 5–15 illustrates the various types of electromagnetic waves in order of decreasing frequency.) Hence, the only property that distinguishes **X-rays** from radio waves is the different frequencies the two types of waves possess. Similarly, the range of colors that make up the visible spectrum can be correlated with frequency. For instance, the lowest frequencies of visi-

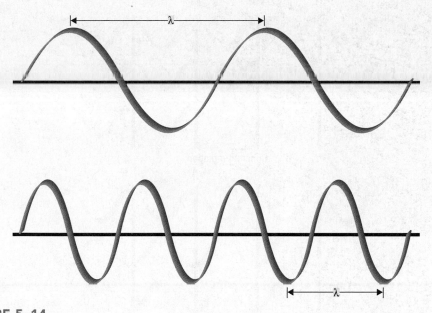

FIGURE 5–14

The frequency of the lower wave is twice that of the upper wave.

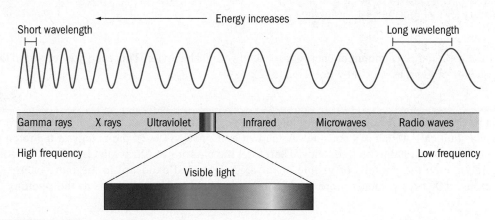

FIGURE 5–15

The electromagnetic spectrum.

ble light are red; waves with a lower frequency fall into the invisible infrared (IR) region. The highest frequencies of visible light are violet; waves with a higher frequency extend into the invisible ultraviolet (UV) region. No definite boundaries exist between any colors or regions of the electromagnetic spectrum; instead, each region is composed of a continuous range of frequencies, each blending into the other.

Ordinarily, light in any region of the electromagnetic spectrum is a collection of waves possessing a range of wavelengths. Under normal circumstances, this light comprises waves that are all out of step with each other (incoherent light). However, scientists can now produce a beam of light that has all of its waves pulsating in unison (see Figure 5–16). This is called **coherent light** or a **laser** (*l*ight *a*mplification by the *s*timulated *e*mission of *r*adiation) beam. Light in this form is very intense and can be focused on a very small area. Laser beams can be focused to pinpoints that are so intense that they can zap microscopic holes in a diamond.

LIGHT AS A PARTICLE   As long as electromagnetic radiation is moving through space, its behavior can be described as that of a continuous wave; however, once radiation is absorbed by a substance, the model of light as a stream of discrete particles must be invoked to best describe its behavior. Here, light is depicted as consisting of energy particles that are known as **photons**. Each

laser
An acronym for *l*ight amplification by *s*timulated emission of radiation; light that has all its waves pulsating in unison

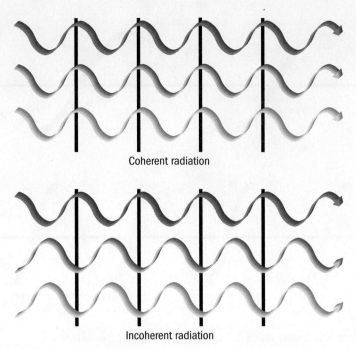

FIGURE 5–16

Coherent and incoherent radiation.

photon

A small packet of electromagnetic radiation energy; each photon contains a unit of energy equal to the product of Planck's constant and the frequency of radiation: $E = hf$

photon has a definite amount of energy associated with its behavior. This energy is related to the frequency of light, as shown by Equation (5–2):

$$E = hf \qquad\qquad (5\text{–}2)$$

where E specifies the energy of the photon, f is the frequency of radiation, and h is a universal constant called Planck's constant. As shown by Equation (5–2), the energy of a photon is directly proportional to its frequency. Therefore, the photons of ultraviolet light will be more energetic than the photons of visible or infrared light, and exposure to the more energetic photons of X-rays presents more danger to human health than exposure to the photons of radio waves.

Absorption of Electromagnetic Radiation

Just as a substance can absorb visible light to produce color, many of the invisible radiations of the electromagnetic spectrum are likewise absorbed. This absorption phenomenon is the basis for spectrophotometry, an important analytical technique in chemical identification. Spectrophotometry measures the quantity of radiation that a particular material absorbs as a function of wavelength or frequency.

We have already observed in the description of color that an object does not absorb all the visible light it is exposed to; instead, it selectively absorbs some frequencies and reflects or transmits others. Similarly, the absorption of other types of electromagnetic radiation by chemical substances is also selective. These key questions must be asked: Why does a particular substance absorb only at certain frequencies and not at others? And are these frequencies predictable? The answers are not simple. Scientists find it difficult to predict with certainty all the frequencies at which any one substance will absorb in a particular region of the electromagnetic spectrum. What is known, however, is that a chemical substance absorbs photons of radiation with a frequency that corresponds to an energy requirement of the substance, as defined by Equation (5–2). Different materials have different energy requirements and therefore absorb at different frequencies. Most important to the analyst is that these absorbed frequencies are measurable and can be used to characterize a material.

The selective absorption of a substance is measured by an instrument called a *spectrophotometer*, which produces a graph or *absorption spectrum* that depicts the absorption of light as a function of wavelength or frequency. The absorption of UV, visible, and IR radiation is particularly applicable for obtaining qualitative data pertaining to the identification of organic substances.

Absorption at a single wavelength or frequency of light is not 100 percent complete—some radiation is transmitted or reflected by the material. Just how much radiation a substance absorbs is defined by a fundamental relationship known as Beer's law, shown in Equation (5–3):

$$A = kc \qquad\qquad (5\text{–}3)$$

Here, A symbolizes the absorption or the quantity of light taken up at a single frequency, c is the concentration of the absorbing material, and k is a proportionality constant. This relationship shows that the quantity of light absorbed at any frequency is directly proportional to the concentration of the absorbing species; the more material you have, the more radiation it will absorb. By defining the relationship between absorbance and concentration, Beer's law permits spectrophotometry to be used as a technique for quantification.

The Spectrophotometer

The spectrophotometer measures and records the absorption spectrum of a chemical substance. The basic components of a simple spectrophotometer are the same regardless of whether it is designed to measure the absorption of UV, visible, or IR radiation. These components are illustrated in Figure 5–17. They include (1) a radiation source, (2) a monochromator or frequency selector, (3) a sample holder, (4) a detector to convert electromagnetic radiation into an electrical signal, and (5) a recorder to produce a record of the signal.

The choice of source will vary with the type of radiation desired. For visible radiation, an ordinary tungsten bulb provides a convenient source of radiation. In the UV region, a hydrogen or deuterium discharge lamp is normally used, and a heated molded rod containing a mixture of rare-earth oxides is a good source of IR light.

The function of the **monochromator** is to select a single wavelength or frequency of light from the source—**monochromatic light.** Some inexpensive spectrophotometers pass the light through colored glass filters to remove all radiation from the beam except for a desired range of wavelengths. More precise spectrophotometers use a prism or diffraction grating to disperse radiation into its component wavelengths or frequencies.[2] The desired wavelength is obtained when the dispersed radiation is focused onto a narrow slit that permits only selected wavelengths to pass through.

monochromator
A device for isolating individual wavelengths or frequencies of light

monochromatic light
Light having a single wavelength or frequency

Most laboratory infrared spectrophotometers use Fourier transform analysis to measure the wavelengths of light at which a material will absorb in the infrared spectrum. This approach does not use any dispersive elements that select single wavelengths or frequencies of light emitted from a source; instead, the heart of a *Fourier transform infrared* (FT-IR) *spectrometer* is the Michelson interferometer. The interferometer uses a beam-splitting prism and two mirrors, one movable and one stationary, to direct light toward a sample. As the wavelengths pass through the sample and reach a detector, they are all measured simultaneously. A mathematical operation, the Fourier transform method, is used to decode the measured signals and record the wavelength data. These Fourier calculations are rapidly carried out by a computer. In a matter of seconds, a computer-operated FT-IR instrument can produce an infrared absorption pattern compatible to one generated by a prism instrument.

Sample preparation varies with the type of radiation being studied. Absorption spectra in the UV and visible regions are usually obtained from samples that have been dissolved in an appropriate solvent. Because the cells holding the solution must be transparent to the light being measured, glass cells are used in the visible region and quartz cells in the ultraviolet region. Practically all substances absorb in some region of the IR spectrum, so sampling techniques must be modified to measure absorption in this spectral region; special cells made out of sodium chloride or potassium bromide are commonly used because they will not absorb light over a wide range of the IR portion of the electromagnetic spectrum.

---

[2] A diffraction grating is made by scratching thousands of parallel lines on a transparent surface such as glass. As light passes through the narrow spacings between the lines, it spreads out and produces a spectrum similar to that formed by a prism.

FIGURE 5–17

Parts of a simple spectrophotometer.

Prism disperses radiation into component wavelengths

(a) Radiation source   Monochromator   Sample cell   Detector   Recorder

Slit allows only selected wavelengths or frequencies of radiation to pass through

(b) Radiation source   Monochromator   Sample cell   Detector   Recorder

Radiation passes through sample, which absorbs certain frequencies

(c) Radiation source   Monochromator   Sample cell   Detector   Recorder

Radiation source   Monochromator   Sample cell   Detector measures absorption of radiation by the sample and converts the radiation into an electrical signal   Recorder

(d)

Recorder translates electrical signal into recording of the absorption spectrum

Radiation source   Monochromator   Sample cell   Detector   Recorder

The absorption spectrum of a chemical substance allows spectrophotometry to be used for identification.

(e)

The detector measures the quantity of radiation that passes through the sample by converting it to an electrical signal. UV and visible spectrophotometers employ photoelectric tube detectors. A signal is generated when the photons strike the tube surface to produce a current that is directly proportional to the intensity of the light transmitted through the sample. When this signal is compared to the intensity of light that is transmitted to the detector in the absence of an absorbing material, the absorbance of a substance can be determined at each wavelength or frequency of light selected. The signal from the detection system is then fed into a recorder, which plots absorbance as a function of wavelength or frequency. Modern spectrophotometers are designed to trace an entire absorption spectrum automatically.

Ultraviolet, Visible, and Infrared Spectrophotometry

Ultraviolet and visible spectrophotometry measure the absorbance of UV and visible light as a function of wavelength or frequency. For example, the UV absorption spectrum of heroin shows a maximum absorption band at a wavelength of 278 nanometers (see Figure 5–18). This shows that the simplicity of a UV spectrum facilitates its use as a tool for determining a material's probable identity. For instance, a white powder may have a UV spectrum comparable to heroin and therefore may be tentatively identified as such. (Fortunately, sugar and starch, common diluents of heroin, do not absorb UV light.) However, this technique will not provide a definitive result; other drugs or materials may have a UV absorption spectrum similar to that of heroin. But this lack of specificity does not diminish the value of the technique because the analyst has quickly eliminated thousands of other possible drugs from consideration and can now proceed to conduct other confirmatory tests, such as thin-layer or gas chromatography, to complete the identification.

In contrast to the simplicity of a UV spectrum, absorption in the **infrared** region provides a far more complex pattern. Figure 5–19 depicts the IR spectra of heroin and secobarbital. Here, the absorption bands are so numerous that each spectrum can provide enough characteristics to identify a substance specifically. **Different materials always have distinctively different infrared spectra; each IR spectrum is therefore equivalent to a "fingerprint" of that substance and no other.** This technique is one of the few tests available to the forensic scientist that can be considered specific in itself for identification. The IR spectra of thousands of organic compounds have been collected, indexed, and cataloged to serve as invaluable references for identifying organic substances.

mycrimekit

WEBEXTRA 5.4
See How a Spectrophotometer Works
http://www.mycrimekit.com

ultraviolet
Invisible long frequencies of light beyond violet in the visible spectrum

infrared
Invisible short frequencies of light before red in the visible spectrum

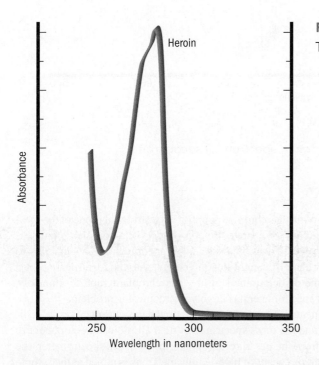

FIGURE 5–18
The ultraviolet spectrum of heroin.

FIGURE 5–19

(a) Infrared spectrum of heroin. (b) Infrared spectrum of secobarbital.

Mass Spectrometry

A previous section discussed the operation of the gas chromatograph. This instrument is one of the most important tools in a crime laboratory. Its ability to separate the components of a complex mixture is unsurpassed. However, gas chromatography (GC) does have one important drawback—its inability to produce specific identification. A forensic chemist cannot unequivocally state the identification of a substance based solely on a retention time as determined by the gas chromatograph. Fortunately, coupling the gas chromatograph to a mass spectrometer has largely overcome this problem.

The separation of a mixture's components is first accomplished on the gas chromatograph. A direct connection between the GC column and the mass spectrometer then allows each component to flow into the spectrometer as it emerges from the gas chromatograph. In the mass spectrometer, the material enters a high-vacuum chamber where a beam of high-energy electrons is aimed at the sample

FIGURE 5–20
How GC/MS works. Left to right, the sample is separated into its components by the gas chromatograph, and then the components are ionized and identified by characteristic fragmentation patterns of the spectra produced by the mass spectrometer.
Courtesy Agilent Technologies, Inc., Palo Alto, Calif.

(a)

(b)

FIGURE 5–21

(a) Mass spectrum of heroin. (b) Mass spectrum of cocaine.

molecules. The electrons collide with the molecules, causing them to lose electrons and to acquire a positive charge (commonly called **ions**). These positively charged molecules or ions are unstable or are formed with excess energy and almost instantaneously decompose into numerous smaller fragments. The fragments then pass through an electric or magnetic field, where they are separated according to their masses. **The unique feature of mass spectrometry is that under carefully controlled conditions, no two substances produce the same fragmentation pattern.** In essence, one can think of this pattern as a "fingerprint" of the substance being examined (see Figure 5–20).

The technique thus provides a specific means for identifying a chemical structure. It is also sensitive to minute concentrations. At present, mass spectrometry finds its widest application in the identification of drugs; however, further research is expected to yield significant applications for identifying other types of physical evidence. Figure 5–21 illustrates the mass spectra of heroin

ion
An atom or molecule bearing a positive or negative charge

and cocaine; each line represents a fragment of a different mass (actually the ratio of mass to charge), and the line height reflects the relative abundance of each fragment. Note how different the fragmentation patterns of heroin and cocaine are. Each mass spectrum is unique to each drug and therefore serves as a specific test for identifying it.

The combination of the gas chromatograph and mass spectrometer is further enhanced when a computer is added to the system. The integrated gas chromatograph/mass spectrometer/computer system provides the ultimate in speed, accuracy, and sensitivity. With the ability to record and store in its memory several hundred mass spectra, such a system can detect and identify substances present in only one-millionth-of-a-gram quantities. Furthermore, the computer can be programmed to compare an unknown spectrum against a comprehensive library of mass spectra stored in its memory. The advent of personal computers and microcircuitry has made it possible to design mass spectrometer systems that can fit on a small table. Such a unit is pictured in Figure 5–22. Research-grade mass spectrometers are found in laboratories as larger floor-model units (see Figure 5–23).

FIGURE 5–22

A tabletop mass spectrometer. (1) The sample is injected into a heated inlet port, and a carrier gas sweeps it into the column. (2) The GC column separates the mixture into its components. (3) In the ion source, a filament wire emits electrons that strike the sample molecules, causing them to fragment as they leave the GC column. (4) The quadrupole, consisting of four rods, separates the fragments according to their mass. (5) The detector counts the fragments passing through the quadrupole. The signal is small and must be amplified. (6) The data system is responsible for total control of the entire GC/MS system. It detects and measures the abundance of each fragment and displays the mass spectrum.
Courtesy Agilent Technologies, Inc., Palo Alto, Calif.

FIGURE 5–23

A scientist injecting a sample into a research-grade mass spectrometer.
Courtesy Geoff Tompkinson/Science Photo Library, Photo Researchers, Inc.

chapter summary >>>>>>>>>>>>>>>>

The proper selection of analytical techniques that will allow the forensic scientist to identify or compare matter can best be understood by categorizing all substances into one of two broad groups: organics and inorganics. In general, organic substances contain carbon. Inorganic materials encompass all other known chemical substances. Another consideration in selecting an analytical technique is the need for either a qualitative or a quantitative determination. The former relates just to the identity of the material, whereas the latter requires the determination of the percentage composition of the components of a mixture.

Chromatography, spectrophotometry, and mass spectrometry are all readily used by a forensic scientist to identify or compare organic materials. Chromatography is a means of separating and tentatively identifying the components of a mixture. Spectrophotometry is the study of the absorption of light by chemical substances. Mass spectrometry characterizes organic molecules by observing their fragmentation pattern after their collision with a beam of high-energy electrons. Gas chromatography (GC) separates mixtures on the basis of their distribution between a stationary liquid phase and a mobile gas phase. In GC, the moving phase is actually a gas called the carrier gas, which flows through a column. The stationary phase is a thin film of liquid contained within the column. After a mixture has traversed the length of the column, it emerges separated into its components. The written record of this separation is called a chromatogram. A direct connection between the GC column and the mass spectrometer allows each component to flow into the mass spectrometer as it emerges from the GC. Fragmentation of each component by high-energy electrons produces a "fingerprint" pattern of the substance being examined.

Other forms of chromatography applicable to forensic science are high-performance liquid chromatography (HPLC) and thin-layer chromatography (TLC). HPLC separates compounds using a stationary phase and a mobile liquid phase and is used with temperature-sensitive compounds. TLC uses a solid stationary phase, usually coated onto a glass plate, and a mobile liquid phase to separate the components of the mixture. A technique analogous to TLC is electrophoresis, in which materials are forced to move across a gel-coated plate under the influence of an electrical potential. In this manner, substances such as proteins and DNA can be separated and characterized.

Most forensic laboratories use ultraviolet (UV) and infrared (IR) spectrophotometers to characterize chemical compounds. In contrast to the simplicity of a UV spectrum, absorption in the infrared region provides a far more complex pattern. Different materials always have distinctively different infrared spectra; each IR spectrum is therefore equivalent to a "fingerprint" of that substance.

review questions

1. Anything that has mass and occupies space is defined as _____.

2. The basic building blocks of all substances are the _____.

3. The number of elements known today is _____.

4. An arrangement of elements by similar chemical properties is accomplished in the _____ table.

5. A(n) _____ is the smallest particle of an element that can exist.

6. Substances composed of two or more elements are called _____.

7. A(n) _____ is the smallest unit of a compound formed by the union of two or more atoms.

8. The physical state that retains a definite shape and volume is a(n) _____.

9. A gas (has, has no) definite shape or volume.

10. During the process of _____, solids go directly to the gaseous state, bypassing the liquid state.

11. The attraction forces between the molecules of a liquid are (greater, less) than those in a solid.

12. Different _____ are separated by definite visible boundaries.

13. Carbon-containing substances are classified as _____.

14. _____ substances encompass all non-carbon-containing materials.

15. A(n) _____ analysis describes the identity of a material, and a(n) _____ analysis relates to a determination of the quantity of a substance.

16. The study of the absorption of light by chemical substances is known as _____.

17. A mixture's components can be separated by the technique of _____.

18. True or False: Henry's law describes the distribution of a volatile chemical compound between its liquid and gas phases. _____

19. The (higher, lower) the solubility of a gas in a liquid, the greater its tendency to remain dissolved in that liquid.

20. True or False: In order for chromatography to occur, one phase must move continuously in one direction over a stationary phase. _____

21. A technique that separates mixtures on the basis of their distribution between a stationary liquid phase and a moving gas phase is _____.

22. The time required for a substance to travel through the gas chromatographic column is a useful identifying characteristic known as _____.

23. Solid materials that are not readily dissolved in solvents for injection into the gas chromatograph can be _____ into numerous gaseous products before entering the gas chromatograph.

24. A major advantage of high-performance liquid chromatography is that the entire process takes place at _____ temperature.

25. A technique that uses a moving liquid phase and a stationary solid phase to separate mixtures is _____.

26. Because most chemical compounds are colorless, the final step of the thin-layer development usually requires that they be _____ by spraying with a chemical reagent.

27. The distance a spot has traveled up a thin-layer plate can be assigned a numerical value known as the _____ value.

28. True or False: Thin-layer chromatography yields the positive identification of a material. _____

29. The migration of materials along a stationary phase under the influence of an electrical potential describes the technique of _____.

30. True or False: Color is a usual indication that substances selectively absorb light. _____

31. The distance between two successive identical points on a wave is known as _____.

32. True or False: Frequency and wavelength are directly proportional to one another. _____

33. Light, X-rays, and radio waves are all members of the _____ spectrum.

34. Red light is (higher, lower) in frequency than violet light.

35. A beam of light that has all of its waves pulsating in unison is called a(n) _____.

36. One model of light depicts it as consisting of energy particles known as _____.

37. True or False: The energy of a light particle (photon) is directly proportional to its frequency. _____

38. Red light is (more, less) energetic than violet light.

39. The selective absorption of electromagnetic radiation by materials (can, cannot) be used as an aid for identification.

40. The amount of radiation a substance will absorb is directly proportional to its concentration as defined by _____ law.

41. The _____ is the instrument used to measure and record the absorption spectrum of a chemical substance.

42. The function of the _____ is to select a single frequency of light emanating from the spectrophotometer's source.

43. An (ultraviolet, infrared) absorption spectrum provides a unique "fingerprint" of a chemical substance.

44. The technique of _____ exposes molecules to a beam of high-energy electrons in order to fragment them.

45. True or False: A mass spectrum is normally considered a specific means for identifying a chemical substance. _____

inorganic analysis

KEY TERMS

alpha particle
atomic mass
atomic number
beta particle
continuous spectrum
electron
electron orbital
emission spectrum
excited state
gamma ray
isotope
line spectrum
neutron
nucleus
proton
radioactivity
X-ray diffraction

Learning Objectives

After studying this chapter you should be able to:

- Describe the usefulness of trace elements for forensic comparison of various types of physical evidence

- Distinguish continuous and line emission spectra

- Understand the parts of a simple emission spectrograph

- List the parts of a simple atomic absorption spectrophotometer

- Define and distinguish protons, neutrons, and electrons

- Define and distinguish atomic number and atomic mass number

- Appreciate the phenomenon of how an atom absorbs and releases energy in the form of light

- Explain the concept of an isotope

- Understand how elements can be made radioactive

- Describe why an X-ray diffraction pattern is useful for chemical identification

Inorganics as Forensic Evidence

In the previous chapter, analytical techniques were described for characterizing a class of matter known as organics. Generally, these materials contain carbon. Although organic substances constitute a substantial portion of the physical evidence submitted to crime laboratories, carbon does not appear among the earth's most abundant elements. Surprisingly, about three-quarters of the weight of the earth's crust is composed of only two elements—oxygen and silicon. In fact, only ten elements make up approximately 99 percent of the earth's crust (see Table 6–1). The remaining elements may almost be considered impurities, although exceedingly important ones. Carbon, the element that is a constituent of most chemical compounds, constitutes less than 0.1 percent of the earth's crust.

Considering these facts, it is certainly reasonable that non-carbon-containing substances—that is, inorganics—are encountered as physical evidence at crime scenes. One only has to consider the prevalence of metallic materials, such as iron, steel, copper, and aluminum, in our society to understand the possibilities of finding tools, coins, weapons, and metal scrapings at crime scenes.

Less well known, but perhaps almost as significant to the criminalist, is the use of inorganic chemicals as pigments in paints and dyes, the incorporation of inorganics into explosive formulations, and the prevalence of inorganic poisons such as mercury, lead, and arsenic.

To appreciate fully the role of inorganic analysis in forensic science, we must first examine its application to the basic objectives of the crime laboratory—identification and comparison of physical evidence. Identification of inorganic evidence is exemplified by a typical request to examine an explosive formulation suspected of containing potassium chlorate, or perhaps to examine a poisonous powder thought to be arsenic. In each case, the forensic scientist must perform tests that will ultimately determine the specific chemical identity of the suspect materials to the exclusion of all others. Only after completing the tests and finding their results identical to previously recorded tests for a known potassium chlorate or a known arsenic can the forensic scientist draw a valid conclusion about the chemical identity of the evidence.

However, comparing two or more objects in order to ascertain their common origin presents a different problem. For example, a criminalist may be asked to determine whether a piece of brass pipe found in the possession of a suspect compares to a broken pipe found at the crime scene. The condition of the two pipes may not allow for comparison by physically fitting together any broken edges. Under these circumstances, the only alternative will be to attempt a comparison through chemical analysis. It is not enough for the analyst to conclude that the pipes are alike because they are brass (an alloy of copper and zinc). After all, hundreds of thousands of brass pipes exist, a situation that is hardly conducive to proving that these two particular pipes were at one time a single unit. The examiner must go a step further to try to distinguish these pipes from all others. Although this may not be possible, a comparison of the pipes' trace elements—that is, elements present in small quantities—will provide a meaningful criterion for at least increasing the probability that the two pipes originated from the same source.

TABLE 6–1

Elemental Abundances as Percentages in the Earth's Crust

Element	Percentage by Weight
Oxygen	47.3
Silicon	27.7
Aluminum	7.9
Iron	4.5
Calcium	3.5
Sodium	2.5
Potassium	2.5
Magnesium	2.2
Titanium	0.5
Hydrogen	0.2
Other elements	1.2

TABLE 6–2

Elemental Analysis of Brass Alloys

Element	High-Tensile Brass (percentage)	Manganese Brass (percentage)
Copper	57.0	58.6
Aluminum	2.8	1 7
Zinc	35.0	33.8
Manganese	2.13	1.06
Iron	1.32	0.90
Nickel	0.48	1.02
Tin	0.64	1.70
Lead	0.17	0.72
Silicon	0.08	Nil

Source: R. L. Williams, "An Evaluation of the SEM with X-Ray Microanalyzer Accessory for Forensic Work," in O. Johari and I. Corvin, eds., *Scanning Electron Microscopy/1971* (Chicago: IIT Research Institute, 1971), p. 541.

Trace Elements

Considering that most of our raw materials originate from the earth's crust, it is not surprising that they are rarely obtained in pure form; instead, they include numerous elemental impurities that usually have to be eliminated through industrial processing. However, in most cases it is not economically feasible to completely exclude all such minor impurities, especially when their presence will have no effect on the appearance or performance of the final product. For this reason, many manufactured products, and even most natural materials, contain small quantities of elements present in concentrations of less than 1 percent.

For the criminalist, the presence of *trace elements* is particularly useful because they provide "invisible" markers that may establish the source of a material or at least provide additional points for comparison. Table 6–2 illustrates how two types of brass alloys can readily be distinguished by their elemental composition. Similarly, the comparison of trace elements present in paint or other types of metallic specimens may provide particularly meaningful data with respect to source or origin. Forensic investigators have examined the evidential value of trace elements present in soil, fibers, and glass, as well as in all types of metallic objects. One example of this application occurred with the examination of the bullet and bullet fragments recovered after the assassination of President Kennedy.

Evidence in the Assassination of President Kennedy

Ever since President Kennedy was killed in 1963, questions have lingered about whether Lee Harvey Oswald was part of a conspiracy to assassinate the president or, as the Warren Commission concluded, a lone assassin. In arriving at its conclusions, the Warren Commission reconstructed the crime as follows: Oswald fired three shots from behind the president while positioned in the Texas School Book Depository building. The president was struck by two bullets, with one bullet totally missing the president's limousine. One bullet hit the president in the back, exited his throat, and then went on to strike Governor Connally, who was sitting in a jump seat in front of the president. The bullet hit Connally first in his back, then exited his chest, struck his right wrist, and temporarily lodged in his left thigh. This bullet was later found on the governor's stretcher at the hospital. A second bullet in the skull fatally wounded the president.

In a room at the Texas School Book Depository, a 6.5-mm Mannlicher-Carcano military rifle was found with Oswald's palm print on it. Also found were three spent 6.5-mm Western Cartridge Co./ Mannlicher-Carcano (WCC/MC) cartridge cases. Oswald, an employee of the depository, had been seen there that morning and also a few minutes after the assassination, disappearing soon thereafter. He was apprehended a few miles from the depository nearly two hours after the shooting.

Critics of the Warren Commission have long argued that evidence exists that would prove Oswald did not act alone. Eyewitness accounts and acoustical data interpreted by some experts

President John F. Kennedy, Governor John Connally of Texas, and Mrs. Jacqueline Kennedy ride through Dallas moments before the assassination. *Courtesy CORBIS-NY*

have been used to advocate the contention that someone else fired at the president from a region in front of the limousine (the so-called grassy knoll). Furthermore, it is argued that the Warren Commission's reconstruction of the crime relied on the assumption that only one bullet caused both the president's throat wound and Connally's back wound. Critics contend that such damage would have deformed and mutilated a bullet. Instead, the recovered bullet showed some flattening, no deformity, and only about 1 percent weight loss.

In 1977, at the request of the U.S. House of Representatives Select Committee on Assassinations, the bullet taken from Connally's stretcher along with bullet fragments recovered from the car and various wound areas were examined for trace element levels.

Lead alloys used for the manufacture of bullets contain an assortment of trace elements. For example, antimony is often added to lead as a hardening agent; copper, bismuth, and silver are other trace elements commonly found in bullet lead. In this case, the bullet and bullet fragments were compared for their antimony and silver content. Previous studies had amply demonstrated that the levels of these two elements are particularly important for characterizing WCC/MC bullets. Bullet lead from this type of ammunition ranges in antimony concentration from 20 to 1,200 parts per million (ppm) and 5 to 15 ppm in silver content.

As can be seen in Table 6–3, the samples designated Q1 and Q9 (the Connally stretcher bullet and fragments from Connally's wrist, respectively) are indistinguishable from one another in antimony and silver content. The samples Q2; Q4, 5; and Q14 (Q4, 5 being fragments from Kennedy's brain, and Q2 and Q14 being fragments recovered from two different areas in the car) also are indistinguishable in antimony and silver content but are different from Q1 and Q9.

The conclusions derived from studying these results are as follows:

1. There is evidence of only two bullets—one composed of 815 ppm antimony and 9.3 ppm silver, the other composed of 622 ppm antimony and 8.1 ppm silver.
2. Both bullets have a composition highly consistent with WCC/MC bullet lead, although other sources cannot entirely be ruled out.

TABLE 6–3

Antimony and Silver Concentrations in the Kennedy Assassination Bullets

	Silver (parts per million)[a]	Antimony (parts per million)	Sample Description
Q1	8.8 ± 0.5	833 ± 9	Connally stretcher bullet
Q9	9.8 ± 0.5	797 ± 7	Fragments from Connally's wrist
Q2	8.1 ± 0.6	602 ± 4	Large fragment from car
Q4, 5	7.9 ± 0.3	621 ± 4	Fragments from Kennedy's brain
Q14	8.2 ± 0.4	642 ± 6	Small fragments found in car

[a]One part per million equals 0.0001 percent.
Source: Reprinted with permission from V. P. Guinn, "JFK Assassination: Bullet Analyses," *Analytical Chemistry*, 51 (1979), 484 A. Copyright 1979, American Chemical Society.

3. The bullet found on the Connally stretcher also damaged Connally's wrist. The absence of bullet fragments from the back wounds of Kennedy and Connally prevented any effort at linking these wounds to the stretcher bullet.

None of these conclusions can totally verify the Warren Commission's reconstruction of the assassination, but the results are at least consistent with the commission's findings. Further, in 2003, an ABC television broadcast showed the results of a ten-year 3-D computer animation study of the events of November 22, 1963. The animation graphically showed that the bullet wounds were completely consistent with Kennedy's and Governor Connally's positions at the time of shooting, and that by following the bullet's trajectory backward they could be found to have originated from a narrow cone including only a few windows of the sixth floor of the School Book Depository.

The analyses on the Kennedy assassination bullets were performed by neutron activation analysis. The remainder of this chapter describes this and other techniques currently used to examine inorganic physical evidence.

The Emission Spectrum of Elements

We have already observed that organic molecules can readily be characterized by their selective absorption of ultraviolet, visible, or infrared radiation. Equally significant to the analytical chemist is the knowledge that elements also selectively absorb and emit light. These observations form the basis of two important analytical techniques designed to determine the elemental composition of materials—*emission spectroscopy* and *atomic absorption spectrophotometry*.

Types of Spectra

The statement that elements emit light should not come as a total surprise, for one need only observe the common tungsten incandescent lightbulb or the glow of a neon light to confirm this observation. When the light emitted from a bulb or from any other light source is passed through a prism, it is separated into its component colors or frequencies. The resulting display of colors is called an **emission spectrum**.

When sunlight or the light from an incandescent bulb is passed through a prism, we have already observed that a range of rainbow colors is produced. This emission spectrum is called a **continuous spectrum** because all the colors merge or blend into one another to form a continuous band. However, not all light sources produce such a spectrum. For example, if the light from a sodium lamp, a mercury arc lamp, or a neon light were passed through a prism, the resultant spectrum would consist not of a continuous band but of several individual colored lines separated by dark spaces. Here, each line represents a definite wavelength or frequency of light that is separate and distinct from all others present in the spectrum. This type of spectrum is called a **line spectrum**. Figure 6–1 shows the line spectra of three elements.

emission spectrum
Light emitted from a source and separated into its component colors or frequencies

continuous spectrum
A type of emission spectrum showing a continuous band of colors all blending into one another

line spectrum
A type of emission spectrum showing a series of lines separated by black areas; each line represents a definite wavelength or frequency

FIGURE 6–1

Some characteristic emission spectra.

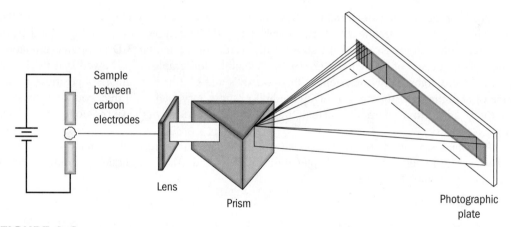

FIGURE 6–2

Parts of a simple carbon arc emission spectrograph.

Heated matter in a solid or liquid state produces a continuous spectrum that is not very indicative of its composition. However, if this same matter is vaporized and "excited" by exposure to high temperature, each element present emits light composed of select frequencies that are characteristic of the element. This spectrum is in essence a "fingerprint" of an element and offers a practical method of identification. Sodium vapor, for example, always shows the same line spectrum, which differs from the spectrum of all other elements.

Carbon Arc Emission Spectrometry

An *emission spectrograph* is an instrument used to obtain and record the line spectra of elements. Essentially, this instrument requires a means for vaporizing and exciting the atoms of elements so that they emit light, a means for separating this light into its component frequencies, and a means of recording the resultant spectrum. A simple carbon arc emission spectrograph is depicted in Figure 6–2.

The specimen under investigation is excited when it is inserted between two carbon electrodes through which a direct current arc is passed. The arc produces enough heat to vaporize and excite the specimen's atoms. The resultant emitted light is collected by a lens and focused onto a prism that disperses it into component frequencies. The separated frequencies are then directed toward a photographic plate, where they are recorded as line images. Normally, a specimen consists of numerous elements; hence, the typical emission spectrum contains many lines. Each element present in the spectrum can be identified when it is compared to a standard chart that shows the position of the principal spectral lines of all the elements. However, forensic analysis more commonly requires

FIGURE 6–3

A comparison of paint chips 1 and 2 by emission spectrographic analysis. A line-for-line comparison shows that the paints have the same elemental composition.

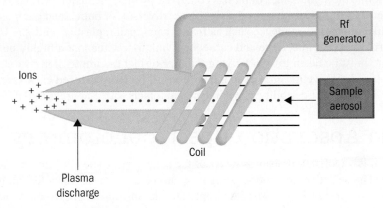

FIGURE 6–4

The creation of charged particles in the torch of an ICP discharge.

simply a rapid comparison of the elemental composition of two or more specimens. This can readily be accomplished when the emission spectra are matched line for line, an approach illustrated in Figure 6–3, in which the emission spectra of two paint chips are shown to be comparable.

Inductively Coupled Plasma Emission Spectrometry (ICP)

Carbon arc emission spectrometry has been supplanted by *inductively coupled plasma (ICP) emission spectrometry*. Like the former, ICP identifies and measures elements through light energy emitted by excited atoms. However, instead of using an electrical arc, the atoms are excited by placing the sample in a hot plasma torch. The torch is designed as three concentric quartz tubes through which argon gas flows. A radio frequency (RF) coil that carries a current is wrapped around the tubes. The RF current creates an intense magnetic field.

THE ICP PROCESS   The process begins when a high-voltage spark is applied to the argon gas flowing through the torch. This strips some electrons from their argon atoms. These electrons are then caught and accelerated in the magnetic field such that they collide with other argon atoms, stripping off still more electrons. The collision of electrons and argon atoms continues in a chain reaction, breaking down the gas into argon atoms, argon ions, and electrons and forming an *inductively coupled plasma discharge*. The discharge is sustained by RF energy that is continuously transferred to it from the coil. The plasma discharge acts like an intense continuous flame generating extremely high temperatures in the range of 7,000–10,000°C. The sample, in the form of an aerosol, is then introduced into the hot plasma, where it collides with the energetic argon electrons generating charged particles (ions) that emit light of characteristic wavelengths corresponding to the identity of the elements present (see Figure 6–4).

APPLICATIONS OF ICP   Two areas of forensic casework in which ICP has been applied are the identification and characterization of mutilated bullets[1] and glass fragments.[2] Mutilated bullets often are not suitable for traditional microscopic comparisons against an exemplar test-fired bullet. In such situations, ICP has been used to obtain an elemental profile of the questioned bullet fragment

[1] R. D. Koons and J. Buscaglia, "Forensic Significance of Bullet Lead Compositions," *Journal of Forensic Sciences* 50 (2005): 341.

[2] S. Montero, A. L. Hobbs, T. A. French, and J. Almirall, "Elemental Analysis of Glass Fragments by ICP-MS as Evidence of Association: Analysis of a Case," *Journal of Forensic Sciences* 48 (2003): 1101.

for comparison against an unfired bullet generally found in the possession of the suspect. For a number of years forensic scientists have taken advantage of significant compositional differences among lead sources for the manufacture of lead-based bullets. Compositional differences in the trace elements that constitute lead bullets are typically reflected in the copper, arsenic, silver, antimony, bismuth, cadmium, and tin profiles of lead bullets. When two or more bullets have comparable elemental compositions, evidence of their similarity may be offered in a court of law.

In this respect, the comparison of lead bullets faces the same quandary as most common types of class physical evidence—how can a forensic analyst explain to a jury that such a finding has meaningful consequences to a criminal inquiry without being able to provide statistical or probability data to support such a contention? Furthermore, the creation of meaningful databases to statistically define the significance of bullets compared by their elemental profiles is currently an unrealistic undertaking. Nevertheless, the significant diversity of bullet lead compositions in our population, like other class evidence such as fibers, hairs, paint, plastics, and glass, makes their chance occurrence at a crime scene and subsequent link to a defendant a highly unlikely event. However, care must be taken to avoid giving the trier of fact the impression that elemental profiles constitute a definitive match. Given the millions of bullets produced each year, one cannot conclusively rule out the possibility of a coincidental match with a non-case-related bullet.

Atomic Absorption Spectrophotometry

When an atom is vaporized, it absorbs many of the same frequencies of light that it emits in an excited state. The selective absorption of light by atoms is the basis for a technique known as *atomic absorption spectrophotometry*. A simple atomic absorption spectrophotometer is illustrated in Figure 6–5.

The Spectrophotometry Process

In atomic absorption spectrophotometry, the specimen is heated to a temperature that is hot enough to vaporize its atoms while leaving a substantial number of atoms in an unexcited state. Normally, the specimen is inserted into an air-acetylene flame to achieve this temperature. The vaporized atoms are then exposed to radiation emitted from a light source. The technique achieves great specificity by using as its radiation source a discharge tube made of the same element being analyzed in the specimen. When the discharge lamp is turned on, it emits only the frequencies of light that are present in the emission spectrum of the element. Likewise, the sample absorbs these frequencies only when it contains the same element. Therefore, to determine the presence of antimony in a specimen, the atomic absorption spectrophotometer must be fitted with a discharge lamp that is constructed of antimony. Under these conditions, the sample will absorb light only when it contains antimony.

Once the radiation has passed through the sample, a monochromator, consisting of a prism or a diffraction grating and a slit, isolates the desired radiation frequency and transmits it to a detector. The detector converts the light into an electrical signal, the intensity of which is observed on a digital recorder.

FIGURE 6–5

Parts of a simple flame atomic absorption spectrophotometer.

The absorption of light by the element of interest is the phenomenon that is being measured in atomic absorption spectrophotometry. The concentration of the absorbing element is directly proportional to the quantity of the light absorbed. The higher the concentration of the element, the more light is absorbed. For this reason, atomic absorption spectroscopy is most useful for accurately determining an element's concentration in a sample. Furthermore, the technique is sufficiently sensitive to find wide application in detecting and quantitating elements that are present at trace levels. However, the technique does have one drawback in that the analyst can determine only one element at a time, each time having to select the proper lamp to match the element under investigation.

Applications of Spectrophotometry

Although atomic absorption spectrophotometry has been used for chemical analysis since 1955, it has not yet found wide application for solving forensic problems. However, a modification in the design of the instrument promises to change this situation. By substituting a heated graphite furnace or a heated strip of metal (tantalum) for the flame, analysts have achieved a more efficient means of atomic volatilization and as a result have substantially increased the sensitivity of the technique. Many elements can now be detected at levels that approach one-trillionth of a gram.

The high sensitivity of "flameless" atomic absorption now equals or surpasses that of most known analytical procedures. Considering the relative simplicity and low cost of the technique, atomic absorption spectrophotometry has become an attractive method for detecting and measuring the smallest levels of trace elements present in physical evidence.

The Origin of Emission and Absorption Spectra

Any proposed theory that attempts to explain the origin of emission and absorption spectra must relate to the fundamental structure of the element—the atom. Scientists now know that the atom is composed of even more elementary particles that are collectively known as *subatomic particles*. The most important subatomic particles are the **proton**, **electron**, and **neutron**. The masses of the proton and neutron are each about 1,837 times the mass of an electron. The proton has a positive electrical charge; the electron has a negative charge equal in magnitude to that of the proton; and the neutron is a neutral particle having neither a positive nor a negative charge. The properties of the proton, neutron, and electron are summarized in the following table:

proton
A positively charged particle that is one of the basic structures in the nucleus of an atom

electron
A negatively charged particle that is one of the fundamental structural units of the atom

neutron
A particle with no electrical charge that is one of the basic structures in the nucleus of an atom

Particle	Symbol	Relative Mass	Electrical Charge
Proton	P	1	+1
Neutron	n	1	0
Electron	e	1/1,837	−1

Atomic Structure

A popular descriptive model of the atom, and the one that will be adopted for the purpose of this discussion, pictures an atom as consisting of electrons orbiting around a central nucleus—an image that is analogous to our solar system, in which the planets revolve around the sun.[3] The **nucleus** of the atom is composed of positively charged protons and neutrons that have no charge. Because the atom has no net electrical charge, the number of protons must always be equal to the number of negatively charged electrons in orbit around the nucleus.

nucleus
The core of an atom containing the protons and neutrons

With this knowledge, we can now begin to describe the atomic structure of the elements; for example, hydrogen has a nucleus consisting of one proton and no neutrons, and it has one orbiting electron. Helium has a nucleus comprising two protons and two neutrons, with two electrons in orbit around the nucleus (see Figure 6–6).

The behavior and properties that distinguish one element from another must be related to the differences in the atomic structure of each element. One such distinction is that each element possesses

---

[3] Actually, the electrons are moving so rapidly around the nucleus as to best be visualized as being in the form of an electron cloud spread out over the surface of the atom.

FIGURE 6–6

The atomic structures of hydrogen and helium.

Hydrogen   Helium

atomic number

The number of protons in the nucleus of an atom; each element has its own unique atomic number

a different number of protons. This number is called the **atomic number** of the element. As we look back at the periodic table illustrated in Figure 5–1, we see that the elements are numbered consecutively. Those numbers represent the atomic number or number of protons associated with each element. **An element is therefore a collection of atoms that all have the same number of protons.** Thus, each atom of hydrogen has one and only one proton, each atom of helium has 2 protons, each atom of silver has 47 protons, and each atom of lead has 82 protons in its nucleus.

Electron Orbitals

electron orbital

The path of electrons as they move around the nuclei of atoms; each orbital is associated with a particular electronic energy level

To explain the origin of atomic spectra, our attention must now focus on the **electron orbitals** of the atom. As electrons move around the nucleus, they are confined to a path from which they cannot stray. This orbital path is associated with a definite amount of energy and is therefore called an *energy level*. Each element has its own set of characteristic energy levels at varying distances from the nucleus. Some levels are occupied by electrons; others are empty.

excited state

The state in which an atom absorbs energy and an electron moves from a lower to a higher energy level

An atom is in its most stable state when all of its electrons are positioned in their lowest possible energy orbitals in the atom. When an atom absorbs energy, such as heat or light, its electrons are pushed into higher-energy orbitals. In this condition, the atom is in an **excited state**. However, because energy levels have fixed values, only a definite amount of energy can be absorbed in moving an electron from one level to another. This is a most important observation, for it means that atoms absorb only a definite value of energy, and all other energy values will be excluded. In atomic absorption spectrophotometry, a photon of light interacts with an electron, causing it to jump into a higher orbital, as shown in Figure 6–7(a). A specific frequency of light is required to cause this transition, and its energy must correspond to the exact energy difference between the two orbitals involved in the transition. This energy difference is expressed by the relationship $E = hf$, where E represents the energy difference between the two orbitals, f is the frequency of absorbed light, and h is a universal constant called Planck's constant. Any energy value that is more or less than this difference will not produce the transition. Hence, an element is selective in the frequency of light it will absorb, and this selectivity is determined by the electron energy levels each element possesses.

In the same manner, if atoms are exposed to intense heat, enough energy is generated to push electrons into unoccupied higher-energy orbitals. Normally, the electron does not remain in this excited state for long, and it quickly falls back to its original energy level. As the electron falls back, it releases energy. An emission spectrum testifies to the fact that this energy loss comes about in the form of light emission [see Figure 6–7(b)]. The frequency of light emitted is again determined by the relationship $E = hf$, where E is the energy difference between the upper and lower energy levels and f is the frequency of emitted light. Because each element has its own characteristic set of energy levels, each emits a unique set of frequency values. The emission spectrum thus provides a "picture" of the energy levels that surround the nucleus of each element.

Thus, we see that as far as atoms are concerned, energy is a two-way street. Energy can be put into the atom at the same time that energy is given off; what goes in must come out. The chemist can study the atom using either approach. Atomic absorption spectrophotometry carefully measures the value and amount of light energy going into the atom; emission spectroscopy collects and measures

FIGURE 6–7

(a) The absorption of light by an atom, causing an electron to jump into a higher orbital.
(b) The emission of light by an atom, caused by an electron falling back to a lower orbital.

(a)   (b)

the various light energies given off. The result is the same: atoms are identified by the existence of characteristic energy levels.

Neutron Activation Analysis

Once scientists realized that it was possible to change the number of subatomic particles in the atom's nucleus, the unleashing of a new source of energy—nuclear energy—was inevitable. This energy has proven so awesome in its power that the survival of civilization will depend on our ability to refrain from using its destructive forces. Of course, this threat does not obscure the fact that controlled nuclear energy promises to be a source of power capable of relieving our dependency on the earth's dwindling reserves of fossil fuels. For the chemist, nuclear chemistry provides a new tool for identifying and quantitating the elements.

Isotopes

Until now, our discussion of subatomic particles has been limited to the proton and electron. However, to understand the principles of nuclear chemistry, we must look at the other important subatomic particle, the neutron. Although the atoms of a single element must have the same number of protons, nothing prevents them from having different numbers of neutrons. The total number of protons and neutrons in a nucleus is known as the **atomic mass** number.

Atoms with the same number of protons but differing solely in the number of neutrons are called **isotopes**. For example, hydrogen consists of three isotopes; besides ordinary hydrogen, which has one proton and no neutrons, two other isotopes exist, deuterium and tritium. Deuterium (or heavy hydrogen) also has one proton but contains one neutron as well. Tritium has one proton and two neutrons in its nucleus. The atomic structures of these isotopes are shown in Figure 6–8. Therefore, all the isotopes of hydrogen have an atomic number of 1 but differ in their atomic mass numbers. Hydrogen has an atomic mass number of 1, deuterium a mass of 2, and tritium a mass of 3. Ordinary hydrogen makes up 99.98 percent of all the hydrogen atoms found in nature.

Radioactivity

Like hydrogen, most elements are known to have two or more isotopes. Tin, for example, has ten isotopes. Many of these isotopes are quite stable, and for all intents and purposes, the isotopes of any one element have indistinguishable properties. Others, however, are not as stable and decompose with time by a process known as *radioactive decay*. **Radioactivity** is the emission of radiation that accompanies the spontaneous disintegration of unstable nuclei. Radioactivity is actually composed of three types of radiation: **alpha particles**, **beta particles**, and **gamma rays**.

Alpha particles are positively charged particles, each with a mass approximately four times that of a hydrogen atom. These particles are helium atoms stripped of their orbiting electrons. Beta particles are actually electrons, and gamma rays are electromagnetic radiations similar to X-rays but of a higher frequency and energy (refer to the electromagnetic spectrum in Figure 5–15). Fortunately, most naturally occurring isotopes are not radioactive, and those that are—radium, uranium, and thorium—are found in such small quantities in the earth's crust that their radioactivity presents no hazard to human survival.

Because of their large mass, alpha particles do not tend to travel far and are not very penetrating; a sheet of paper or your skin easily stops them. However, radioisotopes that emit alpha

atomic mass
The sum of the number of protons and neutrons in the nucleus of an atom

isotope
An atom differing from another atom of the same element in the number of neutrons in its nucleus

radioactivity
The particle and/or gamma-ray radiation emitted by the unstable nucleus of some isotopes

alpha particle
A type of radiation emitted by a radioactive element; the radiation is composed of helium atoms minus their orbiting electrons

beta particle
A type of radiation emitted by a radioactive element; the radiation consists of electrons

gamma ray
A high-energy form of electromagnetic radiation emitted by a radioactive element

Hydrogen   Deuterium   Tritium

FIGURE 6–8
Isotopes of hydrogen.

> > > > > > > > > > > > > > > > > > > >

case study

Death by Radiation Poisoning

In November 2006, Alexander V. Litvinenko lay at death's door in a London hospital. He was in excruciating pain and had symptoms that included hair loss, the inability to make blood cells, and gastrointestinal distress. His organs slowly failed as he lingered for three weeks and then died. British investigators soon confirmed that Litvinenko died from the intake of polonium-210, a radioactive element, in what appeared to be its first use as a murder weapon (see Figure 1).

Litvinenko's death almost immediately set off an international uproar. Litvinenko, a former KGB operative, had become a vocal critic of the Russian spy agency FSB, the domestic successor to the KGB. In 2000, he fled to London where he was granted asylum. Litvinenko continued to voice his criticisms of the Russian spy agency and also became highly critical of Russia's president, Vladimir Putin. Just before his death, he was believed to have compiled, on behalf of a British company looking to invest millions in a project in Russia, an incriminating report regarding the activities of senior Kremlin officials.

Suspicions immediately fell onto Andrei Lugovoi and Dmitri Kovtun, business associates of Mr. Litvinenko. Lugovoi was himself a former KGB officer. On the day he fell ill, Litvinenko met Lugovoi and Kovtun at the Pine Bar of the Millennium Hotel in London. At the meeting, Mr. Litvinenko drank tea out of a teapot later found to be highly radioactive. British officials have accused Lugovoi of

poisoning Litvinenko. The precise nature of the evidence against him has not been made clear, though investigators have linked him and Mr. Kovtun to a trail of polonium-210 radioactivity stretching from hotel rooms, restaurants, bars, and offices in London to Hamburg, Germany, and to British Airways planes that had flown to Moscow. Each man has denied killing Mr. Litvinenko.

Polonium-210 is highly radioactive and very toxic. By weight, it is about 250 million times as toxic as cyanide, so a particle the size of a dust particle could be fatal. It emits a radioactive ray known as an alpha particle. This form of radiation cannot penetrate the skin, so polonium-210 is effective as a poison only if it is swallowed, breathed in, or injected. The particles disperse through the body and first destroy fast-growing cells, like those in bone marrow, blood, hair, and the digestive tract. That would be consistent with Mr. Litvinenko's symptoms. There is no antidote for polonium poisoning.

Polonium does have industrial uses and is produced by commercial or institutional nuclear reactors. Polonium-210 has been found to be ideal for making antistatic devices that remove dust from film and lenses as well as paper and textile plants. Its non-body-penetrating rays produce an electric charge on nearby air. Bits of dust with static attract the charged air, which neutralizes them. Once free of static, the dust is easy to blow or brush away. Manufacturers of such antistatic devices take great pains to make the polonium hard to remove from their products.

FIGURE 1

Alexander Litvinenko, former KGB agent, before and after he became sick.
(left) Courtesy AP Wide World Photos (right) Courtesy Getty Images, Inc.-Getty News

rays are dangerous when ingested. The radioisotope polonium-210, an emitter of alpha particles, was recently implicated in the murder of an ex-KGB agent (see the case study below).

The existence of isotopes would be of little importance to the forensic chemist were it not for the fact that scientists have mastered the techniques for synthesizing radioactive isotopes. If the only distinction between isotopes of an element is the number of neutrons each possesses, is it not reasonable to assume that when atoms are bombarded with neutrons, some neutrons will be captured to make new isotopes? This is exactly what happens in a nuclear reactor. A nuclear reactor is simply a source of neutrons that can be used to bombard the atoms of a specimen, thereby creating radioactive isotopes. When the nucleus of an atom captures a neutron, a new isotope with one additional neutron is formed. In this state, the nuclei are said to be activated, and many immediately begin to decompose by emitting radioactivity.

The Process of Neutron Activation Analysis

To identify the activated isotope, it is necessary to measure the energy of the gamma rays emitted as radioactivity. The gamma rays of each element can be associated with a characteristic energy value. Furthermore, once the element has been identified, its concentration can be measured by the intensity of its gamma-ray radiation; intensity is directly proportional to the concentration of the element in a specimen. The technique of bombarding specimens with neutrons and measuring the resultant gamma-ray radioactivity is known as *neutron activation analysis*. The process is depicted in Figure 6–9.

The major advantage of neutron activation analysis is that it provides a nondestructive method for identifying and quantitating trace elements. A median detection sensitivity of one-billionth of a gram (one nanogram) makes neutron activation analysis one of the most sensitive methods available for the quantitative detection of many elements. Further, neutron activation can simultaneously analyze 20 to 30 elements. A major drawback to the technique is its expense

Each element is associated with a characteristic energy value. Intensity indicates the element concentration in the specimen

FIGURE 6–9

The neutron activation process requires the capture of a neutron by the nucleus of an atom. The new atom is now radioactive and emits gamma rays. A detector permits identification of the radioactive atoms present by measuring the energies and intensities of the gamma rays emitted.

TABLE 6–4

Concentration of Trace Elements in Copper Wire

	Selenium	Gold	Antimony	Silver
Control Wire				
A_1	2.4	0.047	0.16	12.7
A_2	3.5	0.064	0.27	17.2
A_3	2.6	0.050	0.20	13.3
A_4	1.9	0.034	0.21	12.6
Suspect Wire				
B	2.3	0.042	0.15	13.0

Note: Average concentration measured in parts per million.

Source: R. K. H. Chan, "Identification of Single-Stranded Copper Wires by Nondestructive Neutron Activation Analysis," *Journal of Forensic Sciences* 17 (1972), 93. Reprinted by permission of the American Society for Testing and Materials, copyright 1972.

and regulatory requirements. Only a handful of crime laboratories worldwide have access to a nuclear reactor; in addition, sophisticated analyzers are needed to detect and discriminate gamma-ray emissions.

Applications of Neutron Activation Analysis

As far as forensic analysis is concerned, neutron activation has been used to characterize trace elements present in metals, drugs, paint, soil, gunpowder residues, and hair. A typical illustration of its application occurred during the investigation of a theft of copper telegraphic wires in Canada. Four lengths of copper wire (A_1, A_2, A_3, A_4) found at the scene of the theft were compared by neutron activation with a length of copper wire (B) seized at a scrap yard and suspected of being stolen. All were bare, single-strand wire with the same general physical appearance and a diameter of 0.28 centimeter. Prior experiments had revealed that significant variations could be expected in the concentration levels of the trace elements selenium, gold, antimony, and silver for wires originating from different sources. A comparison of these elements present in the wire involved in the theft was undertaken. After exposing the wires to neutrons in a nuclear reactor, neutron activation analysis revealed a match between A_1 and B that was well within experimental error (see Table 6–4). The findings suggested a common origin of the control and suspect wires.

X-Ray Diffraction

Until now, we have discussed methods for detecting and identifying the elements. Emission spectroscopy, atomic absorption, and neutron activation analysis tell us what elements are present in a particular substance, but they do not provide any information as to how the elements are combined into compounds. One way to elicit this information is to aim a beam of X-rays at a crystal and study how the X-rays interact with the atoms that compose the substance under investigation. This technique is known as **X-ray diffraction**.

X-ray diffraction can be applied only to the study of solid, crystalline materials—that is, solids with a definite and orderly arrangement of atoms. For example, sodium chloride (common table salt), pictured in Figure 4–8, is crystalline. Fortunately, many substances, including 95 percent of all inorganic compounds, are crystalline and thus identifiable by X-ray diffraction analysis. The atoms in a crystal can be thought of as being composed of a series of parallel planes. As the X-rays penetrate the crystal, a portion of the beam is reflected by each of the atomic planes. As the reflected beams leave the crystal's planes, they combine with one another to form a series of light and dark bands known as a *diffraction pattern*. Every compound produces a unique diffraction pattern, thus giving analysts a means for "fingerprinting" compounds.

A diagram depicting the X-ray diffraction process is illustrated in Figure 6–10. Diffraction patterns for potassium nitrate and potassium chlorate, two common constituents of homemade explosives, are shown in Figure 6–11. Comparing a questioned specimen with a known X-ray pattern is a rapid and specific way to prove chemical identity.

X-ray diffraction
An analytical technique for identifying crystalline materials

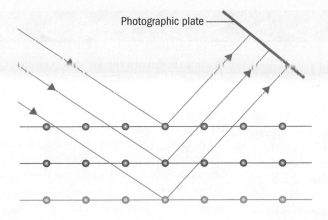

Photographic plate

FIGURE 6–10

A beam of X-rays being reflected off the atomic planes of a crystal. The diffraction patterns that form are recorded on photographic film. These patterns are unique for each crystalline substance.

(a)

(b)

FIGURE 6–11

X-ray diffraction patterns for (a) potassium nitrate and (b) potassium chlorate.

One drawback to X-ray diffraction is its lack of sensitivity. The technique is suitable for identifying the major constituents of a mixture, but it often fails to detect the presence of substances constituting less than 5 percent of a mixture. For this reason, the forensic chemist must use more sensitive techniques—emission spectroscopy, atomic absorption, and neutron activation analysis—to identify trace elements that may be present.

forensic brief

Nuclear Forensics

Nuclear forensics has emerged as a critical profession on the forefront in the war on terrorism. Nuclear forensic scientists are responsible for developing ways to analyze nuclear materials recovered from either intercepted intact nuclear materials or postexplosion debris created as a result of a nuclear explosion. Nuclear forensics can trace its origin to the cold war era, when U.S. planes surreptitiously flew over Soviet airspace sampling airborne particles from the country's nuclear bomb tests. Nuclear forensics matured as a science when the Soviet empire disintegrated and concerns arose over the security of nuclear materials located in states of the former Soviet Union. Fears that these materials might fall into the hands of terrorist organizations engendered scenarios of dirty nuclear bombs attacks on the United States and other Western nations.

Nuclear forensics is becoming an increasingly important tool in the fight against illegal smuggling

(Continued)

forensic brief

Nuclear Forensics (continued)

and trafficking of radiological and nuclear materials. These include materials intended for industrial and medical use, nuclear materials such as those produced in the nuclear fuel cycle of a nuclear power plant (see Figure 1), and much more dangerous nuclear materials that can be used in weapons, such as plutonium and highly enriched uranium. Since the early 1990s, more than two hundred cases of illicitly trafficked nuclear materials have been reported.

In the United States, Lawrence Livermore National Laboratory along with seven other Department of Energy (DOE) national laboratories have been tasked by the FBI and the Department of Homeland Security with developing the nation's technical forensics capability for nuclear and radiological materials. Organizations such as the European Commission's Institute for Transuranium Elements located in Karlsruhe, Germany, have extend nuclear forensic capabilities onto an international scale.

A major focus of nuclear forensics is identifying signatures, which are the physical, chemical, and isotopic characteristics that distinguish one nuclear or radiological material from another. Signatures enable researchers to identify the processes used to initially create a material, which ultimately may yield clues as to the origin of the seized material.

Figure 1
© Royalty-Free/CORBIS

Nuclear forensics can be performed on a broad spectrum of substances. An example is stolen containers of uranium diverted during one of the mining, milling, conversion, enrichment, or fuel fabrication steps used to convert uranium ore to enriched fuel for nuclear power plants; uranium varies in isotopic composition and impurities according to where the uranium was mined and how it was processed. Another example is commercial radioactive materials used in applications such as medical diagnostics and food sterilization.

Researchers analyze the material's chemical and isotopic composition, which includes measuring the amounts of trace elements as well as the ratio of parent isotopes to daughter isotopes. These measurements help determine the source location and sample's age. They also examine the material's morphological characteristics such as shape, size, and texture. Analytical methods include electron microscopy, X-ray diffraction, and mass spectrometry. In addition, as a sample is moved from place to place, it picks up trace evidence such as pollen, hairs, fibers, plant DNA, and fingerprints. These so-called route materials may provide information about who has handled a sample and the path it has traveled.

When comparing a sample's signature against known signatures from uranium mines and fabrication plants, researchers can benefit by assembling a library of nuclear materials of known origin from around the world. Nuclear scientists have developed relationships with domestic suppliers of nuclear materials to assemble such a library. Contracts with major U.S. uranium fuel suppliers have provided researchers with samples and manufacturing data. Forensic scientists are also seeking to obtain samples of uranium products worldwide to analyze the products' isotopic and trace-element content, grain size, and microstructure. Nations with nuclear capabilities are beginning to share information about their nuclear fuel processes and materials. The development of databases is essential to the nuclear forensic scientist's mission of identifying the origin of nuclear materials intercepted in the black market or associated with a terrorist event.

chapter summary

> > > > > > > > > >

Inorganic substances are encountered by forensic scientists as tools, explosives, poisons, and metal scrapings as well as trace components in paints and dyes. Many manufactured products and even most natural materials contain small quantities of elements in concentrations of less than 1 percent. For the criminalist, the presence of these trace elements is particularly useful because they provide "invisible" markers that may establish the source of a material or at least provide additional points for comparison.

Emission spectroscopy, inductively coupled plasma, and atomic absorption spectrophotometry are three techniques available to forensic scientists for determining the elemental composition of materials. An emission spectrograph vaporizes and heats samples to a high temperature so that the atoms present in the material achieve an "excited" state. Under these circumstances, the excited atoms emit light. If the light is separated into its components, one observes a line spectrum. Each element present in the spectrum can be identified by its characteristic line frequencies. In inductively coupled plasma, the sample, in the form of an aerosol, is introduced into a hot plasma, creating charged particles that emit light of characteristic wavelengths corresponding to the identity of the elements present.

In atomic absorption spectrophotometry, the specimen is heated to a temperature that is hot enough to vaporize its atoms while leaving a substantial number of atoms in an unexcited state. The vaporized atoms are then exposed to radiation emitted from a light source specific for a particular element. If the element is present in the material under investigation, a portion of the light is absorbed by the substance. In this manner, many elements can be detected at levels that approach one-trillionth of a gram. Neutron activation analysis measures the gamma-ray frequencies of specimens that have been bombarded with neutrons. This method provides a highly sensitive and nondestructive analysis for simultaneously identifying and quantitating 20 to 30 trace elements. Because this technique requires access to a nuclear reactor, however, it has limited value to forensic analysis.

X-ray diffraction is used to study solid, crystalline materials. As the X-rays penetrate the crystal, a portion of the beam is reflected by each atomic plane. As the reflected beams leave the crystal's planes, they combine with one another to form a series of light and dark bands known as a diffraction pattern. Every compound produces a unique diffraction pattern, thus giving analysts a means for "fingerprinting" inorganic compounds.

review questions

1. The elements _____ and _____ make up 75 percent of the weight of the earth's crust.

2. Only _____ elements make up about 99 percent of the weight of the earth's crust.

3. The presence of _____ elements in materials provides useful "invisible" markers when comparing physical evidence.

4. The knowledge that elements selectively _____ and _____ light provides the basis for important analytical techniques designed to detect the presence of elements in materials.

5. A(n) _____ is a display of colors or frequencies emitted from a light source.

6. True or False: A continuous spectrum consists of a blending of colors. _____

7. A(n) _____ spectrum shows distinct frequencies or wavelengths of light.

8. A line spectrum of an element (is, is not) characteristic of the element.

9. True or False: Matter in a solid or liquid state produces an emission spectrum that is characteristic of its composition. _____

10. The _____ is an instrument used to obtain and record the line spectrum of elements.

11. Excitation of a specimen can be accomplished when it is inserted between two _____ electrodes.

12. The selective absorption of light by atoms is the basis for a technique known as _____.

13. The composition of the discharge lamp (does, does not) have to be taken into consideration when performing an analysis by atomic absorption for a particular element.

14. True or False: One advantage of atomic absorption analysis is that it can simultaneously detect 20 to 30 elements. _____

15. Three important subatomic particles of the atom are the _____, _____, and _____.

16. The proton and electron (are, are not) of approximately equal mass.

17. A proton imparts the nucleus of an atom with a _____ charge.

18. The number of protons (is, is not) always equal to the number of electrons in orbit around the nucleus of an atom.

19. Each atom of the same element always has the same number of _____ in its nucleus.

20. The number of protons in the nucleus of an atom is called the _____.

21. True or False: Each element has its own characteristic set of energy levels. _____

22. True or False: To move an electron from one energy level to the next requires a definite amount of energy. _____

23. As an electron falls from a higher to a lower energy level, it emits _____.

24. The total number of protons and neutrons present in a nucleus is known as the _____.

25. Atoms differing only in the number of neutrons present in their nuclei are called _____.

26. True or False: Deuterium has the greatest number of protons of all the isotopes of hydrogen. _____

27. Radioactivity is composed of the following emissions: _____, _____, and _____.

28. Beta particles are identical to _____.

29. Electromagnetic waves similar to X-rays but of a higher energy are _____.

30. A nuclear reactor is a source of _____.

31. The technique of bombarding specimens with neutrons and measuring the resultant gamma ray emissions is known as _____.

32. As X-rays are reflected off a material's surface, they form a series of light and dark bands known as a(n) _____.

33. X-ray diffraction patterns are obtained from (crystalline, amorphous) substances.

application and critical thinking

1. A forensic analyst at the local crime lab receives pieces of a disfigured bullet from a crime scene. He or she then obtains an exemplar bullet fired by the firearms analyst from the suspect's firearm. What is the next step in analysis?

2. Only a handful of crime laboratories worldwide have access to a nuclear reactor to carry out neutron activation analysis. What are some possible reasons why this is so?

3. If a forensic analyst wanted to analyze a particular sample for the presence of trace amounts of an inorganic substance, would X-ray diffraction be a suitable analytical tool? Why or why not?

further references

Forensic Analysis: Weighing Bullet Lead Evidence. Washington, D.C.: National Academies Press, 2004.

Guinn, V. P., "The Elemental Comparison of Bullet-Lead Evidence Specimens," in S. M. Gerber, ed., *Chemistry and Crime.* Washington, D.C.: American Chemical Society, 1983.

Houck, Max M., ed., *Mute Witnesses: Trace Evidence Analysis.* Burlington, Mass.: Elsevier Academic Press, 2001.

Houck, Max M., ed., *Trace Evidence Analysis—More Cases in Mute Witnesses.* Burlington, Mass.: Elsevier Academic Press, 2004.

Settle, F. A., ed., *Handbook of Instrumental Techniques for Analytical Chemistry.* Upper Saddle River, N.J.: Prentice Hall, 1998.

The Lindbergh Baby Case

On the evening of March 1, 1932, a kidnapper crept up his homemade ladder and stole the baby of Charles and Anne Lindbergh directly from the second-floor nursery of their house in Hopewell, New Jersey. The only evidence of his coming was a ransom note, the ladder, a chisel, and the tragic absence of the infant. A couple of months later, though the $50,000 ransom had been paid, the baby turned up dead in the woods a mile away. There was no additional sign of the killer. Fortunately, when finally studied by wood technologist Arthur Koehler, the abandoned ladder yielded some important investigative clues (see the case study on page 183). By studying the types of wood used and the cutter marks on the wood, Koehler ascertained where the materials might have come from and what specific equipment was used to create them. Koehler traced the wood from a South Carolina mill to a lumberyard in the Bronx, New York. Unfortunately the trail went cold, as the lumberyard did not keep sales records of purchases. The break in the case came in 1934, when Bruno Richard Hauptmann paid for gasoline with a bill that matched a serial number on the ransom money. Koehler showed that microscopic markings on the wood were made by a tool in Hauptmann's possession. Ultimately, handwriting analysis of the ransom note clearly showed it to be written by Hauptmann.

the microscope

Learning Objectives

After studying this chapter you should be able to:

- List and understand the parts of the compound microscope

- Define magnification, field of view, working distance, and depth of focus

- Contrast the comparison and compound microscopes

- Understand the theory and utility of the stereoscopic microscope

- Appreciate how a polarizing microscope is designed to characterize polarized light

- Appreciate how a microspectrophotometer can be used to examine trace physical evidence

- Compare and contrast the image formation mechanism of a light microscope to that of a scanning electron microscope

- Outline some forensic applications of the scanning electron microscope

KEY TERMS

binocular
condenser
depth of focus
eyepiece lens
field of view
microspectro-
    photometer
monocular
objective lens
parfocal
plane-polarized light
polarizer
real image
transmitted
    illumination
vertical or reflected
    illumination
virtual image

Basics of the Microscope

A microscope is an optical instrument that uses a lens or a combination of lenses to magnify and resolve the fine details of an object. The earliest methods for examining physical evidence in crime laboratories relied almost solely on the microscope to study the structure and composition of matter. Even the advent of modern analytical instrumentation and techniques has done little to diminish the usefulness of the microscope for forensic analysis. If anything, the development of the powerful scanning electron microscope promises to add a new dimension to forensic science heretofore unattainable within the limits of the ordinary light microscope.

The earliest and simplest microscope was the single lens commonly referred to as a *magnifying glass*. The handheld magnifying glass makes things appear larger than they are because of the way light rays are refracted, or bent, in passing from the air into the glass and back into the air. The magnified image is observed by looking through the lens, as shown in Figure 7–1. Such an image is known as a **virtual image**; it can be seen only by looking through a lens and cannot be viewed directly. This is distinguished from a **real image**, which can be seen directly, like the image that is projected onto a motion picture screen.

The ordinary magnifying glass can achieve a magnification of about 5 to 10 times. Higher magnifying power is obtainable only with a *compound microscope*, constructed of two lenses mounted at each end of a hollow tube. The object to be magnified is placed under the lower lens, called the **objective lens**, and the magnified image is viewed through the upper lens, known as the **eyepiece lens**. As shown in Figure 7–2, the objective lens forms a real, inverted, magnified image of the object. The eyepiece, acting just like a simple magnifying glass, further magnifies this image into a virtual image, which is what is seen by the eye. The combined magnifying power of both lenses can produce an image magnified up to 1,500 times.

The optical principles of the compound microscope are incorporated into the basic design of different types of light microscopes. The microscopes most applicable for examining forensic specimens are as follows:

1. The compound microscope
2. The comparison microscope
3. The stereoscopic microscope
4. The polarizing microscope
5. The microspectrophotometer

After describing these five microscopes, we will talk about a completely different approach to microscopy, the scanning electron microscope (SEM). This instrument focuses a beam of electrons, instead of visible light, onto the specimen to produce a magnified image. The principle and design of this microscope permit magnifying powers as high as 100,000 times.

virtual image
An image that cannot be seen directly. It can be seen only by a viewer looking through a lens

real image
An image formed by the actual convergence of light rays on a screen

objective lens
The lower lens of a microscope, which is positioned directly over the specimen

eyepiece lens
The lens of a microscope into which the viewer looks; same as the ocular lens

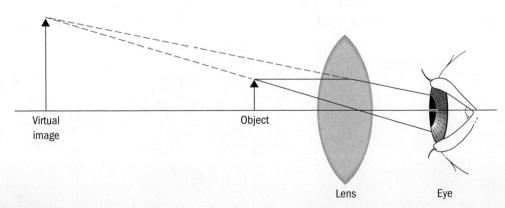

FIGURE 7–1
The passage of light through a lens, showing how magnification is obtained.

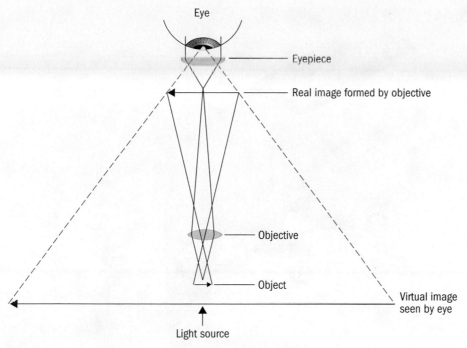

Eye

Eyepiece

Real image formed by objective

Objective

Object

Virtual image
seen by eye

Light source

FIGURE 7–2

The principle of the compound microscope. The passage of light through two lenses forms the virtual image of the object seen by the eye.

The Compound Microscope

The parts of the compound microscope are illustrated in Figure 7–3. Basically, this microscope consists of a mechanical system, which supports the microscope, and an optical system. The optical system illuminates the object under investigation and passes the light through a series of lenses to form an image of the specimen on the retina of the eye. The optical path of light through a compound microscope is shown in Figure 7–4.

Parts of the Compound Microscope

The mechanical system of the compound microscope is composed of six parts:

Base (1).   The support on which the instrument rests.

Arm (2).   A C-shaped upright structure, hinged to the base, that supports the microscope and acts as a handle for carrying.

Stage (3).   The horizontal plate on which the specimens are placed for study. The specimens are normally mounted on glass slides that are held firmly in place on the stage by spring clips.

Body tube (4).   A cylindrical hollow tube on which the objective and eyepiece lenses are mounted at opposite ends. This tube merely serves as a corridor through which light passes from one lens to another.

Coarse adjustment (5).   This knob focuses the microscope lenses on the specimen by raising and lowering the body tube.

Fine adjustment (6).   The movements effected by this knob are similar to those of the coarse adjustment but are of a much smaller magnitude.

The optical system is made up of four parts:

Illuminator (7).   Most modern microscopes use artificial light supplied by a lightbulb to illuminate the specimen being examined. If the specimen is transparent, the light is directed up toward and through the specimen stage from an illuminator built into the base of the microscope. This is known as **transmitted illumination**. When the object is opaque—that is, not transparent—the light source must be placed above the specimen so that it can reflect off the specimen's surface and into the lens system of the microscope. This type of illumination is known as **vertical** or **reflected illumination**.

transmitted illumination
Light that passes up from the condenser and through the specimen

vertical or reflected illumination
Illumination of a specimen from above; in microscopy it is used to examine opaque specimens

FIGURE 7–3

Parts of the compound microscope:
(1) base, (2) arm, (3) stage, (4) body tube,
(5) coarse adjust, (6) fine adjust,
(7) illuminator, (8) condenser, (9) objective
lens, and (10) eyepiece lens.
Courtesy Leica Microsystems, Buffalo, N.Y.,
www.leica-microsystems.com

FIGURE 7–4

Optics of the compound
microscope.
Courtesy Leica Microsystems, Buffalo, N.Y.,
www.leica-microsystems.com

DIALUX

Condenser (8).   The **condenser** collects light rays from the base illuminator and concentrates them on the specimen. The simplest condenser is known as the *Abbé condenser*. It consists of two lenses held together in a metal mount. The condenser also includes an iris diaphragm that can be opened or closed to control the amount of light passing into the condenser.

Objective lens (9).   This is the lens positioned closest to the specimen. To facilitate changing from one objective lens to another, several objectives are mounted on a revolving nosepiece or turret located above the specimen. Most microscopes are **parfocal**, meaning that when the microscope is focused with one objective in position, the other objective can be rotated into place by revolving the nosepiece while the specimen remains very nearly in correct focus.

Eyepiece or ocular lens (10).   This is the lens closest to the eye. A microscope with only one eyepiece is **monocular**; one constructed with two eyepieces (one for each eye) is **binocular**.

Properties of the Compound Microscope

Each microscope lens is inscribed with a number signifying its magnifying power. The image viewed by the microscopist will have a total magnification equal to the product of the magnifying power of the objective and eyepiece lenses. For example, an eyepiece lens with a magnification of 10 times (10×) used in combination with an objective lens of 10× has a total magnification power of 100×. Most forensic work requires a 10× eyepiece in combination with either a 4×, 10×, 20×, or 45× objective. The respective magnifications will be 40×, 100×, 200×, and 450×.

In addition, each objective lens is inscribed with its numerical aperture (N.A.). The ability of an objective lens to resolve details into separate images instead of one blurred image is directly proportional to the numerical aperture value of the objective lens. For example, an objective lens of N.A. 1.30 can separate details at half the distance of a lens with an N.A. of 0.65. The maximum useful magnification of a compound microscope is approximately 1,000 times the N.A. of the objective being used. This magnification is sufficient to permit the eye to see all the detail that can be resolved. Any effort to increase the total magnification beyond this figure will yield no additional detail and is referred to as *empty magnification.*

Although a new student of the microscope may be tempted to immediately choose the highest magnifying power available to view a specimen, the experienced microscopist weighs a number of important factors before choosing a magnifying power. A first consideration must be the size of the specimen area, or the **field of view**, that the examiner wishes to study. As magnifying power increases, the field of view decreases. Thus, it is best to first select a low magnification in which a good general overall view of the specimen is seen and to switch later to a higher power in which a smaller portion of the specimen can be viewed in more detail.

The **depth of focus** is also a function of magnifying power. After a focus has been achieved on a specimen, the depth of focus defines the thickness of that specimen. Areas above and below this region will be blurred and can be viewed only when the focus is readjusted. Depth of focus decreases as magnifying power increases.

The Comparison Microscope

Forensic microscopy often requires a side-by-side comparison of specimens. This kind of examination can best be performed with a comparison microscope, such as the one pictured in Figure 7–5. Basically, the comparison microscope is two compound microscopes combined into one unit. The unique feature of its design is that it uses a bridge incorporating a series of mirrors and lenses to join two independent objective lenses into a single binocular unit. When a viewer looks through the eyepiece lenses of the comparison microscope, a circular field, equally divided into two parts by a fine line, is observed. The specimen mounted under the left-hand objective is seen in the left half of the field, and the specimen under the right-hand objective is observed in the right half of the field. It is important to closely match the optical characteristics of the objective lenses to ensure that both specimens are seen at equal magnification and with minimal but identical lens distortions. Comparison microscopes designed to compare bullets, cartridges, and other opaque objects are equipped with vertical or reflected illumination. Comparison microscopes used to compare hairs or fibers use transmitted illumination.

Figure 7–6 shows the striation markings on two bullets that have been placed under the objective lenses of a comparison microscope. Modern firearms examination began with the

---

condenser
The lens system under the microscope stage that focuses light onto the specimen

parfocal
Describes a microscope such that when an image is focused with one objective in position, the other objective can be rotated into place and the field will remain in focus

monocular
Describes a microscope with one eyepiece

binocular
Describes a microscope with two eyepieces

mycrimekit

WEBEXTRA 7.1
Explore the Concept of Magnification with a Compound Microscope
www.mycrimekit.com

field of view
The area of the specimen that can be seen after it is magnified

depth of focus
The thickness of a specimen that is entirely in focus under a microscope

mycrimekit

WEBEXTRA 7.2
Scan a Sample under the Compound Microscope
www.mycrimekit.com

mycrimekit

WEBEXTRA 7.3
Observe the Concept of Depth of Focus
www.mycrimekit.com

FIGURE 7–5

The comparison microscope—
two independent objective
lenses joined together by an
optical bridge.
Mikael Karlsson\Arresting Images Royalty
Free.

FIGURE 7–6

Photomicrograph taken through a comparison microscope. On the right are the
striation markings on the test-fired bullet, fired through the suspect weapon. On the left
are the markings of the crime-scene bullet.
Courtesy Getty Images Inc.—Hulton Archive

introduction of the comparison microscope, with its ability to give the firearms examiner a side-by-side magnified view of bullets. Bullets that are fired through the same rifle barrel display comparable rifling markings on their surfaces. Matching the majority of striations present on each bullet justifies a conclusion that both bullets traveled through the same barrel.

mycrimekit

WEBEXTRA 7.4
Practice Matching Bullets with the
Aid of a 3-D Interactive Illustration
www.mycrimekit.com

The Stereoscopic Microscope

The details that characterize the structures of many types of physical evidence do not always require examination under very high magnifications. For such specimens, the stereoscopic microscope has proven quite adequate, providing magnifying powers from $10\times$ to $125\times$. This microscope has the advantage of presenting a distinctive three-dimensional image of an object. Also, whereas the image formed by the compound microscope is inverted and reversed (upside-down and backward), the stereoscopic microscope is more convenient because of the prisms in its light path that permit the formation of a right-side-up image. The stereoscopic microscope, shown in Figure 7–7, is actually two monocular compound microscopes properly spaced and aligned to present a three-dimensional image of a specimen to the viewer, who looks through both eyepiece lenses. The light path of a stereoscopic microscope is shown in Figure 7–8.

The stereoscopic microscope is undoubtedly the most frequently used and versatile microscope found in the crime laboratory. Its wide field of view and great depth of focus make it an ideal instrument for locating trace evidence in debris, garments, weapons, or tools. Furthermore, its potentially large *working distance* (the distance between the objective lens and the specimen) makes it quite applicable for the microscopic examination of big, bulky items. When fitted with

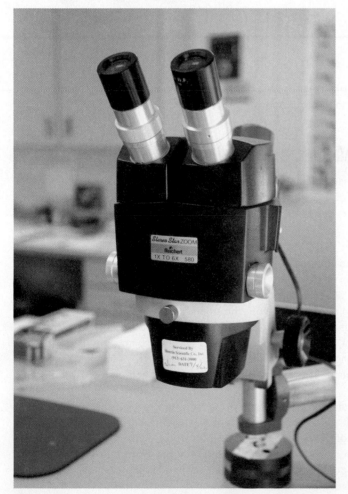

FIGURE 7–7

A stereoscopic microscope.
Courtesy of Mikael Karlsson, Arresting
Images

FIGURE 7–8
Schematic diagram of a stereoscopic microscope. This microscope is actually two separate monocular microscopes, each with its own set of lenses except for the lowest objective lens, which is common to both microscopes.

plane-polarized light
Light confined to a single plane of vibration

polarizer
A device that permits the passage of light waves vibrating in only one plane

vertical illumination, the stereoscopic microscope becomes the primary tool for characterizing physical evidence as diverse as paint, soil, gunpowder residues, and marijuana.

The Polarizing Microscope

Recall from Chapter 5 that light's wavelike motion in space can be invoked to explain many facets of its behavior. The polarizing microscope takes advantage of one of these facts—the fact that light vibrates.

Polarization

The waves that compose a beam of light can be pictured as vibrating in all directions perpendicular to the direction in which the light is traveling. However, when a beam of light passes through certain types of specially fabricated crystalline substances, it emerges vibrating in only one plane. Light that is confined to a single plane of vibration is said to be **plane-polarized**. The device that polarizes light in this manner is called a **polarizer**. A common example of this phenomenon is the passage of sunlight through polarized sunglasses. By transmitting light vibrating in the vertical plane only, these sunglasses eliminate or reduce light glare. Most glare consists of partially polarized light that has been reflected off horizontal surfaces and thus is vibrating in a horizontal plane.

Because polarized light appears no different to the eye from ordinary light, special means must be devised for detecting it. This is accomplished simply by placing a second polarizing crystal, called an *analyzer*, in the path of the polarized beam. As shown in Figure 7–9, if the polarizer and analyzer are aligned parallel to each other, the polarized light passes through and is seen by the eye. If, on the other hand, the polarizer and analyzer are set perpendicular to one another, or are "crossed," no light penetrates, and the result is total darkness or *extinction*.

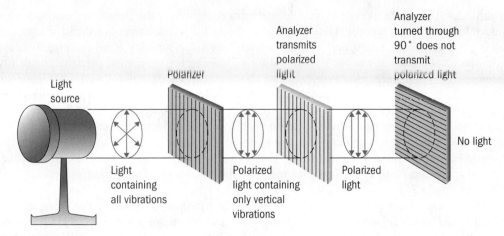

FIGURE 7–9
Polarization of light.

In this manner, a compound or stereoscopic microscope can be outfitted with a polarizer and analyzer to allow the viewer to detect polarized light. Such a microscope is known as a *polarizing microscope*. Essentially, the polarizer is placed between the light source and the sample stage to polarize the light before it passes through the specimen. The polarized light penetrating the specimen must then pass through an analyzer before it reaches the eyepiece and finally the eye. Normally, the polarizer and analyzer are "crossed" so that when no specimen is in place, the field appears dark. However, introducing a specimen that polarizes light reorients the polarized light, allowing it to pass through the analyzer. This result produces vivid colors and intensity contrasts that make the specimen readily distinguishable.

Applications of the Polarized Microscope

The most obvious and important applications of this microscope relate to studying materials that polarize light. For example, as we learned in Chapter 4 (see page 100), many crystalline substances are birefringent; that is, they split a beam of light into two light-ray components of different refractive index values. What makes this observation particularly relevant to our discussion of the polarizing microscope is that the light beams are polarized at right angles to each other. Thus, polarizing microscopy has found wide application for the examination of birefringent minerals present in soil. By using the immersion method and selecting the proper immersion liquids, a refractive index corresponding to each plane of polarized light can be determined. Thus, when a mineral is viewed under polarized light in a liquid that matches one of its refractive indices, the Becke line will no longer be visible. This information, plus observations on crystal color, form, and so on, makes it possible for the microscopist to identify the mineral. Similarly, criminalists use the fact that many synthetic fibers are birefringent to characterize them with a polarizing microscope.

The Microspectrophotometer

From a practical point of view, few instruments in a crime laboratory can match the versatility of the microscope. The microscope's magnifying power is indispensable for finding minute traces of physical evidence. Many items of physical evidence can be characterized by a microscopic examination of their morphological features. Likewise, the microscope can be used to study how light interacts with the material under investigation, or it can be used to observe the effects that other chemical substances have on such evidence. Each of these features allows an examiner to better characterize and identify physical evidence. Recently, linking the microscope to a computerized spectrophotometer has added a new dimension to its capability. This combination has given rise to a new instrument called the **microspectrophotometer**.

In many respects, this is an ideal marriage from the forensic scientist's viewpoint. In Chapter 5, we saw how a chemist can use selective absorption of light by materials to characterize them.

mycrimekit
WEBEXTRA 7.6
Explore the Polarizing Microscope—I
www.mycrimekit.com

mycrimekit
WEBEXTRA 7.7
Explore the Polarizing Microscope—II
www.mycrimekit.com

microspectrophotometer
An instrument that links a microscope to a spectrophotometer

In particular, light in the ultraviolet, visible, and infrared regions of the electromagnetic spectrum is most helpful for this purpose. Unfortunately, in the past, forensic chemists were unable to take full advantage of the capabilities of spectrophotometry for examining trace evidence because most spectrophotometers are not well suited for examining the very small particles frequently encountered as evidence. However, with the development of the microspectrophotometer, a forensic analyst can now view a particle under a microscope while a beam of light is directed at the particle in order to obtain its absorption spectrum. Depending on the type of light employed, an examiner can acquire either a visible or an IR spectral pattern of the substance being viewed under the microscope. The obvious advantage of this approach is to provide the forensic scientist with added information that will characterize trace quantities of evidence. A microspectrophotometer designed to measure the uptake of visible light by materials is shown in Figure 7–10.

Visual comparison of color is usually one of the first steps in examining paint, fiber, and ink evidence. Such comparisons are easily obtained using a comparison microscope. Now, with the use of the microspectrophotometer, not only can the color of materials be compared visually but, at the same time, an absorption spectrum can be plotted for each item under examination to display the exact wavelengths at which it absorbs in the visible-light spectrum. Occasionally colors that appear similar by visual examination show significant differences in their absorption spectra. An example of this approach is shown in Figure 7–11, in which the microspectrophotometer is used to distinguish counterfeit and authentic currency by comparing the spectral patterns of inked lines on currency.

Another emerging technique in forensic science is the use of the infrared microspectrophotometer to examine fibers and paints. The "fingerprint" IR spectrum (see page 137) is unique for each chemical substance. Therefore, obtaining such a spectrum from either a fiber or a paint chip allows the analyst to better identify and compare the type of chemicals from which these materials are manufactured. With a microspectrophotometer, a forensic analyst can view a substance through the microscope and at the same time have the instrument plot the infrared absorption spectrum for that material.

FIGURE 7–10

A visible-light microspectrophotometer.
Courtesy CRAIC Technologies Inc., Altadena, CA. www.microspectra.com

FIGURE 7–11

Two $50 bills are shown at top; one is genuine and the other is counterfeit. Below each bill is a microphotograph of an inked line present on each bill. Each line was examined under a visible-light microspectrophotometer. As shown, the visible absorption spectrum of each line is readily differentiated, thus allowing the examiner to distinguish a counterfeit bill from genuine currency.

Courtesy Peter W. Pfefferli

The Scanning Electron Microscope (SEM)

All the microscopes described thus far use light coming off the specimen to produce a magnified image. The scanning electron microscope is, however, a special case in the family of microscopes (see Figure 7–12). The image is formed by aiming a beam of electrons onto the specimen and studying electron emissions on a closed TV circuit. The beam of electrons is emitted from a hot tungsten filament and is focused by electromagnets onto the surface of the specimen. This

FIGURE 7–12

A scanning electron microscope.
Courtesy Jeol USA Inc., Peabody, Mass., www.jeolusa.com

primary electron beam causes the emission of electrons, known as secondary electrons, from the elements that make up the upper layers of the specimen. Also, 20–30 percent of the primary electrons rebound off the surface. These electrons are known as *backscattered electrons*. The emitted electrons (both secondary and backscattered) are collected and the amplified signal is displayed on a cathode-ray or TV tube. By scanning the primary electron beam across the specimen's surface in synchronization with the cathode-ray tube, it is possible to convert the emitted electrons into an image of the specimen for display on the cathode-ray tube.

The major attractions of the SEM image are its high magnification, high resolution, and great depth of focus. In its usual mode, the SEM has a magnification that ranges from $10\times$ to $100,000\times$. Its depth of focus is some 300 times better than optical systems at similar magnifications, and the resultant picture is almost stereoscopic in appearance. Its great depth of field and magnification are exemplified by the magnification of cystolithic hair on the marijuana leaf, as shown in Figure 7–13. An SEM image of a vehicle's headlight filaments may reveal whether the headlights were on or off at the time of a collision (see Figures 7–14 and 7–15).

Another facet of scanning electron microscopy has been the use of X-ray production to determine the elemental composition of a specimen. X-rays are generated when the electron beam of the scanning electron microscope strikes a target. When the SEM is coupled to an X-ray analyzer, the emitted X-rays can be sorted according to their energy values and used to build up a picture of the elemental distribution in the specimen. Because each element emits X-rays of characteristic energy values, the X-ray analyzer can identify the elements present in a specimen. Furthermore, the element's concentration can be determined by measuring the intensity of the X-ray emission.

FIGURE 7–13

The cystolithic hairs of the marijuana leaf, as viewed with a scanning electron microscope (800×)

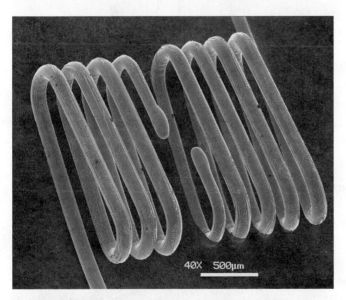

FIGURE 7–14

The melted ends of a hot filament break indicate that the headlights were on when an accident occurred.

Courtesy Jeol USA Inc., Peabody, Mass., www.jeolusa.com

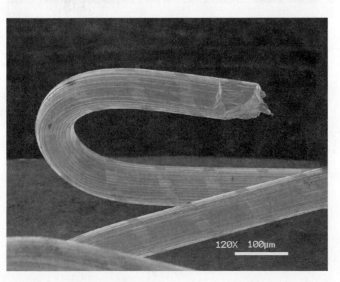

FIGURE 7–15

The sharp ends of a cold filament break indicate that the headlights were off when an accident occurred.

Courtesy Foster and Freeman Limited, Worchester Shire, UK, www.fosterfreemanco.uk

One application of scanning electron microscopy has been to determine whether a suspect has recently fired a gun. In this case, an attempt is made to remove any gunshot particles that remain on a shooter's hands by lifting them off with a piece of adhesive tape. The tape is then examined under the SEM for the presence of particles that may have originated from the bullet primer. These particles can be characterized by their size, shape, and elemental composition. As shown in Figure 7–16, when the sample of gunshot residue is exposed to a beam of electrons from the scanning electron microscope, X-rays are emitted. These X-rays are passed into a detector, where they are converted into electrical signals. These signals are sorted and displayed according to the energies of the emitted X-rays. Through the use of this technique, the elements lead, antimony, and barium, frequently found in most primers, can be rapidly detected and identified.

mycrimekit

WEBEXTRA 7.8
Explore the Scanning Electron Microscope
www.mycrimekit.com

FIGURE 7–16

A schematic diagram of a scanning electron microscope displaying the image of a gunshot residue particle. Simultaneously, an X-ray analyzer detects and displays X-ray emissions from the elements lead (Pb), antimony (Sb), and barium (Ba) present in the particle.
Courtesy Aerospace Corp., El Segundo, Calif.

Forensic Palynology—Pollen and Spores as Evidence

Of the many plant species on earth, more than half a million produce pollen or spores. The pollen or spores produced by each species has a unique type of ornamentation and morphology. This means that pollen or spores can be identified and used to provide links between a crime scene and a person or object if examined by a trained analyst. This technique is called forensic palynology and includes the collection and examination of pollen and spores connected with crime scenes, illegal activities, or terrorism.

In nature, pollen grains are the single-celled male gametophytes (reproductive cells) of seed-bearing plants. The pollen grain wall (*exine*) is durable because it protects and carries "the sperms" needed for plant reproduction. Spores consist of both the male and female gametes of plants such as algae, fungi, mosses, and ferns. Pollen-producing plants are either anemophilous (their pollen is dispersed by wind) or entomophilous (their pollen is carried and dispersed by insects or small animals). Fairly precise geographical locations can often be identified by the presence of different mixtures of airborne pollens produced by anemophilous plants. For example, it may be possible to identify a geographical origin by a profile of the pollen samples retrieved from a suspect's clothing simply by the type and percentages of airborne pollen grains. Entomophilous plants usually produce a small amount of pollen that is very sticky in nature. Therefore, this type of pollen is very rarely deposited on clothing or other objects except by direct contact with the plant. This information is useful when reconstructing the events of a crime because it indicates that the clothing, a vehicle, or other objects may have come into direct contact with plant types found at a crime scene.

Both spores and pollen are microscopic in size and are produced by the adult plants and dispersed by the millions, and both can be analyzed using similar methods and a variety of microscopic techniques. Using a compound light microscope with magnification capabilities up to 1,000×, pollen and spores can usually be identified as coming from a specific plant family or genus, and at times even a unique species. However, often the pollen or spores of related species may appear so similar that identification of the species is possible only with careful analysis using an SEM (see Figure 1).

Unique shapes, aperture type, and surface ornamentation are typically used to identify spore samples. Useful features for characterizing pollen grains include shape, apertures, and wall and surface sculpturing. Shapes of pollen grains include spheres, triangles, ellipses, hexagons, pentagons, and many other geometric variations. *Apertures* are the openings on pollen grains from which the pollen tube grows and carries the sperms to the egg to complete fertilization. Sculpturing of the pollen grain refers to the pattern of the pollen grain surface.

To avoid destruction or contamination, early collection of forensic pollen samples for analysis is

FIGURE 1

Scanning electron micrograph of ragweed pollen at a magnification of 951×.
Dennis Kunkel\Phototake NYC

important and should be completed as soon as possible at a crime scene by a trained palynologist. This kind of expert's first task is to calculate the estimated production and dispersal patterns of spores and pollen (called the *pollen rain*) for the crime scene or area of interest, and then using that information to produce a kind of "pollen fingerprint" of that location.

The information gained from the analysis of pollen and spore evidence has many possible uses. It can link a suspect or object to the crime scene or the victim, prove or disprove a suspect's alibi, include or exclude suspects, track the previous whereabouts of some item or suspect, or indicate the geographical origin of some item. In the past, pollen and spore evidence has also helped locate human remains and concealed burial sites, established the season or time of death of a victim, located the source areas of illegal drugs and fake pharmaceuticals, imprisoned terrorists, and proven the perpetration of illegal poaching or the adulteration of commercial foods.

A case exemplifying the application of forensic palynology to a criminal investigation occurred when a victim was kidnapped, robbed, and then murdered in the eastern part of the American Midwest.[1] The victim's car was stolen, but later abandoned when it got stuck in mud near a busy highway. The next night a drifter was arrested in a nearby town for breaking into a closed store. While in jail awaiting trial, the drifter told a fellow inmate about his car being stuck in the mud and that he would not be in jail but for that mishap. The other prisoner, hoping to work a deal for a lighter sentence, told this story to the sheriff.

During the investigation of the crime scene, one of the law enforcement agents noticed that there was a large field of mature corn (maize, *Zea mays*) growing between the dirt road, where the stolen car had been abandoned in the mud, and the nearby highway leading to the next town. The investigator wondered if traces of torn maize leaves on the suspect's clothing might link him to the crime scene. Fortunately, the drifter's shirt and pants had been removed and stored in sterile paper bags when he was arrested. As with all prisoners in that region, he had been given a pair of orange overalls to wear while in jail.

The shirt and pants were sent to a botanist who was asked to search for traces of maize leaves on the

[1] V. M. Bryant and G. D. Jones, "Forensic Palynology: Current Status of a Rarely Used Technique in the United States of America," *Forensic Science International*, vol. 163, 2006, pp. 183–197.

(continued)

> >

Forensic Palynology—Pollen and Spores as Evidence (continued)

clothing. The botanist was also a palynologist, and thus also collected samples and searched for traces of pollen. The pollen samples provided the best results. The samples collected from the suspect's shirt revealed that the neck and shoulder region of the shirt had high concentrations of fresh maize pollen. The forensic sample collected from the pants also contained maize pollen, but in a lower percentage.

The forensic pollen data indicated that the drifter had recently walked through a maize field similar to the one between the abandoned car and the highway. As he walked through the field, he had brushed against blooming male tassels on the corn plants that were about head high. This accounted for the high amount of maize pollen found on the shoulder and neck area of the shirt. Lesser amounts of maize pollen also fell on his pants as he walked through the field. While the suspect awaited trial, additional evidence and several fingerprints from the victim's farm also linked him to the murder.

chapter summary

> > > > > > > > > > >

A microscope is an optical instrument that uses a lens or a combination of lenses to magnify and resolve the fine details of an object. Various types of microscopes are used to analyze forensic specimens. In the basic compound microscope, the object to be magnified is placed under the lower lens, called the objective lens, and the magnified image is viewed through the upper lens, known as the eyepiece lens. Forensic microscopy often requires side-by-side comparison of specimens. The comparison microscope consists of two independent objective lenses joined together by an optical bridge to a common eyepiece lens. When a viewer looks through the eyepiece lens of the comparison microscope, the objects under investigation are observed side-by-side in a circular field that is equally divided into two parts. Modern firearms examination began with the introduction of the comparison microscope, with its ability to give the firearms examiner a side-by-side magnified view of bullets. The stereoscopic microscope is actually two monocular compound microscopes properly spaced and aligned to present a three-dimensional image of a specimen to the viewer, who looks through both eyepiece lenses. Its large working distance makes it quite applicable for the microscopic examination of big, bulky items.

Light that is confined to a single plane of vibration is said to be plane-polarized. The examination of the interaction of plane-polarized light with matter is made possible with the polarizing microscope. Polarizing microscopy has found wide applications for the study of birefringent materials, that is, materials that have a double refraction. These refractive index data help identify minerals present in a soil sample or the identity of a manufactured fiber. The microspectrophotometer is a spectrophotometer coupled with a light microscope. The examiner studying a specimen under a microscope can simultaneously obtain the visible absorption spectrum or IR spectrum of the material being observed.

Finally, the scanning electron microscope (SEM) bombards a specimen with a beam of electrons instead of light to produce a highly magnified image from $10\times$ to $100,000\times$. The bombardment of the specimen's surface with electrons normally produces X-ray emissions that can be used to characterize elements present in the material under investigation.

review questions

1. A microscope uses a combination of _____ to magnify an image.

2. A type of image that cannot be viewed directly is called a(n) _____ image.

3. A(n) _____ microscope consists of two lenses mounted at each end of a hollow tube.

4. The lens closest to the specimen is called the _____.

5. The lens nearest the viewer's eye is called the _____.

6. The image seen through a compound microscope is (virtual, real).

7. True or False: The coarse and fine adjustments are part of the microscope's mechanical system. _____

8. A transparent specimen is viewed through a microscope using _____ light.

9. An opaque object requires _____ illumination for viewing with a microscope.

10. A(n) _____ collects light rays from the base illuminator and concentrates them on the specimen.

11. A microscope that remains in focus regardless of which objective lens is rotated into place is _____.

12. A microscope with only one eyepiece is _____; one with two eyepieces is _____.

13. Each microscope lens is inscribed with a number signifying its _____.

14. An eyepiece lens of $10\times$ used in combination with an objective lens of $20\times$ has a total magnification power of _____.

15. The ability of an objective lens to resolve details into separate images is directly proportional to its _____.

16. The size of the specimen area in view is known as the _____.

17. As magnification increases, the field of view (increases, decreases).

18. The thickness of a specimen in view is known as the _____.

19. The depth of focus (increases, decreases) with increasing magnification.

20. A side-by-side view of two specimens is best obtained with the _____ microscope.

21. True or False: A bridge is used to join two independent objective lenses into a single binocular unit to form a comparison microscope. _____

22. Two monocular compound microscopes properly spaced and aligned describe the _____ microscope.

23. True or False: The stereoscopic microscope is the least frequently used microscope in a typical crime laboratory. _____

24. The stereoscopic microscope offers a large _____ between the objective lens and the specimen.

25. Light confined to a single plane of vibration is said to be _____.

26. If a polarizer and analyzer are placed (perpendicular, parallel) to each other, no light penetrates.

27. The _____ microscope allows a viewer to detect polarized light.

28. Crystals that are _____ produce two planes of polarized light, each perpendicular to the other.

29. By using the _____, one can view a particle under a microscope while a beam of light is directed at the particle in order to obtain its absorption spectrum.

30. The _____ microscope focuses a beam of electrons on a specimen to produce an image.

31. When a beam of electrons strikes a specimen, _____ are emitted whose energies correspond to elements present in the specimen.

application and critical thinking

1. A forensic biologist must examine the outside of a small leaf and a thin slice of the leaf one cell thick. She has at her disposal a transmitted light microscope and a stereomicroscope (vertical illumination). What instrument should she use for the analysis of each object and why?

2. A trace evidence analyst places crystals of an unidentified white powder onto the stage of a polarizing microscope and observes the crystals through the eyepiece. Under correct focus, some of the crystals show bright colors while others appear very dark and hardly distinguishable. What can be concluded about the contents of the white powder?

3. Numerous red-colored fibers from a sexual assault crime scene are delivered to the crime lab along with red fibers from the suspect's clothing. What instrument should the

trace analyst use to view the fibers and obtain chemical information that could be used to compare the crime-scene and clothing samples?

4. Upon arriving at the crime scene of an attempted homicide, police officers observe a man fleeing the scene and apprehend him. He is suspected to be the shooter in the attempted homicide, and the police wish to test his hands for the presence of compounds consistent with gunshot residue. How should they proceed?

further references

Bartick, E. G., "Infrared Microscopy and Its Forensic Applications," in R. Saferstein, ed., *Forensic Science Handbook*, vol. 3, 2nd edition, Upper Saddle River, N.J.: Prentice Hall, 2010.

"Basic Concepts in Optical Microscopy," http://micro.magnet.fsu.edu/primer/anatomy/anatomy.html.

De Forest, Peter R., "Foundations of Forensic Microscopy," in R. Saferstein, ed., *Forensic Science Handbook*, vol. 1, 2nd ed. Upper Saddle River, N.J.: Prentice Hall, 2002.

Eyring, Michael B., "Visible Microscopical Spectrophotometry in the Forensic Sciences," in R. Saferstein, ed., *Forensic Science Handbook*, vol. 1, 2nd ed. Upper Saddle River, N.J.: Prentice Hall, 2002.

Palenik, S., and C. Palenik, "Microscopy and Microchemistry of Physical Evidence," in R. Saferstein, ed., *Forensic Science Handbook*, vol. 2, 2nd ed. Upper Saddle River, N.J.: Prentice Hall, 2005.

Petraco, N., and T. Kubic, *Basic Concepts in Optical Microscopy for Criminalists, Chemists, and Conservators*. Boca Raton, Fla.: Taylor & Francis, 2004.

Stoney, D. A., and P. M. Dougherty, "The Microscope in Forensic Science," in S. M. Gerber and R. Saferstein, eds., *More Chemistry and Crime*. Washington, D.C.: American Chemical Society, 1997.

case analysis

In the 1930s, the Lindbergh kidnapping case became the latest "trial of the century," marked by sensationalism and continuous media coverage. The key piece of evidence was a homemade ladder left at the scene by the kidnapper. Forensic investigation of the ladder by Arthur Koehler, a wood technologist with the U.S. Forest Products Laboratory, eventually tied the accused kidnapper, Bruno Hauptmann, to the ladder and helped secure his conviction for the crime.

1. What aspects of the ladder rail did Koehler note that helped him determine the source of the wood used to make it? How did Koehler interpret each of these pieces of information to arrive at his conclusions?

2. How did Koehler determine that a belt-driven planer had been used to finish the wood? How did this information help pinpoint the location where the wood was purchased?

3. The wood used to make the rails was very common and used widely throughout the United States. Why did Koehler believe it was milled in the same general area where the kidnapping occurred? How did this information help the investigation?

4. What additional discoveries allowed Koehler to link the wood used in the ladder to Bruno Hauptmann?

Microscopic Trace Evidence— The Overlooked Clue

Arthur Koehler—Wood Detective

Skip Palenik
Walter C. McCrone Associates Inc.

. . . Arthur Koehler . . . wood technologist and chief of the division of silvicultural relations at the U.S. Forest Products Laboratory in Madison, Wisconsin, . . . was born on June 4, 1885, in Mishicot, Wisconsin. His father was a carpenter and young Koehler grew up on a farm with a love of both wood and fine tools. This love naturally led him into forestry and he received a B.S. degree in the subject from the University of Michigan in 1911. . . . Upon graduation he went to work for the U.S. Forest Service in Washington, D.C., and three years later obtained a post at the U.S. Forest Products Laboratory where he served in various capacities until his retirement.

Although his primary responsibilities lay in wood identification and the correlation of microscopic wood structure and end use, Koehler also began to build a reputation as a wood detective after his success in obtaining evidence from wood fragments which were submitted to the laboratory in several cases of local importance. . . . The case which thrust Koehler into the limelight of international publicity, however, was the Lindbergh kidnapping case in which he, by the most painstaking work, traced the kidnap ladder back to the lumberyard from which its constituent parts had been purchased.

Sometime between the hours of 8 and 10 P.M. on the night of March 1, 1932, a kidnapper climbed into the nursery of the newly completed home of Charles and Anne Lindbergh in Hopewell, New Jersey, and abducted their infant son. The only clues left behind were a few indistinct muddy footprints, a ransom note in the nursery, a homemade ladder and a chisel found a short distance from the house. Scarcely two months later, on May 12, the dead body of the child was found, half buried in the woods, about a mile from the Lindbergh home. One of the most intensive manhunts in U.S. history ensued, but failed to uncover any trace of the kidnapper or the ransom money which had been paid.[1]

Shortly after the news of the kidnapping broke in the press Koehler wrote a letter to Colonel Lindbergh offering his services to help with the investigation of the ladder. He never received a reply (which was not surprising considering the flood of mail which arrived at the Lindbergh home in the weeks following the kidnapping). He was not entirely surprised though when his boss, Carlyle P. Winslow, placed before him some slivers of the ladder with the request that the wood be accurately identified.[2] This Koehler did, noting in his report the presence of golden brown, white and black wool fibers which he speculated might be from clothing worn by the kidnapper. That was the last he heard about the ladder for almost a year. During this time it was carried around the country (carefully wrapped in a wool blanket) to various experts including specialists at the National Bureau of Standards.[3] However, after a year of investigation the authorities were no closer to arresting a suspect than they were the day after the crime.

It was almost a year after the kidnapping when Koehler was asked by the head of the U.S. Forest Service, Major Robert Y. Stuart, to travel to Trenton to give the ladder an in-depth examination. Discussions between Colonel Norman Schwarzkopf, who headed the New Jersey State Police (and the kidnap investigation), and Major Stuart had convinced Colonel Schwarzkopf that the ladder might still yield clues about its maker if Koehler were given a chance to examine it thoroughly. Schwarzkopf wasn't too certain about Koehler's ability ("Wasn't he the one who identified the blanket fibers on the wood we sent him?" he asked) but felt he had nothing to lose.

For the first time, Koehler saw the ladder (Figure 1). He was immediately struck by the fact that, although it was cleverly contrived, it was shamefully constructed. Instead of rungs it had cleats, which had been carelessly mortised with a dull chisel. A dull hand plane had been used needlessly in some places and a handsaw had been drawn carelessly across some of the boards.

[1] Waller, George. *Kidnap: The Story of the Lindbergh Case*. Dial Press, New York, 1961.
[2] Koehler, Arthur. "Who Made That Ladder?" as told to Boyden Sparkes. *The Saturday Evening Post*, 297, p. 10, April 20, 1935.
[3] Saylor, Charles Proffer. "Optical Microscopy as Used in Unorthodox Ways," *SPIE*, 104, Multi-disciplinary Microscopy, 31–33, 1977.

FIGURE 1

The ladder used in the kidnapping of the Lindbergh baby.

Alone for four days, Koehler studied the ladder in the police training school in Wilburtha. He then returned to the Forest Products Laboratory with the ladder and closed himself up in a private laboratory with the best optical equipment available.[4] He began by completely dissecting the ladder into its component parts. Each piece was numbered. The cleats were labeled 1 (bottom) through 11 (top). The rails were numbered starting from 12 (bottom left) to 17 (right-hand top). . . . Each mark was noted and indexed. After probing with microscopes, calipers and a variety of lighting and photographic techniques, the ladder slowly began to give up its secrets.

The sheer number of observations, facts and deductions about the origin of the ladder (and its producer) made by Koehler are truly staggering. We are concerned here only with those facts and observations which (1) allowed the parts to be traced and (2) described the carpenter and the previous environment of the ladder. The results were presented not as the subject of a single report but of daily letters to the director of the laboratory. As certain aspects were revealed they were pursued until the object could be traced no further. The most pertinent observations and deductions are listed and described below.

1. Microscopical examination showed four types of wood were used (Table 1). North Carolina pine is a trade name for wood from the southern yellow pine group which grows in commercial stands in the Southern U.S. along the Gulf of Mexico and along the Eastern Seaboard up into New Jersey and southern New York.[5] Douglas fir and ponderosa pine grow in the Western U.S. and birch is found throughout the country.[6]

2. Rails 12 and 13 showed faint marks which gave information about the planer in the mill where the wood was dressed. . . .

TABLE 1

Woods Used in Kidnap Ladder

Cleats	
1–10	Ponderosa pine. 1 × 6-inch boards ripped lengthwise into strips 2¾ inches wide to make cleats.
11	Douglas fir. Grain matched bottom of rail 15.

Side Rails	
12, 13	North Carolina pine. Second growth. Cut from one board originally 14 feet long. Dressed to 3¾ inches in width. Both dressed on same planer.
14, 15	Douglas fir. Dressed on two different planers.
16	North Carolina pine. Narrowed from a wider board as indicated by handsaw and hand-planer marks on edges.
17	Douglas fir. Dressed on different planers than 14 and 15.

Dowel Pins	
	Birch

Figure 2 shows the operation of a mill planer in diagrammatic form. Defects in the cutters allowed the number of knives in the cutters to be determined by counting cutter marks between defect marks. Eight cutter heads dressed the wide surface and six heads the edges. . . .

The lumber went through the planer at a rate of 0.93 inches per complete revolution of the top and bottom cutter heads and 0.86 inches per revolution of the cutter heads that dressed the edges. This was determined by the distance of identical cuts made by a defective knife on each surface. . . .[7] Using the fact that the cutters in mill planers are usually driven at 3600 revolutions per minute it was possible to calculate the speed at which the wood passed into the planer as 258 feet per minute for the edge and 279 feet per minute for the board surfaces. The difference in the speed of the horizontal and vertical heads indicated that the planer was belt driven.

FIGURE 2

Detail of a cutter head illustrating how a defect allowed the number of knives to be determined.

[4] Koehler, Arthur. *The Saturday Evening Post*, 297, p. 84, April 20, 1935.

[5] Isenberg, Irving. *Pulpwoods of the United States and Canada*. Institute of Paper Chemistry, Appleton, Wisc., pp. 19–22, 1951.

[6] Christensen, Donna. *Wood Technology and the Lindbergh Kidnap Case*. Report, May 1971.

[7] Koehler, Arthur. "Techniques Used in Tracing the Lindbergh Kidnapping Ladder," *Am. J. Police Science*, 27, 5 (1937).

3. Rail 16 had four nail holes made by old fashioned square cut 8-penny nails. The holes had no connection with the construction of the ladder and therefore indicated prior use. The nail holes were clean and free from rust indicating inside use. This was confirmed by the general appearance of the rail which, although sapwood, showed no sign of exposure to the weather for any length of time since it was bright and unchecked. Therefore, it must have been nailed down indoors. Since it was low-grade lumber it would not have been used for finish purposes, but for rough construction. The spacing of the nails at 16 and 32 inches was considered significant and the suggestion was made that the rail came from the interior of a barn, garage or attic.

After an initial, futile attempt to trace the birch dowels, Koehler set out to try and trace the North Carolina rails (numbers 12 and 13). Although North Carolina pine grew in a large region it would not be profitable to ship it far, and since the ladder had turned up in New Jersey he felt certain that it had been milled somewhere in the Atlantic States. Using the Southern Lumberman's Directory, a list of 1598 planing mills from Alabama to New York was compiled. A confidential letter from Colonel Schwarzkopf and a two-page description written by Koehler were sent off to all of the mills on the list.

Of all the letters sent, only 25 mills reported having planers which matched the specifications outlined in the letter. Two were immediately excluded since they didn't dress lumber of the requisite size. Samples of 1- × 4-inch wood were requested from each of the remaining 23 mills. A sample received from the M. G. and J. J. Dorn mill of McCormick, South Carolina, showed exactly the marks Koehler was looking for.

A visit to the mill showed that the particular spacing was due to a pulley which had been purchased in September of 1929. The records of the mill showed that forty-six carloads of 1×4 had been shipped north of the Potomac River in the time between the purchases of the pulley and the kidnapping. . . . After personally visiting the final destination of each of the shipments, Koehler and Detective Bornmann finally arrived at a Bronx firm, the National Lumber and Millwork Company. Although the entire shipment had long before been sold, the foreman remembered that some storage bins had been built from some of the wood. The wood matched that from the ladder perfectly (Figures 3 and 4). Examination of wood from shipments before and after the Bronx

FIGURE 3

Comparison of knife marks from mill planer on edges of 1- × 4-inch pine from two shipments from the Dorn mill and a ladder rail.

FIGURE 4

Comparison of knife marks on upper surface of ladder rail and North Carolina pine board located in shipment to the National Lumber and Millwork Company.

carload showed that the belt on the planer had been changed and the knife sharpened. This meant that this shipment was the only one from which the two particular rails from the attic could have come. Whoever built the ladder had purchased part of the wood here!

Koehler was unprepared for the foreman's answer to his request to see the sales records. They had none. They had started selling cash and carry sometime before the Dorn shipment arrived and had no records. Although he had failed to come up with the carpenter's name, the authorities at least now knew the region where the kidnapper lived and bought his wood for the ladder.

Koehler went back to his laboratory and, undaunted, started tracing the Douglas fir rails. At the time a suspect was arrested, he had succeeded in tracing one of the boards to a mill in Bend, Oregon, and another to Spokane, Washington. With the arrest of Richard Hauptmann on September 19, 1934, . . . his role in the case changed from an investigative to a comparative one. In Hauptmann's garage a variety of tools were found whose markings could be compared with those from the ladder. Comparative micrographs of marks made with Hauptmann's plane and plane marks on the ladder showed that his plane was used to plane the cleats (Figure 5). Finally, one of the investigators searching the attic of the suspect's home found that a board had been sawed out of the floor (Figure 6).

Koehler's examination showed that the nail holes in the floor joists and the ladder rail (No. 16) aligned perfectly. A detailed analysis of the grain and wood itself showed that rail 16 and the section of board remaining in the attic were originally all one piece (Figure 7 and Figure 8).

Richard Bruno Hauptmann was convicted and sentenced to death in a sensational trial. Although, in retrospect, there may have been many errors and a good deal of prejudice in the trial itself, the professionalism and objectiveness of Arthur Koehler still stand as an example of science at its best in the service of the law. . . .

FIGURE 5

Comparison of defect marks in Hauptmann's hand-plane with marks on cleats (rungs) from the ladder.

FIGURE 6

Rail 16 fitted into its original position in Hauptmann's attic.

FIGURE 7
Composite photograph by Koehler showing comparison of end grain (growth rings) in board from attic and rail 16.

FIGURE 8
Construction by Koehler showing probable grain pattern of missing piece between attic board and rail 16.

Acknowledgment

The author gratefully acknowledges the invaluable assistance of Dr. Regis Miller and Donna Christensen of the Forest Products Laboratory in Madison, Wisconsin, for making available documents and photographs which were necessary to this article. Additional thanks are due James Gerakaris of McCrone Associates for preparing the drawings of the ladder and mill planer.

Pablo Escobar, Drug Lord

In 1989, *Forbes* magazine listed Pablo Escobar as the seventh richest man in the world. Escobar began his climb to wealth as a teenage car thief in the streets of Medellin, Colombia. He eventually moved into the cocaine-smuggling business. At the peak of his power in the mid-1980s, he was shipping as much as eleven tons of cocaine per flight in jetliners to the United States. Estimates are that the Medellin cartel controlled 80 percent of the world's cocaine market and was taking in about $25 billion annually. Escobar ruthlessly ruled by the gun: murdering, assassinating, and kidnapping. He was responsible for killing three presidential candidates in Colombia as well as the storming of the Colombian Supreme Court, which resulted in the murder of half the justices. All the while, Escobar curried favor with the Colombian general public by cultivating a Robin Hood image and distributing money to the poor. In 1991, hoping to avoid extradition to the United States, Escobar turned himself in to the Colombian government and agreed to be sent to prison. However, the prison compound could easily be mistaken for a country club. There he continued his high-flying lifestyle, trafficking by telephone and even murdering a few associates. When the Colombian government attempted to move Escobar to another jail, he escaped, again fearing extradition to the United States. Pressured by the U.S. government, Colombia organized a task force dedicated to apprehending Escobar. The manhunt for Escobar ended on December 2, 1993, when he was cornered on the roof of one of his hideouts. A shootout ensued and Escobar was fatally wounded by a bullet behind his ear.

drugs

Learning Objectives

After studying this chapter you should be able to:

- Compare and contrast psychological and physical dependence

- Name and classify the commonly abused drugs

- List and define the schedules of the Controlled Substances Act

- Describe the laboratory tests normally used to perform a routine drug identification analysis

- Explain the testing procedures used for forensic identification of marijuana

- Understand the proper collection and preservation of drug evidence

KEY TERMS

anabolic steroids
analgesic
confirmation
depressant
hallucinogen
microcrystalline tests
narcotic
physical dependence
psychological
    dependence
screening test
stimulant

A *drug* can be defined as a natural or synthetic substance that is used to produce physiological or psychological effects in humans or other higher-order animals. However, this colorless clinical definition does not really tell us what drugs are; in their modern context, drugs mean something different to each person. To some, drugs are a necessity for sustaining and prolonging life; to others, drugs provide an escape from the pressures of life; to still others, they are a means of ending it.

Considering the wide application and acceptance of drugs in our society, it was perhaps inevitable that a segment of our population would abuse them. During the 1960s, successive waves of hallucinogens, amphetamines, and barbiturates found their way out of laboratories, pharmacies, and medicine chests and into the streets. During this decade, marijuana became the most widely used illicit drug in the United States, and alcohol consumption continued to rise—today 90 million Americans drink alcohol regularly, and 10 million of these are hopelessly addicted or have severe problems in coping with their drinking habits. In the 1970s, heroin addiction emerged as a national problem, and today the United States is in the midst of an epidemic of cocaine abuse.

Drug abuse has grown from a problem generally associated with members of the lower end of the socioeconomic ladder to one that cuts across all social and ethnic classes of society. Today, approximately 23 million people in the United States use illicit drugs, including about a half million heroin addicts and nearly six million users of cocaine.

In the United States, more than 75 percent of the evidence evaluated in crime laboratories is drug related. The deluge of drug specimens has forced the expansion of existing crime laboratories and the creation of new ones. For many concerned forensic scientists, the crime laboratory's preoccupation with drug evidence represents a serious distraction from time that could be devoted to evaluating evidence related to homicides and other types of serious crimes. However, the increasing caseloads associated with drug evidence have justified the expansion of forensic laboratory services. This expansion has increased the overall analytical capabilities of crime laboratories.

Drug Dependence

In assessing the potential danger of drugs, society has become particularly conscious of their effects on human behavior. In fact, the first drugs to be regulated by law in the early years of the twentieth century were those deemed to have "habit-forming" properties. The early laws were aimed primarily at controlling opium and its derivatives, cocaine, and later marijuana. Today, it is known that the ability of a drug to induce dependence after repeated use is submerged in a complex array of physiological and social factors.

Dependence on drugs exists in numerous patterns and in all degrees of intensity, depending on the nature of the drug, the route of administration, the dose, the frequency of administration, and the individual's rate of metabolism. Furthermore, nondrug factors play an equally crucial role in determining the behavioral patterns associated with drug use. The personal characteristics of the user, his or her expectations about the drug experience, society's attitudes and possible responses, and the setting in which the drug is used are all major determinants of drug dependence.

The question of how to define and measure a drug's influence on the individual and its danger to society is difficult to assess. To this end, the nature and significance of drug dependence must be considered from two overlapping points of view: the interaction of the drug with the individual, and the drug's impact on society. It will be useful when discussing the nature of the drug experience to approach the problem from two distinctly different aspects of human behavior—**psychological dependence** and **physical dependence**.

Psychological Dependence

The common denominator that characterizes all types of repeated drug use is the creation of a psychological dependence for continued use of the drug. It is important to discard the unrealistic image that all drug users are hopeless "addicts" who are social dropouts. Most users present quite a normal appearance and remain both socially and economically integrated in the life of the community.

The reasons why some people abstain from drugs while others become moderately or heavily involved are difficult if not impossible to delineate. Psychological needs arise from numerous

psychological dependence
Conditioned use of a drug caused by underlying emotional needs

physical dependence
Physiological need for a drug that has been brought about by its regular use. Dependence is characterized by withdrawal sickness when administration of the drug is abruptly stopped

personal and social factors that stem from the individual's desire to create a sense of well-being and to escape from reality. In some cases, the individual may be seeking relief from personal problems or stressful situations, or he or she may be trying to sustain a physical and emotional state that permits an improved level of performance. Whatever the reasons, the underlying psychological needs and the desire to fulfill them create a conditioned pattern of drug abuse.

The intensity of the psychological dependence associated with a drug's use is difficult to define and largely depends on the nature of the drug used. For drugs such as alcohol, heroin, amphetamines, barbiturates, and cocaine, continued use is likely to result in a high degree of involvement. Other drugs, such as marijuana and codeine, appear to have a considerably lower potential for the development of psychological dependence. However, this does not imply that repeated abuse of drugs deemed to have a low potential for psychological dependency is safe or will always produce low psychological dependence. We have no precise way of measuring or predicting the impact of drug abuse on the individual. Even if a system could be devised for controlling the many possible variables affecting a user's response, the unpredictability of the human personality would still have to be considered; the personal inadequacies of the drug user represent the underlying motivation for drug use.

Our general knowledge of alcohol consumption should warn us of the fallacy of generalizing when attempting to describe the danger of drug abuse. Obviously, not all alcohol drinkers are psychologically addicted to the drug; most are "social" drinkers who drink in reasonable amounts and on an irregular basis. Many people have progressed beyond this stage and consider alcohol a necessary crutch for dealing with life's stresses and anxieties. However, alcohol abusers exhibit a wide range of behavioral patterns, and to a large extent the degree of psychological dependency must be determined individually. Likewise, it would be fallacious to generalize that all users of marijuana can at worst develop a low degree of dependency on the drug. A wide range of factors also influence marijuana's effect, and heavy users of the drug expose themselves to the danger of developing a high degree of psychological dependency.

Physical Dependence

Whereas emotional well-being is the primary motive leading to repeated and intensive use of a drug, certain drugs, when taken in sufficient dose and frequency, are capable of producing physiological changes that encourage their continued use. Once the user abstains from such a drug, severe physical illness follows. The desire to avoid this *withdrawal sickness* or *abstinence syndrome* ultimately causes physical dependence, or addiction. Hence, for the addict who is accustomed to receiving large doses of heroin, the thought of abstaining and encountering body chills, vomiting, stomach cramps, convulsions, insomnia, pain, and hallucinations is a powerful inducement for continued drug use.

Interestingly, some of the more widely abused drugs have little or no potential for creating physical dependence. Drugs such as marijuana, LSD, and cocaine create strong anxieties when their repeated use is discontinued; however, no medical evidence attributes these discomforts to physiological reactions that accompany withdrawal sickness. On the other hand, use of alcohol, heroin, and barbiturates can result in development of physical dependency.

Physical dependency develops only when the drug user adheres to a regular schedule of drug intake; that is, the interval between doses must be short enough so that the effects of the drug never wear off completely. For example, the interval between injections of heroin for the drug addict probably does not exceed six to eight hours. Beyond this time the addict begins to experience the uncomfortable symptoms of withdrawal. Many heroin users avoid taking the drug regularly for fear of becoming physically addicted to its use. Similarly, the risk of developing physical dependence on alcohol becomes greatest when the consumption is characterized by a continuing pattern of daily use in large quantities.

Table 8–1 categorizes some of the more commonly abused drugs according to their effect on the body and summarizes their tendency to produce psychological dependency and to induce physical dependency with repeated use.

Societal Aspects of Drug Use

The social impact of drug dependence is directly related to the extent to which the user has become preoccupied with the drug. Here, the most important element is the extent to which drug use has become interwoven in the fabric of the user's life. The more frequently the drug satisfies

TABLE 8–1

The Potential of Some Commonly Abused Drugs to Produce Dependency with Regular Use

Drug	Psychological Dependence	Physical Dependence
Narcotics		
Morphine	High	Yes
Heroin	High	Yes
Methadone	High	Yes
Codeine	Low	Yes
Depressants		
Barbiturates (short-acting)	High	Yes
Barbiturates (long-acting)	Low	Yes
Alcohol	High	Yes
Methaqualone (Quaalude)	High	Yes
Meprobamate (Miltown, Equanil)	Moderate	Yes
Diazepam (Valium)	Moderate	Yes
Chlordiazepoxide (Librium)	Moderate	Yes
Stimulants		
Amphetamines	High	?
Cocaine	High	No
Caffeine	Low	No
Nicotine	High	Yes
Hallucinogens		
Marijuana	Low	No
LSD	Low	No
Phencyclidine (PCP)	High	No

the person's need, the greater the likelihood that he or she will become preoccupied with its use, with a consequent neglect of individual and social responsibilities. Personal health, economic relationships, and family obligations may all suffer as the drug-seeking behavior increases in frequency and intensity and dominates the individual's life. The extreme of drug dependence may lead to behavior that has serious implications for the public's safety, health, and welfare.

Drug dependence in its broadest sense involves much of the world's population. As a result, a complex array of individual, social, cultural, legal, and medical factors ultimately influence society's decision to prohibit or to impose strict controls on a drug's distribution and use. Invariably, society must weigh the beneficial aspects of the drug against the ultimate harm its abuse will do to the individual and to society as a whole. Obviously, many forms of drug dependence do not carry sufficient adverse social consequences to warrant their prohibition, as illustrated by the widespread use of such drug-containing substances as tobacco and coffee. Although heavy and prolonged use of these drugs may eventually damage body organs and injure an individual's health, there is no evidence that they result in antisocial behavior, even with prolonged or excessive use. Hence, society is willing to accept widespread use of these substances.

We are certainly all aware of the disastrous failure in the United States to prohibit the use of alcohol during the 1920s and the current debate on whether marijuana should be legalized. Each of these issues emphasizes the delicate balance between individual desires and needs and society's concern with the consequences of drug abuse; moreover, this balance is continuously subject to change and reevaluation.

Types of Drugs

Narcotic Drugs

The term **narcotic** is derived from the Greek word *narkotikos*, which implies a state of lethargy or sluggishness. Pharmacologists classify narcotic drugs as substances that bring relief from pain and produce sleep. Unfortunately, "narcotic" has come to be popularly associated with any drug

narcotic

An analgesic or pain-killing substance that depresses vital body functions such as blood pressure, pulse rate, and breathing rate; regular administration of narcotics produces physical dependence that is socially unacceptable. As a consequence of this incorrect usage, many drugs are improperly called narcotics.

Furthermore, this confusion has produced legal definitions that are at variance with the pharmacological actions of many drugs. For example, until the early 1970s, most drug laws in the United States incorrectly designated marijuana as a narcotic; even now, many drug-control laws in the United States, including the federal law, classify cocaine as a narcotic drug. Pharmacologically, cocaine is actually a powerful central nervous system stimulant, possessing properties opposite to those normally associated with the depressant effects of a narcotic.

OPIATES   Medical professionals apply the term *opiate* to most of the drugs properly classified as narcotics. Narcotic drugs are **analgesics**—that is, they relieve pain by depressing the central nervous system. Regular use of a narcotic drug leads to physical dependence, with all of its dire consequences. The source of most analgesic narcotics is opium, a gummy, milky juice exuded through a cut made in the unripe pod of the poppy (*Papaver somniferum*), a plant grown mostly in parts of Asia. Opium is brownish in color and has a morphine content ranging from 4 to 21 percent.

Although morphine is readily extracted from opium, for reasons that are not totally known, most addicts prefer to use one of its derivatives, *heroin*. Heroin is made rather simply by reacting morphine with acetic anhydride or acetyl chloride (see Figure 8–1). Heroin's high solubility in water makes its street preparation for intravenous administration rather simple, for only by injection are heroin's effects almost instantaneously felt and with maximum sensitivity. To prepare the drug for injection, the addict frequently dissolves it in a small quantity of water in a spoon. The process can be speeded up by heating the spoon over a candle or several matches. The solution is then drawn into a syringe or eyedropper for injection beneath the skin. Figure 8–2 shows some of the paraphernalia typically associated with street administration of heroin. Besides being a powerful analgesic, heroin produces a "high" that is accompanied by drowsiness and a deep sense of well-being; however, the effect is short, generally lasting only three to four hours. Regular use of heroin—or any other narcotic drug—invariably leads to physical dependence, with all of its dire consequences.

The content of a typical heroin bag is an excellent example of the uncertainty attached to buying illicit drugs. For many years into the 1960s and early 1970s, the average bag contained 15 to 20 percent heroin. Currently, the average purity of heroin obtained in the illicit U.S. market is

analgesic
A drug or substance that lessens or eliminates pain

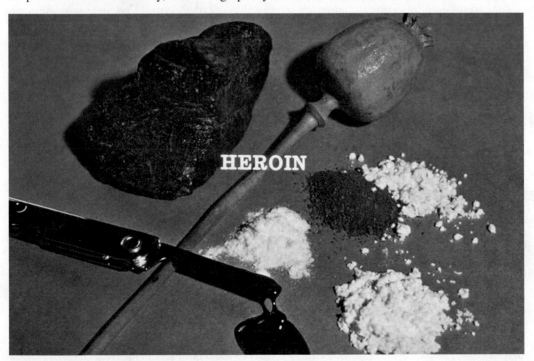

FIGURE 8–1

The opium poppy and its derivatives. Shown are the poppy plant, crude and smoking opium, codeine, heroin, and morphine.
Courtesy Pearson Education/PH College.

FIGURE 8–2

Heroin paraphernalia.
Courtesy Drug Enforcement Administration.

approximately 35 percent. The addict rarely knows or cares what comprises the other 65 percent or so of the material. Traditionally, quinine has been the most common diluent of heroin. Like heroin, it has a bitter taste and was probably originally used to obscure the actual potency of a heroin preparation for those who wished to taste-test the material before buying it. Other diluents commonly added to heroin are starch, lactose, procaine (Novocain), and mannitol.

Codeine is also present in opium, but it is usually prepared synthetically from morphine. It is commonly used as a cough suppressant in prescription cough syrup. Codeine, only one-sixth as strong as morphine, is not an attractive street drug for addicts.

SYNTHETIC OPIATES   A number of narcotic drugs are not naturally derived from opium. However, because they have similar physiological effects on the body as the opium narcotics, they are also commonly referred to as opiates.

In 1995, the U.S. Food and Drug Administration approved for use the pain-killing drug *OxyContin*. The active ingredient in OxyContin is oxycodone, a synthetic closely related to morphine and heroin in its chemical structure. OxyContin is an analgesic narcotic that has effects similar to those of heroin. It is prescribed to a million patients for treatment of chronic pain, with doctors writing close to seven million OxyContin prescriptions each year. The drug is compounded with a time-release formulation that the manufacturer initially believed would reduce the risk of abuse and addiction. This has not turned out to be the case. It is estimated that close to a quarter of a million individuals abuse the drug.

Because it is a legal drug that is diverted from legitimate sources, OxyContin is obtained differently than illegal drugs. Pharmacy robberies, forged prescriptions, and theft from patients with a legitimate prescription are ways in which abusers access OxyContin. Some abusers visit numerous doctors and receive prescriptions even though their medical condition may not warrant it.

Methadone is another well-known synthetic opiate. In the 1960s, scientists discovered that a person receiving methadone periodically in oral doses of 80 to 120 milligrams a day would not get high if he or she then took heroin or morphine. Clearly, although methadone is a narcotic pharmacologically related to heroin, its administration appears to eliminate the addict's desire for heroin while producing minimal side effects. Critics of the controversial methadone maintenance programs claim that methadone use is just substituting one narcotic drug for another, and supporters argue that this is the only known treatment for keeping the addict off heroin and offering some hope for eventual abstention from narcotics.

Physicians are increasingly prescribing methadone for pain relief. Unfortunately, in recent years, the wide availability of the drug for legitimate medical purposes has led to greater quantities

FIGURE 8–3

Several rolled marijuana cigarettes lie on a pile of crushed dried marijuana leaves next to a tobacco cigarette.
Courtesy U.S. Department of Justice, Drug Enforcement Administration.

of the drug being diverted into the illicit market. Methadone is being abused increasingly and is causing an alarming number of overdoses and deaths.

Hallucinogens

Hallucinogens are drugs that can cause marked alterations in mood, attitude, thought processes, and perceptions. Perhaps the most popular and controversial member of this class of drugs is marijuana.

MARIJUANA Marijuana easily qualifies as the most widely used illicit drug in the United States today. For instance, more than 43 million Americans have tried marijuana, according to the latest surveys, and almost half that number may be regular users. Marijuana is a preparation derived from the plant *Cannabis*. Most botanists believe there is only one species of the plant, *Cannabis sativa L*. The marijuana preparation normally consists of crushed leaves mixed in varying proportions with the plant's flower, stem, and seed. See Figure 8–3. The plant secretes a sticky resin known as *hashish*. The resinous material can also be extracted from the plant by soaking in a solvent such as alcohol. On the illicit-drug market, hashish usually appears in the form of compressed vegetation containing a high percentage of resin. See Figure 8–4. A potent form of marijuana is known as *sinsemilla*. This is made from the unfertilized flowering tops of the female *Cannabis* plants, attained by removing all male plants from the growing field at the first sign of their appearance. It follows that the production of sinsemilla requires a great deal of attention and care, and the plant is therefore cultivated on small plots.

History of Marijuana Use Marijuana and its related products have been in use legally and illegally for almost three thousand years. The first reference to the medical use of marijuana is in a pharmacy book written about 2737 B.C. by the Chinese emperor Shen Nung, who recommended it for "female weakness, gout, rheumatism, malaria, beriberi, constipation and absent-mindedness." In China, at that time and even today, the marijuana or hemp plant was also a major source of fiber for the production of rope. Marijuana's mood-altering powers probably did not receive wide attention until about 1000 B.C., when it became an integral part of Hindu culture in India. After A.D. 500, marijuana began creeping westward, and references to it began to appear in Persian and Arabian literature.

hallucinogen
A substance that induces changes in mood, attitude, thought processes, and perceptions

FIGURE 8–4

Blocks of hashish in front of leaves and flowering tops of the marijuana plant.
Courtesy James King-Holmes, Photo Researchers, Inc.

FIGURE 8–5

The marijuana leaf.
SPL\Photo Researchers, Inc.

The plant was probably brought to Europe by Napoleon's soldiers when they returned from Egypt in the early years of the 19th century. In Europe, the drug excited the interest of many physicians who foresaw its application for the treatment of a wide range of ailments. At this time, it also found some use as a painkiller and mild sedative. In later years, these applications were either forgotten or ignored.

Marijuana was first introduced into the United States around 1920. The weed was smuggled by Mexican laborers across the border into Texas. American soldiers also brought the plant in from the ports of Havana, Tampico, and Veracruz. Although its use was confined to a small segment of the population, its popularity quickly spread from the border and Gulf states into most of the major U.S. cities. By 1937, the federal government and 46 states had laws prohibiting the use or possession of marijuana. Under most of these laws, marijuana was subject to the same rigorous penalties applicable to morphine, heroin, and cocaine and was often erroneously designated a "narcotic."

Physical and Pharmacological Characteristics   Marijuana is a weed that grows wild under most climatic conditions. The plant grows to a height of 5 to 15 feet and is characterized by an odd number of leaflets on each leaf. Normally, each leaf contains five to nine leaflets, all having serrated or sawtooth edges, as shown in Figure 8–5.

In 1964, scientists isolated the chemical substance largely responsible for the hallucinogenic properties of marijuana. This substance is known as *tetrahydrocannabinol*, or THC. Its discovery has allowed researchers to measure the potency of marijuana preparations and has permitted studies related to measuring the effect of marijuana's potency on individuals. The THC content of *Cannabis* varies in different parts of the plant, generally decreasing in the following sequence: resin, flowers, and leaves. Little THC is found in the stem, roots, or seeds. The potency and resulting effect of the drug fluctuate, depending on the relative proportion of these plant parts in the marijuana mixture.

The potency of marijuana depends on its form. Marijuana in the form of loose vegetation has an average THC content of about 3–4.5 percent. The more potent sinsemilla form averages about 6–12 percent in THC content, whereas hashish preparations average about 2–8 percent. Another form of hashish is known as *liquid hashish* or *hashish oil*. Hashish in this form is normally a viscous substance, dark green with a tarry consistency. Liquid hashish is produced by efficiently extracting the THC-rich resin from the marijuana plant with an appropriate solvent. Liquid hashish typically varies between 8 and 20 percent in THC content. Because of its extraordinary potency, one drop of the material can produce a "high." Ordinarily a drop is placed on a regular cigarette or on a marijuana cigarette before smoking.

Any study that relates to marijuana's effect on humans must consider the potency of the marijuana preparation. An interesting insight into the relationship between dosage level and marijuana's pharmacological effect was presented in the first report of the National Commission of Marijuana and Drug Abuse:

> At low, usual "social" doses the user may experience an increased sense of well-being; initial restlessness and hilarity followed by a dreamy, carefree state of relaxation; alteration of sensory perceptions including expansion of space and time; and a more vivid sense of touch, sight, smell, taste and sound; a feeling of hunger, especially a craving for sweets; and subtle changes in thought formation and expression. To an unknowing observer, an individual in this state of consciousness would not appear noticeably different from his normal state.
>
> At higher, moderate doses these same reactions are intensified but the changes in the individual would still be scarcely noticeable to an observer. . . . At very high doses, psychotomimetic phenomena may be experienced. These include distortion of body image, loss of personal identity, sensory and mental illusions, fantasies and hallucinations.[1]

Effects of Use   No current evidence suggests that experimental or intermittent use causes physical or psychological harm. Marijuana does not cause physical dependency. However, the risk of harm lies instead in heavy, long-term use of the drug, particularly of the more potent preparations. Heavy users can develop a strong psychological dependence on the drug. Some effects of marijuana use

---

[1] *Marijuana—A Signal of Misunderstanding* (Washington, D.C.: U.S. Government Printing Office, 1972), p. 56.

include increased heart rate, dry mouth, reddened eyes, impaired motor skills and concentration, and frequently hunger and an increased desire for sweets. Long-term chronic marijuana use is associated with amotivational syndrome characterized by apathy; impairment of judgment, memory, and concentration; and loss of interest in personal appearance and the pursuit of conventional goals. Accumulating evidence suggests that marijuana has potential medical uses. Two promising areas of research are marijuana's reduction of excessive eye pressure in glaucoma and lessening of nausea caused by powerful anticancer drugs. Marijuana may also be useful as a muscle relaxant.

OTHER HALLUCINOGENS   A substantial number of substances of widely varying chemical compositions have become part of the drug culture because of their hallucinogenic properties. These include lysergic acid diethylamide (LSD), mescaline, phencyclidine (PCP), psilocybin, and methylenedioxymethamphetamine, also known as MDMA or Ecstasy.

LSD is synthesized from lysergic acid, a substance derived from ergot, which is a type of fungus that attacks certain grasses and grains. Its hallucinogenic effects were first described by the Swiss chemist Albert Hofmann after he accidentally ingested some of the material in his laboratory in 1943. The drug is very potent; as little as 25 micrograms is enough to start vivid visual hallucinations that can last for about 12 hours. The drug also produces marked changes in mood, leading to laughing or crying at the slightest provocation. Feelings of anxiety and tension almost always accompany LSD use. Although physical dependence does not develop with continued use, the individual user may be prone to flashbacks and psychotic reactions even after use is discontinued.

In recent years, abuse of phencyclidine, commonly called PCP, has grown to alarming proportions. Because this drug can be synthesized by rather simple chemical processes, it is manufactured surreptitiously for the illicit market in so-called clandestine laboratories (see Figure 8–6). These laboratories range from large, sophisticated operations to small labs located in a bathroom. Small-time operators normally have little or no training in chemistry and employ "cookbook" methods to synthesize the drug. Some of the more knowledgeable and experienced operators have been able to achieve clandestine production levels that approach a commercial level of operation.

Phencyclidine is often mixed with other drugs, such as LSD or amphetamine, and is sold as a powder ("angel dust"), capsule, or tablet, or as a liquid sprayed on plant leaves. The drug is smoked, ingested, or sniffed. Following oral intake of moderate doses (1–6 milligrams), the user first experiences feelings of strength and invulnerability, along with a dreamy sense of detachment. However, the user soon becomes unresponsive, confused, and agitated. Depression,

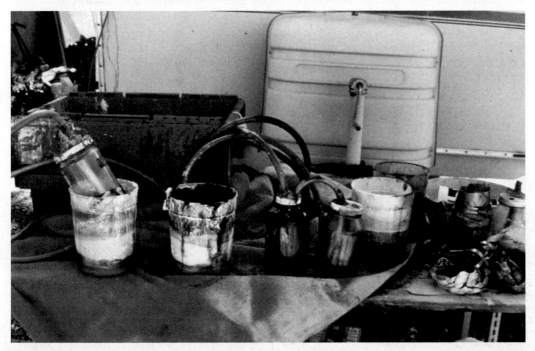

FIGURE 8–6

Scene from a clandestine drug laboratory.
Courtesy Drug Enforcement Administration.

irritability, feelings of isolation, audio and visual hallucinations, and sometimes paranoia accompany PCP use. Severe depression, tendencies toward violence, and suicide accompany long-term daily use of the drug. In some cases, the PCP user experiences sudden schizophrenic behavior days after the drug has been taken.

Depressants

depressant
A substance that depresses the functions of the central nervous system; depressants calm irritability and anxiety and may induce sleep

Depressants are drugs that slow down, or depress, the central nervous system. Several types of drugs fall under this category, including the most widely used drug in the United States—alcohol.

ALCOHOL (ETHYL ALCOHOL)   Many people overlook the fact that alcohol is a drug; its major behavioral effects derive from its depressant action on the central nervous system. In the United States, the alcohol industry annually produces more than one billion gallons of spirits, wine, and beer for which 90 million consumers pay nearly $40 billion. Unquestionably, these and other statistics support the fact that alcohol is the most widely used and abused drug.

The behavioral patterns of alcohol intoxication vary and depend in part on such factors as social setting, amount consumed, and the personal expectation of the individual with regard to alcohol. When alcohol enters the body's bloodstream, it quickly travels to the brain, where it suppresses the brain's control of thought processes and muscle coordination.

Low doses of alcohol tend to inhibit the mental processes of judgment, memory, and concentration. The drinker's personality becomes expansive, and he or she exudes confidence. When taken in moderate doses, alcohol reduces coordination substantially, inhibits orderly thought processes and speech patterns, and slows reaction times. Under these conditions, the ability to walk or drive becomes noticeably impaired. In the next chapter, we examine in greater detail the relationship between alcohol blood levels and driving ability. Higher doses of alcohol may cause the user to become highly irritable and emotional; displays of anger and crying are not uncommon. Extremely high doses may cause an individual to lapse into unconsciousness or even a comatose state that may precede a fatal depression of circulatory and respiratory functions.

BARBITURATES   Barbiturates are commonly referred to as "downers" because they relax, create a feeling of well-being, and produce sleep. Like alcohol, barbiturates suppress the vital functions of the central nervous system. Collectively, barbiturates can be described as derivatives of barbituric acid, which was first synthesized by a German chemist, Adolf von Bayer, more than a hundred years ago. Twenty-five barbiturate derivatives are currently used in medical practice in the United States; however, five—amobarbital, secobarbital, phenobarbital, pentobarbital, and butabarbital—tend to be used for most medical applications. Slang terms for "barbs" usually stem from the color of the capsule or tablet (for example, "yellow jackets," "blue devils," and "reds").

Normally, barbiturate users take these drugs orally. The average sedative dose is about 10–70 milligrams. When taken in this fashion, the drug enters the blood through the walls of the small intestine. Some barbiturates, such as phenobarbital, are absorbed more slowly than others and are therefore classified as long-acting barbiturates. Undoubtedly, the slow action of phenobarbital accounts for its low incidence of abuse. Apparently, barbiturate abusers prefer the faster-acting ones—secobarbital, pentobarbital, and amobarbital. When taken in prescribed amounts, barbiturates are relatively safe, but in instances of extensive and prolonged use, physical dependence can develop. Since the early 1970s, a nonbarbiturate depressant, methaqualone (Quaalude), has appeared on the illicit-drug scene. Methaqualone is a powerful sedative and muscle relaxant that possesses many of the depressant properties of barbiturates.

ANTIPSYCHOTICS AND ANTIANXIETY DRUGS   Although antipsychotics and antianxiety drugs can be considered depressants, they differ from barbiturates in the extent of their actions on the central nervous system. Generally, these drugs produce a relaxing tranquillity without impairing high-thinking faculties or inducing sleep. Antipsychotics such as reserpine and chlorpromazine have been used to reduce the anxieties and tensions of mental patients.

A group of antianxiety drugs is commonly prescribed to deal with the everyday tensions of many healthy people. These drugs include meprobamate (Miltown), chlordiazepoxide (Librium), diazepam (Valium), and Xanax. In the past 45 years, the use of tranquilizers has grown dramatically. Medical evidence shows that these drugs produce psychological and physical dependency with repeated and high levels of usage. For this reason, widespread prescribing of these substances as a means of overcoming the pressures and tensions of life has worried many who fear the creation of a legalized drug culture.

"HUFFING" Since the early 1960s, "huffing," the practice of sniffing materials containing volatile solvents (airplane glue or model cement, for example) has grown in popularity. Within recent years, another dimension has been added to the problem with the increasing number of incidents involving the sniffing of aerosol gas propellants such as freon. All materials used in sniffing contain volatile or gaseous substances that are primarily central nervous system depressants. Although toluene seems to be the most popular solvent to sniff, others can produce comparable physiological effects. These chemicals include naphtha, methyl ethyl ketone (antifreeze), gasoline, and trichloroethylene (dry-cleaning solvent).

The usual immediate effects of sniffing are a feeling of exhilaration and euphoria combined with slurred speech, impaired judgment, and double vision. Finally, the user may experience drowsiness and stupor, with these depressant effects slowly wearing off as the user returns to a normal state. Most experts believe that users become physiologically dependent on the effects achieved by sniffing. There is, however, little evidence to suggest that solvent inhalation is addictive. But sniffers expose themselves to the danger of liver, heart, and brain damage from the chemicals they have inhaled. Even worse, sniffing of some solvents, particularly halogenated hydrocarbons, is accompanied by a significant risk of death.

Stimulants

The term **stimulant** refers to a range of drugs that stimulate, or speed up, the central nervous system.

stimulant
A substance taken to increase alertness or activity

AMPHETAMINES Amphetamines are a group of synthetic drugs that stimulate the central nervous system. They are commonly referred to in the terminology of the drug culture as "uppers" or "speed." Ordinary therapeutic doses of 5–20 milligrams per day, taken orally, provide a feeling of well-being and increased alertness that is followed by a decrease in fatigue and a loss of appetite. However, these apparent benefits of the drug are accompanied by restlessness and instability or apprehension, and once the stimulant effect wears off, depression may set in.

In the United States, the most serious form of amphetamine abuse stems from the intravenous injection of amphetamine or its chemical derivative, methamphetamine (see Figure 8–7). The desire for a more intense amphetamine experience is the primary motive for this route of administration. The initial sensation of a "flash" or "rush," followed by an intense feeling of pleasure, constitutes the principal appeal of the intravenous route for the "speed freak." During a "speed binge," the individual may inject 500–1,000 milligrams of amphetamines every two to three hours. Users have reported experiencing a euphoria that produces hyperactivity, with a feeling of clarity of vision as well as hallucinations. As the effect of the amphetamines wears off, the individual lapses into a period of exhaustion and may sleep continuously for one or two days. Following this, the user often experiences a prolonged period of severe depression, lasting from days to weeks.

A new smokable form of methamphetamine known as "ice" is reportedly in heavy demand in some areas of the United States. Ice is prepared by slow evaporation of a methamphetamine solution to produce large, crystal-clear "rocks." Like crack cocaine (discussed next), ice is smoked and produces effects similar to those of crack cocaine, but the effects last for a longer period of time. Once the effects of ice wear off, users often become depressed and may sleep for days. Chronic users exhibit violent destructive behavior and acute psychosis similar to paranoid schizophrenia. Repeated use of amphetamines leads to a strong psychological dependency, which encourages their continued administration.

COCAINE Between 1884 and 1887, Sigmund Freud created something of a sensation in European medical circles by describing his experiments with a new drug. He reported a substance of seemingly limitless potential as a source of "exhilaration and lasting euphoria" that permitted "intensive mental or physical work [to be] performed without fatigue. . . . It is as though the need for food and sleep was completely banished."

The object of Freud's enthusiasm was cocaine, a drug stimulant extracted from the leaves of *Erythroxylon coca*, a plant grown in tropical Asia and the Andes mountains of South America

FIGURE 8–7

Granular amphetamine beside a razor blade.
Courtesy Cordelia Molloy, Photo Researchers, Inc.

coca leaves and cocaine

FIGURE 8–8

Coca leaves and illicit forms of cocaine.
Courtesy Drug Enforcement Administration.

(see Figure 8–8). At one time, cocaine had wide medical application as a local painkiller or anesthetic. However, this function has now been largely replaced by other drugs, primarily procaine and lidocaine. Cocaine is also a powerful stimulant to the central nervous system, and its effects resemble those caused by the amphetamines—namely, increased alertness and vigor, accompanied by the suppression of hunger, fatigue, and boredom. Most commonly, cocaine is sniffed or "snorted" and is absorbed into the body through the mucous membranes of the nose.

Crack   One form of cocaine that has gained widespread popularity in the drug culture is known as *crack*. The process used to make crack is simple. Ordinary cocaine is mixed with baking soda and water into a solution that is then heated in a pot. This material is then dried and broken into tiny chunks that dealers sell as crack rocks. Crack is freebase cocaine and is sufficiently volatile to be smoked, usually in glass pipes. Crack, like cocaine that is snorted, produces a feeling of euphoria by stimulating a pleasure center in the base of the brain, in an area connected to nerves that are responsible for emotions. Cocaine stimulates this pleasure center to a far greater degree than it would ever normally be stimulated. The result is euphoria—a feeling of increased energy, of being mentally more alert, of feeling really good. The faster the cocaine level rises in the brain, the greater the euphoria, and the surest way to obtain a fast rise in the brain's cocaine level is to smoke crack. Inhaling the cocaine vapor gets a large wallop of the drug to the brain in less than fifteen seconds— about as fast as injecting it and much faster than snorting it. The dark side of crack, however, is that the euphoria fades quickly as cocaine levels drop, leaving the user feeling depressed, anxious, pleasureless. The desire to return to a euphoric feeling is so intense that crack users quickly develop a habit for the drug that is almost impossible to overcome. Only a small percentage of crack abusers will ever be cured of this drug habit.

Effects of Use   In the United States, cocaine abuse is on the rise. Cocaine generates confidence and produces increased alertness, giving a false illusion that one is doing well at an assigned task. However, some regular users of cocaine report accompanying feelings of restlessness, irritability, and anxiety. Cocaine used chronically or at high doses can have toxic effects. Cocaine-related deaths are a result of cardiac arrest or seizures followed by respiratory arrest. Many people are apparently using cocaine to improve their ability to work and to keep going when tired. Although there is no evidence of physical dependency accompanying cocaine's repeated use, abstention from cocaine after prolonged use brings on severe bouts of mental depression, which produce a strong compulsion to resume using the drug. In fact, laboratory experiments with animals have demonstrated that of all the commonly abused drugs, cocaine produces the strongest psychological compulsions for continued use.

The United States spends millions of dollars annually in attempting to control cultivation of the coca leaf in various South American countries and to prevent cocaine trafficking into the United States. Three-quarters of the cocaine smuggled into the United States is refined in clandestine laboratories in Colombia. The profits are astronomical. Peruvian farmers may be paid $200 for enough coca leaves to make one pound of cocaine. The refined cocaine is worth $1,000 when it leaves Colombia and sells at retail in the United States for up to $20,000.

Club Drugs

The term *club drugs* refers to synthetic drugs that are used at nightclubs, bars, and raves (all-night dance parties). Substances that are often used as club drugs include, but are not limited to, MDMA (Ecstasy), GHB (gamma hydroxybutyrate), Rohypnol ("Roofies"), ketamine, and methamphetamine. These drugs have become popular at the dance scene to stimulate the rave experience. A high incidence of use has been found among teens and young adults.

The rave scene supports this type of drug use. Tablets can be easily hidden in various containers, such as Pez dispensers and other items not usually thought of as drug paraphernalia. The rave scene is often depicted as a room filled with people jumping and bouncing in unison for hours to loud rhythmic, trancelike music. The stimulatory effects of some of the club drugs allow for the users to be active for hours.

GHB and Rohypnol are central nervous system depressants that are often connected with drug-facilitated sexual assault, rape, and robbery. Effects accompanying the use of GHB include dizziness, sedation, headache, and nausea. Recreational users have reported euphoria, relaxation, disinhibition, and increased libido. Rohypnol causes muscle relaxation, loss of consciousness, and an inability to remember what happened during the hours after ingesting the drug. This is particularly a concern in a sexual assault because victims are physically unable to resist the attack. Unsuspecting victims become drowsy or dizzy. Effects are even stronger when the drug is combined with alcohol because the user experiences memory loss, blackouts, and disinhibition. Law enforcement agencies have warned multitudes of partygoers that drugs such as Rohypnol and GHB are odorless, colorless, and tasteless and so will remain undetected when slipped into a drink.

Methylenedioxymethamphetamine, also known as MDMA or Ecstasy, is the most popular drug at rave club scenes. Ecstasy is a synthetic, mind-altering drug that exhibits many hallucinogenic and amphetamine-like effects. Ecstasy was originally patented as an appetite suppressant and was later discovered to induce feelings of happiness and relaxation. Recreational drug users find that Ecstasy enhances self-awareness and decreases inhibitions. However, seizures, muscle breakdown, stroke, kidney failure, and cardiovascular system failure often accompany chronic use of Ecstasy. In addition, chronic use of Ecstasy leads to serious damage to the areas of the brain responsible for thought and memory. Ecstasy increases the heart rate and blood pressure; produces muscle tension, teeth grinding, and nausea; and causes psychological difficulties such as confusion, severe anxiety, and paranoia episodes. The drug can cause significant increases in body temperature from the combination of the drug's stimulant effect with the often hot, crowded atmosphere of a rave club.

Ketamine is primarily used in veterinary medicine as an animal anesthetic. When used by humans, the drug can cause euphoria and feelings of unreality accompanied by visual hallucinations. Ketamine can also cause impaired motor function, high blood pressure, amnesia, and mild respiratory depression.

Anabolic Steroids

Anabolic steroids are synthetic compounds that are chemically related to the male sex hormone testosterone. Testosterone has two different effects on the body. It promotes the development of secondary male characteristics (androgen effects), and it accelerates muscle growth (anabolic effects). Efforts to promote muscle growth and to minimize the hormone's androgenic effects have led to the synthesis of numerous anabolic steroids. However, a steroid free of the accompanying harmful side effects of an androgen drug has not yet been developed.

Incidence of steroid abuse first received widespread public attention when both amateur and professional athletes were discovered using these substances to enhance their performance (see Figure 8–9). Interestingly, current research on male athletes given anabolic steroids has generally found little or, at best, marginal evidence of enhanced strength or performance. Although the full extent of anabolic steroid abuse by the general public is not fully known, the U.S. government is sufficiently concerned to regulate the availability of these drugs to the general population and to

anabolic steroids
Steroids that promote muscle growth

FIGURE 8–9

Anabolic steroids: a vial of testosterone and a syringe. Testosterone, the male sex hormone, is sometimes abused by athletes for its protein-building (anabolic) effect.
SPL\Photo Researchers, Inc.

TABLE 8–2

Control Mechanisms of the Controlled Substances Act

Schedule	Registration	Record Keeping	Manufacturing Quotas	Distribution Restrictions	Dispensing Limits
I	Required	Separate	Yes	Order forms	Research use only
II	Required	Separate	Yes	Order forms	Rx: written; no refills
III	Required	Readily retrievable	No, but some drugs limited by schedule II quotas	Records required	Rx: written or oral; with medical authorization refills up to five times in six months
IV	Required	Readily retrievable	No, but some drugs limited by schedule II quotas	Records required	Rx: written or oral; with medical authorization refills up to five times in six months
V	Required	Readily retrievable	No, but some drugs limited by schedule II quotas	Records required	Over-the-counter (Rx drugs limited to MD's order; refills up to five times)

Source: Drug Enforcement Administration, Washington, D.C.

severely punish individuals for illegal possession and distribution of anabolic steroids. In 1991, anabolic steroids were classified as controlled dangerous substances, and the Drug Enforcement Administration was given enforcement power to prevent their illegal use and distribution.

Anabolic steroids are usually taken by individuals who are unfamiliar with the harmful medical side effects. Liver cancer and other liver malfunctions have been linked to steroid use. These drugs also cause masculinizing effects in females, infertility, and diminished sex drive in males. For teenagers, anabolic steroids result in premature halting of bone growth. Anabolic steroids can also cause unpredictable effects on mood and personality, leading to unprovoked acts of anger and destructive behavior. Depression is also a frequent side effect of anabolic steroid abuse.

Drug-Control Laws

Although the previous sections have attempted to classify drugs according to their physiological effects on the body, for practical purposes of law enforcement, the legal community requires a thorough knowledge of drug classification and definitions as they are delineated by drug laws. The medical and legal definitions or classifications of a drug often bear little resemblance. The provisions of drug laws are of particular interest to the criminalist because they may impose specific analytical requirements on drug analysis. For example, the severity of a penalty associated with the manufacture, distribution, possession, and use of a drug may depend on the weight of the drug or its concentration in a mixture. In such cases, the chemist's report must contain all information that is needed to properly charge a suspect under the provisions of the existing law.

The provisions of any drug-control law are an outgrowth of national and local law enforcement requirements and customs, as well as the result of moral and political philosophies. These factors have produced a wide spectrum of national and local drug-control laws. Although their detailed discussion is beyond the intended scope of this book, a brief description of the U.S. federal law known as the Controlled Substances Act will illustrate a legal drug classification system that has been created to prevent and control drug abuse. Many states have modeled their own drug-control laws after this act, an important step in establishing uniform drug-control laws throughout the United States.

Controlled Substances Act

The federal law establishes five schedules of classification (as outlined next) for controlled dangerous substances on the basis of a drug's potential for abuse, potential for physical and psychological dependence, and medical value. This classification system is extremely flexible in that the U.S. attorney general has the authority to add, delete, or reschedule a drug as more information

Import–Export		Security	Manufacturer/ Distributor Reports to Drug Enforcement Administration	Criminal Penalties for Individual Trafficking (First Offense)
Narcotic	Nonnarcotic			
Permit	Permit	Vault/safe	Yes	0–20 years/$1 million
Permit	Permit	Vault/safe	Yes	0–20 years/$1 million
Permit	Declaration	Secure storage area	Yes, narcotic No, nonnarcotic	0–5years/$250,000
Permit	Declaration	Secure storage area	Manufacturer only, narcotic No, nonnarcotic	0–3 years/$250,000
Permit to import; declaration to export	Declaration	Secure storage area	Manufacturer only, narcotic No, nonnarcotic	0–1 year/$100,000

becomes available. In addition, controlled dangerous substances listed in schedules I and II are subject to manufacturing quotas set by the attorney general. For example, eight billion doses of amphetamines were manufactured in the United States in 1971. In 1972, production quotas reduced amphetamine production approximately 80 percent below 1971 levels.

CONTROL MECHANISMS AND PENALTIES   The criminal penalties for unauthorized manufacture, sale, or possession of controlled dangerous substances are related to the schedules as well. The most severe penalties are associated with drugs listed in schedules I and II. For example, for drugs included in schedules I and II, a first offense is punishable by up to 20 years in prison and/or a fine of up to $1 million for an individual or up to $5 million for other than individuals. Table 8–2 summarizes the control mechanisms and penalties for each schedule of the Controlled Substances Act.

Schedule I.   Schedule I drugs are deemed to have a high potential for abuse, have no currently accepted medical use in the United States, and/or lack accepted safety for use in treatment under medical supervision. Drugs controlled under this schedule include heroin, marijuana, methaqualone, and LSD.

Schedule II.   Schedule II drugs have a high potential for abuse, a currently accepted medical use or a medical use with severe restrictions, and a potential for severe psychological or physical dependence. Schedule II drugs include opium and its derivatives not listed in schedule I; cocaine; methadone; phencyclidine (PCP); most amphetamine preparations; and most barbiturate preparations containing amobarbital, secobarbital, and pentobarbital. Dronabinol, the synthetic equivalent of the active ingredient in marijuana, has been placed in schedule II in recognition of its growing medical uses in treating glaucoma and chemotherapy patients.

Schedule III.   Schedule III drugs have less potential for abuse than those in schedules I and II, a currently accepted medical use in the United States, and a potential for low or moderate physical dependence or high psychological dependence. Schedule III controls, among other substances, all barbiturate preparations (except phenobarbital) not covered under schedule II and certain codeine preparations. Anabolic steroids were added to this schedule in 1991.

Schedule IV.   Schedule IV drugs have a low potential for abuse relative to schedule III drugs and have a current medical use in the United States; their abuse may lead to limited dependence relative to schedule III drugs. Drugs controlled in this schedule include propoxyphene (Darvon); phenobarbital; and tranquilizers such as meprobamate (Miltown), diazepam (Valium), and chlordiazepoxide (Librium).

Schedule V.   Schedule V drugs must show low abuse potential, have medical use in the United States, and have less potential for producing dependence than schedule IV drugs. Schedule V controls certain opiate drug mixtures that contain nonnarcotic medicinal ingredients.

Other Provisions of the Act

The Controlled Substances Act stipulates that an offense involving a controlled substance analog, a chemical substance substantially similar in chemical structure to a controlled substance, shall trigger penalties as if it were a controlled substance listed in schedule I. This section is designed to combat the proliferation of so-called designer drugs. *Designer drugs* are substances that are chemically related to some controlled drugs and are pharmacologically potent. These substances are manufactured by skilled individuals in clandestine laboratories, with the knowledge that their products will not be covered by the schedules of the Controlled Substances Act. For instance, fentanyl is a powerful narcotic that is commercially marketed for medical use and is also listed as a controlled dangerous substance. This drug is about 100 times as potent as morphine. Currently, a number of substances chemically related to fentanyl have been synthesized by underground chemists and sold on the street. The first such substance encountered was sold under the street name "China White." These drugs have been responsible for more than a hundred overdose deaths in California and nearly 20 deaths in western Pennsylvania. As designer drugs, such as China White, are identified and linked to drug abuse, they are placed in appropriate schedules.

The Controlled Substances Act also reflects an effort to decrease the prevalence of clandestine drug laboratories designed to manufacture controlled substances. The act regulates the manufacture and distribution of *precursors*, the chemical compounds used by clandestine drug laboratories to synthesize drugs of abuse. Targeted precursor chemicals are listed in the definition section of the Controlled Substances Act. Severe penalties are provided for a person who possesses a listed precursor chemical with the intent to manufacture a controlled substance or who possesses or distributes a listed chemical knowing, or having reasonable cause to believe, that the listed chemical will be used to manufacture a controlled substance. In addition, precursors to PCP, amphetamines, and methamphetamines are enumerated specifically in schedule II, making them subject to regulation in the same manner as other schedule II substances.

Drug Identification

One only has to look into the evidence vaults of crime laboratories to appreciate the assortment of drug specimens that confront the criminalist. The presence of a huge array of powders, tablets, capsules, vegetable matter, liquids, pipes, cigarettes, cookers, and syringes is testimony to the vitality and sophistication of the illicit-drug market. If outward appearance is not evidence enough of the difficult analytical chore facing the forensic chemist, consider the complexity of the drug preparations themselves. Usually these contain active drug ingredients of unknown origin and identity, as well as additives—for example, sugar, starch, and quinine—that dilute their potency and stretch their value on the illicit-drug market. Do not forget that illicit-drug dealers are not hampered by governmental regulations that ensure the quality and consistency of a product.

When a forensic chemist picks up a drug specimen for analysis, he or she can expect to find just about anything, so all contingencies must be prepared for. The analysis must leave no room for error because its results will have a direct bearing on the process of determining the guilt or innocence of a defendant. There is no middle ground in drug identification—either the specimen is a specific drug or it is not—and once a positive conclusion is drawn, the chemist must be prepared to support and defend the validity of the results in a court of law.

The Analytical Process

The challenge or difficulty of forensic drug identification comes in selecting analytical procedures that will ensure a specific identification of a drug. Presented with a substance of unknown origin and composition, the forensic chemist must develop a plan of action that will ultimately yield the drug's identity. This plan, or scheme of analysis, is divided into two phases.

screening test
A test that is nonspecific and preliminary in nature

SCREENING   First, faced with the prospect that the unknown substance may be any one of a thousand or more commonly encountered drugs, the analyst must employ **screening tests** to reduce these possibilities to a small and manageable number. This objective is often accomplished by subjecting the material to a series of color tests that produce characteristic colors for the more commonly encountered illicit drugs. Even if these tests produce negative results, their value lies in having excluded certain drugs from further consideration.

CONFIRMATION   Once the number of possibilities has been substantially reduced, the second phase of the analysis is devoted to pinpointing and confirming the drug's identity. In an era in which crime laboratories receive voluminous quantities of drug evidence, it is impractical to subject a drug to all of the chemical and instrumental tests available. Indeed, it is more realistic to view these techniques as a large analytical arsenal. The chemist, aided by training and experience, must choose tests that will most conveniently furnish the identity of a particular drug.

Forensic chemists often use a specific test (such as infrared spectrophotometry or mass spectrometry) to identify a drug substance to the exclusion of all other known chemical substances. A single test that identifies a substance is known as a **confirmation**. The analytical scheme sometimes consists of a series of nonspecific or presumptive tests. Each test in itself is insufficient to prove the drug's identity; however, the proper analytical scheme encompasses a combination of test results that characterize one and only one chemical substance—the drug under investigation. Furthermore, experimental evidence must confirm that the probability of any other substance responding in an identical manner to the scheme selected is so small as to be beyond any reasonable scientific certainty.

confirmation
A single test that specifically identifies a substance

QUANTITATIVE VS. QUALITATIVE DETERMINATION   Another consideration in selecting an analytical technique is the need for either a *qualitative* or a *quantitative* determination. The former relates just to the identity of the material, whereas the latter refers to the percentage combination of the components of a mixture. Hence, a qualitative identification of a powder may reveal the presence of heroin and quinine, whereas a quantitative analysis may conclude the presence of 10 percent heroin and 90 percent quinine.

Obviously, a qualitative identification must precede any attempt at quantitation, for little value is served by attempting to quantitate a material without first determining its identity. Essentially, a qualitative analysis of a material requires the determination of numerous properties using a variety of analytical techniques. On the other hand, a quantitative measurement is usually accomplished by precise measurement of a single property of the material.

Forensic chemists normally rely on several tests for a routine drug-identification scheme: color tests, microcrystalline tests, chromatography, spectrophotometry, and mass spectrometry.

Color Tests

Many drugs yield characteristic colors when brought into contact with specific chemical reagents. Not only do these tests provide a useful indicator of a drug's presence, but they are also used by investigators in the field to examine materials suspected of containing a drug (see Figure 8–10).[2] However, color tests are useful for screening purposes only and are never taken as conclusive identification of unknown drugs.

Five primary color test reagents are as follows:

1. *Marquis*   (2 percent formaldehyde in sulfuric acid). The reagent turns purple in the presence of heroin and morphine and most opium derivatives. Marquis also becomes orange-brown when mixed with amphetamines and methamphetamines.
2. *Dillie-Koppanyi*   (1 percent cobalt acetate in methanol is first added to the suspect material, followed by 5 percent isopropylamine in methanol). This is a valuable screening test for barbiturates, in whose presence the reagent turns violet-blue in color.
3. *Duquenois-Levine*   (solution A is a mixture of 2 percent vanillin and 1 percent acetaldehyde in ethyl alcohol; solution B is concentrated hydrochloric acid; solution C is chloroform). This is a valuable color test for marijuana, performed by adding solutions A, B, and C, respectively, to the suspect vegetation. A positive result is shown by a purple color in the chloroform layer.
4. *Van Urk*   (1 percent solution of p-dimethylaminobenzaldehyde in 10 percent concentrated hydrochloric acid and ethyl alcohol). The reagent turns blue-purple in the presence of LSD. However, owing to the extremely small quantities of LSD in illicit preparations, this test is difficult to conduct under field conditions.
5. *Scott Test*   (solution A is 2 percent cobalt thiocyanate dissolved in water and glycerine [1:1]; solution B is concentrated hydrochloric acid; solution C is chloroform). This is a color test for cocaine. A powder containing cocaine turns solution A blue. Upon addition of B, the blue color is transformed to a clear pink color. Upon addition of C, if cocaine is present, the blue color reappears in the chloroform layer.

---

[2] Field-color test kits for drugs can be purchased from various commercial manufacturers.

FIGURE 8–10

A field color test kit for cocaine. The suspect drug is placed in the plastic pouch. Tubes containing chemicals are broken open and the color of the chemical reaction is observed.

Courtesy Tri-Tech, Inc., Southport, N.C., www.tritechusa.com.

(a)   (b)

FIGURE 8–11

(a) A photomicrograph of a cocaine crystal formed in platinum chloride (400×).
(b) A photomicrograph of a methamphetamine crystal formed in gold chloride (400×).
Courtesy San Bernardino County Sheriff's Department.

Microcrystalline Tests

microcrystalline tests

Tests to identify specific substances by the color and morphology of the crystals formed when the substance is mixed with specific reagents

A technique considerably more specific than color tests is the **microcrystalline test**. A drop of a chemical reagent is added to a small quantity of the drug on a microscopic slide. After a short time, a chemical reaction ensues, producing a crystalline precipitate. The size and shape of the crystals, under microscope examination, are highly characteristic of the drug. Crystal tests for cocaine and methamphetamine are illustrated in Figure 8–11.

Over the years, analysts have developed hundreds of crystal tests to characterize the most commonly abused drugs. These tests are rapid and often do not require the isolation of a drug from its diluents; however, because diluents can sometimes alter or modify the shape of the crystal, the examiner must develop experience in interpreting the results of the test.

Most color and crystal tests are largely empirical—that is, scientists do not fully understand why they produce the results that they do. From the forensic chemist's point of view, this is not important. When the tests are properly chosen and are used in proper combination, their results constitute an analytical scheme that is characteristic for one and only one drug.

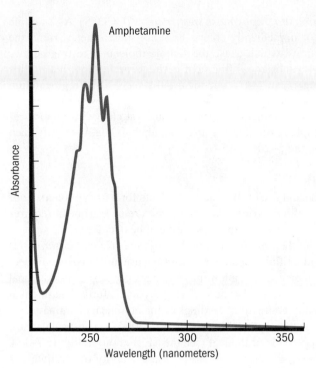

FIGURE 8–12
Ultraviolet spectrum of
amphetamine.

Chromatography

Thin-layer and gas chromatography are especially well suited to the needs of the drug analyst because they separate drugs from their diluents while providing for their tentative identification. The basic principles of these techniques have already been described in Chapter 5.

Because chromatography requires a comparison of either R_f or retention-time values between questioned and known drugs, the analyst must have some clue to the identity of the illicit material before using these techniques. Hence, in a typical drug analysis, chromatography accompanies and complements color and crystal tests.

Spectrophotometry

Selective absorption of UV and IR light by drugs provides a valuable technique for characterizing drugs. The ultraviolet spectrum is not conclusive for positive identification of a drug because other materials may produce an indistinguishable spectrum. Nevertheless, UV spectrophotometry is often a useful technique for establishing the *probable* identity of a drug. For example, if an unknown substance yields a UV spectrum that resembles that of amphetamine (see Figure 8–12), thousands of substances are immediately eliminated from consideration, and the analyst can begin to identify the material from a relatively small number of possibilities. A comprehensive collection of UV drug spectra provides a ready index that can rapidly be searched in order to tentatively identify a drug or, failing that, at least to exclude certain drugs from consideration.

Infrared spectrophotometry is one of the few analytical techniques that can specifically identify a substance. The pattern of an infrared spectrum is unique for each compound and can thus serve as a "fingerprint" of the compound. The combination of preliminary screening tests with a final verification by infrared spectrophotometry offers an ideal approach to drug identification. Unfortunately, the technique does present some problems because the substance to be identified must be as pure as possible. This requirement often necessitates lengthy purification steps to prepare the sample for IR analysis. The IR spectra of heroin and secobarbital were shown in Figure 5–19.

Mass Spectrometry

The technique of chromatography is particularly suited for analyzing illicit drugs because it can readily separate a drug from other substances that may be present in the drug preparation. Chromatography does, however, have the drawback of not being able to provide a specific identification of the material under investigation. This deficiency has been overcome by linking the gas chromatograph to a mass spectrometer (see the discussion on pages 138–140) to yield a very powerful combination known as *gas chromatography/mass spectrometry* (GC/MS). As a sample emerges from the gas chromatograph, it immediately enters the mass spectrometer. Here, the sample is exposed to high-energy electrons, which cause the sample molecules to fragment or break apart. With few exceptions, no two substances fragment in the same fashion; hence, this fragmentation pattern serves as a "fingerprint" of a chemical substance. The fragmentation patterns of heroin and cocaine were shown in Figure 5–21.

With data obtained from a GC/MS determination, a forensic analyst can, with one instrument, separate the components of a complex drug mixture and then unequivocally identify each substance present in the mixture (see Figure 5–20).

The Identification of Marijuana

Enforcement of laws prohibiting the sale and use of marijuana accounts for a high percentage of drug arrests in the United States. Any trial or hearing involving a seizure of marijuana requires identification of the material before the issue of guilt or innocence can be decided.

Unlike most other drugs received by the crime laboratory, marijuana (*Cannabis sativa L.*) possesses botanical features that impart identifiable characteristics. Because most marijuana specimens consist of small leaf fragments, their identification must be partially based on botanical features observed under the microscope by a trained expert. This approach is further augmented with a chemical test that will independently confirm the findings of the botanical examination.

The identification of marijuana by microscopic methods depends largely on observing short hairs shaped like "bear claws" on the upper side of the leaf (see the SEM photo in Figure 7–13). These hairs are known as *cystolithic hairs*. Further verification of the identity of marijuana is confirmed by the presence of longer, nonglandular hairs on the opposite side of the leaf.

The Duquenois-Levine color test, described earlier in this chapter, is a highly but not totally specific test for marijuana. However, when used in combination with a botanical examination, the results constitute a specific identification of marijuana. In addition, the analyst may be unable to obtain a microscopic identification of the marijuana leaf, as in the case of hashish or hashish oil. Here, the color test has to be supplemented by another examination, preferably thin-layer chromatography. This method involves separating chemical constituents found in the suspect resin on a thin-layer plate. The separated components are compared on the same plate to those obtained from a known marijuana extract, as shown in Figure 5–10. In this manner, a positive TLC comparison, used in conjunction with the Duquenois-Levine color test, constitutes a specific identification for marijuana.

Collection and Preservation of Drug Evidence

Preparation of drug evidence for submission to the crime laboratory is normally a relatively simple task, accomplished with minimal precautions in the field. The field investigator is responsible for ensuring that the evidence is properly packaged and labeled for delivery to the laboratory. Considering the countless forms and varieties of drug evidence seized, it is not practical to prescribe any single packaging procedure for fulfilling these requirements. Generally, common sense is the best guide in such situations, keeping in mind that the package must prevent the loss and/or cross-contamination of the contents. Often, the original container in which the drug was seized will suffice to meet these requirements. Specimens suspected of containing volatile solvents, such as those involved in glue-sniffing cases, must be packaged in an airtight container to prevent evaporation of the solvent.

All packages must be marked with sufficient information to ensure identification by the officer in future legal proceedings and to establish the chain of custody.

To aid the drug analyst, the investigator should supply any background information that may relate to a drug's identity. Analysis time can be markedly reduced when this information is at the disposal of the chemist. For the same reason, the results of drug-screening tests used in the field must also be transmitted to the laboratory. Although these tests may indicate the presence of a drug and may help the officer establish probable cause to search and arrest a suspect, they do *not* offer conclusive evidence of a drug's identity.

Virtual Forensics Lab

Drug Identification
To perform a virtual drug identification lab, go to www.pearsoncustom.com/us/vlm/.

chapter summary   > > > > > > > > > > >

A drug can be defined as a natural or synthetic substance that is used to produce physiological or psychological effects in humans or other higher-order animals.

Narcotic drugs are analgesics, meaning they relieve pain by depressing the central nervous system. Regular use of a narcotic drug leads to physical dependence. The most common source of narcotic drugs is opium. Morphine is readily extracted from opium and is used to synthesize heroin. Opiates, which include methadone and OxyContin (oxycodone), are not derived from opium or morphine, but they have the same physiological effects on the body as do opium narcotics. Another class of drugs is hallucinogens; marijuana is the most well-known member of this class. Hallucinogens cause marked changes in mood, attitude, thought processes, and perceptions. Marijuana is the most controversial drug in this class because its long-term effects on health are still largely unknown. Other hallucinogens include LSD, mescaline, PCP, psilocybin, and MDMA (Ecstasy).

Depressants are another class of drugs. These include alcohol (ethanol), barbiturates, tranquilizers, and various substances that can be sniffed, such as airplane glue and model cement. Stimulants include amphetamines, sometimes known as "uppers" or "speed," and cocaine, which in its freebase form is known as *crack*. The term *club drugs* refers to synthetic drugs that are used at nightclubs, bars, and raves (all-night dance parties). Substances that are often used as club drugs include, but are not limited to, MDMA (Ecstasy), GHB (gamma hydroxybutyrate), Rohypnol ("Roofies"), ketamine, and methamphetamine. Yet another category of drugs is anabolic steroids, which are synthetic compounds that are chemically related to the male sex hormone testosterone. Anabolic steroids are often abused by individuals who want to accelerate muscle growth. Federal law establishes five schedules of classification for controlled dangerous substances on the basis of a drug's potential for abuse, potential for physical and psychological dependence, and medical value.

Faced with the prospect that the unknown substance may be any one of a thousand or more commonly encountered drugs, the analyst must employ screening tests to reduce these possibilities to a small and manageable number. This objective is often accomplished by subjecting the material to a series of color tests that produce characteristic colors for the more commonly encountered illicit drugs. Once this preliminary analysis is completed, a confirmation is pursued. Forensic chemists use a specific test to identify a drug substance to the exclusion of all other known chemical substances. Typically infrared spectrophotometry or mass spectrometry is used to specifically identify a drug substance.

review questions

1. True or False: Underlying emotional factors are the primary motives leading to the repeated use of a drug. _____

2. Drugs such as alcohol, heroin, amphetamines, barbiturates, and cocaine can lead to a (high, low) degree of psychological dependence with repeated use.

3. The development of (psychological, physical) dependence on a drug is shown by withdrawal symptoms such as convulsions when the user stops taking the drug.

4. True or False: Abuse of barbiturates can lead to physical dependency. _____

5. True or False: Repeated use of LSD leads to physical dependency. _____

6. Physical dependency develops only when the drug user adheres to a(n) _____ schedule of drug intake.

7. Narcotic drugs are _____ that _____ the central nervous system.

8. _____ is a gummy, milky juice exuded through a cut made in the unripe pod of the opium poppy.

9. The primary constituent of opium is _____.

10. _____ is a chemical derivative of morphine made by reacting morphine with acetic anhydride.

11. A legally manufactured drug that is chemically related to heroin and heavily abused is _____.

12. True or False: Methadone is classified as a narcotic drug, even though it is not derived from opium or morphine. _____

13. Drugs that cause marked alterations in mood, attitude, thought processes, and perceptions, are called _____.

14. _____ is the sticky resin extracted from the marijuana plant.

15. The active ingredient of marijuana largely responsible for its hallucinogenic properties is _____.

16. True or False: The potency of a marijuana preparation depends on the proportion of the various plant parts in the mixture. _____

17. The marijuana preparation with the highest THC content is _____.

18. LSD is a chemical derivative of _____, a chemical obtained from the ergot fungus that grows on certain grasses and grains.

19. The drug phencyclidine is often manufactured for the illicit-drug market in _____ laboratories.

20. Alcohol (stimulates, depresses) the central nervous system.

21. _____ are called "downers" because they depress the central nervous system.

22. Phenobarbital is an example of a (short-, long-) acting barbiturate.

23. _____ is a powerful sedative and muscle relaxant that possesses many of the depressant properties of barbiturates.

24. _____ are drugs used to relieve anxiety and tension without inducing sleep.

25. True or False: Glue sniffing stimulates the central nervous system. _____

26. _____ are a group of synthetic drugs that stimulate the central nervous system.

27. The most severe form of amphetamine abuse stems from its (oral, intravenous) administration.

28. An increasing percentage of amphetamines available on the illicit-drug market originate from _____ drug laboratories.

29. _____ is extracted from the leaf of the coca plant.

30. Traditionally, cocaine is _____ into the nostrils.

31. True or False: Cocaine is a powerful central nervous system depressant. _____

32. The two drugs usually associated with drug-facilitated sexual assaults are _____ and _____.

33. _____ steroids are designed to promote muscle growth but have harmful side effects.

34. The federal drug-control law is known as _____.

35. Federal law establishes _____ schedules of classification for the control of dangerous drugs.

36. Drugs that have no accepted medical use are placed in schedule _____.

37. Librium and Valium are listed in schedule _____.

38. True or False: Color tests are used to identify drugs conclusively. _____

39. The _____ color test reagent turns purple in the presence of heroin.

40. The _____ color test reagent turns orange-brown in the presence of amphetamines.

41. The Duquenois-Levine test is a valuable color test for _____.

42. The _____ test is a widely used color test for cocaine.

43. _____ tests tentatively identify drugs by the size and shape of crystals formed when the drug is mixed with specific reagents.

44. A(n) _____ provides a means of separating drugs from their diluents while making a tentative identification.

45. The pattern of a(n) _____ absorption spectrum is unique for each drug and thus is a specific test for identification.

46. The gas chromatograph, in combination with the _____, can separate the components of a drug mixture and then unequivocally identify each substance present in the mixture.

47. Microscopic identification of marijuana largely depends on observing short hairs on the leaf known as _____ hairs.

48. All packages containing drugs must be marked for identification by the police officer before being sent to the laboratory in order to maintain the _____.

application and critical thinking

1. An individual who has been using a drug for an extended period of time suddenly finds himself unable to secure more of the drug. He acts nervous and irritable and is hyperactive. He seems almost desperate to find more of the drug, but experiences no sickness, pain, or other outward physical discomfort. Based on his behavior, what drugs might he possibly have been using? Explain your answer.

2. Following are descriptions of behavior that are characteristic among users of certain classes of drugs. For each description, indicate the class of drug (narcotics, stimulants, and so on) for which the behavior is most characteristic. For each description, also name at least one drug that produces the described effects.

   a. Slurred speech, slow reaction time, impaired judgment, reduced coordination

   b. Intense emotional responses, anxiety, altered sensory perceptions

   c. Alertness, feelings of strength and confidence, rapid speech and movement, decreased appetite

   d. Drowsiness, intense feeling of well-being, relief from pain

3. Following are descriptions of four hypothetical drugs. According to the Controlled Substances Act, under which drug schedule would each substance be classified?

a. This drug has a high potential for psychological dependence, it currently has accepted medical uses in the United States, and the distributor is not required to report to the U.S. Drug Enforcement Administration.

b. This drug has medical use in the United States, is not limited by manufacturing quotas, and may be exported without a permit.

c. This drug must be stored in a vault or safe, requires separate record keeping, and may be distributed with a prescription.

d. This drug may not be imported or exported without a permit, is subject to manufacturing quotas, and currently has no medical use in the United States.

4. A police officer stops a motorist who is driving erratically and notices a bag of white powder on the front seat of the car that he suspects contains heroin. The officer brings the bag to you, a forensic scientist in the local crime lab. Name one screening test that you might perform to determine the presence of heroin. Assuming the powder tests positive for heroin, what should you do next?

further references

Bono, J. P., "Criminalistics—Introduction to Controlled Substances," in S. B. Karch, ed., *Drug Abuse Handbook*, 2nd ed. Boca Raton, Fla.: Taylor & Francis, 2007.

Christian, D. R., Jr., "Analysis of Controlled Substances," in S. H. James and J. J. Nordby, eds., *Forensic Science: An Introduction to Scientific and Investigative Techniques*, 3rd ed. Boca Raton, Fla.: Taylor & Francis, 2009.

Siegel, J. A., "Forensic Identification of Controlled Substances," in R. Saferstein, ed., *Forensic Science Handbook*, vol. 2, 2nd ed. Upper Saddle River, N.J.: Prentice Hall, 2005.

Smith, F., and J. A. Siegel, eds., *Handbook of Forensic Drug Analysis*. Boca Raton, Fla.: Taylor & Francis, 2005.

Harold Shipman, Dr. Death

Kathleen Grundy's sudden death in 1998 was shocking news to her daughter, Angela Woodruff. Mrs. Grundy, an 81-year-old widow, was believed to be in good health when her physician, Dr. Harold Shipman, visited her a few hours before her demise. Some hours later, when friends came to her home to check on her whereabouts, they found Mrs. Grundy lying on a sofa fully dressed and dead. Dr. Shipman pronounced her dead and informed her daughter that an autopsy was not necessary. A few days later, Mrs. Woodruff was surprised to learn that a will had surfaced leaving all of Mrs. Grundy's money to Dr. Shipman. The will was immediately recognized as a forgery and led to the exhumation of Mrs. Grundy's body. A toxicological analysis of the remains revealed a lethal quantity of morphine. In retrospect, there was good reason to suspect that Dr. Shipman was capable of foul play. In the 1970s, he was asked to leave a medical practice because of a drug abuse problem and charges that he obtained drugs by forgery and deception. However, Dr. Shipman was quickly back to practicing medicine. By 1998, local undertakers became suspicious at the number of his patients who were dying. What is more, they all seemed to be elderly women who were found sitting in a chair or lying fully clothed on a bed. As police investigated, the horror of Dr. Shipman's deeds became apparent. One clinical audit estimated that Dr. Shipman killed at least 236 of his patients over a 24-year period. Most of the deaths were attributed to fatal doses of heroin or morphine. Toxicological analysis on seven exhumed bodies clearly showed significant quantities of morphine. Convicted of murder, Dr. Shipman hanged himself in his jail cell in 2004.

forensic toxicology

KEY TERMS

absorption
acid
alveoli
anticoagulant
artery
base
capillary
excretion
fuel cell detector
metabolize
oxidation
pH scale
preservative
vein

Learning Objectives

After studying this chapter you should be able to:

- Explain how alcohol is absorbed into the bloodstream, transported throughout the body, and eliminated by oxidation and excretion

- Understand the process by which alcohol is excreted in the breath via the lungs

- Understand the concepts of infrared and fuel cell breath-testing devices for alcohol testing

- Describe commonly employed field sobriety tests to assess alcohol impairment

- List and contrast laboratory procedures for measuring the concentration of alcohol in the blood

- Relate the precautions to be taken to properly preserve blood in order to analyze its alcohol content

- Understand the significance of implied-consent laws and the *Schmerber* v. *California* case to traffic enforcement

- Describe techniques that forensic toxicologists use to isolate and identify drugs and poisons

- Appreciate the significance of finding a drug in human tissues and organs to assessing impairment

- Understand the drug recognition expert program and how to coordinate it with a forensic toxicology result

It is no secret that in spite of the concerted efforts of law enforcement agencies to prevent distribution and sale of illicit drugs, thousands die every year from intentional or unintentional administration of drugs, and many more innocent lives are lost as a result of the erratic and frequently uncontrollable behavior of individuals under the influence of drugs. But one should not automatically attribute these occurrences to the wide proliferation of illicit-drug markets. For example, in the United States alone, drug manufacturers produce enough sedatives and antidepressants each year to provide every man, woman, and child with about 40 pills. All of the statistical and medical evidence shows ethyl alcohol, a legal over-the-counter drug, to be the most heavily abused drug in Western countries.

Because the uncontrolled use of drugs has become a worldwide problem affecting all segments of society, the role of the toxicologist has taken on new and added significance. Toxicologists detect and identify drugs and poisons in body fluids, tissues, and organs. Their services are required not only in such legal institutions as crime laboratories and medical examiners' offices; they also reach into hospital laboratories—where the possibility of identifying a drug overdose may represent the difference between life and death—and into various health facilities responsible for monitoring the intake of drugs and other toxic substances. Primary examples include performing blood tests on children exposed to leaded paints or analyzing the urine of addicts enrolled in methadone maintenance programs.

The role of the forensic toxicologist is limited to matters that pertain to violations of criminal law. However, the responsibility for performing toxicological services in a criminal justice system varies considerably throughout the United States. In systems with a crime laboratory independent of the medical examiner, this responsibility may reside with one or the other or may be shared by both. Some systems, however, take advantage of the expertise residing in governmental health department laboratories and assign this role to them. Nevertheless, whatever facility handles this work, its caseload will reflect the prevailing popularity of the drugs that are abused in the community. In most cases, this means that the forensic toxicologist handles numerous requests relating to the determination of the presence of alcohol in the body.

All of the statistical and medical evidence shows that ethyl alcohol—a legal, over-the-counter substance—is the most heavily abused drug in Western countries. Forty percent of all traffic deaths in the United States, nearly 17,500 fatalities per year, are alcohol related, along with more than 2 million injuries each year requiring hospital treatment. This highway death toll, as well as the untold damage to life, limb, and property, shows the dangerous consequences of alcohol abuse. Because of the prevalence of alcohol in the toxicologist's work, we will begin by taking a closer look at how the body processes and responds to alcohol.

The Fate of Alcohol in the Body

The subject of the analysis of alcohol immediately confronts us with the primary objective of forensic toxicology—the detection and isolation of drugs in the body to determine their influence on human behavior. In the case of alcohol, however, the problem is further complicated by practical considerations. The predominant role of the automobile in our society has mandated the imposition of laws to protect the public from the drinking driver. This has meant that toxicologists have had to devise rapid and specific procedures for measuring the degree of alcohol intoxication. The methods used must be suitably designed to test hundreds of thousands of motorists annually without causing them undue physical harm or unreasonable inconvenience, while at the same time providing a reliable diagnosis that can be supported and defended within the framework of the legal system.

Measuring Intoxication

Alcohol, or ethyl alcohol, is a colorless liquid normally diluted with water and consumed as a beverage. Logically, the most obvious measure of intoxication would be the amount of liquor a person has consumed. Unfortunately, most arrests are made after the fact, when such information is not available to legal authorities; furthermore, even if these data could be collected, numerous related factors, such as body weight and the rate of alcohol's **absorption** into the body, are so variable that it would be impossible to prescribe uniform standards that would yield reliable alcohol intoxication levels.

Like any other depressant, alcohol primarily affects the central nervous system, particularly the brain. The extent of the depression is proportional to the concentration of alcohol within the nerve

absorption
Passage of alcohol across the wall of the stomach and small intestine into the bloodstream

cells. The nerve functions most susceptible to alcohol are found in the surface areas of the forebrain. Later, as the person absorbs alcohol to a greater extent, the functions of the central and rear portions of the brain are affected. The nerve functions that are most resistant, and the last to fail, are centered in the brain's medulla, which regulates such vital functions as respiration and heart activity.

Theoretically, for a true determination of the quantity of alcohol impairing an individual's normal body functions, it would be best to remove a portion of brain tissue and analyze it for alcohol content. For obvious reasons, this cannot be done on living subjects. Consequently toxicologists concentrate on the blood, which provides the medium for circulating alcohol throughout the body, carrying it to all tissues, including the brain. Fortunately, experimental evidence supports this approach and shows blood-alcohol concentration to be directly proportional to the concentration of alcohol in the brain. From the medicolegal point of view, blood-alcohol levels have become the accepted standard for relating alcohol intake to its effect on the body.

Absorption and Distribution

Alcohol appears in the blood within minutes after it has been consumed and slowly increases in concentration while it is being absorbed from the stomach and the small intestine into the bloodstream. When all the alcohol has been absorbed, a maximum alcohol level is reached in the blood, and the postabsorption period begins. Then the alcohol concentration slowly decreases until a zero level is again reached.

Many factors determine the rate at which alcohol is absorbed into the bloodstream, including the total time taken to consume the drink, the alcohol content of the beverage, the amount consumed, and the quantity and type of food present in the stomach at the time of drinking. With so many variables, it is difficult to predict just how long the absorption process will require. For example, beer is absorbed more slowly than an equivalent concentration of alcohol in water, apparently because of the carbohydrates present in beer. Also, alcohol consumed on an empty stomach is absorbed faster than an equivalent amount of alcohol taken when there is food in the stomach. The longer the total time required for complete absorption to occur, the lower the peak alcohol concentration in the blood (see Figure 9–1). Depending on a combination of factors, maximum blood-alcohol concentration may not be reached until two or three hours have elapsed from the time of consumption. However, under normal social drinking conditions, it takes anywhere from 30 to 90 minutes from the time of the final drink until the absorption process is completed.

During the absorption phase, alcohol slowly enters the body's bloodstream and is carried to all parts of the body. When the absorption period is completed, the alcohol becomes distributed

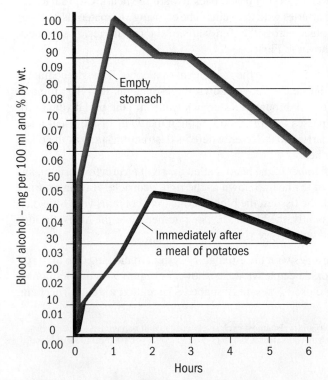

FIGURE 9–1

Blood-alcohol concentrations after ingestion of 2 ounces of pure alcohol mixed in 8 ounces of water (equivalent to about 5 ounces of 80-proof vodka).
Courtesy U.S. Department of Transportation, Washington, D.C.

uniformly throughout the watery portions of the body—that is, throughout about two-thirds of the body volume. Fat, bones, and hair are low in water content and therefore contain little alcohol, whereas alcohol concentration in the rest of the body is fairly uniform. Hence, if blood is not available, as in some postmortem situations, a medical examiner can select a water-rich organ or fluid—for example, the brain, cerebrospinal fluid, or vitreous humor—for determining the body's alcohol content to a reasonable degree of accuracy.

Elimination

As the alcohol is circulated by the bloodstream, the body begins to eliminate it. Alcohol is eliminated through two mechanisms—**oxidation** and **excretion**. Nearly all of the alcohol (95–98 percent) consumed is eventually oxidized to carbon dioxide and water. Oxidation takes place almost entirely in the liver. Here, in the presence of the enzyme alcohol dehydrogenase, the alcohol is converted into acetaldehyde and then to acetic acid. The acetic acid is subsequently oxidized in practically all parts of the body to carbon dioxide and water.

The remaining alcohol is excreted unchanged in the breath, urine, and perspiration. Most significantly, the amount of alcohol exhaled in the breath is in direct proportion to the concentration of alcohol in the blood. This observation has had a tremendous impact on the technology and procedures used for blood-alcohol testing. The development of instruments to reliably measure breath for its alcohol content has made possible the testing of millions of people in a rapid, safe, and convenient manner.

The fate of alcohol in the body is therefore relatively simple—namely, absorption into the bloodstream, distribution throughout the body's water, and finally, elimination by oxidation and excretion. The elimination or "burn-off" rate of alcohol varies in different individuals; 0.015 percent w/v (weight per volume) per hour seems to be average once the absorption process is complete.[1] However, this figure is an average that varies by as much as 30 percent among individuals.

Alcohol in the Circulatory System

The extent to which an individual may be under the influence of alcohol is usually determined by measuring the quantity of alcohol present in the blood system. Normally, this is accomplished in one of two ways: (1) by direct chemical analysis of the blood for its alcohol content or (2) by measurement of the alcohol content of the breath. In either case, the significance and meaning of the results can better be understood when the movement of alcohol through the circulatory system is studied.

Humans, like all vertebrates, have a closed circulatory system, which consists basically of a heart and numerous arteries, capillaries, and veins. An **artery** is a blood vessel carrying blood away from the heart, and a **vein** is a vessel carrying blood back toward the heart. **Capillaries** are tiny blood vessels that interconnect the arteries with the veins. The exchange of materials between the blood and the other tissues takes place across the thin walls of the capillaries. A schematic diagram of the circulatory system is shown in Figure 9–2.

INGESTION AND ABSORPTION   Let us now trace the movement of alcohol through the human circulatory system. After alcohol is ingested, it moves down the esophagus into the stomach. About 20 percent of the alcohol is absorbed through the stomach walls into the portal vein of the blood system. The remaining alcohol passes into the blood through the walls of the small intestine. Once in the blood, the alcohol is carried to the liver, where its destruction starts as the blood (carrying the alcohol) moves up to the heart.

The blood enters the upper right chamber of the heart, called the right atrium (or auricle), and is forced into the lower right chamber of the heart, known as the right ventricle. Having returned to the heart from its circulation through the tissues, the blood at this time contains very little oxygen and much carbon dioxide. Consequently, the blood must be pumped up to the lungs, through the pulmonary artery, to be replenished with oxygen.

AERATION   The respiratory system bridges with the circulatory system in the lungs, so that oxygen can enter the blood and carbon dioxide can leave it. As shown in Figure 9–3, the pulmonary artery branches into capillaries lying close to tiny pear-shaped sacs called **alveoli.** The lungs

---

oxidation

The combination of oxygen with other substances to produce new products

excretion

Elimination of alcohol from the body in an unchanged state; alcohol is normally excreted in breath and urine

artery

A blood vessel that carries blood away from the heart

vein

A blood vessel that transports blood toward the heart

capillary

A tiny blood vessel across whose walls exchange of materials between the blood and the tissues takes place; receives blood from arteries and carries it to veins

alveoli

Small sacs in the lungs through whose walls air and other vapors are exchanged between the breath and the blood

---

[1] In the United States, laws that define blood-alcohol levels almost exclusively use the unit *percent weight per volume*—percent w/v. Hence, 0.015 percent w/v is equivalent to 0.015 grams of alcohol per 100 milliliters of blood, or 15 milligrams of alcohol per 100 milliliters.

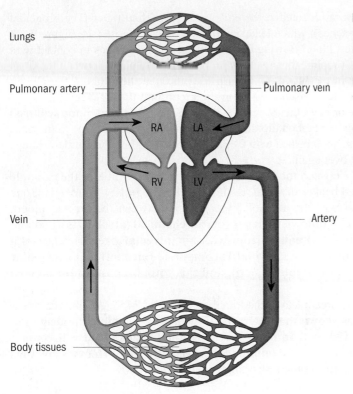

Lungs

Pulmonary artery

Pulmonary vein

Vein

Artery

Body tissues

FIGURE 9–2

Simplified diagram of the human circulatory system. Dark vessels contain oxygenated blood; light vessels contain deoxygenated blood.

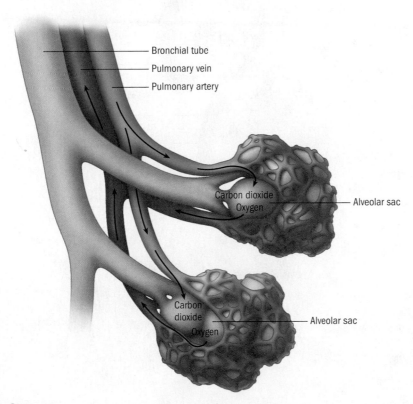

Bronchial tube
Pulmonary vein
Pulmonary artery

Carbon dioxide
Oxygen
Alveolar sac

Carbon dioxide
Oxygen
Alveolar sac

FIGURE 9–3

Gas exchange in the lungs. Blood flows from the pulmonary artery into vessels that lie close to the walls of the alveoli sacs. Here the blood gives up its carbon dioxide and absorbs oxygen. The oxygenated blood leaves the lungs via the pulmonary vein and returns to the heart.

contain about 250 million alveoli, all located at the ends of the bronchial tubes. The bronchial tubes connect to the windpipe (trachea), which leads up to the mouth and nose (see Figure 9–4). At the surface of the alveolar sacs, blood flowing through the capillaries comes in contact with fresh oxygenated air in the sacs. A rapid exchange now proceeds to take place between the fresh air in the sacs and the spent air in the blood. Oxygen passes through the walls of the alveoli into the blood while carbon dioxide is discharged from the blood into the air (Figure 9–3[a]). If, during this exchange, alcohol or any other volatile substance is in the blood, it too will pass into the alveoli. During breathing, the carbon dioxide and alcohol are expelled through the nose and mouth, and the alveoli sacs are replenished with fresh oxygenated air breathed into the lungs, allowing the process to begin all over again.

The distribution of alcohol between the blood and alveolar air is similar to the example of a gas dissolved in an enclosed beaker of water, as described on page 124. Here again, one can use Henry's law to explain how the alcohol divides itself between the air and blood. Henry's law may now be restated as follows: **When a volatile chemical (alcohol) is dissolved in a liquid (blood) and is brought to equilibrium with air (alveolar breath), there is a fixed ratio between the concentration of the volatile compound (alcohol) in air (alveolar breath) and its concentration in the liquid (blood), and this ratio is constant for a given temperature.**

The temperature at which the breath leaves the mouth is normally 34°C. **At this temperature, experimental evidence has shown that the ratio of alcohol in the blood to alcohol in alveoli air is approximately 2,100 to 1. In other words, 1 milliliter of blood will contain nearly the same amount of alcohol as 2,100 milliliters of alveolar breath. Henry's law thus becomes a basis for relating breath to blood-alcohol concentration.**

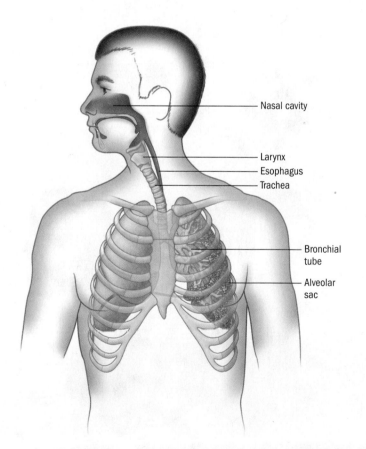

Nasal cavity

Larynx
Esophagus
Trachea

Bronchial tube

Alveolar sac

FIGURE 9–4

The respiratory system. The trachea connects the nose and mouth to the bronchial tubes. The bronchial tubes divide into numerous branches that terminate in the alveoli sacs in the lungs.

RECIRCULATION AND DISTRIBUTION   Now let's return to the circulating blood. After emerging from the lungs, the oxygenated blood is rushed back to the upper left chamber of the heart (left atrium) by the pulmonary vein. When the left atrium contracts, it forces the blood through a valve into the left ventricle, which is the lower left chamber of the heart. The left ventricle then pumps the freshly oxygenated blood into the arteries, which carry the blood to all parts of the body. Each of these arteries, in turn, branches into smaller arteries, which eventually connect with the numerous tiny capillaries embedded in the tissues. Here the alcohol moves out of the blood and into the tissues. The blood then runs from the capillaries into tiny veins that fuse to form larger veins. These veins eventually lead back to the heart to complete the circuit.

During absorption, the concentration of alcohol in the arterial blood is considerably higher than the concentration of alcohol in the venous blood. One typical study revealed a subject's arterial blood-alcohol level to be 41 percent higher than the venous level 30 minutes after the last drink.[2] This difference is thought to exist because of the rapid diffusion of alcohol into the body tissues from venous blood during the early phases of absorption. Because the administration of a blood test requires drawing venous blood from the arm, this test is clearly to the advantage of a subject who may still be in the absorption stage. However, once absorption is complete, the alcohol becomes equally distributed throughout the blood system.

Testing for Intoxication

From a practical point of view, the idea of drawing blood from a vein to test motorists suspected of being under the influence of alcohol simply does not provide a convenient method for monitoring drivers. The need to transport the suspect to a location where a medically qualified person can draw blood would be costly and time consuming, considering the hundreds of tests that the average police department must conduct every year. The methods used must be designed to test hundreds of thousands of motorists annually without causing them undue physical harm or unreasonable inconvenience, while providing a reliable diagnosis that can be supported and defended within the framework of the legal system. This means that toxicologists have had to devise rapid and specific procedures for measuring a driver's degree of alcohol intoxication that can be easily administered in the field.

Breath Testing for Alcohol

The most widespread method for rapidly determining alcohol intoxication is breath testing. A breath tester is simply a device for collecting and measuring the alcohol content of alveolar breath. As we saw earlier, alcohol is expelled unchanged in the breath of a person who has been drinking. A breath test measures the alcohol concentration in the pulmonary artery by measuring its concentration in alveolar breath. Thus, breath analysis provides an easily obtainable specimen along with a rapid and accurate result.

Breath-test results obtained during the absorption phase may be higher than results obtained from a simultaneous analysis of venous blood. However, the former are more reflective of the concentration of alcohol reaching the brain and therefore more accurately reflect the effects of alcohol on the subject. Again, once absorption is complete, the difference between a blood test and a breath test should be minimal.

BREATH-TEST INSTRUMENTS   The first widely used instrument for measuring the alcohol content of alveolar breath was the *Breathalyzer*, developed in 1954 by R. F. Borkenstein, who was a captain in the Indiana State Police. Starting in the 1970s, the Breathalyzer was phased out and replaced by other instruments for measuring the alcoholic content of alveolar breath. Like the Breathalyzer, they assume that the ratio of alcohol in the blood to alcohol in alveolar breath is 2,100 to 1 at a mouth temperature of 34°C. Unlike the Breathalyzer, modern breath testers are free of chemicals. These devices include infrared light absorption devices and **fuel cell detectors**.

fuel cell detector
A detector in which chemical reactions produce electricity

---

[2] R. B. Forney et al., "Alcohol Distribution in the Vascular System: Concentrations of Orally Administered Alcohol in Blood from Various Points in the Vascular System and in Rebreathed Air during Absorption," *Quarterly Journal of Studies on Alcohol* 25 (1964): 205.

(a)   (b)

FIGURE 9–5

(a) An infrared breath-testing instrument—the Data Master DMT. (b) A subject blowing into the DMT breath tester.
Courtesy National Patent Analytical Systems, Inc., Mansfield, Ohio, www.npas.com

An evidential testing instrument that incorporates the principle of infrared light absorption is shown in Figure 9–5. In principle, these instruments operate no differently from the spectrophotometers described on pages 135–138. Any alcohol in the subject's breath is passed into the instrument's breath chamber. As shown in Figure 9–6, a beam of infrared light is aimed through the chamber. A filter is used to select a wavelength of infrared light that alcohol will absorb. As the infrared light passes through the chamber, it interacts with the alcohol, which causes the light to decrease in intensity. The decrease in light intensity is measured by a photoelectric detector that gives a signal proportional to the concentration of alcohol present in the collected breath sample. This information is processed by an electronic microprocessor, and the percent blood-alcohol concentration is displayed on a digital readout. Also, the blood-alcohol level is printed on a card to produce a permanent record of the test result. Most infrared breath testers aim a second infrared beam into the same chamber to check for acetone or other chemical interferences on the breath. If the instrument detects differences in the relative response of the two infrared radiations that do not conform to ethyl alcohol, the operator is immediately informed of the presence of an "interferant."

Another approach for measuring alcohol in breath is to use a fuel cell detector. A fuel cell like the one in Figure 9–7 converts a fuel and an oxidant into an electrical current. In evidential breath-testing devices that use this concept, breath alcohol is the fuel and atmospheric oxygen is the oxidant. Alcohol is converted in the fuel cell into acetic acid, generating a current that is proportional to the quantity of alcohol present in the breath.

Infrared and fuel-cell-based breath testers are microprocessor controlled so that all an operator has to do is press a start button and the instrument automatically moves through a sequence of steps that produce a printout of the subject's test results. These instruments also perform self-diagnostic tests to ascertain whether the instrument is in proper operating condition.

CONSIDERATIONS IN BREATH TESTING   An important feature of these instruments is that they can be connected to an external alcohol standard or simulator in the form of either a liquid or a gas. The liquid simulator comprises a known concentration of alcohol in water. It is heated to a controlled temperature and the vapor formed above the liquid is pumped into the instrument. Dry-gas standards typically consist of a known concentration of alcohol mixed with an inert gas and compressed in cylinders. The external standard is automatically sampled by the breath-test instrument before and/or after the subject's breath sample is taken and recorded. Thus the operator can check the accuracy of the instrument against the known alcohol standard.

The key to the accuracy of a breath-testing device is to ensure that the unit measures the alcohol in the alveolar breath (deep-lung breath) of the subject. This is typically accomplished by programming the unit to accept no less than 1.5 liters of breath from the subject. Also, the subject must blow for a minimum time (such as 6 seconds) with a minimum breath flow rate (such as 3 liters per minute).

Another feature of these instruments is the *slope detector*. As the subject blows into the instrument, the breath-alcohol concentration initially will rise steadily as a function of time. The

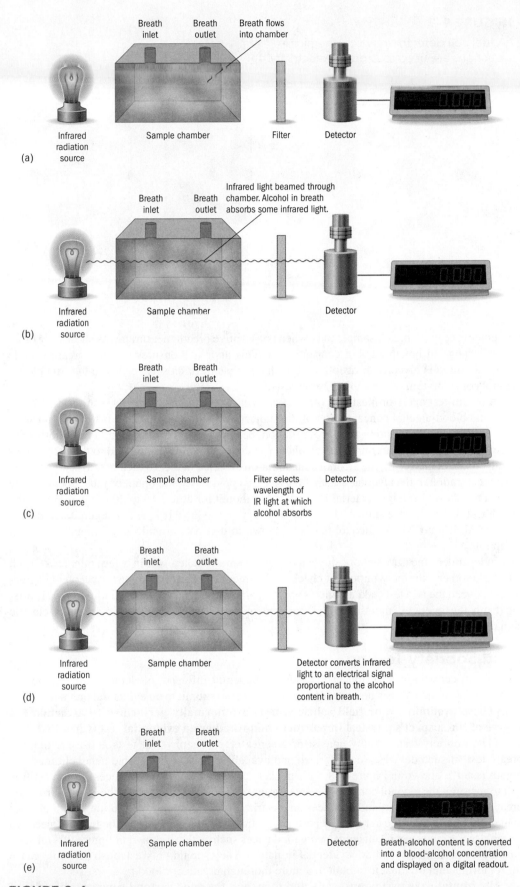

(a) Infrared radiation source | Sample chamber | Filter | Detector
Breath inlet | Breath outlet | Breath flows into chamber

(b) Infrared radiation source | Sample chamber | Detector
Breath inlet | Breath outlet
Infrared light beamed through chamber. Alcohol in breath absorbs some infrared light.

(c) Infrared radiation source | Sample chamber | Filter selects wavelength of IR light at which alcohol absorbs | Detector
Breath inlet | Breath outlet

(d) Infrared radiation source | Sample chamber | Detector converts infrared light to an electrical signal proportional to the alcohol content in breath.
Breath inlet | Breath outlet

(e) Infrared radiation source | Sample chamber | Detector | Breath-alcohol content is converted into a blood-alcohol concentration and displayed on a digital readout.
Breath inlet | Breath outlet

FIGURE 9–6

Schematic diagram of an infrared breath-testing instrument.

FIGURE 9–7

A fuel cell detector in which chemical reactions are used to produce electricity.

instrument accepts a breath sample only when consecutive breath measurements show little or no rate of change in breath-alcohol concentration. This approach ensures that the breath sample being measured is alveolar or deep-lung breath and thus most closely relates to the true blood-alcohol concentration of the subject being tested.

A breath-test operator must take other steps to ensure that the breath-test result truly reflects the actual blood-alcohol concentration of the subject. A major consideration is to avoid measuring "mouth alcohol" resulting from regurgitation, belching, or recent intake of an alcoholic beverage. Also, the recent gargling of an alcohol-containing mouthwash can lead to the presence of mouth alcohol. As a result, the alcohol concentration detected in the exhaled breath is higher than the concentration in the alveolar breath. To avoid this possibility, the operator must not allow the subject to take any foreign material into his or her mouth for at lest 15 to 20 minutes before the breath test. Likewise, the subject should be observed not to have belched or regurgitated during this period of time. Mouth alcohol has been shown to dissipate after 15 to 20 minutes from its inception.

Independent measurement of duplicate breath samples taken within a few minutes of each other is another extremely important check of the integrity of the breath test. Acceptable agreement between the two tests taken minutes apart significantly reduces the possibility of errors arising from the operator, mouth alcohol, instrument component failures, and spurious electric signals.

Field Sobriety Testing

A police officer who suspects that an individual is under the influence of alcohol usually conducts a series of preliminary tests before ordering the suspect to submit to an evidential breath or blood test. **These preliminary, or field sobriety, tests are normally performed to ascertain the degree of the suspect's physical impairment and whether an evidential test is justified.**

Field sobriety tests usually consist of a series of psychophysical tests and a preliminary breath test (if such devices are authorized and available for use). A portable handheld roadside breath tester is shown in Figure 9–8. This pocket-sized device weighs 5 ounces and uses a fuel cell to measure the alcohol content of a breath sample. The fuel cell absorbs the alcohol from the breath sample, oxidizes it, and produces an electrical current proportional to the breath-alcohol content. This instrument can typically perform for three to five years before the fuel cell needs to be replaced. Breath-test results obtained with devices such as those shown in Figure 9–8 must be considered preliminary and nonevidential in nature. They should only establish probable cause for requiring an individual to submit to a more thorough breath or blood test.

Horizontal-gaze nystagmus, walk and turn, and the one-leg stand constitute a series of reliable and effective psychophysical tests. Horizontal-gaze nystagmus is an involuntary jerking of the eye as it moves to the side. A person experiencing nystagmus is usually unaware that the

(a)   (b)

FIGURE 9–8

(a) The Alco-Sensor FST. (b) A subject blowing into the roadside tester device.
Courtesy Intoximeters, Inc., St. Louis, Mo., www.intox.com

Eye looking straight ahead

45

FIGURE 9–9

When a person's blood-alcohol level is in the range of 0.10 percent, jerking of the eye during the horizontal-gaze nystagmus test begins before the eyeball has moved 45 degrees to the side.

jerking is happening and is unable to stop or control it. The subject being tested is asked to follow a penlight or some other object with his or her eye as far to the side as the eye can go. The more intoxicated the person is, the less the eye has to move toward the side before jerking or nystagmus begins. Usually, when a person's blood-alcohol concentration is in the range of 0.10 percent, the jerking begins before the eyeball has moved 45 degrees to the side (see Figure 9–9). Higher blood-alcohol concentration causes jerking at smaller angles. Also, if the suspect has taken a drug that also causes nystagmus (such as phencyclidine, barbiturates, and other depressants), the nystagmus onset angle may occur much earlier than would be expected from alcohol alone.

Walk and turn and the one-leg stand are divided-attention tasks, testing the subject's ability to comprehend and execute two or more simple instructions at one time. The ability to understand and simultaneously carry out more than two instructions is significantly affected by increasing blood-alcohol levels. Walk and turn requires the suspect to maintain balance while standing heel-to-toe and at the same time listening to and comprehending the test instructions. During the walking stage, the suspect must walk a straight line, touching heel-to-toe for nine steps, then turn around on the line and repeat the process. The one-leg stand requires the suspect to maintain balance while standing with heels together listening to the instructions. During the balancing stage, the suspect must stand on one foot while holding the other foot several inches off the ground for 30 seconds; simultaneously, the suspect must count out loud during the 30-second time period.

FIGURE 9–10

Gas chromatogram showing ethyl alcohol (ethanol) in whole blood.
Courtesy Varian Inc., Palo Alto, Calif.

Ethanol

Time (minutes)

Analyzing Blood for Alcohol

Gas chromatography offers the toxicologist the most widely used approach for determining alcohol levels in blood. Under proper gas chromatographic conditions, alcohol can be separated from other volatiles in the blood. By comparing the resultant alcohol peak area to ones obtained with known blood-alcohol standards, the investigator can calculate the alcohol level with a high degree of accuracy (see Figure 9–10).

Another procedure for alcohol analysis involves the oxidation of alcohol to acetaldehyde. This reaction is carried out in the presence of the enzyme alcohol dehydrogenase and the coenzyme nicotin-amide-adenine dinucleotide (NAD). As the oxidation proceeds, NAD is converted into another chemical species, NADH. The extent of this conversion is measured spectrophotometrically and is related to alcohol concentration. This approach to blood-alcohol testing is normally associated with instruments used in a clinical or hospital setting. On the other hand, forensic laboratories normally use gas chromatography for determining blood-alcohol content.

Collection and Preservation of Blood

Blood must always be drawn under medically accepted conditions by a qualified individual. It is important to apply a nonalcoholic disinfectant before the suspect's skin is penetrated with a sterile needle or lancet, to negate any argument that an alcoholic disinfectant may have inadvertently contributed to a falsely high blood-alcohol result. Nonalcoholic disinfectants such as aqueous benzalkonium chloride (Zepiran), aqueous mercuric chloride, or povidone-iodine (Betadine) are recommended for this purpose.

Once blood is removed from an individual, it is best preserved sealed in an airtight container after adding an anticoagulant and a preservative. The blood should be stored in a refrigerator until delivery to the toxicology laboratory. The addition of an **anticoagulant,** such as EDTA or potassium oxalate, prevents clotting; a **preservative,** such as sodium fluoride, inhibits the growth of microorganisms capable of destroying alcohol.

One study performed to determine the stability of alcohol in blood removed from living individuals found that the most significant factors affecting alcohol's stability in blood are storage temperature, the presence of a preservative, and the time of storage.[3] Not a single blood specimen

anticoagulant
A substance that prevents coagulation or clotting of blood

preservative
A substance that stops the growth of microorganisms in blood

[3] G. A. Brown et al., "The Stability of Ethanol in Stored Blood," *Analytica Chemica Acta* 66 (1973): 271.

examined showed an increase in alcohol level with time. Failure to keep the blood refrigerated or to add sodium fluoride resulted in a substantial decline in alcohol concentration. Longer storage times also reduced blood-alcohol levels. Hence, failure to adhere to any of the proper preservation requirements for blood works to the benefit of the suspect and to the detriment of society.

Collection of postmortem blood samples for alcohol determination requires added precautions as compared to collection from living subjects. Ethyl alcohol may be generated in a deceased individual as a result of bacterial action. Therefore, it is best to collect a number of blood samples from different body sites. For example, blood may be removed from the heart and from the femoral (leg) and cubital (arm) veins. Each sample should be placed in a clean, airtight container containing an anticoagulant and sodium fluoride preservative and should be refrigerated. Blood-alcohol levels attributed solely to alcohol consumption should result in nearly similar results for all blood samples collected from the same person. Alternatively, collection of vitreous humor and urine is recommended. Vitreous humor and urine usually do not suffer from postmortem ethyl alcohol production to any significant extent.

Alcohol and the Law

Constitutionally, every state in the United States is charged with establishing and administering statutes regulating the operation of motor vehicles. Although such an arrangement might encourage diverse laws defining permissible blood-alcohol levels, this has not been the case. Both the American Medical Association and the National Safety Council have exerted considerable influence in persuading the states to establish uniform and reasonable blood-alcohol standards.

Blood-Alcohol Laws

Between 1939 and 1964, 39 states and the District of Columbia enacted legislation that followed the recommendations of the American Medical Association and the National Safety Council in specifying that a person with a blood-alcohol concentration in excess of 0.15 percent w/v was to be considered under the influence of alcohol.[4] However, continued experimental studies have since shown a clear correlation between drinking and driving impairment for blood-alcohol levels much below 0.15 percent w/v. As a result of these studies, in 1960 the American Medical Association and in 1965 the National Safety Council recommended lowering the presumptive level at which an individual was considered to be under the influence of alcohol to 0.10 percent w/v. In 2000, U.S. federal law established 0.08 percent as the *per se* blood-alcohol level, meaning that any individual meeting or exceeding this blood-alcohol level shall be deemed intoxicated. No other proof of alcohol impairment is necessary. The 0.08 percent level applies only to noncommercial drivers, as the federal government has set the maximum allowable blood-alcohol concentration for commercial truck and bus drivers at 0.04 percent.

Several Western countries have also set 0.08 percent w/v as the blood-alcohol level above which it is an offense to drive a motor vehicle. Those countries include Canada, Italy, Switzerland, and the United Kingdom. Finland, France, Germany, Ireland, Japan, the Netherlands, and Norway have a 0.05 percent limit. Australian states have adopted a 0.05 percent blood-alcohol concentration level. Sweden has lowered its blood-alcohol concentration limit to 0.02 percent.

As shown in Figure 9–11, one is about four times as likely to become involved in an automobile accident at the 0.08 percent level as a sober individual. At the 0.15 percent level, the chances are 25 times as much for involvement in an automobile accident compared to a sober driver. The reader can *estimate* the relationship of blood-alcohol levels to body weight and the quantity of 80-proof liquor consumed by referring to Figure 9–12.

Constitutional Issues

The Fifth Amendment to the U.S. Constitution guarantees all citizens protection against *self-incrimination*—that is, against being forced to make an admission that would prove one's own guilt in a legal matter. To prevent a person's refusal to take a test for alcohol intoxication on the constitutional grounds of self-incrimination, the National Highway Traffic Safety Administration

---

[4] 0.15 percent w/v is equivalent to 0.15 grams of alcohol per 100 milliliters of blood, or 150 milligrams per 100 milliliters.

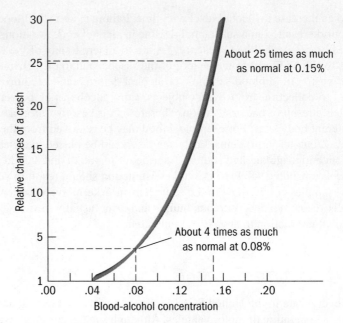

FIGURE 9–11

Diagram of increased driving risk in relation to blood-alcohol concentration.
Courtesy U.S. Department of Transportation, Washington, D.C.

How to Tell What Your Blood Alcohol Level Is After Drinking

"Empty stomach"

Body weight (lb.)	Ounces of 80-proof liquor consumed	Maximum blood-alcohol concentration (% by weight)

"Full stomach"

Body weight (lb.)	Ounces of 80-proof liquor consumed	Maximum blood-alcohol concentration (% by weight)

FIGURE 9–12

To use this diagram, lay a straightedge across your weight and the number of ounces of liquor you've consumed on an empty or full stomach. The point where the edge hits the right-hand column is your maximum blood-alcohol level. The rate of elimination of alcohol from the bloodstream is approximately 0.015 percent per hour. Therefore, to calculate your actual blood-alcohol level, subtract 0.015 from the number in the right-hand column for each hour from the start of drinking.

(NHTSA) recommended an "implied consent" law. By 1973, all the states had complied with this recommendation. In accordance with this statute, operating a motor vehicle on a public highway automatically carries with it the stipulation that the driver must either submit to a test for alcohol intoxication if requested or lose his or her license for some designated period—usually six months to one year.

The leading case relating to the constitutionality of collecting a blood specimen for alcohol testing, as well as for obtaining other types of physical evidence from a suspect without consent, is *Schmerber* v. *California*.[5] While being treated at a Los Angeles hospital for injuries sustained in an automobile collision, Schmerber was arrested for driving under the influence of alcohol. A physician took a blood sample from Schmerber at the direction of the police, over the objection of the defendant. On appeal to the U.S. Supreme Court, the defendant argued that his privilege against self-incrimination had been violated by the introduction of the results of the blood test at his trial. The Court ruled against the defendant, reasoning that the Fifth Amendment only prohibits compelling a suspect to give "testimonial" evidence that may be self-incriminating; being compelled to furnish "physical" evidence, such as fingerprints, photographs, measurements, and blood samples, the Court ruled, was not protected by the Fifth Amendment.

The Court also addressed the question of whether Schmerber was subjected to an unreasonable search and seizure by the taking of a blood specimen without a search warrant. The Court upheld the blood removal, reasoning in this case that the police were confronted with an emergency situation. By the time police officials would have obtained the warrant, the blood levels would have declined significantly as a result of natural body elimination processes. In effect, the evidence would have been destroyed. The Court also emphasized that the blood specimen was taken in a medically accepted manner and without unreasonable force.

This opinion in no way condones warrantless taking of blood for alcohol or drug testing under all circumstances. The reasonableness of actions a police officer may take to compel an individual to yield evidence can be judged only on a case-by-case basis.

The Role of the Toxicologist

Once the forensic toxicologist ventures beyond the analysis of alcohol, he or she encounters an encyclopedic maze of drugs and poisons. Even a cursory discussion of the problems and handicaps imposed on toxicologists is enough to develop a sense of appreciation for their accomplishments and ingenuity.

The toxicologist is presented with body fluids and/or organs and asked to examine them for the presence of drugs and poisons. If he or she is fortunate, which is not often, some clue to the type of toxic substance present may develop from the victim's symptoms, a postmortem pathological examination, an examination of the victim's personal effects, or the nearby presence of empty drug containers or household chemicals. Without such supportive information, the toxicologist must use general screening procedures with the hope of narrowing thousands of possibilities to one.

If this task does not seem monumental, consider that the toxicologist is not dealing with drugs at the concentration levels found in powders and pills. By the time a drug specimen reaches the toxicology laboratory, it has been dissipated and distributed throughout the body. Whereas the drug analyst may have gram or milligram quantities of material to work with, the toxicologist must be satisfied with nanogram or at best microgram amounts, acquired only after careful extraction from body fluids and organs.

Furthermore, the body is an active chemistry laboratory, and no one can appreciate this observation more than a toxicologist. Few substances enter and completely leave the body in the same chemical state. The drug that is injected is not always the substance extracted from the body tissues. Therefore, a thorough understanding of how the body alters or **metabolizes** the chemical structure of a drug is essential in detecting its presence.

It would, for example, be futile and frustrating to search exhaustively for heroin in the human body. This drug is almost immediately metabolized to morphine on entering the bloodstream. Even with this information, the search may still prove impossible unless the examiner also knows that only a small percentage of morphine is excreted unchanged in urine. For the most part, morphine becomes chemically bonded to body carbohydrates before elimination in urine. Thus,

mycrimekit™

WEBEXTRA 9.1
Calculate Your Blood-Alcohol Level
www.mycrimekit.com

mycrimekit™

WEBEXTRA 9.2
See How Alcohol Affects Your Behavior
www.mycrimekit.com

metabolize
To transform a chemical in the body to another chemical to facilitate its elimination from the body

[5]384 U.S. 757 (1966).

forensics at work

Celebrity Toxicology

Michael Jackson:
The Demise of a Superstar

A call to 911 had the desperate tone of urgency. The voice of a young man implored an ambulance to hurry to the home of pop star Michael Jackson. The unconscious performer was in cardiac arrest and was not responding to CPR. The 50-year-old Jackson was pronounced dead upon arrival at a regional medical center. When the initial autopsy results revealed no signs of foul play, rumors immediately began to swirl around a drug-related death. News media coverage showed investigators carrying bags full of drugs and syringes out of the Jackson residence. So it came as no surprise that the forensic toxicology report accompanying Jackson's autopsy showed that the entertainer had died of a drug overdose.

Apparently Jackson had become accustomed to receiving sedatives to help him sleep. Early on the morning of his death, his physician gave Mr. Jackson a tab of valium. At 2 a.m., he administered the sedative lorazepam, and at 3 a.m. the physician administered another sedative, midazolam. Those drugs were administered again at 5 a.m. and 7:30 a.m., but Mr. Jackson still was unable to sleep. Finally, at about 10:40 a.m., Jackson's doctor gave him 25 milligrams of propofol, at which point Mr. Jackson went to sleep. Propofol is a powerful sedative used primarily in the maintenance of surgical anesthesia. All of the drugs administered to Jackson were sedatives, which can act in concert to depress the activities of the central nervous system. Therefore, it comes as no surprise that this drug cocktail resulted in cardiac arrest and death.

Justin Sullivan/Pool\AP Wide World Photos

Accidental Overdose:
The Tragedy of Anna Nicole Smith

Rumors exploded in the media when former model, Playboy playmate, reality television star, and favorite tabloid subject Anna Nicole Smith was found unconscious in her hotel room at the Seminole Hard Rock

successful detection of morphine requires that its extraction be planned in accordance with a knowledge of its chemical fate in the body.

Another example of how one needs to know how a drug metabolizes itself in the body is exemplified by the investigation of the death of Anna Nicole Smith. In her case, the sedative chloral hydrate was a major contributor to her death, and its presence was detected by its active metabolite, trichloroethanol (see Forensics at Work).

Last, when and if the toxicologist has surmounted all of these obstacles and has finally detected, identified, and quantitated a drug or poison, he or she must assess the substance's toxicity. Fortunately, there is published information relating to the toxic levels of most drugs; however, when such data are available, their interpretation must assume that the victim's physiological behavior agrees with that of the subjects of previous studies. In some cases, such an assumption may not be entirely valid without knowing the subject's case history. No experienced toxicologist would be surprised to find an individual tolerating a toxic level of a drug that would have killed most other people.

forensics at work

Manuel Balce Ceneta/PA Photos\Landov Media

Final Pathological Diagnoses

I. Acute Combined Drug Intoxication
   A. Toxic/legal drug:
      Chloral Hydrate (Noctec)
      1. Trichloroethanol (TCE) 75 mg/L (active metabolite)
      2. Trichloroacetic acid (TCA) 85 mg/L (inactive metabolite)
   B. Therapeutic drugs:

1. Diphenhydramine (Benadryl)	0.11 mg/L
2. Clonazepam (Klonopin)	0.04 mg/L
3. Diazepam (Valium)	0.21 mg/L
4. Nordiazepam (metabolite)	0.38 mg/L
5. Temazepam (metabolite)	0.09 mg/L
6. Oxazepam	0.09 mg/L
7. Lorazepam	0.022 mg/L

   C. Other non-contributory drugs present (atropine, topiramate, ciprofloxacin, acetaminophen)

Hotel & Casino in Hollywood, Florida. She was taken to Memorial Legal Hospital, where she was declared dead at the age of 39. Analysis of Smith's blood postmortem revealed an array of prescribed medications. Most pronounced was a toxic level of the sedative chloral hydrate. A part of the contents of the toxicology report from Smith's autopsy are shown here.

Although many of the drugs present were detected at levels consistent with typical doses of the prescribed medications, it was their presence in combination with chloral hydrate that exacerbated the toxic level of chloral hydrate. The lethal combination of these prescription drugs caused failure of both her circulatory and respiratory systems and resulted in her death. The investigators determined that the overdose of chloral hydrate and other drugs was accidental and not a suicide. This was due to the non-excessive levels of most of the prescription medications and the discovery of a significant amount of chloral hydrate still remaining in its original container; had she intended to kill herself she would have likely downed it all. Anna Nicole Smith was a victim of accidental overmedication.

Collection and Preservation of Toxicological Evidence

Toxicology is made infinitely easier once it is recognized that the toxicologist's capabilities are directly dependent on the input received from the attending physician, medical examiner, and police investigator. It is a tribute to forensic toxicologists, who must often labor under conditions that do not afford such cooperation, that they can achieve such a high level of proficiency.

Generally, with a deceased person, the medical examiner decides what biological specimens must be shipped to the toxicology laboratory for analysis. However, a living person suspected of being under the influence of a drug presents a completely different problem, and few options are available. When possible, both blood and urine are taken from any suspected drug user. The entire urine void is collected and submitted for toxicological analysis. Preferably, two consecutive voids should be collected in separate specimen containers.

When a licensed physician or registered nurse is available, a sample of blood should also be collected. The amount of blood taken depends on the type of examination to be conducted. Comprehensive toxicological tests for drugs and poisons can conveniently be carried out on a minimum of 10 cc of blood. A determination solely for the presence of alcohol will require much less—approximately 5 cc of blood. However, many therapeutic drugs, such as tranquilizers and barbiturates, when taken in combination with a small, nonintoxicating amount of alcohol, produce behavioral patterns resembling alcohol intoxication. For this reason, the toxicologist must be given an adequate amount of blood so he or she will have the option of performing a comprehensive analysis for drugs in cases of low alcohol concentrations.

Techniques Used in Toxicology

For the toxicologist, the upsurge in drug use and abuse has meant that the overwhelming majority of fatal and nonfatal toxic agents are drugs. Not surprisingly, a relatively small number of drugs—namely, those discussed in Chapter 8—comprise nearly all the toxic agents encountered. Of these, alcohol, marijuana, and cocaine normally account for 90 percent or more of the drugs encountered in a typical toxicology laboratory.

ACIDS AND BASES   Like the drug analyst, the toxicologist must devise an analytical scheme to detect, isolate, and identify a toxic substance. The first chore is to selectively remove and isolate drugs and other toxic agents from the biological materials submitted as evidence. Because drugs constitute a large portion of the toxic materials found, a good deal of effort must be devoted to their extraction and detection. The procedures are numerous, and a useful description of them would be too detailed for this text. We can best understand the underlying principle of drug extraction by observing that many drugs fall into the categories of **acids** and **bases.**

Although several definitions exist for these two classes, a simple one states that an acid is a compound that sheds a hydrogen ion (or a hydrogen atom minus its electron) with reasonable ease. Conversely, a base is a compound that can pick up a hydrogen ion shed by an acid. The idea of acidity and basicity can be expressed in terms of a simple numerical value that relates to the concentration of the hydrogen ion (H^+) in a liquid medium such as water. Chemists use the **pH scale** to do this. This scale runs from 0 to 14:

$$pH = 0 \quad 1 \quad 2 \quad 3 \quad 4 \quad 5 \quad 6 \quad 7 \quad 8 \quad 9 \quad 10 \quad 11 \quad 12 \quad 13 \quad 14$$
$$\leftarrow \text{ Increasing acidity — Neutral — Increasing basicity } \rightarrow$$

Normally, water is neither acidic nor basic—in other words, it is neutral, with a pH of 7. However, when an acidic substance—for example, sulfuric acid or hydrochloric acid—is added to the water, it adds excess hydrogen ions, and the pH value becomes less than 7. The lower the number, the more acidic the water. Similarly, when a basic substance—for example, sodium hydroxide or ammonium hydroxide—is added to water, it removes hydrogen ions, thus making water basic. The more basic the water, the higher its pH value.

By controlling the pH of a water solution into which blood, urine, or tissues are dissolved, the toxicologist can conveniently control the type of drug that is recovered. For example, acidic drugs are easily extracted from an acidified water solution (pH less than 7) with organic solvents such as chloroform. Similarly, basic drugs are readily removed from a basic water solution (pH greater than 7) with organic solvents. This simple approach gives the toxicologist a general technique for extracting and categorizing drugs. Some of the more commonly encountered drugs may be classified as follows:

Acid Drugs	Basic Drugs
Barbiturates	Phencyclidine
Acetylsalicylic acid (aspirin)	Methadone
	Amphetamines
	Cocaine

SCREENING AND CONFIRMATION   Once the specimen has been extracted and divided into acidic and basic fractions, the toxicologist can identify the drugs present. The strategy for identifying abused drugs entails a two-step approach: *screening* and *confirmation* (see Figure 9–13). A screening test is normally employed to give the analyst quick insight into the likelihood that a specimen contains a drug substance. This test allows a toxicologist to examine a large number of specimens within a short period of time for a wide range of drugs. Any positive results from a screening test are tentative at best and must be verified with a confirmation test.

acid
A compound capable of donating a hydrogen ion (H^+) to another compound

base
A compound capable of accepting a hydrogen ion (H^+)

pH scale
A scale used to express the basicity or acidity of a substance; a pH of 7 is neutral, whereas lower values are acidic and higher values are basic

FIGURE 9–13

Biological fluids and tissues are extracted for acidic and basic drugs by controlling the pH of a water solution in which they are dissolved. Once this is accomplished, the toxicologist analyzes for drugs by using screening and confirmation test procedures.

FIGURE 9–14

The combination of the gas chromatograph and the mass spectrometer enables forensic toxicologists to separate the components of a drug mixture and provides specific identification of a drug substance.

The three most widely used screening tests are thin-layer chromatography (TLC), gas chromatography (GC), and immunoassay. The techniques of GC and TLC have already been described on pages 125–127 and 128–131, respectively. Immunoassay has proven to be a useful screening tool in toxicology laboratories. Its principles are very different from any of the analytical techniques we have discussed so far. Basically, immunoassay is based on specific drug antibody reactions. We will learn about this concept in Chapter 10. The primary advantage of immunoassay is its ability to detect small concentrations of drugs in body fluids and organs. In fact, this technique provides the best approach for detecting the low drug levels normally associated with smoking marijuana.

The necessity of eliminating the possibility that a positive screening test may be due to a substance's having a close chemical structure to an abused drug requires the toxicologist to follow up a positive screening test with a confirmation test. Because of the potential impact of the results of a drug finding on an individual, only the most conclusive confirmation procedures should be used. **Gas chromatography/mass spectrometry is generally accepted as the confirmation test of choice.** The combination of gas chromatography and mass spectrometry provides the toxicologist with a one-step confirmation test of unequaled sensitivity and specificity (see pages 138–140). As shown in Figure 9–14, the sample is separated into its components by the gas chromatograph. When the separated sample component leaves the column of the gas chromatograph, it enters the mass spectrometer, where it is bombarded with high-energy electrons. This bombardment causes the sample to break up into fragments, producing a fragmentation pattern or mass spectrum for each sample. For most compounds, the mass spectrum represents a unique "fingerprint" pattern that can be used for identification.

There is tremendous interest in drug-testing programs conducted not only in criminal matters but for industry and government as well. Urine testing for drugs is becoming common for job applicants and employees in the workplace. Likewise, the U.S. military has an extensive drug urine-testing program for its members. Many urine-testing programs rely on private laboratories to perform the analyses. In any case, when the test results form the basis for taking action against an individual, both a screening and confirmation test must be incorporated into the testing protocol to ensure the integrity of the laboratory's conclusions.

DETECTING DRUGS IN HAIR   When a forensic toxicological examination on a living person is required, practicality limits available specimens to blood and urine. Most drugs remain in the bloodstream for about 24 hours; in urine, they normally are present up to 72 hours. However, it may be necessary to go further back in time to ascertain whether a subject has been abusing a drug. If so, the only viable alternative to blood and urine is head hair.

Hair is nourished by blood flowing through capillaries located close to the hair root. Drugs present in blood diffuse through the capillary walls into the base of the hair and become permanently entrapped in the hair's hardening protein structure. As the hair continues to grow, the drug's location on the hair shaft becomes a historical marker for delineating drug intake. Given that the average human head hair grows at the rate of 1 centimeter per month, analyzing segments of hair for drug content may define the timeline for drug use, dating it back over a period of weeks, months, or even years, depending on the hair's length.

However, caution is required in interpreting the timeline. The chronology of drug intake may be distorted by drugs penetrating the hair's surface as a result of environmental exposure, or drugs may enter the hair's surface through sweat. Nevertheless, drug hair analysis is the only viable approach for measuring long-term abuse of a drug.

Detecting Nondrug Poisons

Although forensic toxicologists devote most of their efforts to detecting drugs, they also test for a wide variety of other toxic substances. Some of these are rare elements, not widely or commercially available. Others are so common that virtually everyone is exposed to nontoxic amounts of them every day.

HEAVY METALS   The forensic toxicologist only occasionally encounters a group of poisons known as *heavy metals*. These include arsenic, bismuth, antimony, mercury, and thallium. To screen for many of these metals, the investigator may dissolve the suspect body fluid or tissue in a hydrochloric acid solution and insert a copper strip into the solution (the Reinsch test). The appearance of a silvery or dark coating on the copper indicates the presence of a heavy metal. Such a finding must be confirmed by the use of analytical techniques suitable for inorganic analysis—namely, atomic absorption spectrophotometry, emission spectroscopy, or X-ray diffraction.

CARBON MONOXIDE   Unlike heavy metals, *carbon monoxide* still represents one of the most common poisons encountered in a forensic laboratory. When carbon monoxide enters the human body, it is primarily absorbed by the red blood cells, where it combines with hemoglobin to form carboxyhemoglobin. An average red blood cell contains about 280 million molecules of hemoglobin. Oxygen normally combines with hemoglobin, which transports the oxygen throughout the body. However, if a high percentage of the hemoglobin combines with carbon monoxide, not enough is left to carry sufficient oxygen to the tissues, and death by asphyxiation quickly follows.

There are two basic methods for measuring the concentration of carbon monoxide in the blood. Spectrophotometric methods examine the visible spectrum of blood to determine the amount of carboxyhemoglobin relative to oxyhemoglobin or total hemoglobin; also, a volume of blood can be treated with a reagent to liberate the carbon monoxide, which is then measured by gas chromatography.

The amount of carbon monoxide in blood is generally expressed as *percent saturation*. This represents the extent to which the available hemoglobin has been converted to carboxyhemoglobin. The transition from normal or occupational levels of carbon monoxide to toxic levels is not sharply defined. It depends, among other things, on the age, health, and general fitness of each individual. In a healthy middle-aged individual, a carbon monoxide blood saturation greater than 50–60 percent is considered fatal. However, in combination with alcohol or other depressants, fatal levels may be significantly lower. For instance, a carbon monoxide saturation of 35–40 percent may prove fatal in the presence of a blood-alcohol concentration of 0.20 percent w/v. Interestingly,

> > > > > > > > > > > > > > > > > > >

Joann Curley: Caught by a Hair

A vibrant young woman named Joann Curley rushed to the Wilkes-Barre (Pennsylvania) General Hospital—her husband, Bobby, was having an attack and required immediate medical attention. Bobby was experiencing a burning sensation in his feet, numbness in his hands, a flushed face, and intense sweating. He was diagnosed with Guillain-Barré syndrome, an acute inflammation of the nervous system that accounted for all of Bobby's symptoms. After being discharged, Bobby experienced another bout of debilitating pain and numbness. He was admitted to another hospital, the larger and more capable Hershey Medical Center in Hershey, Pennsylvania. There doctors observed extreme alopecia, or hair loss.

Test results of Bobby's urine showed high levels of the heavy metal thallium in his body. Thallium, a rare and highly toxic metal that was used decades ago in substances such as rat poison and to treat ringworm and gout, was found in sufficient quantities to cause Bobby's sickness. The use of thallium was banned in the United States in 1984. Now, at least, Bobby could be treated. However, before Bobby's doctors could treat him for thallium poisoning, he experienced cardiac arrest and slipped into a coma. Joann Curley made the difficult decision to remove her husband of 13 months from life support equipment. He died shortly thereafter.

Bobby Curley was an electrician and, for five months before his death, he worked in the chemistry department at nearby Wilkes University. Authorities suspected that Bobby had been accidentally exposed to thallium there among old chemicals and laboratory equipment. The laboratory was searched and several old bottles of powdered thallium salts were discovered in a storage closet. After testing of the air and surfaces, these were eliminated as possible sources for exposure. This finding was supported by the discovery that none of Bobby's co-workers had any thallium in their systems. The next most logical route of exposure was in the home; thus, the Curley kitchen was sampled. Of the hundreds of items tested, three thermoses were found to contain traces of thallium.

Investigators also learned that Bobby had changed his life insurance to list his wife, Joann, as the beneficiary of his $300,000 policy. Based on this information, police consulted a forensic toxicologist in an effort to glean as much from the physical evidence in Bobby Curley's body as possible. The toxicologist conducted segmental analysis of Bobby's hair, an analytical method based on the predictable rate of hair growth on the human scalp: an average of 1 centimeter per month. Bobby had approximately 5 inches (12.5 centimeters) of hair, which represents almost twelve months of hair growth. Each section tested represented a specific period of time in Bobby's final year of his life.

The hair analysis proved that Bobby Curley was poisoned with thallium long before he began working at Wilkes University. The first few doses were small, which probably barely made him sick at the time. Gradually, over a year or more, Bobby was receiving more doses of thallium until he finally succumbed to a massive dose three or four days before his death. After careful scrutiny of the timeline, investigators concluded that only Joann Curley had access to Bobby during each of these intervals. She also had motive, in the amount of $300,000.

Presented with the timeline and the solid toxicological evidence against her, Joann Curley pleaded guilty to murder. As part of her plea agreement, she provided a forty-page written confession of how she haphazardly dosed Bobby with some rat poison she found in her basement. She admitted that she murdered him for the money she would receive from Bobby's life insurance policy.

---

chain smokers may have a constant carbon monoxide level of 8–10 percent from the carbon monoxide in cigarette smoke.

Inhaling automobile fumes is a relatively common way to commit suicide. A garden or vacuum cleaner hose is often used to connect the tailpipe with the vehicle's interior, or the engine is allowed to run in a closed garage. A level of carbon monoxide sufficient to cause death accumulates in five to ten minutes in a closed single-car garage.

The level of carbon monoxide in the blood of a victim found dead at the scene of a fire is significant in ascertaining whether foul play has occurred. High levels of carbon monoxide in the blood prove that the victim breathed the combustion products of the fire and was alive when the fire began. Many attempts at covering up a murder by setting fire to a victim's house or car have been uncovered in this manner.

Significance of Toxicological Findings

Once a drug is found and identified, the toxicologist assesses its influence on the behavior of the individual. Interpreting the results of a toxicology find is one of the toxicologist's more difficult chores. Recall that many of the world's countries have designated a specific blood-alcohol level at which an individual is deemed under the influence of alcohol. These levels were established as a result of numerous studies conducted over several years to measure the effects of alcohol levels on driving performance. However, no such legal guidelines are available to the toxicologist who must judge how a drug other than alcohol affects an individual's performance or physical state.

For many drugs, blood concentration levels are readily determined and can be used to *estimate* the pharmacological effects of the drug on the individual. Often, when dealing with a living person, the toxicologist has the added benefit of knowing what a police officer may have observed about an individual's behavior and motor skills, as well as the outcome of a drug influence evaluation conducted by a police officer trained to be a drug recognition expert (discussed shortly). For a deceased person, drug levels in various body organs and tissues provide additional information about the individual's state at the time of death. However, before conclusions can be drawn about a drug-induced death, other factors must also be considered, including the age, physical condition, and tolerance of the drug user.

With prolonged use of a drug, an individual may become less responsive to a drug's effects and tolerate blood-drug concentrations that would kill a casual drug user. Therefore, knowledge of an individual's history of drug use is important in evaluating drug concentrations. Another consideration is additive or synergistic effects of the interaction of two or more drugs, which may produce a highly intoxicated or comatose state even though none of the drugs alone is present at high or toxic levels. The combination of alcohol with tranquilizers or narcotics is a common example of a potentially lethal drug combination.

The presence of a drug present in urine is a poor indicator of how extensively an individual's behavior or state is influenced by the drug. Urine is formed outside the body's circulatory system, and consequently drug levels can build up in it over a long period. Some drugs are found in the urine one to three days after they have been taken and long after their effects on the user have disappeared. Nevertheless, the value of this information should not be discounted. Urine drug levels, like blood levels, are best used by law enforcement authorities and the courts to corroborate other investigative and medical findings regarding an individual's condition. Hence, for an individual who is arrested for suspicion of being under the influence of a drug, a toxicologist's determinations supplement the observations of the arresting officer, including the results of a drug influence evaluation (discussed next).

For a deceased person, the responsibility for establishing a cause of death rests with the medical examiner or coroner. However, before a conclusive determination is made, the examining physician depends on the forensic toxicologist to demonstrate the presence or absence of a drug or poison in the tissues or body fluids of the deceased. Only through the combined efforts of the toxicologist and the medical examiner (or coroner) can society be assured that death investigations achieve high professional and legal standards.

The Drug Recognition Expert

Whereas recognizing alcohol-impaired performance is an expertise generally accorded to police officers by the courts, recognizing drug-induced intoxication is much more difficult and generally not part of police training. During the 1970s, the Los Angeles Police Department developed and tested a series of clinical and psychophysical examinations that a trained police officer could use to identify and differentiate between types of drug impairment. This program has evolved into a national program to train police as *drug recognition experts*. Normally, a three- to five-month training program is required to certify an officer as a drug recognition expert (DRE).

The DRE program incorporates standardized methods for examining suspects to determine whether they have taken one or more drugs. The process is systematic and standard; to ensure that each subject has been tested in a routine fashion, each DRE must complete a standard Drug Influence Evaluation form (see Figure 9–15). The entire drug evaluation takes approximately 30 to 40 minutes. The components of the 12-step process are summarized in Table 9–1.

The DRE evaluation process can suggest the presence of the following seven broad categories of drugs:

1. Central nervous system depressants
2. Central nervous system stimulants
3. Hallucinogens

FIGURE 9–15

Drug Influence Evaluation form.

4. Dissociative anesthetics (includes phencyclidine and its analogs)
5. Inhalants
6. Narcotic analgesics
7. Cannabis

The DRE program is not designed to be a substitute for toxicological testing. The toxicologist can often determine that a suspect has a particular drug in his or her body. But the toxicologist often cannot infer with reasonable certainty that the suspect was impaired at a specific time. On the other hand, the DRE can supply credible evidence that the suspect was impaired at a specific time and that the nature of the impairment was consistent with a particular family of drugs. But the DRE program usually cannot determine which specific drug was ingested. Proving drug intoxication requires a coordinated effort and the production of competent data from both the DRE and the forensic toxicologist.

Virtual Forensics Lab

Analysis of Blood Alcohol by Gas Chromatography
To perform a virtual blood-alcohol analysis, go to www.pearsoncustom.com/us/vlm/

TABLE 9–1

Components of the Drug Recognition Process

1. *The Breath-Alcohol Test.* By obtaining an accurate and immediate measurement of the suspect's blood-alcohol concentration, the drug recognition expert (DRE) can determine whether alcohol may be contributing to the suspect's observable impairment and whether the concentration of alcohol is sufficient to be the sole cause of that impairment.

2. *Interview with the Arresting Officer.* Spending a few minutes with the arresting officer often enables the DRE to determine the most promising areas of investigation.

3. *The Preliminary Examination.* This structured series of questions, specific observations, and simple tests provides the first opportunity to examine the suspect closely. It is designed to determine whether the suspect is suffering from an injury or from another condition unrelated to drug consumption. It also affords an opportunity to begin assessing the suspect's appearance and behavior for signs of possible drug influence.

4. *The Eye Examination.* Certain categories of drugs induce nystagmus, an involuntary, spasmodic motion of the eyeball. Nystagmus is an indicator of drug-induced impairment. The inability of the eyes to converge toward the bridge of the nose also indicates the possible presence of certain types of drugs.

5. *Divided-Attention Psychophysical Tests.* These tests check balance and physical orientation and include the walk and turn, the one-leg stand, the Romberg balance, and the finger-to-nose.

6. *Vital Signs Examinations.* Precise measurements of blood pressure, pulse rate, and body temperature are taken. Certain drugs elevate these signs; others depress them.

7. *Dark Room Examinations.* The size of the suspect's pupils in room light, near-total darkness, indirect light, and direct light is checked. Some drugs cause the pupils to either dilate or constrict.

8. *Examination for Muscle Rigidity.* Certain categories of drugs cause the muscles to become hypertense and quite rigid. Others may cause the muscles to relax and become flaccid.

9. *Examination for Injection Sites.* Users of certain categories of drugs routinely or occasionally inject their drugs. Evidence of needle use may be found on veins along the neck, arms, and hands.

10. *Suspect's Statements and Other Observations.* The next step is to attempt to interview the suspect concerning the drug or drugs he or she has ingested. Of course, the interview must be conducted in full compliance of the suspect's constitutional rights.

11. *Opinions of the Evaluator.* Using the information obtained in the previous ten steps, the DRE can make an informed decision about whether the suspect is impaired by drugs and, if so, what category or combination of categories is the probable cause of the impairment.

12. *The Toxicological Examination.* The DRE should obtain a blood or urine sample from the suspect for laboratory analysis in order to secure scientific, admissible evidence to substantiate his or her conclusions.

chapter summary >>>>>>>>>>>

Toxicologists detect and identify the presence of drugs and poisons in body fluids, tissues, and organs. A major branch of forensic toxicology deals with the measurement of alcohol in the body for matters that pertain to violations of criminal law. Alcohol appears in the blood within minutes after it has been taken by mouth and slowly increases in concentration while it is being absorbed from the stomach and the small intestine into the bloodstream. When all the alcohol has been absorbed, a maximum alcohol level is reached in the blood and the postabsorption period begins. Then the alcohol concentration slowly decreases until a zero level is again reached. Alcohol is eliminated from the body through oxidation and excretion. Oxidation takes place almost entirely in the liver, whereas alcohol is excreted unchanged in the breath, urine, and perspiration. The extent to which an individual is under the influence of alcohol is usually determined by measuring the quantity of alcohol in the blood or the breath. Breath testers that operate on the principle of infrared light absorption are becoming increasingly popular within the law enforcement community.

Many types of breath testers analyze a set volume of breath. The sampled breath is exposed to infrared light. The degree of interaction of the light with alcohol in the breath sample allows the instrument to measure a blood-alcohol concentration in breath. These breath-testing devices operate on the principle that the ratio between the concentration of alcohol in deep-lung or alveolar breath and its concentration in blood is fixed. Most breath-test devices have set the ratio of alcohol in the blood to alcohol in alveolar air at 2,100 to 1.

Law enforcement officers typically use field sobriety tests to estimate a motorist's degree of physical impairment by alcohol and whether an evidential test for alcohol is justified. The horizontal-gaze nystagmus test, walk and turn, and the one-leg stand are all reliable and effective psychophysical tests.

Gas chromatography is the most widely used approach for determining alcohol levels in blood. Blood must always be drawn under medically accepted conditions by a qualified individual. A nonalcoholic disinfectant must be applied before the suspect's skin is penetrated with a sterile needle or lancet. Once blood is removed from an individual, it is best preserved sealed in an airtight container after adding an anticoagulant and a preservative.

The forensic toxicologist must devise an analytical scheme to detect, isolate, and identify toxic drug substances. Once the drug has been extracted from appropriate biological fluids, tissues, and organs, the forensic toxicologist can identify the drug substance. The strategy for identifying abused drugs entails a two-step approach: screening and confirmation. A screening test gives the analyst quick insight into the likelihood that a specimen contains a drug substance. Positive results from a screening test are tentative at best and must be verified with a confirmation test. The most widely used screening tests are thin-layer chromatography, gas chromatography, and immunoassay. Gas chromatography/mass spectrometry is generally accepted as the confirmation test of choice. Once the drug is extracted and identified, the toxicologist may be required to judge the drug's effect on an individual's natural performance or physical state. The Drug Recognition Expert program incorporates standardized methods for examining automobile drivers suspected of being under the influence of drugs. But the DRE program usually cannot determine which specific drug was ingested. Hence, reliable data from both the DRE and the forensic toxicologist are required to prove drug intoxication.

review questions

1. The most heavily abused drug in the Western world is _____.

2. True or False: Toxicologists are employed only by crime laboratories. _____

3. The amount of alcohol in the blood (is, is not) directly proportional to the concentration of alcohol in the brain.

4. True or False: Blood levels have become the accepted standard for relating alcohol intake to its effect on the body. _____

5. Alcohol consumed on an empty stomach is absorbed (faster, slower) than an equivalent amount of alcohol taken when there is food in the stomach.

6. Under normal drinking conditions, alcohol concentration in the blood peaks in _____ to _____ minutes.

7. In the postabsorption period, alcohol is distributed uniformly among the _____ portions of the body.

8. Alcohol is eliminated from the body by _____ and _____.

9. Ninety-five to 98 percent of the alcohol consumed is _____ to carbon dioxide and water.

10. Oxidation of alcohol takes place almost entirely in the _____.

11. The amount of alcohol exhaled in the _____ is directly proportional to the concentration of alcohol in the blood.

12. Alcohol is eliminated from the blood at an average rate of _____ percent w/v.

13. Alcohol is absorbed into the blood from the _____ and _____.

14. A(n) _____ carries blood away from the heart; a(n) _____ carries blood back to the heart.

15. The _____ artery carries deoxygenated blood from the heart to the lungs.

16. Alcohol passes from the blood capillaries into the _____ sacs in the lungs.

17. One milliliter of blood contains the same amount of alcohol as approximately _____ milliliters of alveolar breath.

18. When alcohol is being absorbed into the blood, the alcohol concentration in venous blood is (higher, lower) than that in arterial blood.

19. Most modern breath testers use _____ radiation to detect and measure alcohol in the breath.

20. To avoid the possibility of "mouth alcohol," the operator of a breath tester must not allow the subject to take any foreign materials into the mouth for _____ minutes before the test.

21. Alcohol can be separated from other volatiles in blood and quantitated by the technique of _____.

22. Roadside breath testers that use a(n) _____ detector are becoming increasingly popular with the law enforcement community.

23. True or False: Portable handheld roadside breath testers for alcohol provide evidential test results. _____

24. Usually, when a person's blood-alcohol concentration is in the range of 0.10 percent, horizontal-gaze nystagmus begins before the eyeball has moved _____ degrees to the side.

25. When drawing blood for alcohol testing, the suspect's skin must first be wiped with a(n) _____ disinfectant.

26. Failure to add a preservative, such as sodium fluoride, to blood removed from a living person may lead to a(n) (decline, increase) in alcohol concentration.

27. Most states have established _____ percent w/v as the impairment limit for blood-alcohol concentration.

28. In the case of _____, the Supreme Court ruled that taking nontestimonial evidence, such as a blood sample, did not violate a suspect's Fifth Amendment rights.

29. Heroin is changed upon entering the body into _____.

30. The body fluids _____ and _____ are both desirable for the toxicological examination of a living person suspected of being under the influence of a drug.

31. A large number of drugs can be classified chemically as _____ and _____.

32. Water with a pH value (less, greater) than 7 is basic.

33. Barbiturates are classified as _____ drugs.

34. Drugs are extracted from body fluids and tissues by carefully controlling the _____ of the medium in which the sample has been dissolved.

35. The technique of _____ is based on specific drug antibody reactions.

36. Both _____ and _____ tests must be incorporated into the drug-testing protocol of a toxicology laboratory to ensure the correctness of the laboratory's conclusions.

37. The gas _____ combines with hemoglobin in the blood to form carboxyhemoglobin, thus interfering with the transportation of oxygen in the blood.

38. The amount of carbon monoxide in blood is usually expressed as _____.

39. True or False: Blood levels of drugs can alone be used to draw definitive conclusions about the effects of a drug on an individual. _____

40. Interaction of alcohol and barbiturates in the body can produce a(n) _____ effect.

41. The level of a drug present in the urine is by itself a (good, poor) indicator of how extensively an individual is affected by a drug.

42. Urine and blood drug levels are best used by law enforcement authorities and the courts to _____ other investigative and medical findings pertaining to an individual's condition.

43. The _____ program incorporates standardized methods for examining suspects to determine whether they have taken one or more drugs.

application and critical thinking

1. Answer the following questions about driving risk associated with drinking and blood-alcohol concentration:

   a. Randy is just barely legally intoxicated. How much more likely is he to have an accident than someone who is sober?

   b. Marissa, who has been drinking, is 15 times as likely to have an accident as her sober friend, Christine. What is Marissa's approximate blood-alcohol concentration?

   c. After several drinks, Charles is ten times as likely to have an accident as a sober person. Is he more or less intoxicated than James, whose blood-alcohol level is 0.10?

   d. Under the original blood-alcohol standards recommended by NHTSA, a person considered just barely legally intoxicated was how much more likely to have an accident than a sober individual?

2. Following is a description of four individuals who have been drinking. Rank them from highest to lowest blood-alcohol concentration:

   a. John, who weighs 200 pounds and has consumed eight 8-ounce drinks on a full stomach

   b. Frank, who weighs 170 pounds and has consumed four 8-ounce drinks on an empty stomach

   c. Gary, who weighs 240 pounds and has consumed six 8-ounce drinks on an empty stomach

   d. Stephen, who weighs 180 pounds and has consumed six 8-ounce drinks on a full stomach

3. Following is a description of four individuals who have been drinking. In which (if any) of the following countries would each be considered legally drunk: the United States, Australia, Sweden?

   a. Bill, who weighs 150 pounds and has consumed three 8-ounce drinks on an empty stomach

   b. Sally, who weighs 110 pounds and has consumed three 8-ounce drinks on a full stomach

   c. Rich, who weighs 200 pounds and has consumed six 8-ounce drinks on an empty stomach

   d. Carrie, who weighs 140 pounds and has consumed four 8-ounce drinks on a full stomach

4. You are a forensic scientist who has been asked to test two blood samples. You know that one sample is suspected of containing barbiturates and the other contains no drugs; however, you cannot tell the two samples apart. Describe how you would use the concept of pH to determine which sample contains barbiturates. Explain your reasoning.

5. You are investigating an arson scene and you find a corpse in the rubble, but you suspect that the victim did not die as a result of the fire. Instead, you suspect that the victim was murdered earlier, and that the blaze was started to cover up the murder. How would you go about determining whether the victim died before the fire?

further references

Benjamin, David M., "Forensic Pharmacology," in R. Saferstein, ed., *Forensic Science Handbook*, vol. 3, 2nd ed., Upper Saddle River, N.J.: Prentice Hall, 2010.

Caplan, Y. H., and J. R. Zettl, "The Determination of Alcohol in Blood and Breath," in R. Saferstein, ed., *Forensic Science Handbook*, vol. 1, 2nd ed., Upper Saddle River, N.J.: Prentice Hall, 2002.

Couper, F. J., and B. K. Logan, *Drugs and Human Performance*. Washington, D.C.: National Highway Traffic Safety Administration, 2004, http://www.nhtsa.dot.gov/people/injury/research/job185drugs/technical-page.htm.

Fenton, John J., *Toxicology: A Case-Oriented Approach*. Boca Raton, Fla.: Taylor & Francis, 2002.

Garriott, James C., ed., *Medicolegal Aspects of Alcohol*, 5th ed. Tucson, Ariz.: Lawyers & Judges, 2009.

Levine, B., ed., *Principles of Forensic Toxicology*, 2nd ed. Washington, D.C.: AACC Press, 2006.

Ropero-Miller, J.D. and Goldberger, B.A., eds., *Handbook of Workplace Drug Testing*, 2nd ed. Washington, D.C.: AACC Press, 2009.

The Green River Killer

This case takes its name from the Green River, which flows through Washington state and empties into Puget Sound in Seattle. In 1982, within six months the bodies of five females were discovered in or near the river. Most of the victims were known prostitutes who were strangled and apparently raped. As police focused their attention on an area known as Sea-Tac Strip, a haven for prostitutes, girls mysteriously disappeared with increasing frequency. By the end of 1986, the body count in the Seattle region rose to 40, all of whom were believed to have been murdered by the Green River Killer. As the investigation pressed on into 1987, the police renewed their interest in one suspect, Gary Ridgway, a local truck painter. Ridgway had been known to frequent the Sea-Tac Strip. Interestingly, in 1984 Ridgway had actually passed a lie detector test. Now with a search warrant in hand, police searched the Ridgway residence and also obtained hair and saliva samples from Ridgway. Again, insufficient evidence caused Ridgway to be released from custody. With the exception of one killing in 1998, the murder spree stopped in 1990, and the case remained dormant for nearly ten years. But the advent of DNA testing brought renewed vigor to the investigation. In 2001, semen samples collected from three early victims of the Green River Killer were compared to Ridgway's saliva that had been collected in 1987. The DNA profiles matched and the police had their man. An added forensic link to Ridgway was made by the location of minute amounts of spray paint on the clothing of six victims that compared to paints collected from Ridgway's workplace. Ridgway avoided the death penalty by confessing to the murders of 48 women.

forensic serology

Learning Objectives

After studying this chapter you should be able to:

- List the A-B-O antigens and antibodies found in the blood for each of the four blood types: A, B, AB, and O

- Understand and describe how whole blood is typed

- List and describe forensic tests used to characterize a stain as blood

- Understand the concept of antigen–antibody interactions and how it is applied to species identification and drug identification

- Explain the differences between monoclonal and polyclonal antibodies

- Contrast chromosomes and genes

- Learn how the Punnett square is used to determine the genotypes and phenotypes of offspring

- List the laboratory tests necessary to characterize seminal stains

- Explain how suspect blood and semen stains are to be properly preserved for laboratory examination

- Describe the proper collection of physical evidence in a rape investigation

KEY TERMS

acid phosphatase
agglutination
allele
antibody
antigen
antiserum
aspermia
chromosome
deoxyribonucleic
    acid (DNA)
egg
erythrocyte
gene
genotype
hemoglobin
heterozygous
homozygous
hybridoma cells
locus
luminol
monoclonal antibodies
oligospermia
phenotype
plasma
polyclonal antibodies
precipitin
serology
serum
sperm
X chromosome
Y chromosome
zygote

In 1901, Karl Landsteiner announced one of the most significant discoveries of the 20th century—the typing of blood—a finding that 29 years later earned him a Nobel Prize. For years physicians had attempted to transfuse blood from one individual to another. Their efforts often ended in failure because the transfused blood tended to coagulate in the body of the recipient, causing instantaneous death. Landsteiner was the first to recognize that all human blood was not the same; instead, he found that blood is distinguishable by its group or type. Out of Landsteiner's work came the classification system that we call the *A-B-O system*. Now physicians had the key for properly matching the blood of a donor to a recipient. One blood type cannot be mixed with a different blood type without disastrous consequences. This discovery, of course, had important implications for blood transfusion and the millions of lives it has since saved. Meanwhile, Landsteiner's findings had opened up a completely new field of research in the biological sciences. Others began to pursue the identification of additional characteristics that could further differentiate blood. By 1937, the Rh factor in blood was demonstrated, and shortly thereafter, numerous blood factors or groups were discovered. More than a hundred different blood factors have been shown to exist. However, the ones in the A-B-O system are still the most important for properly matching a donor and recipient for a transfusion.

Until the early 1990s, forensic scientists focused on blood factors, such as A-B-O, as offering the best means for linking blood to an individual. What made these factors so attractive to the forensic scientist was that in theory no two individuals, except for identical twins, could be expected to have the same combination of blood factors. In other words, blood factors are controlled genetically and have the potential of being a highly distinctive feature for personal identification. What makes this observation so relevant is the high frequency of occurrence of bloodstains at crime scenes, especially crimes of the most serious nature—that is, homicides, assaults, and rapes. Consider, for example, a transfer of blood between the victim and assailant during a struggle; that is, the victim's blood is transferred to the suspect's garment, or vice versa. If the criminalist could individualize human blood by identifying all of its known factors, the result would be evidence of the strongest kind for linking the suspect to the crime scene.

The advent of DNA technology has dramatically altered the approach of forensic scientists toward individualization of bloodstains and other biological evidence. The search for genetically controlled blood factors in bloodstains has been abandoned in favor of characterizing biological evidence by select regions of our **deoxyribonucleic acid (DNA)**. The individualization of dried blood and other biological evidence, now a reality, has significantly altered the role that crime laboratories play in criminal investigations. As we will learn in the next chapter, the high sensitivity of DNA analysis has even altered the type of materials collected from crime scenes in the search for DNA. The next chapter is devoted to discussing recent breakthroughs in associating blood and semen stains with a single individual through characterization of DNA. This chapter focuses on underlying biological concepts that forensic scientists historically relied on as they sought to characterize and individualize biological evidence before the dawning of the age of DNA.

The Nature of Blood

The word *blood* actually refers to a highly complex mixture of cells, enzymes, proteins, and inorganic substances. The fluid portion of blood is called **plasma**. Plasma is composed principally of water and accounts for 55 percent of blood content. Suspended in the plasma are solid materials consisting chiefly of cells—that is, red blood cells (**erythrocytes**), white blood cells (leukocytes), and platelets. The solid portion of blood accounts for 45 percent of its content. Blood clots when a protein in the plasma known as *fibrin* traps and enmeshes the red blood cells. If one were to remove the clotted material, a pale yellowish liquid known as **serum** would be left.

Obviously, considering the complexity of blood, any discussion of its function and chemistry would have to be extensive, extending beyond the scope of this text. It is certainly far more relevant at this point to concentrate our discussion on the blood components that are directly pertinent to the forensic aspects of blood identification—the red blood cells and the blood serum.

Antigens and Antibodies

Functionally, red blood cells transport oxygen from the lungs to the body tissues and in turn remove carbon dioxide from tissues by transporting it back to the lungs, where it is exhaled. However, for reasons unrelated to the red blood cell's transporting mission, on the surface of each cell

DNA
Abbreviation for deoxyribonucleic acid—the molecules carrying the body's genetic information; DNA is double stranded in the shape of a double helix

plasma
The fluid portion of unclotted blood

erythrocyte
A red blood cell

serum
The liquid that separates from the blood when a clot is formed

are millions of characteristic chemical structures called **antigens**. Antigens impart blood-type characteristics to the red blood cells. Blood antigens are grouped into systems depending on their relationship to one another. More than 15 blood antigen systems have been identified to date; of these, the A-B-O and Rh systems are the most important.

If an individual is type A, this simply indicates that each red blood cell has A antigens on its surface; similarly, all type B individuals have B antigens; and the red blood cells of type AB contain both A and B antigens. Type O individuals have neither A nor B antigens on their cells. Hence, the presence or absence of the A and B antigens on the red blood cells determines a person's blood type in the A-B-O system.

Another important blood antigen has been designated as the Rh factor, or D antigen. People with the D antigen are said to be *Rh positive*; those without this antigen are *Rh negative*. In routine blood banking, the presence or absence of the three antigens—A, B, and D—must be determined in testing for the compatibility of the donor and recipient.

Serum is important because it contains certain proteins known as **antibodies. The fundamental principle of blood typing is that for every antigen, there exists a specific antibody.** Each antibody symbol contains the prefix *anti-*, followed by the name of the antigen for which it is specific. Hence, anti-A is specific only for A antigen, anti-B for B antigen, and anti-D for D antigen. The serum-containing antibody is referred to as the **antiserum**, meaning a serum that reacts against something (antigens).

An antibody reacts only with its specific antigen and no other. Thus, if serum containing anti-B is added to red blood cells carrying the B antigen, the two immediately combine, causing the antibody to attach itself to the cell. Antibodies are normally *bivalent*—that is, they have two reactive sites. This means that each antibody can simultaneously be attached to antigens located on two different red blood cells. This creates a vast network of cross-linked cells usually seen as clumping or **agglutination** (see Figure 10–1).

Let's look a little more closely at this phenomenon. In normal blood, shown in Figure 10–2(a), antigens on red blood cells and antibodies coexist without destroying each other because the antibodies present are not specific toward any of the antigens. However, suppose a foreign serum added to the blood introduces a new antibody. The occurrence of a specific antigen–antibody reaction immediately causes the red blood cells to link together, or agglutinate, as shown in Figure 10–2(b).

Evidently, nature has taken this situation into account because when we examine the serum of type A blood, we find anti-B and no anti-A. Similarly, type B blood contains only anti-A, type O blood has both anti-A and anti-B, and type AB blood contains neither anti-A nor anti-B. The antigen and antibody components of normal blood are summarized in the following table:

Blood Type	Antigens on Red Blood Cells	Antibodies in Serum
A	A	Anti-B
B	B	Anti-A
AB	AB	Neither anti-A nor anti-B
O	Neither A nor B	Both anti-A and anti-B

The reasons for the fatal consequences of mixing incompatible blood during a transfusion should now be quite obvious. For example, transfusing type A blood into a type B patient will cause the natural anti-A in the blood of the type B patient to react promptly with the incoming A antigens, resulting in agglutination. In addition, the incoming anti-B of the donor will react with the B antigens of the patient.

Blood Typing

The term **serology** is used to describe a broad scope of laboratory tests that use specific antigen and serum antibody reactions. The most widespread application of serology is the typing of whole blood for its A-B-O identity. In determining the A-B-O blood type, only two antiserums are needed—anti-A and anti-B. For routine blood typing, both of these antiserums are commercially available.

Table 10–1 summarizes how the identity of each of the four blood groups is established when the blood is tested with anti-A and anti-B serum. Type A blood is agglutinated by anti-A serum;

antigen
A substance, usually a protein, that stimulates the body to produce antibodies against it

antibody
A protein that destroys or inactivates a specific antigen; antibodies are found in the blood serum

antiserum
Blood serum that contains specific antibodies

agglutination
The clumping together of red blood cells by the action of an antibody

serology
The study of antigen–antibody reactions

FIGURE 10–1

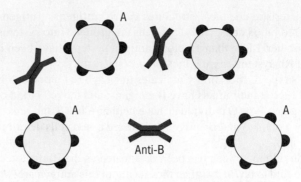

Red blood cells containing A antigens
do not combine with B antibodies

Red blood cells containing B antigens
are agglutinated or clumped together
in the presence of B antibodies

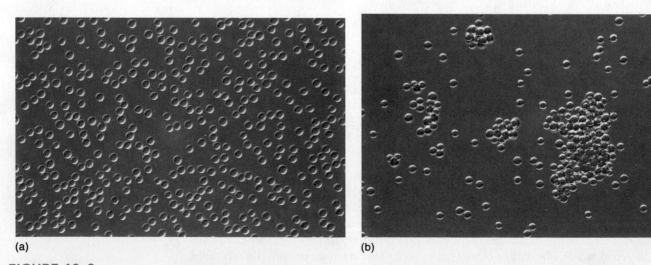

(a) (b)

FIGURE 10–2

(a) Microscopic view of normal red blood cells (500×). (b) Microscopic view of agglutinated red blood cells (500×).
Courtesy J. C. Revy, Phototake NYC

TABLE 10–1

Identification of Blood with Known Antiserum

Anti-A Serum + Whole Blood	Anti-B Serum + Whole Blood	Antigen Present	Blood Type
+	−	A	A
−	+	B	B
+	+	A and B	AB
−	−	Neither A nor B	O

Note: + shows agglutination; − shows absence of agglutination.

TABLE 10–2

Identification of Blood with Known Cells

A Cells + Blood	B Cells + Blood	Antibody Present	Blood Type
+	−	Anti-A	B
−	+	Anti-B	A
+	+	Both anti-A and anti-B	O
−	−	Neither anti-A nor anti-B	AB

Note: + shows agglutination; − shows absence of agglutination.

type B blood is agglutinated by anti-B serum; type AB blood is agglutinated by both anti-A and anti-B; and type O blood is not agglutinated by either the anti-A or anti-B serum.

The identification of natural antibodies present in blood offers another route to the determination of blood type. Testing blood for the presence of anti-A and anti-B requires using red blood cells that have known antigens. Again, these cells are commercially available. Hence, when A cells are added to a blood specimen, agglutination occurs only in the presence of anti-A. Similarly, B cells agglutinate only in the presence of anti-B. All four A-B-O types can be identified in this manner by testing blood with known A and B cells, as summarized in Table 10–2.

The population distribution of blood types varies with location and race throughout the world. In the United States, a typical distribution is as follows:

O	A	B	AB
43%	42%	12%	3%

Immunoassay Techniques

The concept of a specific antigen–antibody reaction is finding application in other areas unrelated to the blood typing of individuals. Most significantly, this approach has been extended to the detection of drugs in blood and urine. Antibodies that react with drugs do not naturally exist; however, they can be produced in animals such as rabbits by first combining the drug with a protein and injecting this combination into the animal. This drug–protein complex acts as an antigen stimulating the animal to produce antibodies (see Figure 10–3). The recovered blood serum of the animal will contain antibodies that are specific or nearly specific to the drug.

Drug   Protein carrier   Drug antibodies

FIGURE 10–3

Several immunological assay techniques are commercially available for detecting drugs through an antigen–antibody reaction. One such technique, the *enzyme-multiplied immunoassay technique (EMIT)*, has gained widespread popularity among toxicologists because of its speed and high sensitivity for detecting drugs in urine.

Enzyme-Multiplied Immunoassay Technique (EMIT)

A typical EMIT analysis begins by adding to a subject's urine antibodies that bind to a particular type or class of drug being looked for. This is followed by adding to the urine a chemically labeled version of the drug. As shown in Figure 10–4, a competition will ensue between the labeled and unlabeled drug (if it's present in the subject's urine) to bind with the antibody. If this competition does occur in a person's urine, it signifies that the urine screen test was positive for the drug being tested. For example, to check someone's urine for methadone, the analyst would add methadone antibodies and chemically labeled methadone to the urine. Any methadone present in the urine immediately competes with the labeled methadone to bind with the methadone antibodies. The quantity of chemically labeled methadone left uncombined is then measured, and this value is related to the concentration of methadone originally present in the urine.

One of the most frequent uses of EMIT in forensic laboratories has been for screening the urine of suspected marijuana users. The primary pharmacologically active agent in marijuana is tetrahydrocannabinol, or THC. To facilitate the elimination of THC, the body converts it to a series of substances called *metabolites* that are more readily excreted. The major THC metabolite found in urine is a substance called *THC-9-carboxylic acid*. Antibodies against this metabolite are prepared for EMIT testing. Normally the urine of marijuana users contains a very small quantity of THC-9-carboxylic acid (less than one-millionth of a gram); however, this level is readily detected by EMIT.

The greatest problem with detecting marijuana in urine is interpretation. Although smoking marijuana will result in the detection of THC metabolite, it is difficult to determine when the individual actually used marijuana. In individuals who smoke marijuana frequently, detection is possible within two to five days after the last use of the drug. However, some individuals may yield positive results up to thirty days after the last use of marijuana.

Currently, thousands of individuals regularly submit to urinalysis tests for the presence of drugs of abuse. These individuals include military personnel, transportation industry employees, police and corrections personnel, and subjects requiring preemployment drug screening. Immunoassay testing for drugs has proven quite suitable for handling the large volume of

FIGURE 10–4

In the EMIT assay, a drug that may be present in a urine specimen will compete with added labeled drugs for a limited number of antibody binding sites. The labeled drugs are indicated by an asterisk. Once the competition for antibody sites is completed, the number of remaining unbound labeled drug is proportional to the drug's concentration in urine.

specimens that must be rapidly analyzed for drug content on a daily basis. Testing laboratories have access to many commercially prepared sera arising from animals being injected with any one of a variety of drugs. A particular serum that has been added to a urine specimen is designed to interact with opiates, cannabinoids, cocaine, amphetamines, phencyclidine, barbiturates, methadone, or other drugs. A word of caution: immunoassay is only presumptive in nature, and its result must be confirmed by additional testing. Specifically, the confirmation test of choice is gas chromatography-mass spectrometry, which is described in more detail in Chapter 9.

Monoclonal Antibodies

As we have seen in the previous section, when an animal such as a rabbit or mouse is injected with an antigen, the animal responds by producing antibodies designed to bind to the invading antigen. However, the process of producing antibodies designed to respond to foreign antigens is complex. For one, an antigen typically has structurally different sites to which an antibody may bind. So when the animal is actively producing attack antibodies, it produces a series of different antibodies, all of which are designed to attack some particular site on the antigen of interest. These antibodies are known as **polyclonal antibodies.** However, the disadvantage of polyclonal antibodies is that an animal can produce antibodies that vary in composition over time. As a result, different batches of polyclonals may vary in their specificity and their ability to bind to a particular antigen site.

As the technologies associated with forensic science have grown in importance, a need has developed, in some instances, to have access to antibodies that are more uniform in their composition and attack power than the traditional polyclonals. This is best accomplished by adopting a process in which an animal will produce antibodies designed to attack one and only one site on an antigen. Such antibodies are known as **monoclonal antibodies**. How can such monoclonals be produced? The process begins by injecting a mouse with the antigen of interest. In response, the mouse's spleen cells will produce antibodies to fight off the invading antigen. The spleen cells are removed from the animal and are fused to fast-growing blood cancer cells to produce **hybridoma cells**. The hybridoma cells are then allowed to multiply and are screened for their specific antibody activity. The hybridoma cells that bear the antibody activity of interest are then selected and cultured. The rapidly multiplying cancer cells linked to the selected antibody cells produce identical monoclonal antibodies in a limitless supply (see Figure 10–5).

Monoclonal antibodies are being incorporated into commercial forensic test kits with increasing frequency. Many immunoassay test kits for drugs of abuse are being formulated with monoclonal antibodies. Also, a recently introduced test for seminal material that incorporates a monoclonal antibody has found wide popularity in crime laboratories (see page 236).

As a side note, in 1999 the U.S. Food and Drug Administration approved a monoclonal drug treatment for cancer. Rituxin is a nontoxic monoclonal antibody designed to attack and destroy cancerous white blood cells containing an antigen designated as CD20. Other monoclonal drug treatments are in the pipeline. Monoclonals are finally beginning to fulfill their long-held expectation as medicine's version of the "magic bullet."

polyclonal antibodies
Antibodies produced by injecting animals with a specific antigen; a series of antibodies are produced responding to a variety of different sites on the antigen

monoclonal antibodies
A collection of identical antibodies that interact with a single antigen site

hybridoma cells
Fused spleen and tumor cells; used to produce identical monoclonal antibodies in a limitless supply

Forensic Characterization of Bloodstains

The criminalist must answer the following questions when examining dried blood: (1) Is it blood? (2) From what species did the blood originate? (3) If the blood is of human origin, how closely can it be associated with a particular individual?

Color Tests

The determination of blood is best made by means of a preliminary color test. For many years, the most commonly used test for this purpose was the *benzidine color test*; however, because benzidine has been identified as a known carcinogen, its use has generally been discontinued, and the chemical phenolphthalein is usually substituted in its place (this test is also known as the *Kastle-Meyer color test*).[1] Both the benzidine and Kastle-Meyer color tests are based on the

---

[1] S. Tobe et al., "Evaluation of Six Presumptive Tests for Blood, Their Specificity, Sensitivity, and Effect on High Molecular-Weight DNA," *Journal of Forensic Sciences* 52 (2007): 102–109.

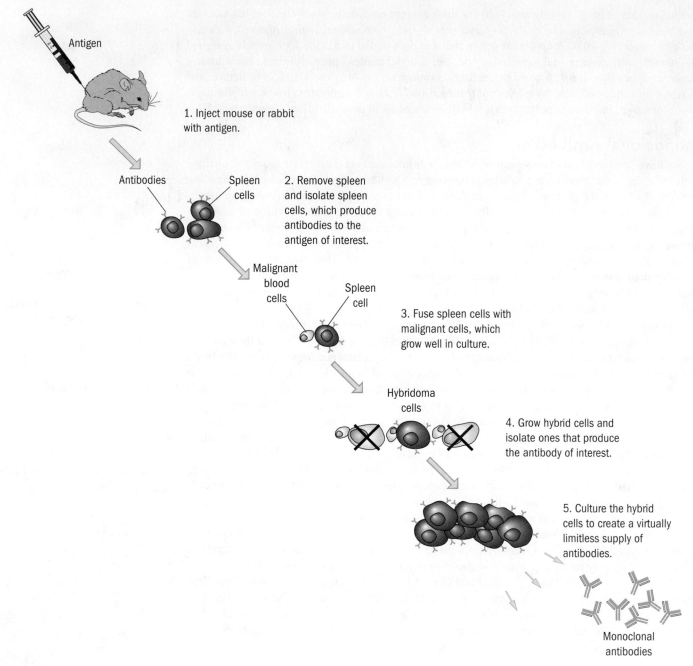

Antigen

1. Inject mouse or rabbit with antigen.

Antibodies

Spleen cells

2. Remove spleen and isolate spleen cells, which produce antibodies to the antigen of interest.

Malignant blood cells

Spleen cell

3. Fuse spleen cells with malignant cells, which grow well in culture.

Hybridoma cells

4. Grow hybrid cells and isolate ones that produce the antibody of interest.

5. Culture the hybrid cells to create a virtually limitless supply of antibodies.

Monoclonal antibodies

FIGURE 10–5

Steps required to produce monoclonal antibodies.

hemoglobin

A red blood cell protein that transports oxygen in the bloodstream; it is responsible for the red color of blood

observation that blood **hemoglobin** possesses peroxidase-like activity. Peroxidases are enzymes that accelerate the oxidation of several classes of organic compounds by peroxides. When a bloodstain, phenolphthalein reagent, and hydrogen peroxide are mixed together, the blood's hemoglobin causes the formation of a deep pink color.

The Kastle-Meyer test is not a specific test for blood; some vegetable materials, for instance, may turn Kastle-Meyer pink. These substances include potatoes and horseradish. However, it is unlikely that such materials will be encountered in criminal situations, and thus from a practical point of view, a positive Kastle-Meyer test is highly indicative of blood. Field investigators have found Hemastix strips a useful presumptive field test for blood. Designed as a urine dipstick test for blood, the strip can be moistened with distilled water and placed in contact with a suspect bloodstain. The appearance of a green color is indicative of blood.

(a)   (b)

FIGURE 10–6

(a) A section of a linoleum floor photographed under normal light. This floor was located in the residence of a missing person. (b) Same section of the floor shown in part (a) after spraying with luminol. A circular pattern was revealed. Investigators concluded that the circular blood pattern was left by the bottom of a bucket carried about during the cleaning up of the blood. A small clump of sponge, blood, and hair was found near where this photograph was taken.

Courtesy North Carolina State Bureau of Investigation

Luminol and Bluestar

Another important presumptive identification test for blood is the **luminol** test.[2] Unlike the benzidine and Kastle-Meyer tests, the reaction of luminol with blood produces light rather than color. By spraying luminol reagent onto a suspect item, investigators can quickly screen large areas for bloodstains. The sprayed objects must be located in a darkened area while being viewed for the emission of light (luminescence); any bloodstains produce a faint blue glow. A relatively new product, Bluestar, is now available to be used in place of luminol (http://www.bluestar-forensic .com). Bluestar is easy to mix in the field. Its reaction with blood can be observed readily without having to create complete darkness. The luminol and Bluestar tests are extremely sensitive—capable of detecting bloodstains diluted to as little as 1 in 100,000. For this reason, spraying large areas such as carpets, walls, flooring, or the interior of a vehicle may reveal blood traces or patterns that would have gone unnoticed under normal lighting conditions (see Figure 10–6). It is important to note that luminol and Bluestar do not interfere with any subsequent DNA testing.[3]

luminol
The most sensitive chemical test that is capable of presumptively detecting bloodstains diluted to as little as 1 in 100,000; its reaction with blood emits light and thus requires the result to be observed in a darkened area

Microcrystalline Tests

The identification of blood can be made more specific if microcrystalline tests are performed on the material. Several tests are available; the two most popular ones are the *Takayama* and *Teichmann tests*. Both of these depend on the addition of specific chemicals to the blood so that characteristic crystals with hemoglobin derivatives will form. Crystal tests are far less sensitive than color tests for blood identification and are more susceptible to interference from contaminants that may be present in the stain.

Precipitin Test

Once the stain has been characterized as blood, the serologist determines whether the stain is of human or animal origin. For this purpose, the standard test used is the **precipitin** test. Precipitin tests are based on the fact that when animals (usually rabbits) are injected with human blood, antibodies form that react with the invading human blood to neutralize its presence. The investigator can recover these antibodies by bleeding the animal and isolating the blood serum. This

precipitin
An antibody that reacts with its corresponding antigen to form a precipitate

---

[2] The luminol reagent is prepared by mixing 0.1 grams 3-amino-phthalhydrazide and 5.0 grams sodium carbonate in 100 milliliters distilled water. Before use, 0.7 grams sodium perborate is added to the solution.

[3] A. M. Gross et al., "The Effect of Luminol on Presumptive Tests and DNA Analysis Using the Polymerase Chain Reaction," *Journal of Forensic Sciences* 44 (1999): 837.

serum contains antibodies that specifically react with human antigens. For this reason, the serum is known as *human antiserum*. In the same manner, by injecting rabbits with the blood of other known animals, virtually any kind of animal antiserum can be produced. Currently, antiserums are commercially available for humans and for a variety of commonly encountered animals—for example, dogs, cats, and deer.

A number of techniques have been devised for performing precipitin tests on bloodstains. The classic method is to layer an extract of the bloodstain on top of the human antiserum in a capillary tube. Human blood, or for that matter, any protein of human origin in the extract, reacts specifically with antibodies present in the antiserum, as indicated by the formation of a cloudy ring or band at the interface of the two liquids (see Figure 10–7).

Another version of the precipitin test, called *gel diffusion*, takes advantage of the fact that antibodies and antigens diffuse or move toward one another on an agar gel–coated plate. The extracted bloodstain and the human antiserum are placed in separate holes opposite each other on the gel. If the blood is of human origin, a line of precipitation will form where the antigens and antibodies meet. Similarly, the antigens and antibodies can be induced to move toward one another under the influence of an electrical field. In the *electrophoretic method* (see pages 131–132), an electrical potential is applied to the gel medium; a specific antigen–antibody reaction is denoted by a line of precipitation formed between the hole containing the blood extract and the hole containing the human antiserum (see Figure 10–8).

The precipitin test is very sensitive and requires only a small amount of blood for testing. Human bloodstains dried for 10 to 15 years and longer may still give a positive precipitin reaction. Even extracts of tissue from mummies four to five thousand years old have given positive reactions with this test. Furthermore, human bloodstains diluted by washing in water and left with only a faint color may still yield a positive precipitin reaction (see Figure 10–9).

Once it has been determined that the bloodstain is of human origin, an effort must be made to associate or disassociate the stain with a particular individual. Until the mid-1990s, routine characterization of bloodstains included the determination of A-B-O types; however, the widespread use of DNA profiling or typing has relegated this subject to one of historical interest only.

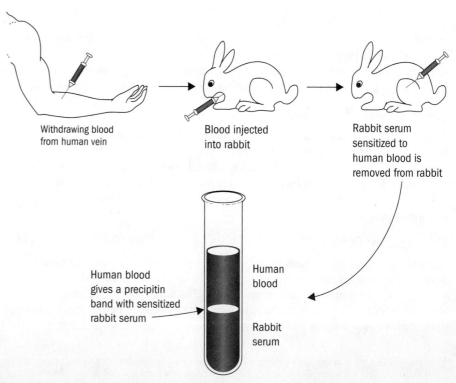

FIGURE 10–7

The precipitin test.

Semen extract
and anti-p30 are
added to their
respective wells

Antigen and antibody
move toward
each other

Formation of a visible
precipitation line midway
between the wells shows
the presence of p30 in the

FIGURE 10–8

Antigens and antibodies moving toward one another under the influence of an electrical potential.

1:128   1:2

1:256   1:4

1:512   1:8

1:1024   1:16

1:2048   1:32

1:4096   1:64

FIGURE 10–9

Results of the precipitin test of dilutions of human serum up to 1 in 4,096 against a human antiserum. A reaction is visible for blood dilutions up to 1 in 256.

Courtesy Millipore Corp., Biomedical, Acton, Mass.

Principles of Heredity

All of the antigens and polymorphic enzymes and proteins that have been described in previous sections are genetically controlled traits. That is, they are inherited from parents and become a permanent feature of a person's biological makeup from the moment he or she is conceived. Determining the identity of these traits, then, not only provides us with a picture of how one individual compares to or differs from another, but gives us an insight into the basic biological substances that determine our overall makeup as human beings and the mechanism by which those substances are transmitted from one generation to the next.

Genes and Chromosomes

Hereditary material is transmitted via microscopic units called **genes**. The gene is the basic unit of heredity. Each gene by itself or in concert with other genes controls the development of a specific characteristic in the new individual; the genes determine the nature and growth of virtually every body structure.

The genes are positioned on **chromosomes**, threadlike bodies that appear in the nucleus of every body cell. See Figure 10–10. All nucleated human cells contain 46 chromosomes, mated in 23 pairs. The only exceptions are the nucleated human reproductive cells, the **egg** and **sperm**, which contain only 23 unmated chromosomes. During fertilization, a sperm and egg combine so that each contributes chromosomes to form the new cell (**zygote**). Hence, the new individual begins life properly with 23 mated chromosome pairs. Because the genes are positioned on the chromosomes, the new individual inherits genetic material from each parent.

Actually, two dissimilar chromosomes are involved in the determination of sex. The egg cell always contains a long chromosome known as the **X chromosome**; but the sperm cell may

gene
A unit of inheritance consisting of a DNA segment located on a chromosome

mycrimekit

WEBEXTRA 10.2
Learn about the Chromosomes Present in Our Cells
www.mycrimekit.com

chromosome
A rodlike structure in the cell nucleus, along which the genes are located; it is composed of DNA surrounded by other material, mainly proteins

egg
The female reproductive cell

sperm
The male reproductive cell

zygote
The cell arising from the union of an egg and a sperm cell

FIGURE 10–10

Computer-enhanced photomicrograph image of human chromosomes.

Courtesy Alfred Pasieka, Science Photo Library, Photo Researchers, Inc.

X chromosome

The female sex chromosome

Y chromosome

The male sex chromosome

locus

The physical location of a gene on a chromosome

allele

Any of several alternative forms of a gene located at the same point on a particular pair of chromosomes; for example, the genes determining the blood types A and B are alleles

homozygous

Having two identical allelic genes on two corresponding positions of a pair of chromosomes

heterozygous

Having two different allelic genes on two corresponding positions of a pair of chromosomes

contain either a short chromosome, known as the **Y chromosome**, or a long X chromosome. When an X-carrying sperm fertilizes an egg, the new cell is XX and develops into a female. A Y-carrying sperm produces an XY fertilized egg and develops into a male. Because the sperm cell ultimately determines the nature of the chromosome pair, we can say that the father biologically determines the sex of the child.

ALLELES   Just as chromosomes come together in pairs, so do the genes they bear. The position a gene occupies on a chromosome is its **locus**. Genes that govern a given characteristic are similarly positioned on the chromosomes inherited from the mother and father. Thus, a gene for eye color on the mother's chromosome will be aligned with a gene for eye color on the corresponding chromosome inherited from the father. Alternative forms of genes that influence a given characteristic and are aligned with one another on a chromosome pair are known as **alleles**.

Another simple example of allele genes in humans is that of blood types belonging to the A-B-O system. Inheritance of the A-B-O type is best described by a theory that uses three genes designated A, B, and O. A gene pair made up of two similar genes—for example, AA and BB— is said to be **homozygous**; a gene pair made up of two different genes—AO, for example—is said to be **heterozygous**. If the chromosome inherited from the father carries the A gene and the chromosome inherited from the mother carries the same gene, the offspring would have an AA combination. Similarly, if one chromosome contains the A gene and the other has the O gene, the genetic makeup of the offspring would be AO.

DOMINANT AND RECESSIVE GENES   When an individual inherits two similar genes from his or her parents, there is no problem in determining the blood type of that person. Hence, an AA combination will always be type A, a BB type B, and an OO type O. However, when two different genes are inherited, one gene will be dominant. It can be said that the A and B genes are *dominant* and that the O gene is always *recessive*—that is, its characteristics remain hidden. For instance, with an AO combination, A is always dominant over O, and the individual will be typed as A. Similarly, a BO combination is typed as B. In the case of AB, the genes are codominant, and the individual's blood type will be AB. The recessive characteristics of O appear only when both recessive genes are present. Hence, the combination OO is typed simply as O.

GENOTYPES AND PHENOTYPES   A pair of allele genes together constitutes the **genotype** of the individual. However, no laboratory test can determine an individual's A-B-O genotype. For example, a person's outward characteristic, or **phenotype**, may be type A, but this does not tell us whether his or her genotype is AA or AO. The genotype can be determined only by studying the family history of the individual. If the genotypes of both parents are known, that of their possible offspring can be forecast.

An easy way to figure this out is to construct a *Punnett square*. To do this, write along a horizontal line the two genes of the male parent, and in the vertical column write the two kinds of female genes present, as shown. In our example, we assume the male parent is type O and therefore has to be an OO genotype; the female parent is type AB and can be only an AB genotype:

Next, write in each box the corresponding gene contributed from the female and then from the male. The squares will contain all the possible genotype combinations that the parents can produce in their offspring:

Hence, in this case, 50 percent of the offspring are likely to be AO and the other 50 percent BO. These are the only genotypes possible from this combination. Because O is recessive, 50 percent of the offspring will probably be type A and 50 percent type B. **From this example, we can see that no blood group gene can appear in a child unless it is present in at least one of the parents.**

Paternity Testing

Although the genotyping of blood factors has useful applications for studying the transmission of blood characteristics from one generation to the next, it has no direct relevance to criminal investigations. It does, however, have important implications in disputed-paternity cases, which are normally encountered in civil, not criminal, courts.

Many cases of disputed paternity can be resolved when the suspected parents and the offspring are related according to their blood group systems. For instance, in the previous example, had the child been type AB, the suspected father would have been cleared. A type O father and a type AB mother cannot have a type AB child. On the other hand, if the child had been type A or type B, the most that could be said is that the suspect may have been the father; this does not mean that he *is* the father, just that he is not excluded based on blood typing. Obviously, many other males also have type O blood. Of course, the more blood group systems that are tested, the better the chances of excluding an innocent male from involvement. Conversely, if no discrepancies are found between offspring and suspect father, the more certain one can be that the suspect is indeed the father. In fact, routine paternity testing involves characterizing blood factors other than A-B-O. Currently, paternity testing laboratories have implemented DNA test procedures that can raise the odds of establishing paternity beyond 99 percent.

genotype
The particular combination of genes present in the cells of an individual

phenotype
The physical manifestation of a genetic trait such as shape, color, and blood type

mycrimekit™
WEBEXTRA 10.4
See How Genes Position Themselves on a Chromosome Pair
www.mycrimekit.com

mycrimekit™
WEBEXTRA 10.5
See How Genes Define Our Genetic Makeup
www.mycrimekit.com

Forensic Characterization of Semen

Many cases received in a forensic laboratory involve sexual offenses, making it necessary to examine exhibits for the presence of seminal stains.

The normal male releases 2.5 to 6 milliliters of seminal fluid during an ejaculation. Each milliliter contains 100 million or more spermatozoa, the male reproductive cells. Forensic examination of articles for seminal stains can actually be considered a two-step process. First, before any tests can be conducted, the stain must be located. Considering the number and soiled condition of outer garments, undergarments, and possible bedclothing submitted for examination, this may prove to be an arduous task. Once located, the stain will have to be subjected to tests that will prove its identity; it may even be tested for the blood type of the individual from whom it originated.

Testing for Seminal Stains

Often, seminal stains are readily visible on a fabric because they exhibit a stiff, crusty appearance. However, reliance on such appearance for locating the stain is at best unreliable and is useful only when the stain is present in a rather obvious area. Certainly, if the fabric has been washed or contains only minute quantities of semen, visual examination of the article offers little chance of detecting the stain. The best way to locate and characterize a seminal stain is to perform the *acid phosphatase color test.*

acid phosphatase
An enzyme found in high concentration in semen

ACID PHOSPHATASE TEST   Acid phosphatase is an enzyme that is secreted by the prostate gland into seminal fluid. Its concentrations in seminal fluid are up to 400 times greater than those found in any other body fluid. Its presence can easily be detected when it comes in contact with an acidic solution of sodium alpha naphthylphosphate and Fast Blue B dye. Also, 4-methyl umbelliferyl phosphate (MUP) fluoresces under UV light when it comes in contact with acid phosphatase.

The utility of the acid phosphatase test is apparent when it becomes necessary to search numerous garments or large fabric areas for seminal stains. If a filter paper is simply moistened with water and rubbed lightly over the suspect area, acid phosphatase, if present, is transferred to the filter paper. Then, when a drop or two of the sodium alpha naphthylphosphate and Fast Blue B solution are placed on the paper, the appearance of a purple color indicates the acid phosphatase enzyme. In this manner, any fabric or surface can be systematically searched for seminal stains.

If it is necessary to search extremely large areas—for example, a bedsheet or carpet—the article can be tested in sections, narrowing the location of the stain with each successive test. Alternatively, the garment under investigation can be pressed against a suitably sized piece of moistened filter paper. The paper is then sprayed with MUP solution. Semen stains appear as strongly fluorescent areas under UV light. A negative reaction can be interpreted as meaning the absence of semen. Although some vegetable and fruit juices (such as cauliflower and watermelon), fungi, contraceptive creams, and vaginal secretions give a positive response to the acid phosphatase test, none of these substances normally reacts with the speed of seminal fluid. A reaction time of less than 30 seconds is considered a strong indication of the presence of semen.

MICROSCOPIC EXAMINATION OF SEMEN   Semen can be unequivocally identified by the presence of spermatozoa. When spermatozoa are located through a microscope examination, the stain is definitely identified as having been derived from semen. Spermatozoa are slender, elongated structures 50–70 microns long, each with a head and a thin flagellate tail (see Figure 10–11). The criminalist can normally locate them by immersing the stained material in a small volume of water. Rapid stirring of the liquid transfers a small percentage of the spermatozoa present into the water. A drop of the water is dried onto a microscope slide, then stained and examined under a compound microscope at a magnification of approximately 400×.[4]

Considering the extremely large number of spermatozoa found in seminal fluid, one would think the chance of locating one would be very good; however, this is not always true. One reason is that spermatozoa are bound tightly to cloth materials.[5] Also, spermatozoa are extremely

[4] J. P. Allery et al., "Cytological Detection of Spermatozoa: Comparison of Three Staining Methods," *Journal of Forensic Sciences* 46 (2001): 349.
[5] In one study, only a maximum of 4 sperm cells out of 1,000 could be extracted from a cotton patch and observed under the microscope. Edwin Jones (Ventura County Sheriff's Department, Ventura, Calif.), personal communication.

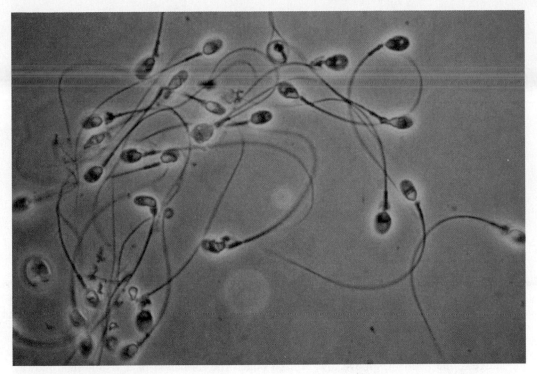

FIGURE 10–11

Photomicrograph of human spermatozoa (300×).
Courtesy John Walsh, Photo Researchers, Inc.

| Antigen and antibody are added to their respective wells | Antigen and antibody move toward each other | Antigen and antibody have formed a visible precipitin line in the gel between the wells |

FIGURE 10–12

brittle when dry and easily disintegrate if the stain is washed or when the stain is rubbed against another object, as can happen frequently in the handling and packaging of this type of evidence. Furthermore, sexual crimes may involve males who have an abnormally low sperm count, a condition known as **oligospermia**, or they may involve individuals who have no spermatozoa at all in their seminal fluid (**aspermia**). Significantly, aspermatic individuals are increasing in numbers because of the growing popularity of vasectomies.

PROSTATE-SPECIFIC ANTIGEN (PSA)   Forensic analysts often must examine stains or swabs that they suspect contain semen (because of the presence of acid phosphatase) but that yield no detectable spermatozoa. How, then, can one unequivocally prove the presence of semen? The solution to this problem came with the discovery in the 1970s of a protein called *p30* or *prostate specific antigen (PSA)*. Under the analytical conditions employed in forensic laboratories, p30 is unique to seminal plasma.

When p30 is isolated and injected into a rabbit, it stimulates the production of polyclonal antibodies (anti-p30). The sera collected from these immunized rabbits can then be used to test suspected semen stains. As shown in Figure 10–12, the stain extract is placed in one well of an electrophoretic plate and the anti-p30 in an opposite well. When an electric potential is applied,

oligospermia
An abnormally low sperm count

aspermia
The absence of sperm; sterility in males

FIGURE 10–13

An antibody–antigen–antibody sandwich or complex is seen as a colored band. This signifies the presence of PSA in the extract of a stain and positively identifies human semen.

the antigens and antibodies move toward each other. The formation of a visible line midway between the two wells shows the presence of p30 in the stain and proves that the stain was seminal in nature.

A more elegant approach to identifying PSA (p30) involves placing an extract of a questioned sample on a porous membrane in the presence of a monoclonal PSA antibody that is linked to a dye. If PSA is present in the extract, a PSA antigen–monoclonal PSA antibody complex forms. This complex then migrates along the membrane, where it interacts with a polyclonal PSA antibody embedded in the membrane. The antibody–antigen–antibody "sandwich" that forms will be apparent by the presence of a colored line (see Figure 10–13). This monoclonal antibody technique is about a hundred times more sensitive for detecting PSA than the one described in the previous paragraph.[6]

Once the material under examination is proven to be semen, the next task is to attempt to associate the semen as closely as possible with a single individual. As we will learn in Chapter 11, forensic scientists can link seminal material to one individual with DNA technology. Just as important is the knowledge that this technology can exonerate many of those wrongfully accused of sexual assault.

Collection and Preservation of Rape Evidence

Seminal constituents on a rape victim are important evidence that sexual intercourse has taken place, but their absence does not necessarily mean that a rape did not occur. Physical injuries such as bruises or bleeding tend to confirm that a violent assault did take place. Furthermore, the forceful physical contact between victim and assailant may result in a transfer of physical evidence—blood, semen, hairs, and fibers. The presence of such physical evidence will help forge a vital link in the chain of circumstances surrounding a sexual crime.

Collection and Handling

To protect this kind of evidence, all the outer and undergarments from the involved parties should be carefully removed and packaged separately in paper (not plastic) bags. Place a clean bedsheet

[6] J. Kearsey, H. Louie, and H. Poon, "Validation Study of the Onestep ABAcard® PSA Test Kit for RCMP Casework," *Canadian Society of Forensic Science Journal* 34 (2001): 63; S. J. Denison, E. M. Lopes, L. D'Costa, and J. C. Newman, "Positive Prostate-Specific Antigen (PSA) Results in Semen-Free Samples," *Canadian Society of Forensic Science Journal* 37 (2004): 197.

on the floor and lay a clean paper sheet over it. The victim must remove her shoes before standing on the paper. Have the person disrobe while standing on the paper in order to collect any loose foreign material falling from the clothing. Collect each piece of clothing as it is removed and place the items in separate paper bags to avoid cross-contamination of physical evidence. Carefully fold the paper sheet so that all foreign materials are contained inside.

If it is deemed appropriate, bedding or the object on which the assault took place should be submitted to the laboratory for processing. Items suspected of containing seminal stains must be handled carefully. Folding an article through the stain may cause it to flake off, as will rubbing the stained area against the surface of the packaging material. If, under unusual circumstances, it is not possible to transport the stained article to the laboratory, the stained area should be cut out and submitted with an unstained piece as a substrate control.

In the laboratory, analysts try to link seminal material to a donor(s) using DNA typing. Because an individual may transfer his or her DNA types to a stain through perspiration, investigators must handle stained articles with care, minimizing direct personal contact. The evidence collector must wear disposable latex gloves when such evidence must be touched.

The rape victim must undergo a medical examination as soon as possible after the assault. At this time, the appropriate items of physical evidence are collected by trained personnel. Evidence collectors should have an evidence-collection kit from the local crime laboratory (see Figures 10–14, 10–15, and 10–16).

The following items of physical evidence are to be collected:

1. *Pubic combings.*   Place a paper towel under the buttocks and comb the pubic area for loose or foreign hairs.
2. *Pubic hair standard/reference samples.*   Cut 15 to 20 full-length hairs from the pubic area at the skin line.
3. *External genital dry-skin areas.*   Swab with at least one dry swab and one moistened swab.

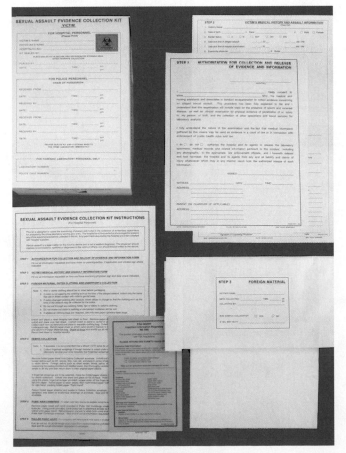

FIGURE 10–14

Victim rape collection kit showing the kit envelope, kit instructions, medical history and assault information forms, and foreign-materials collection bag.
Courtesy Tri-Tech, Inc., Southport, N.C., www.tritechusa.com

FIGURE 10–15

Victim rape collection kit showing collection bags for outer clothing, underpants, debris, pubic hair combings, pubic hair standard/reference samples, vaginal swabs, and rectal swabs.

Courtesy Tri-Tech, Inc., Southport, N.C., www.tritechusa.com

FIGURE 10–16

Victim collection rape kit showing collection bags for oral swabs and smear, pulled head hair standard/reference, known saliva sample, known blood samples, and anatomical drawings.

Courtesy Tri-Tech, Inc., Southport, N.C., www.tritechusa.com

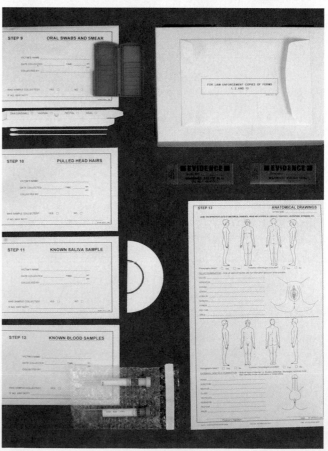

4. ***Vaginal swabs and smear.***   Using two swabs simultaneously, carefully swab the vaginal area and let the swabs air-dry before packaging. Using two additional swabs, repeat the swabbing procedure and smear the swabs onto separate microscope slides, allowing them to air dry before packaging.

5. ***Cervix swabs.***   Using two swabs simultaneously, carefully swab the cervix area and let the swabs air-dry before packaging.

6. ***Rectal swabs and smear.***   To be taken when warranted by case history. Using two swabs simultaneously, swab the rectal canal, smearing one of the swabs onto a microscope slide. Allow both samples to air-dry before packaging.

7. ***Oral swabs and smear.***   To be taken if oral–genital contact occurred. Use two swabs simultaneously to swab the buccal area and gum line. Using both swabs, prepare one smear slide. Allow both swabs and the smear to air-dry before packaging.

8. ***Head hairs.***   Cut at skin line a minimum of five full-length hairs from each of the following scalp locations: center, front, back, left side, and right side. It is recommended that a total of at least 50 hairs be cut and submitted to the laboratory.

9. ***Blood sample.***   Collect at least 20 milliliters in a vacuum tube containing the preservative EDTA. The blood sample can be used for DNA typing as well as for toxicological analysis if required.

10. ***Fingernail scrapings.***   Scrape the undersurface of the nails with a dull object over a piece of clean paper to collect debris. Use separate paper, one for each hand.

11. ***All clothing.***   Package as described earlier.

12. ***Urine specimen.***   Collect 30 milliliters or more of urine from the victim for the purpose of conducting a drug toxicological analysis for Rohypnol, GHB, and other substances associated with drug-facilitated sexual assaults (see pages 200–201).

Often during the investigation of a sexual assault, the victim reports that a perpetrator engaged in biting, sucking, or licking of areas of the victim's body. As we will learn in the next chapter, the tremendous sensitivity associated with DNA technology offers investigators the opportunity to identify a perpetuator's DNA types from saliva residues collected off the skin. The most efficient way to recover saliva residues from the skin is to first swab the suspect area with a rotating motion using a cotton swab moistened with distilled water. A second, dry swab is then rotated over the skin to recover the moist remains on the skin's surface from the wet swab. The swabs are air-dried and packaged together as a single sample.[7]

If a suspect is apprehended, the following items are routinely collected:

1. *All clothing* and any other items believed to have been worn at the time of assault.
2. *Pubic hair combings.*
3. *Pulled head and pubic hair standard/reference samples.*
4. *Penile swab* within twenty-four hours of assault when appropriate to case history.
5. A blood sample or buccal swab (see page 287) for DNA-typing purposes.

The advent of DNA profiling has forced investigators to rethink what items are evidential with respect to a sexual assault. As we will learn in Chapter 11, DNA levels in the range of one-billionth of a gram are now routinely characterized in crime laboratories. In the past, scant attention was paid to the underwear recovered from a male who was suspected of being involved in a sexual assault. From a practical point of view, the presence of seminal constituents on a man's underwear had little or no investigative value. Today, the high sensitivity of DNA analysis has created new areas of investigation. Experience now tells us that it is possible to establish a link between a victim and her assailant by analyzing biological material recovered from the interior front surface of a male suspect's underwear. This is especially important when investigations have failed to yield the presence of a suspect's DNA on exhibits recovered from the victim.

ANALYZING SEMINAL CONSTITUENTS   The persistence of seminal constituents in the vagina may become a factor when trying to ascertain the time of an alleged sexual attack. Although the

---

[7] D. Sweet et al., "An Improved Method to Recover Saliva from Human Skin: The Double Swab Technique," *Journal of Forensic Sciences* 42 (1997): 320.

> >

forensic brief

A common mode of DNA transfer occurs when skin cells from the walls of the victim's vagina are transferred onto the suspect during intercourse. Subsequent penile contact with the inner surface of the suspect's underwear often leads to the recovery of the female victim's DNA from the underwear's inner surface. The power of DNA is aptly illustrated in a case in which the female victim of a rape had consensual sexual intercourse with a male partner prior to being assaulted by a different male. DNA extracted from the inside front area of the suspect's underwear revealed a female DNA profile matching that of the victim. The added bonus in this case was finding male DNA on the same underwear that matched that of the consensual partner.

Source: Gary G. Verret, "Sexual Assault Cases with No Primary Transfer of Biological Material from Suspect to Victim: Evidence of Secondary and Tertiary Transfer of Biological Material from Victim to Suspect's Undergarments," *Proceedings of the Canadian Society of Forensic Science*, Toronto, Ontario, November 2001.

mycrimekit

WEBEXTRA 10.6
Step into the Role of the First Responding Officer at a Sexual Assault Scene
www.mycrimekit.com

mycrimekit

WEBEXTRA 10.7
Assume the Duties of an Evidence-Collection Technician at a Sexual Assault Scene
www.mycrimekit.com

Virtual Forensics Lab

Conduct an Analysis of a Bloodstain
To perform a virtual lab analysis of a bloodstain, go to www.pearsoncustom.com/us/vlm/

presence of spermatozoa in the vaginal cavity provides evidence of intercourse, important information regarding the time of sexual activity can be obtained from the knowledge that motile or living sperm generally survive up to four to six hours in the vaginal cavity of a living person. However, a successful search for motile sperm requires a microscopic examination of a vaginal smear immediately after it is taken from the victim.

A more extensive examination of vaginal collections is later made at a forensic laboratory. Nonmotile sperm may be found in a living female for up to three days after intercourse and occasionally up to six days later. However, intact sperm (sperm with tails) are not normally found 16 hours after intercourse but have been found as late as 72 hours after intercourse. The likelihood of finding seminal acid phosphatase in the vaginal cavity markedly decreases with time following intercourse, with little chance of identifying this substance 48 hours after intercourse.[8] Hence, with the possibility of the prolonged persistence of both spermatozoa and acid phosphatase in the vaginal cavity after intercourse, investigators should determine when and if voluntary sexual activity last occurred before the sexual assault. This information will be useful for evaluating the significance of finding these seminal constituents in the female victim. Blood or buccal swabs for DNA analysis are to be taken from any consensual partner having sex with the victim within 72 hours before the assault.

Another significant indicator of recent sexual activity is p30. This semen marker normally is not detected in the vaginal cavity beyond 24 hours following intercourse.[9]

---

[8] Anne Davies and Elizabeth Wilson, "The Persistence of Seminal Constituents in the Human Vagina," *Forensic Science* 3 (1974): 45.

[9] J. Kearsey, H. Louie, and H. Poon, "Validation Study of the Onestep ABAcard® PSA Test Kit for RCMP Casework," *Canadian Society of Forensic Science Journal* 34 (2001): 63.

chapter summary > > > > > > > > > > > >

The term *serology* describes a broad scope of laboratory tests that use specific antigen and serum antibody reactions. An antibody reacts or agglutinates only with its specific antigen. The identity of each of the four A-B-O blood groups can be established by testing the blood with anti-A and anti-B sera. The concept of specific antigen–antibody reactions has been applied to immunoassay techniques for detecting drugs of abuse in blood and urine. When an animal is injected with an antigen, its body produces a series of different antibodies, all of which are designed to attack some particular site on the antigen of interest. This collection of antibodies is known as *polyclonal antibodies*. Alternately, a more uniform and specific collection of antibodies designed to combine with a single antigen site can be manufactured. Such antibodies are known as *monoclonals*.

The criminalist must answer the following questions when examining dried blood: (1) Is it blood? (2) From what species did the blood originate? (3) If the blood is of human origin, how closely can it be associated to a particular individual? The determination of blood is best made by means of a preliminary color test. A positive result from the Kastle-Meyer color test is highly indicative of blood. Alternatively, the luminol and Bluestar tests are used to search out trace amounts of blood located at crime scenes. The precipitin test uses antisera normally derived from rabbits that have been injected with the blood of a known animal to determine the species origin of a questioned bloodstain. Before the advent of DNA typing, bloodstains were linked to a source by A-B-O typing. This approach has now been supplanted by the newer DNA technology.

Many cases sent to a forensic laboratory involve sexual offenses, making it necessary to examine exhibits for the presence of seminal stains. The best way to locate and characterize a seminal stain is to perform the acid phosphatase color test. Semen can be unequivocally identified by the presence of either spermatozoa or p30, a protein unique to seminal plasma. Forensic scientists can link seminal material to an individual by DNA typing. The rape victim must undergo a medical examination as soon as possible after the assault. At that time clothing, hairs, and vaginal and rectal swabs can be collected for subsequent laboratory examination. If a suspect is apprehended within 24 hours of the assault, it may be possible to detect the victim's DNA on the male's underwear or on a penile swab of the suspect.

review questions

1. Karl Landsteiner discovered that blood can be classified by its _____.

2. True or False: No two individuals, except for identical twins, can be expected to have the same combination of blood types or antigens. _____

3. _____ is the fluid portion of unclotted blood.

4. The liquid that separates from the blood when a clot is formed is called the _____.

5. _____ transport oxygen from the lungs to the body tissues and carry carbon dioxide back to the lungs.

6. On the surface of red blood cells are chemical substances called _____, which impart blood type characteristics to the cells.

7. Type A individuals have _____ antigens on the surface of their red blood cells.

8. Type O individuals have (both A and B, neither A nor B) antigens on their red blood cells.

9. The presence or absence of the _____ and _____ antigens on the red blood cells determines a person's blood type in the A-B-O system.

10. The D antigen is also known as the _____ antigen.

11. Serum contains proteins known as _____, which destroy or inactivate antigens.

12. An antibody reacts with (any, only a specific) antigen.

13. True or False: Agglutination describes the clumping together of red blood cells by the action of an antibody. _____

14. Type B blood contains _____ antigens and anti-_____ antibodies.

15. Type AB blood has (both anti-A and anti-B, neither anti-A nor anti-B) antigens.

16. A drug–protein complex can be injected into an animal to form specific _____ for that drug.

17. The term _____ describes the study of antigen–antibody reactions.

18. Type AB blood (is, is not) agglutinated by both anti-A and anti-B serum.

19. Type B red blood cells agglutinate when added to type (A, B) blood.

20. Type A red blood cells agglutinate when added to type (AB, O) blood.

21. An immunological assay technique used to detect the presence of minute quantities of drugs in blood and urine is _____.

22. The distribution of type A blood in the United States is approximately (42, 15) percent.

23. The distribution of type AB blood in the United States is approximately (12, 3) percent.

24. (All, Most) blood hemoglobin has peroxidase-like activity.

25. For many years, the most commonly used color test for identifying blood was the _____ color test.

26. _____ reagent reacts with blood, causing it to luminesce.

27. Blood can be characterized as being of human origin by the _____ test.

28. Antigens and antibodies (can, cannot) be induced to move toward each other under the influence of an electrical field.

29. Antibodies designed to interact with a specific antigen site are (monoclonal, polyclonal).

30. True or False: Hybridoma cells are used to produce antigens designed to attack one and only one site on an antibody. _____

31. The basic unit of heredity is the _____.

32. Genes are positioned on threadlike bodies called _____.

33. All nucleated cells in the human body, except the reproductive cells, have _____ pairs of chromosomes.

34. The sex of an offspring is always determined by the (mother, father).

35. Genes that influence a given characteristic and are aligned with one another on a chromosome pair are known as _____.

36. When a pair of allelic genes is identical, the genes are said to be (homozygous, heterozygous).

37. A (phenotype, genotype) is an observable characteristic of an individual.

38. The combination of genes present in the cells of an individual is called the _____.

39. A gene (will, will not) appear in a child when it is present in one of the parents.

40. A type B individual may have the genotype _____ or the genotype _____.

41. A type AB mother and type AB father will have offspring of what possible genotypes? _____

42. A type AB mother and type AB father will have offspring of what possible phenotypes? _____

43. The _____ color test is used to locate and characterize seminal stains.

44. Semen is unequivocally identified by the microscopic appearance of _____.

45. Males with a low sperm count have a condition known as (oligospermia, aspermia).

46. The protein _____ is unique to seminal plasma.

47. True or False: DNA may be transferred to an object through the medium of perspiration. _____

48. True or False: Seminal constituents may remain in the vagina for up to six days after intercourse. _____

application and critical thinking

1. Police investigating the scene of a sexual assault recover a large blanket that they believe may contain useful physical evidence. They take it to the laboratory of forensic serologist Scott Alden, asking him to test it for the presence of semen. Noticing faint pink stains on the blanket, Scott asks the investigating detective if he is aware of anything that might recently have been spilled on the blanket. The detective reports that an overturned bowl of grapes and watermelon was found at the scene, as well as a broken glass that had contained wine. After the detective departs, Scott chooses and administers what he considers the best test for analyzing the piece of evidence in his possession. Three minutes after completion of the test, the blanket shows a positive reaction. What test did Scott choose and what was his conclusion? Explain your answer.

2. Criminalist Cathy Richards is collecting evidence from the victim of a sexual assault. She places a sheet on the floor, asks the victim to disrobe, and places the clothing in a paper bag. After collecting pubic combings and pubic hair samples, she takes two vaginal swabs, which she allows to air-dry before packaging. Finally, Cathy collects blood, urine, and scalp hair samples from the victim. What mistakes, if any, did she make in collecting this evidence?

further references

Jones, E. L., Jr., "The Identification and Individualization of Semen Stains," in R. Saferstein, ed., *Forensic Science Handbook*, vol. 2, 2nd ed. Upper Saddle River, N.J.: Prentice Hall, 2005.

Shaler, R. C., "Modern Forensic Biology," in R. Saferstein, ed., *Forensic Science Handbook*, vol. 1, 2nd ed. Upper Saddle River, N.J.: Prentice Hall, 2002.

Virkler, K., and I. K. Lednev, "Analysis of Body Fluids for Forensic Purposes: From Laboratory Testing to Non-Destructive Rapid Confirmatory Identification at a Crime Scene," *Forensic Science International* 188 (2009): 1.

O. J. Simpson—A Mountain of Evidence

On June 12, 1994, police arrived at the home of Nicole Simpson only to view a horrific scene. The bodies of O. J. Simpson's estranged wife and her friend Ron Goldman were found on the path leading to the front door of Nicole's home. Both bodies were covered in blood and had suffered deep knife wounds. Nicole's head was nearly severed from her body. This was not a well-planned murder. A trail of blood led away from the murder scene. Blood was found in O. J. Simpson's Bronco. Blood drops were on O. J.'s driveway and in the foyer of his home. A blood-soaked sock was located in O. J. Simpson's bedroom, and a bloodstained glove rested outside his residence.

As DNA was extracted and profiled from each bloodstained article, a picture emerged that seemed to irrefutably link Simpson to the murders. A trail of DNA leaving the crime scene was consistent with O. J.'s profile, as was the DNA found entering Simpson's home. Simpson's DNA profile was found in the Bronco along with that of both victims. The glove contained the DNA profiles of Nicole and Ron, and the sock had Nicole's DNA profile. At trial, the defense team valiantly fought back. Miscues in evidence collection were craftily exploited. The defense strategy was to paint a picture of not only an incompetent investigation, but one that was tinged with dishonest police planting evidence. The strategy worked. O. J. Simpson was acquitted of murder.

chapter 11

DNA: the indispensable forensic science tool

Learning Objectives

After studying this chapter you should be able to:

- Name the parts of a nucleotide and explain how they are linked together to form DNA

- Understand the concept of base pairing as it relates to the double-helix structure of DNA

- Contrast DNA strands that code for the production of proteins with strands that contain repeating base sequences

- Explain the technology of polymerase chain reaction (PCR) and how it applies to forensic DNA typing

- Understand the structure of an STR

- Describe the difference between nuclear and mitochondrial DNA

- Understand the use of DNA computerized databases in criminal investigation

- List the necessary procedures for the proper preservation of bloodstained evidence for laboratory DNA analysis

KEY TERMS

amelogenin gene
amino acids
buccal cells
chromosome
complementary base pairing
deoxyribonucleic acid (DNA)
electrophoresis
epithelial cells
human genome
hybridization
low copy number
mitochondria
multiplexing
nucleotide
picogram
polymer
polymerase chain reaction (PCR)
primer
proteins
replication
restriction fragment length polymorphisms (RFLPs)
sequencing
short tandem repeat (STR)
substrate control
tandem repeat
touch DNA
Y-STRs

DNA

Abbreviation for deoxyribonucleic acid—the molecules carrying the body's genetic information; DNA is double stranded in the shape of a double helix

The discovery of **deoxyribonucleic acid (DNA)**, the deciphering of its structure, and the decoding of its genetic information were turning points in our understanding of the underlying concepts of inheritance. Now, with incredible speed, as molecular biologists unravel the basic structure of genes, we can create new products through genetic engineering and develop diagnostic tools and treatments for genetic disorders.

For a number of years, these developments were of seemingly peripheral interest to forensic scientists. All that changed when, in 1985, what started out as a more or less routine investigation into the structure of a human gene led to the discovery that portions of the DNA structure of certain genes are as unique to each individual as fingerprints. Alec Jeffreys and his colleagues at Leicester University, England, who were responsible for these revelations, named the process for isolating and reading these DNA markers *DNA fingerprinting*. As researchers uncovered new approaches and variations to the original Jeffreys technique, the terms *DNA profiling* and *DNA typing* came to be applied to describe this relatively new technology.

This discovery caught the imagination of the forensic science community because forensic scientists have long desired to link with certainty biological evidence such as blood, semen, hair, or tissue to a single individual. Although conventional testing procedures had gone a long way toward narrowing the source of biological materials, individualization remained an elusive goal. Now DNA typing has allowed forensic scientists to accomplish this goal. The technique is still relatively new, but in the few years since its introduction, DNA typing has become routine in public crime laboratories and has been made available to interested parties through the services of a number of skilled private laboratories. In the United States, courts have overwhelmingly admitted DNA evidence and accepted the reliability of its scientific underpinnings.

What Is DNA?

chromosome

A rodlike structure in the cell nucleus, along which the genes are located; it is composed of DNA surrounded by other material, mainly proteins

Inside each of 60 trillion cells in the human body are strands of genetic material called **chromosomes**. Arranged along the chromosomes, like beads on a thread, are nearly 25,000 genes. **The gene is the fundamental unit of heredity. It instructs the body cells to make proteins that determine everything from hair color to our susceptibility to diseases.** Each gene is actually composed of DNA specifically designed to carry out a single body function.

Interestingly, although DNA was first discovered in 1868, scientists were slow to understand and appreciate its fundamental role in inheritance. Painstakingly, researchers developed evidence that DNA was probably the substance by which genetic instructions are passed from one generation to the next. But the major breakthrough in comprehending how DNA works did not occur until the early 1950s, when two researchers, James Watson and Francis Crick, deduced the structure of DNA. It turns out that DNA is an extraordinary molecule skillfully designed to carry out the task of controlling the genetic traits of all living cells, plant and animal.

Structure of DNA

polymer

A substance composed of a large number of atoms; these atoms are usually arranged in repeating units, or monomers

Before examining the implications of Watson and Crick's discovery, let's see how DNA is constructed. DNA is a **polymer**. As we will learn in Chapter 12, a polymer is a very large molecule made by linking a series of repeating units.

nucleotide

The unit of DNA consisting of one of four bases—adenine, guanine, cytosine, or thymine—attached to a phosphate–sugar group

NUCLEOTIDES   In the case of DNA, the repeating units are known as **nucleotides**. A nucleotide is composed of a sugar molecule, a phosphorus-containing group, and a nitrogen-containing molecule called a *base*. Figure 11–1 shows how nucleotides can be strung together to form a DNA strand. In this figure, S designates the sugar component, which is joined with a phosphate group to form the backbone of the DNA strand. Projecting from the backbone are the bases.

The key to understanding how DNA works is to appreciate the fact that only four types of bases are associated with DNA: adenine, cytosine, guanine, and thymine. To simplify our discussion of DNA, we will designate each of these bases by the first letter of their names. Hence, *A* will stand for adenine, *C* will stand for cytosine, *G* will stand for guanine, and *T* will represent thymine.

Again, notice in Figure 11–1 how the bases project from the backbone of DNA. Also, although this figure shows a DNA strand of four bases, keep in mind that in theory there is no limit to the length of the DNA strand; in fact, a DNA strand can be composed of a long chain with millions of bases. The information just discussed was well known to Watson and Crick by the time they set about detailing the structure of DNA. Their efforts led to the discovery that the DNA molecule is actually composed of two DNA strands coiled into a *double helix*. This can be thought of as resembling two wires twisted around each other.

As these researchers manipulated scale models of DNA strands, they realized that the only way the bases on each strand could be properly aligned with each other in a double-helix configuration was to place base *A* opposite *T* and *G* opposite *C*. Watson and Crick had solved the puzzle of the double helix and presented the world with a simple but elegant picture of DNA (see Figure 11–2).

COMPLEMENTARY BASE PAIRING   The only arrangement possible in the double-helix configuration was the pairing of bases *A* to *T* and *G* to *C*, a concept that has become known as **complementary base pairing.** Although *A–T* and *G–C* pairs are always required, there are no restrictions on how the bases are to be sequenced on a DNA strand. Thus, one can observe the sequences *T–A–T–T* or *G–T–A–A* or *G–T–C–A*. When these sequences are joined with their complements in a double-helix configuration, they pair as follows:

```
T A T T        G T A A        G T C A
| | | |        | | | |        | | | |
A T A A        C A T T        C A G T
```

Any base can follow another on a DNA strand, which means that the possible number of different sequence combinations is staggering! Consider that the average human chromosome has DNA containing 100 million base pairs. All of the human chromosomes taken together contain

FIGURE 11–1

How nucleotides can be linked to form a DNA strand. S designates the sugar component, which is joined with phosphate groups (P) to form the backbone of DNA. Projecting from the backbone are four bases: *A*, adenine; *G*, guanine; *T*, thymine; and *C*, cytosine.

complementary base pairing
The specific pairing of base A with T and base C with G in double-stranded DNA

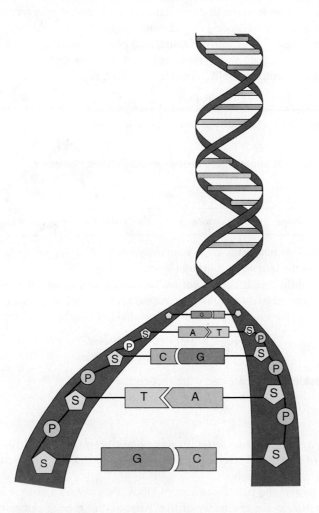

FIGURE 11–2

A representation of a DNA double helix. Notice how bases *G* and *C* pair with each other, as do bases *A* and *T*. This is the only arrangement in which two DNA strands can align with each other in a double-helix configuration.

proteins
Polymers of amino acids that play basic roles in the structures and functions of living things

amino acids
The building blocks of proteins; there are twenty common amino acids; amino acids are linked to form a protein; the types of amino acids and the order in which they're linked determine the character of each protein

about 3 billion base pairs. From these numbers, we can begin to appreciate the diversity of DNA and hence the diversity of living organisms. DNA is like a book of instructions. The alphabet used to create the book is simple enough: *A, T, G,* and *C.* The order in which these letters are arranged defines the role and function of a DNA molecule.

DNA at Work

The inheritable traits that are controlled by DNA arise out of its ability to direct the production of complex molecules called **proteins.** Proteins are actually made by linking a combination of **amino acids.** Although thousands of proteins exist, they can all be derived from a combination of up to 20 known amino acids. The sequence of amino acids in a protein chain determines the shape and function of the protein. Let's look at one example: The protein hemoglobin is found in our red blood cells. It carries oxygen to our body cells and removes carbon dioxide from these cells. One of the four amino acid chains of "normal" hemoglobin is shown in Figure 11–3(a). Studies of individuals with sickle-cell anemia show that this inheritable disorder arises from the presence of "abnormal" hemoglobin in their red blood cells. An amino acid chain for "abnormal" hemoglobin is shown in Figure 11–3(b). Note that the sole difference between "normal" and "abnormal" or sickle-cell hemoglobin arises from the substitution of one amino acid for another in the protein chain.

The genetic information that determines the amino acid sequence for every protein manufactured in the human body is stored in DNA in a genetic code that relies on the sequence of bases along the DNA strand. The alphabet of DNA is simple—*A, T, G,* and *C*—but the key to deciphering the genetic code is to know that each amino acid is coded by a sequence of three bases. Thus, the amino acid alanine is coded by the combination *C–G–T;* the amino acid aspartate is coded by the combination *C–T–A;* and the amino acid phenylalanine is coded by the combination *A–A–A.* With this code in hand, we can now see how the amino acid sequence in a protein chain is determined by the structure of DNA. Consider the DNA segment

$$–C–G–T–C–T–A–A–A–A–C–G–T–$$

The triplet code contained within this segment translates into

$$[C–G–T] – [C–T–A] – [A–A–T] – [C–G–T]$$
$$\textit{alanine} \quad \textit{aspartate} \quad \textit{phenylalanine} \quad \textit{alanine}$$

or the protein chain

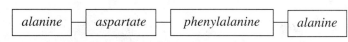

Interestingly, this code is not restricted to humans. Almost all living cells studied to date use the same genetic code as the language of protein synthesis.[1]

If we look at the difference between "normal" and sickle-cell hemoglobin (see Figure 11–3), we see that the latter is formed by substituting one amino acid (valine) for another (glutamate). Within the DNA segment that codes for the production of normal hemoglobin, the letter sequence is

$$–[C–C–T]–[G–A–G]–[G–A–G]–$$
$$\textit{proline} \quad \textit{glutamate} \quad \textit{glutamate}$$

Individuals with sickle-cell disease carry the sequence

$$–[C–C–T]–[G–T–G]–[G–A–G]–$$
$$\textit{proline} \quad \textit{valine} \quad \textit{glutamate}$$

Thus, we see that a single base or letter change (*T* has been substituted for *A* in valine) is the underlying cause of sickle-cell anemia, demonstrating the delicate chemical balance between health and disease in the human body.

As scientists unravel the base sequences of DNA, they obtain a greater appreciation for the roles that proteins play in the chemistry of life. Already the genes responsible for hemophilia,

Figure table (left column)

	Normal hemoglobin	Sickle-cell hemoglobin
1	valine	valine
2	histidine	histidine
3	leucine	leucine
4	threonine	threonine
5	proline	proline
6	glutamate	valine
7	glutamate	glutamate
	(a)	(b)

FIGURE 11–3

(a) A string of amino acids composes one of the protein chains of hemoglobin.
(b) Substitution of just one amino acid for another in the protein chain results in sickle-cell hemoglobin.

---

[1] Instructions for assembling proteins are actually carried from DNA to another region of the cell by ribonucleic acid (RNA). RNA is directly involved in the assembly of the protein using the genetic code it received from DNA.

Duchenne muscular dystrophy, and Huntington's disease have been located. Once scientists have isolated a disease-causing gene, they can determine the protein that the gene has directed the cell to manufacture. By studying these proteins—or the absence of them—scientists will be able to devise a treatment for genetic disorders.

A 13-year project to determine the order of bases on all 23 pairs of human chromosomes (also called the **human genome**) is now complete. Knowing where on a specific chromosome DNA codes for the production of a particular protein is useful for diagnosing and treating genetic diseases. This information is crucial for understanding the underlying causes of cancer. Also, comparing the human genome with that of other organisms will help us understand the role and implications of evolution.

Polymerase Chain Reaction (PCR)

Once the double-helix structure of DNA was discovered, how DNA duplicated itself before cell division became apparent. The concept of base pairing in DNA suggests the analogy of positive and negative photographic film. Each strand of DNA in the double helix has the same information; one can make a positive print from a negative or a negative from a positive.

DNA Replication

The synthesis of new DNA from existing DNA begins with the unwinding of the DNA strands in the double helix. Each strand is then exposed to a collection of free nucleotides. Letter by letter, the double helix is re-created as the nucleotides are assembled in the proper order, as dictated by the principle of base pairing (A with T and G with C). The result is the emergence of two identical copies of DNA where before there was only one (see Figure 11–4). A cell can now pass on its genetic identity when it divides.

Many enzymes and proteins are involved in unwinding the DNA strands, keeping the two DNA strands apart, and assembling the new DNA strands. For example, DNA *polymerases* are enzymes that assemble a new DNA strand in the proper base sequence determined by the original or parent DNA strand. DNA polymerases also "proofread" the growing DNA double helices for mismatched base pairs, which are replaced with correct bases.

Until recently, the phenomenon of DNA **replication** appeared to be only of academic interest to forensic scientists interested in DNA for identification. However, this changed when researchers perfected the technology of using DNA polymerases to copy a DNA strand located outside a living cell. This relatively new laboratory technique is known as **polymerase chain reaction (PCR).** Put simply, PCR is a technique designed to copy or multiply DNA strands.

The PCR Process

In PCR, small quantities of DNA or broken pieces of DNA found in crime-scene evidence can be copied with the aid of a DNA polymerase. The copying process can be accomplished in an automated fashion using a DNA Thermal Cycler (see Figure 11–5). Each cycle of the PCR technique results in a doubling of the DNA, as shown in Figure 11–4. Within a few hours, 30 cycles can multiply DNA a billionfold. Once DNA copies are in hand, they can be analyzed by any of the methods of modern molecular biology. The ability to multiply small bits of DNA opens new and exciting avenues for forensic scientists to explore. It means that sample size is no longer a limitation in characterizing DNA recovered from crime-scene evidence.

PCR is the outgrowth of knowledge gained from an understanding of how DNA strands naturally replicate within a cell. The most important feature of PCR is knowing that an enzyme called *DNA polymerase* can be directed to synthesize a specific region of DNA. In a relatively straightforward manner, PCR can be used to repeatedly duplicate or amplify a strand of DNA millions of times. As an example, let's consider a segment of DNA that we want to duplicate by PCR:

$$-G–T–C–T–C–A–G–C–T–T–\textbf{C–C–A–G}-$$

$$-\textbf{C–A–G}–A–G–T–C–G–A–A–G–G–T–C-$$

human genome
The total DNA content found within the nucleus of a human cell; it is composed of approximately three billion base pairs of genetic information

replication
The synthesis of new DNA from existing DNA

polymerase chain reaction (PCR)
A technique for replicating or copying a portion of a DNA strand outside a living cell; this technique leads to millions of copies of the DNA strand

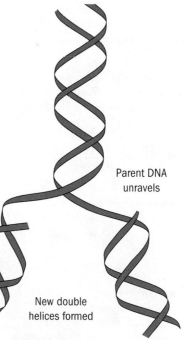

Parent DNA unravels

New double helices formed

FIGURE 11–4

Replication of DNA. The strands of the original DNA molecule are separated, and two new strands are assembled.

FIGURE 11–5

The DNA Thermal Cycler, an instrument that automates the rapid and precise temperature changes required to copy a DNA strand. Within a matter of hours, DNA can be multiplied a millionfold.
Courtesy Applied Biosystems, Foster City, Calif.

primer

A short strand of DNA used to target a region of DNA for replication by PCR

hybridization

The process of joining two complementary strands of DNA to form a double-stranded molecule

mycrimekit™

WEBEXTRA 11.2
Polymerase Chain Reaction
www.mycrimekit.com

tandem repeat

A region of a chromosome that contains multiple copies of a core DNA sequence that are arranged in a repeating fashion

To perform PCR on this DNA segment, short sequences of DNA on each side of the region of interest must be identified. In the example shown here, the short sequences are designated by boldface letters in the DNA segment. These short DNA segments must be available in a pure form known as a **primer** if the PCR technique is going to work.

The first step in the PCR process is to heat the DNA strands to about 94°C. At this temperature, the double-stranded DNA molecules separate completely:

$$-G{-}T{-}C{-}T{-}C{-}A{-}G{-}C{-}T{-}T{-}C{-}C{-}A{-}G-$$

$$-C{-}A{-}G{-}A{-}G{-}T{-}C{-}G{-}A{-}A{-}A{-}G{-}G{-}T{-}C-$$

The second step is to add the primers to the separated strands and allow the primers to combine or **hybridize** with the strands by lowering the test-tube temperature to about 60°C.

$$-G{-}T{-}C{-}T{-}C{-}A{-}G{-}C{-}T{-}T{-}C{-}C{-}A{-}G-$$

$$C{-}A{-}G{-}A$$

$$C{-}C{-}A{-}G$$

$$-C{-}A{-}G{-}A{-}G{-}T{-}C{-}G{-}A{-}A{-}A{-}G{-}G{-}T{-}C-$$

The third step is to add the DNA polymerase and a mixture of free nucleotides (*G*, *A*, *T*, *C*) to the separated strands. When the test tube is heated to 72°C, the polymerase enzyme directs the rebuilding of a double-stranded DNA molecule, extending the primers by adding the appropriate bases, one at a time, resulting in the production of two complete pairs of double-stranded DNA segments.

$$-G{-}T{-}C{-}T{-}C{-}A{-}G{-}C{-}T{-}T{-}C{-}C{-}A{-}G-$$

$$C{-}A{-}G{-}A{-}G{-}T{-}C{-}G{-}A{-}A{-}A{-}G{-}G{-}T{-}C-$$

$$-G{-}T{-}C{-}T{-}C{-}A{-}G{-}C{-}T{-}T{-}C{-}C{-}A{-}G$$

$$-C{-}A{-}G{-}A{-}G{-}T{-}C{-}G{-}A{-}A{-}A{-}G{-}G{-}T{-}C-$$

This completes the first cycle of the PCR technique, and the outcome is a doubling of the number of DNA strands—that is, from one to two. The cycle of heating, cooling, and strand rebuilding is then repeated, resulting again in a doubling of the DNA strands. On completion of the second cycle, four double-stranded DNA molecules will have been created from the original double-stranded DNA sample. Typically, 28 to 32 cycles are carried out to yield almost a billion copies of the original DNA molecule. Each cycle takes less than two minutes to perform.

From the forensic scientist's viewpoint, PCR offers another distinct advantage in that it can amplify minute quantities of DNA, thus overcoming the limited sample-size problem often associated with crime-scene evidence. With PCR, less than one-billionth of a gram of DNA is required for analysis. Consequently, PCR can characterize DNA extracted from small quantities of blood, semen, and saliva.

DNA Typing

Geneticists have discovered that portions of the DNA molecule contain sequences of letters that are repeated numerous times. In fact, more than 30 percent of the human genome is composed of repeating segments of DNA. These repeating sequences, or **tandem repeats,** seem to act as filler or spacers between the coding regions of DNA. Although these repeating segments do not seem to affect our outward appearance or control any other basic genetic function, they are nevertheless part of our genetic makeup, inherited from our parents in the manner illustrated by the Punnett square (page 254). The origin and significance of these tandem repeats is a mystery, but to forensic scientists they offer a means of distinguishing one individual from another through DNA typing.

Forensic scientists first began applying DNA technology to human identity in 1985. From the beginning, attention has focused on the tandem repeats of the genome. These repeats can be visualized as a string of connected boxes with each box having the same core sequence of DNA

G–C–T G–G–T G–C–T G–G–C C–T–C
Fifteen–base core

FIGURE 11–6

A DNA segment consisting of a series of repeating DNA units. In this illustration, the 15-base core can repeat itself hundreds of times. The entire DNA segment is typically hundreds to thousands of bases long.

bases (see Figure 11–6). All humans have the same type of repeats, but there is tremendous variation in the number of repeats that each of us has.

Restriction Fragment Length Polymorphisms (RFLPs)

Up until the mid-1990s, the forensic community aimed its efforts at characterizing repeat segments known as **restriction fragment length polymorphisms (RFLPs).** These repeats are cut out of the DNA double helix by a restriction enzyme that acts like a pair of scissors. A number of different RFLPs were selected by the forensic science community for performing DNA typing. Typically a core sequence is 15 to 35 bases long and repeats itself up to one thousand times.

RFLP DNA typing has the distinction of being the first scientifically accepted protocol in the United States used for the forensic characterization of DNA. However, its utility has been short lived. New technology incorporating PCR has supplanted RFLP. In its short history, perhaps RFLP's most startling impact related to the impeachment trial of President Bill Clinton. The whole complexion of the investigation regarding the relationship of the president with a White House intern, Monica Lewinsky, changed when it was revealed that Ms. Lewinsky possessed a dress that she claimed was stained with the president's semen. The FBI Laboratory was asked to compare the DNA extracted from the dress stain with that of the president. An RFLP match was obtained between the president's DNA and the stain. The combined frequency of occurrence for the seven DNA types found was nearly one in eight trillion, an undeniable link. The dress and a copy of the FBI DNA report are shown in Figure 11–7.

Why couldn't the PCR technology be applied to RFLP DNA typing? Simply put, the RFLP strands are too long, often containing thousands of bases. PCR is best used with DNA strands that are no longer than a couple of hundred bases. The obvious solution to this problem is to characterize DNA strands that are much shorter than RFLPs. Another advantage in moving to shorter DNA strands is that they would be expected to be more stable and less subject to degradation brought about by adverse environmental conditions. The long RFLP strands tend to break apart under adverse conditions not uncommon at crime scenes.

restriction fragment length polymorphisms (RFLPs)
Different fragment lengths of base pairs that result from cutting a DNA molecule with restriction enzymes

Short Tandem Repeats (STRs)

Currently, **short tandem repeat (STR)** analysis has emerged as the most successful and widely used DNA-profiling procedure. STRs are locations (loci) on the chromosome that contain short sequence elements that repeat themselves within the DNA molecule. They serve as helpful markers for identification because they are found in great abundance throughout the human genome.

STRs normally consist of repeating sequences of three to seven bases; the entire strand of an STR is also very short, less than 450 bases long. These strands are significantly shorter than those encountered in other DNA-typing procedures. This means that STRs are much less susceptible to degradation and are often recovered from bodies or stains that have been subject to extreme decomposition. Also, because of their shortness, STRs are an ideal candidate for multiplication by PCR, thus overcoming the limited-sample-size problem often associated with crime-scene evidence. Only the equivalent of 18 DNA-containing cells is needed to obtain a DNA profile. For instance, STR has been used to identify the origin of saliva residue on envelopes, stamps, soda cans, and cigarette butts.

To understand the utility of STRs in forensic science, let's look at one commonly used STR known as TH01. This DNA segment contains the repeating sequence *A–A–T–G*. Seven TH01 variants have been identified in the human genome. These variants contain five to eleven repeats of *A–A–T–G*. Figure 11–8 illustrates two such TH01 variants, one containing six repeats and the other containing eight repeats of *A–A–T–G*.

short tandem repeat (STR)
A region of a DNA molecule that contains short segments consisting of three to seven repeating base pairs

---

FEDERAL BUREAU OF INVESTIGATION
WASHINGTON, D. C. 20535

Report of Examination

Examiner Name:	▓▓▓▓▓▓▓	Date:	08/17/98
Unit:	DNA Analysis 1	Phone No.:	202-324-4409
FBI File No.:	29D-OIC-LR-35063	Lab No.:	980730002 S BO
			980803100 S BO

Results of Examinations:

Deoxyribonucleic acid (DNA) profiles for the genetic loci D2S44, D17S79, D1S7, D4S139, D10S28, D5S110 and D7S467 were developed from HaeIII-digested high molecular weight DNA extracted from specimens K39 and Q3243-1(a semen stain removed from specimen Q3243). Based on the results of these seven genetic loci, specimen K39 (CLINTON) is the source of the DNA obtained from specimen Q3243-1, to a reasonable degree of scientific certainty.

No DNA-RFLP examinations were conducted on specimen Q3243-2 (a semen stain removed from specimen Q3243).

BLACK — 1,440,000,000,000
CAUC — 7,870,000,000,000
SEH — 3,140,000,000,000
SWH — 943,000,000,000

DNAU1 - Page 1 of 1

This Report Is Furnished For Official Use Only

Q3243

FIGURE 11–7

The dress and the FBI Report of Examination for a semen stain located on the dress.

electrophoresis

A technique for separating molecules through their migration on a support medium while under the influence of an electrical potential

During a forensic examination, TH01 is extracted from biological materials and amplified by PCR as described earlier. The ability to copy an STR means that extremely small amounts of the molecule can be detected and analyzed. Once the STRs have been copied or amplified, they are separated by **electrophoresis,** a process discussed in Chapter 5 (see pages 131–132). By examining the distance the STR has migrated on the electrophoretic plate, one can determine the number of A–A–T–G repeats in the STR. Every person has two STR types for TH01, one inherited from each parent. Thus, for example, one may find in a semen stain TH01 with six repeats and eight repeats. This combination of TH01 is found in approximately 3.5 percent of the population.

When examining an STR DNA pattern, one merely needs to look for a match between band sets. For example in, Figure 11–9, DNA extracted from a crime-scene stain matches the DNA

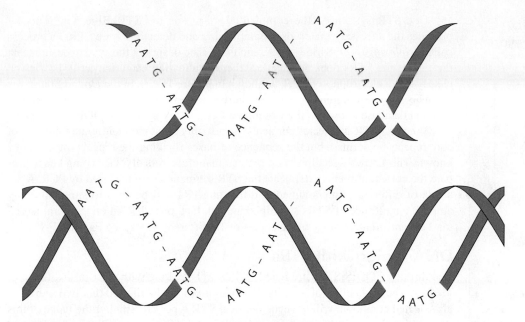

FIGURE 11–8

Variants of the short tandem repeat TH01. The upper DNA strand contains six repeats of the sequence *A–A–T–G*; the lower DNA strand contains eight repeats of the sequence *A–A–T–G*. This DNA type is designated as TH01 6,8.

FIGURE 11–9

A DNA profile pattern of a suspect and its match to crime-scene DNA. From left to right, lane 1 is a DNA standard marker; lane 2 is the crime-scene DNA; and lanes 3 to 5 are control samples from suspects 1, 2, and 3, respectively. Crime-scene DNA matches suspect 2.

Courtesy Edvotek, The Biotechnology Education Company www.edvotek.com

recovered from one of three suspects. When comparing only one STR, only a limited number of people in a population would have the same STR fragment pattern as the suspect. However, by using additional STRs, a high degree of discrimination or complete individualization can be achieved.

Multiplexing

What makes STRs so attractive to forensic scientists is that hundreds of different types of STRs are found in human genes. The more STRs one can characterize, the smaller the percentage of the population from which these STRs can emanate. This gives rise to the concept of **multiplexing.** Using PCR technology, one can simultaneously extract and amplify a combination of different STRs.

multiplexing
A technique that simultaneously detects more than one DNA marker in a single analysis

FIGURE 11–10

A triplex system containing three loci: FGA, vWA, and D3S1358, indicating a match between the questioned and the standard/reference stains.

One STR system on the commercial market is the STR Blue Kit.[2] This kit provides the necessary materials for amplifying and detecting three STRs (a process called *triplexing*)—D3S1358, vWA, and FGA. The design of the system ensures that the size of the STRs does not overlap, thereby allowing each marker to be viewed clearly on an electrophoretic gel, as shown in Figure 11–10. In the United States, the forensic science community has standardized on thirteen STRs for entry into a national database known as the Combined DNA Index System (CODIS).

When an STR is selected for analysis, not only must the identity and number of core repeats be defined, but the sequence of bases flanking the repeats must also be known. This knowledge allows commercial manufacturers of STR-typing kits to prepare the correct primers to delineate the STR segment to be amplified by PCR. Also, a mix of different primers aimed at different STRs will be used to simultaneously amplify a multitude of STRs (multiplexing). In fact, one STR kit on the commercial market can simultaneously make copies of 15 different STRs (see Figure 11–11).

DNA Typing with STRs

The thirteen CODIS STRs are listed in Table 11–1 along with their probabilities of identity. The probability of identity is a measure of the likelihood that two individuals selected at random will have an identical STR type. The smaller the value of this probability, the more discriminating the STR. A high degree of discrimination and even individualization can be attained by analyzing a combination of STRs (multiplexing). Because STRs occur independently of each other, the probability of biological evidence having a particular combination of STR types is determined by the product of their frequency of occurrence in a population. This combination is referred to as the *product rule* (see p. 64). Hence, the greater the number of STRs characterized, the smaller the frequency of occurrence of the analyzed sample in the general population.

FIGURE 11–11

STR profile for 15 loci.

Courtesy H. Edward Grotjan, Ph.D.

[2] Applied Biosystems, 850 Lincoln Centre Drive, Foster City, Calif. 94404.

TABLE 11–1

The Thirteen CODIS STRs and Their Probability of Identities

STR	African American	U.S. Caucasian
D3S1358	0.094	0.075
vWA	0.063	0.062
FGA	0.033	0.036
TH01	0.109	0.081
TPOX	0.090	0.195
CSF1PO	0.081	0.112
D5S818	0.112	0.158
D13S317	0.136	0.085
D7S820	0.080	0.065
D8S1179	0.082	0.067
D21S11	0.034	0.039
D18S51	0.029	0.028
D16S539	0.070	0.089

Source: *The Future of Forensic DNA Testing: Predictions of the Research and Development Working Group.* Washington, D.C.: National Institute of Justice, Department of Justice, 2000, p. 41.

The combination of the first three STRs shown in Table 11–1 typically produces a frequency of occurrence of about 1 in 5,000. A combination of the first six STRs typically yields a frequency of occurrence in the range of 1 in two million for the Caucasian population, and if the top nine STRs are determined in combination, this frequency declines to about 1 in one billion. The combination of all 13 STRs shown in Table 11–1 typically produces frequencies of occurrence that measure in the range of 1 in 575 trillion for Caucasian Americans and 1 in 900 trillion for African Americans. Importantly, several commercially available kits allow forensic scientists to profile STRs in the kinds of combinations cited here.

Capillary Electrophoresis

The separation of STRs can typically be carried out on a flat gel-coated electrophoretic plate, as described earlier. However, the need to reduce analysis time and to automate sampling and data collection has led to the emergence of *capillary electrophoresis* as the preferred technology for characterization of STRs. Capillary electrophoresis is carried out in a thin glass column rather than on the surface of a coated-glass plate.

As illustrated in Figure 11–12, each end of the column is immersed in a reservoir of buffer liquid that also holds electrodes (coated with platinum) to supply high-voltage energy. The column is coated with a gel polymer, and the DNA-containing sample solution is injected into one end of the column by applying a high voltage to an electrode immersed in the DNA solution. The STR fragments then move through the column under the influence of an electrical potential at a speed that is related to the length of the STR fragments. The other end of the column is connected to a detector that tracks the separated STRs as they emerge from the column. As the DNA peaks pass through the detector, they are recorded on a display known as an *electropherogram*, as shown in Figure 11–11.

Sex Identification Using STRs

Manufacturers of commercial STR kits typically used by crime laboratories provide one additional piece of useful information along with STR types: the sex of the DNA contributor. The focus of attention here is the **amelogenin gene** located on both the X and Y chromosomes. This gene, which is actually the gene for tooth pulp, has an interesting characteristic in that it is shorter by six bases in the X chromosome than in the Y chromosome. Hence, when the amelogenin gene is amplified by PCR and separated by electrophoresis, males, who have an X and a Y chromosome, show two bands; females, who have two X chromosomes, have just one band. Typically, these results are obtained in conjunction with STR types.

Another tool in the arsenal of the DNA analyst is the ability to type STRs located on the Y chromosome. The Y chromosome is male specific and is always paired with the X chromosome.

amelogenin gene
A genetic locus useful for determining gender

MiniSTRs

The forensic science community turned to STRs when it became apparent that short segments of DNA would be required to meet the requirements of PCR. Commercial manufacturers of DNA-typing kits prepared a series of 13 STRs for compatibility with the CODIS DNA database that ranged in length from 100 to 450 bases. One obvious benefit in working with short DNA segments was the likelihood that useful information could be extracted even from fragmented DNA. This often proved to be the case, but not always. On occasion, degraded DNA is encountered that is so badly damaged that traditional STR analysis is not possible. Prolonged exposure of DNA to extreme environmental elements, such as temperature extremes, humidity, or microbial activity, can lead to such degradation. An approach to dealing with this problem is to further shorten the STR strands that emerge form the PCR process.

The approach that has been taken to accomplish this task is to create new primers that can be positioned closer to the STR repeat region (see Figure 1). The shorter STR products (called *amplicons*) that now emerge from PCR increase the chances of char-acterizing badly fragmented strands of DNA. These smaller amplicons are called "miniSTRs." One manufacturer of STR kits has produced a miniSTR kit designed to amplify eight miniSTRs, seven of which are totally compatible with the CODIS database. The miniSTRs range in size from 71 to 250 bases. A DNA analyst suspecting a degraded sample now has the option, if sample size permits, of running both traditional STR and miniSTR determinations, or just the latter.

The advent of miniSTRs means that forensic scientists can now analyze samples that were once thought to be of no value. One of the first benefactors of miniSTR technology was the identification of a number of victims from the Waco Branch Davidian fire. Also, a number of World Trade Center victims were identified by miniSTR technology. Another focus of attention has been human hair. In the past, extracting nuclear DNA out of the hair shaft has been enormously difficult; the number of STRs in hair has been found to be very low as well as highly degraded. However, one study has demonstrated that miniSTRs may overcome some of the difficulties in obtaining partial profiles from the degraded DNA present in shed hair.[3]

FIGURE 1

Appropriate primers are positioned close to the repeat units of a DNA segment in order to initiate the PCR process that will create short or miniSTRs.

Y-STRs

Short tandem repeats located on the human Y chromosome

Although more than 400 **Y-STRs** have been identified, only a small number of them are being used for forensic applications. One commercial kit allows for the characterization of 17 Y chromosome STRs. When can it be advantageous to seek out Y-STR types? Generally, Y-STRs are useful for analyzing blood, saliva, or a vaginal swab that is a mix originating from more than one male. For example, Y-STRs prove useful when multiple males are involved in a sexual assault. Further simplifying the analysis is that any DNA in the mixture that originates from a female will not show.

[3] K. E. Opel et al., "Evaluation and Quantification of Nuclear DNA from Human Telogen Hairs," *Journal of Forensic Sciences* 53 (2008): 853.

FIGURE 11–12

Capillary electrophoresis technology has evolved from the traditional flat gel electrophoresis approach. The separation of DNA segments is carried out on the interior wall of a glass capillary tube that is kept at a constant voltage. The size of the DNA fragments determines the speed at which they move through the column. This figure illustrates the separation of three sets of STRs (triplexing).

mycrimekit

WEBEXTRA 11.3
See the 13 CODIS STRs and Their
Chromosomal Positions
www.mycrimekit.com

mycrimekit

WEBEXTRA 11.4
See How to Calculate the Frequency
of Occurrence of a DNA Profile
www.mycrimekit.com

mycrimekit

WEBEXTRA 11.5
Understand the Operational Principles of Capillary Electrophoresis
www.mycrimekit.com

mycrimekit

WEBEXTRA 11.6
See the Electropherogram Record
from One Individual's DNA
www.mycrimekit.com

mycrimekit

WEBEXTRA 11.7
An Animation Depicting Y-STRs
www.mycrimekit.com

Keep in mind that STR types derived from the Y chromosome originate only from this single male chromosome. A female subject, or one with an XX chromosome pattern, does not contribute any DNA information. Also, unlike a conventional STR type that is derived from two chromosomes and typically shows two bands or peaks, a Y-STR has only one band or peak for each STR type.

For example, the traditional STR DNA pattern may prove to be overly complex in the case of a vaginal swab containing the semen of two males. Each STR type would be expected to show four bands, two from each male. Also complicating the appearance of the DNA profile may be the presence of DNA from skin cells emanating from the walls of the vagina. In this circumstance, homing in on the Y chromosome greatly simplifies the appearance and interpretation of the DNA profile. Thus, when presented with a DNA mixture of two males and one female, each STR type would be expected to show six bands. However, the same mixture subjected to Y-STR analysis would show only two bands (one band for each male) for each Y-STR type.

Significance of DNA Typing

STR DNA typing has become an essential and basic investigative tool in the law enforcement community. The technology has progressed at a rapid rate and in only a few years has surmounted numerous legal challenges to become vital evidence for resolving violent crimes and sex offenses. DNA evidence is impartial, implicating the guilty and exonerating the innocent.

In a number of well-publicized cases, DNA evidence has exonerated individuals who have been wrongly convicted and imprisoned. The importance of DNA analyses in criminal investigations has also placed added burdens on crime laboratories to improve their quality-assurance procedures and to ensure the correctness of their results. In several well-publicized instances, the accuracy of DNA tests conducted by government-funded laboratories has been called into question.

The Combined DNA Index System (CODIS)

Perhaps the most significant investigative tool to arise from a DNA-typing program allows crime laboratories to compare DNA types recovered from crime-scene evidence to those of convicted sex offenders and other convicted criminals. This capability is of tremendous value to investigators in cases in which the police have not been able to identify a suspect. All 50 states have legislatively mandated collection of DNA samples from convicted offenders of particular crimes and establishment of DNA databases for law enforcement purposes. CODIS (Combined DNA Index System) is a computer software program developed by the FBI that maintains local, state, and national databases of DNA profiles from convicted offenders, unsolved crime-scene evidence, arrestees, and profiles of missing people. CODIS software enables local, state, and national crime laboratories to compare DNA profiles electronically. Thousands of matches have linked serial crimes to each other and have solved crimes by allowing investigators to match crime-scene evidence to known convicted offenders. As mentioned earlier, in the United States the forensic science community has currently standardized on 13 STRs for entry into CODIS.

Currently, more than 170 public law enforcement laboratories across the United States participate in CODIS. In addition, CODIS is used by more than 40 law enforcement laboratories in more than 25 countries for their own DNA database inquiries. As previously mentioned, state laws now require the acquisition of DNA profiles from all convicted offenders. These profiles are continually added to state and national DNA data banks and have proven to be invaluable investigative resources for law enforcement. CODIS has produced more than 95,000 hits.

Mitochondrial DNA

Typically, when one describes DNA in the context of a criminal investigation, the subject is assumed to be the DNA in the nucleus of a cell. Actually, a human cell contains two types of DNA—nuclear and mitochondrial. The first constitutes the 23 pairs of chromosomes in the nuclei of our

> >

Familial DNA—Expanding the DNA Database

In 1984, Deborah Sykes was raped and stabbed to death as she walked to work in Winston-Salem, North Carolina. A month later, Darryl Hunt, then 19 years old, was arrested and eventually convicted of the crime. Hunt insisted that he was innocent, and by 1990, DNA testing of semen found on Sykes proved that he was not its source. Nevertheless, North Carolina prosecutors ignored this new evidence and he remained in jail. Finally, a search against Darryl Hunt's STR profile in the North Carolina DNA database revealed a close but not perfect match to a genetic profile already in the database, that of his brother. Upon further investigation, that man, Willard Brown, confessed to Sykes's murder in 2003, and Hunt was finally freed from prison.

In this case, DNA profiling exonerated an innocent man and helped lead the police to the real culprit. The Sykes case illustrates how the contents of a criminal DNA database can be dramatically expanded to aid the police in identifying criminals by searching the database for near matches.

Typically, the CODIS database is used to find exact matches with crime-scene DNA. However, taking into account the facts that the 13 STR loci that constitute U.S. offender DNA databases are genetically inherited and that each individual's DNA profile is genetically determined by one's parents creates opportunities to use the database's raw data to search out close relatives. DNA profiles of related individuals are likely to show a higher proportion of shared STR loci as compared to unrelated individuals. Hence, searching the database for profiles that have a high degree of commonality may lead to the identification of a close relative of the perpetrator. Interestingly, studies have shown that a person's chances of committing a crime increase if a parent or sibling had previously done so. A 1999 U.S. Department of Justice survey found that 46 percent of jail inmates had at least one close relative who had also been incarcerated.

The potential for improving the effectiveness of DNA database searches is considerable. Familial searches of a DNA database would dramatically increase the size of the database by three or more times because every profile that is entered would, in effect, contain genetic information about the STR alleles of the donor's parents, siblings, and children. One study estimates that using familial DNA searches could increase the "cold hit" rates by 40 percent. Considering the fact that there have been about 95,000 cold hits in the United States, familial DNA has the potential for identifying thousands of additional criminal suspects.

The concept of familial DNA searching has been routinely adopted in the United Kingdom. In the United States, the FBI notifies investigators about close matches it finds using its current software, but the agency has no current plans to modify its search algorithms to optimize the database's capacity to ferret out near or close matches. This leaves it up to the states to decide whether to release identifying information about an offender whose DNA closely matches a crime scene sample from another state. Challengers to familial database searching have cited it as a violation of constitutional protections against unreasonable search and seizure. A number of mixed state court decisions have failed to produce a consensus on the constitutionality of familial DNA database searches.

---

cells. Each parent contributes to the genetic makeup of these chromosomes. Mitochondrial DNA (mtDNA), on the other hand, is found outside the nucleus of the cell and is inherited solely from the mother.

MITOCHONDRIA   **Mitochondria** are cell structures found in all human cells. They are the power plants of the body, providing about 90 percent of the energy that the body needs to function. A single mitochondrion contains several loops of DNA, all of which are involved in energy generation. Further, because each cell in our bodies contains hundreds to thousands of mitochondria, there are hundreds to thousands of mtDNA copies in a human cell. This compares to just one set of nuclear DNA located in that same cell. Thus, forensic scientists are offered enhanced sensitivity and the opportunity to characterize mtDNA when nuclear DNA is significantly degraded, such as

mitochondria
Small structures located outside the nucleus of a cell; these structures supply energy to the cell; maternally inherited DNA is found in each mitochondrion

in charred remains, or when nuclear DNA may be present in a small quantity (such as in a hair shaft). Interestingly, when authorities cannot obtain a reference sample from an individual who may be long deceased or missing, an mtDNA reference sample can be obtained from any maternally related relative. However, all individuals of the same maternal lineage will be indistinguishable by mtDNA analysis.

Although mtDNA analysis is significantly more sensitive than nuclear DNA profiling, forensic analysis of mtDNA is more rigorous, time consuming, and costly than nuclear DNA profiling. For this reason, only a handful of public and private forensic laboratories receive evidence for this type of determination. The FBI Laboratory has imposed strict limitations on the type of cases in which it will apply mtDNA technology.

SEQUENCING   As was previously discussed, nuclear DNA is composed of a continuous linear strand of nucleotides (*A*, *T*, *G*, and *C*). On the other hand, mtDNA is constructed in a circular or loop configuration. Each loop contains enough (approximately 16,569) *A*, *T*, *G*, and *C* to make up 37 genes involved in mitochondrial energy generation. Two regions of mtDNA have been found to be highly variable in the human population. These two regions have been designated hypervariable region I (HV1) and hypervariable region II (HV2), as shown in Figure 11–13. As indicated previously, the process for analyzing HV1 and HV2 is tedious. It involves generating many copies of these DNA hypervariable regions by PCR and then determining the order of the *A–T–G–C* bases constituting the hypervariable regions. This process is known as **sequencing.** The FBI Laboratory, the Armed Forces DNA Identification Laboratory, and other laboratories have collaborated to compile an mtDNA population database containing the base sequences from HV1 and HV2.

sequencing

A procedure used to determine the order of the base pairs that constitute DNA

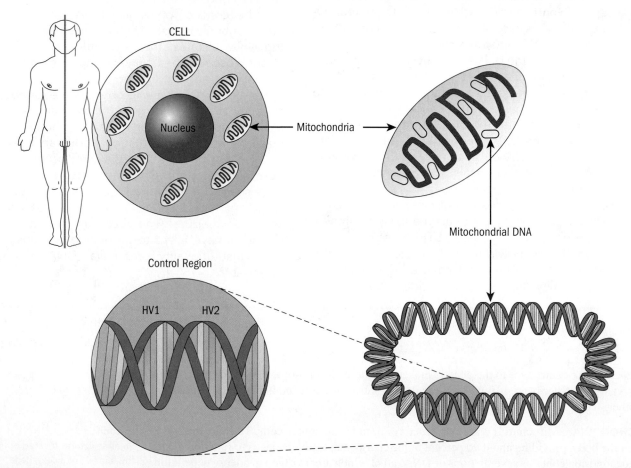

FIGURE 11–13

Every cell in the body contains hundreds of mitochondria, which provide energy to the cell. Each mitochondrion contains numerous copies of DNA shaped in the form of a loop. Distinctive differences between individuals in their mitochondrial DNA makeup are found in two specific segments of the control region on the DNA loop known as HV1 and HV2.

Once the sequences of the hypervariable regions from a case sample are obtained, most laboratories simply report the number of times these sequences appear in the mtDNA database maintained by the FBI. The mtDNA database contains about five thousand sequences. This approach permits an assessment of how common or rare an observed mtDNA sequence is in the database. Interestingly, many of the sequences that have been determined in casework are unique to the existing database, and many types are present at frequencies no greater than 1 percent in the database. Thus it is often possible to demonstrate how uncommon a particular mitochondrial DNA sequence is. However, even under the best circumstances, mtDNA typing does not approach STR analysis in its discrimination power. Thus, mtDNA analysis is best reserved for samples for which nuclear DNA typing is simply not possible.

The first time mtDNA was admitted as evidence in a U.S. court was in 1996 in the case of *State of Tennessee* v. *Paul Ware*. Here, mtDNA was used to link two hairs recovered from the crime scene to the defendant. Interestingly, in this case, blood and semen evidence was absent. Mitochondrial DNA analysis also plays a key role in the identification of human remains. An abundant amount of mtDNA is generally found in skeletal remains. Importantly, mtDNA reference samples are available from family members sharing the same mother, grandmother, great-grandmother, and so on. One of the most publicized cases performed on human remains was the identification of the individual buried in the tomb of the Vietnam War's unknown soldier. The remains lying in the tomb were believed to belong to First Lt. Michael J. Blassie, whose A-37 warplane was shot down near An Loc, South Vietnam, in 1972. In 1984, the U.S. Army Central Identification Laboratory failed to identify the remains by physical characteristics, personal artifacts, or blood-typing results from hairs. The remains were subsequently placed in the tomb. In 1998, at the insistence of the Blassie family, the remains were disinterred for the purpose of performing mtDNA analysis and comparing the results to references from seven families thought to be associated with the case. The remains in the tomb were subsequently analyzed and confirmed to be consistent with DNA from Lt. Blassie's family.

mycrimekit

WEBEXTRA 11.9
Look into the Structure of
Mitochondrial DNA and See
How It Is Used for DNA Typing
www.mycrimekit.com

Collection and Preservation of Biological Evidence for DNA Analysis

Since the early 1990s, the advent of DNA profiling has vaulted biological crime-scene evidence to a stature of importance that is eclipsed only by the fingerprint. In fact, the high sensitivity of DNA determinations has even changed the way police investigators define biological evidence.

forensic brief

In the fall of 1979, a 61-year-old patient wandered away from a U.S. Department of Veterans Affairs medical facility. Despite an extensive search, authorities never located the missing man. More than ten years later, a dog discovered a human skull in a wooded area near the facility. DNA Analysis Unit II of the FBI Laboratory received the case in the winter of 1999. The laboratory determined that the mitochondrial DNA profile from the missing patient's brother matched the mitochondrial DNA profile from the recovered skull and provided the information to the local medical examiner. Subsequently, the remains were declared to be those of the missing patient and returned to the family for burial.

Source: FBI Law Enforcement Bulletin 78 (2002): 21.

forensics at work

The JonBenét Ramsey Murder Case

Point–Counterpoint

Point

July 9, 2008

Boulder District Attorney Mary T. Lacy issues the following announcement with regard to the investigation of the murder of JonBenét Ramsey.

On December 25–26, 1996, JonBenét Ramsey was murdered in the home where she lived with her mother, father and brother. Despite a long and intensive investigation, the death of JonBenét remains unsolved.

The murder has received unprecedented publicity and has been shrouded in controversy. That publicity has led to many theories over the years in which suspicion has focused on one family member or another. However, there has been at least one persistent stumbling block to the possibility of prosecuting any Ramsey family members for the death of JonBenét—DNA.

As part of its investigation of the JonBenét Ramsey homicide, the Boulder Police identified genetic material with apparent evidentiary value. Over time, the police continued to investigate DNA, including taking advantage of advances in the science and methodology. One of the results of their efforts was that they identified genetic material and a DNA profile from drops of JonBenét's blood located in the crotch of the underwear she was wearing at the time her body was discovered. That genetic profile belongs to a male and does not belong to anyone in the Ramsey family.

The police department diligently compared that profile to a very large number of people associated with the victim, with her family, and with the investigation, and has not identified the source, innocent or otherwise, of this DNA. The Boulder Police and prosecutors assigned to this investigation in the past also worked conscientiously with laboratory analysts to obtain better results through new approaches and additional tests as they became available. Those efforts ultimately led to the discovery of sufficient genetic markers from this male profile to enter it into the national DNA data bank.

In December of 2002, the Boulder District Attorney's Office, under Mary T. Lacy, assumed responsibility for the investigation of the JonBenét Ramsey homicide. Since then, this office has worked with the Boulder Police Department to continue the investigation of this crime.

In early August of 2007, District Attorney Lacy attended a Continuing Education Program in West Virginia sponsored by the National Institute of Justice on Forensic Biology and DNA. The presenters discussed successful outcomes from a new methodology described as "touch DNA." One method for sampling for touch DNA is the "scraping method." In this process, forensic scientists scrape a surface where there is no observable stain or other indication of possible DNA in an effort to recover for analysis any genetic material that might nonetheless be present. This methodology was not well known in this country until recently and is still used infrequently.

In October of 2007, we decided to pursue the possibility of submitting additional items from the JonBenét Ramsey homicide to be examined using this methodology. We checked with a number of Colorado sources regarding which private laboratory to use for this work. Based upon multiple recommendations, including that of the Boulder Police Department, we contacted the Bode Technology Group located near Washington, D.C., and initiated discussions with the professionals at that laboratory. First Assistant District Attorney Peter Maguire and Investigator Andy Horita spent a full day with staff members at the Bode facility in early December of 2007.

The Bode Technology laboratory applied the "touch DNA" scraping method to both sides of the waist area of the long johns that JonBenét Ramsey was wearing over her underwear when her body was discovered. These sites were chosen because evidence supports the likelihood that the perpetrator removed and/or replaced the long johns, perhaps by handling them on the sides near the waist.

On March 24, 2008, Bode informed us that they had recovered and identified genetic material from both sides of the waist area of the long johns. The unknown male profile previously identified from the inside crotch area of the underwear matched the DNA recovered from the long johns at Bode.

We consulted with a DNA expert from a different laboratory, who recommended additional investigation into the remote possibility that the DNA might have come from sources at the autopsy when this clothing was removed. Additional samples were obtained and then analyzed by the Colorado Bureau of Investigation to assist us in this effort. We received those results on June 27th of this year and are, as a result, confidant that this DNA did not come from innocent sources at the autopsy. As mentioned above, extensive DNA testing had previously excluded people connected to the family and to the investigation as possible innocent sources.

I want to acknowledge my appreciation for the efforts of the Boulder Police Department, Bode Technology

Group, the Colorado Bureau of Investigation, and the Denver Police Department Forensic Laboratory for the great work and assistance they have contributed to this investigation.

The unexplained third party DNA on the clothing of the victim is very significant and powerful evidence. It is very unlikely that there would be an innocent explanation for DNA found at three different locations on two separate items of clothing worn by the victim at the time of her murder. This is particularly true in this case because the matching DNA profiles were found on genetic material from inside the crotch of the victim's underwear and near the waist on both sides of her long johns, and because concerted efforts that might identify a source, and perhaps an innocent explanation, were unsuccessful.

It is therefore the position of the Boulder District Attorney's Office that this profile belongs to the perpetrator of the homicide.

DNA is very often the most reliable forensic evidence we can hope to find during a criminal investigation. We rely on it often to bring to justice those who have committed crimes. It can likewise be reliable evidence upon which to remove people from suspicion in appropriate cases.

The Boulder District Attorney's Office does not consider any member of the Ramsey family, including John, Patsy, or Burke Ramsey, as suspects in this case. We make this announcement now because we have recently obtained this new scientific evidence that adds significantly to the exculpatory value of the previous scientific evidence. We do so with full appreciation for the other evidence in this case.

Local, national, and even international publicity has focused on the murder of JonBenét Ramsey. Many members of the public came to believe that one or more of the Ramseys, including her mother or her father or even her brother, were responsible for this brutal homicide. Those suspicions were not based on evidence that had been tested in court; rather, they were based on evidence reported by the media.

It is the responsibility of every prosecutor to seek justice. That responsibility includes seeking justice for people whose reputations and lives can be damaged irreparably by the lingering specter of suspicion. In a highly publicized case, the detrimental impact of publicity and suspicion on people's lives can be extreme. The suspicions about the Ramseys in this case created an ongoing living hell for the Ramsey family and their friends, which added to their suffering from the unexplained and devastating loss of JonBenét.

For reasons including those discussed above, we believe that justice dictates that the Ramseys be treated only as victims of this very serious crime. We will accord them all the rights guaranteed to the victims of violent crimes under the law in Colorado and all the respect and sympathy due from one human being to another. To the extent that this office has added to the distress suffered by the Ramsey family at any time or to any degree, I offer my deepest apology.

We prefer that any tips related to this ongoing investigation be submitted in writing or via electronic mail to BoulderDA.org, but they can also be submitted to our tip line at (303) 441–1636.

This office will make no further statements.

Counterpoint

Last year, then–Boulder, Colorado, District Attorney Mary Keenan Lacy, who had been "investigating" the Ramsey case for the last few years, wrote a letter to JonBenét's father John, apologizing for having believed he or his wife, the late Patsy, or their son Burke (then nine) had anything to do with their daughter's 1996 death. Lacy indicated that recent tests from the Bode Laboratory of Virginia revealed that their "new methodology" of touch DNA found a match that proves an intruder was culpable of the slaying in which the six-year-old was molested, strangled and given a fractured skull.

There has always been unmatched, unknown male DNA—likely from saliva—in the inside crotch of the child's underpants. A minute amount, too degraded to get a proper DNA profile, was mixed with her blood when someone stuck her oh-so-slightly with the pointed end of a broken paintbrush on the night of her death. Because the DNA was so insignificant, it was theorized to have come from someone coughing during the manufacturing process, then the blood drops on top rehydrated it. If the DNA and blood were deposited at the same time, they would have degraded at the same rate—but here the blood sample was robust.

Lacy wrote that the lab discovered that sloughed-off skin cells on the waist area of the long johns JonBenét wore over her underpants can be matched to the underpants' DNA.

That was great news for people who want to believe there was an intruder with no link to the family members. No one imagines a parent could harm a child in such a brutal and horrendous fashion. Only problem is, adults—including parents—kill kids all the time. While

(Continued)

forensics at work

The JonBenét Ramsey Murder Case (continued)

this murder is unique in its application and renown, from an investigative point of view it's just another homicide that has to be dissected to be understood. Anyone looking rationally at the evidence here, and assessing it as a whole, cannot be pleased with Lacy's letter to Ramsey or the fact that she cleared the most credible suspects in the case. At the least it sets a terrible precedent where other people "under the umbrella of suspicion" in other cases will demand the same treatment if their investigations take a long time to reach a courtroom. Just because someone isn't on trial, or a case has gone cold, doesn't mean that the right people aren't firmly under the microscope of authorities.

Mary Lacy left office in January, 2009, and the new DA, or any in the future, can retract her pronouncement. Frankly it will take a brave person to go against the sea of public opinion by individuals who want to blame a bogeyman. One note of encouragement is the case has been returned to the Boulder police, who are better equipped to investigate than the DA's office ever was. The case had been moved to Lacy's predecessor when the Ramsey family complained that the police spotlight on them was unfair. As we all know, there's no statute of limitations on homicide.

This doesn't take Lacy off the hook, as I see it. Here are some facts of the case which were ignored by her reckless decision. . . .

Touch DNA is nothing new to law enforcement, although Bode has only tested for it for about three years. For some ten years, the FBI lab at Quantico and other labs have used it to capture skin cells from inside masks or gloves, and from guns or knives.

Neither Lacy nor Bode will make available their test results so independent experts can critically review the information. If scientific evidence is to be used to make an argument, proof should be offered. Perhaps some media outlet will file a lawsuit to compel the documents.

What Lacy and Bode have said is that the mystery man's DNA is on the waist area, and that the DNA doesn't match any Ramsey family member. Nothing is stated about where and how much Ramsey DNA was discovered. Patsy dressed the child in those long johns before putting her to bed, and the waistband is precisely what John's two hands touched when he carried his daughter's stiff body in a vertical position upstairs from the basement where she was found deceased. And since DNA can survive multiple launderings, we can't pinpoint when that touch DNA was left on the waistband.

Boulder County Coroner Dr. John Meyer's autopsy report is the Rosetta Stone to this case. It explains the type and order of JonBenét's injuries—asphyxiation by a ligature, then a head blow. It does not reveal who killed the girl. Due to the three-page phony ransom note that many analysts believe was penned by Patsy, the working strategy was to consider Mrs. Ramsey as the perpetrator of all the insults inflicted upon the tot. But while there might have been enough evidence for an arrest, there was not enough for a conviction—and among insiders there was debate about who—if anyone in the household—did what. Without a clear through-line that police and prosecutors could agree upon, what chance would a jury have to find its way to a guilty verdict?

What the autopsy report states without equivocation is that the child suffered vaginal injuries that were "chronic," meaning they predated the murder by days or weeks. We're talking repeated digital penetration that eroded—not ruptured—her hymen. Also, the opening of her vagina was twice the size of a similar aged child's. These factors would have been testified to by at least three pediatric gynecological physicians, had the case gone to trial. This unknown pedophile would have needed on-going intimate access to JonBenét before the night she died. Mary Lacy's early prosecutorial career was as a sex crimes expert, so why didn't she recognize the nature of this little girl's injuries?

If some accident led to JonBenét being strangled, then hit violently in the head, a normal reaction would have been for her caretakers to rush her to a hospital.

---

picogram
One-trillionth of a gram, or 0.000000000001 gram

low copy number
Fewer than 18 DNA-bearing cells

Just how sensitive is STR profiling? Forensic analysts using currently accepted protocols can reach sensitivity levels as low as 125 **picograms.** Interestingly, a human cell has an estimated 7 picograms of DNA, which means that only 18 DNA-bearing cells are needed to obtain an STR profile. However, modifications in the technology can readily extend the level of detection down to 9 cells. A quantity of DNA that is below the normal level of detection is defined as a **low copy number.** With this technology in hand, the horizon of the criminal investigator extends beyond the traditional dried blood or semen stain to include stamps and envelopes licked with saliva, a cup or can that has touched a person's lips, chewing gum, the sweat band of a hat, or a bedsheet

But that didn't happen, I surmise, because her pre-existing genital injuries would have been noticed. And so, a ridiculous—and sadly, effective—cover-up ensued.

Mary Lacy was responsible for the 2006 debacle where she had arrested and brought back from Thailand a false confessor named John Mark Karr. When the underpants' DNA excluded him from being the perpetrator she let him go and publicly stated: "The DNA could be an artifact. It isn't necessarily the killer's. There's a probability that it's the killer's. But it could be something else."

She added: "No one is really cleared of a homicide until there's a conviction in court, beyond a reasonable doubt. And I don't think you will get any prosecutor, unless they were present with the person at the time of the crime, to clear someone."

What made her change her thinking when she cleared the Ramseys?

More to the point, where are the intruder's skin cells from the rope around the child's neck, the paintbrush, the spoon and bowl of pineapple she ate from just before she died, the white blanket that covered her, the flashlight believed to have hit her head, and the pen and paper used in the bogus ransom note? And where is the intruder's touch DNA on the waistband of JonBenét's underpants? Did the stranger pull down her long johns, then command her to pull down her own panties? Are we to believe he then put on gloves—or maybe a whole scuba suit, since there were no unidentified footprints, finger- or handprints, hairs or fibers?

Woven inside the rope around the neck, which was wrapped around a piece of a broken paintbrush, were fibers from the distinctive jacket Patsy wore that evening—and, allegedly, inside the underpants were fibers from the wool sweater John had on. Patsy's fibers were also in the tote where the paintbrush came from and on the sticky side of the piece of duct tape that covered JonBenét's mouth—a length of tape so small it could have been easily flicked aside by her

tongue if it had been placed on her mouth while she was alive.

Lacy wrote that autopsy personnel were swabbed and tested for a DNA match, and thus excluded. But what about crime scene workers or lab technicians? And how many markers are in the touch DNA profile? The underpants' DNA was not enough to get a proper match through CODIS, the federal database. That didn't stop Lacy from sending it through on a regular basis—such busywork has little prospect of ending with a match, but it makes it seem as if something is being done.

Years ago, there was a civil suit in this case wherein a federal judge issued a statement that said, based on her reading of the material submitted to her, there was a higher likelihood of an intruder being the killer than a family member. At that time, Mary Lacy read a statement that suggested the Ramseys were innocent, based on the judicial ruling—though not clearing them. That statement was reportedly dictated to her by a Ramsey associate. What only those close to the case know is that one side of the civil suit completely abandoned its case, never offering paperwork, so the only information the judge had was that which came from the Ramsey camp. Ergo, an easy decision for the judge to make. Since then, Ramsey advisers have pummeled Lacy to clear the family entirely and eventually it happened. The Ramsey case isn't alone. The parents of a missing and presumed dead British three-year-old have used the media and spinmeisters that include members of the Ramseys' own team, and a duped public which has contributed millions of bucks, to petition for their names to be cleared.

It's egregious when an officer of the court misrepresents scientific evidence to win political favor. Mary Lacy was right to offer up an apology. But it should have been to JonBenét and not her family.

Source: Dawna Kaufmann, investigative journalist Co-author with Cyril H. Wecht, MD, JD, of *A Question of Murder.*

---

containing dead skin cells. Likewise, skin or **epithelial cells** transferred onto the surface of a weapon, the interior of a glove, or a pen have yielded DNA results.[4]

The phenomenon of transferring DNA via skin cells onto the surface of an object has come to be called **touch DNA.** Again, keep in mind that, in theory, only 18 skin cells deposited on an object are required to obtain a DNA profile.

The ultimate sensitivity goal in forensic DNA analysis is profiling DNA extracted from one human cell. Such an accomplishment seems close to fruition. Researchers have reported obtaining

epithelial cells
The outer layer of skin cells; these DNA-bearing cells often fall off or are rubbed off onto objects retrieved from crime scenes

touch DNA
DNA from skin cells transferred onto the surface of an object by simple contact

[4] R. A. Wickenheiser, "Trace DNA: A Review, Discussion of Theory, and Application of the Transfer of Trace Qualities through Skin Contact," *Journal of Forensic Sciences* 47 (2002): 442.

STR profiles from one or two cells and have successfully profiled DNA from single dermal-ridge fingerprints.[5] Although it's premature to imply that this technology, or a comparable one, is eligible for admission in criminal trials, one cannot exclude its use in criminal and forensic intelligence investigations. Table 11–2 illustrates the power of DNA as a creator of physical evidence.

Collection of Biological Evidence

However, before investigators become enamored with the wonders of DNA, they should first realize that the crime scene must be treated in the traditional manner. Before the collection of evidence begins, biological evidence should be photographed close up and its location relative to the entire crime scene recorded through notes, sketches, and photographs. If the shape and position of bloodstains may provide information about the circumstances of the crime, an expert must immediately conduct an on-the-spot evaluation of the blood evidence. The significance of the position and shape of bloodstains can best be ascertained when the expert has an on-site overview of the entire crime scene and can better reconstruct the movement of the individuals involved. No attempt should be made to disturb the blood pattern before this phase of the investigation is completed.

The evidence collector must handle all body fluids and biologically stained materials with a minimum amount of personal contact. All body fluids must be assumed to be infectious; hence, wearing disposable latex gloves while handling the evidence is required. Latex gloves also significantly reduce the possibility that the evidence collector will contaminate the evidence. These gloves should be changed frequently during the evidence-collection phase of the investigation. Safety considerations and avoidance of contamination also call for the wearing of face masks, shoe covers, and possibly coveralls.

Blood has great evidential value when a transfer between a victim and suspect can be demonstrated. For this reason, all clothing from both victim and suspect should be collected and sent to the laboratory for examination. This procedure must be followed even when the presence of blood on a garment does not appear obvious to the investigator. Laboratory search procedures are far

TABLE 11–2

Location and Sources of DNA at Crime Scenes

Evidence	Possible Location of DNA on the Evidence	Source of DNA
Baseball bat or similar weapon	Handle, end	Sweat, skin, blood, tissue
Hat, bandanna or mask	Inside	Sweat, hair, dandruff
Eyeglasses	Nose or ear pieces, lens	Sweat, skin
Facial tissue, cotton swab	Surface area	Mucus, blood, sweat, semen, ear wax
Dirty laundry	Surface area	Blood, sweat, semen
Toothpick	Tips	Saliva
Used cigarette	Cigarette butt	Saliva
Stamp or envelope	Licked area	Saliva
Tape or ligature	Inside/outside surface	Skin, sweat
Bottle, can, or glass	Sides, mouthpiece	Saliva, sweat
Used condom	Inside/outside surface	Semen, vaginal or rectal cells
Blanket, pillow, sheet	Surface area	Sweat, hair, semen, urine, saliva
"Through and through" bullet	Outside surface	Blood, tissue
Bite mark	Person's skin or clothing	Saliva
Fingernail, partial fingernail	Scrapings	Blood, sweat, tissue

Source: National Institute of Justice, U.S. Department of Justice.

---

[5] E. K. Hanson and J. Ballantyne, "Whole Genome Amplification Strategy for Forensic Genetic Analysis Using Single or Few Cell Equivalents of Genomic DNA," *Analytical Biochemistry* 346 (2005): 246.

more revealing and sensitive than any that can be conducted at the crime scene. In addition, blood should also be searched for in less-than-obvious places. For example, the criminal may have wiped his or her hands on materials not readily apparent to the investigator. Investigators should look for towels, handkerchiefs, or rags that may have been used and then hidden, and should also examine floor cracks or other crevices that may have trapped blood.

Packaging of Biological Evidence

Biological evidence should not be packaged in plastic or airtight containers because accumulation of residual moisture could contribute to the growth of DNA-destroying bacteria and fungi. **Each stained article should be packaged separately in a paper bag or a well-ventilated box.** If feasible, the entire stained article should be packaged and submitted for examination. If this is not possible, dried blood is best removed from a surface with a sterile cotton-tipped swab lightly moistened with distilled water from a dropper bottle. A portion of the unstained surface material near the recovered stain must likewise be removed or swabbed and placed in a separate package. This is known as a **substrate control**. The forensic examiner may use the substrate swab to confirm that the results of the tests performed were brought about by the stain and not by the material on which it was deposited. However, this practice is normally not necessary when DNA determinations are carried out in the laboratory. One point is critical, and that is that the collected swabs must not be packaged in a wet state. After the collection is made, the swab must be air-dried for approximately five to ten minutes. Then it is best to place it in a swab box (see Figure 11–14), which has a circular hole to allow air circulation. The swab box can then be placed in a paper or manila envelope.

All packages containing biological evidence should be refrigerated or stored in a cool location out of direct sunlight until delivery to the laboratory. However, one common exception is blood mixed with soil. Microbes present in soil rapidly degrade DNA. Therefore, blood in soil must be stored in a clean glass or plastic container and immediately frozen.

substrate control
An unstained object adjacent to an area on which biological material has been deposited

buccal cells
Cells derived from the inner cheek lining

Obtaining DNA Reference Specimens

Biological evidence attains its full forensic value only when an analyst can compare each of its DNA types to known DNA samples collected from victims and suspects. For this purpose, at least 7 milliliters (7 cc) of whole blood should be drawn from individuals by a qualified medical person. The blood sample should be collected in a sterile vacuum tube containing the preservative *EDTA* (ethylenediamine tetraacetic acid). In addition to serving as a preservative, EDTA inhibits the activity of enzymes that degrade DNA. The tubes must be kept refrigerated (not frozen) while awaiting transportation to the laboratory. In addition to blood, other options exist for obtaining standard/reference DNA specimens. The least intrusive method for obtaining a DNA standard/reference, one that nonmedical personnel can readily use, is the *buccal swab*. Cotton swabs are placed in the subject's mouth and the inside of the cheek is vigorously swabbed, resulting in the transfer of **buccal cells** onto the swab.

With the increasing need for collection and analysis of DNA samples in forensic investigations, collection and long-term storage of DNA has become an important consideration. FTA paper is a type of commercially available filter paper loaded with a mix of reagents on which DNA samples can be stored. The card has been impregnated with a chemical that protects DNA from bacterial enzyme breakdown. The fibers of the paper can entrap the DNA for more than ten years without refrigeration. Figure 11–15 illustrates the collection of a buccal swab and its transfer onto an FTA card for storage.

If an individual is not available to give a DNA standard/reference sample, some interesting alternatives are available to evidence collectors, including a toothbrush, combs and hairbrushes, a razor, soiled laundry, used cigarette butts, and earplugs. Any of these items may contain a sufficient quantity of DNA for typing purposes. Interestingly, as investigators worked to identify the remains of victims of the World Trade Center attack on September 11, 2001, the families of the missing were requested to supply the New York City DNA Laboratory with these types of items in an effort to match recovered DNA with human remains.

FIGURE 11–14

Air-dried swabs are placed in a swab box for delivery to the forensic laboratory.
Courtesy Tri-Tech, Inc., Southport, N.C., www.tritechusa.com

(1)

(2)

(3)

(4)

FIGURE 11–15

(1) A buccal swab is collected by rubbing each cheek for 15 seconds. (2) A protective film is peeled off the FTA card. (3) The swab is snapped in place against the FTA paper. (4) The FTA card is removed from the collection device and stored.

Courtesy GE Healthcare Bio-Sciences Corp. (GEHC), Piscataway, N.J., www.whatman.com

mycrimekit

WEBEXTRA 11.10
DNA Forensics
www.mycrimekit.com

mycrimekit

WEBEXTRA 11.11
Step into the Role of the First Responding Officer at a Burglary Scene
www.mycrimekit.com

Contamination of DNA Evidence

One key concern during the collection of a DNA-containing specimen is contamination. Contamination can occur by introducing foreign DNA through coughing or sneezing onto a stain during the collection process, or there can be a transfer of DNA when items of evidence are incorrectly placed in contact with each other during packaging. Fortunately, an examination of DNA band patterns in the laboratory readily reveals the presence of contamination. For example, with an STR, one will expect to see a two-band pattern. More than two bands suggest a mixture of DNA from more than one source.

Crime-scene investigators can take some relatively simple steps to minimize contamination of biological evidence:

1. Change gloves before handling each new piece of evidence.
2. Collect a substrate control for possible subsequent laboratory examination.

3. Pick up small items of evidence such as cigarette butts and stamps with clean forceps. Disposable forceps are to be used so that they can be discarded after a single evidence collection.

4. Always package each item of evidence in its own well-ventilated container.

A common occurrence at crime scenes is to suspect the presence of blood but not be able to observe any with the naked eye. In these situations, the common test of choice is luminol (see page 249). Interestingly, luminol does not inhibit the ability to detect and characterize STRs.[6] Therefore, luminol can be used to locate traces of blood and areas that have been washed nearly free of blood without compromising the potential for DNA typing.

mycrimekit

WEBEXTRA 11.12
Assume the Duties of an Evidence Collection Technician at a Burglary Scene
www.mycrimekit.com

Virtual Forensics Lab

DNA
To perform a virtual DNA lab, go to www.pearsoncustom.com/us/vlm/

forensic brief

A woman alleged that she had been held against her will and sexually assaulted by a male friend in an apartment. During the course of the assault, a contact lens was knocked from the victim's eye. After the assault, she escaped, but because she was afraid of the threats made by her attacker, she did not report the assault to the police for three days. When the police examined the apartment, they noted that it had been thoroughly cleaned. A vacuum cleaner bag was seized for examination, and several pieces of material resembling fragments of a contact lens were discovered within the bag.

In the laboratory, approximately 20 nanograms of human DNA was recovered from the contact lens fragments. Cells from both the eyeball and the interior of the eyelids are naturally replaced every 6 to 24 hours. Therefore, both are potential sources for the DNA found. The DNA profile originating from the fragments matched the victim, thus corroborating the victim's account of the crime. The estimated population frequency of occurrence for the nine matching STRs are approximately 1 in 850 million. The suspect subsequently pleaded guilty to the offense.

STR Locus	Victim's DNA Type	Contact Lens
D3S1358	15,18	15,18
FGA	24, 25	24, 25
vWA	17,17	17,17
TH01	6, 7	6, 7
F13A1	5, 6	5, 6
fes/fps	11,12	11,12
D5S818	11,12	11,12
D13S317	11,12	11,12
D7S820	10,12	10,12

Source: R. A. Wickenheiser and R. M. Jobin, "Comparison of DNA Recovered from a Contact Lens Using PCR DNA Typing," *Canadian Society of Forensic Science Journal* 32 (1999): 67.

[6] A. M. Gross et al., "The Effect of Luminol on Presumptive Tests and DNA Analysis Using the Polymerase Chain Reaction," *Journal of Forensic Sciences* 44 (1999): 837.

chapter summary

> > > > > > > > > > >

Portions of the DNA structure are as unique to each individual as fingerprints. The gene is the fundamental unit of heredity. Each gene is actually composed of DNA specifically designed to control the genetic traits of our cells. DNA is constructed as a very large molecule made by linking a series of repeating units called nucleotides. Four types of bases are associated with the DNA structure: adenine (*A*), guanine (*G*), cytosine (*C*), and thymine (*T*). The bases on each strand are properly aligned in a double-helix configuration. As a result, adenine pairs with thymine and guanine pairs with cytosine. This concept is known as base pairing. The order of the bases is what distinguishes different DNA strands.

Portions of the DNA molecule contain sequences of bases that are repeated numerous times. To a forensic scientist, these tandem repeats offer a means of distinguishing one individual from another through DNA typing. Length differences associated with relatively short repeating DNA strands are called short tandem repeats (STRs) and form the basis for the current DNA-typing procedure. They serve as useful markers for identification because they are found in great abundance throughout the human genome. STRs normally consist of repeating sequences 3 to 7 bases long, and the entire strand of an STR is also very short, less than 450 bases long. This means that STRs are much less susceptible to degradation and may often be

recovered from bodies or stains that have been subjected to decomposition. Also, because of their shortness, STRs are ideal candidates for multiplication by PCR, in which STR strands are multiplied over a billionfold. PCR is responsible for the ability of STR typing to detect the genetic material of as few as 18 DNA-bearing cells. The more STRs one can characterize, the smaller the percentage of the population from which a particular combination of STRs can emanate. This gives rise to the concept of multiplexing. Using the technology of PCR, one can simultaneously extract and amplify a combination of different STRs. Currently, U.S. crime laboratories have standardized on 13 STRs. With STR analysis, as few as 125 picograms of DNA are required.

Another type of DNA used for individual characterization is mitochondrial DNA. Mitochondrial DNA is located outside the cell's nucleus and is inherited from the mother. However, mitochondrial DNA typing does not approach STR analysis in its discrimination power and thus is best reserved for samples, such as hair, for which STR analysis may not be possible.

Bloodstained evidence should not be packaged in plastic or airtight containers because accumulation of residual moisture could contribute to the growth of blood-destroying bacteria and fungi. Each stained article should be packaged separately in a paper bag or in a well-ventilated box.

review questions

1. The fundamental unit of heredity is the _____.

2. Each gene is actually composed of _____, specifically designed to carry out a single body function.

3. A(n) _____ is a very large molecule made by linking a series of repeating units.

4. A(n) _____ is composed of a sugar molecule, a phosphorus-containing group, and a nitrogen-containing molecule called a base.

5. DNA is actually a very large molecule made by linking a series of _____ to form a natural polymer.

6. _____ different bases are associated with the makeup of DNA.

7. Watson and Crick demonstrated that DNA is composed of two strands coiled into the shape of a(n) _____.

8. The structure of DNA requires the pairing of base A to _____ and base G to _____.

9. The base sequence *T–G–C–A* can be paired with the base sequence _____ in a double-helix configuration.

10. The inheritable traits that are controlled by DNA arise out of DNA's ability to direct the production of _____.

11. _____ are derived from a combination of up to 20 known amino acids.

12. The production of an amino acid is controlled by a sequence of _____ bases on the DNA molecule.

13. True or False: Enzymes known as DNA polymerase assemble new DNA strands into a proper base sequence during replication. _____

14. True or False: DNA can be copied outside a living cell. _____

15. True or False: All of the letter sequences in DNA code for the production of proteins. _____

16. In STR DNA typing, a typical DNA pattern shows (two, three) bands.

17. True or False: Specimens amenable to DNA typing are blood, semen, body tissues, and hair. _____

18. Short DNA segments containing repeating sequences of three to seven bases are called _____.

19. True or False: The longer the DNA strand, the less susceptible it is to degradation. _____

20. The short length of STRs allows them to be replicated by _____.

21. True or False: Enzymes known as DNA polymerases assemble new DNA strands into a proper base sequence based off the template strand during replication. _____

22. DNA evidence at a crime scene can be copied by the processes of the _____ with the aid of a DNA polymerase and specific primers.

23. Used as markers for identification purposes, _____ are locations on the chromosome that contain short sequences that repeat themselves within the DNA molecule and in great abundance throughout the human genome.

24. (CODIS, AFIS) maintains local, state, and national databases of DNA profiles from convicted offenders, unsolved crime-scene evidence, and profiles of missing people.

25. Amazingly, the sensitivity of STR profiling requires only _____ DNA-bearing cells to obtain an STR profile.

26. During evidence collection, all body fluids must be assumed to be _____ and handled with latex-gloved hands.

27. The concept of (CODIS, multiplexing) involves simultaneous detection of more than one DNA marker.

28. DNA fragments can be separated and identified by (gas chromatography, capillary electrophoresis).

29. The amelogenin gene shows two bands for a (male, female) and one band for a (male, female).

30. Y-STR typing is useful when one is confronted with a DNA mixture containing more than one (male, female) contributor.

31. Mitochondrial DNA is inherited from the (mother, father).

32. True or False: Mitochondrial DNA is more plentiful in the human cell than is nuclear DNA. _____

33. (Two, Four) regions of mitochondrial DNA have been found to be highly variable in the human population.

34. True or False: Polymerase chain reaction is a part of the process used in the forensic analysis of RFLP, STRs, and mitochondrial DNA. _____

35. The national DNA database in the United States has standardized on _____ STRs for entry into the database.

36. True or False: Y-STR data is normally entered into the CODIS database collection. _____.

37. Small amounts of blood are best submitted to a crime laboratory in a (wet, dry) condition.

38. True or False: Airtight packages make the best containers for blood-containing evidence. _____

39. Whole blood collected for DNA-typing purposes must be placed in a vacuum containing the preservative _____.

40. A typical STR DNA type emanating from a single individual shows a (one, two, three)-band pattern.

application and critical thinking

1. The following sequence of bases is located on one strand of a DNA molecule:

   C–G–A–A–T–C–G–C–A–A–T–C–G–A–C–C–T–G

   List the sequence of bases that will form complementary pairs on the other strand of the DNA molecule.

2. A woman reports being mugged by a masked assailant, whom she scratched on the arm during a brief struggle. The victim gives the police a good description of her attacker, but she is not sure whether the attacker was male or female. Describe the steps and procedures you would use to determine the sex of the attacker. How will you know whether the attacker is male or female?

3. Police discover a badly decomposed body buried in an area where a man disappeared some years before. The case was never solved, nor was the victim's body ever recovered. As the lead investigator, you suspect that the newly discovered body is that of the victim. What is your main challenge in using DNA typing to determine whether your suspicion is correct? How would you go about using DNA technology to test your theory?

4. You are a forensic scientist performing DNA typing on a blood sample sent to your laboratory. While performing an STR analysis on the sample, you notice a four-band pattern. What conclusion should you draw? Why?

further references

Butler, J. M., *Forensic DNA Typing*, 3rd ed. Burlington, Mass.: Elsevier Academic Press, 2010.

Inman, K., and N. Rudin, *An Introduction to Forensic DNA Analysis*, 2nd ed. Boca Raton, Fla.: Taylor & Francis, 2002.

Isenberg, A. R., "Forensic Mitochondrial DNA Analysis," in R. Saferstein, ed., *Forensic Science Handbook*, vol. 2, 2nd ed. Upper Saddle River, N.J.: Prentice Hall, 2005.

Isenberg, A. R., and J. M. Moore, "Mitochondrial DNA Analysis at the FBI Laboratory," *Forensic Science Communications* 1, no. 2 (1999), http://www.fbi.gov/hq/lab/fsc/backissu/july1999/dnalist.htm.

Kobilinsky, L., "Deoxyribonucleic Acid Structure and Function—A Review," in R. Saferstein, ed., *Forensic Science Handbook*, vol. 3, 2nd ed.., Upper Saddle River, N.J.: Prentice Hall, 2010.

The Forensic Community's Response to September 11

On September 11, Brion Smith was home in Frederick, Md., enjoying a vacation day when the news flashed across his television screen—the World Trade Center (WTC) buildings had been struck by two hijacked airplanes. Minutes later, a third plane struck the Pentagon while a fourth later crashed in a field in Somerset County, Pa. Acting on impulse, Smith, chief deputy medical examiner for the DNA Division of the Office of the Armed Forces Medical Examiner (OAFME), immediately gathered his things and headed in to work. "Your first inclination, of course, is to go to the crash site," he says, "however, a DNA person has little utility outside of the laboratory.". . .

Wilder Damian Smith
Staff editor for *Analytical Chemistry*

World Trade Center

Marie Samples, an assistant director in the Department of Forensic Biology in the Office of Chief Medical Examiner (OCME) in New York, was sitting in a management meeting when a co-worker poked his head in and delivered the horrific news. "When someone tells you that the WTCs have just collapsed, you don't ever fathom that happening," says Samples. "I don't think it sunk in with me until I got home."

Overseeing mass tragedies is nothing new to the OCME. In 1990, the lab handled the Happy Land Social Club fire in which 87 people died; then in 1993, they handled the *Golden Venture* tragedy in which 286 Chinese immigrants drowned when their boat went aground off the coast of New Jersey. The OCME has about 90 experienced technicians on staff who perform various tasks, including examining physical evidence; conducting DNA extractions; and overseeing DNA quantitation, amplification, and finally, DNA typing.

"Our first thought was that we would be able to handle the samples in-house," says Samples. But as the estimates of the number of bodies at the WTC site continued to pile up—initial reports were as high as 7000—those plans quickly changed. "We've handled big disasters in the past, but this was nothing like we've ever seen," exclaims Samples. Although the OCME has the largest DNA analysis lab in the country, the thought of tackling a project with that many unknown and presumed dead presented other problems for Samples and her lab. "We had two big responsibilities that were clashing," she says,

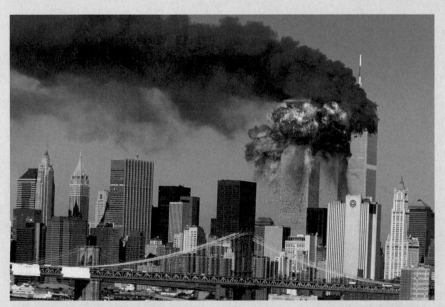

United Flight 175, hijacked by terrorists, crashes into 2 World Trade Center. *Courtesy Robert Clark, Aurora Photos Inc.*

Reprinted in part, with permission, from *Analytical Chemistry*, 74, no. 7 (2002), 190A. Copyright © 2002 by the American Chemical Society and reprinted by permission of the copyright owner.

"our commitment to serve the criminal justice system in New York for the cases we normally handle—sexual assaults, homicides, etc.—and our role as a support lab for the medical examiners in determining the cause of death." She goes on to say, "We knew we couldn't do both of them well at the same time, so we decided to contract out the DNA typing work."

As the search and rescue mission for the victims of the WTC collapse became a recovery mission, more problems faced the forensic community. At Ground Zero—the name given to the site of the collapsed WTC buildings—literally millions of human remains were lying scattered deep beneath the tons of twisted metal and shattered cement. "We have to remember that when those towers fell, they turned into giant shredders," says Kevin McElfresh, a senior scientist with BODE Technologies. The smoldering fires, the exposure to the outside weather, and the estimated amount of time it would take to remove the debris—a year, by some calculations—also presented problems for the chemists. "At least in the [1999] Swiss Air crash, the remains were in the water at the bottom of the ocean in four degree water; even though they were down there for three months, we were still able to extract DNA to generate full profiles," says Benoit Leclair, senior scientist with Myriad Genetics. . . .

Some 7 months later, remains were still being collected and taken to Fresh Kills, an abandoned 3000-acre landfill on Staten Island, N.Y., that has been reincarnated as the country's largest "rake-and-sift" DNA lab. There, workers meticulously pick through bits of concrete, rocks, and other rubble in search of the tiniest remnants of human tissue, teeth, and even hair to aid in the identification process. The OCME extracts the DNA from each of the remains recovered, and those extracts are then shipped off to the respective companies for DNA typing and profiling.

To handle the profiling, the OCME contracted the services of three companies: Myriad Genetics, Celera Genomics, and BODE Technologies. Blood and tissue samples recovered from the site are being sent to Myriad Genetics, based in Salt Lake City, Utah. The company is using the technique of short tandem repeats (STR) on the recovered tissues. "I would refer to this as data mining," says Leclair. STR is a technique that focuses on 13 loci found over the 23 pairs of chromosomes that make up a human's genome. After polymerase chain reaction (PCR) amplification, the newly formed DNA fragments are separated by capillary electrophoresis. Myriad had worked with the New York State Police prior to September 11, performing similar analysis on New York's rape kits.

When blood and tissue samples are not available from the WTC site for DNA typing, forensic scientists often have to turn to another source: bones. BODE Technical Group, a Virginia-based company, is overseeing the bone analysis of the victims. Its lab has about 70 employees, and one of its two specialized units is devoted to forensic analysis. The company participated in the forensic identification of the 88 victims in the Alaska Air crash in 2000. Currently, it has received over 7000 samples from the WTC site.

When the tissue samples are severely burned or degraded, a process called mitochondrial DNA (mtDNA) analysis often has to be done; because this was the case with some of the recovered remains from Ground Zero, the OCME contracted the Rockville, Md., company Celera Genomics to oversee the mtDNA analyses of the WTC victims. However, Celera, a business under the Applera Corp., was an unusual choice. "Unlike BODE and Myriad," says Heather Kowalski, Celera's director of corporate communications, "[Celera] didn't have a forensic part to our business before this tragedy

occurred." Celera is known mainly for its work on the Human Genome Project and as a high-throughput sequencing company.

In preparation for the incoming samples, Celera built four new forensic laboratories in the span of two months and hired Rhonda Roby to oversee the forensics program. Before that, Roby worked as a forensic scientist for Applied Biosystems (AB), which is also a business unit of Applera, and which has a Human Identification Group and experience working with the forensic community. Despite the novelty of the project, Roby wasn't intimidated. "As scientists, we knew we had something to offer, and Applera wanted to do it right," says Roby. "Celera offers expertise in high-throughput sequencing and bioinformatics capabilities, and Applied Biosystems offers expertise as the inventors of the sequencing chemistry, software and instruments, and a team of forensic scientists from the Human Identification Group."

Quality Control

After DNA profiles are obtained, the results are then shipped back to the New York State Police Laboratory in Albany, N.Y. There, the information is stored in a specially modified version of the FBI's Combined DNA Index System (CODIS) database.

The original CODIS database stores the DNA information of convicted felons and is used to match that information in prosecution cases. This new version of the database uses the same DNA comparison software, but only for purposes of matching the September 11 DNA profiles to those of the recovered victims' blood samples submitted by their relatives, and to the DNA information obtained from the victims' toothbrushes, hair, soiled laundry, and used cigarette butts. Also, as part of the OCME's quality control efforts, BODE is also repeating 5% of the mtDNA analysis that Celera conducts.

Sample Analysis

Medical and legal issues have to be considered when determining how much of a sample is needed to yield identifying information.

Ground Zero. *Courtesy AP/Wide World Photos*

The condition of the recovered body parts determines which type of analysis—nuclear (nucDNA) or mtDNA—is performed.

NucDNA analysis is the most commonly used because it's faster, the genome is found in the cell's nucleus, and the DNA has alleles from each parent. In nucDNA analysis, the DNA fragments are analyzed and amplified using PCR. The profile from the nucDNA is then obtained and used to match and verify a victim. However, this type of analysis usually requires a lot of sample. "The problem," says Smith, "is that despite having a large amount of sample, sometimes there are only three grams of usable tissue available for analysis; and that is often totally exhausted during analysis."

MtDNA analysis is somewhat different. Mitochondria are abundant in the cell's cytoplasm, but the mtDNA only comes from the mother. The high number of mtDNA genomes in the cell increases the likelihood of successful PCR amplification. However, mtDNA analysis is more difficult to perform than nucDNA, more time consuming, and very expensive.

The second issue facing analysts is more humanitarian. "We can't tell someone, 'The good news was that it was him; the bad news is that he's all gone,'" says Smith. Most families would rather have some remains of their loved one to take home, even if it is just a small piece. "There isn't one of our people that doesn't understand that there is a family in dire need to know what happened to their loved one," says McElfresh. The scientists use every piece of information they can to find answers. "What gets to me the most is that when it's late and you have a set of records in front of you and what you are looking at is the reconstruction of a person's life through the eyes and the contributions of their family," he says. The resolve of the scientists, says Smith, is evident every day. "With this project, I've seen people so driven that they are standing with their eyes shut and you have to tell them to go home," he says.

The Pentagon and Somerset

Civilian plane crashes are normally assigned to the Federal Aviation Administration (FAA) and the National Transportation Safety Board (NTSB). However, the DNA Division of the OAFME—a federal lab based in Rockville, Md., with two forensic facilities—handled the remains from the Pentagon and the Somerset County, Pa., sites. "We [NTSB] don't have DNA analysis capability," says Frank Ciaccio, chief of forensic sciences and a forensic anthropologist for the NTSB.

In 1996, the NTSB established a memorandum of understanding with the Department of Defense that recommends to local coroners that they use the services of the Armed Forces DNA Identification Laboratory (AFDIL)—the first facility of the OAFME—for DNA analysis. Under the terms of that agreement, the Armed Forces Institute of Pathology (AFIP) simply had to be invited to perform the DNA identifications of the crash victims by the local coroner, and that is what happened in the Pentagon and Somerset cases.

Previously, the AFDIL had performed DNA casework on the victims of the 1999 Egypt Air and the 2000 Alaska Air plane crashes. The AFDIL has 30 technicians divided into 6 teams that specialize in mtDNA analysis and a smaller group that handles all the nucDNA casework. The mtDNA section of the AFDIL was created in 1991 and has been instrumental in the identification of the recovered remains of American servicemen from the Korean War. To date, the AFDIL has received over 2000 samples for typing from the Pentagon and Somerset crashes.

The second OAFME facility, called the Armed Forces Repository of Specimen Samples for the Identification of Remains, houses blood-stained cards for all active duty, reserve, and National Guard military personnel. These filter paper cards are refrigerated and contain each person's name, social security number, date of birth, and two quarter-size spots of blood. In the Pentagon and Somerset crashes, about 50 of the victims were active duty American servicemen.

Were They Prepared?

"We have the largest DNA lab in the country, and even we couldn't handle [the WTC] caseload," says Samples. "It's hard for a lab to try to prepare for something along the lines of New York when it isn't likely to happen." (Samples's lab also had 12 new lab technicians start work on September 10.)

Learning from previous crashes, Smith's lab implemented a few critical changes. "We found that by having a DNA collection team [at the crash site], they could collect the tissue sample after it has been taken from the body and tag it with a number and bar code onsite before it gets back to the lab," he says. Creating better software in the chain of custody was also important. "For the Pentagon and Somerset crashes we set up two computer systems, one at the Dover Air Force Base and the other in Somerset County for the Pennsylvania crash."

Smith believes experience is the best teacher. "The thing we were missing in the Egypt and Alaska Air crashes was how to compare hundreds of DNA profiles obtained from the evidence with hundreds of DNA reference profiles," he says. "The hardest part of the project was sorting, comparing, matching, and reporting the data, so there was clearly a role for automation."

Need for New Technology

Although forensic technology has advanced, Leclair believes it still is always a step behind the last disaster. "We have the DNA typing tools to tackle a disaster such as Swiss Air only as a result of the TWA 800 disaster," states Leclair. Back in the late 1980s, DNA analysis was all done using a variable number of tandem repeats or restriction fragment-length polymorphisms, which required an enormous amount of sample and analysis time.

Today, most labs are using PCR to analyze DNA. "PCR has been the biggest addition to forensic technology," says McElfresh. "I can't imagine dealing with something the magnitude of this [WTC buildings and Pentagon] with that old technology."

But the tragedies of September 11, say some forensic scientists, should be a wake-up call to the community. "Considering the magnitude of the New York disaster, one can readily see the need for powerful bioinformatics tools," states Leclair.

Roby believes that robotics and more advanced automation are the technologies of the future for forensics. "What may come out of [September 11] is that we are using robotic systems and automation, and we may be able to advance forensic sciences with the scientific technology that is available in other areas with these systems," she says. Samples agrees. "We had thought about using the robotics system before, but our caseload had never justified using them."

Justifying new technology, and finding the time to develop it, seem to be the biggest obstacles. "I think the forensic community could have handled the caseload of the WTC buildings without robotics and automation," says Roby, "but the question is how long would it have taken?"

The Sam Sheppard Case: A Trail of Blood

Convicted in 1954 of bludgeoning his wife to death, Dr. Sam Sheppard achieved celebrity status when the storyline of TV's *The Fugitive* was apparently modeled on his efforts to seek vindication for the crime he professed not to have committed. Dr. Sheppard, a physician, claimed he was dozing on his living room couch when his pregnant wife, Marilyn, was attacked. Sheppard's story was that he quickly ran upstairs to stop the carnage, but was knocked unconscious briefly by the intruder. The suspicion that fell on Dr. Sheppard was fueled by the revelation that he was having an adulterous affair. At trial, the local coroner testified that a pool of blood on Marilyn's pillow contained the impression of a "surgical instrument." After Sheppard had been imprisoned for ten years, the U.S. Supreme Court set aside his conviction due to the "massive, pervasive, and prejudicial publicity" that had attended his trial.

In 1966, the second Sheppard trial commenced. This time, the same coroner was forced to back off from his insistence that the bloody outline of a surgical instrument was present on Marilyn's pillow. However, a medical technician from the coroner's office now testified that blood on Dr. Sheppard's watch was from blood spatter, indicating that Dr. Sheppard was wearing the watch in the presence of the battering of his wife. The defense countered with the expert testimony of eminent criminalist Dr. Paul Kirk. Dr. Kirk concluded that blood spatter marks in the bedroom showed the killer to be left-handed. Dr. Sheppard was right-handed.

Dr. Kirk further testified that Sheppard stained his watch while attempting to obtain a pulse reading. After less than 12 hours of deliberation, the jury failed to convict Sheppard. But the ordeal had taken its toll. Four years later Sheppard died, a victim of drug and alcohol abuse.

crime-scene reconstruction: bloodstain pattern analysis

Learning Objectives

After studying this chapter, you should be able to:

- Define crime-scene reconstruction

- Discuss the information that can be gained from bloodstain pattern analysis about the events involved in a violent crime

- Explain how surface texture, directionality, and angle of impact affect the shape of individual bloodstains

- Calculate the angle of impact of a bloodstain using its dimensions

- Describe the classifications of low-, medium-, and high-velocity impact spatter and appreciate how these classifications should be used

- Discuss the methods to determine the area of convergence and area of origin for impact spatter patterns

- Understand how various blood pattern types are created and which features of each pattern can be used to aid in reconstructing events at a crime scene

- Describe the methods for documenting bloodstain patterns at a crime scene

KEY TERMS

angle of impact
area of convergence
area of origin
arterial spray
back spatter
cast-off
crime-scene
   reconstruction
drip trail pattern
expirated blood
   pattern
flows
forward spatter
high-velocity spatter
impact spatter
low-velocity spatter
medium-velocity
   spatter
satellite spatter
skeletonization
transfer pattern
void

Fundamentals of Crime-Scene Reconstruction

Previous discussions dealing with the processes of identification and comparison have stressed laboratory work routinely performed by forensic scientists. However, there is another dimension to the role that forensic scientists play during the course of a criminal investigation: participating in a team effort to reconstruct events that occurred before, during, and after the commission of a crime.

Law enforcement personnel must take proper action to enhance all aspects of the crime-scene search so as to optimize the crime-scene reconstruction. First, and most important, is securing and protecting the crime scene. Protecting the scene is a continuous endeavor from the beginning to the end of the search. Evidence that can be invaluable to reconstructing the crime can be unknowingly altered or destroyed by people trampling through the scene, rendering the evidence useless. The issue of possible contamination of evidence will certainly be attacked during the litigation process and could make the difference between a guilty and not-guilty verdict.

Before processing the crime scene for physical evidence, the investigator should make a preliminary examination of the scene as it was left by the perpetrator. Each crime scene presents its own set of circumstances. The investigator's experience and the presence or absence of physical evidence become critical factors in reconstructing a crime. The investigator captures the nature of the scene as a whole by performing an initial walk-through of the crime scene and contemplating the events that took place. Using the physical evidence available to the naked eye, he or she can hypothesize about what occurred, where it occurred, and when it occurred. During the walk-through, the investigator's task is to document observations and formulate how the scene should ultimately be processed. As the collection of physical evidence begins, any and all observations should be recorded through photographs, sketches, and notes. By carefully collecting physical evidence and thoroughly documenting the crime scene, the investigator can begin to unravel the sequence of events that took place during the commission of the crime.

Often reconstruction requires the involvement of law enforcement personnel, a medical examiner, and/or a criminalist. All of these professionals contribute unique perspectives to develop the crime-scene reconstruction. Was more than one person involved? How was the victim killed? Were actions taken to cover up what took place? The positioning of the victim in a crime scene can often reveal pertinent information for the investigation. Trained medical examiners can examine the victim at a crime scene and determine whether the body has been moved after death by evaluating the livor distribution within the body (see pages 72–73). For example, if livor has developed in areas other than those closest to the ground, the medical examiner can reason that the victim was probably moved after death. Likewise, the examiner can determine whether the victim was clothed after death because livor will not develop in areas of the body that are restricted by clothing.

A criminalist or trained crime-scene investigator can also bring special skills to the reconstruction of events that occurred during the commission of a crime. For example, a criminalist using a laser beam to plot the approximate bullet path in trajectory analysis can help determine the probable position of the shooter relative to that of the victim (see Figure 12–1). Other skills that a criminalist may employ during a crime-scene reconstruction analysis include determining the direction of impact of projectiles penetrating glass objects (see pages 107–108); locating gunshot residues deposited on the victim's clothing for the purpose of estimating the distance of a shooter from a target (see pages 427–430); searching for primer residues deposited on the hands of a suspect shooter (see pages 431–434); and, as we will see from the discussion that follows, analyzing blood spatter patterns.

Crime-scene reconstruction is the method used to support a likely sequence of events at a crime scene by observing and evaluating physical evidence and statements made by individuals involved with the incident. The evidence may also include information obtained from reenactments. Therefore, reconstructions have the best chance of being accurate when investigators use proper documentation and collection methods for all types of evidence.

crime-scene reconstruction
The method used to support a likely sequence of events at a crime scene by the observation and evaluation of physical evidence and statements made by individuals involved with the incident

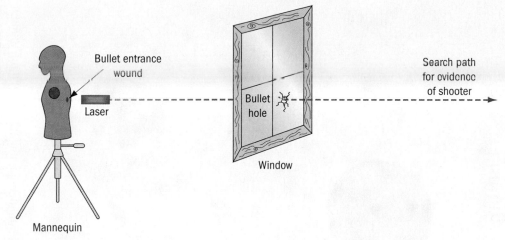

FIGURE 12–1

A laser beam is used to determine the search area for the position of a shooter who has fired a bullet through a window and wounded a victim. The bullet path is determined by lining up the victim's bullet wound with the bullet hole present in the glass pane.

General Features of Bloodstain Formation

Crimes involving violent contact between individuals are frequently accompanied by bleeding and resultant bloodstain patterns. Crime-scene analysts have come to appreciate that bloodstain patterns deposited on floors, walls, ceilings, bedding, and other relevant objects can provide valuable insights into events that occurred during the commission of a violent crime. The information one is likely to uncover as a result of bloodstain pattern interpretation includes the following:

- The direction from which blood originated
- The angle at which a blood droplet struck a surface
- The location or position of a victim at the time a bloody wound was inflicted
- The movement of a bleeding individual at the crime scene
- The minimum number of blows that struck a bleeding victim
- The approximate location of an individual delivering blows that produced a bloodstain pattern

The crime-scene investigator must not overlook the fact that the location, distribution, and appearance of bloodstains and spatters may be useful for interpreting and reconstructing the events that accompanied the bleeding. A thorough analysis of the significance of the position and shape of blood patterns with respect to their origin and trajectory is exceedingly complex and requires the services of an examiner who is experienced in such determinations. Most important, the interpretation of bloodstain patterns necessitates a carefully planned control experiment using surface materials comparable to those found at the crime scene. This chapter presents the basic principles and common deductions behind bloodstain pattern analysis to give the reader general knowledge to use at the crime scene.

Surface Texture

Surface texture is of importance in the interpretation of bloodstain patterns arising from blood dripping off an object. Comparisons between standards and unknowns are valid only when identical surfaces are used. In general, harder and nonporous surfaces (such as glass or smooth tile) result in less spatter. Rough surfaces, such as carpeting or wood, usually result in irregularly shaped stains with serrated edges, possibly with **satellite spatter** (see Figure 12–2).

Direction and Angle of Impact

An investigator may discern the direction of travel of blood striking an object by studying the stain's shape. As the stain becomes more elliptical in shape, its direction of impact becomes more

satellite spatter

Small droplets of blood that are distributed around the perimeter of a drop or drops of blood and were produced as a result of the blood impacting the target surface

(a)   (b)

FIGURE 12–2

(a) A bloodstain from a single drop of blood that struck a glass surface after falling 24 inches. (b) A bloodstain from a single drop of blood that struck a cotton muslin sheet after falling 24 inches.
(a) Courtesy A. Y. Wonder; (b) Courtesy, A. Y. Wonder

FIGURE 12–3

A bloodstain pattern produced by drops of blood that were traveling from left to right.
Courtesy A. Y. Wonder

discernible because the pointed end of a bloodstain faces its direction of travel. Also, the distorted or disrupted edge of an elongated stain indicates the direction of travel of the blood. In Figure 12–3, the bloodstain pattern was produced by several drops of blood that were traveling from left to right before striking a flat, level surface.

It is possible to determine the impact angle of blood on a flat surface by measuring the degree of circular distortion of the stain. A drop deposited at an **angle of impact** of about 90 degrees (directly vertical to the surface) will be approximately circular in shape with no tail or buildup of

angle of impact
The acute angle formed between the path of a blood drop and the surface that it contacts

FIGURE 12–4
The higher pattern is of a single drop of human blood that fell 24 inches and struck hard, smooth cardboard at 50 degrees. On this drop the irregular edge shows the direction. The lower pattern is of a single drop of human blood that fell 24 inches and struck hard, smooth cardboard at 15 degrees. On this drop the tail shows the direction.
Courtesy A. Y. Wonder

blood. However, as the angle of impact deviates from 90 degrees, the stain becomes elongated in shape. Buildup of blood will show up in the larger angles, whereas longer and longer tails will appear as the angle of impact becomes smaller (see Figure 12–4).

Impact Bloodstain Spatter Patterns

One of the most common type of bloodstain pattern found at a crime scene is **impact spatter.** This pattern occurs when an object impacts a source of blood. The spatter projected outward and away from the source, such as an exit wound, is called a **forward spatter. Back spatter,** sometimes called *blowback spatter*, consists of the blood projected backward from a source, such as an entrance wound, potentially being deposited on the object or person creating the impact. Impact spatter patterns consist of many drops radiating in direct lines from the origin of blood to the target (see Figure 12–5).

Investigators have derived a common classification system of impact spatter from the velocity of a blood droplet. In general, as the force of the impact on the source of blood increases, so does the velocity of the blood drops emanating from the source. It is also generally true that as both the force and velocity of impact increase, the diameter of the resulting blood drops decreases.

Classifying Impact Spatter

LOW-VELOCITY SPATTER   An impact pattern consisting of large separate or compounded drops with diameters of 3 millimeters or more is known as **low-velocity spatter.** This kind of spatter is

mycrimekit
WEBEXTRA 12.1
See How Bloodstain Spatter Patterns Are Formed
www.mycrimekit.com

impact spatter
A bloodstain pattern produced when an object makes forceful contact with a source of blood, projecting drops of blood outward from the source

forward spatter
Blood that travels away from the source in the same direction as the force that caused the spatter

back spatter
Blood directed back toward the source of the force that caused the spatter

low-velocity spatter
An impact spatter pattern created by a force traveling at 5 feet per second or less and producing drops with diameters greater than 3 millimeters

Determining the Angle of Impact of Bloodstains

The distorted or disrupted edge of an elongated stain indicates the direction of travel of the blood drop. One may establish the location or origin of bloodshed by determining the directionality of the stain and the angle at which blood came into contact with the landing surface. To determine the angle of impact, calculate the stain's length-to-width ratio and apply the formula

$$\text{Sin } A = \frac{\text{width of blood stain}}{\text{length of blood stain}}$$

where A = the angle of impact.

For example, suppose the width of a stain is 11 mm and the length is 22 mm.

$$\text{Sin } A = \frac{11 \text{ mm}}{22 \text{ mm}} = 0.50$$

A scientific calculator with trigonometric functions will calculate that a sine of 0.50 corresponds to a 30-degree angle.

Note: There is a 5-degree error factor with this formula. This means that calculations are good to plus or minus 5 degrees of the actual value of the angle of impact. The measurements for length and width should be made with a ruler, micrometer, or photographic loupe.

FIGURE 12–5

Impact spatter produced by a series of body blows. The arrows show the blood drops' linear direction of travel from the origin of impact for each of numerous blows.
Courtesy A. Y. Wonder

medium-velocity spatter
An impact spatter pattern created by a force traveling at 5 to 25 feet per second and producing drops with diameters between 1 and 3 millimeters

high-velocity spatter
An impact spatter pattern created by a force traveling at 100 feet per second or faster and producing drops with diameters less than 1 millimeter

normally produced by minimal force. Typically, the drops hit the surface at a speed of less than 5 feet per second.

MEDIUM-VELOCITY SPATTER   A pattern consisting of small drops with diameters from 1 to 3 millimeters is classified as **medium-velocity spatter.** This type of impact spatter is normally associated with blunt-force trauma to an individual. Drops of medium-velocity spatter hit the surface at 5 to 25 feet per second.

HIGH-VELOCITY SPATTER   Very fine drops with diameters of less than 1 millimeter are classified as **high-velocity spatter.** Here the drops hit the surface at 100 feet per second or faster. Gunshot exit wounds or explosions commonly produce this type of spatter. However, because the drops are very small, they may not travel far; they may fall to the floor or ground where investigative personnel could overlook them.

Using droplet size to classify impact patterns by velocity is a useful tool for giving investigators insight into the general nature of a crime. However, the velocity at which blood strikes a surface by itself cannot illuminate the specific events that produced the spatter pattern. For example, beatings can produce high-velocity spatter or patterns that look more like low-velocity spatter. In general, one should use velocity categories very cautiously and for descriptive purposes only in evaluating impact spatter patterns.

As we will learn, blood spatter patterns can arise from a number of distinctly different sources. Illustrations of patterns emanating from impact (just discussed), cast-off (on page 306), and arterial spray (on page 307) are shown in Figure 12–6.

(a)

(b)

(c)

FIGURE 12–6

(a) The action associated with producing impact spatter. (b) The action associated with producing cast-off spatter. (c) The action associated with producing arterial spray spatter.

Courtesy of A. Y. Wonder

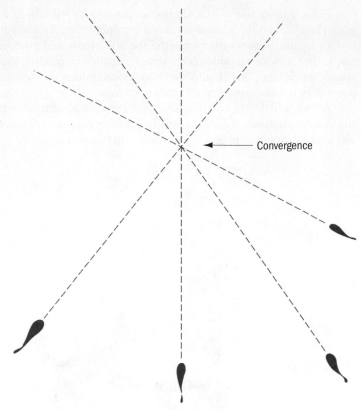

FIGURE 12–7

An illustration of stain convergence on a two-dimensional plane. Convergence represents the area from which the stains emanated.

Courtesy Judith Bunker, J. L. Bunker & Assoc., Ocoee, Fla.

← Convergence

Origin-of-Impact Patterns

Impact spatter patterns can offer investigators clues that help determine the origin of the blood source and the position of the victim at the time of the impact.

area of convergence

The area on a two-dimensional plane where lines traced through the long axis of several individual bloodstains meet; this approximates the two-dimensional place from which the bloodstains were projected

AREA OF CONVERGENCE   The **area of convergence** is the area on a two-dimensional plane from which the drops originated. This can be established by drawing straight lines through the long axis of several individual bloodstains, following the line of their tails. The intersection of these lines is the area of convergence, and the approximate area of origin will be on a line straight out from this area. Figure 12–7 illustrates how to draw lines to find an area of convergence.

An object hitting a source of blood numerous times will never produce exactly the same pattern each time. One may therefore determine the number of impacts by drawing the area of convergence for groups of stains from separate impacts.

area of origin

The location in three-dimensional space that blood that produced a bloodstain originated from; the location of the area of convergence and the angle of impact for each bloodstain is used to approximate this area

AREA OF ORIGIN   It may also be important to determine the **area of origin** of a bloodstain pattern, the area in a three-dimensional space from which the blood was projected. This will show the position of the victim or suspect in space when the stain-producing event took place. The distribution of the drops in an impact pattern gives a general idea of the distance from the blood source to the bloodstained surface. Impact patterns produced at a distance close to the surface will appear as clustered stains. As the distance from the surface increases, so do the distribution and distance between drops.

A common method for determining the area of origin at the crime scene is called the *string method*. Figure 12–8 illustrates the steps in the string method:

1. Find the area of convergence for the stain pattern.
2. Place a pole or stand as an axis coming from the area of convergence.
3. Attach one end of a string next to each droplet. Place a protractor next to each droplet and lift the string until it lines up with the determined angle of impact of the drop. Keeping the string in line with the angle, attach the other end of the string to the axis pole.
4. View the area of origin of the drops where the strings appear to meet. Secure the strings at this area.

This method produces an approximation of the area of origin with an error of 2 feet.

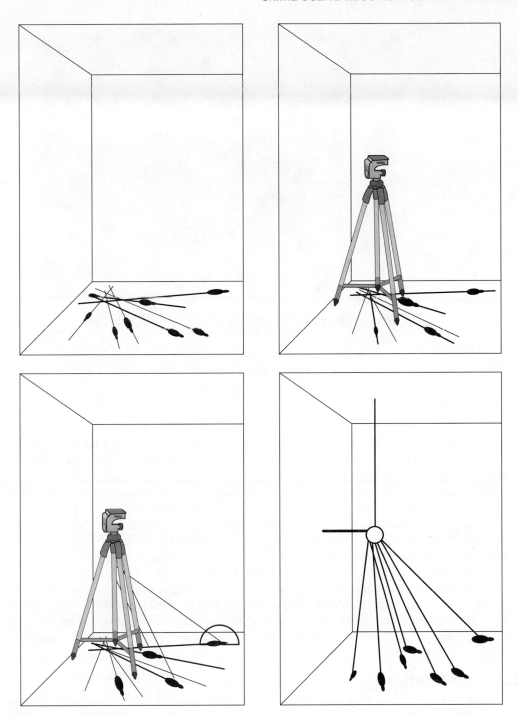

FIGURE 12–8

An illustration of the string method used at a crime scene to determine the area of origin of blood spatter.

Source: Bloodstain Pattern Evidence by Anita Y. Wonder, p. 47. Copyright Elsevier, 2007

More Bloodstain Spatter Patterns

Gunshot Spatter

A shooting may leave a distinct gunshot spatter pattern. This may be characterized by both forward spatter from an exit wound and back spatter from an entrance wound. However, the gunshot produces only back spatter if the bullet does not exit the body. If the victim is close enough to a

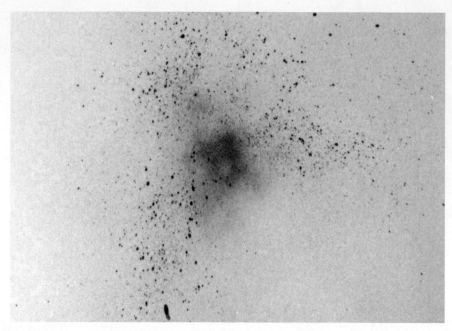

FIGURE 12–9

The high-velocity spatter from the cone-shaped deposit of gunshot spatter.
Courtesy A. Y. Wonder

FIGURE 12–10

Back spatter bloodstains entering the muzzle of a weapon discharged in close proximity to a victim.
Courtesy Ralph R. Ristenbatt III and Robert Shaler

cast-off

A bloodstain pattern that is created when blood is flung from a blood bearing object in motion onto a surface

vertical surface when suffering a gunshot wound, the blood will be expelled both forward and backward. This will leave a pattern of very fine drops radiating out in a cone-shaped pattern characteristic of high-velocity spatter (see Figure 12–9).

The location of the injury, the size of the wound created, and the distance between the victim and the muzzle of the weapon all affect the amount of back spatter that occurs. Finding high-velocity spatter containing the victim's blood on a suspect can help investigators place the suspect in the vicinity when the gun was discharged. Back spatter created by a firearm discharge generally contains fewer and smaller atomized stains than does forward spatter. A muzzle blast striking an entrance wound will cause the formation of atomized blood.

Depending on the distance from the victim at which the gun was discharged, some back spatter may strike the gunman and enter the gun muzzle. This is called the *drawback effect*. Blood within the muzzle of a gun can place the weapon in the vicinity of the gunshot wound. The presence of blowback spatter on a weapon's muzzle is consistent with the weapon being close to the victim at the time of firing (see Figure 12–10).

Cast-Off Spatter

A **cast-off** pattern is created when a blood-covered object flings blood in an arc onto a nearby surface. This kind of pattern commonly occurs when a person pulls a bloody fist or weapon back between delivering blows to a victim (see Figure 12–6[b]). The bloodstain tails will point in the direction that the object was moving.

The width of the cast-off pattern created by a bloody object may help suggest the kind of object that produced the pattern. The sizes of the drops are directly related to the size of the point from which they were propelled. Drops propelled from a small or pointed surface will be smaller and the pattern more linear; drops propelled from a large or blunt surface will be larger and the pattern wider. The volume of blood deposited on an object from the source also affects the size and number of drops in the cast-off pattern. The less blood on the object, the smaller the stains produced. The pattern may also suggest whether the blow that caused the pattern was directed from right to left or left to right. The pattern will point in the direction of the backward thrust, which will be opposite the direction of the blow. This could suggest which hand the assailant used to deliver the blows.

Cast-off patterns may also show the *minimum* number of blows delivered to a victim. Each blow should be marked by an upward-and-downward or forward-and-backward arc pattern

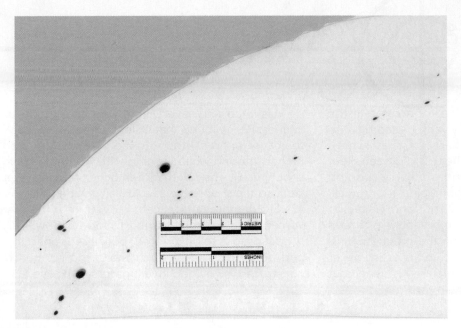

FIGURE 12–11

The castoff pattern created from one backward and one forward motion of an overhand swing. The larger drops are away from the victim because they're made when the weapon holds the greatest amount of blood. The smaller spatters are directed toward the victim.

Source: Bloodstain Pattern Evidence by Anita Y. Wonder, p. 295. Copyright Elsevier, 2007

FIGURE 12–12
Arterial spray spatter found at a crime scene where a victim suffered injury to an artery.
Courtesy Norman H. Reeves, Bloodstain Pattern Analysis, Tucson, Ariz., www.bloody1.com

(see Figure 12–11). By counting and pairing the patterns, one can estimate the minimum number of blows. An investigator should take into consideration that the first blow would only cause blood to pool to the area; it would not produce a cast-off pattern. Also, some blows may not come into contact with blood and so will not produce a pattern. The medical examiner is in the best position to estimate the number of blows a victim received.

Arterial Spray Spatter

Arterial spray spatter is created when a victim suffers an injury to a main artery or the heart. The pressure of the continuing pumping of blood causes blood to spurt out of the injured area (see Figure 12–6[c]). Commonly, the pattern shows large spurted stains for each time the heart pumps. Some radial spikes, satellite spatter, or flow patterns may be evident because of the large volume of blood being expelled with each spurt. Drops may also be seen on the surface in fairly uniform size and shape and in parallel arrangement (see Figure 12–12).

    The lineup of the stains shows the victim's movement. Any vertical arcs or waves in the line show fluctuations in blood pressure. The larger arterial stains are at the end of the overall pattern. The initial breach can produce a mist effect from the initial pressure. Then, as the pressure drops, larger blood deposits occur because arterial pressure is not causing them to break up. Arterial patterns can also be differentiated because the oxygenated blood spurting from the artery tends to be a brighter red color than blood expelled from impact wounds.

Expired Blood Patterns

A pattern created by blood that is expelled from the mouth or nose from an internal injury is called an **expired blood pattern.** If the blood that creates such a pattern is under great pressure, it produces very fine high-velocity spatter. Expired blood at very low velocities produces a stain cluster with irregular edges (see Figure 12–13). The presence of bubbles of oxygen in the drying drops can differentiate a pattern created by expired blood from other types of bloodstains. Expired blood also may be lighter in color when compared to impact spatter as a result of dilution by saliva. The presence of expired blood gives an important clue as to the injuries suffered and the events that took place at a crime scene.

arterial spray
A characteristic bloodstain pattern containing spurts that resulted from blood exiting under pressure from an arterial injury

expired blood pattern
A pattern created by blood that is expelled out of the nose, mouth, or respiratory system as a result of air pressure and/or airflow

forensics at work

Stephen Scher banged on the door of a cabin in the woods outside Montrose, Pennsylvania. According to Scher, his friend, Marty Dillon, had just shot himself while chasing after a porcupine. The two had been skeet shooting at Scher's cabin, enjoying a friendly sporting weekend, when Dillon spotted a porcupine and took off out of sight. Scher heard a single shot and waited to hear his friend's voice. After a few moments, he chased after Dillon and found him lying on the ground near a tree stump, bleeding from a wound in his chest. Scher administered CPR after locating his dying friend, but

he was unable to save Dillon, who later died from his injuries. Police found that Dillon's untied boot had been the cause of his shotgun wound. They determined that he had tripped while running with his loaded gun and shot himself. The grief-stricken Scher aroused no suspicion, so the shooting was ruled an accident.

Shortly thereafter, Scher moved from the area, divorced his wife, and married Dillon's widow. This was too suspicious to be ignored; police reopened the case and decided to reconstruct the crime scene. The reconstruction provided investigators with several pieces

FIGURE 12–13

An example of expirated blood expelled with two wheezes from the mouth.
Courtesy A. Y. Wonder

Void Patterns

void

An area within a deposited spatter pattern that is clear of spatter, caused by an object or person blocking the area at the time of the spatter's deposition

A **void** is created when an object blocks the deposition of blood spatter onto a target surface or object (see Figure 12–14). The spatter is deposited onto the object or person instead. The blank space on the surface or object may give a clue as to the size and shape of the missing object or person. Once the object or person is found, the missing piece of the pattern should fit in, much like a puzzle piece, with the rest of the pattern. Voids may be applicable for establishing the body position of the victim or assailant at the time of the incident.

of blood evidence that pointed to Scher as Dillon's murderer.

Police noticed that Scher's boots bore the unmistakable spray of high-velocity impact blood spatter, evidence that he was standing within an arm's length of Dillon when Dillon was shot. This pattern of bloodstains cannot be created while administering CPR, as Scher claimed had happened. The spatter pattern also clearly refuted Scher's claim that he did not witness the incident. In addition, the tree stump near Dillon's body bore the same type of blood spatter, in a pattern that indicated Dillon was *seated on the stump* and not running when he was shot. Finally, Dillon's ears were free of the high-velocity blood spatter that covered his face, but blood was on his hearing protectors found nearby. This is a clear indication that he was wearing his hearing protectors when he was shot and they were removed before investigators arrived. This and other evidence resulted in Scher's conviction for the murder of his longtime friend, Marty Dillon.

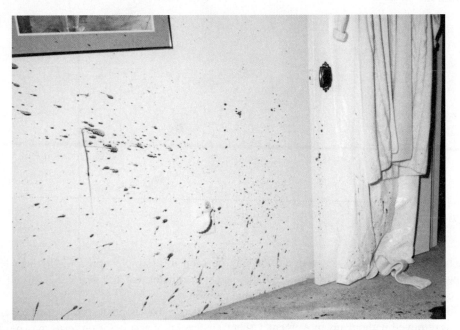

FIGURE 12–14

A void pattern is found behind the door where the surface of the door blocked the deposition of spatter on that area. This void, and the presence of spatter on the door, shows that the door was open when the spatter was deposited.

Courtesy Norman H. Reeves, Bloodstain Pattern Analysis, Tucson, Ariz., www.bloody1.com

Other Bloodstain Patterns

Not all bloodstains at a crime scene appear as spatter patterns. The circumstances of the crime often create other types of stains that can be useful to investigators.

Contact/Transfer Patterns

When an object with blood on it touches one that does not have blood on it, this produces a contact or **transfer pattern.** Examples of transfers with features include fingerprints (see Figure 12–15), handprints, footprints, footwear prints, tool prints, and fabric prints in blood. These may provide further leads by offering individual characteristics.

transfer pattern

A bloodstain pattern created when a surface that carries wet blood comes in contact with a second surface; recognizable imprints of all or a portion of the original surface or the direction of movement may be observed

FIGURE 12–15

A transfer pattern consisting of bloody fingerprints with apparent ridge detail.
Courtesy Lawrence A. Presley, Arcadia University

FIGURE 12–16

A series of swipe patterns moving from right to left.
Courtesy A. Y. Wonder

The size and general shape of a tool may be seen in a simple transfer. This can lead to narrowing the possible tools by class characteristics. A transfer that shows a very individualistic feature may help point to the tool that made the pattern.

Simple transfer patterns are produced when the object makes contact with the surface and the object is removed without any movement. Other transfers known as *swipe patterns* may be caused by movement of the bloody object across a surface. Generally, the swipe pattern will lighten and "feather" as the pattern moves away from the initial contact point (see Figure 12–16). The direction of separate bloody transfers, such as footwear prints in blood, may show the movement of the suspect, victim, or others through the crime scene after the blood was present. The first transfer pattern will be dark and heavy with blood, whereas subsequent transfers will be increasingly lighter in color. As the transfers get lighter, less and less of the transferring object's surface will deposit visible traces of blood. Bloody shoe imprints may also suggest whether the wearer was running or walking. Running typically produces imprints with more space between them and more satellite or drop patterns between each imprint.

Flows

flow pattern
A bloodstain pattern formed by the movement of small or large amounts of blood as a result of gravity's pull

Patterns made by drops or large amounts of blood flowing by the pull of gravity are called **flows.** Flows may be formed by single drops or large volumes of blood coming from an actively bleeding wound or blood deposited on a surface such as from an arterial spurt. Clotting of the blood's solid parts may occur when a flow extends onto an absorbent surface.

The flow direction may show movements of objects or bodies while the flow was still in progress or after the blood had dried. Figure 12–17 illustrates a situation in which movement of the surface while the flow was still in progress led to a specific pattern.

FIGURE 12–17

The flow pattern suggests that the victim was upright and then fell while blood flowed. The assailant claimed the victim was stabbed while sleeping.
Source: Bloodstain Pattern Evidence by Anita Y. Wonder, p. 98. Copyright Elsevier, 2007

Interruption of a flow pattern may be helpful in assessing the sequence and passage of time between the flow and its interruption. If a flow found on an object or body does not appear consistent with the direction of gravity, one may surmise that the object or body was moved after the blood had dried.

Pools

A pool of blood occurs when blood collects in a level (not sloped) and undisturbed place. Blood that pools on an absorbent surface may be absorbed throughout the surface and diffuse, creating a pattern larger than the original pool. This often occurs to pools on beds or sofas.

The approximate drying time of a pool of blood is related to the environmental condition of the scene. By experimentation, an analyst may be able to reasonably estimate the drying times of stains of different sizes. Small and large pools of blood can aid in reconstruction by providing an estimation of the amount of time that elapsed since the blood was deposited. Considering the drying time of a blood pool can yield information about the timing of events that accompanied the incident.

The edges of a stain will dry to the surface, producing a phenomenon called **skeletonization** (see Figure 12–18). This usually occurs within 50 seconds of deposition of drops, and longer for larger volumes of blood. If the central area of the pooled bloodstain is altered by wiping, the skeletonized perimeter will be left intact. This can be used to interpret whether movement or activity occurred shortly after the pool was deposited, or whether the perimeter had time to skeletonize before the movement occurred. This may be important for classifying the source of the original stain.

Drip Trail Patterns

A **drip trail pattern** is a series of drops that are separate from other patterns, formed by blood dripping off an object or injury. The stains form a kind of line or path usually made by the suspect after injuring or killing the victim, or they can show the movement of a wounded victim. It may simply show movement, lead to a discarded weapon, or provide identification of the suspect by his or her own blood. Investigators often see this type of pattern in stabbings during which the suspect cuts himself or herself as a result of the force necessary to stab the victim. Figure 12–19 shows a drip trail pattern away from the center of action at a crime scene.

skeletonization
The process by which the edges of a stain dry to the surface in a specific period of time (dependent on environmental and surface conditions); skeletonization remains apparent even after the rest of the bloodstain has been disturbed from its original position

drip trail pattern
A pattern of bloodstains formed by the dripping of blood off a moving surface or person in a recognizable pathway separate from other patterns

FIGURE 12–18

Skeletonization is shown in a bloodstain that was disturbed after the edges had time to skeletonize.

Courtesy Norman H. Reeves, Bloodstain Pattern Analysis, Tucson, Ariz., www.bloody1.com

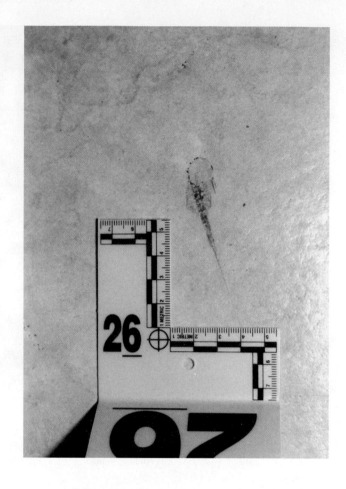

FIGURE 12–19

A drip trail pattern leads away from the center of the mixed bloodstain pattern.

Courtesy Norman H. Reeves, Bloodstain Pattern Analysis, Tucson, Ariz., www.bloody1.com

The shape of the stains in a drip trail pattern can help investigators determine the direction and speed at which a person was moving. The tails of the drops in a trail pattern point in the direction the person was moving. More circular stains are found where the person was moving slowly enough to not form tails. This information may be helpful in reconstruction.

Documenting Bloodstain Pattern Evidence

Blood spatter patterns of any kind can provide a great deal of information about the events that took place at a crime scene. For this reason, investigators should note, study, and photograph each pattern and drop. This must be done to accurately record the location of specific patterns and to distinguish the stains from which laboratory samples were taken. The photographs and sketches can also point out specific stains used in determining the direction of force, angle of impact, and area of origin.

Just as in general crime-scene photography, the investigator should create photographs and sketches of the overall pattern to show the orientation of the pattern to the scene. The medium-range documentation should include pictures and sketches of the whole pattern and the relationships among individual stains within the pattern. The close-up photographs and sketches should show the dimensions of each individual stain. Close-up photographs should be taken with a scale of some kind apparent in the photograph.

Two common methods of documenting bloodstain patterns place attention on the scale of the patterns. The *grid method* involves setting up a grid of squares of known dimensions over the entire pattern using string and stakes (see Figure 12–20). All overall, medium-range, and close-up photographs are taken with and without the grid. The second method, called the *perimeter ruler method*, involves setting up a rectangular border of rulers around the pattern and then placing a small ruler next to each stain. In this method, the large rulers show scale in the overall and medium-range photos, whereas the small rulers show scale in the close-up photographs (see Figure 12–21). Some investigation teams use tags in close-up photographs to show evidence numbers or other details.

An area-of-origin determination should be calculated whenever possible. All measurements of stains and calculations of angle of impact and point of origin should be recorded in crime-scene notes. Especially important stains can be roughly sketched within the notes.

Only some jurisdictions have a specialist on staff to decipher patterns either at the scene or from photographs at the lab. Therefore, it is important that all personnel be familiar with patterns to properly record and document them for use in reconstruction.

Virtual Forensics Lab

Blood Spatter Evidence
To perform a virtual lab analysis of blood spatter evidence, go to www.pearsoncustom.com/us/vlm/

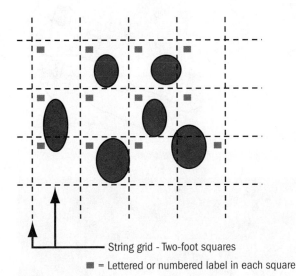

String grid - Two-foot squares

■ = Lettered or numbered label in each square

FIGURE 12–20

The grid method may be used for photographing bloodstain pattern evidence.
Source: R. R. Ogle, Jr., *Crime Scene Investigation and Reconstruction*, 2nd ed., Prentice Hall, Upper Saddle River, N.J., 2007

Measurement rulers

Small metric rulers

Areas with bloodstain patterns

FIGURE 12–21

The perimeter ruler method may be used for photographing bloodstain pattern evidence.
Source: R. R. Ogle, Jr., *Crime Scene Investigation & Reconstruction*, 2nd ed., Prentice Hall, Upper Saddle River, N.J., 2007

forensics at work

An elderly male was found lying dead on his living room floor. He had been beaten about the face and head, then stabbed in the chest and robbed. The reconstruction of bloodstains found on the interior front door and the adjacent wall documented that the victim was beaten about the face with a fist and struck on the back of the head with his cane. A three-dimensional diagram and photograph illustrating the evidential bloodstain patterns is shown in Figure 1(a) and 1(b).

A detail photograph of bloodstains next to the interior door is shown in Figure 2. Arrow 1 in Figure 2 points to the cast-off pattern directed left to right as blood was flung from the perpetrator's fist while inflicting blows. Arrow 2 in Figure 2 points to three transfer impression patterns directed left to right as the perpetrator's bloodstained hand contacted the wall and as the fist blows were being inflicted on the victim. Arrow 3 in Figure 2 points to blood flow from the victim's wounds as he slumped against the wall.

Figure 3 contains a series of laboratory test patterns created to evaluate the patterns contained within Figure 2.

Figure 4 shows how the origin of individual impact spatter patterns located on the wall and door and emanating from the bleeding victim can be documented by the determination of separate areas of convergence.

FIGURE 1

A three-dimensional diagram illustrating bloodstain patterns that were located, documented, and reconstructed.
The Institute of Applied Forensic Technology, Ocoee, Florida

FIGURE 2

Positions of bloodstain patterns arising from blows that were inflicted on the victim's face.
The Institute of Applied Forensic Technology, Ocoee, Florida

A suspect was apprehended three days later, and he was found to have an acute fracture of the right hand. When he was confronted with the bloodstain evidence, the suspect admitted striking the victim, first with his fist, then with a cane, and finally stabbing him with a kitchen knife. The suspect pleaded guilty to three first-degree felonies.

(a)

(b)

(c)

(d)

FIGURE 3

(a) A laboratory test pattern showing an impact spatter. The size and shape of the stains demonstrate a forceful impact 90 degrees to the target. (b) A laboratory test pattern illustrating a cast-off pattern directed left to right from an overhead swing. (c) A laboratory test pattern showing a repetitive transfer impression pattern produced by a bloodstained hand moving left to right across the target. (d) A laboratory test pattern illustrating vertical flow patterns. The left pattern represents a stationary source; the right pattern was produced by left-to-right motion.

The Institute of Applied Forensic Technology, Ocoee, Florida

(a) Patterns A, B, C

(b) Patterns E and F

(c) Patterns G and H

FIGURE 4

(a) A convergence of impact spatter patterns associated with beating with a fist. (b) The convergence of impact spatter associated with the victim falling to the floor while bleeding from the nose. (c) The convergence of impact spatter associated with the victim while face down at the door, being struck with a cane.

The Institute of Applied Forensic Technology, Ocoee, Florida

chapter summary

> > > > > > > > > > >

Physical evidence left behind at a crime scene, properly handled and preserved, plays a crucial role in reconstructing the events that took place surrounding the crime. Crime-scene reconstruction relies on the combined efforts of medical examiners, criminalists, and law enforcement personnel to recover physical evidence and to sort out the events surrounding the occurrence of a crime.

The location, distribution, and appearance of bloodstains and spatters may be useful for interpreting and reconstructing the events that produced the bleeding. An investigator or bloodstain pattern analyst can decipher from individual bloodstains the directionality and angle of impact of the blood when it impacted the surface of deposition. In addition, bloodstain patterns, consisting of many individual bloodstains, may convey to the analyst the location of victims or suspects, the movement of bleeding individuals, and the number of blows delivered.

Surface texture and an individual stain's shape, size, and location must be considered when determining the direction and angle of impact of the bloodstain. Surface texture can greatly affect the shape of a bloodstain. The directionality of an individual bloodstain may be shown by the stain's tail or the accumulation of blood because the tail or accumulation appears on the side opposite the force. The angle of impact of a bloodstain can be approximated by the shape of the bloodstain, or it can be more effectively estimated using the width-to-length ratio of the stain.

An impact spatter pattern occurs when an object impacts a source of blood producing forward spatter projected forward from the source and back spatter projected backward from the source. Patterns created by impact spatter can be classified as low-velocity (>3 mm drops), medium-velocity (1–3 mm drops), or high-velocity (<1 mm drops). These classifications are for descriptive purposes only and should not be used to determine the kind of force that produced the pattern. The area of convergence of an impact spatter pattern is the area the individual stains emanated from on a two-dimensional plane. The area of origin of a bloodstain pattern in three-dimensional space may represent the position of the victim or suspect when the stain-producing event took place.

Gunshot spatter consists of very fine spatter originating from both forward spatter from an exit wound and back spatter from an entrance wound, or only back spatter if the bullet did not exit the body. Blood cast off from an object, typically a weapon or fist between delivering blows to a victim, may form an arc pattern on a nearby surface. The features of the pattern can suggest the kind of object that created it and the minimum number of blows delivered by the object. The characteristic spurts present in an arterial spray spatter are created by the continuing pumping of blood from an arterial injury. Expired blood expelled from the mouth or nose may at first appear to be fine high-velocity or large low-velocity impact spatter. It may feature bubbles of oxygen in the drying drops or possibly be mixed with saliva. A void, where an object (or person) blocks the deposition of blood spatter onto a target surface or object, may give a clue as to the size and shape of the missing object or person.

Transfer patterns, created when an object with blood on it makes simple contact with a surface, may reveal the shape or texture characteristics of the object. Because the direction of flows originating from either a single drop or a large amount of blood is caused by gravity, the direction of a pattern may suggest the original position of the surface when the flow was formed. A drip trail pattern shows a path of drops separate from other patterns; it is formed by single blood drops dripping off an object or injury. The presence of skeletonization of the perimeter of a bloodstain suggests that the stain was disturbed after the edges had had sufficient time to skeletonize.

The precise appearance and location of each bloodstain at a crime scene is important. Therefore, each bloodstain pattern located at a crime scene must be properly documented in notes, photographs, and sketches. Medium-range and close-up photographs should be recorded using either the grid method or perimeter ruler method to show the orientation and relative size of the pattern and individual stains.

review questions

1. _____ is the method used to support a likely sequence of events at a crime scene by the observation and evaluation of physical evidence and statements made by individuals involved with the incident.

2. Reconstructing the circumstances of a crime scene is a team effort that may include the help of law enforcement personnel, medical examiners, and _____.

3. Violent contact between individuals at a crime scene frequently produces bleeding and results in the formation of _____.

4. The proper interpretation of bloodstain patterns necessitates carefully planned _____ using surface materials comparable to those found at the crime scene.

5. Bloodstain patterns may convey to the analyst the location and movements of _____ or _____ during the commission of a crime.

6. True or False: Harder and less porous surfaces result in less spatter, whereas rough surfaces result in stains with more spatter and serrated edges. _____

7. Generally, bloodstain diameter (increases, decreases) with height. _____

8. The _____ and _____ of blood striking an object may be discerned by the stain's shape.

9. A drop of blood that strikes a surface at an angle of impact of approximately 90 degrees will be close to (elliptical, circular) in shape. _____

10. The angle of impact of an individual bloodstain can be estimated using the ratio of _____ divided by _____.

11. _____ is the most common type of blood spatter found at a crime scene and is produced when an object forcefully contacts a source of blood.

12. True or False: Forward spatter consists of the blood projected backward from the source, and back spatter is projected outward and away from the source. _____

13. The classification system of impact spatter is based on the size of drops resulting from the velocity of the blood drops produced, and patterns can be classified as _____, _____, or _____ impact spatter.

14. True or False: The velocity classification system is a good way to classify impact patterns and to determine the kind of force that produced them. _____

15. The _____ is the point on a two-dimensional plane from which the drops originated.

16. The _____ of a bloodstain pattern in a three-dimensional space illustrates the position of the victim or suspect when the stain-producing event took place.

17. The _____ method is used at the crime scene to determine the area of origin.

18. A(n) _____ is created by contact between a bloody object and a surface.

19. Movement of a bloody object across a surface, (lightens, darkens) as the pattern moves away from the point of contact.

20. True or False: Footwear transfer patterns created by an individual who was running typically show imprints with more space between them compared to those of an individual who was walking. _____

21. True or False: The direction of a flow pattern may show movements of objects or bodies while the flow was still in progress or after the blood had dried. _____

22. The approximate drying time of a(n) _____ of blood determined by experimentation is related to the environmental condition of the scene and may suggest how much time has elapsed since its deposition.

23. The edges of a bloodstain generally _____ within 50 seconds of deposition and are left intact even if the central area of a bloodstain is altered by a wiping motion.

24. A(n) _____ pattern commonly originates from repeated strikes from weapons or fists and is characterized by an arc pattern of separate drops showing directionality.

25. True or False: Characteristics of a cast-off pattern arc cannot give clues as to the kind of object that was used to produce the pattern. _____

26. When an injury is suffered to an artery, the pressure of the continuing pumping of blood projects blood out of the injured area in spurts creating a pattern known as _____.

27. If a(n) _____ pattern is found at a scene, it may show movement, lead to a discarded weapon, or provide identification of the suspect by his or her own blood.

28. A bloodstain pattern created by _____ features bubbles of oxygen in the drying drops and may be lighter in color when compared to impact spatter.

29. The shape and size of the blank space, or _____, created when an object blocks the deposition of spatter onto a surface and is then removed may give a clue as to the size and shape of the missing object or person.

30. True or False: Each bloodstain pattern found at a crime scene should be noted, studied, and photographed. _____

31. When documenting bloodstain patterns, the _____ involves setting up a grid of squares of known dimensions over the entire pattern and taking overview, medium-range, and close-up photographs with and without the grid.

32. The _____ method of bloodstain documentation involves setting up a border of rulers around the pattern and then placing a small ruler next to each stain to show relative position and size in photographs.

33. True or False: The pointed end of a bloodstain always faces toward its direction of travel. _____

application and critical thinking

1. After looking at the bloodstains in the figure, answer the following questions:

   a. Which three drops struck the surface closest to a 90-degree angle? Explain your answer.

   b. Which three drops struck the surface farthest from a 90-degree angle? Explain your answer.

   c. In what direction were drops 2 and 7 traveling when they struck the surface? Explain your answer.

2. Investigator Priscilla Wright arrives at a murder scene and finds the body of a victim who suffered a gunshot wound, but she sees no blood spatter on the wall or floor behind it. What should she conclude from this observation?

3. Investigator Terry Martin arrives at an assault scene and finds a cast-off pattern consisting of tiny drops of blood in a very narrow linear arc pattern on a wall near the victim. What does this tell him about the weapon used in the crime?

further references

Bevel, Tom, and Ross Gardner, *Bloodstain Pattern Analysis: With an Introduction to Crime Scene Reconstruction*, 3rd ed. Boca Raton, Fla.: CRC Press, 2008.

James, Stuart H., Paul E. Kish, and T. P. Sutton, *Principles of Bloodstain Pattern Analysis: Theory and Practice*. Boca Raton, Fla.: CRC Press, 2005.

Wonder, A. Y., *Blood Dynamics*. Burlington, Mass.: Elsevier Academic Press, 2001.

Wonder, A. Y., *Bloodstain Pattern Evidence: Objective Approaches and Case Applications*. Burlington, Mass.: Elsevier Academic Press, 2007.

Jeffrey MacDonald: Fatal Vision

The grisly murder scene that confronted police on February 17, 1970, is one that cannot be wiped from memory. Summoned to the Fort Bragg residence of Captain Jeffrey MacDonald, a physician, police found the bludgeoned body of MacDonald's wife. She had been repeatedly knifed, and her face was smashed to a pulp. MacDonald's two children, ages 2 and 5, had been brutally and repeatedly knifed and battered to death. Suspicion quickly fell on MacDonald. To the eyes of investigators, the murder scene had a staged appearance. MacDonald described a frantic effort to subdue four intruders who had slashed at him with an ice pick. However, the confrontation left MacDonald with minor wounds and no apparent defense wounds on his arms. MacDonald then described how he had covered his slashed wife with his blue pajama top. Interestingly, when the body was removed blue threads were observed under the body. In fact, blue threads matching the pajama top turned up throughout the house—nineteen in one child's bedroom, including one beneath her fingernail, and two in the other child's bedroom. Eighty-one blue fibers were recovered from the master bedroom, and two were located on a bloodstained piece of wood outside the house. Later forensic examination showed that the 48 ice pick holes in the pajama top were smooth and cylindrical, a sign that the top was stationary when it was slashed. Also, folding the pajama top demonstrated that the 48 holes actually could have been made by 21 thrusts of an ice pick. This coincided with the number of wounds that MacDonald's wife sustained. As described in the book *Fatal Vision*, which chronicled the murder investigation, when MacDonald was confronted with adulterous conduct, he replied, "You guys are more thorough than I thought." MacDonald is currently serving three consecutive life sentences.

hairs, fibers, and paint

KEY TERMS

anagen phase
catagen phase
cortex
cuticle
follicular tag
macromolecule
manufactured fibers
medulla
mitochondrial DNA
molecule
monomer
natural fibers
nuclear DNA
polymer
telogen phase

Learning Objectives

After studying this chapter you should be able to:

- Recognize and understand the cuticle, cortex, and medulla areas of hair

- List the three phases of hair growth

- Appreciate the distinction between animal and human hairs

- List hair features that are useful for the microscopic comparison of human hairs

- Explain the proper collection of forensic hair evidence

- Describe and understand the role of DNA typing in hair comparisons

- Understand the differences between natural and manufactured fibers

- List the properties of fibers that are most useful for forensic comparisons

- Describe the proper collection of fiber evidence

- List the most useful examinations for performing a forensic comparison of paint

- Describe the proper collection and preservation of forensic paint evidence

The trace evidence transferred between individuals and objects during the commission of a crime, if recovered, often corroborates other evidence developed during the course of an investigation. Although in most cases physical evidence cannot by itself positively identify a suspect, laboratory examination may narrow the origin of such evidence to a group that includes the suspect. Using many of the instruments and techniques described in the previous three chapters, the crime laboratory has developed a variety of procedures for comparing and tracing the origins of physical evidence. This chapter and those that follow discuss how to apply these techniques to the analysis of the types of physical evidence most often encountered at crime scenes. We begin with a discussion of hairs, fibers, and paint.

Morphology of Hair

Hair is encountered as physical evidence in a wide variety of crimes. However, any review of the forensic aspects of hair examination must start with the observation that it is not yet possible to individualize a human hair to any single head or body through its morphology. Over the years, criminalists have tried to isolate the physical and chemical properties of hair that could serve as individual characteristics of identity. Partial success has finally been achieved by isolating and characterizing the DNA present in hair. The importance of hair as physical evidence cannot be underemphasized. Its removal from the body often denotes physical contact between a victim and perpetrator and hence a crime of a serious or violent nature. When hair is properly collected at the crime scene and submitted to the laboratory along with enough standard/reference samples, it can provide strong corroborative evidence for placing an individual at a crime site.

The first step in the forensic examination of hair logically starts with its color and structure, or morphology, and, if warranted, progresses to the more detailed DNA extraction, isolation, and characterization.

Hair is an appendage of the skin that grows out of an organ known as the *hair follicle*. The length of a hair extends from its root or bulb embedded in the follicle, continues into the shaft, and terminates at the tip end. The shaft, which is composed of three layers—the **cuticle**, **cortex**, and **medulla**—is subjected to the most intense examination by the forensic scientist (see Figure 13–1).

Cuticle

Two features that make hair a good subject for establishing individual identity are its resistance to chemical decomposition and its ability to retain structural features over a long period of time. Much of this resistance and stability is attributed to the cuticle, the outside covering of the hair.

cuticle
The scale structure covering the exterior of the hair

cortex
The main body of the hair shaft

medulla
A cellular column running through the center of the hair

FIGURE 13–1
Cross section of skin showing hair growing out of a tubelike structure called the follicle.

The cuticle is formed by overlapping scales that always point toward the tip end of each hair. The scales form from specialized cells that have hardened (*keratinized*) and flattened in progressing from the follicle. The scales of most animal hair can best be described as looking like shingles on a roof. Although the scale pattern is not a useful characteristic for individualizing human hair, the variety of patterns formed by animal hair makes it an important feature for species identification. Figure 13–2 shows the scale patterns of some animal hairs and of a human hair as viewed by the scanning electron microscope. Another method of studying the scale pattern of hair is to make a cast of its surface. This is done by embedding the hair in a soft medium, such as clear nail polish or softened vinyl. When the medium has hardened, the hair is removed, leaving a clear, distinct impression of the hair's cuticle, ideal for examination with a compound microscope.

Cortex

Contained within the protective layer of the cuticle is the cortex. The cortex is made up of spindle-shaped cortical cells aligned in a regular array, parallel to the length of the hair. The cortex derives its major forensic importance from the fact that it is embedded with the pigment granules that give hair its color. The color, shape, and distribution of these granules provide important points of comparison among the hairs of different individuals.

The structural features of the cortex are examined microscopically after the hair has been mounted in a liquid medium with a refractive index close to that of the hair. Under these conditions, the amount of light reflected off the hair's surface is minimized, and the amount of light penetrating the hair is optimized.

(a)   (b)   (c)

(d)   (e)   (f)

FIGURE 13–2
Scale patterns of various types of hair. (a) Human head hair (600×), (b) dog (1250×), (c) deer (120×), (d) rabbit (300×), (e) cat (2000×), and (f) horse (450×).

| Continuous | Interrupted | Fragmented |

FIGURE 13–3
Medulla patterns.

Medulla

The medulla is a collection of cells that looks like a central canal running through a hair. In many animals, this canal is a predominant feature, occupying more than half of the hair's diameter. The *medullary index* measures the diameter of the medulla relative to the diameter of the hair shaft and is normally expressed as a fraction. For humans, the index is generally less than one-third; for most other animals, the index is one-half or greater.

The presence and appearance of the medulla vary from individual to individual and even among the hairs of a given individual. Not all hairs have medullae, and when they do exist, the degree of medullation can vary. In this respect, medullae may be classified as being continuous, interrupted, fragmented, or absent (see Figure 13–3). Human head hairs generally exhibit no medullae or have fragmented ones; they rarely show continuous medullation. One noted exception is the Mongoloid race, whose members usually have head hairs with continuous medullae. Also, most animals have medullae that are either continuous or interrupted.

Another interesting feature of the medulla is its shape. Humans, as well as many animals, have medullae that give a nearly cylindrical appearance. Other animals exhibit medullae that have a patterned shape. For example, the medulla of a cat can best be described as resembling a string of pearls, whereas members of the deer family show a medullary structure consisting of spherical cells occupying the entire hair shaft. Figure 13–4 illustrates medullary sizes and forms for a number of common animal hairs and a human head hair.

A searchable database on CD-ROM of the 35 most common animal hairs encountered in forensic casework is commercially available.[1] This database allows an examiner to rapidly search for animal hairs based on scale patterns and/or medulla type using a PC. A typical screen presentation arising from such a data search is shown in Figure 13–5.

Root

The root and other surrounding cells within the hair follicle provide the tools necessary to produce hair and continue its growth. Human head hair grows in three developmental stages, and the shape and size of the hair root is determined by the growth phase in which the hair happens to be. The three phases of hair growth are the **anagen**, **catagen**, and **telogen phases**.

In the anagen phase, which may last up to six years, the root is attached to the follicle for continued growth, giving the root bulb a flame-shaped appearance (Figure 13–6[a]). When pulled from the root, some hairs in the anagen phase have a **follicular tag**. With the advent of DNA analysis, this follicular tag is important for individualizing hair.

Hair continues to grow, but at a decreasing rate, during the catagen phase, which can last anywhere from two to three weeks. In the catagen phase, roots typically take on an elongated appearance (Figure 13–6[b]) as the root bulb shrinks and is pushed out of the hair follicle.

Once hair growth ends, the telogen phase begins and the root takes on a club-shaped appearance (Figure 13–6[c]). Over two to six months, the hair is pushed out of the follicle, causing the hair to be naturally shed.

Identification and Comparison of Hair

Most often the prime purpose for examining hair evidence in a crime laboratory is to establish whether the hair is human or animal in origin or to determine whether human hair retrieved at a crime scene compares with hair from a particular individual. Although animal hair can normally be distinguished from human hair with little difficulty, human hair comparisons must be undertaken

anagen phase
The initial growth phase during which the hair follicle actively produces hair

catagen phase
A transition stage between the anagen and telogen phases of hair growth

telogen phase
The final growth phase in which hair naturally falls out of the skin

follicular tag
A translucent piece of tissue surrounding the hair's shaft near the root; it contains the richest source of DNA associated with hair

[1] J. D. Baker and D. L. Exline, *Forensic Animal Hair Atlas: A Searchable Database on CD-ROM*. RJ Lee Group, Inc., 350 Hochberg Rd., Monroeville, Pa. 15146.

FIGURE 13–4

Medulla patterns for various types of hair. (a) Human head hair (400×), (b) dog (400×), (c) deer (500×), (d) rabbit (450×), (e) cat (400×), and (f) mouse (500×).

with extreme caution and with an awareness of hair's tendency to exhibit variable morphological characteristics, not only from one person to another but also within a single individual.

Considerations in Hair Examination

A careful microscopic examination of hair reveals morphological features that can distinguish human hair from animal hair. The hair of various animals also differs enough in structure that the examiner can often identify the species. Before reaching such a conclusion, however, the examiner must have access to a comprehensive collection of reference standards and the accumulated

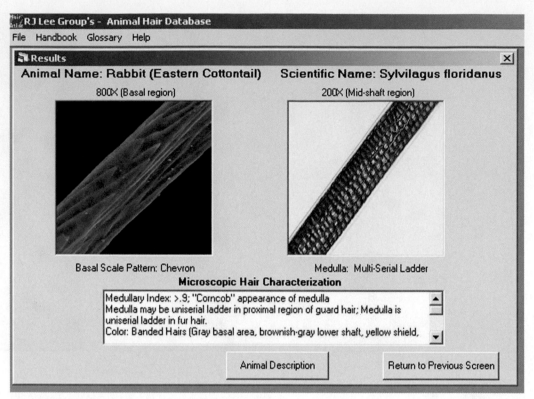

FIGURE 13–5

Information on rabbit hair contained within the *Forensic Animal Hair Atlas*.
Courtesy RJ Lee Group, Inc. Monroeville, Pa.

FIGURE 13–6

Hair roots in the (a) anagen phase, (b) catagen phase, and (c) telogen phase (100×).
Courtesy Charles A. Linch

experience of hundreds of prior hair examinations. Scale structure, medullary index, and medullary shape are particularly important in hair identification.

The most common request when hair is used as forensic evidence is to determine whether hair recovered at the crime scene compares to hair removed from a suspect. In most cases, such a comparison relates to hair obtained from the scalp or pubic area. Ultimately, the evidential value of the comparison depends on the degree of probability with which the examiner can associate the hair in question with a particular individual.

HAIR CHARACTERISTICS   In making a hair comparison, a comparison microscope is an invaluable tool that allows the examiner to view the questioned and known hair together, side by side. Any variations in the microscopic characteristics will thus be readily observed. Because hair from any part of the body exhibits a range of characteristics, it is necessary to have an adequate number of known hairs that are representative of all of its features when making a comparison.

In comparing hair, the criminalist is particularly interested in matching the color, length, and diameter. Other important features are the presence or absence of a medulla and the distribution, shape, and color intensity of the pigment granules in the cortex. A microscopic examination may also distinguish dyed or bleached hair from natural hair. A dyed color is often present in the cuticle as well as throughout the cortex. Bleaching, on the other hand, tends to remove pigment from the hair and to give it a yellowish tint. If hair has grown since it was last bleached or dyed, the natural-end portion will be quite distinct in color. An estimate of the time since dyeing or bleaching can be made because *hair grows approximately one centimeter per month*. Other significant but less frequent features may be observed in hair. For example, morphological abnormalities may be present because of certain diseases or deficiencies. Also, the presence of fungal and nit infections can further link a hair specimen to a particular individual.

POTENTIAL FOR ERROR   Although microscopic comparison of hairs has long been accepted as an appropriate approach for including and excluding questioned hairs against standard/reference hairs, many forensic scientists have long recognized that this approach is subjective and is highly dependent on the skills and integrity of the analyst as well as the hair morphology being examined. However, until the advent of DNA analysis, the forensic science community had no choice but to rely on the microscope to carry out hair comparisons.

Any lingering doubts about the necessity of augmenting microscopic hair examinations with DNA analysis evaporated with the publication of an FBI study describing significant error rates associated with microscopic comparison of hairs.[2] Hair evidence submitted to the FBI for DNA analysis between 1996 and 2000 was examined both microscopically and by DNA analysis. Approximately 11 percent of the hairs (9 out of 80) in which FBI hair examiners found a positive microscopic match between questioned and standard/reference hairs were found to be nonmatches when they were later subjected to DNA analysis. The course of events is clear; microscopic hair comparisons must be regarded by police and courts as presumptive in nature, and all positive microscopic hair comparisons must be confirmed by DNA determinations.

Questions Concerning Hair Examination

A number of questions may be asked to further ascertain the present status of forensic hair examinations.

CAN THE BODY AREA FROM WHICH A HAIR ORIGINATED BE DETERMINED?   Normally, it is easy to determine the body area from which a hair came. For example, scalp hairs generally show little diameter variation and have a more uniform distribution of pigment color when compared to other body hairs. Pubic hairs are short and curly, with wide variations in shaft diameter, and usually have continuous medullae. Beard hairs are coarse, are normally triangular in cross section, and have blunt tips acquired from cutting or shaving.

CAN THE RACIAL ORIGIN OF HAIR BE DETERMINED?   In many instances, the examiner can distinguish hair originating from members of different races; this is especially true of Caucasian and Negroid head hair. Negroid hairs are normally kinky, containing dense, unevenly distributed pigments. Caucasian hairs are usually straight or wavy, with very fine to coarse pigments that are more evenly distributed when compared to Negroid hair. Sometimes a cross-sectional examination of hair may aid in the identification of race.

Cross-sections of hair from Caucasians are oval to round in shape, whereas cross-sections of Negroid hair are flat to oval in shape. However, all of these observations are general in nature, with many possible exceptions. The criminalist must approach the determination of race from hair with caution and a good deal of experience.

---

[2] M. M. Houk and B. Budowle, "Correlation of Microscopic and Mitochondrial DNA Hair Comparisons," *Journal of Forensic Sciences* 47 (2002): 964.

> > > > > > > > > > > > > > > > > > >

The Central Park Jogger Case Revisited

On April 19, 1989, a young woman left her apartment around nine p.m. to jog in New York's Central Park. Nearly five hours later, she was found comatose lying in a puddle of mud in the park. She had been raped, her skull was fractured, and she had lost 75 percent of her blood. When the woman recovered, she had no memory of what happened to her. The brutality of the crime sent shock waves through the city and seemed to fuel a national perception that crime was running rampant and unchecked through the streets of New York.

Already in custody at the station house of the Central Park Precinct was a group of 14- and 15-year-old boys who had been rounded up leaving the park earlier in the night by

A courtroom sketch of the trial proceeding in the Central Park Jogger case.
AP Wide World Photos

police who suspected that they had been involved in a series of random attacks.

Over the next two days, four of the teenagers gave videotape statements, which they later recanted, admitting to participating in the attack. Ultimately, five of the teenagers were charged with the crime. Interestingly, none of the semen collected from the victim could be linked to any of the defendants. However, according to the testimony of a forensic analyst, two head hairs collected from the clothing of one of the defendants microscopically compared to those of the victim, and a third hair collected from the same defendant's T-shirt microscopically compared to the victim's pubic hair. Besides these three hairs, a fourth hair was found microscopically similar to the victim's. This hair was recovered from the clothing of Steven Lopez, who was originally charged with rape but not prosecuted for the crime. Hairs were the only pieces of physical evidence offered by the district attorney to directly link any of the teenagers to the crime. The hairs were cited by the district attorney as a way for the jury to know that the videotaped confessions of the teenagers were reliable. The five defendants were convicted and ultimately served from 9 to 13 years.

Matias Reyes was arrested in August 1989, more than three months after the jogger attack. He pleaded guilty to murdering a pregnant woman, raping three others, and committing a robbery. He was sentenced to 33 years to life. In January 2002, Reyes confessed to the Central Park attack. Follow-up tests revealed that Reyes's DNA compared to semen recovered from the jogger's body and her sock. Other DNA tests showed that the hairs offered into evidence at the original trial did not come from the victim, and so could not be used to link the teenagers to the crime as the district attorney had argued.

After an 11-month reinvestigation of the original charges, a New York State Supreme Court judge dismissed all the convictions against the five teenage suspects in the Central Park jogger case.

CAN THE AGE AND SEX OF AN INDIVIDUAL BE DETERMINED FROM A HAIR SAMPLE?   The age of an individual cannot be learned from a hair examination with any degree of certainty except with infant hair. Infant hairs are fine, are short in length, have fine pigment, and are rudimentary in character. Although the presence of dye or bleach on the hair may offer some clue to sex, present hairstyles make these characteristics less valuable than they were in the past. The recovery of nuclear DNA either from tissue adhering to hair or from the root structure of the hair will allow a determination of whether the hair originated from a male or female (see page 275).

IS IT POSSIBLE TO DETERMINE WHETHER HAIR WAS FORCIBLY REMOVED FROM THE BODY?   A microscopic examination of the hair root may establish whether the hair fell out or was pulled out of the skin. A hair root with follicular tissue (root sheath cells) adhering to it, as shown in Figure 13–7, indicates a hair that has been pulled out either by a person or by brushing or combing. Hair naturally falling off the body has a bulbous-shaped root free of any adhering tissue. However, the absence of sheath cells cannot always be relied on for correctly judging whether hair has been forcibly pulled from the body. In some cases the root of a hair is devoid of any adhering tissue even when it has been pulled from the body. Apparently, an important consideration is how quickly

FIGURE 13–7
Forcibly removed head hair, with follicular tissue attached.

the hair is pulled out of the head. Hairs pulled quickly from the head are much more likely to have sheath cells compared to hairs that have been removed slowly from the scalp.[3]

ARE EFFORTS BEING MADE TO INDIVIDUALIZE HUMAN HAIR?   As we learned in Chapter 11, forensic scientists are routinely isolating and characterizing individual variations in DNA. Forensic hair examiners can link human hair to a particular individual by characterizing the **nuclear DNA** in the hair root or in follicular tissue adhering to the root (see Figure 13–7). Recall that the follicular tag is the richest source of DNA associated with hair. In the absence of follicular tissue, an examiner must extract DNA from the hair root. The growth phase of hair (see page 324) is a useful predictor of the likelihood of successfully typing DNA in human hair.[4] Examiners have a higher rate of success in extracting DNA from hair roots in the anagen phase or from anagen-phase hairs entering the catagen phase of growth. Telogen-phase hairs have an inadequate amount of DNA for successful typing. Because most hairs are naturally shed and are expected to be in the telogen stage, these observations do not portend well for hairs collected at crime scenes. However, some crime scenes are populated with forcibly removed hairs that are expected to be rich sources for nuclear DNA.

When a questioned hair does not have adhering tissue or a root structure amenable to the isolation of nuclear DNA, there is an alternative—**mitochondrial DNA**. Unlike the nuclear DNA described earlier, which is located in the nuclei of practically every cell in our body, mitochondrial DNA is found in cellular material outside the nucleus. Interestingly, unlike nuclear DNA, which is passed down to us from both parents, mitochondrial DNA is transmitted only from mother to child. Importantly, many more copies of mitochondrial DNA are located in our cells as compared to nuclear DNA. For this reason, the success rate of finding and typing mitochondrial DNA is much greater from samples, such as hair, that have limited quantities of nuclear DNA. Hairs 1–2 centimeters long can be subjected to mitochondrial analysis with extremely high odds of success. This subject is discussed in greater detail in Chapter 11.

CAN DNA INDIVIDUALIZE A HUMAN HAIR?   In some cases, the answer is yes. As we learned in Chapter 11, nuclear DNA produces frequency of occurrences as low as one in billions or trillions. On the other hand, mitochondrial DNA cannot individualize human hair, but its diversity within the human population often permits exclusion of a significant portion of a population as potential contributors of a hair sample. Ideally, the combination of a positive microscopic comparison and an association through nuclear or mitochondrial DNA analysis provides a strong and meaningful link between a questioned hair and standard/reference hairs. However, a word of caution: mitochondrial DNA cannot distinguish microscopically similar hairs from different individuals who are maternally related.

Collection and Preservation of Hair Evidence

When questioned hairs are submitted to a forensic laboratory for examination, they must always be accompanied by an adequate number of standard/reference samples from the victim of the crime and from individuals suspected of having deposited hair at the crime scene. We have learned that

nuclear DNA
DNA present within the nucleus of a cell; this form of DNA is inherited from both parents

mitochondrial DNA
DNA present in small structures (mitochondria) outside the nucleus of a cell; mitochondria supply energy to the cell; this form of DNA is inherited maternally (from the mother)

---

[3] L. A. King, R. Wigmore, and J. M. Twibell, "The Morphology and Occurrence of Human Hair Sheath Cells," *Journal of the Forensic Science Society* 22 (1982): 267.
[4] C. A. Linch et al., "Evaluation of the Human Hair Root for DNA Typing Subsequent to Microscopic Comparison," *Journal of Forensic Sciences* 43 (1998): 305.

hair from different parts of the body varies significantly in its physical characteristics. Likewise, hair from any one area of the body can also have a wide range of characteristics. For this reason, the questioned and standard/reference hairs must come from the same area of the body; one cannot, for instance, compare head hair to pubic hair. It is also important that the collection of standard/reference hair be carried out in a way to ensure a representative sampling of hair from any one area of the body.

Forensic hair comparisons generally involve either head hair or pubic hair. Collecting 50 full-length hairs from all areas of the scalp normally ensures a representative sampling of head hair. Likewise, a minimum collection of 24 full-length pubic hairs should cover the range of characteristics present in this type of hair. In rape cases, care must first be taken to comb the pubic area with a clean comb to remove all loose foreign hair present before the victim is sampled for standard/reference hair. The comb should then be packaged in a separate envelope.

Because a hair may show variation in color and other morphological features over its entire length, the entire hair length is collected. This requirement is best accomplished by either pulling the hair out of the skin or clipping it at the skin line. During an autopsy, hair samples are collected from a victim of suspicious death as a matter of routine. Because the autopsy may occur early in an investigation, the need for hair standard/reference samples may not always be apparent. However, one should never rule out the possible involvement of hair evidence in subsequent investigative findings. Failure to make this simple collection at an opportune time may result in complicated legal problems at a later date.

Types of Fibers

Just as hair left at a crime scene can serve as identification, the same logic can reasonably be extended to the fibers that compose our fabrics and garments. Fibers may become important evidence in incidents that involve personal contact—such as homicide, assault, or sexual

forensic brief

The murder of Ennis Cosby, son of entertainer Bill Cosby, at first appeared unsolvable. It was a random act. When his car tire went flat, he pulled off the road and called a friend on his cellular phone to ask for assistance. Shortly thereafter, an assailant demanded money and, when Cosby didn't respond quickly enough, shot him once in the temple. Acting on a tip from a friend of the assailant, police investigators later found a .38 revolver wrapped in a blue cap miles from the crime scene. Mikail Markhasev was arrested and charged with murder. At trial, the district attorney introduced firearms evidence to show that the recovered gun had fired the bullet aimed at Cosby. However, a single hair also recovered from the hat dramatically linked Markhasev to the crime. Los Angeles Police Department forensic analyst Harry Klann identified six DNA markers from the follicular tissue adhering to the hair root that matched Markhasev's DNA. This particular DNA profile is found in one out of 15,500 members of the general population. Upon hearing all the evidence, the jury deliberated and convicted Markhasev of murder.

Bill Cosby and his son Ennis Cosby.
Courtesy Andrea Mohin, The New York Times

offenses—in which cross-transfers may occur between the clothing of suspect and victim. Similarly, the force of impact between a hit-and-run victim and a vehicle often leaves fibers, threads, or even whole pieces of clothing adhering to parts of the vehicle. Fibers may also become fixed in screens or glass broken in the course of a breaking-and-entering attempt.

Regardless of where and under what conditions fibers are recovered, their ultimate value as forensic evidence depends on the criminalist's ability to narrow their origin to a limited number of sources or even to a single source. Unfortunately, mass production of garments and fabrics has limited the value of fiber evidence in this respect, and only under the most unusual circumstances does the recovery of fibers at a crime scene provide individual identification with a high degree of certainty.

For centuries, humans depended on natural sources derived from plants and animals for textile fibers. Early in the 20th century, the first manufactured fiber—rayon—became a practical reality, followed in the 1920s by the introduction of cellulose acetate. Since the late 1930s, scientists have produced dozens of new fibers. In fact, the development of fibers, fabrics, finishes, and other textile-processing techniques has made greater advances since 1900 than in the five thousand years of recorded history before the 20th century. Today, such varied items as clothing, carpeting, draperies, wigs, and even artificial turf attest to the predominant role that manufactured fibers have come to play in our culture and environment.

For the purpose of discussing the forensic examination of fibers, it is convenient to classify them into two broad groups: *natural* and *manufactured*.

Natural Fibers

Natural fibers are wholly derived from animal or plant sources. Animal fibers constitute most of the natural fibers encountered in crime laboratory examinations. These include hair coverings from such animals as sheep (wool), goats (mohair, cashmere), camels, llamas, alpacas, and vicuñas; fur fibers include those obtained from animals such as mink, rabbit, beaver, and muskrat.

natural fibers
Fibers derived entirely from animal or plant sources

Forensic examination of animal fibers uses the same procedures discussed in the previous section for the forensic examination of animal hairs. Identification and comparison of such fibers relies solely on a microscopic examination of color and morphological characteristics. Again, a sufficient number of standard/reference specimens must be examined to establish the range of fiber characteristics of the suspect fabric.

By far the most prevalent plant fiber is cotton. The wide use of undyed white cotton fibers in clothing and other fabrics has made its evidential value almost meaningless, although the presence of dyed cotton in a combination of colors has, in some cases, enhanced its evidential significance. The microscopic view of cotton fiber shown in Figure 13–8 reveals its most distinguishing feature—a ribbonlike shape with twists at irregular intervals.

Manufactured Fibers

Beginning with the introduction of rayon in 1911 and the development of nylon in 1939, **manufactured fibers** have increasingly replaced natural fibers in garments and fabrics. Today, such fibers are marketed under hundreds of different trade names. To reduce consumer confusion, the U.S. Federal Trade Commission has approved "generic" or family names for the grouping of all manufactured fibers. Many of these generic classes are produced by several manufacturers and are sold under a confusing variety of trade names. For example, in the United States, polyesters are marketed under names that include Dacron, Fortrel, and Kodel. In England, polyesters are called Terylene. Table 13–1 lists major generic fibers, along with common trade names and their characteristics and applications.

manufactured fibers
Fibers derived from either natural or synthetic polymers; the fibers are typically made by forcing the polymeric material through the holes of a spinneret

The first machine-made fibers were manufactured from raw materials derived from cotton or wood pulp. These materials are processed, and pure cellulose is extracted from them. Depending on the type of fiber desired, the cellulose may be chemically treated and dissolved in an appropriate solvent before it is forced through the small holes of a spinning jet or spinneret to produce the fiber. Fibers manufactured from natural raw materials in this manner are classified as *regenerated fibers* and commonly include rayon, acetate, and triacetate, all of which are produced from regenerated cellulose.

Most of the fibers currently manufactured are produced solely from synthetic chemicals and are therefore classified as *synthetic fibers*. These include nylons, polyesters, and acrylics. The

FIGURE 13–8
Photomicrograph of cotton fiber (450×).

polymer
A substance composed of a large number of atoms; these atoms are usually arranged in repeating units or monomers

creation of synthetic fibers became a reality only when scientists developed a method of synthesizing long-chained molecules called **polymers**.

In 1930, chemists discovered an unusual characteristic of one of the polymers under investigation. When a glass rod in contact with viscous material in a beaker was slowly pulled away, the substance adhered to the rod and formed a fine filament that hardened as soon as it entered the cool air. Furthermore, the cold filaments could be stretched several times their extended length to produce a flexible, strong, and attractive fiber. The first synthetic fiber was improved and then marketed as nylon. Since then, fiber chemists have successfully synthesized new polymers and have developed more efficient methods for manufacturing them. These efforts have produced a multitude of synthetic fibers.

Polymers

The polymer is the basic chemical substance of all synthetic fibers. Indeed, an almost unbelievable array of household, industrial, and recreational products is manufactured from polymers; these include plastics, paints, adhesives, and synthetic rubber. Polymers exist in countless forms and varieties and with the proper treatment can be made to assume different chemical and physical properties.

molecule
Two or more atoms held together by chemical bonds

As we have already observed, chemical substances are composed from basic structural units called **molecules**. The molecules of most materials are composed of just a few atoms; for example, water, H_2O, has 2 atoms of hydrogen and 1 atom of oxygen. The heroin molecule, $C_{21}H_{23}O_5N$, contains 21 atoms of carbon, 23 atoms of hydrogen, 5 atoms of oxygen, and 1 atom of nitrogen. Polymers, on the other hand, are formed by linking a large number of molecules, so that it is not unusual for a polymer to contain thousands or even millions of atoms. This is why polymers are often referred to as **macromolecules**, or "big" molecules.

macromolecule
A molecule with a high molecular mass

monomer
The basic unit of structure from which a polymer is constructed

Simply, a polymer can be pictured as resembling a long, repeating chain, with each link representing the basic structure of the polymer (see Figure 13–9). The repeating molecular units in the polymer, called **monomers**, are joined end to end, so that thousands are linked to form a long chain. What makes polymer chemistry so fascinating is the countless possibilities for linking different molecules. By simply varying the chemical structure of the basic molecules, or monomers, and by devising numerous ways to weave them together, chemists have created polymers that exhibit different properties. This versatility enables polymer chemists to synthesize glues, plastics, paints, and fibers.

TABLE 13–1

Major Generic Fibers

Major Generic Fiber	Characteristics	Major Domestic and Industrial Uses
Acetate	• Luxurious feel and appearance • Wide range of colors and lusters • Excellent drapability and softness • Relatively fast-drying • Shrink-, moth-, and mildew-resistant	*Apparel:* Blouses, dresses, foundation garments, lingerie, linings, shirts, slacks, sportswear *Fabrics:* Brocade, crepe, double knits, faille, knitted jerseys, lace, satin, taffeta, tricot *Home Furnishings:* Draperies, upholstery *Other:* Cigarette filters, fiberfill for pillows, quilted products
Acrylic	• Soft and warm • Wool-like • Retains shape • Resilient • Quick-drying • Resistant to moths, sunlight, oil, and chemicals	*Apparel:* Dresses, infant wear, knitted garments, skiwear, socks, sportswear, sweaters *Fabrics:* Fleece and pile fabrics, facing fabrics in bonded fabrics, simulated furs, jerseys *Home Furnishings:* Blankets, carpets, draperies, upholstery *Other:* Auto tops, awnings, hand-knitting and craft yarns, industrial and geotextile fabrics
Aramid	• Does not melt • Highly flame resistant • Great strength • Great resistance to stretch • Maintains shape and form at high temperatures	Hot-gas filtration fabrics, protective clothing, military helmets, protective vests, structural composites for aircraft and boats, sailcloth, tires, ropes and cables, mechanical rubber goods, marine and sporting goods
Bicomponent	• Thermal bonding • Self-bulking • Very fine fibers • Unique cross-sections • The functionality of special polymers or additives at reduced cost	Uniform distribution of adhesive; fiber remains a part of structure and adds integrity; customized sheath materials to bond various materials; wide range of bonding temperatures; cleaner, environmentally friendly (*no effluent*); recyclable; lamination/molding/densification of composites
Lyocell	• Soft, strong, absorbent • Good dyeability • Fibrillates during wet processing to produce special textures	Dresses, slacks, and coats
Rayon	• Highly absorbent • Soft and comfortable • Easy to dye • Versatile • Good drapability	*Apparel:* Blouses, coats, dresses, jackets, lingerie, linings, millinery, rainwear, slacks, sports shirts, sportswear, suits, ties, work clothes *Home Furnishings:* Bedspreads, blankets, carpets, curtains, draperies, sheets, slipcovers, tablecloths, upholstery *Other:* Industrial products, medical-surgical products, nonwoven products, tire cord
Spandex	• Can be stretched 500 percent without breaking • Can be stretched repeatedly and recover original length • Lightweight • Stronger and more durable than rubber • Resistant to body oils	*Articles* (in which stretch is desired): Athletic apparel, bathing suits, delicate laces, foundation garments, golf jackets, ski pants, slacks, support and surgical hose

(Continued)

TABLE 13–1

Major Generic Fibers (Continued)

Major Generic Fiber	Characteristics	Major Domestic and Industrial Uses
Melamine	• White and dyeable • Flame resistance and low thermal conductivity • High-heat dimensional stability • Processable on standard textile equipment	*Fire-Blocking Fabrics:* Aircraft seating, fire blockers for upholstered furniture in high-risk occupancies (e.g., to meet California TB 133 requirements) *Protective Clothing:* Firefighters' turnout gear, insulating thermal liners, knit hoods, molten metal splash apparel, heat-resistant gloves *Filter Media:* High-capacity, high-efficiency, high-temperature baghouse air filters
Modacrylic	• Soft • Resilient • Abrasion and flame resistant • Quick-drying • Resists acids and alkalies • Retains shape	*Apparel:* Deep-pile coats, trims, linings, simulated fur, wigs and hairpieces *Fabrics:* Fleece fabrics, industrial fabrics, knit-pile fabric backings, nonwoven fabrics *Home Furnishings:* Awnings, blankets, carpets, flame-resistant draperies and curtains, scatter rugs *Other:* Filters, paint rollers, stuffed toys
Nylon	• Exceptionally strong • Supple • Abrasion resistant • Lustrous • Easy to wash • Resists damage from oil and many chemicals • Resilient • Low in moisture absorbency	*Apparel:* Blouses, dresses, foundation garments, hosiery, lingerie and underwear, raincoats, ski and snow apparel, suits, windbreakers *Home Furnishings:* Bedspreads, carpets, draperies, curtains, upholstery *Other:* Air hoses, conveyor and seat belts, parachutes, racket strings, ropes and nets, sleeping bags, tarpaulins, tents, thread, tire cord, geotextiles
Olefin	• Unique wicking properties that make it very comfortable • Abrasion resistant • Quick-drying • Resistant to deterioration from chemicals, mildew, perspiration, rot, and weather • Sensitive to heat • Soil resistant • Strong; very lightweight • Excellent colorfastness	*Apparel:* Pantyhose, underwear, knitted sports shirts, men's half-hose, men's knitted sportswear, sweaters *Home Furnishings:* Carpet and carpet backing, slipcovers, upholstery *Other:* Dye nets, filter fabrics, laundry and sandbags, geotextiles, automotive interiors, cordage, doll hair, industrial sewing thread
Polyester	• Strong • Resistant to stretching and shrinking • Resistant to most chemicals • Quick-drying • Crisp and resilient when wet or dry • Wrinkle and abrasion resistant • Retains heat-set pleats and creases • Easy to wash	*Apparel:* Blouses, shirts, career apparel, children's wear, dresses, half-hose, insulated garments, ties, lingerie and underwear, permanent-press garments, slacks, suits *Home Furnishings:* Carpets, curtains, draperies, sheets and pillowcases *Other:* Fiberfill for various products, fire hose, power belting, ropes and nets, tire cord, sail, V-belts
PBI	• Extremely flame-resistant • Outstanding comfort factor combined with thermal and chemical stability properties • Will not burn or melt • Low shrinkage when exposed to flame	Suitable for high-performance protective apparel such as firefighters' turnout coats, astronaut space suits, and applications in which fire resistance is important

Source: American Fiber Manufacturers Assoc. Inc., Washington, D.C., http://www.fibersource.com/f-tutor/q-guide.htm.

Monomer

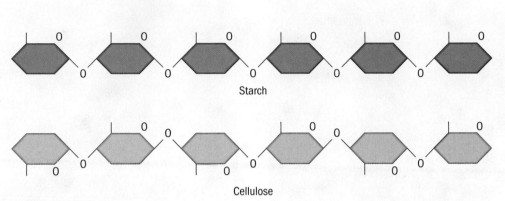

Starch

Cellulose

FIGURE 13-10

Starch and cellulose are natural carbohydrate polymers consisting of a large number of repeating units or monomers.

It would be a mistake to give the impression that all polymers are synthesized in the chemical laboratory. Indeed, this is far from true, for nature has produced polymers that humans have not yet been able to copy. For example, the proteins that form the basic structure of animal hairs, as well as of all living matter, are polymers, composed of thousands of amino acids linked in a highly organized arrangement and sequence. Similarly, cellulose, the basic ingredient of wood and cotton, and starch are both natural polymers built by the combination of several thousand carbohydrate monomers, as shown in Figure 13–10. Hence, the synthesis of manufactured fibers merely represents an extension of chemical principles that nature has successfully used to produce hair and vegetable fibers.

Identification and Comparison of Manufactured Fibers

The evidential value of fibers lies in the criminalist's ability to trace their origin. Obviously, if the examiner is presented with fabrics that can be exactly fitted together at their torn edges, it is a virtual certainty that the fabrics were of common origin. However, more often the criminalist obtains a limited number of fibers for identification and comparison. Generally, in these situations, the possibilities for obtaining a physical match are nonexistent, and the examiner must resort to a side-by-side comparison of the standard/reference and crime-scene fibers.

Microscopic Examination

The first and most important step in the examination is a microscopic comparison for color and diameter using a comparison microscope. Unless these two characteristics agree, there is little reason to suspect a match. Other morphological features that could be present to aid in the comparison are lengthwise striations on the surface of some fibers and the pitting of the fiber's surface with delustering particles (usually titanium dioxide) added in the manufacturing process to reduce shine (Figure 13–11).

The cross-sectional shape of a fiber may also help characterize the fiber (Figure 13–12).[5] In the Wayne Williams case (see Chapter 3), unusually shaped yellow-green fibers discovered on a number of the murder victims were ultimately linked to a carpet in the Williams home. This fiber

---

[5] S. Palenik and C. Fitzsimons, "Fiber Cross-Sections: Part I," *Microscope* 38 (1990): 187.

(a)   (b)

FIGURE 13–11

Photomicrographs of synthetic fibers: (a) cellulose triacetate (450×) and (b) olefin fiber embedded with titanium dioxide particles (450×).

Round   Trilobal

Multi-lobed

Dumbbell   Flat

FIGURE 13–12

Cross-sectional shapes of fibers.

FIGURE 13–13

A scanning electron photomicrograph of the cross section of a nylon fiber removed from a sheet used to transport the body of a murder victim. The fiber, associated with a carpet in Wayne Williams's home, was manufactured in 1971 in relatively small quantities.
Courtesy Federal Bureau of Investigation, Washington, D.C.

was a key element in proving Williams's guilt. A photomicrograph of this unusually shaped fiber is shown in Figure 13–13.

Dye Composition

Although two fibers may seem to have the same color when viewed under the microscope, compositional differences may exist in the dyes that were applied to them during their manufacture. In fact, most textile fibers are impregnated with a mixture of dyes selected to obtain a desired shade or color. The significance of a fiber comparison is enhanced when the forensic examiner can show that the questioned and standard/reference fibers have the same dye composition.

The visible-light microspectrophotometer (pages 173–175) is a convenient way for analysts to compare the colors of fibers through spectral patterns. This technique is not limited by sample size—a fiber as small as one millimeter or less in length can be examined by this type of microscope. The examination is nondestructive and is carried out on fibers simply mounted on a microscope slide.

A more detailed analysis of the fiber's dye composition can be obtained through a chromatographic separation of the dye constituents. To accomplish this, small strands of fibers are compared for dye content by first extracting the dye off each fiber with a suitable solvent and then spotting the dye solution onto a thin-layer chromatography plate. The dye components of the questioned and standard/reference fibers are separated on the thin-layer plate and compared side by side for similarity.[6]

Chemical Composition

Once this phase of the analysis is complete, and before any conclusion can be reached that two or more fibers compare, they must be shown to have the same chemical composition. In this respect, tests are performed to confirm that all of the fibers involved belong to the same broad generic class. Additionally, the comparison will be substantially enhanced if it can be demonstrated that all of the fibers belong to the same subclassification within their generic class. For example, at least four different types of nylon are available in commercial and consumer markets, including nylon 6, nylon 6-10, nylon 11, and nylon 6-6. Although all types of nylon have many properties in common, each may differ in physical shape, appearance, and dyeability because of modifications in basic chemical structure. Similarly, a study of more than two hundred different samples of acrylic fibers revealed that they could actually be divided into 24 distinguishable groups on the basis of their polymeric structure and microscopic characteristics.[7]

[6] D. K. Laing et al., "The Standardisation of Thin-Layer Chromatographic Systems for Comparisons of Fibre Dyes," *Journal of the Forensic Science Society* 30 (1990): 299.
[7] M. C. Grieve, "Another Look at the Classification of Acrylic Fibres, Using FTIR Microscopy," *Science & Justice* 35 (1995): 179.

Textile chemists have devised numerous tests for determining the class of a fiber. However, unlike the textile chemist, the criminalist frequently does not have the luxury of having a substantial quantity of fabric to work with and must therefore select tests that will yield the most information with the least amount of material. Only a single fiber may be available for analysis, and often this may amount to no more than a minute strand recovered from a fingernail scraping of a homicide or rape victim.

Other Properties for Examination

A most useful physical property of fibers, from the criminalist's point of view, is that many manufactured fibers exhibit double refraction or birefringence (see page 100). Synthetic fibers are manufactured by melting a polymeric substance or dissolving it in a solvent and then forcing it through the fine holes of a spinneret. The polymer emerges as a fine filament, with its molecules aligned parallel to the length of the filament (see Figure 13–14). Just as the regular arrangement of atoms produces a crystal, so will the regular arrangement of the fiber's polymers cause crystallinity in the finished fiber. This crystallinity makes a fiber stiff and strong and gives it the optical property of double refraction.

Polarized white light passing through a synthetic fiber is split into two rays that are perpendicular to each other, causing the fiber to display polarization or interference colors when viewed under a polarizing microscope (see Figure 13–15). Depending on the class of fiber, each polarized plane of light has a characteristic index of refraction. This value can be determined by immersing the fiber in a fluid with a comparable refractive index and observing the disappearance of the Becke line under a polarizing microscope. Table 13–2 lists the two refractive indices

FIGURE 13–14

In the production of manufactured fibers, the bulk polymer is forced through small holes to form a filament in which all the polymers are aligned in the same direction.

FIGURE 13–15

A photomicrograph of nylon fibers displaying interference colors when observed between the crossed polars of a polarizing microscope (50×).
Courtesy William Randle, Missouri State Highway Patrol Crime Laboratory, Jefferson City, Mo.

TABLE 13–2

Refractive Indices of Common Textile Fibers

Fiber	Refractive Index		
	Parallel	Perpendicular	Birefringence
Acetate	1.478	1.477	0.001
Triacetate	1.472	1.471	0.001
Acrylic	1.524	1.520	0.004
Nylon			
Nylon 6	1.568	1.515	0.053
Nylon 6-6	1.582	1.519	0.063
Polyester			
Dacron	1.710	1.535	0.175
Kodel	1.642	1.540	0.102
Modacrylic	1.536	1.531	0.005
Rayon			
Cuprammonium rayon	1.552	1.520	0.032
Viscose rayon	1.544	1.520	0.024

Note: The listed values are for specific fibers, which explains the highly precise values given. In identification work, such precision is not practical; values within 0.02 or 0.03 of those listed will suffice.

of some common classes of fibers, along with their birefringence. The virtue of this technique is that a single fiber, microscopic in size, can be analyzed in a nondestructive manner.

The polymers that compose a manufactured fiber, just as in any other organic substance, selectively absorb infrared light in a characteristic pattern. Infrared spectrophotometry thus provides a rapid and reliable method for identifying the generic class, and in some cases the subclasses, of fibers. The infrared microspectrophotometer combines a microscope with an infrared spectrophotometer (see pages 173–174). Such a combination makes possible the infrared analysis of a small single-strand fiber while it is being viewed under a microscope.[8]

Significance of a Match

Once a fiber match has been determined, the question of the significance of such a finding is bound to be raised. In reality, no analytical technique permits the criminalist to associate a fiber strand definitively to any single garment. Furthermore, except in the most unusual circumstances, no statistical databases are available for determining the probability of a fiber's origin. Considering the mass distribution of synthetic fibers and the constantly changing fashion tastes of our society, it is highly unlikely that such data will be available in the foreseeable future. Nevertheless, one should not discount or minimize the significance of a fiber association.

An enormous variety of fibers exist in our society. By simply looking at the random individuals we meet every day, we can see how unlikely it is to find two different people wearing identically colored fabrics (with the exception of blue denims or white cottons). There are thousands of different-colored fibers in our environment. Combine this with the fact that forensic scientists compare not only the color of fibers but also their size, shape, microscopic appearance, chemical composition, and dye content, and one can now begin to appreciate how unlikely it is to find two indistinguishable colored fibers emanating from randomly selected sources.

Furthermore, the significance of a fiber association increases dramatically if the analyst can link two or more distinctly different fibers to the same object. Likewise, the associative value of fiber evidence is dramatically enhanced if it is accompanied by other types of physical evidence linking a person or object to a crime.

As with most class evidence, the significance of a fiber comparison is dictated by the circumstances of the case; by the location, number, and nature of the fibers examined; and, most important, by the judgment of an experienced examiner.

[8] M. W. Tungol et al., "Analysis of Single Polymer Fibers by Fourier Transform Infrared Microscopy: The Results of Case Studies," *Journal of Forensic Sciences* 36 (1992): 1027.

forensics at work

Fatal Vision Revisited

Dr. Jeffrey MacDonald was convicted in 1979 of murdering his wife and two young daughters. The events surrounding the crime and the subsequent trial were recounted in Joe McGinniss's best-selling book *Fatal Vision*. The focus of MacDonald's defense was that intruders entered his home and committed these violent acts. Eleven years after this conviction, MacDonald's attorneys filed a petition for a new trial, claiming the existence of "critical new" evidence.

The defense asserted that wig fibers found on a hairbrush in the MacDonald residence were evidence that an intruder dressed in a wig entered the MacDonald home on the day of the murder. Subsequent examination of this claim by the FBI Laboratory focused on a blond fall frequently worn by MacDonald's wife. Fibers removed from the fall were shown to clearly match fibers on the hairbrush. The

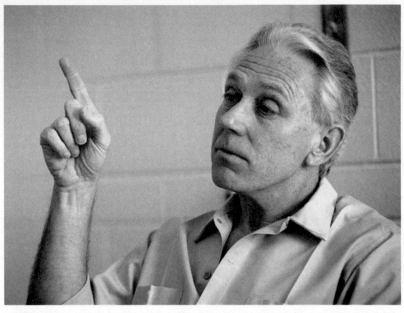

Jeffrey MacDonald in 1995 at Sheridan, Oregon, Federal Correctional Institution.
Courtesy AP Wide World Photos

FIGURE 13–16

A fiber comparison made with an infrared spectrophotometer. The infrared spectrum of a fiber from Mrs. MacDonald's fall compares to a fiber recovered from a hairbrush in the MacDonald home. These fibers were identified as modacrylics, the most common type of synthetic fiber used in the manufacture of human hair goods.
Courtesy SA Michael Malone, FBI Laboratory, Washington, D.C.

examination included the use of infrared microspec-trophotometry to demonstrate that the suspect wig fibers were chemically identical to fibers found in the composition of the MacDonald fall (see Figure 13–16). Hence, although wig fibers were found at the crime scene, the source of these fibers could be accounted for—they came from Mrs. MacDonald's fall.

Another piece of evidence cited by MacDonald's lawyers was a bluish-black woolen fiber found on the body of Mrs. MacDonald. They claimed that this fiber compared to a bluish-black woolen fiber recovered from the club used to assault her. These wool fibers were central to MacDonald's defense that the "intruders" wore dark-colored clothing. Initial examination showed that the fibers were microscopically indistinguishable. However, the FBI also compared the two wool fibers by visible-light microspectrophotometry. Comparison of their spectra clearly showed that their dye compositions differed, providing no evidence of outside intruders (see Figure 13–17). Ultimately, the U.S. Supreme Court denied the merits of MacDonald's petition for a new trial.

Source: B. M. Murtagh and M. P. Malone, "Fatal Vision Revisited," *The Police Chief* (June 1993): 15.

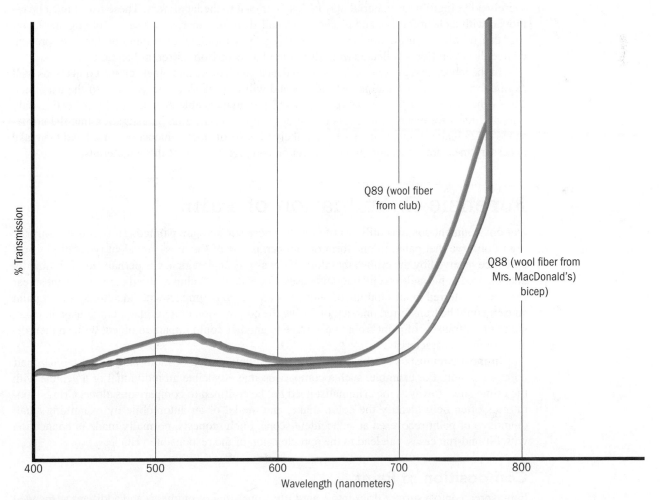

FIGURE 13–17

The visible-light spectrum for the woolen fiber recovered from Mrs. MacDonald's body is clearly different from that of the fiber recovered from the club used to assault her.
Courtesy SA Michael Malone, FBI Laboratory, Washington, D.C.

Collection and Preservation of Fiber Evidence

As criminal investigators have become more aware of the potential contribution of trace physical evidence to the success of their investigations, they have placed greater emphasis on conducting thorough crime-scene searches for evidence of forensic value. Their skill and determination at carrying out these tasks is tested when it comes to the collection of fiber-related evidence. Fiber evidence can be associated with virtually any type of crime. It cannot usually be seen with the naked eye and thus can be easily overlooked by someone not specifically looking for it.

An investigator committed to optimizing the laboratory's chances for locating minute strands of fibers seeks to identify and preserve potential "carriers" of fiber evidence. Relevant articles of clothing should be packaged carefully in paper bags. Each article must be placed in a separate bag to avoid cross-contamination of evidence. Scrupulous care must be taken to prevent articles of clothing from different people or from different locations from coming into contact. Such articles must not even be placed on the same surface before packaging. Likewise, carpets, rugs, and bedding are to be folded carefully to protect areas suspected of containing fibers. Car seats should be carefully covered with polyethylene sheets to protect fiber evidence, and knife blades should be covered to protect adhering fibers. If a body is thought to have been wrapped at one time in a blanket or carpet, adhesive tape lifts of exposed body areas may reveal fiber strands.

Occasionally the field investigator may need to remove a fiber from an object, particularly if loosely adhering fibrous material may be lost in transit to the laboratory. These fibers must be removed with a clean forceps and placed in a small sheet of paper, which, after folding and labeling, can be placed inside another container. Again, scrupulous care must be taken to prevent contact between fibers collected from different objects or from different locations.

In the laboratory, the search for fiber evidence on clothing and other relevant objects, as well as in debris, is time consuming and tedious and will test the skill and patience of the examiner. The crime-scene investigator can reduce this task to manageable proportions by collecting only relevant items for examination. It is essential from the onset of an investigation that the crime-scene investigator pinpoint areas where a likely transfer of fiber evidence occurred and then take necessary measures to ensure proper collection and preservation of these materials.

Forensic Examination of Paint

Our environment contains millions of objects whose surfaces are painted. Thus, it is not surprising to observe that paint, in one form or another, is one of the most prevalent types of physical evidence received by the crime laboratory. Paint as physical evidence is perhaps most frequently encountered in hit-and-run and burglary cases. For example, a chip of dried paint or a paint smear may be transferred to the clothing of a hit-and-run victim on impact with an automobile, or paint smears could be transferred onto a tool during the commission of a burglary. Obviously, in many situations a transfer of paint from one surface to another could impart an object with an identifiable forensic characteristic.

In most circumstances, the criminalist must compare two or more paints to establish their common origin. For example, such a comparison may associate an individual or a vehicle with the crime site. However, the criminalist need not be confined to comparisons alone. Crime laboratories often help identify the color, make, and model of an automobile by examining small quantities of paint recovered at an accident scene. Such requests, normally made in connection with hit-and-run cases, can lead to the apprehension of the responsible vehicle.

Composition of Paint

Paint spread onto a surface dries into a hard film consisting of pigments and additives suspended in a binder. Pigments impart color and hiding (or opacity) to paint and are usually mixtures of different inorganic and organic compounds added to the paint by the manufacturer to produce specific colors and properties. The binder provides the support medium for the pigments and additives and is a polymeric substance. Paint is thus composed of a binder and pigments, as well as other additives, all dissolved or dispersed in a suitable solvent. After the paint has been applied to a surface, the solvent evaporates, leaving behind a hard polymeric binder and any pigments that were suspended in it.

One of the most common types of paint examined in the crime laboratory is finishes from automobiles. One interesting fact that is helpful in forensic characterization of automotive paint is that manufacturers apply a variety of coatings to the body of an automobile. This adds significant diversity to automobile paint and contributes to the forensic significance of automobile paint comparisons. The automotive finishing system for steel usually consists of at least four organic coatings:

Electrocoat primer.   The first layer applied to the steel body of a car is the electrocoat primer. The primer, consisting of epoxy-based resins, is electroplated onto the steel body of the automobile to provide corrosion resistance. The resulting coating is uniform in appearance and thickness. The color of these electrodeposition primers ranges from black to gray.

Primer surfacer.   Originally responsible for corrosion control, the surfacer usually follows the electrocoat layer and is applied before the basecoat. Primer surfacers are epoxy-modified polyesters or urethanes. The function of this layer is to completely smooth out and hide any seams or imperfections because the colorcoat will be applied on this surface. This layer is highly pigmented. Color pigments are used to minimize color contrast between primer and topcoats. For example, a light-gray primer may be used under pastel shades of a colored topcoat; a red oxide may be used under a dark-colored topcoat.

Basecoat.   The next layer of paint on a car is the basecoat or colorcoat. This layer provides the color and aesthetics of the finish and represents the "eye appeal" of the finished automobile. The integrity of this layer depends on its ability to resist weather, UV radiation, and acid rain. Most commonly, an acrylic-based polymer comprises the binder system of basecoats. Interestingly, the choice of automotive pigments is dictated by toxic and environmental concerns. Thus, the use of lead, chrome, and other heavy-metal pigments has been abandoned in favor of organic-based pigments. There is also a growing trend toward pearl luster or mica pigments. Mica pigments are coated with layers of metal oxide to generate interference colors. Also, the addition of aluminum flakes to automotive paint imparts a metallic look to the paint's finish.

Clearcoat.   An unpigmented clearcoat is applied to improve gloss, durability, and appearance. Most clearcoats are acrylic based, but polyurethane clearcoats are increasing in popularity. These topcoats provide outstanding etch resistance and appearance.

Microscopic Examination of Paint

The microscope has traditionally been and remains the most important instrument for locating and comparing paint specimens. Considering the thousands of paint colors and shades, it is quite understandable why color, more than any other property, imparts paint with its most distinctive forensic characteristics. Questioned and known specimens are best compared side by side under a stereoscopic microscope for color, surface texture, and color layer sequence. See Figure 13–18.

The importance of layer structure for evaluating the evidential significance of paint evidence cannot be overemphasized. When paint specimens possess colored layers that match in number and sequence of colors, the examiner can begin to relate the paints to a common origin. How many layers must be matched before the criminalist can conclude that the paints come from the same source? There is no one accepted criterion. Much depends on the uniqueness of each layer's color and texture, as well as the frequency with which the particular combination of colors under investigation is observed to occur. Because no books or journals have compiled this type of information, the criminalist is left to his or her own experience and knowledge when making this decision.

Unfortunately, most paint specimens presented to the criminalist do not have a layer structure of sufficient complexity to allow them to be individualized to a single source. See Figure 13–19. However, the diverse chemical composition of modern paints provides additional points of comparison between specimens. Specifically, a thorough comparison of paint must include a chemical analysis of the paint's pigments, its binder composition, or both.

Analytical Techniques Used in Paint Comparison

The wide variation in binder formulations in automobile finishes provides particularly significant information. More important, paint manufacturers make automobile finishes in hundreds of varieties; this knowledge is most helpful to the criminalist who is trying to associate a paint chip with one car as distinguished from the thousands of similar models that have been produced in any one year. For

FIGURE 13–18

A stereoscopic microscope comparison of two automotive paints. The questioned paint on the left has a layer structure consistent with the control paint on the right.
Courtesy Leica Microsystems, Inc., Buffalo, N.Y., www.leica-microsystems.com

FIGURE 13–19

Red paint chips peeling off a wall revealing underlying layers.
Courtesy Jack Hollingsworth, Getty Images, Inc. - Photodisc/Royalty Free

instance, there are more than a hundred automobile production plants in the United States and Canada. Each can use one paint supplier for a particular color or vary suppliers during a model year. Although a paint supplier must maintain strict quality control over a paint's color, the batch formulation of any paint binder can vary, depending on the availability and cost of basic ingredients.

CHARACTERIZATION OF PAINT BINDERS Pyrolysis gas chromatography has proven to be a particularly invaluable technique for distinguishing most paint formulations. In this process, paint chips as small as 20 micrograms are decomposed by heat into numerous gaseous products and are sent through a gas chromatograph. As shown in Figure 13–20, the polymer chain is decomposed by a heated filament, and the resultant products are swept into and through a gas chromatograph column. The separated decomposition products of the polymer emerge and are recorded. The pattern of this chromatogram or "pyrogram" distinguishes one polymer from another. The result is

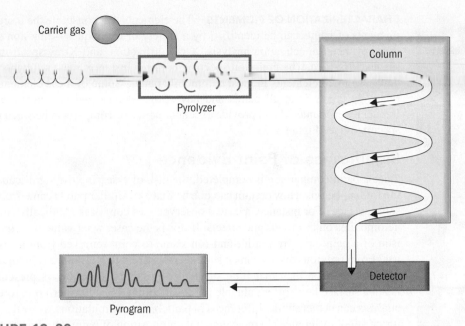

FIGURE 13–20

Schematic diagram of pyrolysis gas chromatography.

FIGURE 13–21

Paint pyrograms of acrylic enamel paints. (a) Paint from a Ford model and (b) paint from a Chrysler model.
Courtesy Varian Inc., Palo Alto, Calif.

a pyrogram that is sufficiently detailed to reflect the chemical makeup of the binder. Figure 13–21 illustrates how the patterns produced by paint pyrograms can differentiate acrylic enamel paints removed from two different automobiles. Infrared spectrophotometry is still another analytical technique that provides information about the binder composition of paint.[9] Binders selectively absorb infrared radiation to yield a spectrum that is highly characteristic of a paint specimen.

[9] P. G. Rodgers et al., "The Classification of Automobile Paint by Diamond Window Infrared Spectrophotometry, Part I: Binders and Pigments," *Canadian Society of Forensic Science Journal* 9 (1976): 1; T. J. Allen, "Paint Sample Presentation for Fourier Transform Infrared Microscopy," *Vibration Spectroscopy* 3 (1992): 217.

FIGURE 13–22

Automotive color chart of various car models.
Courtesy Damian Dovanganes, AP Wide World Photos

CHARACTERIZATION OF PIGMENTS   The elements that constitute the inorganic pigments of paints can be identified by a variety of techniques—emission spectroscopy, neutron activation analysis, X-ray diffraction, and X-ray spectroscopy (pages 176–178). The emission spectrograph, for instance, can simultaneously detect 15 to 20 elements in most automobile paints. Some of these elements are relatively common to all paints and have little forensic value; others are less frequently encountered and provide excellent points of comparison between paint specimens (see Figure 6–3).

Significance of Paint Evidence

Once a paint comparison is completed, the task of assessing the significance of the finding begins. How certain can one be that two similar paints came from the same surface? For instance, a casual observer sees countless identically colored automobiles on our roads and streets. If this is the case, what value is a comparison of a paint chip from a hit-and-run scene to paint removed from a suspect car? From previous discussions it should be apparent that far more is involved in paint comparison than matching surface paint colors. Paint layers present beneath a surface layer offer valuable points of comparison. Furthermore, forensic analysts can detect subtle differences in paint binder formulations, as well as major or minor differences in the elemental composition of paint. Obviously, these properties cannot be discerned by the naked eye.

The significance of a paint comparison was convincingly demonstrated from data gathered at the Centre of Forensic Sciences, Toronto, Canada.[10] Paint chips randomly taken from 260 vehicles located in a local wreck yard were compared by color, layer structure, and, when required, by infrared spectroscopy. All were distinguishable except for one pair. In statistical terms, these results signify that if a crime-scene paint sample and a paint standard/reference sample removed from a suspect car compare by the previously discussed tests, the odds against the crime-scene paint originating from another randomly chosen vehicle are approximately 33,000 to 1. Obviously, this type of evidence is bound to forge a strong link between the suspect car and the crime scene.

Crime laboratories are often asked to identify the make and model of a car from a very small amount of paint left behind at a crime scene. Such information is frequently of use in a search for an unknown car involved in a hit-and-run incident. Often, the questioned paint can be identified when its color is compared to color chips representing the various makes and models of manufactured cars. However, in many cases it is not possible to state the exact make or model of the car in question because any one paint color can be found on more than one car model. For example, General Motors may use the same paint color for several production years on cars in its Cadillac, Buick, and Chevrolet lines.

Color charts for automobile finishes are available from various paint manufacturers and refinishers (see Figure 13–22). Starting with the 1974 model year, the Law Enforcement Standards Laboratory at the National Institute of Standards and Technology collected and disseminated to crime laboratories auto paint color samples from U.S. domestic passenger cars. This collection was distributed by Collaborative Testing Services, McLean, Virginia, through 1991. Since 1975, the Royal Canadian Mounted Police Forensic Laboratories have been systematically gathering color and chemical information on automotive paints. This computerized database, known as PDQ (Paint Data Query), allows an analyst to obtain information on paints related to automobile make, model, and year. The database contains such parameters as automotive paint layer colors, primer colors, and binder composition (see Figure 13–23). A number of U.S. laboratories have access to PDQ.[11] Also some laboratories maintain an in-house collection of automobile paints associated with various makes and models (see Figure 13–24).

[10] G. Edmondstone, J. Hellman, K. Legate, G. L. Vardy, and E. Lindsay, "An Assessment of the Evidential Value of Automotive Paint Comparisons," *Canadian Society of Forensic Science Journal* 37 (2004): 147.

[11] J. L. Buckle et al., "PDQ—Paint Data Queries: The History and Technology behind the Development of the Royal Canadian Mounted Police Laboratory Services Automotive Paint Database," *Canadian Society of Forensic Science Journal* 30 (1997): 199. An excellent discussion of the PDQ database is also available in A. Beveridge, T. Fung, and D. MacDougall, "Use of Infrared Spectroscopy for the Characterisation of Paint Fragments," in B. Caddy, ed., *Forensic Examination of Glass and Paint* (New York: Taylor & Francis, 2001), pp. 222–233.

(a)

(b)

FIGURE 13–23

(a) Home screen for PDQ database. (b) Partial list of auto paints contained in the PDQ database.

Courtesy Royal Canadian Mounted Police

Collection and Preservation of Paint Evidence

As has already been noted, paint chips are most likely to be found on or near people or objects involved in hit-and-run incidents. The recovery of loose paint chips from a garment or from the road surface must be done with the utmost care to keep the paint chip intact. Paint chips may be picked

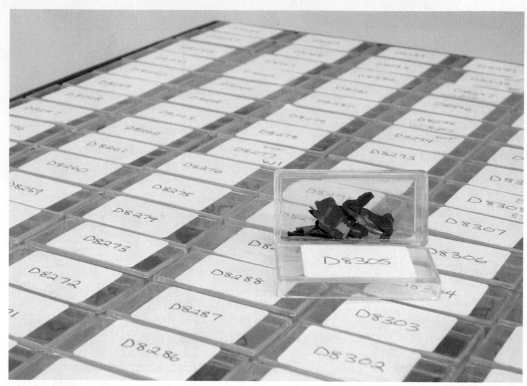

FIGURE 13–24

A crime laboratory's automotive paint library. Paints were collected at an automobile impound yard and then cataloged for rapid retrieval and examination.
Royal Canadian Mounted Police

up with a tweezers or scooped up with a piece of paper. Paper druggist folds and glass or plastic vials make excellent containers for paint. If the paint is smeared on or embedded in garments or objects, the investigator should not attempt to remove it; instead, it is best to package the whole item carefully and send it to the laboratory for examination.

When a transfer of paint occurs in hit-and-run situations, such as to the clothing of a pedestrian victim, uncontaminated standard/reference paint must always be collected from an undamaged area of the vehicle for comparison in the laboratory. It is particularly important that the collected paint be close to the area of the car that was suspected of being in contact with the victim. This is necessary because other portions of the car may have faded or been repainted. Standard/reference samples are always removed so as to include all the paint layers down to the bare metal. This is best accomplished by removing a painted section with a clean scalpel or knife blade. Samples ¼ inch square are sufficient for laboratory examination. Each paint sample should be separately packaged and marked with the exact location of its recovery. When a cross-transfer of paint occurs between two vehicles, again all of the layers, including the foreign as well as the underlying original paints, must be removed from each vehicle. A standard/reference sample from an adjacent undamaged area of each vehicle must also be taken in such cases. Carefully wipe the blade of any knife or scraping tool used before collecting each sample, to avoid cross-contamination of paints.

Tools used to enter buildings or safes often contain traces of paints as well as other substances such as wood and safe insulation. Care must be taken not to lose this type of trace evidence. The scene investigator should not try to remove the paint; instead, he or she should package the tool for laboratory examination. Standard/reference paint should be collected from all surfaces suspected of having been in contact with the tool. Again, all layers of paint must be included in the sample.

When the tool has left its impression on a surface, standard/reference paint is collected from an uncontaminated area adjacent to the impression. No attempt should be made to collect the paint from the impression itself. If this is done, the impression may be permanently altered and its evidential value lost.

chapter summary

> > > > > > > > > > >

Hair is an appendage of the skin that grows out of an organ known as the hair follicle. The length of a hair extends from its root or bulb embedded in the follicle, continues into a shaft, and terminates at a tip end. The shaft, which is composed of three layers—the cuticle, cortex, and medulla—is subjected to the most intense examination by the forensic scientist. The comparison microscope is an indispensable tool for comparing these morphological characteristics. When comparing strands of hair, the criminalist is particularly interested in matching the color, length, and diameter. A careful microscopic examination of hair reveals morphological features that can distinguish human hair from the hair of animals. Scale structure, medullary index, and medullary shape are particularly important in hair identification. Other important features for comparing hair are the presence or absence of a medulla and the distribution, shape, and color intensity of the pigment granules present in the cortex. However, microscopic hair examinations tend to be subjective and highly dependent on the skills and integrity of the analyst. Recent major breakthroughs in DNA profiling have extended this technology to the individualization of human hair. The probability of detecting DNA in hair roots is more likely for hair being examined in its anagen or early growth phase as opposed to its catagen or telogen phases. Often, when hair is forcibly removed a follicular tag, a translucent piece of tissue surrounding the hair's shaft near the root, may be present. This has proven to be a rich source of DNA associated with hair. Also, mitochondrial DNA can be extracted from the hair shaft. As a rule, all positive microscopic hair comparisons must be confirmed by DNA analysis.

The quality of fiber evidence depends on the ability of the criminalist to identify the origin of the fiber or at least to narrow the possibilities to a limited number of sources. Microscopic comparisons between questioned and standard/reference fibers are initially undertaken for color and diameter characteristics. Other morphological features that could be important in comparing fibers are striations on the surface of the fiber, the presence of delustering particles, and the cross-sectional shape of the fiber. The visible-light microspectrophotometer provides a convenient way to compare the colors of fibers through spectral patterns. Infrared spectrophotometry is a rapid and reliable tool for identifying the generic class of fibers, as is the polarizing microscope.

Paint spread onto a surface dries into a hard film consisting of pigments and additives suspended in the binder. One of the most common types of paint examined in the crime laboratory is finishes from automobiles. Automobile manufacturers normally apply a variety of coatings to the body of an automobile. Hence, the wide diversity of automotive paint contributes to the forensic significance of an automobile paint comparison. Questioned and known specimens are best compared side by side under a stereoscopic microscope for color, surface texture, and color layer sequence. Pyrolysis gas chromatography and infrared spectrophotometry are invaluable techniques for distinguishing most paint binder formulations, adding further significance to a forensic paint comparison.

review questions

1. Hair is an appendage of the skin, growing out of an organ known as the _____.

2. The three layers of the hair shaft are the _____, the _____, and the _____.

3. True or False: The scales of most animal hairs can be described as looking like shingles on a roof. _____

4. The _____ contains the pigment granules that impart color to hair.

5. The central canal running through many hairs is known as the _____.

6. The diameter of the medulla relative to the diameter of the hair shaft is the _____.

7. Human hair generally has a medullary index of less than _____; the hair of most animals has an index of _____ or greater.

8. Human head hairs generally exhibit (continuous, absent) medullae.

9. If a medulla exhibits a patterned shape, the hair is (human, animal) in origin.

10. The three stages of hair growth are the _____, _____, and _____ phases.

11. A single hair (can, cannot) be individualized to one person by microscopic examination.

12. In making hair comparisons, it is best to view the hairs side by side under a(n) _____ microscope.

13. _____ hairs are short and curly, with wide variation in shaft diameter.

14. It (is, is not) possible to determine when hair was last bleached or dyed.

15. True or False: The age and sex of the individual from whom a hair sample has been taken can be determined through an examination of the hair's morphological features. _____

16. Hair forcibly removed from the body (always, often) has follicular tissue adhering to its root.

17. Microscopic hair comparisons must be regarded by police and courts as presumptive in nature, and all positive microscopic hair comparisons must be confirmed by _____ typing.

18. True or False: Currently, DNA typing can individualize a single hair. _____

19. A(n) _____ hair root is a likely candidate for DNA typing.

20. A minimum collection of _____ full-length hairs normally ensures a representative sampling of head hair.

21. A minimum collection of _____ full-length pubic hairs is recommended to cover the range of characteristics present in this region of the body.

22. _____ fibers are derived totally from animal or plant sources.

23. The most prevalent natural plant fiber is _____.

24. True or False: Regenerated fibers, such as rayon and acetate, are manufactured by chemically treating cellulose and passing it through a spinneret. _____

25. Fibers manufactured solely from synthetic chemicals are classified as _____.

26. True or False: Polyester was the first synthetic fiber. _____

27. _____ are composed of a large number of atoms arranged in repeating units.

28. The basic unit of the polymer is called the _____.

29. _____ are polymers composed of thousands of amino acids linked in a highly organized arrangement and sequence.

30. True or False: A first step in the forensic examination of fibers is to compare color and diameter. _____

31. The microspectrophotometer employing _____ light is a convenient way for analysts to compare the colors of fibers through spectral patterns.

32. The dye components removed from fibers can be separated and compared by _____ chromatography.

33. Synthetic fibers possess the physical property of _____ because they are crystalline.

34. The microspectrophotometer employing _____ light provides a rapid and reliable method for identifying the generic class of a single fiber.

35. Normally, fibers possess (individual, class) characteristics.

36. The two most important components of dried paint from the criminalist's point of view are the _____ and the _____.

37. The most important physical property of paint in a forensic comparison is _____.

38. Paints can be individualized to a single source only when they have a sufficiently detailed _____.

39. The _____ layer provides corrosion resistance for the automobile.

40. "Eye appeal" of the automobile comes from the _____ layer.

41. Pyrolysis gas chromatography is a particularly valuable technique for characterizing paint's (binder, pigments).

42. Emission spectroscopy can be used to identify the (inorganic, organic) components of paint's pigments.

43. True or False: Paint samples removed for examination must always include all of the paint layers. _____

application and critical thinking

1. Indicate the phase of growth of each of the following hairs:

   a. The root is club-shaped

   b. The hair has a follicular tag

   c. The root bulb is flame-shaped

   d. The root is elongated

2. A criminalist studying a dyed sample hair notices that the dyed color ends about 1.5 centimeters from the tip of the hair. Approximately how many weeks before the examination was the hair dyed? Explain your answer.

3. Following are descriptions of several hairs; based on these descriptions, indicate the likely race of the person from whom the hair originated:

   a. Evenly distributed, fine pigmentation

   b. Continuous medullation

   c. Dense, uneven pigmentation

   d. Wavy with a round cross-section

4. Criminalist Pete Evett is collecting fiber evidence from a murder scene. He notices fibers on the victim's shirt and trousers, so he places both of these items of clothing in a

plastic bag. He also sees fibers on a sheet near the victim, so he balls up the sheet and places it in separate plastic bag. Noticing fibers adhering to the windowsill from which the attacker gained entrance, Pete carefully removes it with his fingers and places it in a regular envelope. What mistakes, if any, did Pete make while collecting this evidence?

5. You are investigating a hit-and-run accident and have identified a suspect vehicle. Describe how you would collect paint to determine whether the suspect vehicle was involved in the accident. Be sure to indicate the tools you would use and the steps you would take to prevent cross contamination.

further references

Bisbing, R. E., "The Forensic Identification and Association of Human Hair," in R. Saferstein, ed., *Forensic Science Handbook*, vol. 1, 2nd ed., Upper Saddle River, N.J.: Prentice Hall, 2002.

Caddy, B., ed., *Forensic Examination of Glass and Paint*. Boca Raton, Fla.: Taylor & Francis, 2001.

Deedrick, D. W., "Hairs, Fibers, Crime, and Evidence," *Forensic Science Communications* 2, no. 3 (2000), http://www.fbi.gov/hq/lab/fsc/backissu/july2000/deedrick.htm.

Deedrick, D. W., and S. L. Koch, "Microscopy of Hair Part I: A Practical Guide and Manual for Human Hairs," *Forensic Science Communications* 6, no. 1 (2004), http://www.fbi.gov/hq/lab/fsc/backissu/jan2004/research/2004_01_research01b.htm.

Deedrick, D. W., and S. L. Koch, "Microscopy of Hair Part II: A Practical Guide and Manual for Animal Hairs," *Forensic Science Communications* 6, no. 3 (2004), http://www.fbi.gov/hq/lab/fsc/backissu/july2004/research/2004_03_research02.htm.

Eyring, M. B., and B. D. Gaudette, "The Forensic Aspects of Textile Fiber Examination," in R. Saferstein, ed., *Forensic Science Handbook*, vol. 2, 2nd ed., Upper Saddle River, N.J.: Prentice Hall, 2005.

Ogle, R. R., Jr., and M. J. Fox, *Atlas of Human Hair: Microscopic Characteristics*. Boca Raton, Fla.: Taylor & Francis, 1999.

Oien, C.T., "Forensic Hair Comparison: Background Information for Interpretation," *Forensic Science Communications* 11, no. 2 (2009), www.fbi.gov/hq/lab/fsc/backissu/april2009/review/2009_04_review02.htm

Petraco, N., and P. R. De Forest, "A Guide to the Analysis of Forensic Dust Specimens," in R. Saferstein, ed., *Forensic Science Handbook*, vol. 3, 2nd ed., Upper Saddle River, N.J.: Prentice Hall, 2010.

Robertson, J., and M. Grieve, eds., *Forensic Examination of Fibres*, 2nd ed., Boca Raton, Fla.: Taylor & Francis, 1999.

Thornton, J. L., "Forensic Paint Examination," in R. Saferstein, ed., *Forensic Science Handbook*, vol. 1, 2nd ed., Upper Saddle River, N.J.: Prentice Hall, 2002.

Debora Green—Poisoning the American Dream

On the face of it, the Farrar family had it all. Dr. Debora Green, a nonpracticing oncologist, and her husband, Dr. Michael Farrar, had an opulent home in an exclusive Kansas City suburb. Michael, a cardiologist, had a successful practice that enabled Debora to stay home to raise their three loving children, Tim, Kate, and Kelly.

In late 1995, Michael Farrar was hospitalized for a mysterious illness. Michael entered a revolving door of excruciating stomach pain and recovery, framed in the context of his failing marriage. Unknown to outsiders, Michael had initially asked Debora for a divorce in 1994.

Michael's suspicion of foul play was aroused when he found a large number of castor bean packets in Debora's purse. She had used the castor beans to poison Michael's food; they contain ricin, a deadly poison.

On the night of October 24, 1995, the Green house became engulfed in flames and was destroyed. Michael Farrar was sleeping elsewhere while the couple were beginning a legal separation preceding their divorce. Their daughter Kate, then 10 years old, escaped the fire by exiting her bedroom window, scaling the garage roof, and jumping to safety into the arms of her mother, who was standing outside the house. Their son Tim, 13, and daughter Kelly, 6, were killed in the blaze that consumed their home.

Dave Kaup/AP Wide World Photos

Fire investigators quickly realized that they were confronting a criminal case of arson. Unconnected fires had occurred in various rooms of the house. Throughout the first floor of the house, pour patterns were obvious where someone had spread accelerants—flammable substances used to spread the fire more quickly—on the floors. Heavy soaking of the carpet on the stairways leading to the children's rooms would have created a wall of fire effectively blocking the children's escape route. This arsonist was also a murderer.

Police arrested Debora and charged her with two counts of first-degree murder and aggravated arson. Psychological evaluation of the defendant concluded that she had a schizoid personality that was masked by a high degree of intelligence. Debora Green is currently serving a life sentence in a Missouri prison. Her psychotic behavior became the subject of Ann Rule's novel *Bitter Harvest*.

forensic aspects of fire investigation

Learning Objectives

After studying this chapter you should be able to:

- List the conditions necessary to initiate and sustain combustion

- Understand the three mechanisms of heat transfer

- Recognize the telltale signs of an accelerant-initiated fire

- Describe how to collect physical evidence at the scene of a suspected arson

- Describe laboratory procedures used to detect and identify hydrocarbon residues

KEY TERMS

accelerant
combustion
endothermic reaction
energy
exothermic reaction
flammable range
flash point
glowing combustion
heat of combustion
hydrocarbon
ignition temperature
modus operandi
oxidation
pyrolysis
spontaneous
   combustion

Forensic Investigation of Arson

Arson often presents complex and difficult circumstances to investigate. Normally these incidents are committed at the convenience of a perpetrator who has thoroughly planned the criminal act and has left the crime scene long before any official investigation is launched. Furthermore, proving commission of the offense is more difficult because of the extensive destruction that frequently dominates the crime scene. The contribution of the criminalist is only one aspect of a comprehensive and difficult investigative process that must establish a motive, the **modus operandi**, and a suspect.

The criminalist's function is limited; usually he or she is expected only to detect and identify relevant chemical materials collected at the scene and to reconstruct and identify igniters. Although a chemist can identify trace amounts of gasoline or kerosene in debris, no scientific test can determine whether an arsonist has used a pile of rubbish or paper to start a fire. Furthermore, a fire can have many accidental causes, including faulty wiring, overheated electric motors, improperly cleaned and regulated heating systems, and cigarette smoking—which usually leave no chemical traces. Thus, the final determination of the cause of a fire must consider numerous factors and requires an extensive on-site investigation. The ultimate determination must be made by an investigator whose training and knowledge have been augmented by the practical experiences of fire investigation.

modus operandi
An offender's pattern of operation

The Chemistry of Fire

Humankind's early search to explain the physical concepts underlying the behavior of matter always bestowed a central and fundamental role on fire. To ancient Greek philosophers, fire was one of the four basic elements from which all matter was derived. The medieval alchemist thought of fire as an instrument of transformation, capable of changing one element into another. One ancient recipe expresses its mystical power as follows: "Now the substance of cinnabar is such that the more it is heated, the more exquisite are its sublimations. Cinnabar will become mercury, and passing through a series of other sublimations, it is again turned into cinnabar, and thus it enables man to enjoy eternal life."

Today, we know of fire not as an element of matter but as a transformation process during which oxygen is united with some other substance to produce noticeable quantities of heat and light (a flame). Therefore, any insight into why and how a fire is initiated and sustained must begin with the knowledge of the fundamental chemical reaction of fire—**oxidation**.

Oxidation

oxidation
The combination of oxygen with other substances to produce new substances

In a simple description of oxidation, oxygen combines with other substances to produce new products. Thus, we may write the chemical equation for the burning of methane gas, a major component of natural gas, as follows:

$$CH_4 \ + \ 2O_2 \ \longrightarrow \ CO_2 \ + \ 2H_2O$$

methane   oxygen   yields   carbon dioxide   water

However, not all oxidation proceeds in the manner that one associates with fire. For example, oxygen combines with many metals to form oxides. Thus, iron forms a red-brown iron oxide, or rust, as follows (see Figure 14–1):

$$4Fe \ + \ 3O_2 \ \longrightarrow \ 2Fe_2O_3$$

iron   oxygen   yields   iron oxide

Yet chemical equations do not give us a complete insight into the oxidation process. We must consider other factors to understand all of the implications of oxidation or, for that matter, any other chemical reaction. Methane burns when it unites with oxygen, but merely mixing methane and oxygen does not produce a fire. Nor, for example, does gasoline burn when it is simply exposed to air. However, lighting a match in the presence of any one of these fuel–air mixtures (assuming proper proportions) produces an instant fire.

What are the reasons behind these differences? Why do some oxidations proceed with the outward appearances that we associate with a fire, but others do not? Why do we need a match to

FIGURE 14–1

Rust forming on iron is an example of oxidation.
Courtesy Nicholas Gissing/Debut Art, Ltd

initiate some oxidations, but others proceed at room temperature? The explanation lies in a fundamental but abstract concept—energy.

Energy

Energy can be defined as the ability or potential of a system or material to do work. Energy takes many forms, such as heat energy, electrical energy, mechanical energy, nuclear energy, light energy, and chemical energy. For example, when methane is burned, the stored chemical energy in methane is converted to energy in the form of heat and light. This heat may be used to boil water or to provide high-pressure steam to turn a turbine. This is an example of converting chemical energy to heat energy to mechanical energy. The turbine can then be used to generate electricity, transforming mechanical energy to electrical energy. Electrical energy may then be used to turn a motor. In other words, energy can enable work to be done; heat is energy.

energy
The ability or potential of a system or material to do work

    The quantity of heat from a chemical reaction comes from the breaking and formation of chemical bonds. Methane is a molecule composed of one carbon atom bonded with four hydrogen atoms:

$$
\begin{array}{c}
\mathrm{H} \\
| \\
\mathrm{H - C - H} \\
| \\
\mathrm{H}
\end{array}
$$

An oxygen molecule forms when two atoms of the element oxygen bond:

$$\mathrm{O = O}$$

In chemical changes, atoms are not lost but merely redistributed during the chemical reaction; thus, the products of methane's oxidation will be carbon dioxide:

$$\mathrm{O = C = O}$$

and water:

$$H—O—H$$

This rearrangement, however, means that the chemical bonds holding the atoms together must be broken and new bonds formed. We now have arrived at a fundamental observation in our dissection of a chemical reaction—that molecules must absorb energy to break apart their chemical bonds, and that they liberate energy when their bonds are re-formed.

The amount of energy needed to break a bond and the amount of energy liberated when a bond is formed are characteristic of the type of chemical bond involved. Hence, a chemical reaction involves a change in energy content; energy is going in and energy is given off. The quantities of energies involved are different for each reaction and are determined by the participants in the chemical reaction.

Combustion

All oxidation reactions, including the **combustion** of methane, are examples of reactions in which more energy is liberated than is required to break the chemical bonds between atoms. Such reactions are said to be **exothermic**. The excess energy is liberated as heat, and often as light, and is known as the **heat of combustion**. Table 14–1 summarizes the heats of combustion of some important fuels in fire investigation.

Although we will not be concerned with them, some reactions require more energy than they eventually liberate. These reactions are known as **endothermic reactions**.

Thus, all reactions require an energy input to start them. We can think of this requirement as an invisible energy barrier between the reactants and the products of a reaction (see Figure 14–2). The higher this barrier, the more energy required to initiate the reaction. Where does this initial energy come from? There are many sources of energy; however, for the purpose of this discussion we need to look at only one—heat.

combustion
Rapid combination of oxygen with another substance, accompanied by production of noticeable heat and light

exothermic reaction
A chemical transformation in which heat energy is liberated

heat of combustion
The heat liberated during combustion

endothermic reaction
A chemical transformation in which heat energy is absorbed from the surroundings

TABLE 14–1

Heats of Combustion of Fuels

Fuel	Heat of Combustion[a]
Crude oil	19,650 Btu/gal
Diesel fuel	19,550 Btu/lb
Gasoline	19,250 Btu/lb
Methane	995 Btu/cu ft
Natural gas	128–1,868 Btu/cu ft
Octane	121,300 Btu/gal
Wood	7,500 Btu/lb
Coal, bituminous	11,000–14,000 Btu/lb
Anthracite	13,351 Btu/lb

[a] A Btu (British thermal unit) is defined as the quantity of heat required to raise the temperature of 1 pound of water 1°F at or near its point of maximum density.

Source: John D. DeHaan, *Kirk's Fire Investigation*, 2nd ed. Upper Saddle River, N.J.: Prentice Hall, 1983.

$$CH_4 + 2O_2 \qquad CO_2 + 2H_2O$$

FIGURE 14–2

An energy barrier must be hurdled before reactants such as methane and oxygen can combine with one another to form the products of carbon dioxide and water.

TABLE 14–2

Ignition Temperatures of Some Common Fuels

Fuel	Ignition Temperature, °F
Acetone	869
Benzene	928
Fuel oil #2	495
Gasoline (low octane)	536
Kerosene (fuel oil #1)	410
n-Octane	428
Petroleum ether	550
Turpentine	488

Source: John D. DeHaan, *Kirk's Fire Investigation*, 4th ed. Upper Saddle River, N.J.: Prentice Hall, 1997.

HEAT   The energy barrier in the conversion of iron to rust is relatively small, and it can be surmounted with the help of heat energy in the surrounding environment at normal outdoor temperatures. Not so for methane or gasoline; these energy barriers are quite high, and a high temperature must be applied to start the oxidation of these fuels. Hence, before any fire can result, the temperature of these fuels must be raised enough to exceed the energy barrier. Table 14–2 shows that this temperature, known as the **ignition temperature**, is quite high for common fuels.

Once combustion starts, enough heat is liberated to keep the reaction going by itself. In essence, the fire becomes a chain reaction, absorbing a portion of its own liberated heat to generate even more heat. The fire burns until either the oxygen or the fuel is exhausted.

Normally, a lighted match provides a convenient igniter of fuels. However, the fire investigator must also consider other potential sources of ignition—for example, electrical discharges, sparks, and chemicals—while reconstructing the initiation of a fire. All of these sources have temperatures higher than the ignition temperature of most fuels.

SPEED OF REACTION   Although the liberation of energy explains many important features of oxidation, it does not explain all characteristics of the reaction. Obviously, although all oxidations liberate energy, not all are accompanied by a flame; witness the oxidation of iron to rust. Therefore, one other important consideration will make our understanding of oxidation and fire complete: the rate or speed at which the reaction takes place.

A chemical reaction, such as oxidation, takes place when molecules combine or collide with one another. The faster the molecules move, the greater the number of collisions between them and the faster the rate of reaction. Many factors influence the rate of these collisions. In our description of fire and oxidation, we consider only two: the physical state of the fuel and the temperature.

Physical State of Fuel   A fuel achieves a reaction rate with oxygen sufficient to produce a flame only when it is in the gaseous state because only in this state can molecules collide frequently enough to support a flaming fire. This remains true whether the fuel is a solid such as wood, paper, cloth, or plastic, or a liquid such as gasoline or kerosene.

For example, the conversion of iron to rust proceeds slowly because the iron atoms cannot achieve a gaseous state. The combination of oxygen with iron is thus restricted to the surface area of the metal exposed to air, a limitation that severely reduces the rate of reaction. On the other hand, the reaction of methane and oxygen proceeds rapidly because all the reactants are in the gaseous state. The speed of the reaction is reflected by the production of noticeable quantities of heat and light (a flame).

Fuel Temperature   How, then, does a liquid or solid maintain a gaseous reaction? In the case of a liquid fuel, the temperature must be high enough to vaporize the fuel. The vapor that forms burns when it mixes with oxygen and combusts as a flame. The **flash point** is the *lowest* temperature at which a liquid gives off sufficient vapor to form a mixture with air that will support combustion. Once the flash point is reached, the fuel can be ignited by some outside source of temperature to start a fire. The ignition temperature of a fuel is always considerably higher than the flash point.

ignition temperature
The minimum temperature at which a fuel spontaneously ignites

flash point
The minimum temperature at which a liquid fuel produces enough vapor to burn

FIGURE 14-3

Intense heat causes solid fuels such as wood to decompose into gaseous products, a process called *pyrolysis*.

Courtesy David Trood/Image Bank/Getty Images

For example, gasoline has a flash point of −50°F; however, an ignition temperature of 495°F is needed to start a gasoline fire.

With a solid fuel such as wood, the process of generating vapor is more complex. A solid fuel burns only when exposed to heat intense enough to decompose the solid into gaseous products. This chemical breakdown of solid material is known as **pyrolysis**. The gaseous products of pyrolysis combine with oxygen to produce a fire (see Figure 14–3). Here again, fire can be described as a chain reaction. A match or other source of heat initiates the pyrolysis of the solid fuel, the gaseous products react with oxygen in the air to produce heat and light, and this heat in turn pyrolyzes more solid fuel into volatile gases.

Typically, the rate of a chemical reaction increases when the temperature is raised. The magnitude of the increase varies from one reaction to another and also from one temperature range to another. For most reactions, a 10°C (18°F) rise in temperature doubles or triples the reaction rate. This observation explains in part why burning is so rapid. As the fire spreads, it raises the temperature of the fuel–air mixture, thus increasing the rate of reaction; this in turn generates more heat, again increasing the rate of reaction. Only when the fuel or oxygen is depleted does this vicious cycle come to a halt.

THE FUEL–AIR MIX   As we have seen from our discussion about gaseous fuel, air (oxygen) and sufficient heat are the basic ingredients of a flaming fire. There is also one other consideration—the gas fuel–air mix. A mixture of gaseous fuel and air burns only if its composition lies within certain limits. If the fuel concentration is too low (lean) or too great (rich), combustion does not occur. The concentration range between the upper and lower limits is called the **flammable range**. For example, the flammable range for gasoline is 1.3–6.0 percent. Thus, in order for a gasoline–air mix to burn, gasoline must make up at least 1.3 percent, and no more than 6 percent, of the mixture.

GLOWING COMBUSTION   Although a flaming fire can be supported only by a gaseous fuel, in some instances a fuel can burn without a flame. Witness a burning cigarette or the red glow of hot

pyrolysis
The decomposition of solid organic matter by heat

flammable range
The entire range of possible gas or vapor fuel concentrations in air that are capable of burning

FIGURE 14–4
Red-hot charcoals are an example of glowing combustion.
Courtesy Paul Sisul/Stone/Getty Images

charcoals (see Figure 14–4). These are examples of **glowing combustion** or *smoldering*. Here combustion occurs on the surface of a solid fuel in the absence of heat high enough to pyrolyze the fuel. Interestingly, this phenomenon generally ensues long after the flames have gone out. Wood, for example, tends to burn with a flame until all of its pyrolyzable components have been expended; however, wood's carbonaceous residue continues to smolder long after the flame has extinguished itself.

glowing combustion
Combustion on the surface of a solid fuel in the absence of heat high enough to pyrolyze the fuel

SPONTANEOUS COMBUSTION   One interesting phenomenon often invoked by arson suspects as the cause of a fire is **spontaneous combustion**. Actually, the conditions under which spontaneous combustion can develop are rather limited and rarely account for the cause of a fire. Spontaneous combustion is the result of a natural heat-producing process in poorly ventilated containers or areas. For example, hay stored in barns provides an excellent growing medium for bacteria whose activities generate heat. If the hay is not properly ventilated, the heat builds to a level that supports other types of heat-producing chemical reactions in the hay. Eventually, as the heat rises, the ignition temperature of hay is reached, spontaneously setting off a fire.

spontaneous combustion
A fire caused by a natural heat-producing process in the presence of sufficient air and fuel

Another example of spontaneous combustion involves the ignition of improperly ventilated containers containing rags soaked with certain types of highly unsaturated oils, such as linseed oil. Heat can build up to the point of ignition as a result of a slow heat-producing chemical oxidation between the air and the oil. Of course, storage conditions must encourage the accumulation of the heat over a prolonged period of time. However, spontaneous combustion does not occur with hydrocarbon lubricating oils, and it is not expected to occur with most household fats and oils.

In summary, three requirements must be satisfied to initiate and sustain combustion:

1. A fuel must be present.
2. Oxygen must be available in sufficient quantity to combine with the fuel.
3. Heat must be applied to initiate the combustion, and sufficient heat must be generated to sustain the reaction.

Heat Transfer

Consider how a structural fire begins. The typical scenario starts with heat ignition at a single location. It may be an arsonist lighting a gasoline-soaked rag, a malfunctioning electric appliance sparking, or an individual falling asleep while smoking a cigarette in bed. How does a flame initially confined to a single location spread to engulf an entire structure? Understanding the anatomy of a fire begins with comprehending how heat travels through a burning structure.

The previous section stressed the importance of the role of heat in generating sufficient fuel vapors to support combustion, as well as the requirement that the heat source be hot enough to ignite the fuel's vapor. Once the fire begins, the heat generated by the fuel's reaction with air is fed back into the fuel–air mix to keep the chemical reaction going.

As a fire progresses, the heat created by the combustion process tends to move from a high-temperature region to one at a lower temperature. Understanding heat transfer from one location to another is important for reconstructing the origin of a fire, as well as for understanding why and how fire spreads through a structure. The three mechanisms of heat transfer are conduction, radiation, and convection.

CONDUCTION   Movement of heat through a solid object is caused by a process called *conduction*, in which electrons and atoms within the heated object collide with one another. Heat always travels from hot areas of a solid to cold ones by conduction. Solids whose atoms or molecules have loosely held electrons are good conductors of heat. Metals have the most loosely held electrons and are therefore excellent conductors of heat. Thus, when you insert one end of a metal object into an open flame, the entire object quickly becomes hot to the touch.

Materials that have electrons firmly attached to their molecules are poor conductors of heat. Poor conductors are called *insulators*. Wood is a good insulator; for that reason, metal objects that are subject to intense heat (such as skillets and saucepans) often have wooden handles (see Figure 14–5).

In reconstructing a fire scene, it's important to keep in mind that heat may be transported through metals such as beams, nails, fasteners, bolts, and other good conductors to a location far from the initial heat source. Any fuel in contact with the conductor may be ignited, creating a new fire location. On the other hand, the conductivity of wood, plastic, and paper is very low, meaning that heat emanating from these surfaces does not spread well and does not cause ignitions far from the initial heat source.

RADIATION   *Radiation* is the transfer of heat energy from a heated surface to a cooler surface by electromagnetic radiation. A hot surface emits electromagnetic radiation of various wavelengths, and in a fire scene the electromagnetic radiation moves in a straight line from one surface to another. Radiant heat plays a key role in understanding how fire spreads throughout a

FIGURE 14–5

The wooden handle on this saucepan is a poor conductor of heat.
Courtesy Topham, The Image Works

FIGURE 14–6
Convection causes flames to rise to the upper floor of a burning structure.
Courtesy Dave Frazier, Danita Delimont Photography

structure. For example, all surfaces that face the fire are exposed to radiant heat and burst into flames when the surface reaches their ignition temperature. In very large fires, nearby structures and vehicles are often ignited at a distance by radiant heat.

CONVECTION   *Convection* is the transfer of heat energy by movement of molecules within a liquid or gas. Water being heated on a stove illustrates the concept of convection. As the water molecules on the bottom of the pot move faster, they spread apart and become less dense, causing them to move upward. Denser, cooler water molecules then migrate to the bottom of the pot. In this way convection currents keep the fluid stirred up as warmer fluid moves away from the heat source and cooler fluid moves toward the heat source. Likewise, warm air expands, becoming less dense and causing it to rise and move toward the cooler surrounding air.

In a structural fire, the gaseous hot products of combustion expand, and convection moves the hot gases to the upper portions of the structure (see Figure 14–6). The convected hot gases become a source of heat, radiating heat energy downward onto all the surfaces below them. The hot surfaces of the exposed objects often pyrolyze or break down, releasing gaseous molecules. The phenomenon known as *flashover* occurs when all the combustible fuels simultaneously ignite, engulfing the entire structure in flame.

Searching the Fire Scene

The arson investigator should begin examining a fire scene for signs of arson as soon as the fire has been extinguished. Most arsons are started with petroleum-based **accelerants** such as gasoline or kerosene. Thus, the presence of containers capable of holding an accelerant arouse suspicions of arson. Discovery of an ignition device ranging in sophistication from a candle to a time-delay device is another indication of possible arson. A common telltale sign of arson is an irregularly

accelerant
Any material used to start or sustain a fire

FIGURE 14–7

Irregularly shaped pattern on the ground resulting from a poured ignitable liquid.

Courtesy Franklin County Crime Scene Unit, N.C.

shaped pattern on a floor or on the ground (see Figure 14–7) resulting from pouring an accelerant onto the surface. In addition to these visual indicators, investigators should look for signs of breaking and entering and theft, and they should begin interviewing any eyewitnesses to the fire.

Timeliness of Investigation

Time constantly works against the arson investigator. Any accelerant residues that remain after a fire is extinguished may evaporate within a few days or even hours. Furthermore, safety and health conditions may necessitate that cleanup and salvage operations begin as quickly as possible. Once this occurs, a meaningful investigation of the fire scene is impossible. Accelerants in soil and vegetation can be rapidly degraded by bacterial action. Freezing samples containing soil or vegetation is an effective way to prevent this degradation.

The need to begin an *immediate* investigation of the circumstances surrounding a fire even takes precedence over the requirement to obtain a search warrant to enter and search the premises. The Supreme Court, explaining its position on this issue, stated in part:

> . . . Fire officials are charged not only with extinguishing fires, but with finding their causes. Prompt determination of the fire's origin may be necessary to prevent its recurrence, as through the detection of continuing dangers such as faulty wiring or a defective furnace. Immediate investigation may also be necessary to preserve evidence from intentional or accidental destruction. And, of course, the sooner the officials complete their duties, the less will be their subsequent interference with the privacy and the recovery efforts of the victims. For these reasons, officials need no warrant to remain in a building for a reasonable time to investigate the cause of a blaze after it has been extinguished. And if the warrantless entry to put out the fire and determine its cause is constitutional, the warrantless seizure of evidence while inspecting the premises for these purposes also is constitutional. . . .

In determining what constitutes a reasonable time to investigate, appropriate recognition must be given to the exigencies that confront officials serving under these conditions, as well as to individuals' reasonable expectations of privacy.[1]

Locating the Fire's Origin

A search of the fire scene must focus on finding the fire's origin, which will prove most productive in any search for an accelerant or ignition device. In searching for a fire's specific point of origin, the investigator may uncover telltale signs of arson such as evidence of separate and unconnected fires or the use of "streamers" to spread the fire from one area to another. For example, the arsonist may have spread a trail of gasoline or paper to cause the fire to move rapidly from one room to another.

There are no fast and simple rules for identifying a fire's origin. Normally a fire tends to move upward, and thus the probable origin is most likely closest to the lowest point that shows the most intense characteristics of burning. Sometimes as the fire burns upward, a V-shaped pattern forms against a vertical wall, as shown in Figure 14–8. Because flammable liquids always flow to the lowest point, more severe burning found on the floor than on the ceiling may indicate the presence of an accelerant. If a flammable liquid was used, charring is expected to be more intense on the bottom of furniture, shelves, and other items rather than the top.

However, many factors can contribute to the deviation of a fire from normal behavior. Prevailing drafts and winds; secondary fires due to collapsing floors and roofs; the physical arrangement of the burning structure; stairways and elevator shafts; holes in the floor, wall, or roof; and the effects of the firefighter in suppressing the fire are all factors that the fire investigator must consider before determining conclusive findings.

Once located, the point of origin should be protected to permit careful investigation. As at any crime scene, nothing should be touched or moved before notes, sketches, and photographs are taken. An examination must also be made for possible accidental causes, as well as

[1] *Michigan v. Tyler*, 436 U.S. 499 (1978).

FIGURE 14–8

Typical V patterns illustrating upward movement of the fire.
Courtesy John Lentini

FIGURE 14–9

Portable hydrocarbon detector.
Courtesy Sirchie Finger Print Laboratories, Inc., Youngsville, N.C., www.sirchie.com

for evidence of arson. The most common materials used by an arsonist to ensure the rapid spread and intensity of a fire are gasoline and kerosene or, for that matter, any volatile flammable liquid.

Searching for Accelerants

Fortunately, only under the most ideal conditions will combustible liquids be entirely consumed during a fire. When the liquid is poured over a large area, a portion of it will likely seep into a porous surface, such as cracks in the floor, upholstery, rags, plaster, wallboards, or carpet. Enough of the liquid may remain unchanged to permit its detection in the crime laboratory. In addition, when a fire is extinguished with water, the evaporation rate of volatile fluids may be slowed because water cools and covers materials through which the combustible liquid may have soaked. Fortunately, water does not interfere with laboratory methods used to detect and characterize flammable liquid residues.

The search for traces of flammable liquid residues may be aided by the use of a sensitive portable vapor detector or "sniffer" (see Figure 14–9). This device can rapidly screen suspect materials for volatile residues by sucking in the air surrounding the questioned sample. The air is passed over a heated filament; if a combustible vapor is present, it oxidizes and immediately increases the temperature of the filament. The rise in filament temperature is then registered as a deflection on the detector's meter.

Of course, such a device is not a conclusive test for a flammable vapor, but it is an excellent screening device for checking suspect samples at the fire scene. Another approach is to use dogs that have been trained to recognize the odor of hydrocarbon accelerants.

Collection and Preservation of Arson Evidence

Two to three quarts of ash and soot debris must be collected at the point of origin of a fire when arson is suspected. The collection should include all porous materials and all other substances thought likely to contain flammable residues. These include such things as wood flooring, rugs, upholstery, and rags.

Packaging and Preservation of Evidence

Specimens should be packaged immediately in airtight containers so possible residues are not lost through evaporation. New, clean paint cans with friction lids are good containers because they are low cost, airtight, unbreakable, and available in a variety of sizes (see Figure 14–10). Wide-mouthed glass jars are also useful for packaging suspect specimens, provided that they have airtight lids. Cans and jars should be filled one-half to two-thirds full, leaving an air space in the container above the debris.

Large bulky samples should be cut to size at the scene as needed so that they will fit into available containers. Plastic polyethylene bags are not suitable for packaging specimens because they react with hydrocarbons and permit volatile hydrocarbon vapors to be depleted. Fluids found in open bottles or cans must be collected and sealed. Even when such containers appear empty, the investigator is wise to seal and preserve them in case they contain trace amounts of liquids or vapors.

Substrate Control

The collection of all materials suspected of containing volatile liquids must be accompanied by a thorough sampling of similar but uncontaminated control specimens from another area of the fire scene. This is known as *substrate control*. For example, if an investigator collects carpeting at the point of origin, he or she must sample the same carpet from another part of the room, where it can be reasonably assumed that no flammable substance was placed.

In the laboratory, the criminalist checks the substrate control to be sure that it is free of any flammables. This procedure reduces the possibility (and subsequent argument) that the carpet was exposed to a flammable liquid such as a cleaning solution during normal maintenance. In addition, laboratory tests on the unburned control material may help analyze the breakdown products from the material's exposure to intense heat during the fire. Common materials such as plastic floor tiles, carpet, linoleum, and adhesives can produce volatile hydrocarbons when they are burned. These breakdown products can sometimes be mistaken for an accelerant.

Igniters and Other Evidence

The scene should also be thoroughly searched for igniters. The most common igniter is a match. Normally the match is completely consumed during a fire and is impossible to locate. However, there have been cases in which, by force of habit, matches have been extinguished and tossed

FIGURE 14–10

Various sizes of paint cans suitable for collecting debris at fire scenes.
Courtesy Sirchie Finger Print Laboratories, Inc., Youngsville, N.C., www.sirchie.com

aside only to be recovered later by the investigator. This evidence may prove valuable if the criminalist can fit the match to a book found in the possession of a suspect.

Arsonists can construct many other types of devices to start a fire. These include burning cigarettes, firearms, ammunition, a mechanical match striker, electrical sparking devices, and a "Molotov cocktail"—a glass bottle containing flammable liquid with a cloth rag stuffed into it and lit as a fuse. Relatively complex mechanical devices are much more likely to survive the fire for later discovery. The broken glass and wick of the Molotov cocktail, if recovered, must be preserved as well.

One important piece of evidence is the clothing of the suspect perpetrator. If this individual is arrested within a few hours of initiating the fire, residual quantities of the accelerant may still be present in the clothing. As we will see in the next section, the forensic laboratory can detect extremely small quantities of accelerants, making the examination of a suspect's clothing a feasible investigative approach. Each item of clothing should be placed in a separate airtight container, preferably a new, clean paint can.

Analysis of Flammable Residues

Criminalists are nearly unanimous in judging the gas chromatograph to be the most sensitive and reliable instrument for detecting and characterizing flammable residues. Most arsons are initiated by petroleum distillates, such as gasoline and kerosene, that are composed of a complex mixture of **hydrocarbons**. The gas chromatograph separates the hydrocarbon components of these liquids and produces a chromatographic pattern characteristic of a particular petroleum product.

hydrocarbon
Any compound consisting of only carbon and hydrogen

The Headspace Technique

Before accelerant residues can be analyzed, they first must be recovered from the debris collected at the scene. The easiest way to recover accelerant residues from fire-scene debris is to heat the airtight container in which the sample is sent to the laboratory. When the container is heated, any volatile residue in the debris is driven off and trapped in the container's enclosed airspace. The vapor or *headspace* is then removed with a syringe, as shown in Figure 14–11.

When the vapor is injected into the gas chromatograph, it is separated into its components, and each peak is recorded on the chromatogram. One way of classifying ignitable liquids is by their boiling point range, which is related to the number of carbon molecules that are present in the mixture of hydrocarbons that make up an ignitable fuel. A common classification system characterizes ignitable liquids based on their boiling point ranges and number of carbon molecules as light, medium, and heavy petroleum distillates. Figure 14–12 illustrates examples of chromatograms for light, medium, and heavy petroleum distillates. The identity of the volatile residue is determined when the pattern of the resultant chromatogram is compared to patterns produced by known petroleum products. For example, in Figure 14–13, a gas chromatographic analysis of debris recovered from a fire site shows a chromatogram similar to a known gasoline standard, thus proving the presence of gasoline.

In the absence of any recognizable pattern, the individual peaks can be identified when the investigator compares their retention times to known hydrocarbon standards (such as hexane, benzene, toluene, and xylenes). The brand name of a gasoline sample cannot currently be determined by gas chromatography or any other technique. Fluctuating gasoline markets and exchange agreements among the various oil companies preclude this possibility.

Vapor Concentration

One major disadvantage of the headspace technique is that the size of the syringe limits the volume of vapor that can be removed from the container and injected into the gas chromatograph. To overcome this deficiency, many crime laboratories augment the headspace technique with a method called *vapor concentration*. One setup for this analysis is shown in Figure 14–14.

A charcoal-coated strip, similar to that used in environmental monitoring badges, is placed within the container holding the debris that has been collected from the fire scene.[2] The container

FIGURE 14–11

Removal of vapor from an enclosed container for gas chromatographic analysis.

[2] R. T. Newman et al., "The Use of Activated Charcoal Strips for Fire Debris Extractions by Passive Diffusion. Part 1: The Effects of Time, Temperature, Strip Size, and Sample Concentration," *Journal of Forensic Sciences* 41 (1996): 361.

FIGURE 14–12

Chromatograms of ignitable liquids: (a) light petroleum distillate, (b) medium petroleum distillate, and (c) heavy petroleum distillate.

is then heated to about 60°C for about one hour. At this temperature, a significant quantity of accelerant vaporizes into the container airspace. The charcoal absorbs the accelerant vapor with which it comes into contact. In this manner, over a short period of time a significant quantity of the accelerant will be trapped and concentrated onto the charcoal strip.

Once the heating procedure is complete, the analyst removes the charcoal strip from the container and recovers the accelerant from the strip by washing it with a small volume of solvent (carbon disulfide). The solvent is then injected into the gas chromatograph for analysis. The major advantage of using vapor concentration with gas chromatography is its sensitivity. By absorbing the accelerant into a charcoal strip, the forensic analyst can increase the sensitivity of accelerant detection at least a hundredfold over that of the conventional headspace technique.

An examination of Figure 14–13 shows that identifying an accelerant such as gasoline by gas chromatography is an exercise in pattern recognition. Typically a forensic analyst compares the pattern generated by the sample to chromatograms from accelerant standards obtained under the same conditions. The pattern of gasoline, as with many other accelerants, can easily

FIGURE 14–13

(*top*) Gas chromatograph of vapor from a genuine gasoline sample. (*bottom*) Gas chromatograph of vapor from debris recovered at a fire site. Note the similarity of the known gasoline to vapor removed from the debris.

be placed in a searchable library. An invaluable reference known as the Ignitable Liquids Reference Collection (ILRC) is found on the Internet at http://ilrc.ucf.edu. The ILRC is a useful collection showing chromatographic patterns for approximately five hundred ignitable liquids.

Gas Chromatography/Mass Spectrometry

On occasion, discernible patterns are not attainable by gas chromatography. This may be due to a combination of accelerants, or to the mixing of accelerant residue with heat-generated breakdown products of materials burning at the fire scene. Under such conditions, a gas chromatographic pattern can be difficult if not impossible to interpret. In these cases, gas chromatography

FIGURE 14–14

Apparatus for accelerant recovery by vapor concentration. The vapor in the enclosed container is exposed to charcoal, a chemical absorbent, where it is trapped for later analysis.

FIGURE 14–15

Chromatogram of a residue sample collected at a fire scene (a) shows a pattern somewhat like that of gasoline (b). However, a definitive conclusion that the unknown contained gasoline could be obtained only after extraneous peaks were eliminated from the unknown by the use of GC/MS (c).

Virtual Forensics Lab

Arson Detection—The Recovery of Flammable Liquids

To perform a virtual arson detection lab, go to www.pearsoncustom.com/us/vlm/

combined with mass spectrometry (discussed in Chapter 5) has proven valuable for solving difficult problems in the detection of accelerant residues.

Complex chromatographic patterns can be simplified by passing the separated components emerging from the gas chromatographic column through a mass spectrometer. As each component enters the mass spectrometer, it is fragmented into a collection of ions. The analyst can then control which ions will be detected and which will go unnoticed. In essence, the mass spectrometer acts as a filter allowing the analyst to see only the peaks associated with the ions selected for a particular accelerant. In this manner, the chromatographic pattern can be simplified by eliminating extraneous peaks that may obliterate the pattern.[3] The process is illustrated in Figure 14–15.

[3] M. W. Gilbert, "The Use of Individual Extracted Ion Profiles versus Summed Extracted Ion Profiles in Fire Debris Analysis," *Journal of Forensic Sciences* 43 (1998): 871.

chapter summary

> > > > > > > > > > >

When a fire occurs, oxygen combines with a fuel to produce noticeable quantities of heat and light (flames). Three requirements must be satisfied to initiate and sustain combustion: (1) a fuel must be present, (2) oxygen must be available in sufficient quantity to combine with the fuel, and (3) sufficient heat must be applied to initiate the combustion and generated to sustain the reaction. A fuel achieves a reaction rate with oxygen sufficient to sustain a fire only when it is in the gaseous state.

As a fire progresses, the heat created by the combustion process tends to move from a high-temperature region to one at a lower temperature. Heat transfer during a fire can occur in a number of ways. Conduction is movement of heat through an object caused by electrons and atoms colliding within the heated object. Radiation is the transfer of heat energy from a heated surface to a cooler surface by electromagnetic radiation. Convection is the transfer of heat energy by movement of molecules within a liquid or gas.

The arson investigator must begin examining a fire scene for signs of arson as soon as the fire has been extinguished. Some telltale signs of arson include evidence of separate and unconnected fires, the use of "streamers" to spread the fire from one area to another, and evidence of severe burning found on the floor as opposed to the ceiling of a structure.

The search of the fire scene must focus on finding the fire's origin. There are no fast and simple rules for identifying a fire's origin. Normally a fire tends to move upward, and thus the probable origin is most likely closest to the lowest point that shows the most intense characteristics of burning. Sometimes as the fire burns upward, a V-shaped pattern forms against a vertical wall. At the suspect point of origin of a fire, porous materials should be collected and stored in airtight containers.

In the laboratory, the gas chromatograph is the most sensitive and reliable instrument for detecting and characterizing flammable residues. Most arsons are initiated by petroleum distillates such as gasoline and kerosene. The gas chromatograph separates the hydrocarbon components and produces a chromatographic pattern characteristic of a particular petroleum product. By comparing select gas chromatographic peaks recovered from fire-scene debris to known flammable liquids, a forensic analyst may be able to identify the accelerant used to initiate the fire.

review questions

1. True or False: The absence of chemical residues always rules out the possibility of arson. _____

2. The combination of oxygen with other substances to produce new chemical products is called _____.

3. True or False: All oxidation reactions produce noticeable quantities of heat and light. _____

4. _____ is the capacity for doing work.

5. Burning methane for the purpose of heating water to produce steam in order to drive a turbine is an example of converting _____ energy to _____ energy.

6. The quantity of heat evolved from a chemical reaction arises out of the _____ and _____ of chemical bonds.

7. Molecules must (absorb, liberate) energy to break their bonds and (absorb, liberate) energy when their bonds are re-formed.

8. All oxidation reactions (absorb, liberate) heat.

9. Reactions that liberate heat are said to be _____.

10. Excess heat energy liberated by an oxidation reaction is called the _____.

11. A chemical reaction in which heat is absorbed from the surroundings is said to be _____.

12. True or False: All reactions require an energy input to start them. _____

13. The minimum temperature at which a fuel burns is known as the _____ temperature.

14. A fuel achieves a sufficient reaction rate with oxygen to produce a flame only in the (gaseous, liquid) state.

15. The lowest temperature at which a liquid fuel produces enough vapor to burn is the _____.

16. _____ is the chemical breakdown of a solid material to gaseous products.

17. _____ is a phenomenon in which a fuel burns without the presence of a flame.

18. The rate of a chemical reaction (increases, decreases) as the temperature rises.

19. _____ describes a fire caused by a natural heat-producing process.

20. A fire moves away from the original point of ignition because the _____ created by the combustion process tends to move from a high-temperature region to one at a lower temperature.

21. Electrons and atoms within a solid object exposed to heat collide with one another, causing movement of heat through the object in a process called _____.

22. In a process known as _____, a heated surface emits electromagnetic radiation of various wavelengths that moves in a straight line from one surface to another, helping the fire to spread throughout a structure.

23. True or False: An immediate search of a fire scene can commence without obtaining a search warrant. _____

24. A search of the fire scene must focus on finding the fire's _____.

25. True or False: The probable origin of a fire is most likely closest to the lowest point that shows the most intense characteristics of burning. _____

26. The collection of debris at the origin of a fire should include all (porous, nonporous) materials.

27. _____ containers must be used to package all materials suspected of containing hydrocarbon residues.

28. The most sensitive and reliable instrument for detecting and characterizing flammable residues is the (gas chromatograph, infrared spectrophotometer).

29. The identity of a volatile petroleum residue is determined by the (size, pattern) of its gas chromatogram.

30. True or False: The major advantage of using the vapor concentration technique in combination with gas chromatography is its extreme sensitivity for detecting volatile residues from fire-scene evidence. _____

31. True or False: A forensic analyst typically compares the gas chromatographic pattern generated from a fire-scene sample to a library of patterns in order to identify the accelerant. _____

32. The criminalist (can, cannot) identify gasoline residues by brand name.

33. Complex chromatographic patterns can be simplified by passing the components emerging from the gas chromatographic column through a(n) _____.

application and critical thinking

1. Indicate which method of heat transfer is most likely to be responsible for each of the following:
   a. Ignition of papers in the room where a fire starts
   b. Ignition of electrical wiring in a room adjoining the fire's point or origin
   c. Ignition of roof timbers
   d. Ignition of a neighboring house

2. It is late August in Houston, Texas, and you are investigating a fire that occurred at a facility that stores motor oils and other lubricating oils. A witness points out a man who allegedly ran from the structure about the same time that the fire started. You question the man, who turns out to be the owner of the facility. He tells you that he was checking his inventory when barrels of waste motor oil stored in an unventilated back room spontaneously burst into flames. The owner claims that the fire spread so rapidly that he had to flee the building before he could call 911. After speaking with several employees, you learn that the building has no air conditioning and that the oil had been stored for almost a year in the cramped back room. You also learn from a detective assisting on the case that the owner increased his insurance coverage on the facility within the past three months. Should you believe the owner's story, or should you suspect arson? On what do you base your conclusion?

3. Criminalist Mick Mickelson is collecting evidence from a fire scene. He gathers about a quart of ash and soot debris from several rooms surrounding the point of origin. He stores the debris in a new, clean paint can, filled about three-quarters full. Seeing several pieces of timber that he believes may contain accelerant residues, he cuts them and places them in airtight plastic bags. A short time later, a suspect is arrested and Mick searches him for any signs of an igniter or accelerants. He finds a cigarette lighter on the suspect and seizes it for evidence before turning the suspect over to the police. What mistakes, if any, did Mick make in collecting evidence?

further references

Almirall, J. R., and K. G. Furton, eds., *Fire Scene Evidence*. Boca Raton, Fla.: Taylor & Francis, 2004.

DeHaan, John D., *Kirk's Fire Investigation*, 6th ed. Upper Saddle River, N.J.: Prentice Hall, 2006.

Icove, David J., and John D. DeHaan, *Forensic Fire Scene Reconstruction*. Upper Saddle River, N.J.: Pearson Prentice Hall, 2004.

Lentini, J. J., *Scientific Protocols for Fire Investigation*. Boca Raton, Fla.: Taylor & Francis, 2006.

Midkiff, C. R., "Arson and Explosive Investigation," in R. Saferstein, ed., *Forensic Science Handbook*, vol. 1, 2nd ed. Upper Saddle River, N.J.: Prentice Hall, 2002.

NFPA 921 Guide for Fire and Explosion Investigations. Quincy, Mass.: National Fire Protection Association, 2008.

Stuffer, Eric, Julia A. Dolan, and Reta Newman, *Fire Debris Analysis*. Burlington, Mass.: Academic Press, 2008.

The Oklahoma City Bombing

It was the biggest act of mass murder in U.S. history. On a sunny spring morning in April 1995, a Ryder rental truck pulled into the parking area of the Alfred P. Murrah federal building in Oklahoma City. The driver stepped down from the truck's cab and casually walked away. Minutes later, the truck exploded into a fireball, unleashing enough energy to destroy the building and kill 168 people, including 19 children and infants in the building's day care center.

Later that morning, an Oklahoma Highway Patrol officer pulled over a beat-up 1977 Mercury Marquis being driven without a license plate. On further investigation, the driver, Timothy McVeigh, was found to be in possession of a loaded firearm and charged with transporting a firearm. At the explosion site, remnants of the Ryder truck were located and the truck was quickly traced to a renter—Robert Kling, an alias for Timothy McVeigh. Coincidentally, the rental agreement and McVeigh's driver's license both used the address of McVeigh's friend, Terry Nichols. Investigators later recovered McVeigh's fingerprint on a receipt for 2,000 pounds of ammonium nitrate, a basic explosive ingredient. Forensic analysts also located PETN residues on the clothing McVeigh wore on the day of his arrest. PETN is a component of detonating cord. After three days of deliberation, a jury declared McVeigh guilty of the bombing and sentenced him to die by lethal injection.

forensic investigation of explosions

Learning Objectives

After studying this chapter you should be able to:

- Understand how explosives are classified

- List some common commercial, homemade, and military explosives

- Describe how to collect physical evidence at the scene of an explosion

- Describe laboratory procedures used to detect and identify explosive residues.

KEY TERMS

black powder
deflagration
detonating cord
detonation
explosion
high explosive
low explosive
oxidizing agent
primary explosive
safety fuse
secondary explosive
smokeless powder
  (double-base)
smokeless powder
  (single-base)

Explosions and Explosives

The ready accessibility of potentially explosive laboratory chemicals, dynamite, and, in some countries, an assortment of military explosives has provided the criminal element of society with a lethal weapon. Unfortunately for society, explosives have become an attractive weapon to criminals bent on revenge, destruction of commercial operations, or just plain mischief.

Although politically motivated bombings have received considerable publicity worldwide, in the United States most bombing incidents are perpetrated by isolated individuals rather than by organized terrorists. These incidents typically involve homemade explosives and incendiary devices. The design of such weapons is limited only by the imagination and ingenuity of the bomber.

Like arson investigation, bomb investigation requires close cooperation of a group of highly specialized individuals trained and experienced in bomb disposal, bomb-site investigation, forensic analysis, and criminal investigation. The criminalist must detect and identify explosive chemicals recovered from the crime scene as well as identify the detonating mechanisms. This special responsibility concerns us for the remainder of this chapter.

The Chemistry of Explosions

explosion
A chemical or mechanical action caused by combustion, accompanied by creation of heat and rapid expansion of gases

Like fire, an **explosion** is the product of combustion accompanied by the creation of gases and heat. However, the distinguishing characteristic of an explosion is the rapid rate of the reaction. The sudden buildup of expanding gas pressure at the origin of the explosion produces the violent physical disruption of the surrounding environment.

Our previous discussion of the chemistry of fire referred only to oxidation reactions that rely on air as the sole source of oxygen. However, we need not restrict ourselves to this type of situation. For example, explosives are substances that undergo a rapid exothermic oxidation reaction, producing large quantities of gases. This sudden buildup of gas pressure constitutes an explosion. Detonation occurs so rapidly that oxygen in the air cannot participate in the reaction; thus, many explosives must have their own source of oxygen.

oxidizing agent
A substance that supplies oxygen to a chemical reaction

Chemicals that supply oxygen are known as **oxidizing agents**. One such agent is found in black powder, a *low explosive*, which is composed of a mixture of the following chemical ingredients:

75 percent potassium nitrate (KNO_3)
15 percent charcoal (C)
10 percent sulfur (S)

In this combination, oxygen containing potassium nitrate acts as an oxidizing agent for the charcoal and sulfur fuels. As heat is applied to black powder, oxygen is liberated from potassium nitrate and simultaneously combines with charcoal and sulfur to produce heat and gases (symbolized by ↑), as represented in the following chemical equation:

$$3C \quad + \quad S \quad + \quad 2KNO_3 \quad \rightarrow$$
carbon sulfur potassium nitrate yields

$$3CO_2\uparrow \quad + \quad N_2\uparrow \quad + \quad K_2S$$
carbon dioxide nitrogen potassium sulfide

Some explosives have their oxygen and fuel components combined within one molecule. For example, the chemical structure of nitroglycerin, the major constituent of dynamite, combines carbon, hydrogen, nitrogen, and oxygen:

$$
\begin{array}{ccccc}
H & & H & & H \\
| & & | & & | \\
H - C & - & C & - & C - H \\
| & & | & & | \\
NO_2 & & NO_2 & & NO_2
\end{array}
$$

When nitroglycerin detonates, large quantities of energy are released as the molecule decomposes, and the oxygen recombines to produce large volumes of carbon dioxide, nitrogen, and water.

Consider, for example, the effect of confining an explosive charge to a relatively small, closed container. On detonation, the explosive almost instantaneously produces large volumes of gases that exert enormously high pressures on the interior walls of the container. In addition, the heat energy released by the explosion expands the gases, causing them to push on the walls with an even greater force. If we could observe the effects of an exploding lead pipe in slow motion, we would first see the pipe's walls stretch and balloon under pressures as high as several hundred tons per square inch. Finally, the walls would fragment and fly outward in all directions. This flying debris or shrapnel constitutes a great danger to life and limb in the immediate vicinity.

On release from confinement, the gaseous products of the explosion suddenly expand and compress layers of surrounding air as they move outward from the origin of the explosion. This blast effect, or outward rush of gases, at a rate that may be as high as 7,000 miles per hour creates an artificial gale that can overthrow walls, collapse roofs, and disturb any object in its path. If a bomb is sufficiently powerful, more serious damage will be inflicted by the blast effect than by fragmentation debris (see Figure 15–1).

Types of Explosives

The speed at which explosives decompose varies greatly from one to another and permits their classification as *high* and *low explosives*. In a low explosive, this speed is called the speed of **deflagration** (burning). It is characterized by very rapid oxidation that produces heat, light, and a subsonic pressure wave. In a high explosive, it is called the speed of detonation. **Detonation** refers to the creation of a supersonic shock wave within the explosive charge. This shock wave breaks the chemical bonds of the explosive charge, leading to the new instantaneous buildup of heat and gases.

LOW EXPLOSIVES Low explosives, such as black and smokeless powders, decompose relatively slowly at rates up to 1,000 meters per second. Because of their slow burning rates, they produce a propelling or throwing action that makes them suitable as propellants for ammunition or skyrockets. However, the danger of this group of explosives must not be underestimated because, when any one of them is confined to a relatively small container, it can explode with a force as lethal as that of any known explosive.

Black Powder and Smokeless Powder The most widely used explosives in the low-explosive group are black powder and smokeless powder. The popularity of these two explosives is enhanced by their accessibility to the public. Both are available in any gun store, and black powder can easily be made from ingredients purchased at any chemical supply house as well.

Black powder is a relatively stable mixture of potassium nitrate or sodium nitrate, charcoal, and sulfur. Unconfined, it merely burns; thus it commonly is used in safety fuses that carry a flame to an explosive charge. A **safety fuse** usually consists of black powder wrapped in a fabric or plastic casing. When ignited, a sufficient length of fuse will burn at a rate slow enough to allow a person adequate time to leave the site of the pending explosion. Black powder, like any other low explosive, becomes explosive and lethal only when it is confined.

The safest and most powerful low explosive is **smokeless powder**. This explosive usually consists of nitrated cotton or nitrocellulose (**single-base powder**) or nitroglycerin mixed with nitrocellulose (**double-base powder**). The powder is manufactured in a variety of grain sizes and shapes, depending on the desired application (see Figure 15–2).

Chlorate Mixtures The only ingredients required for a low explosive are fuel and a good oxidizing agent. The oxidizing agent potassium chlorate, for example, when mixed with sugar, produces a popular and accessible explosive mix. When confined to a small container—for example, a pipe—and ignited, this mixture can explode with a force equivalent to a stick of 40 percent dynamite.

Some other commonly encountered ingredients that may be combined with chlorate to produce an explosive are carbon, sulfur, starch, phosphorus, and magnesium filings. Chlorate mixtures may also be ignited by the heat generated from a chemical reaction. For instance, sufficient heat can be generated to initiate combustion when concentrated sulfuric acid comes in contact with a sugar–chlorate mix.

FIGURE 15–1

A violent explosion.

deflagration

A very rapid oxidation reaction accompanied by the generation of a low-intensity pressure wave that can disrupt the surroundings

detonation

An extremely rapid oxidation reaction accompanied by a violent disruptive effect and an intense, high-speed shock wave

low explosive

An explosive with a velocity of detonation less than 1,000 meters per second

black powder

Normally, a mixture of potassium nitrate, carbon, and sulfur in the ratio 75/15/10

safety fuse

A cord containing a core of black powder, used to carry a flame at a uniform rate to an explosive charge

smokeless powder (single-base)

An explosive consisting of nitrocellulose

smokeless powder (double-base)

An explosive consisting of a mixture of nitrocellulose and nitroglycerin

FIGURE 15–2

Samples of smokeless powders.

Courtesy of ATF (Bureau of Alcohol, Tobacco, Firearms & Explosives)

high explosive

An explosive with a velocity of detonation greater than 1,000 meters per second

primary explosive

A high explosive that is easily detonated by heat, shock, or friction

secondary explosive

A high explosive that is relatively insensitive to heat, shock, or friction

Gas–Air Mixtures   Another form of low explosive is created when a considerable quantity of natural gas escapes into a confined area and mixes with a sufficient amount of air. If ignited, this mixture results in simultaneous combustion and sudden production of large volumes of gases and heat. In a building, walls are forced outward by the expanding gases, causing the roof to fall into the interiors, and objects are thrown outward and scattered in erratic directions with no semblance of pattern.

Mixtures of air and a gaseous fuel explode or burn only within a limited concentration range. For example, the concentration limits for methane in air range from 5.3 to 13.9 percent. In the presence of too much air, the fuel becomes too diluted and does not ignite. On the other hand, if the fuel becomes too concentrated, ignition is prevented because there is not enough oxygen to support the combustion.

Mixtures at or near the upper concentration limit ("rich" mixtures) explode; however, some gas remains unconsumed because there is not enough oxygen to complete the combustion. As air rushes back into the origin of the explosion, it combines with the residual hot gas, producing a fire that is characterized by a *whoosh* sound. This fire is often more destructive than the explosion that preceded it. Mixtures near the lower end of the limit ("lean" mixtures) generally cause an explosion without accompanying damage due to fire.

HIGH EXPLOSIVES   **High explosives** include dynamite, TNT, PETN, and RDX. They detonate almost instantaneously at rates of 1,000–8,500 meters per second, producing a smashing or shattering effect on their target. High explosives are classified into two groups—primary and secondary explosives—based on their sensitivity to heat, shock, or friction.

Primary explosives are ultrasensitive to heat, shock, or friction, and under normal conditions they detonate violently instead of burning. For this reason, they are used to detonate other explosives through a chain reaction and are often referred to as *primers*. Primary explosives provide the major ingredients of blasting caps and include lead azide, lead styphnate, and diazodinitrophenol (see Figure 15–3). Because of their extreme sensitivity, these explosives are rarely used as the main charge of a homemade bomb.

Secondary explosives are relatively insensitive to heat, shock, or friction, and they normally burn rather than detonate when ignited in small quantities in open air. This group comprises most high explosives used for commercial and military blasting. Some common examples of secondary explosives are dynamite, TNT (trinitrotoluene), PETN (pentaerythritol tetranitrate), RDX (cyclotrimethylenetrinitramine), and tetryl (2,4,6-trinitrophenylmethylnitramine).

Dynamite   It is an irony of history that the prize most symbolic of humanity's search for peace—the Nobel Peace Prize—should bear the name of the developer of one of our most lethal discoveries—dynamite. In 1867, the Swedish chemist Alfred Nobel, searching for a method to desensitize nitroglycerin, found that when kieselguhr, a variety of diatomaceous earth, absorbed a large portion of nitroglycerin, it became far less sensitive but still retained its explosive force. Nobel later decided to use pulp as an absorbent because kieselguhr was a heat-absorbing material.

This so-called pulp dynamite was the beginning of what is now known as the straight dynamite series. These dynamites are used when a quick shattering action is desired. In addition to nitroglycerine and pulp, present-day straight dynamites also include sodium nitrate (which furnishes oxygen for complete combustion) and a small percentage of a stabilizer, such as calcium carbonate.

All straight dynamite is rated by strength; the strength rating is determined by the weight percentage of nitroglycerin in the formula. Thus, a 40 percent straight dynamite contains 40 percent nitroglycerin, a 60 percent grade contains 60 percent nitroglycerin, and so forth. However, the relative blasting power of different strengths of dynamite is not directly proportional to their strength ratings. A 60 percent straight dynamite, rather than being three times as strong as a 20 percent, is only one and one-half times as strong (see Figure 15–4).

Ammonium Nitrate Explosives   In recent years, nitroglycerin-based dynamite has all but disappeared from the industrial explosives market. Commercially, these explosives have been replaced mainly by ammonium nitrate–based explosives, that is, water gels, emulsions, and ANFO explosives. These explosives mix oxygen-rich ammonium nitrate with a fuel to form a low-cost, stable explosive.

FIGURE 15–3

Blasting caps. The left and center caps are initiated by an electrical current; the right cap is initiated by a safety fuse.

Typically, water gels have a consistency resembling that of set gelatin or gel-type toothpaste. They are characterized by their water-resistant nature and are employed for all types of blasting under wet conditions. These explosives are based on formulations of ammonium nitrate and sodium nitrate gelled with a natural polysaccharide such as guar gum. Commonly, a combustible material such as aluminum is mixed into the gel to serve as the explosive's fuel.

Emulsion explosives differ from gels in that they consist of two distinct phases, an oil phase and a water phase. In these emulsions, a droplet of a supersaturated solution of ammonium nitrate is surrounded by a hydrocarbon serving as a fuel. A typical emulsion consists of water, one or more inorganic nitrate oxidizers, oil, and emulsifying agents. Commonly, emulsions contain micron-sized glass, resin, or ceramic spheres known as *microspheres* or *microballoons*. The size of these spheres controls the explosive's sensitivity and detonation velocity.

Ammonium nitrate soaked in fuel oil is an explosive known as *ANFO*. Such commercial explosives are inexpensive and safe to handle and have found wide applications in blasting operations in the mining industry. Ammonium nitrate in the form of fertilizer makes a readily obtainable ingredient for homemade explosives. Indeed, in an incident related to the 1993 bombing of New York City's World Trade Center, the FBI arrested five men during a raid on their hideout in New York City, where they were mixing a "witches' brew" of fuel oil and an ammonium nitrate–based fertilizer.

TATP   *Triacetone triperoxide* (TATP) is a homemade explosive that has been used as an improvised explosive by terrorist organizations in Israel and other Middle Eastern countries. It is prepared by reacting the common ingredients of acetone and hydrogen peroxide in the presence of an acid catalyst such as hydrochloric acid.

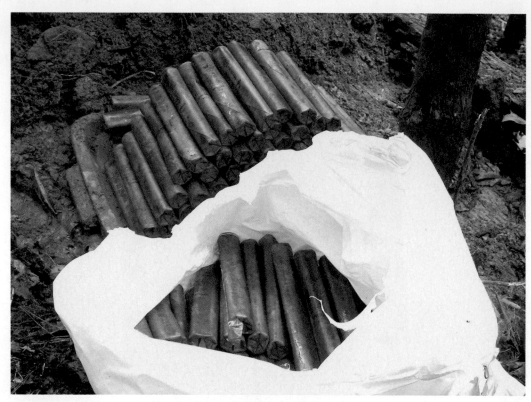

FIGURE 15–4
Sticks of dynamite.
U.S. Department of Justice\AP Wide World Photos

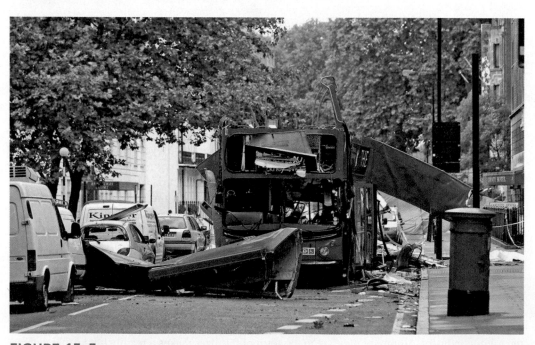

FIGURE 15–5
A London bus destroyed by a TATP-based bomb.
Courtesy AP Wide World Photos

TATP is a friction- and impact-sensitive explosive that is extremely potent when confined in a container such as a pipe. The 2005 London transit bombings were caused by TATP-based explosives and provide ample evidence that terrorist cells have moved TATP outside the Middle East. A London bus destroyed by one of the TATP bombs is shown in Figure 15–5.

A plot to blow up ten international plane flights leaving Britain for the United States with a "liquid explosive" apparently involved plans to smuggle the peroxide-based TATP explosive onto the planes. This plot has prompted authorities to prohibit airline passengers from carrying liquids and gels onto planes.

Military High Explosives   No discussion of high explosives would be complete without a mention of military high explosives. In many countries outside the United States, the accessibility of high explosives to terrorist organizations makes them common constituents of homemade bombs. RDX, the most popular and powerful military explosive, is often encountered in the form of a pliable plastic of doughlike consistency known as *composition C–4* (a U.S. military designation).

TNT was produced and used on an enormous scale during World War II and may be considered the most important military bursting charge explosive. Alone or in combination with other explosives, it has found wide application in shells, bombs, grenades, demolition explosives, and propellant compositions (see Figure 15–6). Interestingly, military "dynamite" contains no nitroglycerin but is actually composed of a mixture of RDX and TNT. Like other military explosives, TNT is rarely encountered in bombings in the United States.

PETN is used by the military in TNT mixtures for small-caliber projectiles and grenades. Commercially, the chemical is used as the explosive core in a **detonating cord** or *primacord*. Instead of the slower-burning safety fuse, a detonating cord is often used to connect a series of explosive charges so that they will detonate simultaneously.

Detonators   Unlike low explosives, bombs made of high explosives must be detonated by an initiating explosion. In most cases, detonators are blasting caps composed of copper or aluminum cases filled with lead azide as an initiating charge and PETN or RDX as a detonating charge. Blasting caps can be initiated by means of a burning safety fuse or by an electrical current.

Homemade bombs camouflaged in packages, suitcases, and the like, are usually initiated with an electrical blasting cap wired to a battery. An unlimited number of switching-mechanism designs have been devised for setting off these devices; clocks and mercury switches are favored. Bombers sometimes prefer to employ outside electrical sources. For instance, most automobile bombs are detonated when the ignition switch of a car is turned on.

detonating cord
A cordlike explosive containing a core of high-explosive material, usually PETN; also called primacord

FIGURE 15–6
Military explosives in combat use.
Courtesy Getty Images/Time Life Pictures

forensics at work

Liquid Explosives

In 2006, security agencies in the United States and Great Britain uncovered a terrorist plot to use liquid explosives to destroy commercial airlines operating between the two countries. Of the hundreds of types of explosives, most are solid. Only about a dozen are liquid. But some of those liquid explosives can be readily purchased and others can be made from hundreds of different kinds of chemicals that are not difficult to obtain. After the September 11 attacks, worries about solid explosives became the primary concern. In 2001, Richard Reid was arrested for attempting to destroy an American Airlines flight out of Paris. Authorities later found a high explosive with a TATP detonator hidden in the lining of his shoe. It is therefore not surprising that terrorists turned to liquids in this latest plot. A memo issued by federal security officials about the plot to blow up ten international planes highlighted a type of liquid explosive based on peroxide.

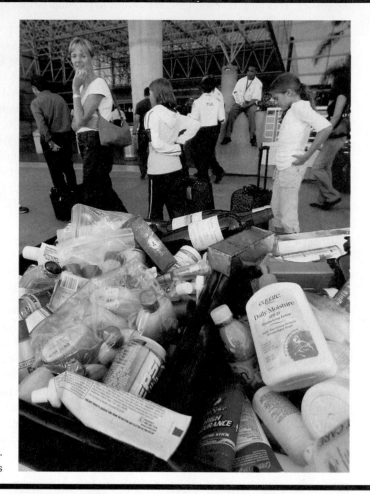

Gels discarded by airline passengers before boarding.
Stefano Paltera, AP Wide World Photos

Collection and Analysis of Evidence of Explosives

The most important step in the detection and analysis of explosive residues is the collection of appropriate samples from the explosion scene. Invariably, undetonated residues of the explosive remain at the site of the explosion. The detection and identification of these explosives in the laboratory depends on the bomb-scene investigator's skill and ability to recognize and sample the areas most likely to contain such materials.

Detecting and Recovering Evidence of Explosives

The most obvious characteristic of a high or contained low explosive is the presence of a crater at the origin of the blast. Once the crater has been located, all loose soil and other debris must immediately be removed from the interior of the hole and preserved for laboratory analysis. Other good sources of explosive residues are objects located near the origin of detonation. Wood, insulation, rubber, and other soft materials that are readily penetrated often collect traces of the explosive. However, nonporous objects near the blast must not be overlooked. For instance, residues can be

The most common peroxide-based explosive is TATP (triacetone triperoxide), which is made up of acetone and hydrogen peroxide, two widely available substances. TATP can be used as a detonator or a primary explosive and has been used in Qaeda-related bomb plots and by Palestinian suicide bombers. TATP itself is a white powder made up of crystals that form when acetone and hydrogen peroxide are mixed together, usually with a catalyst added to speed the chemical reactions. Acetone is the main ingredient in nail polish remover, while hydrogen peroxide is a popular antiseptic. When the two main ingredients are mixed, they form a white powder that can be easily detonated using an electrical spark.

Commercially available hydrogen peroxide, however, is not concentrated enough to create TATP. The solution sold in stores contains about 3 percent hydrogen peroxide, compared to the approximately 70 percent concentration need for TATP. However, hydrogen peroxide solutions of up to 30 percent can be obtained from chemical supply houses. According to explosives experts, a mixture of 30 percent hydrogen peroxide and acetone can create a fire hot enough to burn though the fuselage of an aircraft.

In theory, scientists know how to detect peroxide-based explosives. The challenge is to design machines that can perform scans quickly and efficiently on thousands of passengers passing through airport security checks. Current scanning machines at airports are designed to detect nitrogen containing chemicals and are not designed to detect peroxide-containing explosive ingredients. Since 9/11, security experts have worried about the possibility of liquid explosives in the form of liquids and gels getting onto airliners.

Without the luxury of waiting for newly designed scanning devices capable of ferreting out dangerous liquids to be in place at airports, the decision was made to use a common-sense approach—that is, to restrict the types and quantities of liquids that a passenger can carry onto a plane.

found on the surfaces of metal objects near the site of an explosion. Material blown away from the blast's origin should also be recovered because it, too, may retain explosive residues.

The entire area must be systematically searched, with great care given to recovering any trace of a detonating mechanism or any other item foreign to the explosion site. Wire-mesh screens are best used for sifting through debris. All personnel involved in searching the bomb scene must take appropriate measures to avoid contaminating the scene, including dressing in disposable gloves, shoe covers, and overalls.

ION MOBILITY SPECTROMETER   In pipe-bomb explosions, particles of the explosive are frequently found adhering to the pipe cap or to the pipe threads, as a result of either being impacted into the metal by the force of the explosion or being deposited in the threads during the construction of the bomb. One approach for screening objects for the presence of explosive residues in the field or the laboratory is the ion mobility spectrometer (IMS).[1] A portable IMS is shown in Figure 15–7.

[1] T. Keller et al., "Application of Ion Mobility Spectrometry in Cases of Forensic Interest," *Forensic Science International* 161 (2006): 130.

FIGURE 15–7

A portable ion mobility spectrometer used to rapidly detect and tentatively identify trace quantities of explosives. Courtesy GE Ion Track, Wilmington, Mass. 01887

This handheld detector uses a vacuum to collect explosive residues from suspect surfaces. Alternatively, the surface suspected of containing explosive residues is wiped down with a Teflon-coated fiberglass disc and the collected residues are then drawn into the spectrometer off the disc. Once in the IMS, the explosive residues are vaporized by the application of heat. These vaporized substances are exposed to a beam of electrons or beta rays emitted by radioactive nickel and converted into electrically charged molecules or ions. The ions are then allowed to move through a tube (drift region) under the influence of an electric field. A schematic diagram of an IMS is shown in Figure 15–8.

The preliminary identification of an explosive residue can be made by noting the time it takes the explosive to move through the tube. Because ions move at different speeds depending on their size and structure, they can be characterized by the speed at which they pass through the tube. Used as a screening tool, this method rapidly detects a full range of explosives, even at low detection levels. However, all results need to be verified through confirmatory tests.

The IMS can detect plastic explosives as well as commercial and military explosives. More than 10,000 portable and full-size IMS units are currently used at airport security checkpoints, and more than 50,000 handheld IMS analyzers have been deployed for chemical-weapons monitoring in various armed forces.

COLLECTION AND PACKAGING   All materials collected for examination by the laboratory must be placed in airtight sealed containers and labeled with all pertinent information. Soil and other soft loose materials are best stored in metal airtight containers such as clean paint cans. Debris and articles collected from different areas are to be packaged in separate airtight containers. Plastic bags should not be used to store evidence suspected of containing explosive residues. Some explosives can actually escape through the plastic. Sharp-edged objects should not be allowed to pierce the sides of a plastic bag. It is best to place these types of items in metal containers.

Analysis of Evidence of Explosives

When the bomb-scene debris and other materials arrive at the laboratory, everything is first examined microscopically to detect particles of unconsumed explosive. Portions of the recovered debris and detonating mechanism, if found, are carefully viewed under a low-power stereoscopic microscope in a painstaking effort to locate particles of the explosive. Black powder and smokeless powder are relatively easy to locate in debris because of their characteristic shapes and colors

Sample is drawn into ionization chamber

Sample is bombarded by radioactive particles emitted by an isotope of nickel to form ions

Drift rings

Collection electrode

Shutter

(a)

Ionization chamber

Drift region

Sample is converted into ions of different sizes and structures

Drift rings

Collection electrode

Shutter

(b)

Ionization chamber

Drift region

Explosive substances can be characterized by the speed at which they move through the electric field

Drift rings

Collection electrode

Shutter

(c)

Ionization chamber

Drift region

Ions separate as they move through an electric field

FIGURE 15–8

Schematic diagram of an ion mobility spectrometer. A sample is introduced into an ionization chamber, where bombardment with radioactive particles emitted by an isotope of nickel converts the sample to ions. The ions move into a drift region where ion separation occurs based on the speed of the ions as they move through an electric field.

TABLE 15–1

Color Spot Tests for Common Explosives

Substance	Reagent		
	Greiss[a]	Diphenylamine[b]	Alcoholic KOH[c]
Chlorate	No color	Blue	No color
Nitrate	Pink to red	Blue	No color
Nitrocellulose	Pink	Blue-black	No color
Nitroglycerin	Pink to red	Blue	No color
PETN	Pink to red	Blue	No color
RDX	Pink to red	Blue	No color
TNT	No color	No color	Red
Tetryl	Pink to red	Blue	Red-violet

[a] Greiss reagent: Solution 1—Dissolve 1 g sulfanilic acid in 100 mL 30% acetic acid. Solution 2—Dissolve 0.5 g N-(1-napthyl) ethylenediamine in 100 mL methyl alcohol. Add solutions 1 and 2 and a few milligrams of zinc dust to the suspect extract.

[b] Diphenylamine reagent: Dissolve 1 g diphenylamine in 100 mL concentrated sulfuric acid.

[c] Alcoholic KOH reagent: Dissolve 10 g of potassium hydroxide in 100 mL absolute alcohol.

(see Figure 15–2). However, dynamite and other high explosives present the microscopist with a much more difficult task and often must be detected by other means.

Following microscopic examination, the recovered debris is thoroughly rinsed with acetone. The high solubility of most explosives in acetone ensures their quick removal from the debris. When a water-gel explosive containing ammonium nitrate or a low explosive is suspected, the debris should be rinsed with water so that water-soluble substances (such as nitrates and chlorates) will be extracted. Table 15–1 lists a number of simple color tests the examiner can perform on the acetone and water extracts to screen for the presence of organic and inorganic explosives, respectively.

SCREENING AND CONFIRMATION TESTS   Once collected, the acetone extract is concentrated and analyzed using color spot tests, thin-layer chromatography (TLC), high-performance liquid chromatography (HPLC; see pages 127–128), and gas chromatography/mass spectrometry. The presence of an explosive is indicated by a well-defined spot on a TLC plate with an R_f value corresponding to a known explosive—for example, nitroglycerin, RDX, or PETN.

The high sensitivity of HPLC also makes it useful for analyzing trace evidence of explosives. HPLC operates at room temperature and hence does not cause explosives, many of which are temperature sensitive, to decompose during their analysis. When a water-gel explosive containing ammonium nitrate or a low explosive is suspected, the debris should be rinsed with water so that water-soluble substances (such as nitrates and chlorates) will be extracted.

When sufficient quantities of explosives are recoverable, confirmatory tests may be performed by either infrared spectrophotometry or X-ray diffraction. The former produces a unique "fingerprint" pattern for an organic explosive, as shown by the IR spectrum of RDX in Figure 15–9. The latter provides a unique diffraction pattern for inorganic substances such as potassium nitrate and potassium chlorate, shown in Figure 6–11.

TAGGANTS   An explosive "taggant" program has been proposed to further enhance a bomb-scene investigator's chances of recovering useful evidence at a postexplosion scene. Under this proposal, tiny color-coded chips the size of sand grains would be added to commercial explosives during their manufacture. Some of these chips would be expected to survive an explosion and be capable of recovery at explosion scenes. To aid in their recovery, the chips are made both fluorescent and magnetic sensitive. Hence, investigators can search for taggants at the explosion site with magnetic tools and ultraviolet light.

The taggant chip is arranged in a color sequence that indicates where the explosive was made and when it was produced (see Figure 15–10). With this knowledge, the explosive can be traced through its distribution chain to its final legal possessor. The taggant colors are readily observed and are read with the aid of a low-power microscope.

FIGURE 15–9

Infrared spectrum of RDX.

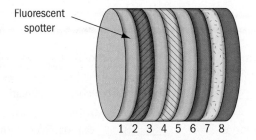

FIGURE 15–10

Cross-section of a taggant. The color sequence of the recovered taggant is observed with the aid of a low-power microscope. The colors are then matched to a color code to yield information about the plant of manufacture, production lot, and purchasers of the explosive material.

There are no plans to institute a taggant program for commercial explosives in the United States. In Europe, only Switzerland has adopted a taggant program; thus, it is extremely doubtful that taggants will be found in any significant number of bombing incidents in the foreseeable future. Interestingly, the International Civil Aviation Organization has mandated that a volatile taggant be added to plastic explosives during their manufacture in order to facilitate the detection of these explosives. Programs are now under way to tag commercial C–4 with the volatile chemical known as DMNB (2,3-dimethyl-2,3-dinitrobutane).

chapter summary

> > > > > > > > > > >

Explosives are substances that undergo a rapid oxidation reaction with the production of large quantities of gases. This sudden buildup of gas pressure constitutes an explosion. The speed at which explosives decompose permits their classification as high or low explosives.

The most widely used low explosives are black powder and smokeless powder. Among the high explosives, primary explosives are ultrasensitive to heat, shock, or friction and provide the major ingredients found in blasting caps. Secondary explosives normally constitute the main charge of a high explosive.

Among the high explosives, nitroglycerin-based dynamite has all but disappeared from the industrial explosives market and has been replaced by ammonium nitrate–based explosives (such as water gels, emulsions, and ANFO explosives). In many countries outside the United States, the accessibility of military high explosives to terrorist organizations makes them common constituents of homemade bombs. RDX is the most popular and powerful of the military explosives.

The entire bomb site must be systematically searched with great care given to recovering any trace of a detonating mechanism or any other item foreign to the explosion site. Objects located at or near the origin of the explosion must be collected for laboratory examination.

Typically, in the laboratory, debris collected at explosion scenes is examined microscopically for unconsumed explosive particles. Recovered debris may also be thoroughly rinsed with organic solvents and analyzed by testing procedures that include color spot tests, thin-layer chromatography, high-performance liquid chromatography, and gas chromatography/mass spectrometry.

review questions

1. Oxidizing agents supply _____ to a chemical reaction.

2. Three ingredients of black powder are _____, _____, and _____.

3. Rapid combustion accompanied by the creation of large volumes of gases describes a(n) _____.

4. Explosives that decompose at relatively slow rates are classified as _____ explosives.

5. _____ explosives detonate almost instantaneously to produce a smashing or shattering effect.

6. The most widely used low explosives are _____ and _____.

7. A low explosive becomes explosive and lethal only when it is _____.

8. True or False: Air and a gaseous fuel burn when mixed at any concentration range. _____

9. High explosives can be classified as either _____ or _____ explosives.

10. The blasting power of different dynamite strengths (is, is not) in direct proportion to the weight percentage of nitroglycerin.

11. True or False: The most common commercial explosives incorporate ammonium nitrate. _____

12. The most widely used explosive in the military is _____.

13. The explosive core in detonating cord is _____.

14. A high explosive is normally detonated by a(n) _____ explosive contained within a blasting cap.

15. An obvious characteristic of a high explosive is the presence of a(n) _____ at the origin of the blast.

16. The most important step in detecting explosive residues is the _____ of appropriate samples from the explosion scene.

17. To screen objects for the presence of explosive residues in the field or the laboratory, the investigator may use a handheld _____.

18. Unconsumed explosive residues may be detected in the laboratory through a careful _____ examination of the debris.

19. Debris recovered from the site of an explosion is routinely rinsed with _____ in an attempt to recover high-explosive residues.

20. Once collected, the acetone extract is initially analyzed by _____, _____, and _____.

21. The technique of _____ produces a unique absorption spectrum for an organic explosive.

22. The technique of _____ provides a unique diffraction pattern for the identification of the inorganic constituents of explosives.

23. True or False: Debris and articles at an explosion scene that are collected from different areas are to be packaged in separate airtight containers._____

24. True or False: In the absence of airtight metal containers, plastic bags can be used to store evidence suspected of containing explosive residues._____

application and critical thinking

1. The following pieces of evidence were found at separate explosion sites. For each item, indicate whether the explosion was more likely caused by low or high explosives, and explain your answer:
   a. Lead azide residues
   b. Nitrocellulose residues
   c. Ammonium nitrate residues
   d. Scraps of primacord
   e. Potassium chlorate residues

2. Which color test or tests would you run first on a suspect sample to test for evidence of each of the following explosives? Explain your answers.
   a. Tetryl
   b. TNT
   c. Chlorate
   d. Nitrocellulose

3. Criminalist Matt Weir is collecting evidence from the site of an explosion. Arriving on the scene, he immediately proceeds to look for the crater caused by the blast. After finding the crater, he picks through the debris at the site by hand, looking for evidence of detonators or foreign materials. Matt collects loose soil and debris from the immediate area, placing the smaller bits in paper folded into a druggist fold. Larger items he stores in plastic bags for transportation to the laboratory. What mistakes, if any, did Matt make in collecting and storing this evidence?

further references

Thurman, J. T., *Practical Bomb Scene Investigation*. Boca Raton, Fla.: Taylor & Francis, 2006.

Yinon, J., *Forensic and Environmental Detection of Explosives*. West Sussex, England: Wiley, 1999.

headline news

James Earl Ray: Conspirator or Lone Gunman?

Since his arrest in 1968 for the assassination of Dr. Martin Luther King, Jr., endless speculation has swirled around the motives and connections of James Earl Ray. Ray was a career criminal who was serving time for armed robbery when he escaped from the Missouri State Prison almost one year before the assassination. On April 3, 1968, Ray arrived in Memphis, Tennessee. The next day he rented a room at Bessie Brewer's Rooming House, across the street from the Lorraine Motel where Dr. King was staying.

At 6:00 p.m., Dr. King left his second-story motel room and stepped onto the balcony of the Lorraine Motel. As King turned toward his room, a shot rang out, striking the civil rights activist. Nothing could be done to revive him, and Dr. King was pronounced dead at 7:05 p.m. As the assailant ran on foot from Bessie Brewer's, he left a blanket-covered package in front of a nearby building and then drove off in a white Mustang. The package was later shown to contain a high-powered rifle equipped with a scope, a radio, some clothes, a pair of binoculars, a couple of beer cans, and a receipt for the binoculars. Almost a week after the shooting, the white Mustang was found abandoned in Atlanta, Georgia.

Fingerprints later identified as James Earl Ray's were found in the Mustang, on the rifle, on the binoculars, and on a beer can. In 1969, Ray entered a guilty plea in return for a sentence of ninety-nine years. Although a variety of conspiracy theories surround this crime, the indisputable fact is that a fingerprint put the rifle that killed Martin Luther King, Jr., in the hands of James Earl Ray.

fingerprints

Learning Objectives

After studying this chapter you should be able to:

- Know the common ridge characteristics of a fingerprint

- List the three major fingerprint patterns and their respective subclasses

- Distinguish visible, plastic, and latent fingerprints

- Describe the concept of an automated fingerprint identification system (AFIS)

- List the techniques for developing latent fingerprints on porous and nonporous objects

- Describe the proper procedures for preserving a developed latent fingerprint

KEY TERMS

anthropometry
arch
digital imaging
fluoresce
iodine fuming
latent fingerprint
livescan
loop
ninhydrin
Physical Developer
pixel
plastic print
portrait parlé
ridge characteristics
   (minutiae)
sublimation
superglue fuming
visible print
whorl

History of Fingerprinting

Since the beginnings of criminal investigation, police have sought an infallible means of human identification. The first systematic attempt at personal identification was devised and introduced by a French police expert, Alphonse Bertillon, in 1883. The Bertillon system relied on a detailed description (**portrait parlé**) of the subject, combined with full-length and profile photographs and a system of precise body measurements known as **anthropometry**.

The use of anthropometry as a method of identification rested on the premise that the dimensions of the human bone system remained fixed from age 20 until death. Skeleton sizes were thought to be so extremely diverse that no two individuals could have exactly the same measurements. Bertillon recommended routine taking of eleven measurements of the human anatomy. These included height, reach, width of head, and length of the left foot (see Figure 1–2).

For two decades, this system was considered the most accurate method of identification. But in the first years of the new century, police began to appreciate and accept a system of identification based on the classification of finger ridge patterns known as *fingerprints*. Today, the fingerprint is the pillar of modern criminal identification.

Early Use of Fingerprints

Evidence exists that the Chinese used the fingerprint to sign legal documents as far back as three thousand years ago. However, whether this practice was performed for ceremonial custom or as a means of personal identity remains a point of conjecture lost to history. In any case, the examples of fingerprinting in ancient history are ambiguous, and the few that exist did not contribute to the development of fingerprinting techniques as we know them today.

Several years before Bertillon began work on his system, William Herschel, an English civil servant stationed in India, started the practice of requiring Indian citizens to sign contracts with the imprint of their right hand, which was pressed against a stamp pad for the purpose. The motives for Herschel's requirement remain unclear; he may have envisioned fingerprinting as a means of personal identification or just as a form of the Hindu custom that a trace of bodily contact was more binding than a signature on a contract. In any case, he did not publish anything about his activities until after a Scottish physician, Henry Fauld, working in a hospital in Japan, published his views on the potential application of fingerprinting to personal identification.

In 1880, Fauld suggested that skin ridge patterns could be important for the identification of criminals. He told about a thief who left his fingerprint on a whitewashed wall, and how in comparing these prints with those of a suspect, he found that they were quite different. A few days later another suspect was found whose fingerprints compared with those on the wall. When confronted with this evidence, the individual confessed to the crime.

Fauld was convinced that fingerprints furnished infallible proof of identification. He even offered to set up, at his own expense, a fingerprint bureau at Scotland Yard to test the practicality of the method. But his offer was rejected in favor of the Bertillon system. This decision was reversed less than two decades later.

Early Classification of Fingerprints

The extensive research into fingerprinting conducted by another Englishman, Francis Galton, provided the needed impetus that made police agencies aware of its potential application. In 1892, Galton published his classic textbook *Finger Prints*, the first book of its kind on the subject. In his book, he discussed the anatomy of fingerprints and suggested methods for recording them. Galton also proposed assigning fingerprints to three pattern types—loops, arches, and whorls. Most important, the book demonstrated that no two prints were identical and that an individual's prints remained unchanged from year to year. At Galton's insistence, the British government adopted fingerprinting as a supplement to the Bertillon system.

The next step in the development of fingerprint technology was the creation of classification systems capable of filing thousands of prints in a logical and searchable sequence. Dr. Juan Vucetich, an Argentinian police officer fascinated by Galton's work, devised a workable concept in 1891. His classification system has been refined over the years and is still widely used today in most Spanish-speaking countries. In 1897, another classification system was proposed by an Englishman, Sir Edward Richard Henry. Four years later, Henry's system was adopted by Scotland

portrait parlé
A verbal description of a perpetrator's physical characteristics and dress provided by an eyewitness

anthropometry
A system of identification of individuals by measurement of parts of the body, developed by Alphonse Bertillon

Yard. Today, most English-speaking countries, including the United States, use some version of Henry's classification system to file fingerprints.

Adoption of Fingerprinting

Early in the 20th century, Bertillon's measurement system began to fall into disfavor. Its results were highly susceptible to error, particularly when the measurements were taken by people who were not thoroughly trained. The method was dealt its most severe and notable setback in 1903 when a convict, Will West, arrived at Fort Leavenworth prison. A routine check of the prison files startlingly revealed that a William West, already in the prison, could not be distinguished from the new prisoner by body measurements or even by photographs. In fact, the two men looked just like twins, and their measurements were practically the same. Subsequently, fingerprints of the prisoners clearly distinguished them.

In the United States, the first systematic and official use of fingerprints for personal identification was adopted by the New York City Civil Service Commission in 1901. The method was used for certifying all civil service applications. Several American police officials received instruction in fingerprint identification at the 1904 World's Fair in St. Louis from representatives of Scotland Yard. After the fair and the Will West incident, fingerprinting began to be used in earnest in all major cities of the United States. In 1924, the fingerprint records of the Bureau of Investigation and Leavenworth were merged to form the nucleus of the identification records of the new Federal Bureau of Investigation. The FBI has the largest collection of fingerprints in the world. By the beginning of World War I, England and practically all of Europe had adopted fingerprinting as their primary method of identifying criminals.

In 1999, the admissibility of fingerprint evidence was challenged in the case of *United States* v. *Byron C. Mitchell* in the Eastern District of Pennsylvania. The defendant's attorneys argued that fingerprints could not be proven unique under the guidelines cited in *Daubert* (see pages 16–17). Government experts vigorously disputed this claim. After a four-and-a-half-day *Daubert* hearing, the judge upheld the admissibility of fingerprints as scientific evidence and ruled that (1) human friction ridges are unique and permanent and (2) human friction ridge skin arrangements are unique and permanent.

Fundamental Principles of Fingerprints

First Principle: A Fingerprint Is an Individual Characteristic; No Two Fingers Have Yet Been Found to Possess Identical Ridge Characteristics

The acceptance of fingerprint evidence by the courts has always been predicated on the assumption that no two individuals have identical fingerprints. Early fingerprint experts consistently referred to Galton's calculation, showing the possible existence of 64 billion different fingerprints, to support this contention. Later, researchers questioned the validity of Galton's figures and attempted to devise mathematical models to better approximate this value. However, no matter what mathematical model one refers to, the conclusions are always the same: the probability for the existence of two identical fingerprint patterns in the world's population is extremely small.

Not only is this principle supported by theoretical calculations, but just as important, it is verified by the millions of individuals who have had their prints classified during the past 110 years— no two have ever been found to be identical. The FBI has nearly 50 million fingerprint records in its computer database and has yet to find an identical image belonging to two different people.

RIDGE CHARACTERISTICS The individuality of a fingerprint is not determined by its general shape or pattern but by a careful study of its **ridge characteristics** (also known as **minutiae**). The identity, number, and relative location of characteristics such as those illustrated in Figure 16–1 impart individuality to a fingerprint. If two prints are to match, they must reveal characteristics that not only are identical but have the same relative location to one another in a print. In a judicial proceeding, a point-by-point comparison must be demonstrated by the expert, using charts similar to the one shown in Figure 16–2, in order to prove the identity of an individual.

If an expert were asked to compare the characteristics of the complete fingerprint, no difficulty would be encountered in completing such an assignment; the average fingerprint has as

ridge characteristics (minutiae)

Ridge endings, bifurcations, enclosures, and other ridge details, which must match in two fingerprints in order for their common origin to be established

FIGURE 16–1

Fingerprint ridge characteristics.
Courtesy Sirchie Fingerprint Laboratories, Youngsville, N.C., www.sirchie.com

1. *Bifurcation*	5. *Bifurcation*	9. *Ridge ending*
2. *Ridge ending*	6. *Bifurcation*	10. *Short ridge*
3. *Enclosure*	7. *Bifurcation*	11. *Bifurcation*
4. *Ridge ending*	8. *Ridge ending*	12. *Ridge ending*

FIGURE 16–2

A fingerprint exhibit illustrating the matching ridge characteristics between the crime-scene print and an inked impression of one of the suspect's fingers.

many as 150 individual ridge characteristics. However, most prints recovered at crime scenes are partial impressions, showing only a segment of the entire print. Under these circumstances, the expert can compare only a small number of ridge characteristics from the recovered print to a known recorded print.

RIDGE COMPARISONS   For years, experts have debated how many ridge comparisons are necessary to identify two fingerprints as the same. Numbers that range from 8 to 16 have been suggested as being sufficient to meet the criteria of individuality. However, the difficulty in establishing such a minimum is that no comprehensive statistical study has ever been undertaken to determine the frequency of occurrence of different ridge characteristics and their relative locations. Until such a study is undertaken and completed, no meaningful guidelines can be established for defining the uniqueness of a fingerprint.

In 1973, the International Association for Identification, after a three-year study of this question, concluded that "no valid basis exists for requiring a predetermined minimum number of friction ridge characteristics which must be present in two impressions in order to establish positive identification." Hence, the final determination must be based on the experience and knowledge of the expert, with the understanding that others may profess honest differences of opinion on the uniqueness of a fingerprint if the question of minimal number of ridge characteristics exists. In 1995, members of the international fingerprint community at a conference in Israel issued the Ne'urim Declaration, which supported the 1973 International Association for Identification resolution.

Second Principle: A Fingerprint Remains Unchanged During an Individual's Lifetime

Fingerprints are a reproduction of friction skin ridges found on the palm side of the fingers and thumbs. Similar friction skin can also be found on the surface of the palms and soles of the feet. Apparently, these skin surfaces have been designed by nature to provide our bodies with a firmer grasp and a resistance to slippage. A visual inspection of friction skin reveals a series of lines corresponding to hills (ridges) and valleys (grooves). The shape and form of the skin ridges are what one sees as the black lines of an inked fingerprint impression.

STRUCTURE OF THE SKIN   Skin is composed of layers of cells. Those nearest the surface make up the outer portion of the skin known as the *epidermis*, and the inner skin is known as the *dermis*. A cross section of skin (see Figure 16–3) reveals a boundary of cells separating the epidermis and dermis. The shape of this boundary, made up of *dermal papillae*, determines the form and pattern of the ridges on the surface of the skin. Once the dermal papillae develop in the human fetus, the ridge patterns remain unchanged throughout life except to enlarge during growth.

Each skin ridge is populated by a single row of pores that are the openings for ducts leading from the sweat glands. Through these pores, perspiration is discharged and deposited on the surface of the skin. Once the finger touches a surface, perspiration, along with oils that may have been picked up by touching the hairy portions of the body, is transferred onto that surface, thereby leaving an impression of the finger's ridge pattern (a fingerprint). Prints deposited in this manner are invisible to the eye and are commonly referred to as **latent fingerprints**.

CHANGING FINGERPRINTS   Although it is impossible to change one's fingerprints, there has been no lack of effort on the part of some criminals to obscure them. If an injury reaches deeply

latent fingerprint
A fingerprint made by the deposit of oils and/or perspiration; it is invisible to the naked eye

Ridge island
Sweat pores
Epidermis
Papillae
Dermis
Duct of sweat gland
Sweat gland
Nerves of touch

FIGURE 16–3
Cross-section of human skin.

FIGURE 16–4

The right index finger impression of John Dillinger, before scarification on the left and afterward on the right. Comparison is proved by the 14 matching ridge characteristics.
Courtesy Institute of Applied Science, Youngsville, N.C.

enough into the skin and damages the dermal papillae, a permanent scar will form. However, for this to happen, such a wound would have to penetrate 1 to 2 millimeters beneath the skin's surface. Indeed, efforts at intentionally scarring the skin can only be self-defeating, for it would be totally impossible to obliterate all of the ridge characteristics on the hand, and the presence of permanent scars merely provides new characteristics for identification.

Perhaps the most publicized attempt at obliteration was that of the notorious gangster John Dillinger, who tried to destroy his own fingerprints by applying a corrosive acid to them. Prints taken at the morgue after he was shot to death, compared with fingerprints recorded at the time of a previous arrest, proved that his efforts had been fruitless (see Figure 16–4).

Third Principle: Fingerprints Have General Ridge Patterns That Permit Them to Be Systematically Classified

All fingerprints are divided into three classes on the basis of their general pattern: **loops**, **whorls**, and **arches**. Sixty to 65 percent of the population have loops, 30 to 35 percent have whorls, and about 5 percent have arches. These three classes form the basis for all ten-finger classification systems presently in use.

loop
A class of fingerprints characterized by ridge lines that enter from one side of the pattern and curve around to exit from the same side of the pattern

LOOPS   A typical loop pattern is illustrated in Figure 16–5. A loop must have one or more ridges entering from one side of the print, recurving, and exiting from the same side. If the loop opens toward the little finger, it is called an *ulnar loop*; if it opens toward the thumb, it is a *radial loop*. The pattern area of the loop is surrounded by two diverging ridges known as *type lines*. The ridge point at or nearest the type-line divergence and located at or directly in front of the point of divergence is known as the *delta*. To many, a fingerprint delta resembles the silt formation that builds up as a river flows into the entrance of a lake—hence, the analogy to the geological formation known as a delta. All loops must have one delta. The *core*, as the name suggests, is the approximate center of the pattern.

whorl
A class of fingerprints that includes ridge patterns that are generally rounded or circular in shape and have two deltas

WHORLS   Whorls are actually divided into four distinct groups, as shown in Figure 16–6: plain, central pocket loop, double loop, and accidental. All whorl patterns must have type lines and at least two deltas. A plain whorl and a central pocket loop have at least one ridge that makes a complete circuit. This ridge may be in the form of a spiral, oval, or any variant of a circle. If an imaginary line drawn between the two deltas contained within these two patterns touches any one of the spiral ridges, the pattern is a plain whorl. If no such ridge is touched, the pattern is a central pocket loop.

arch
A class of fingerprints characterized by ridge lines that enter the print from one side and flow out the other side

ARCHES   Arches, the least common of the three general patterns, are subdivided into two distinct groups: plain arches and tented arches, as shown in Figure 16–7. The plain arch is the simplest of all fingerprint patterns; it is formed by ridges entering from one side of the print and

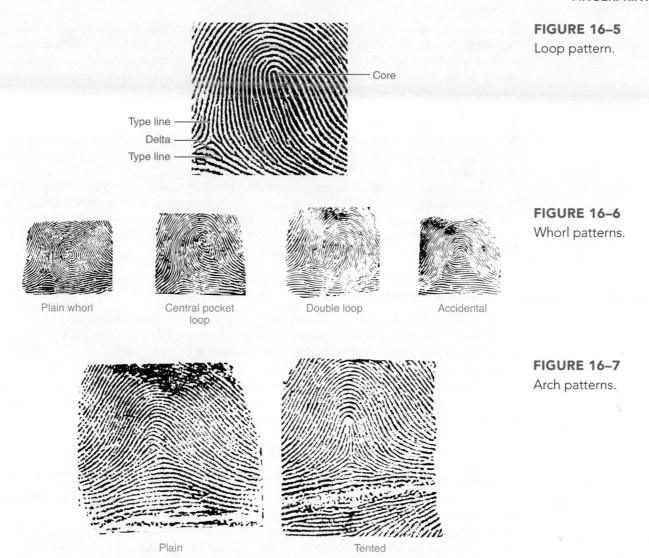

FIGURE 16–5
Loop pattern.

FIGURE 16–6
Whorl patterns.

FIGURE 16–7
Arch patterns.

exiting on the opposite side. Generally, these ridges tend to rise in the center of the pattern, forming a wavelike pattern. The tented arch is similar to the plain arch except that instead of rising smoothly at the center, there is a sharp upthrust or spike, or the ridges meet at an angle that is less than 90 degrees.[1] Arches do not have type lines, deltas, or cores.

OTHER PATTERNS As the name implies, the double loop is made up of two loops combined into one fingerprint. Any whorl classified as an accidental either contains two or more patterns (not including the plain arch) or is a pattern not covered by other categories. Hence, an accidental may consist of a combination loop and plain whorl or loop and tented arch.

With a knowledge of basic fingerprint pattern classes, we can now begin to develop an appreciation for fingerprint classification systems. However, the subject is far more complex than can be described in a textbook of this nature. The student seeking a more detailed treatment of the subject would do well to consult the references cited at the end of the chapter.

Classification of Fingerprints

The original Henry system, as it was adopted by Scotland Yard in 1901, converted ridge patterns on all ten fingers into a series of letters and numbers arranged in the form of a fraction. However, the system as it was originally designed could accommodate files of up to only 100,000 sets of

---

[1] A tented arch is also any pattern that resembles a loop but lacks one of the essential requirements for classification as a loop.

prints; thus, as collections grew in size, it became necessary to expand the capacity of the classification system. In the United States, the FBI, faced with the problem of filing ever-increasing numbers of prints, expanded its classification capacity by modifying and extending the original Henry system. These modifications are collectively known as the *FBI system* and are used by most agencies in the United States today.

The Primary Classification

Although we will not discuss all of the different divisions of the FBI system, a description of just one part, the primary classification, will provide an interesting insight into the process of fingerprint classification.

The primary classification is part of the original Henry system and provides the first classification step in the FBI system. Using this classification alone, all of the fingerprint cards in the world could be divided into 1,024 groups. The first step in obtaining the primary classification is to pair up fingers, placing one finger in the numerator of a fraction, the other in the denominator. The fingers are paired in the following sequence:

$$\frac{\text{R. Index}}{\text{R. Thumb}} \quad \frac{\text{R. Ring}}{\text{R. Middle}} \quad \frac{\text{L. Thumb}}{\text{R. Little}} \quad \frac{\text{L. Middle}}{\text{L. Index}} \quad \frac{\text{L. Little}}{\text{L. Ring}}$$

The presence or absence of the whorl pattern is the basis for determination of the primary classification. If a whorl pattern is found on any finger of the first pair, it is assigned a value of 16; on the second pair, a value of 8; on the third pair, a value of 4; on the fourth pair, a value of 2; and on the last pair, a value of 1. Any finger with an arch or loop pattern is assigned a value of 0.

After values for all ten fingers are obtained in this manner, they are totaled, and 1 is added to both the numerator and denominator. The fraction thus obtained is the primary classification. For example, if the right index and right middle fingers are whorls and all the others are loops, the primary classification is

$$\frac{16 + 0 + 0 + 0 + 0 + 1}{0 + 8 + 0 + 0 + 0 + 1} = \frac{17}{8}$$

Approximately 25 percent of the population falls into the 1/1 category; that is, all their fingers have either loops or arches.

A fingerprint classification system cannot in itself unequivocally identify an individual; it merely provides the fingerprint examiner with a number of candidates, all of whom have an indistinguishable set of prints in the system's file. The identification must always be made by a final visual comparison of the suspect print's and file print's ridge characteristics; only these features can impart individuality to a fingerprint. Although ridge patterns impart class characteristics to the print, the type and position of ridge characteristics give it its individual character.

Automated Fingerprint Identification Systems

The Henry system and its subclassifications have proven to be a cumbersome system for storing, retrieving, and searching for fingerprints, particularly as fingerprint collections grow in size. Nevertheless, until the emergence of fingerprint computer technology, this manual approach was the only viable method for the maintenance of fingerprint collections. Since 1970, technological advances have made possible the classification and retrieval of fingerprints by computers. Automated Fingerprint Identification Systems (AFISs) have proliferated throughout the law enforcement community.

In 1999, the FBI initiated full operation of the Integrated Automated Fingerprint Identification System (IAFIS), the largest AFIS in the United States, which links state AFIS computers with the FBI database. This database contains nearly 50 million fingerprint records. However, an AFIS can come in all sizes ranging from the FBI's to independent systems operated by cities, counties, and other agencies of local government (see Figure 16–8). Unfortunately, these local systems often are not linked to the state's AFIS system because of differences in software configurations.

How AFIS Works

The heart of AFIS technology is the ability of a computer to scan and digitally encode fingerprints so that they can be subject to high-speed computer processing. **The AFIS uses automatic scanning devices that convert the image of a fingerprint into digital minutiae that contain data showing ridges at their points of termination (ridge endings) and the branching of ridges into two ridges (bifurcations).** The relative position and orientation of the minutiae are also determined, allowing the computer to store each fingerprint in the form of a digitally recorded geometric pattern.

The computer's search algorithm determines the degree of correlation between the location and relationship of the minutiae for both the search and file prints. In this manner, a computer can make thousands of fingerprint comparisons in a second; for example, a set of ten fingerprints can be searched against a file of 500,000 ten-finger prints (ten-prints) in about eight-tenths of a second. During the search for a match, the computer uses a scoring system that assigns prints to each of the criteria set by an operator. When the search is complete, the computer produces a list of file prints that have the closest correlation to the search prints. All of the selected prints are then examined by a trained fingerprint expert, who makes the final verification of the print's identity. Thus, the AFIS makes no final decisions on the identity of a fingerprint, leaving this function to the eyes of a trained examiner.

The speed and accuracy of ten-print processing by AFIS have made possible the search of single latent crime-scene fingerprints against an entire file's print collection. Before the AFIS, police were usually restricted to comparing crime-scene fingerprints against those of known suspects. The impact of the AFIS on no-suspect cases has been dramatic. Minutes after California's AFIS network received its first assignment, the computer scored a direct hit by identifying an individual who had committed 15 murders, terrorizing the city of Los Angeles. Police estimate that it would have taken a single technician, manually searching the city's 1.7 million print cards,

FIGURE 16–8

An AFIS system designed for use by local law enforcement agencies.
Courtesy AFIX Technologies Inc., Pittsburg, KS 66762, www.afix.net

FIGURE 16–9

A side-by-side comparison of a latent print against a file fingerprint is conducted in seconds, and their similarity rating (SIM) is displayed on the upper-left portion of the screen.
Courtesy Sirchie Fingerprint Laboratories, Youngsville, N.C., www.sirchie.com

67 years to come up with the perpetrator's prints. With the AFIS, the search took approximately 20 minutes. In its first year of operation, San Francisco's AFIS computer conducted 5,514 latent fingerprint searches and achieved 1,001 identifications—a hit rate of 18 percent. This compares to the previous year's average of 8 percent for manual latent-print searches.

As an example of how an AFIS computer operates, one system has been designed to automatically filter out imperfections in a latent print, enhance its image, and create a graphic representation of the fingerprint's ridge endings and bifurcations and their direction. The print is then computer searched against file prints. The image of the latent print and a matching file print are then displayed side by side on a high-resolution video monitor, as shown in Figure 16–9. The matching latent and file prints are then verified and charted by a fingerprint examiner at a video workstation.

The stereotypical image of a booking officer rolling inked fingers onto a standard ten-print card for ultimate transmission to a database has, for the most part, been replaced with digital-capture devices (**livescan**) that eliminate ink and paper. The livescan captures the image on each finger and the palms as they are lightly pressed against a glass platen. These livescan images can then be sent to the AFIS database electronically, so that within minutes the booking agency can enter the fingerprint record into the AFIS database and search the database for previous entries of the same individual. See Figure 16–10.

livescan
An inkless device that captures the digital images of fingerprints and palm prints and electronically transmits the images to an AFIS

FIGURE 16–10
Livescan technology enables law enforcement to print and compare a subject's fingerprints rapidly, without inking the fingerprints.
Courtesy MorphoTrak, Inc.

Considerations with AFIS

AFIS has fundamentally changed the way criminal investigators operate, allowing them to spend less time developing suspect lists and more time investigating the suspects generated by the computer. However, investigators must be cautioned against overreliance on a computer. Sometimes a latent print does not make a hit because of the poor quality of the file print. To avoid these potential problems, investigators must still print all known suspects in a case and manually search these prints against the crime-scene prints.

AFIS computers are available from several different suppliers. Each system scans fingerprint images and detects and records information about minutiae (ridge endings and bifurcations); however, they do not all incorporate exactly the same features, coordinate systems, or units of measure to record fingerprint information. These software incompatibilities often mean that, although state systems can communicate with the FBI's IAFIS, they may not communicate with each other directly. Likewise, local and state systems frequently cannot share information with each other. Many of these technical problems will be resolved as more agencies follow transmission standards developed by the National Institute of Standards and Technology and the FBI.

forensic brief

The Night Stalker

Richard Ramirez committed his first murder in June 1984. His victim was a 79-year-old woman who was stabbed repeatedly and sexually assaulted and then had her throat slashed. It would be eight months before Ramirez murdered again. In the spring, Ramirez began a murderous rampage that resulted in 13 additional killings and 5 rapes.

His modus operandi was to enter a home through an open window, shoot the male residents, and savagely rape his female victims. He scribed a pentagram on the wall of one of his victims and the words *Jack the Knife*, and was reported by another to force her to "swear to Satan" during the assault. His identity still unknown, the news media dubbed him the "Night Stalker." As the body count continued to rise, public hysteria and a media frenzy prevailed.

The break in the case came when the license plate of what seemed to be a suspicious car related to a sighting of the Night Stalker was reported to the police. The police determined that the car had been stolen and eventually located it, abandoned in a parking lot. After processing the car for prints, police found one usable partial fingerprint. This fingerprint was entered into the Los Angeles Police Department's brand-new AFIS computerized fingerprint system.

The Night Stalker was identified as Richard Ramirez, who had been fingerprinted following a traffic violation some years before. Police searching the home of one of his friends found the gun used

Richard Ramirez, the Night Stalker.

to commit the murders, and jewelry belonging to his victims was found in the possession of Ramirez's sister. Ramirez was convicted of murder and sentenced to death in 1989. He remains on death row.

forensics at work

The Mayfield Affair

On March 11, 2004, a series of ten explosions at four sites occurred on commuter trains traveling to or near the Atocha train station in Madrid, Spain. The death toll from these explosions was nearly 200, with more than 1,500 injured. On the day of the attack, a plastic bag was found in a van previously reported as stolen. The bag contained copper detonators like those used on the train bombs. On March 17, the FBI received electronic images of latent fingerprints that were recovered from the plastic bag. A search was initiated on the FBI's IAFIS. A senior fingerprint examiner encoded seven minutiae points from the high-resolution image of one suspect latent fingerprint and initiated an IAFIS search matching the print to Brandon Mayfield.

Mayfield's prints were in the FBI's central database because they had been taken when he joined the military, where he served for eight years before being honorably discharged as a second lieutenant. After a visual comparison of the suspect and file prints, the examiner concluded a "100 percent match." The identification was verified by a retired FBI fingerprint examiner with more than 30 years of experience who was under contract with the bureau, as well as by a court-appointed independent fingerprint examiner (see Figure 16–11).

Mayfield, age 37, a Muslim convert, was arrested on May 6 on a material witness warrant. The U.S. Attorney's Office came up with a list of Mayfield's potential ties to Muslim terrorists, which they included in the affidavit they presented to the federal judge who ordered his arrest and detention. The document also said that, although no travel records were found for Mayfield, "It is believed that Mayfield may have traveled under a false or fictitious name." On May 24, after the Spaniards had linked the print from the plastic bag to an Algerian national, Mayfield's case was thrown out. The FBI issued him a highly unusual official apology, and his ordeal became a stunning embarrassment to the U.S. government.

As part of its corrective-action process, the FBI formed an international committee of distinguished latent-print examiners and forensic experts. Their task was to review the analysis performed by the FBI Laboratory and make recommendations that would help prevent this type of error in the future. The committee came up with some startling findings and observations (available at www.fbi.gov/hq/lab/fsc/backissu/jan2005/special_report/2005_special_report.htm).

The committee members agreed that "the quality of the images that were used to make the erroneous identification was not a factor. . . . [T]he identification is filled with dissimilarities that were easily observed when a detailed analysis of the latent print was conducted."

They further stated,

the power of the IAFIS match, coupled with the inherent pressure of working an extremely high-profile case, was thought to have influenced the initial examiner's judgment and subsequent examination. . . . The apparent mindset of the initial examiner after reviewing the results of the IAFIS search was that a match did exist; therefore, it would be reasonable to assume that the other characteristics must match as well. In the absence of a detailed analysis of the print, it can be a short distance from finding only seven characteristics sufficient for plotting, prior to the automated search, to the position of 12 or 13 matching characteristics once the mind-set of identification has become dominant. . . .

Once the mind-set occurred with the initial examiner, the subsequent examinations were tainted. . . . because of the inherent pressure of such a high-profile case, the power of an IAFIS match in conjunction with the similarities in the candidate's print, and the knowledge of the previous examiners' conclusions (especially since the initial examiner was a highly respected supervisor with many years of experience), it was concluded that subsequent examinations were incomplete and inaccurate. To disagree was not an expected response. . . . when the individualization had been made by the examiner, it

Methods of Detecting Fingerprints

visible print
A fingerprint made when the finger deposits a visible material such as ink, dirt, or blood onto a surface

plastic print
A fingerprint impressed in a soft surface

Through common usage, the term *latent fingerprint* has come to be associated with any fingerprint discovered at a crime scene. Sometimes, however, prints found at the scene of a crime are quite visible to the eye, and the word *latent* is a misnomer. Actually, there are three kinds of crime-scene prints: **visible prints** are made by fingers touching a surface after the ridges have been in contact with a colored material such as blood, paint, grease, or ink; **plastic prints** are ridge impressions left on a soft material such as putty, wax, soap, or dust; and *latent* or *invisible prints* are impressions caused by the transfer of body perspiration or oils present on finger ridges to the surface of an object.

(a)

(b)

FIGURE 16–11

(a) Questioned print recovered in connection with the Madrid bombing investigation. (b) File print of Brandon Mayfield.

(a) Courtesy Sirchie Fingerprint Laboratories, Youngsville, NC, www.sirchie.com, U.S. Department of Justice

became increasingly difficult for others in the agency to disagree.

The committee went on to make a number of quality-assurance recommendations to help avoid a recurrence of this type of error.

The Mayfield incident has also been the subject of an investigation by the Office of the Inspector General (OIG), U.S. Department of Justice (www.usdoj.gov/oig/special/s0601/final.pdf). The OIG investigation concluded that a "series of systemic issues" in the FBI Laboratory contributed to the Mayfield misidentification. The report noted that the FBI has made significant procedural modifications to help prevent similar errors in the future and strongly supported the FBI's

decision to undertake research to develop more objective standards for fingerprint identification.

An internal review of the FBI Latent Print Unit conducted in the aftermath of the Mayfield affair has resulted in the implementation of revisions in training, as well as in the decision-making process when determining the comparative value of a latent print, along with more stringent verification policies and procedures (M. A. Smrz et al., *Journal of Forensic Identification* 56 [2006]: 402–34).

The impact of the Mayfield affair on fingerprint technology as currently practiced and the weight courts will assign to fingerprint matches remain open questions.

Locating Fingerprints

Locating visible or plastic prints at the crime scene normally presents little problem to the investigator because these prints are usually distinct and visible to the eye. Locating latent or invisible prints is obviously much more difficult and requires the use of techniques to make the print visible. Although the investigator can choose from several methods for visualizing a latent print, the choice depends on the type of surface being examined.

Hard and nonabsorbent surfaces (such as glass, mirror, tile, and painted wood) require different development procedures from surfaces that are soft and porous (such as papers, cardboard, and cloth). Prints on the former are preferably developed by the application of a powder or treatment with superglue, whereas prints on the latter generally require treatment with one or more chemicals.

Sometimes the most difficult aspect of fingerprint examination is the location of prints. Recent advances in fingerprint technology have led to the development of an ultraviolet image converter for the purpose of detecting latent fingerprints. This device, called the Reflected Ultraviolet Imaging System (RUVIS), can locate prints on most nonabsorbent surfaces without the aid of chemical or powder treatments (see Figure 16–12).

RUVIS detects the print in its natural state by aiming UV light at the surface suspected of containing prints. When the UV light strikes the fingerprint, the light is reflected back to the viewer, differentiating the print from its background surface. The transmitted UV light is then converted into visible light by an image intensifier. Once the print is located in this manner, the crime-scene investigator can develop it in the most appropriate fashion. See Figure 16–13.

FIGURE 16–12

A Reflected Ultraviolet Imaging System allows an investigator to directly view surfaces for the presence of untreated latent fingerprints.
Courtesy Sirchie Fingerprint Laboratories, Youngsville, N.C., www.sirchie.com

FIGURE 16–13

Using a Reflected Ultraviolet Imaging System with the aid of a UV lamp to search for latent fingerprints.
Courtesy Sirchie Fingerprint Laboratories, Youngsville, N.C., www.sirchie.com

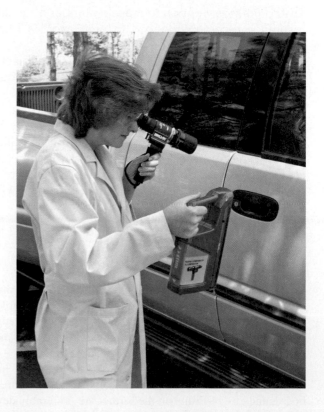

Developing Latent Prints

FINGERPRINT POWDERS   Fingerprint powders are commercially available in a variety of compositions and colors. These powders, when applied lightly to a nonabsorbent surface with a camel's-hair or fiberglass brush, readily adhere to perspiration residues and/or deposits of body oils left on the surface (see Figure 16–14).

Experienced examiners find that gray and black powders are adequate for most latent-print work; the examiner selects the powder that affords the best color contrast with the surface being dusted. Hence, the gray powder, composed of an aluminum dust, is used on dark-colored surfaces. It is also applied to mirrors and metal surfaces that are polished to a mirrorlike finish because these surfaces photograph as black. The black powder, composed basically of black carbon or charcoal, is applied to white or light-colored surfaces.

Other types of powders are available for developing latent prints. A magnetic-sensitive powder can be spread over a surface with a magnet in the form of a Magna Brush. A Magna Brush does not have any bristles to come in contact with the surface, so there is less chance that the print will be destroyed or damaged. The magnetic-sensitive powder comes in black and gray and is especially useful on such items as finished leather and rough plastics, where the minute texture of the surface tends to hold particles of ordinary powder. Fluorescent powders are also used to develop latent fingerprints. These powders fluoresce under ultraviolet light. By photographing the fluorescence pattern of the developing print under UV light, it is possible to avoid having the color of the surface obscure the print.

IODINE FUMING   Of the several chemical methods used for visualizing latent prints, **iodine fuming** is the oldest. Iodine is a solid crystal that, when heated, is transformed into a vapor without passing through a liquid phase; such a transformation is called **sublimation**. Most often, the suspect material is placed in an enclosed cabinet along with iodine crystals (see Figure 16–15). As the crystals are heated, the resultant vapors fill the chamber and combine with constituents of the latent print to make it visible. The reasons why latent prints are visualized by iodine vapors are not yet fully understood. Many believe that the iodine fumes combine with fatty oils; however, there is also convincing evidence that the iodine may actually interact with residual water left on a print from perspiration.[2]

Unfortunately, iodine prints are not permanent and begin to fade once the fuming process is stopped. Therefore, the examiner must photograph the prints immediately on development in order to retain a permanent record. Also, iodine-developed prints can be fixed with a 1 percent solution of starch in water, applied by spraying. The print turns blue and lasts for several weeks to several months.

iodine fuming
A technique for visualizing latent fingerprints by exposing them to iodine vapors

sublimation
A physical change from the solid directly into the gaseous state

FIGURE 16–14

Developing a latent fingerprint on a surface by applying a fingerprint powder with a fiberglass brush.
Courtesy Sirchie Fingerprint Laboratories, Youngsville, N.C., www.sirchie.com

[2] J. Almag, Y. Sasson, and A. Anati, "Chemical Reagents for the Development of Latent Fingerprints II: Controlled Addition of Water Vapor to Iodine Fumes—A Solution to the Aging Problem," *Journal of Forensic Sciences* 24 (1979): 431.

FIGURE 16-15

A heated fuming cabinet.
Courtesy Sirchie Fingerprint Laboratories,
Youngsville, N.C., www.sirchie.com

ninhydrin

A chemical reagent used to develop latent fingerprints on porous materials by reacting with amino acids in perspiration

NINHYDRIN   Another chemical used for visualizing latent prints is **ninhydrin**. The development of latent prints with ninhydrin depends on its chemical reaction to form a purple-blue color with amino acids present in trace amounts in perspiration. Ninhydrin (triketohydrindene hydrate) is commonly sprayed onto the porous surface from an aerosol can. A solution is prepared by mixing the ninhydrin powder with a suitable solvent, such as acetone or ethyl alcohol; a 0.6 percent solution appears to be effective for most applications.

Generally, prints begin to appear within an hour or two after ninhydrin application; however, weaker prints may be visualized after 24 to 48 hours. The development can be hastened if the treated specimen is heated in an oven or on a hot plate at a temperature of 80–100°C. The ninhydrin method has developed latent prints on paper as old as 15 years.

Physical Developer

A silver nitrate–based reagent formulated to develop latent fingerprints on porous surfaces

PHYSICAL DEVELOPER   **Physical Developer** is a third chemical mixture used for visualizing latent prints. Physical Developer is a silver nitrate–based liquid reagent. The procedure for preparing and using Physical Developer is described in Appendix IV. This method has gained wide acceptance by fingerprint examiners, who have found it effective for visualizing latent prints that remain undetected by the previously described methods. Also, this technique is effective for developing latent fingerprints on porous articles that may have been wet at one time.

For most fingerprint examiners, the chemical method of choice is ninhydrin. Its extreme sensitivity and ease of application have all but eliminated the use of iodine for latent-print visualization. However, when ninhydrin fails, development with Physical Developer may provide identifiable results. Application of Physical Developer washes away any traces of proteins from an object's surface; **hence, if one wishes to use all of the previously mentioned chemical development methods on the same surface, it is necessary to first fume with iodine, follow this treatment with ninhydrin, and then apply Physical Developer to the object.**

superglue fuming

A technique for visualizing latent fingerprints on nonporous surfaces by exposing them to cyanoacrylate vapors; named for the commercial product Super Glue.

SUPERGLUE FUMING   In the past, chemical treatment for fingerprint development was reserved for porous surfaces such as paper and cardboard. However, since 1982, a chemical technique known as **superglue fuming** has gained wide popularity for developing latent prints on nonporous surfaces such as metals, electrical tape, leather, and plastic bags.[3] See Figure 16–16.

---

[3] F. G. Kendall and B. W. Rehn, "Rapid Method of Superglue Fuming Application for the Development of Latent Fingerprints," *Journal of Forensic Sciences* 28 (1983): 777.

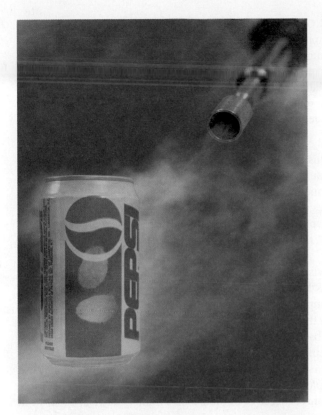

FIGURE 16–16

Superglue fuming a nonporous metallic surface in the search for latent fingerprints.

Courtesy Sirchie Fingerprint Laboratories, Youngsville, N.C., www.sirchie.com

(a)

(b)

FIGURE 16–17

(a) A handheld fuming wand uses disposable cartridges containing cyanoacrylate. The wand is used to develop prints at the crime scene and (b) in the laboratory.

Courtesy Sirchie Fingerprint Laboratories, Youngsville, N.C., www.sirchie.com

Superglue is approximately 98–99 percent cyanoacrylate ester, a chemical that interacts with and visualizes a latent fingerprint. Cyanoacrylate ester fumes can be created when superglue is placed on absorbent cotton treated with sodium hydroxide. The fumes can also be created by heating the glue. The fumes and the evidential object are contained within an enclosed chamber for up to six hours. Development occurs when fumes from the glue adhere to the latent print, usually producing a white-appearing latent print. Interestingly, small enclosed areas, such as the interior of an automobile, have been successfully processed for latent prints with fumes from superglue.

Through the use of a small handheld wand, cyanoacrylate fuming is now easily done at a crime scene or in a laboratory setting. The wand heats a small cartridge containing cyanoacrylate. Once heated, the cyanoacrylate vaporizes, allowing the operator to direct the fumes onto the suspect area (see Figure 16–17).

OTHER TECHNIQUES FOR VISUALIZATION   One of the most exciting and dynamic areas of research in forensic science today is the application of chemical techniques to the visualization of latent fingerprints. Changes are occurring rapidly as researchers uncover a variety of processes applicable to the visualization of latent fingerprints. Interestingly, for many years progress in this field was minimal, and fingerprint specialists traditionally relied on three chemical techniques—iodine, ninhydrin, and silver nitrate—to reveal a hidden fingerprint. Then superglue fuming extended chemical development to prints deposited on nonporous surfaces.

Fluorescence   The first hint of things to come was the discovery that latent fingerprints could be visualized by exposure to laser light. This laser method took advantage of the fact that perspiration contains a variety of components that **fluoresce** when illuminated by laser light. Fluorescence occurs when a substance absorbs light and reemits the light in wavelengths longer than the illuminating source. Importantly, substances that emit light or fluoresce are more readily seen with either the naked eye or through photography than are non-light-emitting materials. The high sensitivity of fluorescence serves as the underlying principle of many of the new chemical techniques used to visualize latent fingerprints.

The earliest use of fluorescence to visualize fingerprints came with the direct illumination of a fingerprint with argon–ion lasers. This laser type was chosen because its blue-green light output induced some of the perspiration components of a fingerprint to fluoresce (see Figure 16–18). The major drawback of this approach is that the perspiration components of a fingerprint are often present in quantities too minute to observe even with the aid of fluorescence. The fingerprint examiner, wearing safety goggles containing optical filters, visually examines the specimen being exposed to the laser light. The filters absorb the laser light and permit the wavelengths at which latent-print residues fluoresce to pass through to the eyes of the wearer. The filter also protects the operator against eye damage from scattered or reflected laser light. Likewise, latent-print residue producing sufficient fluorescence can be photographed by placing this same filter across the lens of the camera. Examination of specimens and photography of the fluorescing latent prints are carried out in a darkened room.

Chemically Induced Fluorescence   The next advancement in latent-fingerprint development occurred with the discovery that fingerprints could be treated with chemicals that would induce fluorescence when exposed to laser illumination. For example, the application of zinc chloride after ninhydrin treatment or the application of the dye rhodamine 6G after superglue fuming caused fluorescence and increased the sensitivity of detection on exposure to laser illumination. The discovery of numerous chemical developers for visualizing fingerprints through fluorescence quickly followed. This knowledge set the stage for the next advance in latent-fingerprint development—the *alternate light source*.

With the advent of chemically induced fluorescence, lasers were no longer needed to induce fingerprints to fluoresce through their perspiration residues. High-intensity light sources or alternate light sources have proliferated and all but replaced laser lights. See Figure 16–19. High-intensity quartz halogen or xenon-arc light sources can be focused on a suspect area through a

fluoresce
To emit visible light when exposed to light of a shorter wavelength

FIGURE 16–18

Schematic depicting latent-print detection with the aid of a laser. A fingerprint examiner, wearing safety goggles containing optical filters, examines the specimen being exposed to the laser light. The filter absorbs the laser light and permits the wavelengths at which latent-print residues fluoresce to pass through to the eyes of the wearer.
Courtesy Federal Bureau of Investigation, Washington, D.C.

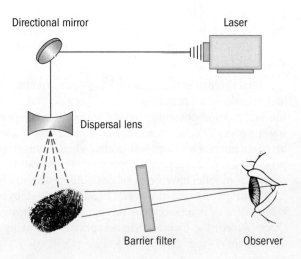

Directional mirror   Laser

Dispersal lens

Barrier filter   Observer

FIGURE 16–19

An alternate light source system incorporating a high-intensity light source.
Courtesy Foster & Freeman Limited, Worcestershire, U.K., www.fosterfreeman.co.uk

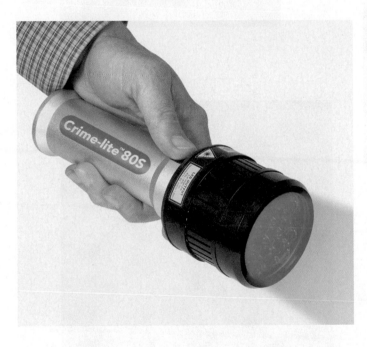

FIGURE 16–20

Lightweight handheld alternate light source that uses an LED light source.
Courtesy Foster & Freeman Limited, Worcestershire, U.K., www.fosterfreeman.co.uk

fiber-optic cable. This light can be passed through several filters, giving the user more flexibility in selecting the wavelength of light to be aimed at the latent print. Alternatively, lightweight, portable alternate light sources that use light-emitting diodes (LEDs) are also commercially available (see Figure 16–20). In most cases, these light sources have proven to be as effective as laser light in developing latent prints, and they are commercially available at costs significantly less than those of laser illuminators. Furthermore, these light sources are portable and can be readily taken to any crime scene.

NEWER CHEMICAL PROCESSES   A large number of chemical treatment processes are available to the fingerprint examiner (see Figure 16–21), and the field is in a constant state of flux. Selection of an appropriate procedure is best left to technicians who have developed their skills through casework experience.

Newer chemical processes include a substitute for ninhydrin called DFO (1,8-diazafluoren-9-one). This chemical visualizes latent prints on porous materials when exposed to an alternate light source. DFO has been shown to develop 2.5 times more latent prints on paper than ninhydrin. A chemical called 1,2-indanedione is also emerging as a potential reagent for the development of latent fingerprints on porous surfaces. 1,2-indanedione gives both good initial color and

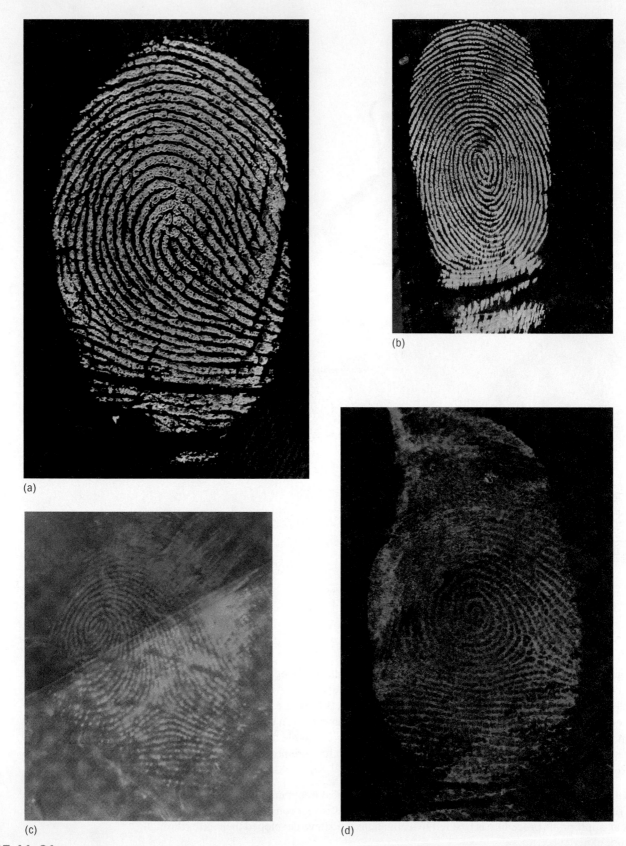

(a)

(b)

(c)

(d)

FIGURE 16–21

(a) Latent fingerprint visualized by cyanoacrylate fuming. (b) Fingerprint treated with cyanoacrylate and rhodamine 6G fluorescent dye. (c) Fingerprint treated with cyanoacrylate and the fluorescent dye combination RAM. (d) A bloody fingerprint detected by laser light after spraying with merbromin and hydrogen peroxide.

Courtesy North Carolina State Bureau of Investigation, Raleigh, N.C.

strong fluorescence when reacted with amino acids derived from prints and thus has the potential to provide in one process what ninhydrin and DFO can do in two different steps.

Dye combinations known as RAM, RAY, and MRM 10, when used in conjunction with superglue fuming, have been effective in visualizing latent fingerprints by fluorescence. A number of chemical formulas useful for latent-print development are listed in Appendix IV.

Studies have demonstrated that common fingerprint-developing agents do not interfere with DNA-testing methods used for characterizing bloodstains.[4] Nonetheless, in cases involving items with material adhering to their surfaces and/or items that will require further laboratory examinations, fingerprint processing should not be performed at the crime scene. Rather, the items should be submitted to the laboratory, where they can be processed for fingerprints in conjunction with other necessary examinations.

Preservation of Developed Prints

Once the latent print has been visualized, it must be permanently preserved for future comparison and possible use in court as evidence. A photograph must be taken before any further attempts at preservation. Any camera equipped with a close-up lens will do; however, many investigators prefer to use a camera specially designed for fingerprint photography. Such a camera comes equipped with a fixed focus to take photographs on a 1:1 scale when the camera's open eye is held exactly flush against the print's surface (see Figure 16–22). In addition, photographs must be taken to provide an overall view of the print's location with respect to other evidential items at the crime scene.

FIGURE 16–22

Camera fitted with an adapter designed to give an approximate 1:1 photograph of a fingerprint.
Courtesy Sirchie Fingerprint Laboratories, Youngsville, N.C., www.sirchie.com

[4] C. Roux et al., "A Further Study to Investigate the Effect of Fingerprint Enhancement Techniques on the DNA Analysis of Bloodstains," *Journal of Forensic Identification* 49 (1999): 357; C. J. Frégeau et al., "Fingerprint Enhancement Revisited and the Effects of Blood Enhancement Chemicals on Subsequent Profiler Plus™ Fluorescent Short Tandem Repeat DNA Analysis of Fresh and Aged Bloody Fingerprints," *Journal of Forensic Sciences* 45 (2000): 354; and P. Grubwieser et al., "Systematic Study on STR Profiling on Blood and Saliva Traces after Visualization of Fingerprints," *Journal of Forensic Sciences* 48 (2003): 733.

FIGURE 16–23

"Lifting" a fingerprint.
Courtesy Sirchie Fingerprint
Laboratories, Youngsville, N.C.,
www.sirchie.com

Once photographs have been secured, one of two procedures is to be followed. If the object is small enough to be transported without destroying the print, it should be preserved in its entirety; the print should be covered with cellophane so it will be protected from damage. On the other hand, prints on large immovable objects that have been developed with a powder can best be preserved by "lifting." The most popular type of lifter is a broad adhesive tape similar to clear adhesive tape. When the powdered surface is covered with the adhesive side of the tape and pulled up, the powder is transferred to the tape. Then the tape is placed on a properly labeled card that provides a good background contrast with the powder.

A variation of this procedure is the use of an adhesive-backed clear plastic sheet attached to a colored cardboard backing. Before it is applied to the print, a celluloid separator is peeled from the plastic sheet to expose the adhesive lifting surface. The tape is then pressed evenly and firmly over the powdered print and pulled up (see Figure 16–23). The sheet containing the adhering powder is now pressed against the cardboard backing to provide a permanent record of the fingerprint.

Digital Imaging for Fingerprint Enhancement

When fingerprints are lifted from a crime scene, they are not usually in perfect condition, making the analysis that much more difficult. Computers have advanced technology in most fields, and fingerprint identification has not been left behind. With the help of digital imaging software, fingerprints can now be enhanced for the most accurate and comprehensive analysis.

Creating Digital Images

digital imaging
A process through which a picture is converted into a series of square electronic dots known as pixels; the picture is manipulated by computer software that changes the numerical value of each pixel

pixel
A square electronic dot that is used to compose a digital image

Digital imaging is the process by which a picture is converted into a digital file. The image produced from this digital file is composed of numerous square electronic dots called **pixels**. Images composed of only black and white elements are referred to as *grayscale images*. Each pixel is assigned a number according to its intensity. The grayscale image is made from the set of numbers to which a pixel may be assigned, ranging from 0 (black) to 255 (white). Once an image is digitally stored, it is manipulated by computer software that changes the numerical value of each pixel, thus altering the image as directed by the user. *Resolution* reveals the degree of detail that can be seen in an image. It is defined in terms of dimensions, such as 800×600 pixels. The larger the numbers, the more closely the digital image resembles the real-world image.

The input of pictures into a digital imaging system is usually done through the use of scanners, digital cameras, and video cameras. After the picture is changed to its digital image, several methods can be employed to enhance the image. The overall brightness of an image, as well as the contrast between the image and the background, can be adjusted through contrast-enhancement methods. One approach used to enhance an image is *spatial filtering*. Several types of filters produce various effects. A low-pass filter is used to eliminate harsh edges by reducing the intensity difference between pixels. A second filter, the high-pass filter, operates by modifying a pixel's numerical value to exaggerate its intensity difference from that of its neighbor. The resulting effect increases the contrast of the edges, thus providing a high contrast between the elements and the background.

Analyzing Digital Images

Frequency analysis, also referred to as *frequency Fourier transform* (FFT), is used to identify periodic or repetitive patterns such as lines or dots that interfere with the interpretation of the image. These patterns are diminished or eliminated to enhance the appearance of the image. Interestingly, the spacings between fingerprint ridges are themselves periodic. Therefore, the contribution of the fingerprint can be identified in FFT mode and then enhanced. Likewise, if ridges from overlapping prints are positioned in different directions, their corresponding frequency information is at different locations in FFT mode. The ridges of one latent print can then be enhanced while the ridges of the other are suppressed.

Color interferences also pose a problem when analyzing an image. For example, a latent fingerprint found on paper currency or a check may be difficult to analyze because of the distracting colored background. With the imaging software, the colored background can simply be removed to make the image stand out (see Figure 16–24). If the image itself is a particular color, such as a ninhydrin-developed print, the color can be isolated and enhanced to distinguish it from the background.

Digital imaging software also provides functions in which portions of the image can be examined individually. With a scaling and resizing tool, the user can select a part of an image and resize it for a closer look. This function operates much like a magnifying glass, helping the examiner view fine details of an image.

An important and useful tool, especially for fingerprint identification, is the compare function. This specialized feature places two images side by side and allows the examiner to chart the common features on both images simultaneously (see Figure 16–25). The zoom function is used in conjunction with the compare tool. As the examiner zooms into a portion of one image, the software automatically zooms into the second image for comparison.

FIGURE 16–24

A fingerprint being enhanced in Adobe Photoshop. In this example, on the left is the original scan of an inked fingerprint on a check. On the right is the same image after using Adobe Photoshop's Channel Mixer to eliminate the green security background.
Courtesy Imaging Forensics, Fountain Valley, Calif., www.imagingforensics.com

Virtual Forensics Lab

Fingerprinting
To perform a virtual fingerprinting lab, go to www.pearsoncustom .com/us/vlm/

Although digital imaging is undoubtedly an effective tool for enhancing and analyzing images, it is only as useful as the images it has to work with. If the details do not exist on the original images, the enhancement procedures are not going to work. The benefits of digital enhancement methods are apparent when weak images are made more distinguishable.

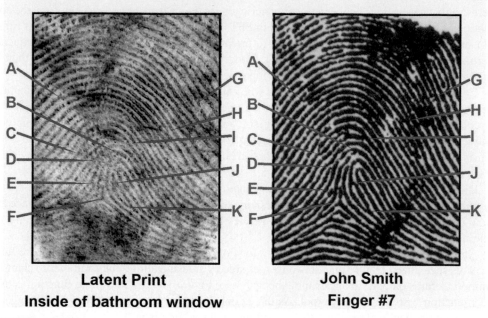

Latent Print
Inside of bathroom window

John Smith
Finger #7

FIGURE 16–25

Current imaging software allows fingerprint analysts to prepare a fingerprint comparison chart. The fingerprint examiner can compare prints side by side and display important features that are consistent between the fingerprints. The time needed to create a display of this sort digitally is about 30 to 60 minutes.
Courtesy Imaging Forensics, Fountain Valley, Calif., www.imagingforensics.com

chapter summary >>>>>>>>>>>>>

Fingerprints are a reproduction of friction skin ridges found on the palm side of the fingers and thumbs. The basic principles underlying the use of fingerprints in criminal investigations are that (1) a fingerprint is an individual characteristic because no two fingers have yet been found to possess identical ridge characteristics, (2) a fingerprint remains unchanged during an individual's lifetime, and (3) fingerprints have general ridge patterns that permit them to be systematically classified. All fingerprints are divided into three classes on the basis of their general pattern: loops, whorls, and arches.

Fingerprint classification systems are based on knowledge of fingerprint pattern classes. The individuality of a fingerprint is not determined by its general shape or pattern, but by a careful study of its ridge characteristics. The expert must demonstrate a point-by-point comparison in order to prove the identity of an individual. AFIS aids this process by converting the image of a fingerprint into digital minutiae that contain data showing ridges at their points of termination (ridge endings) and their branching into two ridges (bifurcations). A single fingerprint can be searched against the FBI AFIS digital database of 50 million fingerprint records in a matter of minutes.

Once the finger touches a surface, perspiration, along with oils that may have been picked up by touching the hairy portions of the body, is transferred onto that surface, thereby leaving an impression of the finger's ridge pattern (a fingerprint). Prints deposited in this manner are invisible to the eye and are commonly referred to as latent or invisible fingerprints.

Visible prints are made when fingers touch a surface after the ridges have been in contact with a colored material such as blood, paint, grease, or ink. Plastic prints are ridge impressions left on a soft material, such as putty, wax, soap, or dust. Latent prints deposited on hard and nonabsorbent surfaces (such as glass, mirror, tile, and painted wood) are preferably developed by the application of a powder; prints on porous surfaces (such as paper and cardboard) generally require treatment with a chemical. Examiners use various chemical methods to visualize latent prints, such as iodine fuming, ninhydrin, and Physical Developer. Superglue fuming develops latent prints on nonporous surfaces, such as metals, electrical tape, leather, and plastic bags. Development occurs when fumes from the glue adhere to the print, usually producing a white latent print.

The high sensitivity of fluorescence serves as the underlying principle of many of the new chemical techniques used to visualize latent fingerprints. Fingerprints are treated with chemicals that induce fluorescence when exposed to a high-intensity light or an alternate light source.

Once the latent print has been visualized, it must be permanently preserved for future comparison and for possible use as court evidence. A photograph must be taken before any further attempts at preservation are made. If the object is small enough to be transported without destroying the print, it should be preserved in its entirety. Prints on large immovable objects that have been developed with a powder are best preserved by "lifting" with a broad adhesive tape.

review questions

1. The first systematic attempt at personal identification was devised and introduced by _____.

2. A system of identification relying on precise body measurements is known as _____.

3. The fingerprint classification system used in most English-speaking countries was devised by _____.

4. True or False: The first systematic and official use of fingerprints for personal identification in the United States was adopted by the New York City Civil Service Commission. _____

5. The individuality of a fingerprint (is, is not) determined by its pattern.

6. A point-by-point comparison of a fingerprint's _____ must be demonstrated in order to prove identity.

7. _____ are a reproduction of friction skin ridges.

8. The form and pattern of skin ridges are determined by the (epidermis, dermal papillae).

9. A permanent scar forms in the skin only when an injury damages the _____.

10. Fingerprints (can, cannot) be changed during a person's lifetime.

11. The three general patterns into which fingerprints are divided are _____, _____, and _____.

12. The most common fingerprint pattern is the _____.

13. Approximately 5 percent of the population has the _____ fingerprint pattern.

14. A loop pattern that opens toward the thumb is known as a(n) (radial, ulnar) loop.

15. The pattern area of the loop is enclosed by two diverging ridges known as _____.

16. The ridge point nearest the type-line divergence is known as the _____.

17. All loops must have (one, two) delta(s).

18. The approximate center of a loop pattern is called the _____.

19. If an imaginary line drawn between the two deltas of a whorl pattern touches any of the spiral ridges, the pattern is classified as a (plain whorl, central pocket loop).

20. The simplest of all fingerprint patterns is the _____.

21. Arches (have, do not have) type lines, deltas, and cores.

22. The presence or absence of the _____ pattern is used as a basis for determining the primary classification in the Henry system.

23. The largest category (25 percent) in the primary classification system is (1/1, 1/2).

24. A fingerprint classification system (can, cannot) unequivocally identify an individual.

25. True or False: Computerized fingerprint search systems match prints by comparing the position of bifurcations and ridge endings. _____

26. A fingerprint left by a person with soiled or stained fingertips is called a(n) _____.

27. _____ fingerprints are impressions left on a soft material.

28. Fingerprint impressions that are not readily visible are called _____.

29. Fingerprints on hard and nonabsorbent surfaces are best developed by the application of a(n) _____.

30. Fingerprints on porous surfaces are best developed with _____ treatment.

31. _____ vapors chemically combine with fatty oils or residual water to visualize a fingerprint.

32. The chemical _____ visualizes fingerprints by its reaction with amino acids.

33. Chemical treatment with _____ visualizes fingerprints on porous articles that may have been wet at one time.

34. True or False: A latent fingerprint is first treated with Physical Developer followed by ninhydrin. _____

35. A chemical technique known as _____ is used to develop latent prints on nonporous surfaces such as metal and plastic.

36. _____ occurs when a substance absorbs light and reemits the light in wavelengths longer than the illuminating source.

37. High-intensity light sources known as _____ are effective in developing latent fingerprints.

38. Once a fingerprint has been visualized, it must be preserved by _____.

39. The image produced from a digital file is composed of numerous square electronic dots called _____.

40. A (high-pass filter, frequency Fourier transform analysis) is used to identify repetitive patterns such as lines or dots that interfere with the interpretation of a digitized fingerprint image.

application and critical thinking

1. Classify each of the prints shown below as loop, whorl, or arch.

2. A description of the types of prints from the fingers of a criminal suspect appears on page 415. Using the FBI system, determine the primary classification of this individual.

3. While searching a murder scene, you find the following items that you believe may contain latent fingerprints. Indicate whether prints on each item should be developed using fingerprint powder or chemicals.

   a. A leather sofa

   b. A mirror

   c. A painted wooden knife handle

   d. Blood-soaked newspapers

   e. A revolver

4. Criminalist Frank Mortimer is using digital imaging to enhance latent fingerprints. Indicate which features of digital imaging he would most likely use for each of the following tasks:

   a. Isolating part of a print and enlarging it for closer examination

   b. Increasing the contrast between a print and the background surface on which it is located

   c. Examining two prints that overlap one another

(1) _____

(2) _____

(3) _____

(4) _____

(5) _____

(6) _____

Finger	Right Hand	Left Hand
Thumb	Whorl	Whorl
Index	Loop	Whorl
Middle	Whorl	Arch
Ring	Whorl	Whorl
Little	Arch	Whorl

further references

Cowger, James E., *Friction Ridge Skin*. Boca Raton, Fla.: Taylor & Francis, 1992.

Komarinski, Peter, *Automated Fingerprint Identification Systems (AFIS)*. Burlington, Mass.: Elsevier Academic Press, 2004.

Lee, H. C., and R. E. Gaensleen, eds., *Advances in Fingerprint Technology*, 2nd ed. Boca Raton, Fla.: Taylor & Francis, 2001.

Lennard, C., M. Margot, C. Stoilovic, and C. Champod, eds., *Fingerprints and Other Ridge Skin Impressions*. Boca Raton, Fla.: Taylor & Francis, 2004.

U.S. Department of Justice, *The Science of Fingerprints*. Washington, D.C.: U.S. Government Printing Office, 1990.

U.S. Department of Justice, *The Fingerprint Sourcebook*, http://www.OJP.usdoj.gov/nij/pubs-sum/225320.htm

The Beltway Snipers

During a three-week period in October 2002, ten people were killed and three others were wounded as two snipers terrorized the region in and around the Baltimore–Washington metropolitan area. The arrest of John Allen Muhammad, 41, and Lee Boyd Malvo, 17, ended the ordeal. The semiautomatic .223-caliber rifle seized from them was ultimately linked by ballistics tests to eight of the ten killings. The car that Muhammad and Malvo were driving had been specially configured with one hole in the trunk through which a rifle barrel could protrude, so that a sniper could shoot from inside a slightly ajar trunk.

The major break in the case came when a friend of Muhammad's called police suggesting that Muhammad and his friend Malvo were the likely snipers. Muhammad's automobile records revealed numerous traffic stops in the Beltway area during the time of the shootings. Another break in the case came when Malvo called a priest to boast of a killing weeks before in Montgomery, Alabama. Investigators traced the claim to a recent liquor store holdup that left one person dead. Fortunately, the perpetrator of this crime left a latent fingerprint at the murder scene. Authorities quickly tracked the print to Malvo, a Jamaican citizen, through his fingerprints on file with the Immigration and Naturalization Service. A description of Muhammad's car was released to the media, leading to tips from alert citizens who noticed the car parked in a rest area with both occupants asleep.

The motive for the shooting spree was believed to be a planned plot to extort $10 million from local and state governments. Muhammad was recently executed, and Malvo is currently serving life imprisonment without parole.

firearms, tool marks, and other impressions

KEY TERMS

bore
breechblock
caliber
choke
distance determination
ejector
extractor
firearms identification
gauge
Greiss test
grooves
lands
rifling

Learning Objectives

After studying this chapter you should be able to:

- Describe techniques for rifling a barrel

- Recognize the class and individual characteristics of bullets and cartridge cases

- Understand the use of the comparison microscope to compare bullets and cartridge cases

- Explain the concept of the NIBIN database

- Explain the procedure for determining how far a weapon was fired from a target

- Identify the laboratory tests for determining whether an individual has fired a weapon

- Explain the forensic significance of class and individual characteristics to the comparison of tool mark, footwear, and tire impressions

- List some common field reagents used to enhance bloody footprints

Just as natural variations in skin ridge patterns and characteristics provide a key to human identification, minute random markings on surfaces can impart individuality to inanimate objects. Structural variations and irregularities caused by scratches, nicks, breaks, and wear permit the criminalist to relate a bullet to a gun; a scratch or abrasion mark to a single tool; or a tire track to a particular automobile. Individualization, so vigorously pursued in all other areas of criminalistics, is frequently attainable in firearms and tool mark examination.

Although a portion of this chapter will be devoted to the comparison of surface features for the purposes of bullet identification, a complete description of the services and capabilities of the modern forensic firearms laboratory cannot be restricted to just this one subject, important as it may be. The high frequency of shooting cases means that the science of **firearms identification** must extend beyond mere comparison of bullets to include knowledge of the operation of all types of weapons, restoration of obliterated serial numbers on weapons, detection and characterization of gunpowder residues on garments and around wounds, estimation of muzzle-to-target distances, and detection of powder residues on hands. Each of these functions will be covered in this chapter.

Bullet and Cartridge Comparisons

The inner surface of the barrel of a gun leaves its markings on a bullet passing through it. These markings are peculiar to each gun. Hence, if one bullet found at the scene of a crime and another test-fired from a suspect's gun show the same markings, the suspect is linked to the crime. Because these inner surface striations are so important for bullet comparison, it is important to know why and how they originate.

The Gun Barrel

The gun barrel is produced from a solid bar of steel that has been hollowed out by drilling. The microscopic drill marks left on the barrel's inner surface are randomly irregular and in themselves impart a uniqueness to each barrel. However, the manufacture of a barrel requires the additional step of impressing its inner surface with spiral **grooves**, a step known as **rifling**. The surfaces of the original **bore** remaining between the grooves are called **lands** (see Figure 17–1). As a fired bullet travels through a barrel, it engages the rifling grooves; these grooves then guide the bullet through the barrel, giving it a rapid spin. This is done because a spinning bullet does not tumble end over end on leaving the barrel, but remains instead on a true and accurate course.

The diameter of the gun barrel, sketched in Figure 17–2, measured between opposite lands, is known as the **caliber** of the weapon. Caliber is normally recorded in hundredths of an inch or in millimeters—for example, .22 caliber and 9 mm. Actually, the term *caliber*, as it is commonly applied, is not an exact measurement of the barrel's diameter; for example, a .38-caliber weapon may actually have a bore diameter that ranges from 0.345 to 0.365 inch.

RIFLING METHODS   Before 1940, barrels were rifled by having one or two grooves at a time cut into the surface with steel hook cutters. The cutting tool was rotated as it passed down the barrel, so that the final results were grooves spiraling either to the right or left. However, as the need for

firearms identification
A discipline mainly concerned with determining whether a bullet or cartridge was fired by a particular weapon; it is not to be confused with ballistics, which is the study of a projectile in motion

grooves
The cut or low-lying portions between the lands in a rifled bore

rifling
The spiral grooves formed in the bore of a firearm barrel that impart spin to the projectile when it is fired

bore
The interior of a firearm barrel

lands
The raised portion between the grooves in a rifled bore

caliber
The diameter of the bore of a rifled firearm; the caliber is usually expressed in hundredths of an inch or millimeters—for example, .22 caliber and 9 mm

FIGURE 17–1

Interior view of a gun barrel, showing the presence of lands and grooves.

FIGURE 17–2

Cross section of a barrel with six grooves. The diameter of the bore is the caliber.

increased speed in the manufacture of weapons became apparent, newer techniques were developed that were far more suitable for the mass production of weapons.

The broach cutter, shown in Figure 17–3, consists of a series of concentric steel rings, with each ring slightly larger than the preceding one. As the broach passes through the barrel, it simultaneously cuts all grooves into the barrel at the required depth. The broach rotates as it passes through the barrel, giving the grooves their desired direction and rate of twist.

In contrast to the broach, the button process involves no cuttings. A steel plug or "button" impressed with the desired number of grooves is forced under extremely high pressures through the barrel. A single pass of the button down the barrel compresses the metal to create lands and grooves on the barrel walls that are negative forms of those on the button. The button rotates to produce the desired direction and rate of twist (see Figure 17–4).

Like the button process, the mandrel rifling or hummer forging process involves no cutting of metal. A mandrel is a rod of hardened steel machined so its form is the reverse impression of

FIGURE 17–3

A segment of a broach cutter.
Courtesy Susan Walsh, AP Wide World Photos

FIGURE 17–4

(top) Cross-section of a .22-caliber rifled barrel. *(bottom)* A button used to produce the lands and grooves in the barrel.
Courtesy New Jersey State Police

the rifling it is intended to produce. The mandrel is inserted into a slightly oversized bore, and the barrel is compressed with hammering or heavy rollers into the mandrel's form.

Every firearms manufacturer chooses a rifling process that is best suited to meet the production standards and requirements of its product. Once the choice is made, however, the class characteristics of the weapon's barrel will remain consistent; each will have the same number of lands and grooves, with the same approximate width and direction of twist. For example, .32-caliber Smith & Wesson revolvers have five lands and grooves twisting to the right. On the other hand, Colt .32-caliber revolvers exhibit six lands and grooves twisting to the left. Although these class characteristics permit the examiner to distinguish one type or brand name of weapon from another, they do not impart individuality to any one barrel; no class characteristic can do this.

If one could cut a barrel open lengthwise, a careful examination of the interior would reveal the existence of fine lines, or *striations*, many running the length of the barrel's lands and grooves. These striations are impressed into the metal as the negatives of minute imperfections found on the rifling cutter's surface, or they are produced by minute chips of steel pushed against the barrel's inner surface by a moving broach cutter. The random distribution and irregularities of these markings are impossible to duplicate exactly in any two barrels. **No two rifled barrels, even those manufactured in succession, have identical striation markings.** These striations form the individual characteristics of the barrel.

COMPARING BULLET MARKINGS   As the bullet passes through the barrel, its surface is impressed with the rifled markings of the barrel. The bullet emerges from the barrel carrying the impressions of the bore's interior surface; these impressions reflect both the class and individual characteristics of the barrel (see Figure 17–5). Because there is no practical way of making a direct comparison between the markings on the fired bullet and those found within a barrel, the examiner must obtain test bullets fired through the suspect barrel for comparison. To prevent damage to the test bullet's markings and to facilitate the bullet's recovery, test firings are normally made into a recovery box filled with cotton or into a water tank.

FIGURE 17–5

A bullet is impressed with the rifling markings of the barrel when it emerges from the weapon.
Courtesy New Jersey State Police

The number of lands and grooves, and their direction of twist, are obvious points of comparison during the initial stages of the examination. Any differences in these class characteristics immediately eliminate the possibility that both bullets traveled through the same barrel. A bullet with five lands and grooves could not possibly have been fired from a weapon of like caliber with six lands and grooves, nor could one having a right twist have come through a barrel impressed with a left twist. If both bullets carry the same class characteristics, the analyst must begin to match the striated markings on both bullets. This can be done only with the assistance of the comparison microscope (see Chapter 7).

Modern firearms identification began with the development and use of the comparison microscope. This instrument is the most important tool at the disposal of the firearms examiner. The test and evidence bullets are mounted on cylindrical adjustable holders beneath the objective lenses of the microscope, each pointing in the same direction (see Figure 17–6). Both bullets are observed simultaneously within the same field of view, and the examiner rotates one bullet until a well-defined land or groove comes into view. Once the striation markings are located, the other bullet is rotated until a matching region is found. Not only must the lands and grooves of the test and evidence bullet have identical widths, but the longitudinal striations on each must coincide. When a matching area is located, the two bullets are simultaneously rotated to obtain additional matching areas around the periphery of the bullets. Figure 17–7 shows a typical photomicrograph of a bullet match as viewed under a comparison microscope.

CONSIDERATIONS IN BULLET COMPARISON   Unfortunately, the firearms examiner rarely encounters a perfect match all around the bullet's periphery. The presence of grit and rust can alter the markings on bullets fired through the same barrel. More commonly, recovered evidence bullets may become so mutilated and distorted on impact as to yield only a small area with intact markings.

Furthermore, striation markings on a barrel are not permanent structures; they are subject to continuing change and alteration through wear as succeeding bullets traverse the length of the barrel. Fortunately, in most cases, these changes are not dramatic and do not prevent the matching of two bullets fired by the same weapon. As with fingerprint comparison, there are no hard-and-fast rules governing the minimum number of points required for a bullet comparison. The final opinion must be based on the judgment, experience, and knowledge of the expert.

Frequently, the firearms examiner receives a spent bullet without an accompanying suspect weapon and is asked to determine the caliber and possible make of the weapon. If a bullet appears not to have lost its metal, its weight may be one factor in determining its caliber. In some instances, the number of lands and grooves, the direction of twist, and the widths of lands and grooves are useful class characteristics for eliminating certain makes of weapons from consideration. For example, a bullet that has five lands and grooves and twists to the right could not come from a weapon manufactured by Colt because Colts are not manufactured with these class characteristics.

Sometimes a bullet has rifling marks that set it apart from most other manufactured weapons, as in the case of Marlin rifles. These weapons are rifled by a technique known as *microgrooving* and may have 8 to 24 grooves impressed into their barrels; few other weapons are manufactured in this fashion. In this respect, the FBI maintains a record known as the *General Rifling Characteristics File*. This file contains listings of class characteristics, such as land and groove width dimensions, for known weapons. It is periodically updated and distributed to the law enforcement community to help identify rifled weapons from retrieved bullets.

As previously discussed, unlike rifled firearms, a shotgun has a smooth barrel. It therefore follows that projectiles passing through a shotgun barrel are not impressed with any characteristic markings that can later be related back to the weapon. Shotguns generally fire small lead balls or pellets contained within a shotgun shell (see Figure 17–8). A paper or plastic wad pushes the pellets through the barrel on ignition of the cartridge's powder charge. By weighing and measuring the diameter of the shot recovered at a crime scene, the examiner can usually determine the size of shot used in the shell. The size and shape of the recovered wad may also reveal the gauge of the shotgun used and, in some instances, may indicate the manufacturer of the fired shell.

The diameter of the shotgun barrel is expressed by the term **gauge**.[1] The higher the gauge number, the smaller the barrel's diameter. For example, a 12-gauge shotgun has a bore diameter of 0.730 inch as contrasted to 0.670 inch for a 16-gauge shotgun. The exception to this rule is the .410-gauge shotgun, which refers to a barrel 0.41 inch in diameter.

---

[1] Originally, the number of lead balls with the same diameter as the barrel would make a pound. For example, a 20-gauge shotgun has an inside diameter equal to the diameter of a lead ball that weighs 1/20 of a pound.

mycrimekit
WEBEXTRA 17.1
Practice Matching Bullets with the Aid of a 3-D Interactive Illustration
www.mycrimekit.com

mycrimekit
WEBEXTRA 17.2
3-D Shotshell Illustrations
www.mycrimekit.com

gauge
Size designation of a shotgun, originally the number of lead balls with the same diameter as the barrel that would make a pound; for example, a 12-gauge shotgun would have a bore diameter of a lead ball 1/12 pound in weight; the only exception is the .410 shotgun, in which bore size is 0.41 inch

FIGURE 17–6

A bullet holder beneath the objective lens of a comparison microscope.
Courtesy Leica Microsystems, Buffalo, N.Y., www.leica-microsystems.com

FIGURE 17–7

Photomicrograph of two bullets through a comparison microscope. The test bullet is on the right; the questioned bullet is on the left.
Courtesy Philadelphia Police Department Laboratory

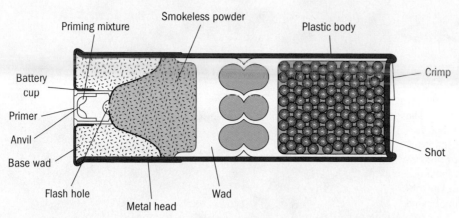

FIGURE 17–8

Cross-section of a loaded shotgun shell.

(a)   (b)

FIGURE 17–9

Comparison microscope photomicrograph showing a match between (a) firing pin impressions and (b) the breechblock markings on two shells.

Courtesy Ronald Welsh, Bureau of Forensic Services, Central Valley Laboratory, Ripon, Calif.

Cartridge Cases

The act of pulling a trigger releases the weapon's firing pin, causing it to strike the primer, which in turn ignites the powder. The expanding gases generated by the burning gunpowder propel the bullet forward through the barrel, simultaneously pushing the spent cartridge case or shell back with equal force against the **breechblock**. As the bullet is marked by its passage through the barrel, the shell is also impressed with markings by its contact with the metal surfaces of the weapon's firing and loading mechanisms. As with bullets, these markings can be reproduced in test-fired cartridges to provide distinctive points of comparison for individualizing a spent shell to a rifled weapon or shotgun.

The shape of the firing pin is impressed into the relatively soft metal of the primer on the cartridge case, revealing the minute distortions of the firing pin. These imperfections may be sufficiently random to individualize the pin impression to a single weapon. Similarly, the cartridge case, in its rearward thrust, is impressed with the surface markings of the breechblock. The breechblock, like any machined surface, is populated with random striation markings that become a highly distinctive signature for individualizing its surface. Other distinctive markings that may appear on the shell as a result of metal-to-metal contact are caused by the **extractor** and **ejector** mechanism and the magazine or clip, as well as by imperfections on the fire chamber walls. Photomicrographs in Figure 17–9 reveal a comparison of the firing pin and breechblock impressions on evidence and test-fired shells.

breechblock
The rear part of a firearm barrel

mycrimekit

WEBEXTRA 17.3
3-D Revolver Cartridge Illustrations
www.mycrimekit.com

extractor
The mechanism in a firearm by which a cartridge of a fired case is withdrawn from the chamber

ejector
The mechanism in a firearm that throws the cartridge or fired case from the firearm

> > > > > > > >

case study

Sacco and Vanzetti

In 1920, two security guards were viciously gunned down by unidentified assailants. The security guards were transporting shoe factory payroll, nearly $16,000 in cash, at the time of the robbery-murder. Eyewitnesses described the assailants as "Italian-looking," one with a full handlebar mustache. The robbers had used two firearms, leaving behind three different brands of shells.

Two suspects were identified and arrested—Nicola Sacco and his friend, the amply mustachioed Bartolomeo Vanzetti. After denying owning any firearms, each was found to be in possession of a loaded pistol. In fact, Sacco's pistol was .32 caliber, the same caliber as the crime-scene bullets. In Sacco's pockets were found 23 bullets matching the brands of the empty shells found at the murder scene.

This case coincided with the "Red Scare," a politically turbulent time in post–World War I America. Citizens feared socialist zealots, and the media played up these emotions. Political maneuvering and the use of the media muddied the waters surrounding the case, and the fact that both suspects belonged to anarchist political groups that advocated revolutionary violence against the government only incited public animosity toward them. Sympathetic socialist organizations attempted to turn Sacco and Vanzetti into martyrs, calling their prosecution a "witch hunt."

The outcome of the trial ultimately depended on whether the prosecution could prove that Sacco's pistol fired the bullets that killed the two security guards. At trial, the ballistics experts testified that the bullets used were no longer in production and they

Sacco and Vanzetti.
Courtesy Corbis/Bettman

could not find similar ammunition to use in test firings—aside from the unused cartridges found in Sacco's pockets. A forensics expert for the prosecution concluded that a visual examination showed that the bullets matched, leading the jury to return a verdict of guilty. Sacco and Vanzetti were sentenced to death.

Because of continued public protests, a committee was appointed in 1927 to review the case. Around this time, Calvin Goddard, at the Bureau of Forensic Ballistics in New York, perfected the comparison microscope for use in forensic firearms investigations. With this instrument, two bullets are viewed side by side to compare the striations imparted to a bullet's surface as it travels through the gun's barrel. The committee asked Goddard to examine the bullets in question. A test-fired bullet from Sacco's weapon was matched conclusively by Goddard to one of the crime-scene bullets. The fates of Sacco and Vanzetti were sealed and they were put to death in 1927.

mycrimekit

WEBEXTRA 17.4
3-D Pistol Cartridge Illustrations
www.mycrimekit.com

mycrimekit

WEBEXTRA 17.5
3-D Rifle Cartridge Illustrations
www.mycrimekit.com

mycrimekit

WEBEXTRA 17.6
View Animations to Illustrate the Firing Process and the Extraction/Ejection Process of a Semiautomatic Pistol
www.mycrimekit.com

Firing pin, breechblock, extractor, and ejector marks may also be impressed onto the surface of the brass portion of shells fired by a shotgun. These impressions provide points for individualizing the shell to a weapon that are just as valuable as cartridge cases discharged from a rifled firearm. Furthermore, in the absence of a suspect weapon, the size and shape of a firing pin impression and/or the position of ejector marks in relationship to extractor and other markings may provide some clue to the type or make of the weapon that may have fired the questioned shell, or at least may eliminate a large number of possibilities.

Automated Firearms Search Systems

The use of firearms, especially semiautomatic weapons, during the commission of a crime has significantly increased throughout the United States. Because of the expense of such firearms, the likelihood that a specific weapon will be used in multiple crimes has risen. The advent of computerized imaging technology has made possible the storage of bullet and cartridge surface characteristics in a manner analogous to the storage of automated fingerprint files (see pages 396–398). Using this concept, crime laboratories can be networked, allowing them to share information on bullets and cartridges retrieved from several jurisdictions.

Search Systems

The effort to build a national computerized database for firearms evidence in the United States had a rather confusing and inefficient start in the early 1990s. Two major federal law enforcement agencies, the FBI and the ATF, offered the law enforcement community competing and incompatible computerized systems.

EARLY SYSTEMS The automated search system developed for the FBI was known as *DRUGFIRE*. This system emphasized the examination of unique markings on the cartridge casings expended by the weapon. The specimen was analyzed through a microscope attached to a video camera. The magnification allowed for a close-up view to identify individual characteristics. The image was captured by a video camera, digitized, and stored in a database. Although DRUGFIRE emphasized cartridge-case imagery, the images of highly characteristic bullet striations could also be stored in a like manner for comparisons.

The *Integrated Ballistic Identification System (IBIS)*, developed for the Bureau of Alcohol, Tobacco, Firearms and Explosives, processed digital microscopic images of identifying features found on both expended bullets and cartridge casings. IBIS incorporated two software programs: Bulletproof, a bullet-analyzing module, and Brasscatcher, a cartridge-case-analyzing module. A schematic diagram of Bulletproof's operation is depicted in Figure 17–10.[2]

FIGURE 17–10

Bulletproof configuration. The sample is mounted on the specimen manipulator and illuminated by the light source from a microscope. The image is captured by a video camera and digitized. This digital image is then stored in a database, available for retrieval and comparison. The search for a match includes analyzing the width of land and groove impressions along with both rifling and individual characteristics. The Brasscatcher software uses the same system configuration but emphasizes the analysis of expended cartridge casings rather than the expended bullets.

Courtesy Forensic Technology (WAI) Inc., Côte St-Luc, Quebec, Canada

[2] R. E. Tontarski, Jr., and R. M. Thompson, "Automated Firearms Evidence Comparison: A Forensic Tool for Firearms Identification—An Update," *Journal of Forensic Sciences* 43 (1998): 641.

NIBIN   In 1999, members of the FBI and ATF joined forces to introduce the *National Integrated Ballistics Information Network (NIBIN)* program to the discipline of firearms examination. NIBIN guides and assists federal, state, and local laboratories interested in housing an automated search system. The new unified system incorporates both DRUGFIRE and IBIS technologies available in prior years. ATF has the overall responsibility for the system sites, whereas the FBI is responsible for the communications network.

Agencies using the new IBIS technology produce database files from bullets and cartridge casings retrieved from crime scenes or test fires from retrieved firearms. More than two hundred law enforcement agencies worldwide have adapted to this technology. The success of the system has been proven with more than 800,000 images compiled; nationwide, law enforcement agencies have connected more than 28,000 bullets and casings to more than one crime (see Figure 17–11).

For example, in a recent case, a Houston security guard was shot and killed during a botched armed robbery. A bullet and .40-caliber Smith & Wesson cartridge casing were recovered and

FIGURE 17–11

Bullets A, B, C, and D were acquired in the IBIS database at different times from different crime scenes. D is a fragmented bullet that had only three land impressions available for acquisition. Upon the entry of bullet D, IBIS found a potential matching candidate in the database: B. On the far right, bullet D is compared to bullet B using the IBIS imaging software. Finally, a forensic firearms examiner using the actual evidence under a conventional comparison microscope will confirm the match between B and D.
Courtesy Forensic Technology WAI Inc.

imaged into NIBIN. Earlier that day, a robbery-turned-double-homicide left two store clerks dead. Again, two bullets and two .40-caliber Smith & Wesson cartridge casings were recovered. Once they were processed into NIBIN, a correlation was found with the murder of the security officer and a separate aggravated robbery that occurred two weeks prior. All three crimes were linked with a firearm believed to be a .40-caliber Smith & Wesson pistol.

Further investigation into the use of a victim's credit card aided police in locating two suspects. In the possession of one suspect was a .40-caliber Smith & Wesson pistol. Once retrieved, the gun was test-fired and imaged into NIBIN. The casing from the test-fired weapon matched the evidence obtained in the robbery and the aggravated robbery-homicides. The associations were verified by traditional firearms examination comparisons performed by a firearms examiner. Before this computerized technology was developed, it would have taken years, or may have been impossible, to link all of these shootings to one single firearm.

In another example, the ATF laboratory in Rockville, Maryland, received 1,466 cartridge casings from the Ovcara mass burial site in Bosnia. After processing and imaging profiles for all casings, the examiners determined that 18 different firearms were used at the site. With the help of NIBIN technology and competent examiners, jurists were able to try and convict an individual for war crimes.

NIBIN serves only as a screening tool for firearms evidence. A computerized system does not replace the skills of the firearms examiner. NIBIN can screen hundreds of unsolved firearms cases and may narrow the possibilities to several firearms. However, the final comparison will be made by the forensic examiner through traditional microscopic methods.

Ballistic Fingerprinting

Participating crime laboratories in the United States are building databases of bullet and cartridge cases found at crime scenes and those fired in tests of guns seized from criminals. As these databases come online and prove their usefulness in solving crimes, law enforcement officials and the political community are scrutinizing the feasibility of scaling this concept up to create a system of *ballistic fingerprinting*. This system would entail the capture and storage of appropriate markings on bullets and cartridges test-fired from handguns and rifles before they are sold to the public. Questions regarding who will be responsible for collecting the images and details of how they will be stored are but two of many issues to be determined. The concept of ballistic fingerprinting is an intriguing one for the law enforcement community and promises to be explored and debated intensely in the future.

Gunpowder Residues

In incidents involving gunshot wounds, it is often necessary to determine the distance from which the weapon was fired. Frequently, in incidents involving a shooting death, the individual apprehended and accused pleads self-defense as the motive for the attack. Such claims are fertile grounds for **distance determinations** because finding the proximity of the parties involved in the incident is necessary to establish the facts of the incident. Similarly, careful examination of the wounds of suicide victims usually reveals characteristics associated with a very close-range gunshot wound. The absence of such characteristics is a strong indication that the wound was not self-inflicted and signals the possibility of foul play.

distance determination
The process of determining the distance between the firearm and a target, usually based on the distribution of powder patterns or the spread of a shot pattern

Distance Determination

Modern ammunition is propelled toward a target by the expanding gases created by the ignition of smokeless powder or nitrocellulose in a cartridge. Under ideal circumstances, all of the powder would be consumed in the process and converted into the rapidly expanding gases. However, in practice the powder is never totally burned. When a firearm is discharged, unburned and partially burned particles of gunpowder in addition to smoke are propelled out of the barrel along with the bullet toward the target. If the muzzle of the weapon is sufficiently close, these products are deposited onto the target. The distribution of gunpowder particles and other discharge residues around the bullet hole permits an assessment of the distance from which a handgun or rifle was fired.

The accuracy of a distance determination varies according to the circumstances of the case. When the investigator is unable to recover a suspect weapon, the best that the examiner can do is to state whether a shot could have been fired within some distance interval from the target. More exact opinions are possible only when the examiner has the suspect weapon in hand and has knowledge of the type of ammunition used in the shooting.

HANDGUNS AND RIFLES   The precise distance from which a handgun or rifle has been fired must be determined by careful comparison of the powder-residue pattern on the victim's clothing or skin against test patterns made when the suspect weapon is fired at varying distances from a target. A white cloth or a fabric comparable to the victim's clothing may be used as a test target (see Figure 17–12). Because the spread and density of the residue pattern vary widely between weapons and ammunition, such a comparison is significant only when it is made with the suspect weapon and suspect ammunition, or with ammunition of the same type and make. By comparing the test and evidence patterns, the examiner may find enough similarity in shape and density on which to judge the distance from which the shot was fired.

Without the weapon, the examiner is restricted to looking for recognizable characteristics around the bullet hole. Such findings are at best approximations made as a result of general observations and the examiner's experience. However, some noticeable characteristics should be sought. For instance, when the weapon is held in contact with or less than 1 inch from the target, a heavy concentration of smokelike vaporous lead usually surrounds the bullet entrance hole. Often, loose fibers surrounding a contact hole show scorch marks from the flame discharge of the weapon, and some synthetic fibers may show signs of being melted as a result of the heat from the discharge. Furthermore, the blowback of muzzle gases may produce a stellate (star-shaped) tear pattern around the hole. Such a hole is invariably surrounded by a rim of a smokelike deposit of vaporous lead (see Figure 17–13).

(a)   (b)

(c)   (d)

FIGURE 17–12

Test powder patterns made with a Glock 9mm luger fired at the following distances: (a) contact, (b) 6 inches, (c) 12 inches, and (d) 18 inches.

Courtesy Michelle D. Miranda, MS, D-ABC

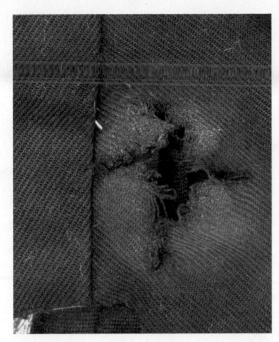

FIGURE 17–13
A contact shot.
Courtesy Michelle D. Miranda, MS, D-ABC

A halo of vaporous lead (smoke) deposited around a bullet hole normally indicates a discharge 12 to 18 inches or less from the target. The presence of scattered specks of unburned and partially burned powder grains without any accompanying soot can often be observed at distances up to approximately 25 inches. Occasionally, however, scattered gunpowder particles are noted at a firing distance as far out as 36 inches. With ball powder ammunition, this distance may be extended to 6 to 8 feet.

Finally, a weapon that has been fired more than 3 feet from a target usually does not deposit any powder residues onto the target's surface. In these cases, the only visual indication that the hole was made by a bullet is a dark ring, known as *bullet wipe*, around the perimeter of the entrance hole. Bullet wipe consists of a mixture of carbon, dirt, lubricant, primer residue, and lead wiped off the bullet's surface as it passes through the target. Again, in the absence of a suspect weapon, these observations are general guidelines for estimating target distances. Numerous factors—barrel length, caliber, type of ammunition, and type and condition of the weapon fired—influence the amount of gunpowder residue deposited on a target.

SHOTGUNS The determination of firing distances involving shotguns must again be related to test firings performed with the suspect weapon, using the same type of ammunition known to be used in the crime. In the absence of a weapon, the muzzle-to-target distance can be estimated by measuring the spread of the discharged shot. With close-range shots varying in distance up to 4 to 5 feet, the shot charge enters the target as a concentrated mass, producing a hole somewhat larger than the bore of the barrel. As the distance increases, the pellets progressively separate and spread out. Generally speaking, the spread in the pattern made by a 12-gauge shotgun increases 1 inch for each yard of distance. Thus, a 10-inch pattern would be produced at approximately 10 yards. Of course, this is only a rule of thumb; normally, a great number of variables can affect the shot pattern. Other factors to consider include the barrel length, the size and quantity of the pellets fired, the quantity of powder charge used to propel the pellets, and the choke of the gun under examination. **Choke** is the degree of constriction placed at the muzzle end of the barrel. The greater the choke, the narrower the shotgun pattern and the faster and farther the pellets will travel.

choke
An interior constriction placed at or near the muzzle end of a shotgun's barrel to control shot dispersion

Powder Residues on Garments

When garments or other evidence relevant to a shooting are received in the crime laboratory, the surfaces of all items are first examined microscopically for gunpowder residue. These particles may be identifiable by their characteristic colors, sizes, and shapes. However, the absence of visual indications does not preclude the possibility that gunpowder residue is present. Sometimes the lack of color contrast between the powder and garment or the presence of heavily encrusted

(a)   (b)

FIGURE 17–14

(a) A shirt bearing a powder stain, photographed under normal light. (b) An infrared photograph of the same shirt.

deposits of blood can obscure the visual detection of gunpowder. Often, an infrared photograph of the suspect area overcomes the problem. Such a photograph may enhance the contrast, thus revealing vaporous lead and powder particles deposited around the hole (see Figure 17–14). In other situations, this may not help, and the analyst must use chemical tests to detect gunpowder residues.

Nitrites are one type of chemical product that results from the incomplete combustion of smokeless (nitrocellulose) powder. One test method for locating powder residues involves transferring particles embedded on the target surface to chemically treated gelatin-coated photographic paper. This procedure is known as the **Greiss test**. The examiner presses the photographic paper onto the target with a hot iron; once the nitrite particles are on the paper, they are made easily visible by chemical treatment.[3] In addition, comparing the developed nitrite pattern to nitrite patterns obtained from test firings at known distances can be useful in determining the shooting distance from the target. A second chemical test is then performed to detect any trace of lead residue around the bullet hole. The questioned surface is sprayed with a solution of sodium rhodizonate, followed by a series of oversprays with acid solutions. This treatment causes lead particles to exhibit a pink color, followed by a blue-violet color.

Greiss test

A chemical test used to develop patterns of gunpowder residues around bullet holes

Primer Residues on the Hands

The firing of a weapon not only propels residues toward the target, but also blows gunpowder and primer residues back toward the shooter (see Figure 17–15). As a result, traces of these residues are often deposited on the firing hand of the shooter, and their detection can provide valuable information as to whether an individual has recently fired a weapon.

[3] P. C. Maiti, "Powder Patterns around Bullet Holes in Bloodstained Articles," *Journal of the Forensic Science Society* 13 (1973): 197.

FIGURE 17–15

When a handgun is fired, gunpowder and primer residues are normally blown back toward the hand of the shooter.
Courtesy Forensic Technology WAI Inc.

Detecting Primer Residues

Early efforts at demonstrating powder residues on the hands centered on chemical tests that could detect unburned gunpowder or nitrates. For many years, the *dermal nitrate test* enjoyed popularity. It required the application of hot paraffin or wax to the suspect's hand with a paintbrush. After drying into a solid crust, the paraffin was removed and tested with diphenylamine. A blue color was taken as an indication of a positive reaction for nitrates (see Table 15–1). However, the dermal nitrate test has fallen into disfavor with law enforcement agencies, owing mainly to its lack of specificity. Common materials such as fertilizers, cosmetics, urine, and tobacco all give positive reactions that are indistinguishable from that obtained for gunpowder by this test.

Efforts to identify a shooter now center on the detection of primer residues deposited on the hand of a shooter at the time of firing. With the exception of most .22-caliber ammunition, primers currently manufactured contain a blend of lead styphnate, barium nitrate, and antimony sulfide. Residues from these materials are most likely to be deposited on the thumb web and the back of the firing hand of a shooter because these areas are closest to gases escaping along the side or back of the gun during discharge. In addition, individuals who handle a gun without firing it may have primer residues deposited on the palm of the hand coming in contact with the weapon.

However, with the handling of a used firearm, the passage of time, and the resumption of normal activities following a shooting, gunshot residues from the back of the hand are frequently redistributed to other areas, including the palms. Therefore, it is not unusual to find higher levels of barium and antimony on the palms than on the backs of the hands of known shooters. Another possibility is the deposition of significant levels of barium and antimony on the hands of an individual who is near a firearm when it is discharged.

Tests for Primer Residues

Determination of whether a person has fired or handled a weapon or has been near a discharged firearm is normally made by measuring the presence and possibly the amount of barium and antimony on the relevant portions of the suspect's hands. A variety of materials and techniques are used for removing these residues. The most popular approach, and certainly the most convenient for the field investigator, requires the application of an adhesive tape or adhesive to the hand's surface in order to remove any adhering residue particles.

SWABBING   Another approach is to remove any residues present by swabbing both the firing and nonfiring hands with cotton that has been moistened with 5 percent nitric acid. The front and back of each hand are separately swabbed. All four swabs, along with a moistened control, are then forwarded to the crime laboratory for analysis (see Appendix II for a detailed description of residue collection procedures).

In any case, once the hands are treated for the collection of barium and antimony, the collection medium must be analyzed for the presence of these elements. High barium and antimony levels on the suspect's hand(s) strongly indicate that the person fired or handled a weapon or was near a firearm when it was discharged. Because these elements are normally present after a firing in small quantities (less than 10 micrograms), only the most sensitive analytical techniques can detect them.

Unfortunately, even though most specimens submitted for this type of analysis have been from individuals strongly suspected of having fired a gun, there has been a low rate of positive findings. The major difficulty appears to be the short time that primer residues remain on the hands. These residues are readily removed by intentional or unintentional washing, rubbing, or wiping of hands. In fact, one study convincingly demonstrated that it is difficult to detect primer residues on cotton hand swabs taken as soon as two hours after firing a weapon.[4] Hence, some laboratories do not accept cotton hand swabs taken from living subjects six or more hours after a firing has occurred.

In cases that involve suicide victims, a higher rate of positives for the presence of gunshot residue is obtained when the hand swabbing is conducted before the person's body is moved or when the hands are protected by paper bags.[5] However, hand swabbing or the application of an adhesive cannot be used to detect firings with most .22-caliber rim-fire ammunition. Such ammunition may contain only barium or neither barium nor antimony in its primer composition.

SEM TESTING   Most laboratories possessing gunshot residue detection capabilities require the application of an adhesive to the shooter's hands.[6] Microscopic primer and gunpowder particles on the adhesive are then located with the aid of a scanning electron microscope (SEM). These particles have a characteristic size and shape that readily distinguish them from other contaminants present on the hands (see Figure 17–16). When the SEM is linked to an X-ray analyzer (see pages 175–178), an elemental analysis of the particles can be conducted. A finding of a select combination of elements (lead, barium, and antimony) confirms that the particles were indeed primer residue (see Figure 17–17). Appendix II contains a detailed description of the SEM residue collection procedure.

The major advantage of the SEM approach for primer residue detection is its enhanced specificity over hand swabbing. The SEM characterizes primer particles by their size and shape as well as by their chemical composition. Unfortunately, the excessive operator time required to search out and characterize gunshot residue has deterred this technique's use. The availability of automated particle search and identification systems for use with scanning electron microscopes may overcome this problem. Results of work performed with automated systems show it to be significantly faster than a manual approach for searching out gunshot residue particles.[7]

---

[4] J. W. Kilty, "Activity after Shooting and Its Effect on the Retention of Primer Residues," *Journal of Forensic Sciences* 29 (1975): 219.

[5] G. E. Reed et al., "Analysis of Gunshot Residue Test Results in 112 Suicides," *Journal of Forensic Sciences* 35 (1990): 62.

[6] G. M. Woiten et al., "Particle Analysis for the Detection of Gunshot Residue, I: Scanning Electron Microscopy/Energy Dispersive X-Ray Characterization of Hand Deposits from Firing," *Journal of Forensic Sciences* 24 (1979): 409.

[7] R. S. White and A. D. Owens, "Automation of Gunshot Residue Detection and Analysis by Scanning Electron Microscopy/Energy Dispersive X-Ray Analysis (SEM/EDX)," *Journal of Forensic Sciences* 32 (1987): 1595; and W. L. Tillman, "Automated Gunshot Residue Particle Search and Characterization," *Journal of Forensic Sciences* 32 (1987): 62.

FIGURE 17–16

An SEM view of gunshot residue particles.

Courtesy Foster and Freeman Limited, Worchester Shine, UK, www.fosterfreeman.co.uk

FIGURE 17–17

Spectrum showing the presence of lead, barium, and antimony in gunshot residue.

Courtesy Jeol USA Inc., Peabody, Mass., www.jeolusa.com

Serial Number Restoration

Today, many manufactured items, including automobile engine blocks and firearms, are impressed with a serial number for identification. Increasingly, the criminalist is asked to restore such a number when it has been removed or obliterated by grinding, rifling, or punching.

Serial numbers are usually stamped on a metal body or frame, or on a plate, with hard steel dies. These dies strike the metal surface with a force that allows each digit to sink into the metal at a prescribed depth. Serial numbers can be restored because the metal crystals in the stamped zone are placed under a permanent strain that extends a short distance beneath the original numbers. When a suitable etching agent is applied, the strained area dissolves faster than the unaltered metal, thus revealing the etched pattern in the form of the original numbers. However, if the zone of strain has been removed, or if the area has been impressed with a different strain pattern, the number usually cannot be restored.

Before any treatment with the etching reagent, the obliterated surface must be thoroughly cleaned of dirt and oil and polished to a mirrorlike finish. The reagent is swabbed onto the surface with a cotton ball. The choice of etching reagent depends on the type of metal surface being worked on. A solution of hydrochloric acid (120 mL), copper chloride (90 g), and water (100 mL) generally works well for steel surfaces.

Collection and Preservation of Firearms Evidence

Firearms

The Hollywood image of an investigator picking up a weapon by its barrel with a pencil or stick in order to protect fingerprints must be avoided. This practice only disturbs powder deposits, rust, or dirt lodged in the barrel, and consequently may alter the striation markings on test-fired bullets. If recovery of latent fingerprints is a primary concern, hold the weapon by the edge of the trigger guard or by the checkered portion of the grip, which usually does not retain identifiable fingerprints.

The most important consideration in handling a weapon is safety. Before any weapon is sent to the laboratory, all precautions must be taken to prevent an accidental discharge of a loaded weapon in transit. In most cases, it will be necessary to unload the weapon. If this is done, a record should first be made of the weapon's hammer and safety position; likewise, the location of all fired and unfired ammunition in the weapon must be recorded.

When a revolver is recovered, the chamber position in line with the barrel should be indicated by a scratch mark on the cylinder. Each chamber is designated with a number on a diagram, and as each cartridge or casing is removed, it should be marked to correspond to the numbered chambers in the diagram. Knowledge of the cylinder position of a cartridge casing may be useful for later determination of the sequence of events, particularly in shooting cases when more than one shot was fired. Place each round in a separate box or envelope. If the weapon is an automatic, the magazine must be removed and checked for prints and the chamber then emptied.

As with any other type of physical evidence recovered at a crime scene, firearms evidence must be marked for identification and a chain of custody must be established. Therefore, when a firearm is recovered, an identification tag should be attached to the trigger guard. The tag should be marked to show appropriate identifying data, including the weapon's serial number, make, and model and the investigator's initials. The firearm itself may be further identified by being marked directly with a sharp-pointed scriber in an inconspicuous area of the weapon—for example, the inside of the trigger guard. This practice will avoid any permanent defacement of the weapon.

When a weapon is recovered from an underwater location, no effort must be made to dry or clean it. Instead, the firearm should be transported to the laboratory in a receptacle containing enough of the same water necessary to keep it submerged. This procedure prevents rust from developing during transport.

Ammunition

Protection of class and individual markings on bullets and cartridge cases must be the primary concern of the field investigator. Thus, extreme caution is needed when removing a lodged bullet from a wall or other object. If the bullet's surface is accidentally scratched during this operation, valuable striation markings could be obliterated. It is best to free bullets from their target by carefully breaking away the surrounding support material while avoiding direct contact with the projectile.

Bullets recovered at the crime scene are scribed with the investigator's initials, on either the base or the nose of the bullet (see Figure 17–18). Again, obliteration of any striation markings on the bullet must be scrupulously avoided. If the bullet is badly deformed and there is no apparent place for identification, it should just be placed in a container that is appropriately marked for identification. In any case, the investigator must protect the bullet by wrapping it in tissue paper before placing it in a pillbox or an envelope for shipment to the crime laboratory.

In handling the bullet, the investigator should be conscious of the possibility that minute traces of evidence, such as paint and fibers, may be adhering to the bullet. Care must be taken to leave these trace materials intact. Similarly, a fired casing must be identified so as to avoid destroying marks impressed on it from the weapon. The investigator's initials should be placed near the outside or inside mouth of the shell (see Figure 17–19). Discharged shells from shotguns are initialed with ink or indelible pencil on the paper or plastic tube remaining on the shell or on the metal nearest the mouth of the shell.

In addition, when semiautomatic or automatic weapons have been fired, the ejection pattern of the casings can help establish the relationship of the suspect to his or her victim. For this reason, the exact location of the place from which a shell casing was recovered is important information that must be noted by the investigator.

In incidents involving shotguns, any wads recovered are to be packaged and sent to the laboratory. An examination of the size and composition of the wad may reveal information about the type of ammunition used and the gauge of the shotgun.

Gunpowder Deposits

The clothing of a firearms victim must be carefully preserved so as to prevent damage or disruption to powder residues deposited around a bullet or shell hole. The cutting or tearing of clothing in the area of the holes must be avoided as the clothing is being removed. All wet clothing should be air-dried out of direct sunlight and then folded carefully so as not to disrupt the area around the bullet hole. Each item should be placed in a separate paper bag.

Tool Marks

A *tool mark* is any impression, cut, gouge, or abrasion caused by a tool coming into contact with another object. Most often, tool marks are encountered at burglary scenes that involve forcible entry into a building or safe. Generally, these marks occur as indented impressions into a softer surface or as abrasion marks caused by the tool cutting or sliding against another object.

Comparing Tool Marks

Typically, an indented impression is left on the frame of a door or window as a result of the prying action of a screwdriver or crowbar. A careful examination of these impressions can reveal important class characteristics—that is, the size and shape of the tool. However, they rarely reveal any significant individual characteristics that could permit the examiner to individualize the mark to a single tool. Such characteristics, when they do exist, usually take the form of discernible random nicks and breaks that the tool has acquired through wear and use (Figure 17–20).

Just as the machined surfaces of a firearm are impressed with random striations during its manufacture, the edges of a pry bar, chisel, screwdriver, knife, or cutting tool likewise display a series of microscopic irregularities that look like ridges and valleys. Such markings are left as a result of the machining processes used to cut and finish tools. The shape and pattern of such minute imperfections are further modified by damage and wear during the life of the tool. Considering the unending variety of patterns that the hills and valleys can assume, it is highly unlikely

FIGURE 17–18

Discharged evidence bullets should be marked on the base or nose. When there is more than one bullet, a number should accompany the initials. *Never* mark bullets on the side.

FIGURE 17–19

Discharged evidence shells should be marked on the outside or inside, as close as possible to the mouth of the shell. Discharged shotgun shells should be marked on the brass, close to the paper or plastic. *Never* mark the shells where the firing pin strikes the primer.

FIGURE 17–20

A comparison of a tool mark with a suspect screwdriver. Note how the presence of nicks and breaks on the tool's edge helps individualize the tool to the mark.

that any two tools will be identical. Hence, these minute imperfections impart individuality to each tool.

If the edge of a tool is scraped against a softer surface, it may cut a series of striated lines that reflect that pattern of the tool's edge. Markings left in this manner are compared in the laboratory through a comparison microscope with test tool marks made from the suspect tool. The result can be a positive comparison, and hence a definitive association of the tool with the evidence mark, when a sufficient quantity of striations match between the evidence and test markings.

One of the major problems associated with tool mark comparisons is the difficulty in duplicating in the laboratory the tool mark left at the crime scene. A thorough comparison requires the preparation of a series of test marks obtained by applying the suspect tool at various angles and pressures to a soft metal surface (lead is commonly used). This approach gives the examiner ample opportunity to duplicate many of the details of the original evidence marking. A photomicrograph of a typical tool mark comparison is illustrated in Figure 17–21.

Collecting Tool Mark Evidence

Whenever practical, the entire object or the part of the object bearing a tool mark should be submitted to the crime laboratory for examination. When removal of the tool mark is impractical, the only recourse is to photograph the marked area to scale and make a cast of the mark. Under these circumstances, liquid silicone casting material has been found to be the most satisfactory for reproducing most of the fine details of the mark. See Figure 17–22. However, even under the most optimum conditions, the clarity of many of the tool mark's minute details will be lost or obscured in a photograph or cast. Of course, this will reduce the chance of individualizing the mark to a single tool.

The crime-scene investigator must never attempt to fit the suspect tool into the tool mark. Any contact between the tool and the marked surface may alter the mark and will, at the least, raise serious questions about the integrity of the evidence. The suspect tool and mark must be packaged in separate containers, with every precaution taken to avoid contact between the tool or mark and another hard surface. Failure to properly protect the tool or mark from damage could result in the destruction of its individual characteristics.

FIGURE 17–21

A photograph of a tool mark comparison seen under a comparison microscope.
Courtesy Leica Microsystems, Buffalo, N.Y., www.leica-microsystems.com

(a)   (b)

FIGURE 17–22

(a) Casting a tool mark impression with a silicone-based putty. (b) Impression alongside suspect tool.
Courtesy Sirchie Fingerprint Laboratories, Youngsville, N.C., www.sirchie.com

Furthermore, the tool or its impression may contain valuable trace evidence. Chips of paint adhering to the mark or tool provide perhaps the best example of how the transfer of trace physical evidence can occur as a result of using a tool to gain forcible entry into a building. Obviously, the presence of trace evidence greatly enhances the evidential value of the tool or its mark and requires special care in handling and packaging the evidence to avoid losing or destroying these items.

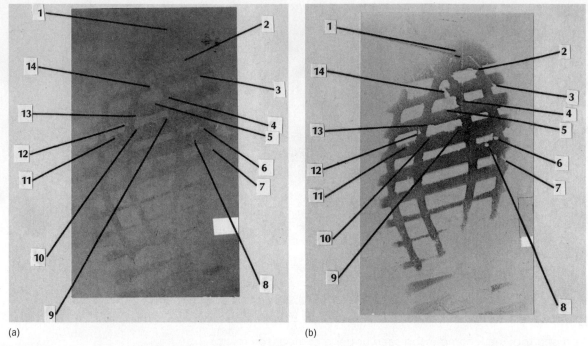

FIGURE 17–23

(a) Impression of shoe found at a crime scene. (b) Test impression made with suspect shoe. A sufficient number of points of comparison exist to support the conclusion that the suspect shoe left the impression at the crime scene.

Other Impressions

From time to time, impressions of another kind are left at a crime scene. This evidence may take the form of a shoe, tire, or fabric impression and may be as varied as a shoe impression left on a piece of paper at the scene of a burglary (Figure 17–23), a hit-and-run victim's garment that has come into violent contact with an automobile (Figure 17–24), or the impression of a bloody shoe print left on a floor or carpet at a homicide scene (Figure 17–25).

Preserving Impressions

The primary consideration in collecting impressions at the crime scene is the preservation of the impression or its reproduction for later examination in the crime laboratory. Before any impression is moved or otherwise handled, it must be photographed (a scale should be included in the picture) to show all the observable details of the impression. Several shots should be taken directly over the impression as well as at various angles around the impression. The skillful use of side lighting for illumination will help highlight many ridge details that might otherwise remain obscured. Photographs should also be taken to show the position of the questioned impression in relation to the overall crime scene.

Although photography is an important first step in preserving an impression, it must be considered merely a backup procedure that is available to the examiner if the impression is damaged before reaching the crime laboratory. Naturally, it is preferable for the examiner to receive the original impression for comparison to the suspect shoe, tire, garment, and so forth. In most cases when the impression is on a readily recoverable item, such as glass, paper, or floor tile, little or no difficulty is presented in transporting the evidence intact to the laboratory.

Lifting Impressions

If an impression is encountered on a surface that cannot be submitted to the laboratory, the investigator may be able to preserve the print in a manner that is analogous to lifting a fingerprint. This is especially true of impressions made in light deposits of dust or dirt. A lifting material large

FIGURE 17–24

A small child was found dead at the edge of a rural road near a railroad crossing, the victim of a hit-and-run driver. A local resident was suspected, but he denied any knowledge of the incident. The investigating officer noted what appeared to be a fabric imprint on the bumper of the suspect's automobile. The weave pattern of the clothing of the deceased was compared with the imprint on the bumper and was found to match. When the suspect was confronted with this information, he admitted his guilt.
Courtesy Centre of Forensic Sciences, Toronto, ON, Canada

enough to lift the entire impression should be used. Carefully place the lifting material over the entire impression. Use a fingerprint roller to eliminate any air pockets before lifting the impression off the surface.

A more exotic approach to lifting and preserving dust impressions involves the use of a portable electrostatic lifting device.[8] The principle employed is similar to that of creating an electrostatic charge on a comb and using the comb to lift small pieces of tissue paper. A sheet of mylar film is placed on top of the dust mark, and the film is pressed against the impression with the aid of a roller. The high-voltage electrode of the electrostatic unit is then placed in contact with the film while the unit's earth electrodes are placed against a metal plate (earth plate) (see Figure 17–26). A charge difference develops between the mylar film and the surface below the dust mark so that the dust is attached to the lifting film. In this manner, dust prints on chairs, walls, floors, and the like, can be transferred to the mylar film. Floor surfaces up to 40 feet long can be covered with a mylar sheet and searched for dust impressions. The electrostatic lifting technique is particularly helpful in recovering barely visible dust prints on colored surfaces. Dust impressions can also be enhanced through chemical development (see Figure 17–27).[9]

---

[8] See R. Milne, "Electrostatic Lifting of Marks at Crime Scenes and the Development of Pathfinder," *Science & Justice* 38 (1998): 135.
[9] B. Glattstein, Y. Shor, N. Levin, and A. Zeichner, "pH Indicators as Chemical Reagents for the Enhancement of Footwear Marks," *Journal of Forensic Sciences* 41 (1996): 23.

(a)   (b)

FIGURE 17–25

An imprint of a shoe was found on the carpet in the home of a homicide victim (b). The suspect's shoe, shown in (a), made the impression. Note the distinctive impression of the hole present in the shoe's sole.
Courtesy of Dade County Crime Lab.

FIGURE 17–26

Electrostatic lifting of a dust impression off a floor using an electrostatic unit.
Courtesy Sirchie Fingerprint Laboratories, Youngsville, N.C., www.sirchie.com

Casting Impressions

When shoe and tire marks are impressed into soft earth at a crime scene, their preservation is best accomplished by photography and casting.[10] Class I dental stone, a form of gypsum, is widely recommended for making casts of shoe and tire impressions. A series of photographs clearly illustrating the steps to be carried out in the casting of an impression are shown in Figure 17–28.

---

[10] D. S. Hilderbrand and M. Miller, "Casting Materials—Which One to Use?" *Journal of Forensic Identification* 45 (1995): 618.

(a)

(b)

FIGURE 17–27

(a) A dust impression of a shoe print on cardboard before enhancement. (b) Shoe print after chemical enhancement with Bromophenol Blue and exposure to water vapor.
Courtesy Division of Identification and Forensic Science (DIFS), Israel Police Headquarters, Jerusalem, Israel

The cast should be allowed to air-dry for 24 to 48 hours before it is shipped to the forensic science laboratory for examination. Figure 17–29 illustrates a cast made from a shoe print in mud. The cast compares to the suspect shoe. An aerosol product known as Snow Impression Wax is available for casting snow impressions.[11] The recommended procedure is to spray three light coats of the wax at an interval of one to two minutes between layers and then let it dry for ten minutes. A viscous mixture of Class I dental stone is then poured onto the wax-coated impression. After the casting material has hardened, the cast can be removed.

A number of chemicals can be used to develop and enhance footwear impressions made with blood. In areas where a bloody footwear impression is very faint or where the subject has tracked through blood leaving a trail of bloody impressions, chemical enhancement can visualize latent or nearly invisible blood impressions (see Figure 17–30). A number of chemical formulas useful for bloody footwear impression development are listed in Appendix V.

A number of blood enhancement chemicals have been examined for their impact on STR DNA typing. None of the chemicals examined had a deleterious effect, on a short-term basis, on the ability to carry out STR DNA typing on the blood.[12]

[11] Available from Sirchie Finger Print Laboratories, Inc., Youngsville, N.C.
[12] C. J. Frégeau et al., "Fingerprint Enhancement Revisited and the Effects of Blood Enhancement Chemicals on Subsequent Profiler Plus™ Fluorescent Short Tandem Repeat DNA Analysis of Fresh and Aged Bloody Fingerprints," *Journal of Forensic Sciences* 45 (2000): 354.

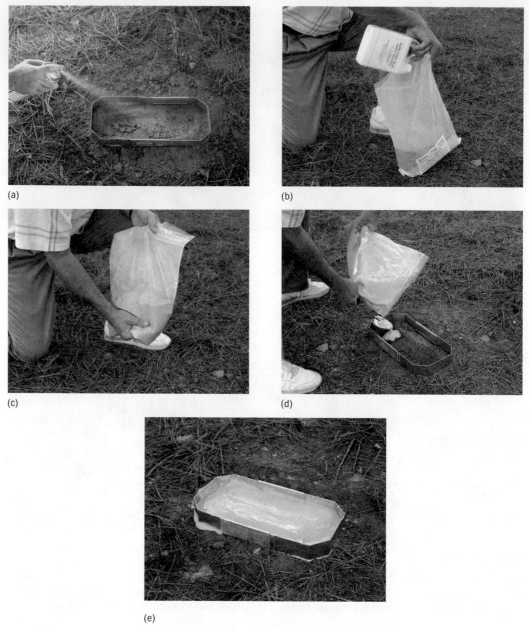

(a)

(b)

(c)

(d)

(e)

FIGURE 17–28

Casting a footwear impression at a crime scene. (a) The impression is hardened using aerosol hairspray. (b) The correct amount of water is added to a known amount of dental stone. (c) The mixture is kneaded by hand until the desired (pancake batter–like) consistency is reached. (d) The dental stone is poured into the impression using a spoon as a medium to disperse the flow. (e) The impression is filled with dental stone and allowed to dry before removal.

Courtesy Sirchie Fingerprint Laboratories, Youngsville, N.C., www.sirchie.com

Comparing Impressions

Whatever the circumstances, the laboratory procedures used for examining any type of impression remain the same. Of course, a comparison is possible only when an item suspected of having made the impression is recovered. Test impressions may be necessary to compare the characteristics of the suspect item with the evidence impression.

The evidential value of the impression is determined by the number of class and individual characteristics that the examiner finds. Agreement with respect to size, shape, or design may

(a) (b) (c)

FIGURE 17–29

(a) Shoe impression in mud. (b) Cast of shoe impression. (c) Shoe suspected of leaving muddy impression.

Courtesy Sirchie Fingerprint Laboratories, Youngsville, N.C., www.sirchie.com

permit the conclusion that the impression could have been made by a particular shoe, tire, or garment; however, one cannot entirely exclude other possible sources from having the same class characteristics. More significant is the existence of individual characteristics arising out of wear, cuts, gouges, or other damage. A sufficient number or the uniqueness of such points of comparison support a finding that both the evidence and test impressions originated from one and only one source.

When tire tread impressions are left at a crime scene, the laboratory can examine the design of the impression and possibly determine the style and/or manufacturer of the tire. This may be particularly helpful to investigators when a suspect tire has not yet been located.

New computer software may be able to help the forensic scientist make shoe print comparisons. For example, an automated shoe print identification system developed in England, called Shoeprint Image Capture and Retrieval (SICAR), incorporates multiple databases to search known and unknown footwear files for comparison against footwear specimens. Shoe print images can be entered into SICAR by either a scanner or a digital camera. This product has a comprehensive shoe sole database (Solemate ™) that includes more than 17,000 footwear entries, representing more than 700 shoe brands, providing investigators with a means for linking a crime scene footwear impression to a particular shoe manufacturer.

Using the SICAR system, an impression from a crime scene can be compared to a reference database to find out what type of shoe caused the imprint. That same impression can also be searched in the suspect and crime databases to reveal whether that shoe print matches the shoes of a person who has been in custody or the shoe prints left behind at another crime scene. When matches are made during the searching process, the images are displayed side by side on the computer screen (see Figure 3–7).

Human bite mark impressions on skin and foodstuffs have proven to be important items of evidence for convicting defendants in a number of homicide and rape cases in recent years. If a sufficient number of points of similarity between test and suspect marks are present, a forensic odontologist may conclude that a bite mark was made by one particular individual (see Figure 17–31).

(a)

(b)

(c)

(d)

FIGURE 17–30

(a) Bloody footprint on cardboard treated with amido black. (b) Bloody footprint treated with Hungarian Red dye. (c) Bloody footprint visualized with leucocrystal violet. (d) Bloody footprint enhanced with patent blue.

(a) Courtesy Dwane S. Hilderbrand and David P. Coy, Scottsdale Police Crime Laboratory, Scottsdale, Ariz.
(b) Courtesy ODV Inc., South Paris, Maine (c–h) Courtesy William Bodziak, FBI Laboratory

(e)

(f)

(g)

(h)

FIGURE 17–30 (Continued)

(e) Bloody foot impression treated with amido black. (f) Bloody footprint visualized with fushin acid dye. (g) Bloody foot impression visualized with tartrazine. (h) Bloody footprint treated with diaminobenzidine.

(a)

(b)

FIGURE 17–31

(a) Bite mark impression on the victim's forearm. (b) Upper dental model from the teeth of the suspect matches the individual teeth characteristics of the bite marks.
Courtesy Haskell Askin, D.D.S., Forensic Odontologist, Brick Town, NJ 08724

> >

case study

The O. J. Simpson Trial—Who Left the Impressions at the Crime Scene?

On the night of June 12, 1994, Nicole Brown—ex-wife of football star O. J. Simpson—and her friend Ron Goldman were brutally murdered on the grounds outside her home in Brentwood, California. O. J. Simpson was arrested for their murders, but professed his innocence. At the crime scene, investigators found bloody shoe impressions along the concrete walkway leading up to the front door of Brown's condominium. These shoe impressions were of extremely high quality and of intricate detail. The news media broadcast countless images of these bloody shoe prints on television, making it obvious to the killer that those shoes would surely link him to the crime.

Famed FBI shoe print examiner William J. Bodziak investigated the footwear evidence from the scene. His first task was to identify the brand of shoe that made the marks. Because the pattern was clear and distinct, with complete toe-to-heel detail, this seemed a simple task at first. Bodziak compared this pattern to the thousands of sole patterns in the FBI's database. None matched. He then went to his reference collection of books and trade show brochures, again with no success.

Bodziak's experience told him that these were expensive, Italian-made casual dress shoes with a sole made from synthetic material. Using this knowledge, he shopped the high-end stores for a similar tread pattern, but still was unable to identify the shoes. He then drew a composite sketch of the sole and faxed the image to law enforcement agencies and shoe manufacturers and distributors worldwide. The owner of the American distributing company for Bruno Magli shoes was the only one to respond.

Further exhaustive investigation revealed that these were extremely rare shoes. There were two styles of shoe bearing this exact sole design. They were available for only two years, and from a mere forty stores in the United States and Puerto Rico. The Lorenzo style shoe had a bootlike upper that came to the ankle. The Lyon style shoe had the lower, more typical dress shoe cut. The impressions were made by a size 12 shoe, and it was later determined that only 299 pairs of size 12 with this tread pattern were sold in the United States.

Simpson flatly denied ever owning these shoes, adding that he would never wear anything so ugly. However, he was known to wear a size 12, and photographs taken almost nine months before the murders show Simpson wearing a pair of black leather Bruno Magli Lorenzo shoes. These shoes were available in several colors, so this narrows the number of shoes matching Simpson's pair of Lorenzos (this size, color, and style) sold in the United States to twenty-nine pairs.

Proving that Simpson owned a pair of shoes that had the exact pattern found printed in blood at the crime scene was an essential component of the case, but it was not done in time to be used during the criminal prosecution. The photographs of Simpson in his Bruno Magli shoes were released after the culmination of the criminal trial, so the jury never heard the direct evidence that Simpson owned these shoes. However, this proved to be an important link uniting Simpson with the crime scene in the civil trial. Although O. J. Simpson was acquitted of the murders of Nicole Brown and Ron Goldman in the criminal trial, he was judged responsible for their murders in the civil court case.

chapter summary >>>>>>>>>>>>>

Structural variations and irregularities caused by scratches, nicks, breaks, and wear permit the criminalist to relate a bullet to a gun, a scratch or abrasion mark to a single tool, or a tire track to a particular automobile.

The manufacture of a barrel requires impressing its inner surface with spiral grooves, a step known as rifling. The surfaces of the original bore remaining between the grooves are called lands. No two rifled barrels, even those manufactured in succession, have identical striation markings. These striations form the individual characteristics of the barrel. The inner surface of the barrel of a gun leaves its striation markings on a bullet passing through it. The number of lands and grooves and their direction of twist are obvious points of comparison during the initial stages of an examination. Any differences in these class characteristics immediately eliminate the possibility that both bullets traveled through the same barrel.

The comparison microscope is the most important tool to a firearms examiner. Two bullets can be observed and compared simultaneously within the same field of view. Not only must the lands and grooves of the test and evidence bullet have identical widths, but the longitudinal striations on each must coincide. The firing pin, breechblock, and ejector and extractor mechanism also offer a highly distinctive signature for individualization of cartridge cases. The advent of computerized imaging technology has made possible the storage of bullet and cartridge surface characteristics in a manner analogous to automated fingerprint files. However, the final comparison will be made by the forensic examiner through traditional microscopic methods.

The distribution of gunpowder particles and other discharge residues around a bullet hole permits an assessment of the distance from which a handgun or rifle was fired. The firing of a weapon not only propels residues toward the target, but also blows gunpowder and primer residues back toward the shooter. As a result, traces of these residues are often deposited on the firing hand of the shooter, and their detection can provide valuable information as to whether an individual has recently fired a weapon. Examiners measure the amount of barium and antimony on the relevant portion of the suspect's hands or characterize the morphology of particles containing these elements to determine whether a person has fired or handled a weapon, or was near a discharged firearm.

Increasingly, the criminalist is asked to restore a serial number that has been obliterated by grinding, rifling, or punching. Restoration of serial numbers is possible through chemical etching because the metal crystals in the stamped zone are placed under a permanent strain that extends a short distance beneath the original numbers.

A tool mark is any impression, cut, gouge, or abrasion caused by a tool coming into contact with another object. Hence any minute imperfections on a tool impart individuality to that tool. The shape and pattern of such imperfections are further modified by damage and wear during the life of the tool. The comparison microscope is used to compare crime-scene tool marks with test impressions made with the suspect tool. When shoe and tire marks are impressed into soft earth at a crime scene, their preservation is best accomplished by photography and casting. In areas where a bloody footwear impression is very faint or where the subject has tracked through blood, leaving a trail of bloody impressions, chemical enhancement can visualize latent or nearly invisible blood impressions. A sufficient number of points of comparison or the uniqueness of such points support a finding that both the questioned and test impressions originated from one and only one source.

review questions

1. The _____ is the original part of the bore left after rifling grooves are formed.

2. The diameter of the gun barrel is known as its _____.

3. True or False: The number of lands and grooves is a class characteristic of a barrel. _____

4. The _____ characteristics of a rifled barrel are formed by striations impressed into the barrel's surface.

5. The most important instrument for comparing bullets is the _____.

6. To make a match between a test bullet and a recovered bullet, the lands and grooves of the test and evidence bullet must have identical widths, and the longitudinal _____ on each must coincide.

7. True or False: It is always possible to determine the make of a weapon by examining a bullet it fired. _____

8. A shotgun has a _____ barrel.

9. The diameter of a shotgun barrel is expressed by the term _____.

10. True or False: Shotgun pellets can be individualized to a single weapon. _____

11. True or False: A cartridge case can be individualized to a single weapon. _____

12. The automated firearms search system developed by the FBI and ATF as a unified system incorporating both DRUGFIRE and IBIS technologies available in prior years is known as _____.

13. True or False: The distribution of gunpowder particles and other discharge residues around a bullet hole permits an approximate determination of the distance from which the gun was fired. _____

14. True or False: Without the benefit of a weapon, an examiner can make an exact determination of firing distance. _____

15. A halo of vaporous lead (smoke) deposited around a bullet hole normally indicates a discharge _____ to _____ inches from the target.

16. If a firearm has been fired more than 3 feet from a target, usually no residue is deposited but a dark ring, known as _____, is observed.

17. As a rule of thumb, the spread in the pattern made by a 12-gauge shotgun increases 1 inch for every _____ of distance from the target.

18. A(n) _____ photograph may help visualize gunpowder deposits around a target.

19. True or False: One test method for locating powder residues involves transferring particles embedded on the target surface to chemically treated photographic paper. _____

20. Current methods for identifying a shooter rely on the detection of _____ residues on the hands.

21. Determining whether an individual has fired a weapon is done by measuring the elements _____ and _____ present on the hands.

22. True or False: Firings with all types of ammunition can be detected by hand swabbings with nitric acid. _____

23. Microscopic primer and gunpowder particles on the adhesives applied to a suspected shooter's hand can be found with a(n) _____.

24. True or False: Restoration of serial numbers is possible because in the stamped zone the metal is placed under a(n) permanent strain that extends beneath the original numbers. _____

25. True or False: It is proper to insert a pencil into the barrel when picking up a crime-scene gun. _____

26. Recovered bullets are initialed on either the _____ or _____ of the bullet.

27. True or False: Because minute traces of evidence such as paint and fibers may be adhering to a recovered bullet, the investigator must take care to remove these trace materials immediately. _____

28. True or False: Cartridge cases are best marked at the base of the shell. _____

29. The clothing of the victim of a shooting must be handled so as to prevent disruption of _____ around bullet holes.

30. A(n) _____ is any impression caused by a tool coming into contact with another object.

31. Tool marks compare only when a sufficient number of _____ match between the evidence and test markings.

32. Objects bearing tool marks should be submitted intact to the crime lab or a(n) _____ should be taken of the tool mark.

33. An imprint may be lifted using lifting sheets or a(n) _____.

34. Shoe and tire marks impressed into soft earth at a crime scene are best preserved by _____ and _____.

35. A wear pattern, cut, gouge, or other damage pattern can impart _____ characteristics to a shoe.

application and critical thinking

1. From each of the following descriptions of bullet holes, use general guidelines to estimate the distance from the shooter to the target.

   a. A few widely scattered gunpowder particles with no soot around the entrance hole

   b. A dark ring around the bullet hole, but no soot or gunpowder particles

   c. A halo of soot surrounding the entrance hole along with scattered specks of powder grains

   d. Scorch marks and melted fibers surrounding the entrance hole

2. You are investigating a shooting involving a 12-gauge shotgun with a moderately high choke. The spread of the pattern made by the pellets measures 12 inches. In your opinion, which of the following is probably closest to the distance from the target to the shooter? Explain your answer and explain why the other answers are likely to be incorrect.

   a. 18 yards

   b. 12 yards

   c. 6 yards

   d. 30 yards

3. Criminalist Ben Baldanza is collecting evidence from the scene of a shooting. After locating the revolver suspected of firing the shots, Ben picks the gun up by the grip, unloads it, and places the ammunition in an envelope. He then attaches an identification tag to the grip. Searching the scene, Ben finds a bullet lodged in the wall. He uses pliers to grab the bullet and pull it from the wall, then inscribes the bullet with his initials and places it in an envelope. What mistakes, if any, did Ben make in collecting this evidence?

4. How would you go about collecting impressions in each of the following situations?
   a. You discover a shoe print in dry dirt.
   b. You discover a tool mark on a windowsill.
   c. You discover tire marks in soft earth.
   d. You discover a shoe print on a loose piece of tile.
   e. You discover a very faint shoe print in dust on a colored linoleum floor.

further references

Bodziak, William J., *Footwear Impression Evidence*, 2nd ed. Boca Raton, Fla.: Taylor & Francis, 1999.

Bodziak, William J., *Tire Tread and Tire Track Evidence: Recovery and Forensic Examination*. Boca Raton, Fla.: Taylor & Francis, 2008

Heard, B.J., *Handbook of Firearms and Ballistics: Examining and Interpreting Forensic Evidence*. 2nd ed. Chichester, West Sussex, U.K., 2008.

An Introduction to Forensic Firearm Identification, http://www.firearmsid.com.

Rowe, Walter F., "Firearms Identification," in R. Saferstein, ed., *Forensic Science Handbook*, vol. 2, 2nd ed., Upper Saddle River, N.J.: Prentice Hall, 2005.

Schehl, S. A., "Firearms and Toolmarks in the FBI Laboratory," *Forensic Science Communications* 2, no. 2 (2000), http://www.fbi.gov/hq/lab/fsc/backissu/april2000/schehl1.htm.

The Unabomber

In 1978, a parcel addressed to a Northwestern University professor exploded as it was being opened by a campus security officer. This was the first of a series of bomb-containing packages sent to universities and airlines. The perpetrator was dubbed UN (university) A (airlines) BOM; hence, *the Unabomber*. The explosives were usually housed in a pipe within a wooden box. The explosive ingredients generally were black powder, smokeless powder, or an ammonium nitrate mix. The box was filled with metal objects to create a shrapnel effect on explosion. The device typically had the initials "FC" punched into it. The first Unabomber fatality came in 1985. The Unabomber surfaced again in 1993, mailing bombs to two university professors. Their injuries were not fatal, but his next two attacks did result in fatalities.

In 1995, the case took an unexpected turn when the Unabomber promised to end his mad spree if his 35,000-page typewritten *Manifesto* sent to the *New York Times* and the *Washington Post* were published. The *Manifesto* proved to be a long, rambling rant against technology, but it offered valuable clues that broke the case. David Kaczynski realized that the *Manifesto*'s writing style and the philosophy it espoused closely resembled that of his brother Ted. Linguistic experts carefully pored over the *Manifesto*'s content. Ted Kaczynski was arrested in Montana in 1996. Inside his ramshackle cabin were writings similar to the *Manifesto*, three manual typewriters, and bomb-making materials. Forensic document examiners matched the typewritten *Manifesto* to one of the typewriters recovered from the cabin.

document examination

KEY TERMS

charred document
erasure
exemplar
indented writings
infrared luminescence
natural variations
obliteration
questioned document

Learning Objectives

After studying this chapter you should be able to:

- Define the term *questioned document*

- Know what common individual characteristics are associated with handwriting

- List some important guidelines for the collection of known writings for comparison to a questioned document

- Recognize some of the class and individual characteristics of printers and photocopiers

- List some of the techniques document examiners use to uncover alterations, erasures, obliterations, and variations in pen inks

Document Examiner

Ordinarily, the work of the document examiner involves examining handwriting and typescript to ascertain the source or authenticity of a questioned document. However, document examination is not restricted to a mere visual comparison of words and letters. The document examiner must know how to use the techniques of microscopy, photography, and even such analytical methods as chromatography to uncover successfully all efforts, both brazen and subtle, designed to change the content or meaning of a document.

Alterations of documents through overwriting, erasures, or the more obvious crossing out of words must be recognized and characterized as efforts to alter or obscure the original meaning of a document. The document examiner uses his or her special skills to reconstruct the written contents of charred or burned paper or to uncover the meaning of indented writings found on a paper pad after the top sheet has been removed.

questioned document
Any document about which some issue has been raised or that is the subject of an investigation

Any object that contains handwritten or typewritten markings whose source or authenticity is in doubt may be referred to as a **questioned document**. Such a broad definition covers all of the written and printed materials we normally encounter in our daily social and business activities. Letters, checks, drivers' licenses, contracts, wills, voter registrations, passports, petitions, and even lottery tickets are the more common specimens received in crime laboratories to be examined. However, we need not restrict our examples to paper documents. Questioned documents may include writings or other markings found on walls, windows, doors, or any other objects.

Document examiners possess no mystical powers or scientific formulas for identifying the authors of writings. They apply knowledge gathered through years of training and experience to recognize and compare the individual characteristics of questioned and known authentic writings. For this purpose, the gathering of documents of known authorship or origin is critical to the outcome of the examination. Collecting known writings may entail considerable time and effort, and their collection may be further hampered by uncooperative or missing witnesses. However, the uniqueness of handwriting makes this type of physical evidence, like fingerprints, one of few definitive individual characteristics available to the investigator, a fact that certainly justifies an extensive investigative effort.

Handwriting Comparisons

Document experts continually testify that no two individuals write exactly alike. This is not to say that there cannot be marked resemblances between two individuals' handwritings because many factors make up the total character of a person's writing.

General Style

Perhaps the most obvious feature of handwriting to the layperson is its general style. As children we all learn to write by attempting to copy letters that match a standard form or style shown to us by our teachers. The style of writing acquired by the learner is that which is fashionable for the particular time and locale. In the United States, for example, the two most widely used systems are the Palmer method, first introduced in 1880, and the Zaner-Bloser method, introduced in about 1895 (see Figure 18–1). To some extent, both of these systems are taught in nearly all 50 states.

The early stages that accompany the learning and practicing of handwriting are characterized by a conscious effort on the part of the student to copy standard letter forms. It is not surprising that many pupils in a handwriting class tend at first to have writing styles that are similar to one another, with minor differences attributable to skill in copying. However, as initial writing skills improve, a child normally reaches the stage where the nerve and motor responses associated with the act of writing become subconscious. The individual's writing now begins to take on innumerable habitual shapes and patterns that distinguish it from all others. The document examiner looks for these unique writing traits.

Variations in Handwriting

The unconscious handwriting of two different individuals can never be identical. Individual variations associated with mechanical, physical, and mental functions make it extremely unlikely that all of these factors can be exactly reproduced by any two people. Thus, variations are expected in

FIGURE 18–1

(top) An example of Zaner-Bloser handwriting; *(bottom)* an example of Palmer handwriting.

Courtesy Robert J. Phillips, Document Examiner, Audubon, New Jersey

angularity, slope, speed, pressure, letter and word spacings, relative dimensions of letters, connections, pen movement, writing skill, and finger dexterity.

Furthermore, many other factors besides pure handwriting characteristics should be considered. The arrangement of the writing on the paper may be as distinctive as the writing itself. Margins, spacings, crowding, insertions, and alignment are all results of personal habits. Spelling, punctuation, phraseology, and grammar can be personal and, if so, combine to individualize the writer.

In a problem involving the authorship of handwriting, all characteristics of both the known and questioned documents must be considered and compared. Dissimilarities between the two writings are a strong indication of two writers, unless these differences can logically be accounted for by the facts surrounding the preparation of the documents. Because any single characteristic, even the most distinctive one, may be found in the handwriting of other individuals, no single handwriting characteristic can by itself be taken as the basis for a positive comparison. The final conclusion must be based on a sufficient number of common characteristics between the known and questioned writings to effectively preclude the chance of their having originated from two different sources.

What constitutes a sufficient number of personal characteristics? Here again, there are no hard-and-fast rules for making such a determination. The expert examiner can make this judgment only in the context of each particular case.

Challenges to Handwriting Comparison

When the examiner receives a reasonable amount of known handwriting for comparison, there is usually little difficulty in finding sufficient evidence to determine the source of a questioned document. Frequently, however, circumstances may prevent a positive conclusion or may permit only the expression of a qualified opinion. Such situations usually develop when an insufficient number of known writings are made available for comparison. Although nothing may be found that definitely points to the questioned and known handwriting being of a different origin, not enough personal characteristics may be present in the known writings that are consistent with the questioned materials.

Difficulties may also arise when the examiner receives questioned writings containing only a few words, all deliberately written in a crude, unnatural form or all very carefully written and thought out so as to disguise the writer's natural style—a situation usually encountered with threatening or obscene letters. It is extremely difficult to compare handwriting that has been very carefully prepared to a document written with such little thought for structural details that it contains only the subconscious writing habits of the writer. However, although it may be relatively easy to change one's writing habits for a few words or sentences, the task of maintaining such an effort grows more difficult with each additional word.

When an adequate amount of writing is available to the examiner, the attempt at total disguise may fail. This was illustrated in the attempt by Clifford Irving to forge letters in the name of the late industrialist Howard Hughes in order to obtain lucrative publishing contracts for Hughes's life story. Figure 18–2 shows the forged signatures of Howard Hughes along with Clifford Irving's known writings. By comparing these signatures, document examiner R. A. Cabbane of the U.S. Postal Inspection Service detected many examples of Irving's personal characteristics in the forged signatures.

For example, note the formation of the letter *r* in the word *Howard* on lines 1 and 3, as compared with the composite on line 6. Observe the manner in which the terminal stroke of the letter *r* tends to terminate with a little curve at the baseline of Irving's writing and the forgery. Notice the way the bridge of the *w* drops in line 1 and also in line 6. Also, observe the similarity in the formation of the letter *g* as it appears on line 1 as compared with the second signature on line 5.

FIGURE 18–2

Forged signatures of Howard Hughes and examples of Clifford Irving's writing.

Reprinted by permission of the American Society for Testing and Materials from the *Journal of Forensic Sciences,* copyright 1975

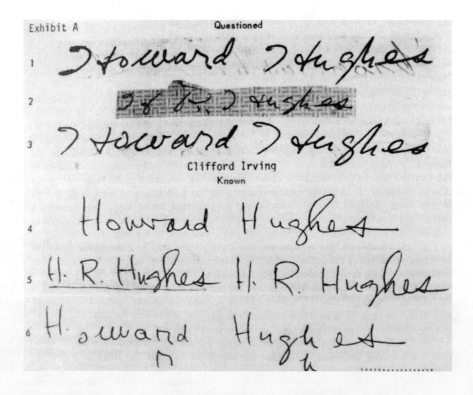

The document examiner must also be aware that writing habits may be altered beyond recognition by the influence of drugs or alcohol. Under these circumstances, it may be impossible to obtain known writings of a suspect written under conditions comparable to those at the time the questioned document was prepared.

Collection of Handwriting Exemplars

It should be fairly obvious by now that collection of an adequate number of known writings (**exemplars**) is most critical for determining the outcome of a comparison. Generally, known writings of the suspect furnished to the examiner should be as similar as possible to the questioned document. This is especially true with respect to the writing implement and paper. Styles and habits may be somewhat altered if a person switches from a pencil to a ballpoint pen or to a fountain pen. The way the paper is ruled, or the fact that it is unruled, may also affect the handwriting of a person who has become particularly accustomed to one type or the other. Known writings should also contain some of the words and combinations of letters present in the questioned document.

DETERMINING AUTHENTICITY   The known writings must be adequate in number to show the examiner the range of **natural variations** in a suspect's writing characteristics. No two specimens of writing prepared by one person are ever identical in every detail. Variation is an inherent part of natural writing. In fact, a signature forged by tracing an authentic signature can often be detected even if the original and tracing coincide exactly because no one ever signs two signatures exactly alike (see Figure 18–3).

Many sources are available to the investigator for establishing the authenticity of the writings of a suspect. An important consideration in selecting sample writings is the age of the genuine document

exemplar
An authentic sample used for comparison purposes, such as handwriting

natural variations
Normal deviations found between repeated specimens of an individual's handwriting or any printing device

FIGURE 18–3

Examples of handwriting from the same individual over an extended period of time.
Courtesy Robert J. Phillips, Document Examiner, Audubon, New Jersey

forensics at work

Hitler's Diaries

In 1981 a spectacular manuscript attributed to Adolf Hitler was disclosed by the brother of an East German general. These documents included Hitler's 27-volume diary and an unknown third volume of his autobiography, *Mein Kampf*. The existence of these works was both culturally and politically significant to the millions who were affected by World War II.

Authentication of the diaries was undertaken by two world-renowned experts, one Swiss and one American.

Both declared that the handwritten manuscripts were identical to the known samples of Adolf Hitler's handwriting that they were given. Bidding wars began for publishing rights, and a major national newspaper in the United States won with a price near $4 million.

The publishing company that originally released the documents to the world market undertook its own investigation, which ultimately revealed a clever but devious plot. The paper on which the diaries were written contained a

relative to the questioned one. It is important to try to find standards that date closely in time to the questioned document. For most typical adults, basic writing changes are comparatively slow. Therefore, material written within two or three years of the disputed writing is usually satisfactory for comparison; as the age difference between the genuine and unknown specimens becomes greater, the standard tends to become less representative.

OBTAINING WRITING SAMPLES   Despite the many potential sources of handwriting exemplars, it may be difficult or impossible to obtain an adequate set of collected standards. In these situations, handwriting may have to be obtained voluntarily or under court order from the suspect. There is ample case law to support the constitutionality of taking handwriting specimens. In the case of *Gilbert* v. *California*,[1] the Supreme Court upheld the taking of handwriting exemplars before the appointment of counsel. The Court also reasoned that handwriting samples are identifying physical characteristics that lie outside the protection privileges of the Fifth Amendment. Furthermore, in the case of *United States* v. *Mara*,[2] the Supreme Court ruled that taking a handwriting sample did not constitute an unreasonable search and seizure of a person and hence did not violate Fourth Amendment rights.

As opposed to nonrequested specimens (written without the thought that they may someday be used in a police investigation), requested writing samples may be consciously altered by the writer. However, the investigator can take certain steps to minimize attempts at deception. The requirement of several pages of writing normally provides enough material that is free of attempts at deliberate disguise or nervousness for a valid comparison. In addition, the writing of dictation yields exemplars that best represent the suspect's subconscious style and characteristics.

Other steps that can be taken to minimize a conscious writing effort, as well as to ensure conditions approximating those of the questioned writing, can be summarized as follows:

1. The writer should be allowed to write sitting comfortably at a desk or table and without distraction.
2. The suspect should not under any conditions be shown the questioned document or be told how to spell certain words or what punctuation to use.
3. The suspect should be furnished a pen and paper similar to those used in the questioned document.
4. The dictated text should be the same as the contents of the questioned document, or at least should contain many of the same words, phrases, and letter combinations found in the document. In handprinting cases, the suspect must not be told whether to use uppercase (capital) or lowercase (small) lettering. If after writing several pages the writer fails to use the desired type of lettering, he or she can then be instructed to include it. Altogether, the text must be no shorter than a page.
5. Dictation of the text should take place at least three times. If the writer is trying to disguise the writing, noticeable variations should appear among the three repetitions. Discovering this, the investigator must insist on continued repetitive dictation of the text.

[1] 388 U.S. 263 (1967).
[2] 410 U.S. 19 (1973).

whitener that didn't exist until 1954, long after Hitler committed suicide. The manuscript binding threads contained viscose and polyester, neither of which was available until after World War II. Further, the inks used in the manuscript were all inconsistent with those in use during the year these pages were allegedly written.

Moreover, the exemplars sent to the Swiss and American experts as purportedly known examples of Hitler's handwriting were actually from the same source as the diaries. Thus, the experts were justified in proclaiming that the documents were authentic because they were written by the same hand—it just wasn't Hitler's. Chemical analysis of the inks later determined that the "Hitler diaries" were in fact less than one year old—spectacular, but fake!

6. Signature exemplars can best be obtained when the suspect is required to combine other writings with a signature. For example, instead of compiling a set of signatures alone, the writer might be asked to fill out completely 20 to 30 separate checks or receipts, each of which includes a signature.
7. Before requested exemplars are taken from the suspect, a document examiner should be consulted and shown the questioned specimens.

Typescript Comparisons

With the emergence of digital technology, document examiners are confronted with a new array of machines capable of creating documents subject to alteration or fraudulent use. Personal computers use daisy wheel, dot-matrix, ink-jet, and laser printers. More and more, the document examiner encounters problems involving these machines, which often produce typed copies that have only inconspicuous defects.

Photocopier, Printer, and Fax Examination

In the cases of photocopiers, fax machines, and computer printers, an examiner may need to identify the make and model of a machine that may have been used in printing a document. Alternatively, the examiner may need to compare a questioned document with test samples printed from a suspect machine. Typically, the examiner generates approximately ten samples through each machine to obtain a sufficient representation of a photocopier's characters. A side-by-side comparison is then made between the questioned document and the printed exemplars to compare markings produced by the machine.

PHOTOCOPIERS   Transitory defect marks originating from random debris on the glass platen, inner cover, or mechanical portions of a copier produce images. These images are often irregularly shaped and sometimes form distinctive patterns. Thus, they become points of comparison as the document examiner attempts to link the document to suspect copiers. The gradual change, shift, or duplication of these marks may aid the examiner in dating the document.

FAX MACHINES   In analyzing computer printouts and faxes, examiners use the same approach for comparing the markings on a questioned document to exemplar documents generated by a suspect machine. These markings include all possible transitory patterns arising from debris and other extraneous materials. Interestingly, fax machines print a header known as the *transmitting terminal identifier* (TTI) at the top of each fax page. For the document examiner, the TTI is an important point of comparison (see Figure 18–4). The header and the document's text should have different type styles. TTIs can be fraudulently prepared and placed in the appropriate position on a fax copy. However, a microscopic examination of the TTI's print quickly reveals significant characteristics that distinguish it from a genuine TTI.

FIGURE 18–4

A fax page showing a transmitting terminal identifier (TTI).

₪001/002

GRIZZLY
RANCH

4456 Grizzly Road, Portola, CA 96122 (530)832-9617 x 1108 (530)832-0501 FAX
www.grizzlyranch.com

FAX

To:	JOE BROWN	From:	DAVID SMITH
		Pages:	2
CC: Sarah Jones		Date:	July 20, 2006
Re: Letter Droft		Fax:	202-555-1272
☐ Urgent	☑ For Review	☐ Please Comment	☐ Please Reply

PLease see ATTACHed
document

In determining the fax machine's model type, the examiner most often begins by analyzing the TTI type style. The fonts of that line are determined by the sending machine. The number of characters, their style, and their position in the header are best evaluated through a collection of TTI fonts organized into a useful database. One such database is maintained by the American Society of Questioned Document Examiners.

COMPUTER PRINTERS   Computer printer model determination requires an extensive analysis of the specific printer technology and type of ink used. Visual and microscopic techniques provide useful information in determining the technology and toner used. Generally, printers are categorized as impact and nonimpact printers by the mechanism of their toner application. Nonimpact printers, such as ink-jet and laser printers, and impact printers, such as thermal and dot-matrix printers, all have characteristic ways of printing documents. Character shapes, toner differentiation, and toner application methods are easily determined with a low-power microscope and help the examiner narrow the possibilities of model type.

When the suspect machine is not available, the examiner may need to analyze the document's class characteristics to identify the make and model of the machine. It is important to identify the printing technology, the type of paper, the type of toner or ink used, the chemical composition of the toner, and the type of toner-to-paper fusing method used in producing the document. Examination of the toner usually involves microscopic analysis to characterize its surface morphology, followed by identification of the inorganic and organic components of the toner. These results separate model types into categories based on their mechanical and printing characteristics. Typically, document examiners access databases to help identify the model type of machine used to prepare a questioned document. The resulting list of possibilities produced by the database hopefully reduces the number of potential machines to a manageable number. Obviously, once a suspect machine is identified, the examiner must perform a side-by-side comparison of questioned and exemplar printouts as described previously.

TYPEWRITERS   One mechanical writing device the document examiner encounters is the typewriter, although it is not as prevalent as it used to be. Examiners are most often asked the following two questions about typewriters: (1) Can the make and model of the typewriter used to type the questioned document be identified? (2) Can a particular suspect typewriter be identified as having prepared the questioned document?

To answer the first question, the examiner must have access to a complete reference collection of past and present typefaces used by typewriter manufacturers. The two most popular typeface sizes are pica (10 letters to the inch) and elite (12 letters to the inch). Although a dozen manufacturers may use a pica or an elite typeface, many of these are readily distinguishable when the individual type character's style, shape, and size are compared.

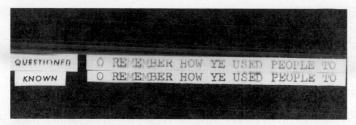

FIGURE 18–5

A portion of a typewriting comparison points to the conclusion that the same machine typed both specimens. Besides the similarity in the design and size of type, note the light impression consistently made by the letter *M*. Also, the letter *E* slants to the right, almost touching *D* in the word *USED* in both specimens.
Courtesy New Jersey State Police

As is true for any mechanical device, use of a typewriter will result in wear and damage to the machine's moving parts. These changes occur both randomly and irregularly, thereby imparting individual characteristics to the typewriter. Variations in vertical and horizontal alignment (characters are too high or low or too far left or right of their correct position) and perpendicular misalignment of characters (characters leaning to the left or to the right), as well as defects in each typeface, are most valuable for proving the identity of a typewriter (see Figure 18–5).

Associating a particular typewriter with a typewritten document requires comparing the questioned document to exemplars prepared from the suspect typewriter. As with handwriting, collection of proper standards is the foundation of such comparisons. In this respect, it is preferable if the investigator can directly supply the document examiner with the questioned typewriter. This arrangement gives the examiner the opportunity to prepare an adequate number of exemplars and also allows direct examination of the machine's typefaces. If the investigator has to prepare standards from the questioned machine, a minimum of one copy in full word-for-word order of the questioned typewriting must be obtained.

Another area of investigation relates to the ribbon. An examination of the type impressions left on a ribbon may reveal the portion of the ribbon on which a particular text was typed.

When the suspect typewriter is not available for examination, the investigator must gather known writings that have been typed on the suspect machine. Ideally, material should be selected that contains many of the same combinations of letters and words found on the questioned document. The individual defects that characterize a typewriter develop and change as the machine is used; some may have changed between the preparation of the questioned and standard material. Hence, if many specimens are available, those prepared near the time of the disputed document should be collected.

Alterations, Erasures, and Obliterations

Documents are often altered or changed after preparation so that their original intent may be hidden or so that a forgery may be perpetrated. Documents can be changed in several ways, and for each way, the application of a special discovery technique is necessary.

Erasures and Alterations

One of the most common ways to alter a document is to try to erase parts of it, using an India rubber eraser, sandpaper, razor blade, or knife to remove writing or type by abrading or scratching the paper's surface. All such attempts at erasure disturb the upper fibers of the paper. These changes are apparent when the suspect area is examined under a microscope using direct light or by allowing the light to strike the paper obliquely from one side (side lighting). Although microscopy may reveal whether an **erasure** has been made, it does not necessarily indicate the original letters or words present. Sometimes so much of the paper has been removed that identifying the original contents is impossible.

In addition to abrading the paper, the perpetrator may also choose to obliterate words with a chemical erasure. In this case, strong oxidizing agents are placed over the ink, producing a colorless reaction product. Although such an attempt may not be noticeable to the naked eye,

erasure

The removal of writing, typewriting, or printing from a document; it is normally accomplished by either chemical means or an abrasive instrument

(a)

(b)

FIGURE 18–6

(a) A 20-dollar bill as it appears under room light. (b) The bill illuminated with ultraviolet light reveals ink writing.
Courtesy Sirchie Fingerprint Laboratories, Youngsville, N.C., www.sirchie.com

examination under the microscope reveals a discoloration on the treated area of the paper. Sometimes examination of the document under ultraviolet or infrared lighting reveals the chemically treated portion of the paper. Interestingly, examination of documents under ultraviolet light may also reveal the presence of fluorescent ink markings that go unnoticed in room light, as seen in Figure 18–6.

Some inks, when exposed to blue-green light, absorb the radiation and reradiate infrared light. This phenomenon is known as **infrared luminescence**. Thus, if an alteration is made to a document with ink differing from the original, it can sometimes be detected by illuminating the document with blue-green light and using infrared-sensitive film to record the light emanating from the document's surface. In this fashion, any differences in the luminescent properties of the inks are observed (see Figure 18–7). Infrared luminescence has also revealed writing that has been erased. Such writings may be recorded by invisible residues of the original ink that remain embedded in the paper even after an erasure.

Another important application of infrared photography arises from the observation that inks may differ in their ability to absorb infrared light. Thus, illuminating a document with infrared light and recording the light reflected off the document's surface with infrared-sensitive film may enable the examiner to differentiate inks of a dissimilar chemical composition (see Figure 18–8).

infrared luminescence

A property exhibited by some dyes that emit infrared light when exposed to blue-green light

Obliterations

Intentional **obliteration** of writing by overwriting or crossing out is seldom used for fraudulent purposes because of its obviousness. Nevertheless, such cases may be encountered in all types of documents. Success at permanently hiding the original writing depends on the material used to cover the writing. If it is done with the same ink as was used to write the original material, recovery will be difficult if not impossible. However, if the two inks are of a different chemical composition, photography with infrared-sensitive film may reveal the original writing. Infrared radiation may pass through the upper layer of writing while being absorbed by the underlying area (see Figure 18–9).

Close examination of a questioned document sometimes reveals crossing strokes or strokes across folds or perforations in the paper that are not in a sequence that is consistent with the natural preparation of the document. Again, these differences can be shown by microscopic or photographic scrutiny.

Infrared photography sometimes reveals the contents of a document that has been accidentally or purposely charred in a fire. Another way to decipher **charred documents** involves reflecting light off the paper's surface at different angles in order to contrast the writing against the charred background (see Figure 18–10).

obliteration

The blotting out or smearing over of writing or printing to make the original unreadable

charred document

Any document that has become darkened and brittle through exposure to fire or excessive heat

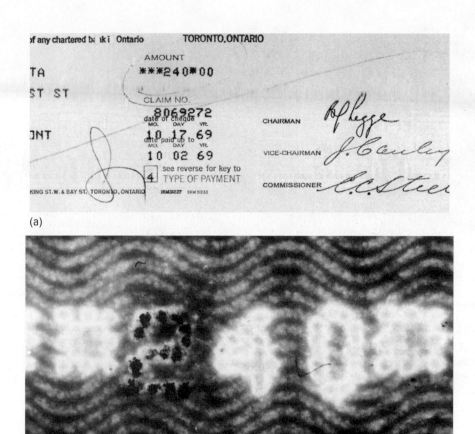

(a)

(b)

FIGURE 18–7

Part of a check stolen from a government agency as it appears to the naked eye is shown in (a). An infrared luminescence photograph was prepared of the amount figures at a magnification of 10× in (b). This clearly shows that the number 2 was added with a different ink. The accused pleaded guilty.

Courtesy Centre of Forensic Sciences, Toronto, Canada

(a)

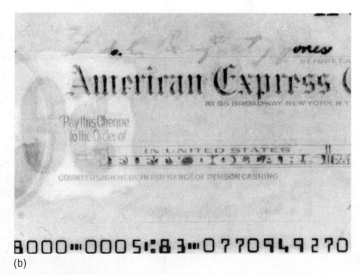

(b)

FIGURE 18–8

(a) This photograph, taken under normal illumination, shows the owner of an American Express check to be "Freda C. Brightly Jones." Actually, this signature was altered. The check initially bore the signature "Fred C. Brightly Jr."
(b) This photograph taken under infrared illumination, using infrared-sensitive film, clearly shows that the check was altered by adding *a* to *Fred* and *ones* to *Jr*. The ink used to commit these changes is distinguishable because it absorbs infrared light, whereas the original ink does not.

Courtesy (a) New Jersey State Police

(a)

(b)

FIGURE 18–9

(a) A photograph showing an area of a document that has been blacked out with a heavy layer of ink overwriting.
(b) In this photograph, the covering ink has been penetrated by infrared photography to reveal the original writing.
Courtesy Centre of Forensic Sciences, Toronto, Canada

Digital image processing is the method by which the visual quality of digital pictures is improved or enhanced. *Digitizing* is the process by which the image is stored in memory. This is commonly done by scanning an image with a flatbed scanner or a digital camera and converting the image by computer into an array of digital intensity values called *pixels*, or picture elements (see page 410). Once the image has been digitized, an image editing program such as Adobe Photoshop is used to adjust the image. An image may be enhanced through lightening, darkening, and color and contrast controls. An example of how the technology is applied to forensic document examination is shown in Figures 18–11 and 18–12.

Other Document Problems

Indented Writings

indented writings

Impressions left on papers positioned under a piece of paper that has been written on

Indented writings are the partially visible depressions on a sheet of paper underneath the one on which the visible writing was done. Such depressions are caused by the application of pressure on the writing instrument and would appear as a carbon copy of a sheet if carbon paper had been inserted between the pages.

Indented writings have proved to be valuable evidence. For example, the top sheet of a bookmaker's records may have been removed and destroyed, but it still may be possible to determine the writing by the impressions left on the pad. These impressions may contain incriminating evidence supporting the charge of illegal gambling activities. When paper is studied under oblique or side lighting, its indented impressions are often readable (see Figure 18–13).

An innovative approach to visualizing indented writings has been developed at the London College of Printing in close consultation with the Metropolitan Police Forensic Science Laboratory.[3] The method involves applying an electrostatic charge to the surface of a polymer film that has been placed in contact with a questioned document, as shown in Figure 18–14. Indented impressions on the document are revealed by applying a toner powder to the charged film. For many documents examined by this process, clearly readable images have been produced from

[3] D. M. Ellen, D. J. Foster, and D. J. Morantz, "The Use of Electrostatic Imaging in the Detection of Indented Impressions," *Forensic Science International* 15 (1980): 53.

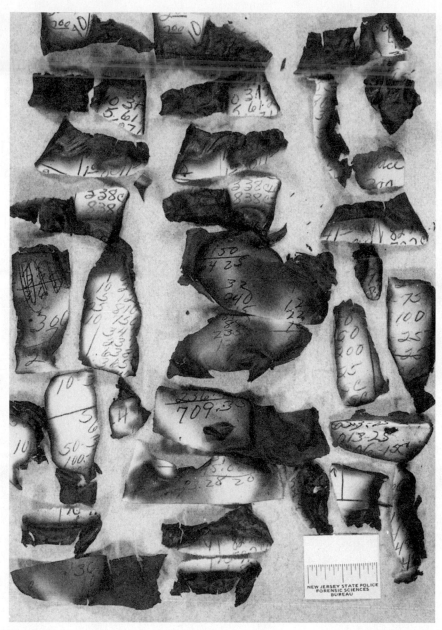

FIGURE 18–10

Decipherment of charred papers seized in the raid of a suspected bookmaking establishment. The charred documents were photographed with reflected light.
Courtesy New Jersey State Police

impressions that could not be seen or were barely visible under normal illumination. An instrument that develops indented writings by electrostatic detection is commercially available and is routinely used by document examiners.

Ink and Paper Comparison

A study of the chemical composition of writing ink present on documents may verify whether known and questioned documents were prepared by the same pen. A nondestructive approach to comparing ink lines is accomplished with a visible microspectrophotometer (see pages 173–175).[4] A case example illustrating the application of this approach to ink analysis appears in Figure 7–11. Thin-layer chromatography is also suitable for ink comparisons. Most commercial inks, especially ballpoint inks, are actually mixtures of several organic dyes. These dyes can be separated on a

---

[4] P. W. Pfefferli, "Application of Microspectrophotometry in Document Examination," *Forensic Science International* 23 (1983): 129.

ORIGINAL

SCREEN

EXCLUSION

CURVES

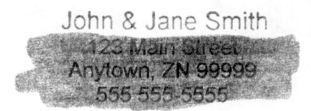

LEVELS

REPLACE COLOR

FIGURE 18–11

This composite demonstrates the various changes that can be applied to a digitized image in order to reveal information that has been obscured. Using a photo editor (Adobe Photoshop), the original was duplicated and pasted as a second layer. Colors were changed in selected areas of the image using the "screen" and "exclusion" options. "Replace color" allows the user to choose a specific color or range of colors and lighten, darken, or change the hue of the colors selected. "Level" and "curves" tools can adjust the lightest and darkest color ranges and optimize contrast, highlights, and shadow detail of the image for additional clarity.

Courtesy Lt. Robert J. Garrett, Middlesex County Prosecutor's Office, N.J.

properly developed thin-layer chromatographic plate. The separation pattern of the component dyes is distinctly different for inks with different dye compositions and thus provides many points of comparison between a known and a questioned ink.

Ink can be removed from paper with a hypodermic needle with a blunted point to punch out a small sample from a written line. About ten plugs or microdots of ink are sufficient for chromatographic analysis. The U.S. Secret Service and the Internal Revenue Service jointly maintain the United States International Ink Library. This collection includes more than 9,200 inks, which date back to the 1920s. Each year new pen and ink formulations from writing pens, ink-jets, and toners are added to the reference collection. These inks have been systematically cataloged according to dye patterns developed by thin-layer chromatography

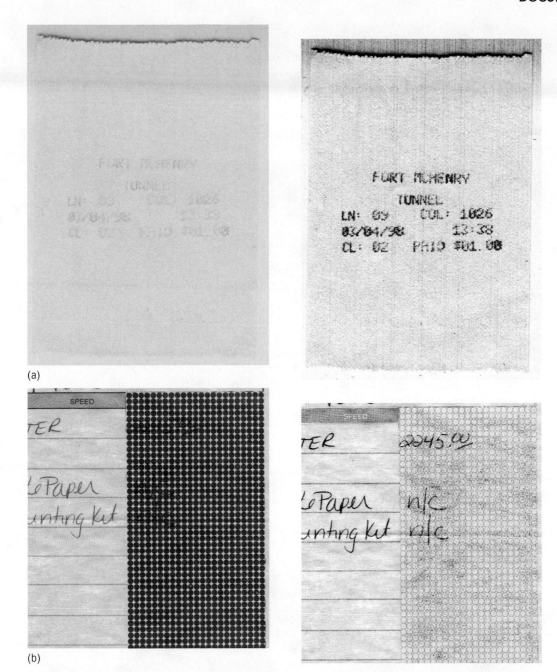

FIGURE 18–12

(a) Receipts have been used in investigations to establish a victim's whereabouts, provide suspects with alibis, and substantiate a host of personal conduct. Unfortunately, many times, because of wear, age, or poor printing at the register, the receipt may be unreadable. This can be corrected using photo-editing software. In this example, the original toll receipt was scanned at the highest color resolution, which allows more than 16 million colors to be reproduced. The image was then manipulated, revealing the printed details, by adjusting the lightest and darkest levels and the color content of the image. (b) Invoices may contain details about a transaction that are important to an investigation. The copy that ships with the merchandise may have that information blocked out. This information may be recovered using digital imaging. The left figure shows the original shipping ticket. The right figure shows the information revealed after replacing the color of the blocking pattern.

Courtesy Lt. Robert J. Garrett, Middlesex County Prosecutor's Office, N.J.

(a)

(b)

FIGURE 18–13

A suspected forger was arrested. In his car, police found written lists of the victims he intended to defraud. Some of these writings are shown in (a). A writing pad found in his house had indentations on the top page of the pad shown in (b). These indentations corresponded to the writings found in the car, further linking the suspect to the writings.

Courtesy Centre of Forensic Sciences, Ministry of Community Safety and Correctional Services, Toronto, ON, Canada

FIGURE 18–14

An electrostatic detection apparatus (ESDA) works by applying an electrostatic charge to a document suspected of containing indented writings. The indentations are then visualized by the application of charge-sensitive toner.

Courtesy Foster & Freeman Limited, Worcestershire, U.K., www.fosterfreeman.co.uk

FIGURE 18-15

Chart demonstrating different TLC patterns
of blue ballpoint inks.
Courtesy U.S. Secret Service Laboratory, Washington, D.C.

(TLC; see Figure 18–15). On several occasions, this approach has been used to prove that a document has been fraudulently backdated. For example, in one instance, it was possible to establish that a document dated 1958 was backdated because a dye identified in the questioned ink had not been synthesized until 1959.

To further aid forensic chemists in ink-dating matters, several ink manufacturers, at the request of the U.S. Treasury Department, voluntarily tag their inks during the manufacturing process. The tagging program allows inks to be dated to the exact year of manufacture by changing the tags annually.

Another area of inquiry for the document examiner is the paper on which a document is written or printed. Paper is often made from cellulose fibers found in wood and fibers recovered from recycled paper products. The most common features associated with a paper examination are general appearance, color, weight, and watermarks. Other areas of examination include fiber identification and the characterization of additives, fillers, and pigments present in the paper product.

Virtual Forensics Lab

Thin-Layer Chromatography of Ink

To perform a virtual thin-layer chromatography lab analyzing ink, go to **www.pearsoncustom.com/us/vlm/**

chapter summary   > > > > > > > > > > > >

Any object with handwriting or print whose source or authenticity is in doubt may be referred to as a questioned document. Document examiners apply knowledge gathered through years of training and experience to recognize and compare the individual characteristics of questioned and known authentic writings. For this purpose, gathering documents of known authorship or origin is critical to the outcome of the examination. Many factors compose the total character of a person's writing. The unconscious handwriting of two different individuals can never be identical. Furthermore, the writing style of one individual may be altered beyond recognition by the influence of drugs or alcohol. The collection of an adequate number of known writings is critical for determining the outcome of a handwriting comparison. Known writing should contain some of the words and combinations of letters present in the questioned document.

The two requests most often made of the examiner in connection with the examination of typewriters and printing devices are to determine whether the make and model of the typewriter and printing devices used to prepare the questioned document can be identified and whether a particular suspect typewriter or printing device can be identified as having prepared the questioned document. The individual type character's style, shape, and size are compared to a complete reference collection of past and present typefaces. As is true for any mechanical device, use of a printing device results in wear and damage to the machine's moving parts. These changes occur both randomly and irregularly, thereby imparting individual characteristics to the printing device. The document examiner has to deal with problems involving business and personal computers, which often produce printed copies that have only subtle defects.

Document examiners must deal with evidence that has been changed in several ways, such as through alterations, erasures, and obliterations. Indented writings have proved to be valuable evidence. It may be possible to determine what was written by the impressions left on a paper pad. Applying an electrostatic charge to the surface of a polymer film that has been placed in contact with a questioned document visualizes indented writings. A study of the chemical composition of writing ink on documents may verify whether known and questioned documents were prepared by the same pen.

review questions

1. Any object that contains handwriting or typescript and whose source or authenticity is in doubt is referred to as a(n) _____.

2. Variations in mechanical, physical, and mental functions make it (likely, unlikely) that the writing of two different individuals can be distinguished.

3. In a problem involving the authorship of handwriting, all characteristics of both the _____ and _____ documents must be considered and compared.

4. True or False: A single handwriting characteristic by itself can be taken as a basis for a positive comparison. _____

5. True or False: Normally, known writings need not contain words and combinations of letters present in the questioned document. _____

6. As the age difference between genuine and unknown specimens becomes greater, the standard tends to become (more, less) representative of the unknown.

7. In the case of _____, the Supreme Court held handwriting to be nontestimonial evidence not protected by Fifth Amendment privileges.

8. When requested writing is being given by a suspect, care must be taken to minimize a(n) _____ writing effort.

9. Random wear and damage to a typewriter impart it with _____ characteristics.

10. Examination of a document under _____ or _____ lighting may reveal chemical erasures of words or numbers.

11. Some inks, when exposed to blue-green light, absorb _____ radiation and emit light.

12. Handwriting containing inks of different chemical compositions may be distinguished by photography with _____ film.

13. _____ writings are partially visible impressions appearing on a sheet of paper underneath the one on which the visible writing was done.

14. Many ink dyes can be separated by the technique of _____ chromatography.

application and critical thinking

1. Criminalist Julie Sandel is investigating a series of threatening notes written in pencil and sent to a local politician. A suspect is arrested and Julie directs the suspect to prepare writing samples to compare to the writing on the notes. She has the suspect sit at a desk in an empty office and gives him a pen and a piece of paper. She begins to read one of the notes and asks the suspect to write the words she dictates. After reading about half a page, she stops, then dictates the same part of the note a second time for the suspect. At one point, the suspect indicates that he does not know how to spell one of the words, so Julie spells it for him. After completing the task, Julie takes the original notes and the dictated writing from the suspect to a document examiner. What mistakes, if any, did Julie make?

2. In each of the following situations, indicate how you would go about recovering original writing that is not visible to the naked eye.

   a. The original words have been obliterated with a different ink than was used to compose the original.

   b. The original words have been obliterated by chemical erasure.

   c. The original writing was made with fluorescent ink.

   d. The original documents have been charred or burned.

3. You have been asked to determine whether a handwritten will, supposedly prepared 30 years ago, is authentic or a modern forgery. What aspects of the document would you examine to make this determination? Explain how you would use thin-layer chromatography to help you come to your conclusion.

further references

Brunelle, Richard L., "Questioned Document Examination," in R. Saferstein, ed., *Forensic Science Handbook*, vol. 1, 2nd ed., Upper Saddle River, N.J.: Prentice Hall, 2002.

Ellen, David, *The Scientific Examination of Documents—Methods and Techniques*, 3rd ed. Boca Raton, Fla.: Taylor & Francis, 2005.

Held, D. A. E., "Handwriting, Typewriting, Shoeprints, and Tire Treads: FBI Laboratory's Questioned Documents Unit," *Forensic Science Communications*, 3, no. 2 (2001), http://www.fbi.gov/hq/lab/fsc/backissu/april2001/held.htm.

Hilton, Ordway, *Scientific Examination of Questioned Documents*, rev. ed. Boca Raton, Fla.: Taylor & Francis, 1992.

Kelly, J. S. Lindblom, B. S., *Scientific Examination of Questioned Documents,* 2nd ed., Boca Raton, Fla.: Taylor & Francis, 2006.

The BTK Killer

Dennis Rader was arrested in February 2005 and charged with committing ten murders since 1974 in the Wichita, Kansas, area. The killer, whose nickname stands for "bind, torture, kill," hadn't murdered since 1991, but resurfaced in early 2004 by sending a letter to a local newspaper taking credit for a 1986 slaying. Included with the letter were a photocopy of the victim's driver's license and three photos of her body. The BTK killer was back to his old habit of taunting the police. Three months later another letter surfaced. This time the letter detailed some of the events surrounding BTK's first murder victims. In 1974, he strangled Joseph and Julie Otero along with two of their children. Shortly after those murders occurred, BTK sent a letter to a local newspaper in which he gave himself the name BTK. In December 2004, a package found in a park contained the driver's license of another BTK victim along with a doll whose hands were bound with pantyhose and that was covered with a plastic bag.

The major break in the case came when BTK sent a message on a floppy disk to a local TV station. "Erased" information on the disk was recovered and restored by forensic computer specialists, and the disk was traced to the Christ Lutheran Church in Wichita. The disk was then quickly linked to Dennis Rader, the church council president. The long odyssey of the BTK killer was finally over.

computer forensics

by Andrew W. Donofrio

Learning Objectives

After studying this chapter you should be able to:

- List and describe the hardware and software components of a computer

- Understand the difference between read-only memory and random-access memory

- Describe how a hard disk drive is partitioned

- Describe the proper procedure for preserving computer evidence at a crime scene

- Understand the difference between and location of visible and latent data

- List the areas of the computer that will be examined to retrieve forensic data

- Relate various areas found on the computer where a user's Internet activities can be investigated

- Describe how e-mails, chat, and instant messages on the Internet can be traced and recovered

- List and describe three locations where investigators may pinpoint the origin of a hacker

KEY TERMS

bit
bookmark
byte
central processing
   unit (CPU)
cluster
cookies
file slack
firewall
hacking
hard disk drive (HDD)
hardware
Internet cache
Internet history
latent data
Message Digest 5
   (MD5)/secure hash
   algorithm (SHA)
motherboard
operating system (OS)
partition
RAM slack
random-access
   memory (RAM)
sector
software
swap file
temporary files
unallocated space
visible data

Andrew W. Donofrio is a detective sergeant with the Prosecutor's Office in Bergen County, New Jersey, and is a leading computer forensics examiner for Bergen County, with more than 18 years' experience in the field of law enforcement. He has conducted more than five hundred forensic examinations of computer evidence and frequently lectures on the subject throughout the state, as well as teaching multiday courses on computer forensics and investigative topics at police academies and colleges in New Jersey. Det. Sgt. Donofrio writes regularly on Internet-related and computer forensics issues for a number of law enforcement publications and has appeared as a guest expert on Internet-related stories on MSNBC.

Since the 1990s, few fields have progressed as rapidly as computer technology. Computers are no longer a luxury, nor are they in the hands of just a select few. Technology and electronic data are a part of everyday life and permeate all aspects of society. Consequently, computers have become increasingly important as sources of evidence in an ever-widening spectrum of criminal activities.

Investigators frequently encounter computers and other digital devices in all types of cases. As homicide investigators sift for clues they may inquire whether the method for a murder was researched on the Internet; whether signs of an extramarital affair can be found in e-mail or remnants of instant messages, which may provide motive for a spouse killing or murder for hire; or whether threats were communicated to the victim before a murder by an obsessed stalker. Arson investigators want to know whether financial records on a computer may provide a motive in an arson-for-profit fire. A burglary investigation would certainly be aided if law enforcement determined that the proceeds from a theft were being sold online—perhaps through eBay or a similar online auction site.

Accessibility to children and the perception of anonymity has given sexual predators a way to seek out child victims online. The vulnerability of computers to hacker attacks is a constant reminder of security issues surrounding digitally stored data. Finally, the fact that computers control most of our critical infrastructure makes technology an appetizing target for would-be terrorists.

Computer forensics involves the preservation, acquisition, extraction, analysis, and interpretation of computer data. Although this is a simple definition, it gets a bit more complicated. Part of this complication arises from technology itself. More and more devices are capable of storing electronic data: cell phones, personal digital assistants (PDAs), iPods, digital cameras, flash memory cards, smart cards, jump drives, and many others. Methods for extracting data from these devices each present unique challenges. However, sound forensic practices apply to all these devices. The most logical place to start to examine these practices is with the most common form of electronic data: the personal computer.

From Input to Output: How Does the Computer Work?

Hardware versus Software

Before we get into the nuts and bolts of computers, we must establish the important distinction between hardware and software. **Hardware** comprises the physical components of the computer: the computer chassis, monitor, keyboard, mouse, hard disk drive, random-access memory (RAM), central processing unit (CPU), and so on (see Figure 19–1). The list is much more extensive, but generally speaking, if it is a computer component or peripheral that you can see, feel, and touch, it is hardware.

Software, conversely, is a set of instructions compiled into a program that performs a particular task. Software consists of programs and applications that carry out a set of instructions on the hardware. Operating systems (Windows, Mac OS, Linux, Unix), word-processing programs (Microsoft Word, WordPerfect), Web-browsing applications (Internet Explorer, Safari, Firefox), and accounting applications (Quicken, QuickBooks, Microsoft Money) are all examples of software.

It is important not to confuse software with the physical media that it comes on. When you buy an application such as Microsoft Office, it comes on a compact disc (CD). The CD containing this suite of applications is typically referred to as software, but this is technically wrong. The CD is external computer media that contains the software; it is a container for and a medium to load the set of instructions onto the hard disk drive (the hardware).

Hardware Components

COMPUTER CASE/CHASSIS   The case is the physical box holding the fixed internal computer components in place. Cases come in many shapes and sizes: a full upright tower chassis, a slim desktop model sitting on the desktop, or an all-in-one monitor/computer case like the iMac. For our purposes, the term *system unit* is probably most appropriate when describing a chassis seized as evidence. The term *system unit* accurately references the chassis, including the motherboard and other internal components.

---

hardware

The physical components of a computer: case, keyboard, monitor, motherboard, RAM, HDD, mouse, and so on; generally speaking, if it is a computer component you can touch, it is hardware

software

A set of instructions compiled into a program that performs a particular task; software consists of programs and applications that carry out a set of instructions on the hardware

External Drive

CD/DVD Drive

Power supply

DVD

Hard Disk Drive

Floppy Disk Drive

Expansion Bus
with Expansion Card

Motherboard

ROM

CPU

RAM

Computer Case/Chasis

FIGURE 19–1

Cutaway diagram of a personal computer showing the tangible hardware components of a computer system.
Courtesy Tim Downs

POWER SUPPLY The term *power supply* is actually a misnomer because it doesn't actually supply power—the power company does that. Rather, a computer's power supply converts power from the wall outlet to a usable format for the computer and its components. Different power supplies have different wattage ratings. The use, or more specifically, the components, of the computer dictate the appropriate power supply.

MOTHERBOARD The main circuit board in a computer (or other electronic devices) is referred to as the **motherboard**. Motherboards contain sockets for chips and slots for add-on cards. Examples of add-on cards are a video card to connect the computer to the monitor, a network card or modem to connect to an internal network or the Internet, and a sound card to connect to speakers. Sockets on the motherboard typically accept things like random-access memory (RAM) or the central processing unit (CPU). The keyboard, mouse, CD-ROM drives, floppy disk drives, monitor, and other peripherals or components connect to the motherboard in some fashion through a direct wired or wireless connection.

SYSTEM BUS Contained on the motherboard, the system bus is a vast complex network of wires that carry data from one hardware device to another. This network is analogous to a complex highway. Data is sent along the bus in the form of ones and zeros (or, more appropriately stated, as electrical impulses representing an "on" or "off" state—this two-state computing is also known as *binary computing*).

READ-ONLY MEMORY (ROM) This rather generic term describes special chips on the motherboard. ROM chips store programs called *firmware*, used to start the boot process and configure a computer's components. Today's ROM chips, termed *flash ROM*, are a combination of two types

motherboard
The main system board of a computer (and many other electronic devices); it delivers power, data, and instructions to the computer's components; every component in the computer connects to the motherboard, either directly or indirectly

of chips used in past motherboard technologies. The first was known as the *system ROM*, which was responsible for booting the system and handling the "assumed" system hardware present in the computer. As the system ROM, generally speaking, could not be altered, and because as technology matured changes to the "assumed" hardware were more common, a different type of chip was introduced. The *complementary metal-oxide semiconductor* (CMOS) was a separate chip that allowed the user to exercise setup control over several system components. Regardless of how this technology is present on the motherboard, it can be referred to as the BIOS, for *basic input-output system*. The operation of the BIOS is relevant to several computer forensic procedures, particularly the boot sequence. It is the set of routines associated with the BIOS in ROM that initiates the booting process and enables the computer to communicate with various devices in the system such as disk drives, keyboard, monitor, and printer. As will become clear later, it is important not to boot the actual computer under investigation to the original hard disk drive. This would cause changes to the data, thus compromising the integrity of evidence. The BIOS allows investigators to control the boot process to some degree.

central processing unit (CPU)
The main chip within the computer; also referred to as the brain of the computer; this microprocessor chip handles most of the operations (code and instructions) of the computer

CENTRAL PROCESSING UNIT (CPU) The **central processing unit (CPU)**, also referred to as a processor, is essentially the brain of the computer. It is the main (and typically the largest) chip that plugs into a socket on the motherboard. The CPU is the part of the computer that actually computes. Basically, all operations performed by the computer are run through the CPU. The CPU carries out the program steps to perform the requested task. That task can range from opening and working in a Microsoft Word document to performing advanced mathematical algorithms. CPUs come in various shapes, sizes, and types. Intel Pentium chips and Advanced Micro Devices (AMD) chips are among the most common.

random-access memory (RAM)
The volatile memory of the computer; when power is turned off, its contents are lost; programs and instructions are loaded into RAM while they are in use

RANDOM-ACCESS MEMORY (RAM) This is one of the most widely mentioned types of computer memory. **Random-access memory (RAM)** takes the burden off the computer's processor and hard disk drive (HDD). If the computer had to access the HDD each time it wanted data, it would run slowly and inefficiently. Instead the computer, aware that it may need certain data at a moment's notice, stores the data in RAM. It is helpful to envision RAM as chips that create a large spreadsheet, with each cell representing a memory address that the CPU can use as a reference to retrieve data. RAM is referred to as *volatile memory* because it is not permanent; its contents undergo constant change and are forever lost once power is taken away from the computer. RAM takes the physical form of chips that plug into the motherboard; SIMMs (single inline memory modules), DIMMs (dual inline memory modules), and SDRAM (synchronous dynamic random-access memory) are just a few of the types of chips. Today's computers come with various denominations of RAM: 2 GB (gigabyte) is the most common.[1]

INPUT DEVICES Input devices are used to get data into the computer or to give the computer instructions. Input devices constitute part of the "user" side of the computer. Examples include the keyboard, mouse, joystick, and scanner.

OUTPUT DEVICES Output devices are equipment through which data is obtained from the computer. Output devices are also part of the "user" side of the computer, and provide the results of the user's tasks. They include the monitor, printer, and speakers.

hard disk drive (HDD)
Typically the main storage location within the computer; consists of magnetic platters contained in a case (usually 3.5" in a desktop computer and 2.5" in a laptop); the HDD is usually where the operating system, applications, and user data are stored

HARD DISK DRIVE (HDD) Generally speaking, the **hard disk drive (HDD)** is the primary component of storage in the personal computer (Figure 19–2). It typically stores the operating system (Windows, Mac OS, Linux, Unix), the programs (Microsoft Word, Internet Explorer, Open Office for Linux, and so on) and data files created by the user (documents, spreadsheets, accounting information, the company database, and so on). Unlike RAM, the HDD is permanent storage and retains its information even after the power is turned off. HDDs work off a controller that is typically part of the motherboard, but sometimes takes the form of an add-on (expansion) card plugged into the motherboard. The most common types of HDD controllers are integrated drive electronics (IDE), small computer system interface (SCSI), and serial ATA (SATA). Each HDD type has a different interface that connects it to the controller. Regardless of the type of controller, the data is basically stored in the same fashion. HDDs are mapped (formatted) and

---

[1] A megabyte (MB) is approximately one million bytes (discussed later in the chapter), a gigabyte (GB) is approximately one billion bytes, or 1,000 megabytes.

FIGURE 19–2

An inside view of the platter and read/write head of a hard disk drive.
Courtesy Corbis RF

have a defined layout. They are logically divided into sectors, clusters, tracks, and cylinders. (See the section titled "How Data Is Stored" for further information).

NETWORK INTERFACE CARD (NIC)   Very rarely do we find a computer today that doesn't have a NIC. Whether they are on a local network or the Internet, when computers need to communicate with each other, they typically do so through a NIC. NICs come in many different forms: add-on cards that plug into the motherboard, hard-wired devices on the motherboard, add-on cards (PCMCIA) for laptops, and universal serial bus (USB) plug-in cards, to name a few. Some are wired cards, meaning they need a physical wired connection to participate on the network, and others are wireless, meaning they receive their data via radio waves.

OTHER COMMON STORAGE DEVICES   Although the HDD is the most common storage device for the personal computer, many others exist. Methods for storing data and the layout of that data can vary from device to device. A CD-ROM, for example, uses a different technology and format for writing data than a floppy disk or USB thumb drive. Fortunately, regardless of the differences among devices, the same basic forensic principles apply for acquiring the data. Common storage devices include the following:

CD-R/RW (COMPACT DISC-RECORD/REWRITE) AND DVD-R/RW (DVD-RECORD/REWRITE)   Compact discs (CDs) and digital video discs (DVDs) are two of the most common forms of storing external data. They are used to store a wide variety of information, such as music, video, and data files. A largely plastic disc with an aluminum layer is read by laser light in the CD/DVD reader. Different CDs are encoded in different ways, making the job of the forensic examiner difficult at times.

FLOPPY DISKS   Though "floppies" are not as common as they once were, forensic examiners still encounter the 3.5-inch floppy disk. Floppy disks can be used to boot an operating system or to store data. They are constructed of hard plastic with a thin plastic disk on the inside. That thin plastic disk is coated with a magnetic iron oxide material. The disk is mapped and stores data in a similar fashion to the hard disk drive. By today's standards, floppy disks don't hold much data.

USB THUMB DRIVES AND SMART MEDIA CARDS   These devices can store a large amount of data—some as much as 64 GB. They are known as solid-state storage devices because they have no moving parts. Smart media cards are typically found in digital cameras and PDAs, whereas USB thumb drives come in many shapes, sizes, and storage capacities.

TAPES   Tapes come in many different formats and storage capacities. Each typically comes with its own hardware reader and sometimes a proprietary application to read and write its contents. Tapes and thumb drives are typically used for backup purposes and consequently have great forensic potential.

Putting It All Together

A person approaches the computer, sits down, and presses the power button. The power supply wakes up and delivers power to the motherboard and all of the hardware connected to the computer. At this point the flash ROM chip on the motherboard (the one that contains the BIOS) conducts a power-on self test (POST) to make sure everything is working properly.

The flash ROM also polls the motherboard to check the hardware that is attached and follows its programmed boot order, thus determining from what device it should boot. Typically the boot device is the HDD, but it can also be a floppy disk, CD, or USB drive. If it is the HDD, the HDD is then sent control. It locates the first sector of its disk (known as the master boot record), determines its layout (partition[s]), and boots an operating system (Windows, Mac OS, Linux, Unix). The person is then presented with a computer work environment, commonly referred to as a desktop.

Now ready to work, the user double-clicks an icon on the desktop, such as a Microsoft Word shortcut, to open the program and begin to type a document. The CPU processes this request, locates the Microsoft Word program on the HDD (using a predefined map of the drive called a *file system table*), carries out the programming instructions associated with the application, loads Microsoft Word into RAM via the system bus, and sends the output to the monitor by way of the video controller, which is either located on or attached to the motherboard.

The user then begins to type, placing the data from the keyboard into RAM. At the end, the user may print the document or simply save it to the HDD for later retrieval. If printed, the data is taken from RAM, processed by the CPU, placed in a format suitable for printing, and sent through the system bus to the external port where the printer is connected. If the document is saved, the data is taken from RAM, processed by the CPU, passed to the HDD controller (IDE, SCSI, or SATA) by way of the system bus, and written to a portion of the HDD. The HDD's file system table is updated so it knows where to retrieve that data later. In actuality, the boot process is more complex than the way it has been described here and requires the forensic examiner to possess an in-depth knowledge of its process.

The preceding example illustrates how three components perform most of the work: the CPU, RAM, and system bus. The example can get even more complicated as the user opens more applications and performs multiple tasks simultaneously (*multitasking*). Several tasks can be loaded into RAM at once, and the CPU is capable of juggling them all. This allows for the multitasking environment and the ability to switch back and forth between applications. All of this is orchestrated by the operating system and is written in the language of the computer—ones and zeros. The only detail missing, and one that is important from a forensic standpoint, is a better understanding of how data is stored on the hard disk drive.

Storing and Retrieving Data

Before beginning to understand how data is stored on a hard disk drive (HDD), it is first important to understand the role of the **operating system (OS)**. An OS, such as Windows, Mac OS, Linux, or Unix, is the bridge between the human user and the computer's electronic components. It provides the user with a working environment and facilitates interaction with the system's components. Each OS supports certain types of file systems that store data in different ways, but some support the methods of others.

Formatting and Partitioning the HDD

Generally speaking, before an OS can write to a HDD it must first be formatted. But even before it can be formatted, a partition must be defined. A **partition** is nothing more than a contiguous set of blocks that are defined and treated as an independent disk. This means that a hard disk drive can hold several partitions, making a single HDD appear as several disks.

Partitioning a drive can be thought of as dividing a container that begins as nothing more than four sides with empty space on the inside. We then cut a hole in the front of it and place inside two drawers containing the hardware to open and close them. We have just created a two-drawer filing cabinet and defined each drawer as contiguous blocks of storage. A partitioning utility such as Disk Manager or fdisk defines the drawer or drawers (partitions) that will later hold the data on the HDD. Just as the style, size, and shape of a filing cabinet drawer can vary, so too can partitions.

After a hard drive is partitioned, it is typically formatted. (At this point it is a high-level format, not to be confused with low-level formatting, which is generally done by the manufacturer of the HDD.) The formatting process initializes portions of the HDD and creates the structure of the file system. The file system can be thought of as the system for storing and locating data on a storage device. Some of the file system types are FAT12 (typically on floppy disks), FAT16 (older DOS and older Windows partitions), FAT32 (Windows file systems), NTFS (most current Windows systems—2000 and XP), EXT2 and EXT3 (Linux systems), and HPFS (some Macintosh systems).

Each of these file systems has a different way of storing, retrieving, and allocating data. So, in summary, a drive is prepared in three processes: low-level formatting (typically done by the manufacturer, dividing the platters into tracks and sectors), partitioning (accomplished through a utility such as fdisk or Disk Manager, defining a contiguous set of blocks), and formatting (initializing portions of the disk and creating the file system structure). Although the process is a bit more technical and detailed, at the conclusion of these steps, the drive is logically defined. We say "logically" because no real divisions are made. If you were to crack open the HDD before or after partitioning and formatting, to the naked eye the platters would look the same.

Mapping the HDD

As shown in Figure 19–3, HDDs contain several platters stacked vertically that are logically divided into sectors, clusters, tracks, and cylinders. **Sectors** are typically 512 bytes in size (a **byte** is eight bits; a **bit** is a single one or zero). **Clusters** are groups of sectors; their size is defined by the file system, but they are always in sector multiples of two. (Although an NTFS partition does permit a one-sector-per-cluster scenario, such a scenario is not usually chosen.) A cluster, therefore, consists of two, four, six, or eight sectors, and so on. (With modern file systems, the user can exercise some control over the number of sectors per cluster.) *Tracks* are concentric circles that are defined around the platter. *Cylinders* are groups of tracks that reside directly above and below each other.

Additionally, the HDD has a file system table (map) of the layout of the defined space in that partition. FAT file systems use a *file allocation table* (which is where the acronym *FAT* comes

sector
The smallest addressable unit of data by a hard disk drive; generally consists of 512 bytes

byte
A group of eight bits

bit
Short for binary digit; taking the form of either a one or a zero, it is the smallest unit of information on a machine

cluster
A group of sectors in multiples of two; cluster size varies from file system to file system and is typically the minimum space allocated to a file

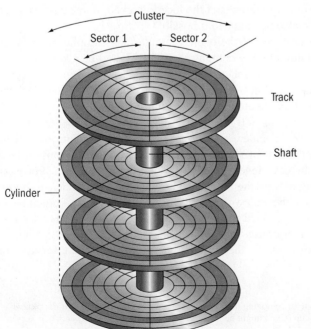

FIGURE 19–3

Partitions of a hard disk drive.

from) to track the location of files and folders (data) on the HDD, whereas NTFS file systems (used by most current Windows systems—Vista and XP) use, among other things, a *master file table (MFT)*. Each file system table tracks data in different ways, and computer forensic examiners should be versed in the technical nuances of the HDDs they examine. It is sufficient for our purposes here, however, to merely visualize the file system table as a map where the data is located. This map uses the numbering of sectors, clusters, tracks, and cylinders to keep track of the data.

One way to envision a partition and file system is as a room full of safe-deposit boxes. The room itself symbolizes the entire partition and the boxes symbolize clusters of data. In order to determine who rented which box, and subsequently where their property is, a central database is needed. This is especially true if a person rented two boxes located in opposite ends of the room (noncontiguous data on the HDD). The database tracking the locations of the safe-deposit boxes is much like a file system table tracking the location of data within the clusters.

This example is also useful to understand the concept of reformatting a HDD. If the database managing the locations of the safe-deposit boxes were wiped out, the property in them would still remain; we just wouldn't know what was where. So too with the hard disk drive. If a user were to wipe the file system table clean—for example, by reformatting it—the data itself would not be gone. Both the database tracking the locations of the safe-deposit boxes and the file system table tracking the location of the data in the cluster are maps—not the actual contents. (Exceptions exist with some file systems, such as an NTFS file system, which stores data for very small files right in its file system table, known as the master file table).

Processing the Electronic Crime Scene

Processing the electronic crime scene has a lot in common with processing a traditional crime scene. The investigator must first ensure that the proper legal requirements (search warrant, consent, and so on) have been met so that the scene can be searched and the evidence seized. The investigator should then devise a plan of approach based on the facts of the case and the physical location. The scene should be documented in as much detail as possible before disturbing any evidence, and before the investigator lays a finger on any computer components. Of course, there are circumstances in which an investigator may have to act quickly and pull a plug before documenting the scene, such as when data is in the process of being deleted.

Documenting the Crime Scene

Crime-scene documentation is accomplished through two actions: sketching and photographing. The electronic crime scene is no different. The scene should be sketched in a floor plan fashion (see Figure 19–4) and then overall photographs of the location taken. In the case of a network, a technical network sketch should also be included if possible.

After photographs have been taken of the overall layout, close-up photographs should be shot. A close-up photograph of any running computer monitor should be taken. All the connections to the main system unit, such as peripheral devices (keyboard, monitor, speakers, mouse, and so on), should be photographed. If necessary, system units should be moved delicately and carefully to facilitate the connections photograph. (See Figure 19–5.) Close-up photographs of equipment serial numbers should be taken if practical.

At this point, investigators must decide whether to perform a live acquisition of the data, perform a system shutdown (as in the case of server equipment), pull the plug from the back of the computer,[2] or a combination thereof. Several factors influence this decision. For example, if encryption is being used and by pulling the plug the data will encrypt, rendering it unreadable without a password or key, pulling the plug would not be prudent. Similarly, if crucial evidentiary data exists in RAM and has not been saved to the HDD, the data will be lost. Hence, if power to the system is discontinued, another option must be considered. Regardless, the equipment will most likely be seized. Exceptions exist in the corporate environment, where servers are fundamental to business operations.

---

[2] Pulling the plug should always be done by removing the plug from the back of the computer. If the plug is removed from the wall, a battery backup (UPS) might be in place, causing an alert to the system and keeping the unit powered on.

FIGURE 19–4

Rough sketch made at a crime scene with necessary measurements included.

After the photographs and sketches are complete, but before disconnecting the peripherals from the computer, a label should be placed on the cord of each peripheral, with a corresponding label placed on the port to which it is connected. A numbering scheme should be devised to identify the system unit if several computers are at the scene (Figure 19–6). The combination of sketching, photographing, and labeling should adequately document the scene, prevent confusion of which component went with which system unit, and facilitate reconstruction if necessary for lab or courtroom purposes.

Forensic Image Acquisition

Now that the items have been seized, the data needs to be obtained for analysis. The number of electronic items that potentially store evidentiary data are too vast to cover in this section. The hard disk drive will be used as an example, but the same "best practices" principles apply for other electronic devices as well.

Throughout the entire process, the computer forensic examiner must use the least intrusive method. The goal in obtaining data from a HDD is to do so without altering even one bit of data.

FIGURE 19–5

Back of a computer showing all connections.

FIGURE 19–6

Back of a computer with each component correlated with its port through the use of a labeling scheme.

Message Digest 5 (MD5)/Secure Hash Algorithm (SHA)

A software algorithm used to "fingerprint" a file or contents of a disk; used to verify the integrity of data; in forensic analysis it is typically used to verify that an acquired image of suspect data was not altered during the process of imaging

Because booting a HDD to its operating system changes many files and could potentially destroy evidentiary data, obtaining data is generally accomplished by removing the HDD from the system and placing it in a laboratory forensic computer so that a forensic image can be created. However, the BIOS of the seized computer sometimes interprets the geometry of the HDD differently than the forensic computer does. In these instances, the image of the HDD must be obtained using the seized computer. Regardless, the examiner must ensure that the drive to be analyzed is in a "write-blocked," read-only state when creating the forensic image. Furthermore, the examiner needs to be able to prove that the forensic image he or she obtained includes every bit of data and caused no changes (writes) to the HDD.

To this end, a sort of fingerprint of the drive is taken before and after imaging. This fingerprint is taken through the use of a **Message Digest 5 (MD5), Secure Hash Algorithm (SHA)**, or similar validated algorithm. Before imaging the drive the algorithm is run and a 32-character alphanumeric string is produced based on the drive's contents. The algorithm is then run against the resulting forensic image; if nothing changed, the same alphanumeric string is produced, thus demonstrating that the image is all-inclusive of the original contents and that nothing was altered in the process.

A forensic image of the data on a HDD (and the same holds true for floppy disks, CDs, DVDs, tapes, flash memory devices, and any other storage medium) is merely an exact duplicate of the entire contents of the drive. In other words, all portions of the drive are copied from the first bit (one or zero) to the last. Why would investigators want to copy what appears to be blank or unused portions of the HDD? The answer is simple: to preserve latent data, discussed later in the chapter. It suffices to say here that data exists in areas of the drive that are, generally speaking, unknown and inaccessible to most end users. This data can be valuable as evidence. Therefore, a forensic image—one that copies every single bit of information on the drive—is necessary.[3] A forensic image differs from a backup or standard copy in that it takes the entire contents, not only data the operating system is aware of.

Many forensic software packages come equipped with a method to obtain the forensic image. The most popular software forensic tools—EnCase, Forensic Toolkit (FTK), Forensic Autopsy (Linux-based freeware), and SMART (Linux-based software by ASR Data)—all include a method to obtain a forensic image. All produce self-contained image files that can then be interpreted and analyzed. They also allow image compression to conserve storage. The fact that self-contained, compressed files are the result of forensic imaging allows many images from different cases to be stored on the same forensic storage drive. This makes case management and storage much easier (see Figure 19–7).

Analysis of Electronic Data

Analysis of electronic data is virtually limitless and bound only to the level of skill of the examiner. The more familiar an examiner is with computers, operating systems, application software, data storage, and a host of other disciplines, the more prepared he or she will be to look for evidentiary data.

Because computers are vast and complex, discussing each area, file, directory, log, or computer process that could potentially contain evidentiary data is beyond the scope of one chapter—and may be beyond the scope of an entire book. What follows are some of the more common areas of analysis. While reading this section, reflect on your own knowledge of computers and consider what other data might be of evidentiary value and where it might be found.

Visible Data

The category of **visible data** includes all information that the operating system is presently aware of and thus is readily accessible to the user. Here we present several common types of visible data considered in many investigations. This list is by no means exhaustive and can include any information that has value as evidence.

visible data

All data that the operating system is presently aware of and thus is readily accessible to the user

---

[3] In this instance, *bit* is both metaphorical and literal. Every bit of information is needed, so we must get it all. So too every bit, as in the smallest unit of data storage—a one or a zero—must be imaged.

FIGURE 19–7

Screen shot of EnCase Software. EnCase is a common forensic software application capable of imaging and assisting in the analysis of data.
Courtesy of Guidance Software, www.guidancesoftware.com

DATA/WORK PRODUCT FILES   One place to find evidence is in documents or files produced by the suspect. This category is extremely broad and can include data from just about any software program. Microsoft Word and WordPerfect word-processing programs typically produce text-based files such as typed documents and correspondence. These programs, and a host of other word-processing programs, have replaced the typewriter. They are common sources of evidence in criminal cases, particularly those involving white-collar crime.

Also relevant in white-collar crime and similar financial investigations are any data related to personal and business finance. Programs such as QuickBooks and Peachtree accounting packages can run the entire financial portion of a small to midsize business. Similarly, it is not uncommon to find personal bank account records in the computer that are managed with personal finance software such as Microsoft Money and Quicken. Moreover, criminals sometimes use these programs as well as spreadsheet applications to track bank accounts stolen from unsuspecting victims. Computer forensic examiners should familiarize themselves with these programs, the ways in which they store data, and methods for extracting and reading the data.

Advances in printer technology have made high-quality color printing both affordable and common in many homes. Although this is a huge benefit for home office workers and those interested in graphic arts, the technology has been used for criminal gain. Counterfeiting and check and document fraud are easily perpetrated by most home computer users. All that is required is a decent ink-jet printer and a scanner. Including the computer, a criminal could set up a counterfeiting operation for less than $1500. Examiners must learn the graphics and photo-editing applications used for nefarious purposes. Being able to recognize the data produced by these applications and knowing how to display the images is key to identifying the evidence.

SWAP FILE DATA   When an application is running, the program and the data being accessed are loaded into RAM. A computer's RAM is much faster than the "read" speed of the hard disk drive, and that's why the programs are loaded here—for fast access and functioning. RAM, however, has its limits. Some computers have 256 MB of RAM, others 512 MB, and still others as much as a gigabyte or two. Regardless of the amount, though, most operating systems (Windows,

Linux, and so on) are programmed to conserve RAM when possible. This is where the **swap file** comes in. The operating system attempts to keep only data and applications that are presently being used in RAM. Other applications that were started, but are currently waiting for user attention, may be swapped out of RAM and written to the swap space on the hard disk drive.[4]

For example, a manager of a retail store may want to type a quarterly report based on sales. The manager starts Microsoft Word and begins his report. Needing to incorporate sales figure data from a particular spreadsheet, he opens Microsoft Excel. Depending on what is running on the computer, the original Word document may be swapped from RAM to the swap space on the HDD to free up space for Excel. As the manager goes back and forth between the programs (and maybe checks his e-mail in between) this swapping continues. Data that is swapped back and forth is sometimes left behind in the swap space. Even as this area is constantly changed, some of the data is orphaned in unallocated space, an area of the HDD discussed later in this chapter.

Swap file or space can be defined as a particular file or even a separate HDD partition, depending on the operating system and file system type (FAT, NTFS, EXT2, and so on). For Windows systems either the swap file *Win386.sys* or *pagefile.sys* is used, depending on the specific Windows version and file system type. Linux systems can create partitions just for swapping data in and out of RAM. Data in the swap space can be read by examining the HDD through forensic software or a utility that provides a binary view, such as Norton Disk Editor or WinHex (see Figure 19–8).

TEMPORARY FILES   Any user who has suffered a sudden loss of power in the middle of typing a document can attest to the value of a **temporary file**. Most programs automatically save a copy of the file being worked on in a temporary file. After typing a document, working on a spreadsheet, or working on a slide presentation, the user can save the changes, thus promoting the temporary copy to an actual file. This is done as a sort of backup on the fly. If the computer experiences a sudden loss of power or other catastrophic failure, the temporary file can be recovered, limiting the amount of data lost. The loss is limited because the temporary file is not updated in real time. Rather, it is updated periodically (typically defaulted to every ten minutes in most programs), depending on the application's settings.

Temporary files can sometimes be recovered during a forensic examination. Additionally, some of the data that may have been orphaned from a previous version may be recoverable, if not the complete file. This is true even when a document has been typed and printed, but never saved. The creation of the temporary file makes it possible for some of this "unsaved" data to be recovered during analysis.

FIGURE 19–8

As a user switches between applications and performs multiple tasks, data is swapped back and forth between RAM and the computer's hard drive. This area on the hard drive is referred to as either *swap space* or a *paging file*

---

[4] Actually, the more appropriate term is probably *paging* as opposed to *swapping*. This is because entire programs are typically not swapped in and out of memory to the swap space; rather, *pages* of memory are placed there.

Another type of temporary file valuable to the computer investigator is the print spool file. When a print job is sent to the printer, a spooling process delays the sending of the data to the printer. This happens so the application can continue to work while the printing takes place in the background. To facilitate this, a temporary print spool file is created; this file typically includes the data to be printed and information specific to the printer. There are different methods for accomplishing this, and thus the files created as a result of this process vary. It is sometimes possible to view the data in a readable format from the files created during the spooling process.

Latent Data

The term **latent data** includes data that are obfuscated (not necessarily intentionally) from a user's view. It includes areas of files and disks that are typically not apparent to the computer user but contain data nonetheless. Latent data are one of the reasons a forensic image of the media is created. If a standard copy were all that was produced, only the logical data (that which the operating system is aware of) would be captured. Getting every bit of data ensures that potentially valuable evidence in latent data is not missed.

latent data
Areas of files and disks that are typically not apparent to the computer user (and often not to the operating system) but contain data nonetheless

Once the all-inclusive forensic image is produced, how is the latent data viewed? Utilities that allow a user to examine a hard disk drive on a binary (ones and zeros) level are the answer. Applications such as Norton Disk Editor and WinHex provide this type of access to a hard disk drive or other computer media. Thus these applications, sometimes also referred to as *hex editors* (for the hexadecimal shorthand of computer language), allow all data to be read on the binary level independent of the operating system's file system table. Utilities such as these can write to the media under examination, thus changing data. Consequently, a software or hardware write-blocker should be used.

A more common option in data forensics is to use specialized forensic examination software. EnCase and Forensic Toolkit for Windows and SMART and Forensic Autopsy for Linux are examples of forensic software. Each allows a search for evidence on the binary level and provides automated tools for performing common forensic processing techniques. Examiners should be cautious, however, about relying too heavily on automated tools. To merely use an automated tool without understanding what is happening in the background and why evidentiary data may exist in particular locations would severely impede the ability to testify to the findings.

SLACK SPACE   Slack space is empty space on a hard disk drive created because of the way the HDD stores files. Recall that, although the smallest unit of data measure is one bit (either a one or a zero), a HDD cannot address or deal with such a small unit. In fact, not even a byte (eight bits) can be addressed. Rather, the smallest unit of addressable space by a HDD is the sector. HDDs typically group sectors in 512-byte increments, whereas CD-ROMs allocate 2,048 bytes per sector.

If the minimum addressable unit of the HDD is 512 bytes, what happens if the file is only 100 bytes? In this instance there are 412 bytes of slack space. It does not end here, however, because of the minimum cluster requirement. As you may recall, clusters are groups of sectors used to store files and folders. The cluster is the minimum storage unit defined and used by the logical partition. It is because of the minimum addressable sector of the HDD and the minimum unit of storage requirement of the volume that we have slack space.

Minimum cluster allocation must be defined in a sector multiple of two. Thus, a cluster must be a minimum of two, four, six, or eight sectors, and so on. Returning to our initial example of the 100-byte file, suppose an HDD has a two-sectors-per-cluster volume requirement. This means that the HDD will isolate a minimum of two 512-byte sectors (a total of 1,024 bytes) of storage space for that 100-byte file. The remaining 924 bytes would be slack space (see Figure 19–9).

To illustrate this point, let us expand on the previous example of safe-deposit boxes. The bank offers safe-deposit boxes of a particular size. This is the equivalent of the HDD's clusters. A person wanting to place only a deed to a house in the box gets the same size box as a person who wants to stuff it full of cash. The former would have empty space should he or she desire to place additional items in the box. This empty space is the equivalent of slack space. But what if the box becomes full and the person needs more space? That person must then get a second box. Similarly, if a file grows to fill one cluster and beyond, a second cluster (and subsequent clusters as needed) is allocated. The remaining space in the second cluster is slack space. This continues as more and more clusters are allocated depending on file size and file growth.

HDD

FIGURE 19–9

Slack space illustrated in a two-sector cluster. Cluster sizes are typically greater than two sectors, but two sectors are displayed here for simplicity.

HDD

FIGURE 19–10

File slack.

RAM slack

The area beginning at the end of the logical file and terminating at the end of that sector; in some older operating systems this area is padded with information in RAM

file slack

The area that begins at the end of the last sector that contains logical data and terminates at the end of the cluster

This example is a bit of an oversimplification because there are actually two types of slack space: RAM slack and file slack. **RAM slack** occupies the space from where the actual (logical) data portion of the file ends to where the first allocated sector in the cluster terminates. **File slack**, therefore, occupies the remaining space of the cluster.

Let us go back to the 100-byte file with the two-sectors-per-cluster minimum requirement. Following the end of the logical data (the end of the 100 bytes), the remaining 412 bytes of that sector is RAM slack; the additional 512 bytes completing the cluster is then file slack. See Figure 19–10 for a visual depiction. The question now becomes: what can I expect to find in slack space and why is this important? The answer: junk—valuable junk.

RAM slack is a concept that was more relevant in older operating systems. Remember that the minimum amount of space the HDD can address is the 512-byte sector. Therefore, if the file size is only 100 bytes, the remaining space must be padded. Some operating systems pad this area with data contained in RAM. This could include Web pages, passwords, data files, or other data that existed in RAM when the file was written. Modern Windows operating systems pad this space with zeros, but some examinations may still yield valuable data in this area.

File slack, on the other hand, can contain a lot of old, orphaned data. To illustrate this point, let's take the 100-byte file example a bit further. Let's say that before the 100-byte file was written to the HDD, occupying one cluster (two sectors totaling 1,024 bytes), a 1,000-byte file occupied this space but was deleted by the user. When a file is "deleted," the data still remains behind, so it is probably a safe bet that data from the original 1,000-byte file remain in the slack space of the new 100-byte file now occupying this cluster. This is just one example of why data exists in file slack and why it may be valuable as evidence.

In one final attempt to illustrate this point, let us again build on our safe-deposit box analogy. Suppose a person rents two safe-deposit boxes, each box representing a sector and the two combined representing a cluster. If that person places the deed to his house in the first box, the remaining space in that box would be analogous to RAM slack. The space in the second box would be the equivalent of file slack. The only difference is that, unlike the empty spaces of the safe-deposit box, the slack space of the file most likely contains data that may be valuable as evidence.

The data contained in RAM and file slack is not really the concern of the operating system. As far as the OS is concerned, this space is empty and therefore ready to be used. Until that happens, however, an examination with one of the aforementioned tools will allow a look into these areas, thus revealing the orphaned data. The same is true for unallocated space.

UNALLOCATED SPACE   Latent evidentiary data also resides in **unallocated space**. What is unallocated space, how does data get in there, and what is done to access this space? If we have an 80-GB hard drive and only half of the hard drive is filled with data, then the other half, or 40 GB, is unallocated space. Returning to our safe-deposit box analogy, if the entire bank of safe-deposit boxes contains 100 boxes, but only 50 are currently in use, then the other 50 would be the equivalent of unallocated space. The HDD's unallocated space typically contains a lot of useful data. The constant shuffling of files on the HDD causes data to become orphaned in unallocated space as the logical portion of the file is rewritten to other places. Some examples of how data is orphaned may help.

> **unallocated space**
> The area of the HDD that the operating system (file system table) sees as empty (containing no logical files) and ready for data; simply stated, it is the unused portion of the HDD, but is not necessarily empty

DEFRAGMENTING   Defragmenting a HDD involves moving noncontiguous data back together. Remember that the HDD has minimum space reservation requirements. Again, if the file requires only 100 bytes of space, the operating system may allocate much more than that for use. If the file grows past what has been allocated for it, another cluster is required. If, however, a different file occupies the next cluster in line, then the operating system will have to find another place for that first file on the drive. In this scenario, the file is said to be *fragmented* because data for the same file is contained in noncontiguous clusters. In the case of the HDD, the shuffling of files causes data to be orphaned in unallocated space.

Ultimately fragmentation of numerous files can degrade the performance of a HDD, causing the read/write heads to have to traverse the platters to locate the data. Defragmenting the HDD takes noncontiguous data and rearranges it so it is in contiguous clusters. Building yet again on our safe-deposit box analogy, if a renter eventually needs to store more property than his original box can hold, the bank will rent him a second box. If, however, all the boxes around his are occupied and the only free one is in another section of the room, then his property is "fragmented." The bank would have to "defrag" the safe-deposit boxes to get the property of users with more than one box into adjacent boxes.

SWAP FILE/SWAP SPACE   Recall that a computer uses the HDD to maximize the amount of RAM by constantly swapping data in and out of RAM to a predetermined location on the HDD, thus freeing valuable RAM. The constant read and write operations of RAM cause a constant change in the swap file—*WIN386.swp* or *pagefile.sys* in Windows—or swap space on a Linux system. Data can become orphaned in unallocated space from this constant swapping to and from the HDD.

DELETED FILES   The deletion of files is another way that data becomes orphaned in unallocated space. Data from deleted files can manifest itself in different ways during a forensic examination. The actions that occur when a file is deleted vary among file systems. What is fairly consistent, though, is that generally speaking the data is not gone. For example, consider what happens when a user or program deletes a file in a Windows operating system with a FAT file system. When a file is deleted, the first character in the file's directory entry (its name) is replaced with the Greek letter sigma. When the sigma replaces the first character, the file is no longer viewable through conventional methods and the operating system views the space previously occupied by the file as available. The data, however, is still there.

This example doesn't account for the actions of the Windows Recycle Bin. When the Windows operating system is set up to merely place the deleted file in the Recycle Bin, the original directory entry is deleted and one is created in the Recycle folder for that particular user. The new Recycle folder entry is linked to another file, the *info* or *info2* file, which includes some additional data, such as the location of the file before its deletion should the user wish to restore it to that location. Detailed discussions of the function of the Recycle Bin are beyond the scope of this chapter, but suffice it to say that even when the Recycle Bin is emptied the data usually remains behind until overwritten. Moreover, Windows NTFS partitions and Linux EXT partitions handle deleted files differently, but in both cases data typically remains.

What if a new file writes data to the location of the original file? Generally speaking, the data is gone. This is, of course, unless the new file only partially overwrites the original. In this instance we return to the unallocated-space orphaned-data scenario: if a file that occupied two clusters is deleted, and a new file overwrites one of the clusters, then the data in the second cluster is orphaned in unallocated space. Of course, yet a third file can overwrite the second cluster entirely, but until then the data remains in unallocated space.

Let us once again look to our safe-deposit box analogy. If, for example, the owner of two safe-deposit boxes stopped renting them, the bank would list them as available. If the owner didn't clean them out, the contents would remain unchanged. If a new owner rented one of the boxes, the contents from the former owner would be replaced with the new owner's possessions. The second box would therefore still contain orphaned contents from its previous owner. The contents would remain in this "unallocated box" space until another renter occupies it.

Forensic Analysis of Internet Data

It's important from the investigative standpoint to be familiar with the evidence left behind from a user's Internet activity. A forensic examination of a computer system reveals quite a bit of data about a user's Internet activity. The data described next would be accessed and examined using the forensic techniques outlined in the previous sections of this chapter.

Internet Cache

Evidence of Web browsing typically exists in abundance on the user's computer. Most Web browsers (Internet Explorer, and Firefox) use a caching system to expedite Web browsing and make it more efficient. This was particularly true in the days of dial-up Internet access. When a user accesses a Web site, such as the *New York Times* home page, the data is fed from that server (in this example the *New York Times*), via the Internet service provider, over whatever type of connection the user has, to his or her computer. If that computer is accessing the Internet via a dial-up connection, the transfer of the *New York Times* home page may take a while because the data transfer rate and capabilities (bandwidth) of the telephone system is limited. Even with the high-speed access of a DSL line or cable connection, conservation of bandwidth is always a consideration. Taking that into account, Web browsers store (cache) portions of the pages visited onto the local hard disk drive. This way, if the page is revisited, portions of it can be reconstructed more quickly from this saved data, rather than having to pull it yet again from the Internet and use precious bandwidth.

Internet cache
Portions of visited Web pages placed on the local hard disk drive to facilitate quicker retrieval once revisited

This **Internet cache** is a potential source of evidence for the computer investigator. Portions of, and in some cases, entire visited Web pages can be reconstructed. Even if deleted, these cached files can often be recovered (see the section on deleted data). Investigators must know how to search for this data within the particular Web browser used by a suspect.

Internet Cookies

cookies
Files placed on a computer from a visited Web site; they are used to track visits and usage of that site

Cookies provide another area where potential evidence can be found. To appreciate the value of cookies you must first understand how they get onto the computer and their intended purpose. **Cookies** are placed on the local hard disk drive by Web sites the user has visited, if the user's Web browser (such as Internet Explorer) is set to allow this to happen. Microsoft Internet Explorer places cookies in a dedicated directory. The Web site uses cookies to track certain information about its visitors. This information can be anything, such as history of visits, purchasing habits, passwords, and personal information used to recognize the user for later visits.

Consider a user who registers for an account at the Barnes and Noble bookstore Web site, then returns to the same site from the same computer a few days later. The site will then display "Welcome, *Your User Name*." This data is retrieved from the cookie file placed on the user's hard disk drive by the Web site during the initial visit and registration with the site.

It is helpful to think of cookies almost like a Caller ID for Web sites. The site recognizes and retrieves information about the visitor, as when a salesperson recognizes the caller from a Caller ID display and quickly pulls the client's file. Cookie files can be a valuable source of evidence. In Internet Explorer, they take the form of plain text files, which can typically be opened with a standard text viewer or word-processing program, revealing part of the data. The existence of the files themselves, regardless of the information contained within, can be of evidentiary value to show a history of Web visits. A typical cookie may resemble the following: rsaferstein@ forensicscience.txt. From this we can surmise that someone using the local computer login *rsaferstein* accessed the forensic science Web site. It is possible that the cookie was placed there by an annoying pop-up ad, but considered against other evidence in the computer data, the presence of this cookie may be of corroborative value.

Internet History

Most Web browsers track the history of Web page visits for the computer user. This is probably done merely for a matter of convenience. Like the "recent calls" list on a cell phone, the **Internet history** provides an accounting of sites most recently visited, with some storing weeks' worth of visits. Users can go back and access sites they recently visited just by going through the browser's history. Most Web browsers store this information in one particular file; Internet Explorer uses the *index.dat* file. On a Windows system, an *index.dat* file is created for each login user name on the computer.

> **Internet history**
> An accounting of Web sites visited; different browsers store this information in different ways

The history file can be located and read with most popular computer forensic software packages. It displays the uniform resource locator (URL) of each Web site, along with the date and time the site was accessed. An investigation involving Internet use almost always includes an examination of Internet history data.

In some respects, the term "*Internet* history" is wrong because it doesn't encompass all of its functions. Several browsers—Internet Explorer, for one—store other valuable evidence independent of Internet access. It is not uncommon to see files accessed over a network listed in the history. Similarly, files accessed on external media, such as floppy disks, CDs, or thumb drives, may also appear in the history. Regardless, the Internet history data is a valuable source of evidence worthy of examination (see Figure 19–11).

Bookmarks and Favorite Places

Another way users can access Web sites quickly is to store them in their **bookmarks** or "Favorite Places." Like a preset radio station, Web browsers allow users to bookmark Web sites for future visits (see Figure 19–12). A lot can be learned from a user's bookmarked sites. You may learn what online news a person is interested in or what type of hobbies he or she has. You may also see that person's favorite child pornography or computer hacking sites bookmarked.

> **bookmark**
> A feature that enables the user to designate favorite sites for fast and easy access

In Internet Explorer the favorite places are kept in a folder with link (shortcut) files to a particular URL. They can be organized in subfolders or grouped by type. The same is true for the Firefox Web browser, except that Firefox bookmarks are stored in a document done in hypertext markup language (HTML), the same language interpreted by Web browsers themselves.

Forensic Investigation of Internet Communications

Computer investigations often begin with or are centered on Internet communication. Whether it is a chat conversation among many people, an instant message conversation between two individuals, or the back-and-forth of an e-mail exchange, human communication has long been a source of evidentiary material. *Regardless of the type, investigators are typically interested in communication.*

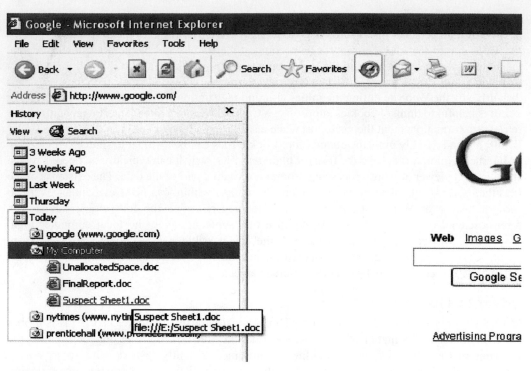

FIGURE 19–11

The Internet history displays more than just Web browsing activity. Here we see Microsoft Word documents and a picture accessed on the current day.

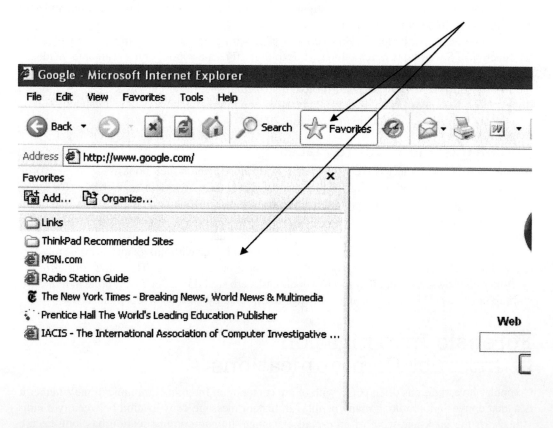

FIGURE 19–12

Bookmarks or favorite places can be saved for quick access in most Web browsers.

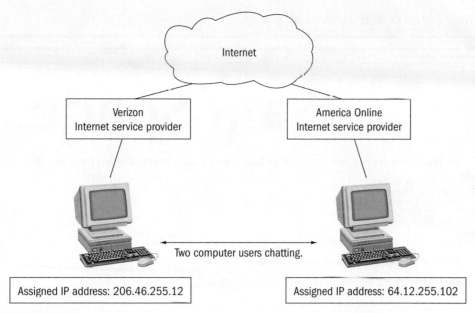

Two computer users chatting.

Assigned IP address: 206.46.255.12

Assigned IP address: 64.12.255.102

FIGURE 19–13

Two computers communicating by sending data to each other's IP address via the Internet. An IP address is assigned to each computer by their respective Internet service providers.

Role of the IP

With all of the computer manufacturers and software developers, some rules are necessary for computers to communicate on a global network. Just as any human language needs rules for people to communicate successfully, so does the language of computers. Computers that participate on the Internet, therefore, must be provided with an address known as an Internet protocol (IP) address from the Internet service provider to which they connect.

IP addresses take the form ###.###.###.###, in which, generally speaking, ### can be any number from 0 to 255. A typical IP address might look like this: 66.94.234.13. Not only do IP addresses provide the means by which data can be routed to the appropriate location, but they also provide the means by which most Internet investigations are conducted (see Figure 19–13). Thus the IP address may lead to the identity of a real person. If an IP address is the link to the identity of a real person, then it is quite obviously valuable for identifying someone on the Internet.

To illustrate, let's assume that a user of the Internet, fictitiously named John Smith, connects to the Internet from his home by way of a Verizon DSL connection. Verizon in this case would be responsible for providing Smith with his IP address. Verizon was issued a bank of IP addresses to service its customers from a regulatory body designed to track the usage of IP addresses (obviously so no two were used at the same time).

Suppose that Smith, while connected to the Internet, decides to threaten an ex-girlfriend by sending her an e-mail telling her he is going to kill her. That e-mail must first pass through Smith's Internet service provider's computers (in this case, Verizon) on its way to its destination—Smith's girlfriend. The e-mail would be stamped by the servers that it passes through, and this stamp would include the IP address given to Smith by Verizon for his session on the Internet.

An investigator responsible for tracking that e-mail would locate the originating IP address stamped in the e-mail header. That IP address could be researched using one of many Internet sites (http://www.samspade.org, http://www.arin.net) to determine which Internet service provider was given this IP as part of a block to service its customers (see Figure 19–14). The investigator then files a subpoena with the Internet service provider (Verizon) asking which of its customers was using that IP address on that date and time.

IP addresses are located in different places for different methods of Internet communications. E-mail has the IP address in the header portion of the mail. This may not be readily apparent and

FIGURE 19-14

Sites such as http://www.samspade.org can be used to track the origins of an IP address.
Courtesy Word to the Wise

may require a bit of configuration to reveal. Each e-mail client is different and needs to be evaluated on a case-by-case basis. For an instant message or chat session, the particular provider (the one providing the chat mechanism—AOL, Yahoo, and so on) would be contacted to provide the user's IP address.

E-Mail, Chat, and Instant Messaging

E-mail can be read by a number of *clients* or software programs. Two of the most popular ways to access, read, and store e-mail in today's Internet environment, however, are Microsoft Outlook and through an Internet browser. Some people even use a combination of the two.

If an e-mail account is linked through Microsoft Outlook, then the e-mail is stored in a compound file (a file with several layers). Typically, a compound file exists for received (inbox), sent, and deleted e-mail. Users can also create new categories (shown as folders in Outlook) and categorize saved e-mail there. Most computer forensic software applications can view (mount) these compound files so that the e-mail can be seen, including any file attachments. These files can also be imported into a clean copy (one not attached to an account) of Microsoft Outlook and the e-mail viewed there. Investigators must also be aware that in a computer network environment, the user's Outlook files may not reside on his or her workstation computer, but rather on a central mail or file server.

Most accounts offer the ability to access e-mail through a Web-based interface as well. This way, users can access their e-mail remotely from other computers. For e-mail accessed through a Web browser, the information presented earlier on Internet-based evidence applies. The Web interface converts the e-mail into a document suitable for reading in a Web browser. Consequently, Web-based e-mail is often found in the Internet cache. This is particularly true of free Internet e-mail providers such as Hotmail and Yahoo.

Much of the evidence from Internet communication is also derived from chat and instant message technology. This is particularly true in the world of child sexual exploitation over the Internet. Various technologies provide chat and instant message services. Most chat and instant message conversations are not saved by the parties involved. Although most of the software does allow for conversation archiving, it is typically turned off by default. Therefore, conversations of this nature typically exist in the volatile memory space of random-access memory (RAM).

Recall that RAM is termed volatile because it holds data only if it has power. Unplugging the computer will cause the data located in RAM to be lost. If, however, chat or instant message conversations are relevant as evidence and the computer was turned off, thus erasing the data in RAM, all may not be lost. Remember that there is an interaction between the computer system's RAM and the hard disk drive. RAM is a commodity and therefore the computer's operating system makes an effort to conserve it as best as possible. This is done by swapping/paging that information back and forth into the swap space/paging file. Therefore remnants of chat conversations are often found in the swap space/paging file during a forensic examination of the hard disk drive. These remnants, however, are typically fragmented, disconnected, and incomplete. Therefore if the chat or instant message is still present on the screen (and thus probably still in RAM), the investigator needs a method by which to preserve and collect it.

A detailed discussion of capturing volatile data from RAM is beyond the scope of this chapter. Suffice it to say that many commercial forensic software packages can capture this data. Similarly, Linux-based tools can accomplish this as well. The examiner may even be able to export the data remotely to another device. Regardless of the method, the data needs to be acquired.

Furthermore, many programs such as America Online Instant Messenger, Yahoo Messenger, and mIRC (Internet Relay Chat) create files regarding the rooms or channels a user chatted in or the screen names with which a user sent instant messages. Each application needs to be researched and the computer forensic examination guided by an understanding of how it functions.

Hacking

Unauthorized computer intrusion, more commonly referred to as **hacking**, is the concern of every computer administrator. Hackers penetrate computer systems for a number of reasons. Sometimes the motive is corporate espionage; other times it is merely for bragging rights within the hacker community. Most commonly, though, a rogue or disgruntled employee with some knowledge of the computer network is looking to cause damage. Whatever the motivation, corporate America frequently turns to law enforcement to investigate and prosecute these cases.

Generally speaking, when investigating an unauthorized computer intrusion, investigators concentrate their efforts in three locations: *log files*, *volatile memory*, and *network traffic*. Logs typically document the IP address of the computer that made the connection. Logs can be located in several locations on a computer network. Most servers on the Internet track connections made to them through the use of logs. Additionally the router (the device responsible for directing data) may contain log files detailing connections.

Similarly, devices known as **firewalls** may contain log files listing computers that were allowed access to the network or an individual system. Firewalls are devices (taking the form of either hardware or software) that permit only requested traffic to enter a computer system (or, more appropriately, a network). In other words, if a user didn't send out a request for Internet traffic from a specific system, the firewall should block its entry. If the log files captured the IP address of the intruder, then revealing the user behind the IP is the same process as for e-mail. Investigating a computer intrusion, however, does get a bit more complicated than this.

Frequently, in cases of unlawful access to a computer network, the perpetrator attempts to cover the tracks of his or her IP address. In these instances, advanced investigative techniques may be necessary to discover the hacker's true identity. When an intrusion is in progress, the investigator may have to capture volatile data (data in RAM). The data in RAM at the time of an intrusion may provide valuable clues to the identity of the intruder, or at least his or her method of attack. As in the case of an instant message or chat conversation, the data in RAM needs to be acquired.

Another standard tactic for investigating intrusion cases is to document all programs installed and running on a system in order to discover malicious software installed by the perpetrator to facilitate entry. The investigator uses specialized software to document running processes, registry entries, open ports, and any installed files.

Additionally, the investigator may want to capture live network traffic as part of the evidence collection and investigation process. Traffic that travels the network does so in the form of data packets. In addition to data, these packets also contain source and destination IP addresses. If the

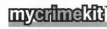

WEBEXTRA 19.1
Follow the Trail of an E-Mail
as It Travels through the Internet
www.mycrimekit.com

hacking
Has various meanings, but is frequently used as a slang term for an unauthorized computer or network intrusion

firewall
Hardware or software designed to protect intrusions into an Internet network

attack requires two-way communication, as in the case of a hacker stealing data, then data needs to be transmitted back to the hacker's computer using the destination IP address. Once this is learned, the investigation can focus on that system. Moreover, the type of data that is being transmitted on the network may be a clue as to what type of attack is being launched, whether any important data is being stolen, or what types of malicious software, if any, are involved in the attack.

chapter summary

> > > > > > > > > > >

Computers have permeated society and are used in countless ways with innumerable applications. Similarly, the role of electronic data in investigative work has realized exponential growth in the last decade. Users of computers and other electronic data storage devices leave footprints and data trails behind. Computer forensics involves the preservation, acquisition, extraction, analysis, and interpretation of computer data. In today's world of technology, many devices are capable of storing data and could thus be grouped into the field of computer forensics.

The central processing unit (CPU) is the brain of the computer—the main chip responsible for doing the actual computing. Random-access memory (RAM) is volatile memory containing data that is forever lost when the power is turned off. Programs are loaded into RAM because of its faster read speed. The hard disk drive (HDD) is typically the primary location of data storage within the computer. Different operating systems map out HDDs differently, and examiners must be familiar with the file system they are examining. Evidence exists in many different locations and in numerous forms on a HDD. This evidence can be grouped into two major categories: visible and latent data.

Visible data is data that the operating system is aware of and consequently is easily accessible to the user. From an evidentiary standpoint, it can encompass any type of user-created data, such as word-processing documents, spreadsheets, accounting records, databases, and pictures. Temporary files, created by programs as a sort of backup on the fly, can also prove valuable as evidence.

Finally, data in the swap space (used to conserve the valuable RAM within the computer system) can yield evidentiary visible data.

Latent data, on the other hand, is data that the operating system typically is not aware of. Evidentiary latent data can exist in both RAM slack and file slack. RAM slack is the area from the end of the logical file to the end of the sector. File slack is the remaining area from the end of the final sector containing logical data to the end of the cluster. Another area where latent data may be found is in unallocated space. Unallocated space is space on a HDD that the operating system sees as empty and ready for data. The constant shuffling of data through deletion, defragmentation, and swapping is one of the ways data is orphaned in latent areas. Finally, when a user deletes files the data typically remains behind. Deleted files are therefore another source of latent data to be examined during forensic analysis.

Investigators seeking a history of an Internet user's destinations can take advantage of the fact that computers store or cache portions of Web pages visited, and Web sites often create cookies to track certain information about Web site visitors. An investigator tracking the origin of an e-mail seeks out the sender's IP address in the e-mail's header. Chat and instant messages are typically located in a computer's random-access memory (RAM). Finding the origin of unauthorized computer intrusions (hacking) requires investigation of a computer's log file, RAM, and network traffic, among other things.

review questions

1. Computer forensics involves the _____, _____, _____, _____, and _____ of computer data.

2. True or False: Hardware comprises the physical components of the computer. _____

3. _____ is a set of instructions compiled into a program that performs a particular task.

4. (ROM, RAM) chips store programs used to start the boot process.

5. The term used to describe the chassis, including the motherboard and any other internal components of a personal computer, is _____.

6. True or False: The motherboard is a complex network of wires that carry data from one hardware device to another. _____

7. True or False: The first thing you should do when you encounter a computer system in a forensic investigation is to connect the power supply and boot the system. _____

8. RAM is referred to as volatile memory because it is not _____.

9. The brain of the computer is referred to as the _____.

10. The _____ is the primary component of storage in the personal computer.

11. Personal computers typically communicate with each other through a(n) _____.

12. The computer's _____ permits the user to manage files and applications.

13. A hard drive's partitions are typically divided into _____, _____, _____, and _____.

14. A(n) _____ is a single one or zero in the binary system and the smallest term in the language of computers.

15. A(n) _____ is a group of eight bits.

16. A group of sectors, always units in multiples of two, is called a(n) _____.

17. An exact duplicate of the entire contents of a hard disk drive is known as a(n) _____.

18. All data readily available to a computer user is known as _____ data.

19. A(n) _____ file is created when data is moved from RAM to the hard disk drive to conserve space.

20. Most programs automatically save a copy of a file being worked on into a(n) _____ file.

21. The existence of _____ data is why a forensic image of the media is created.

22. The smallest unit of addressable space on a hard disk drive is the _____.

23. The two types of slack space are _____ slack and _____ slack.

24. _____ slack is the area from the end of the data portion of the file to the end of the sector.

25. The portion of a disk that does not contain stored data is called _____.

26. True or False: Defragmenting a hard disk drive involves moving noncontiguous data back together. _____

27. True or False: A portion of a "deleted" file may be found in a computer's unallocated space. _____

28. A(n) _____ takes the form of a series of numbers to route data to an appropriate location on the Internet.

29. A user's hard disk drive will _____ portions of Web pages that have been visited.

30. A(n) _____ is placed on a hard disk drive by a Web site to track certain information about its visitors.

31. E-mails have the _____ address of the sender in the header portion of the mail.

32. True or False: Chat and instant messages conducted over the Internet are typically stored in RAM storage. _____

33. When investigating a hacking incident, investigators concentrate their efforts on three locations: _____, _____, and _____.

34. Devices that permit only requested traffic to enter a computer system are known as _____.

application and critical thinking

1. If a file system defines a cluster as six sectors, how many bits of information can be stored on each cluster? Explain your answer.

2. Criminalist Tom Parauda is investigating the scene of a crime involving a computer. After he arrives, he photographs the overall scene and takes close-up shots of all the connections to the single computer involved, as well as photos of the serial numbers of the computer and all peripheral devices. Tom then labels the cord to each peripheral device, then disconnects them from the computer. After making sure that all data in RAM has been saved to the hard disk drive, he unplugs the computer from the wall. What mistakes, if any, did Tom make?

3. You are investigating a case in which an accountant is accused of keeping fraudulent books for a firm. Upon examining his computer, you notice that the suspect uses two different accounting programs that are capable of reading the same types of files. Given this information, where would you probably begin to search for latent data on the computer and why?

4. You are examining two computers to determine the IP address from which several threatening e-mails were sent. The first computer uses Microsoft Outlook as an e-mail client and the second uses a Web-based e-mail client. Where would you probably look first for the IP addresses in each of these computers?

case analysis 1

Suspicious circumstances surrounding the death of Ms. Smith in a home fire led the police to suspect her husband of murder. Evidence later recovered from Mr. Smith's computer proved key in solving the case.

1. What did police hope to prove from examining the Microsoft Word files on Mr. Smith's computer? Why did they believe this would implicate him in his wife's murder?

2. How were the documents titled *insurance1.doc* and *WRL1604.tmp* important to tying Mr. Smith to his wife's death?

case analysis 2

When police seized a laptop from a van parked suspiciously outside a local shopping mall, they discovered a cyber counterfeiting ring that employed modern technology to perpetrate this age-old crime.

1. What physical evidence most strongly implicated the driver of the van in a currency counterfeiting operation? What aspect of this evidence confirmed these suspicions?

2. What files located on the suspect's computer indicated that the suspects were producing more than counterfeit currency? What conclusion did the investigators draw from the existence of these files?

further references

Britz, M. T., *Computer Forensics and Cyber Crime,* 2nd ed. Upper Saddle River, N.J.: Prentice Hall, 2008.

Carrier, B., *File System Forensic Analysis.* Upper Saddle River, N.J.: Addison-Wesley, 2005.

Casey, E., *Digital Evidence and Computer Crimes*, 2nd ed. San Diego: Elsevier Academic Press, 2004.

Kruse, W. G., and J. G. Heiser, *Computer Forensics— Incident Response Essentials.* Boston: Addison-Wesley, 2001.

Leshin, C. B., *Internet Investigations in Criminal Justice.* Upper Saddle River, N.J.: Prentice-Hall, 1997.

Nelson, B., A. Phillips, F. Enfinger, and C. Steuart, *Guide to Computer Forensics and Investigations*, 4th ed. Boston: Thomson Course Technology, 2009.

Proise, C., K. Mandia, and B. Pepe, *Incident Response and Computer Forensics*, 2nd ed. New York: McGraw-Hill, 2003.

Computer Forensic Analysis Answers the Question "Arson or Accident?"

Brief

The home of John Smith was destroyed by a fire, which was later determined to be the result of arson. During the fire, Smith's wife, Jane, died. Investigators learned that insurance policies taken against both the home and the life of Jane Smith were recently increased, so Smith stands to receive a very large monetary settlement. This fact, and problems with his purported alibi at the time of the fire, makes him the primary suspect. Smith has steadfastly denied the existence of the insurance policies and offers that his wife must have recently changed the policies.

Further investigation discloses that the couple did not possess a home computer but that Smith uses a computer at work. After applying for and receiving a search warrant for Smith's workplace, the arson investigator seizes the computer system unit from underneath Smith's desk, which he found in a powered-off condition. During execution of the search warrant, the company's computer administrator tells investigators that the computer was used only by Smith. The computer system unit is submitted for forensic analysis.

Analysis Request

Locate any incriminating or exculpatory evidentiary data with respect to Smith's knowledge of changes in his insurance policy. Locate any evidentiary data with respect to motive for the crimes of arson and/or homicide.

Forensic Image Acquisition

1. The computer system was documented and its chassis was opened and a single IDE/ATA hard disk drive (HDD) was located and documented. The HDD was removed from the system and the computer system unit was booted to the BIOS setup program. The system date and time were verified.
2. The HDD was then placed in a forensic workstation, connected to the system using a hardware write-blocking device to ensure that the suspect HDD was not altered in any way.
3. A forensic image of the HDD was acquired using EnCase Version 5. The integrity of this image was verified using the MD5 algorithm inherent in the EnCase program. A date and time analysis was done on all the files, revealing no dates later than the date of the execution of the search warrant.

Courtesy Peter Arnold Inc.

Analysis

1. Deleted files were recovered.
2. A file signature analysis was run.
3. All files, including dates and times, logical and physical sizes, and complete location path, were documented by the EnCase program.
4. User accounts were documented: two default accounts (*Administrator* and *Guest*, SID 500 and 501, respectively) and one user account (*jsmith*).
5. The operating system and file system type were documented: Windows 2000 using an NTFS partition.
6. Keyword text searches, derived from the text of letters received by the insurance company, were conducted.
7. All Microsoft Word documents were examined.
8. All text documents were examined.
9. Print spool files were examined.

Findings

1. A file titled *insurance1.doc* was located in the directory *C:\Documents and Settings\jsmith\junk*. The directory structure *C:\Documents and Settings\jsmith* coincides with a default directory for the user name *jsmith*, which would have been established with that account. The subdirectory *junk* was then added by a user of the *jsmith* account. The text in this file is the same as the one received by the insurance company requesting an increase in homeowner's insurance.

2. Text found in unallocated space matches sections of text in a second letter received by the insurance company requesting an increase in life insurance for Jane Smith.

3. A file titled *WRL1604.tmp* was found in the directory *C:\Documents and Settings\jsmith\junk*. The file matches that of a temporary Microsoft Word file and contains text matching sections of text in the letter received by the insurance company requesting an increase in life insurance for Jane Smith.

4. A file titled *46127a.SPL* was located in the directory *C:\windows\system32\spool\printers*. This file appears to be a print spool file. This file, when viewed as an Enhanced Meta File (EMF), reveals a document exact in composition and similar in layout to the letter received by the insurance company requesting an increase in life insurance for Jane Smith. An EMF is a type of spool file created during the printing process and can be viewed as a Windows picture file in the forensic software.

Conclusion

Based on the forensic examination of the computer data submitted in this case, it can be stated within a reasonable degree of scientific certainty that a user of this computer had knowledgeable interaction with letters very similar in content, composition, and structure to the evidentiary letters submitted as reference for analysis.

Counterfeiting and Fraud:
A Forensic Computer Investigation

Brief

A detective submits a laptop computer for examination and explains that it was seized in connection with a case of counterfeiting and fraud. According to the detective, patrol officers happened upon a large sport-utility vehicle, occupied by one male driver, parked in the lot of a local mall. According to the officers, the driver and the circumstances appeared suspicious.

After investigating further, the officers located a laptop computer, color printer, and scanner in the rear of the vehicle. All equipment was hooked up and running. Additionally, the officers located gift certificates for one of the stores within the mall, which apparently were printed inside the vehicle. Finally, two $100 bills bearing exactly the same serial number were located in the driver's wallet. In response to questioning, the driver admitted using the system to print bogus gift certificates and counterfeit cash, which he then redeemed inside the mall. Prior to submission at the computer forensics laboratory, the equipment was processed for fingerprints at the state Bureau of Criminal Identification (BCI).

*Courtesy Getty Images,
Inc.—Agence France Presse*

Analysis Request

Locate any evidentiary data with respect to the crimes of counterfeiting and fraud. Demonstrate any connection between the recovered printed documents and the electronic equipment seized from the vehicle.

Forensic Image Acquisition

1. The computer system was documented and its case was opened and a single IDE hard disk drive (HDD) was located and documented. The HDD was removed from the system and the computer system unit was booted to the BIOS setup program. The system date and time were verified.
2. The HDD was then placed in a forensic workstation, connected to the system using a hardware write-blocking device to ensure that the suspect HDD was not altered in any way.
3. A forensic image of the HDD was acquired using EnCase Version 5. The integrity of this image was verified using the MD5 algorithm inherent in the EnCase program. A date and time analysis was done on all the files, revealing no dates later than the date of the execution of the search warrant.

Analysis

1. Deleted files were recovered.
2. A file signature analysis was run.
3. All files, including dates and times, logical and physical sizes, and complete location path, were documented by the EnCase program.
4. The operating system and file system type were documented: Windows XP using an NTFS file system.
5. All graphics files were viewed, including ones previously deleted.
6. A graphics finder script was run against unallocated space. The script searched this area to locate file signatures of known graphics files.
7. All print spool files were located and examined.

Findings

1. A file titled *100front.jpg* was located in the directory *C:\Documents and Settings\user1\My Documents*. This file is an image of the front of a $100 bill. The serial number on this image matched the serial number of the suspected counterfeit $100 bills found on the suspect.

2. A file titled *100back.jpg* was located in the directory *C:\Documents and Settings\user1\My Documents*. This file is an image of the back of a $100 bill.

3. A file titled *GapGiftCert1.jpg* was located in the directory *C:\Documents and Settings\user1\My Documents*. This file is an image of the front of a gift certificate for The Gap, a retail store.

4. A file titled *GapGiftCert2.jpg* was located in the directory *C:\Documents and Settings\user1\My Documents*. This file is an image of the back of a gift certificate for The Gap, a retail store.

5. A file titled *thumbs.db* was located in the directory *C:\Documents and Settings\user1\My Documents*. This file, when viewed as a compound file, displayed several images, namely the images in items 1–4.

6. In the folder *C:\Documents and Settings\User1\My Recent Documents*, link files were found to the following:
   a. *C:\Documents and Settings\user1\My Documents\ 100front.jpg*
   b. *C:\Documents and Settings\user1\My Documents\ 100back.jpg*
   c. *C:\Documents and Settings\user1\My Documents\ GapGiftCert1.jpg*
   d. *C:\Documents and Settings\user1\My Documents\ GapGiftCert2.jpg*

7. The submitted scanner and printer were connected to a laboratory computer system and the aforementioned evidentiary files were copied onto the HDD of that system. Several printouts of the images were made. Additionally, test items were scanned and printed. All exemplars produced from the laboratory computer system were submitted to the state Bureau of Criminal Identification. The original counterfeit currency and gift certificates were also submitted to BCI for comparison to the exemplars. BCI was asked to locate any distinguishing characteristics produced by the printer and scanner submitted in this case.

Conclusion

Based on the forensic examination of the computer data submitted in this case, it can be stated within a reasonable degree of scientific certainty that a user of this computer knowingly produced counterfeit currency and counterfeit gift certificates.

the future

In 1949, Charles O'Hara and James Osterburg, noted criminalistics authors, wrote: "The present position of criminalistics among the sciences may properly be compared with that of chemistry in the nineteenth century." Certainly, in this new millennium, the changes that have taken place since this observation was made have been nothing short of revolutionary. Forensic science may still have many shortcomings, but it has successfully shed the distinction of being a nineteenth-century science.

Crime laboratories have now become the major benefactors of enormous advances in scientific technology. Chromatography and spectrophotometry have already had a tremendous impact on forensic methodology. In a very short span of time, DNA typing has developed into a routine forensic science technique. The future promises even more rapid progress. Mass spectrometry, capillary electrophoresis, and high-performance liquid chromatography, among other developments, are rapidly gaining recognition as essential forensic tools. The scanning electron microscope is already enhancing the application of microscopy to the examination of trace physical evidence. An even more impressive tool is the scanning electron microscope linked to an X-ray microanalyzer. This combination enables forensic scientists to examine very small samples nondestructively while plotting the elemental composition of the specimen in view.

The notion that there is a need for trained and knowledgeable evidence collectors at crime scenes has been a recurring one throughout this text. Once again this requirement must be reiterated. How is the evidence collector or investigator to gain the skill and appreciation for recognizing the value of physical evidence? The trend of events seems to be one of conceding past failings and acknowledging the need for creating specialists to perform evidence-collection functions. In growing numbers, police agencies are training and equipping "evidence-collection technicians" to help criminal investigators retrieve evidence at the crime scene.

If this program is to have a significant impact on investigative procedures, immediate steps must be taken that go beyond mere designation of an evidence-collection unit on a police agency's organization chart. The effectiveness of such a program should not be measured by the number of oversized and overequipped mobile vans at the unit's disposal; instead, a staff of dedicated operators and administrators trained and experienced in evidence collection must be assembled. This unit must be recognized as the essential first step in forensic analysis and must become an integral part, both administratively and functionally, of the total forensic service offered by a law enforcement agency.

The education of evidence collectors and investigators is a critical factor in improving the quality of crime scene investigation. Although continued in-depth training of investigators by forensic scientists is an essential ingredient for the success of such a program, many agencies—for lack of space, time, or desire—have not implemented this training. It is therefore gratifying that colleges and universities are emerging as centers of education for law enforcement personnel. Criminal justice or law enforcement programs provide viable forums for teaching the philosophy and theory of criminal investigation and forensic science. However, academia must strive to supplement, not supplant, police in-service training. Police administrators now have the responsibility for selecting the personnel to perform investigative functions. These administrators cannot abdicate their responsibility to create and foster training programs to ensure competent performance of the investigator's mission.

Whether a college degree will someday be required by all police departments is still a subject of debate, but the trend is certainly in that direction. More than a thousand higher education institutions in the United States offer some sort of law enforcement program. Future generations of criminal investigators and police administrators will be recruited from the ranks of these students. Participation in these programs offers the forensic scientist a unique opportunity to teach, develop, and put into practice the philosophy that science is an integral part of criminal investigation.

Of course education alone will not guarantee the success of the criminal investigator or evidence collector. Experience, perceptive skill, persistence, and precise judgment are all essential ingredients to the makeup of the successful investigator and evidence collector. Combine all of these characteristics with a careful selection process designed to choose only those who qualify for this role, and the result will be substantial enhancement of the quality of criminal investigative services.

Certainly it is not the case that crime laboratories are not being used or that forensic scientists have difficulty justifying a full day's work. On the contrary, these facilities are overworked and understaffed. The demand imposed on them just to complete the examination of drug and blood-alcohol evidence is enough to inundate and preoccupy all but the larger crime laboratories. Most facilities are drowning in a "sea" of drugs. Furthermore, the disproportionate burden placed on the skills, time, and equipment of the laboratory by drug and blood-alcohol evidence has had a detrimental effect on the capacity of the law enforcement system to process physical evidence generated by more serious or violent crimes.

The solution to the problem may seem obvious: more people, larger facilities, and, of course, more money. But crime laboratories must stand in line with other components of the criminal justice system because skyrocketing crime rates have overburdened our police, courts, and correctional institutions. In light of public and political outcries, criminal justice administrators have sought programs geared to producing quick and dramatic reductions in crime rates. In this atmosphere, hiring more scientists or buying a mass spectrometer or a gas chromatograph may hardly seem the best way to reduce crime.

The solution is not a crash program for building crime laboratories or, for that matter, a crash program aimed at improving one segment of the criminal justice community at the expense of the others. Reduction of crime will come about only with a balanced approach to criminal justice, as well as alleviation of social injustices. We must keep the future role of the crime laboratory in its proper perspective while examining the goals and performance that we expect from all components of our criminal justice system.

The size and effectiveness of a crime laboratory directly mirror the capability of the investigative agencies that it serves. If all or even most of the burglaries, homicides, assaults, rapes, and other types of major offenses were investigated with the thoroughness expected of a proper criminal investigation, the quantity of physical evidence collected would require the existence of better staffed and better equipped crime laboratories.

An important impetus behind the expansion of crime laboratory services in the United States has been DNA profiling. The advent of DNA profiling has placed tremendous pressures on crime laboratory services. Laws passed to mandate entry into a DNA database for many convicted offenders and, in some jurisdictions, arrestees, has imposed tremendous workloads on crime laboratories that must also cope with an overwhelming variety of evidence collected at crime scenes for DNA analysis. The high-profile nature of DNA investigations has pressured government officials to expand crime laboratory facilities and to hire adequate staff to deal with the influx of biological evidence.

Although the commitment of police to improve the quality of crime-scene investigation is essential, it must be accompanied by a simultaneous effort to improve the caliber of crime laboratory services. Certainly, thorough collection of crime-scene evidence will require more forensic scientists to handle the increasing caseloads. However, forensic scientists should not be lulled into a false sense of security by believing that the tremendous strides made in the development of analytical instruments and techniques are sufficient to meet the needs and goals of their profession. Progress can be expected only if crime laboratories are staffed with trained and knowledgeable scientists.

Fortunately more colleges and universities are offering courses and degree programs in forensic science or criminalistics. These institutions are beginning to serve as fertile training grounds for new forensic scientists. Although many of these individuals have textbook knowledge of the techniques used in forensic analysis, few arrive at the crime laboratory possessing an understanding of the practical aspects of criminal investigation. This deficiency necessitates a prolonged and time-consuming period of intensive training under the direction of trained criminalists. Not only must the new criminalist learn to apply specialized skills to the responsibilities and objectives of a working crime laboratory, he or she must also acquire a familiarity with all phases of crime laboratory operation.

The extent and depth of versatility expected of the forensic scientist are usually determined by the size of the crime laboratory's staff. Scientists in smaller laboratories are often expected to be generalists, performing a wide variety of tasks in order to fulfill the varied objectives of the laboratory. Their counterparts in larger facilities enjoy the luxury of working in specialized areas, relying on a teamwork approach to provide the spectrum of scientific skills needed for the comparison or identification of physical evidence.

In addition to his or her technical responsibilities, the newly trained criminalist must discover and master the role of expert witness. A good courtroom demeanor and the ability to communicate thoughts and ideas in clear, concise terms are absolutely essential if the scientist's examination and conclusions are to be properly and effectively presented at a hearing or in a courtroom.

The current momentum of forensic research could very well falter unless individuals who possess relevant knowledge and skills are attracted to careers in forensic science. The recognition by a sufficient number of colleges and universities of the need to foster undergraduate and graduate programs in this field is essential for ensuring an ample supply of scientists to meet the anticipated personnel needs of the profession. Furthermore, the establishment of forensic education programs, especially at the graduate level, should be accompanied by the formulation of new academic research programs dedicated to investigating fertile areas of research that are pertinent to the expanding role of forensic science in criminal justice. In a university environment, these research programs can be pursued in an atmosphere unaffected by the pressures of everyday casework, a burden that currently weighs heavily on the working forensic scientist.

The prospects for significant technological advances in forensic science in the near future are great. In fact, the computer-aided search of single latent fingerprints is already a reality in most jurisdictions. The ability to search, in a matter of minutes, files comprising millions of prints in order to ascertain a probable match to a latent fingerprint represents the most significant contribution that forensic science has made to criminal investigation since the introduction of the fingerprint itself. Jurisdictions using this approach have reported startling increases in arrests.

Computerized technology is also helping investigators link multiple unrelated shooting cases to a single firearm. The automated search system NIBIN (see pp. 426–427) allows the surface characteristics of a bullet or cartridge case to be scanned and stored in a computerized database that is networked throughout various regions of the United States. An investigator can search the database for entries bearing similar characteristics to the evidential bullet or cartridge case. If a match is made, multiple crimes may be linked and associated with a single firearm.

Almost every week we read in newspapers that researchers are developing new products with their ability to manipulate genes. The ability of scientists to penetrate DNA, the basic building block of genes, provides investigators with a powerful forensic tool to individualize blood, semen, and hair. The FBI has initiated an aggressive forensic research program to develop this technology, along with an ambitious technical training program to instruct personnel of state and local crime laboratories throughout the United States in the use of this technology. DNA typing has already progressed to the level that all states are routinely DNA typing offenders involved in sex-related and other crimes. The technology of DNA profiling has progressed so rapidly that today blood and semen stains recovered from crime scenes are as revealing of human identity as a fingerprint. CODIS is a computer software program developed and maintained by the FBI that links local, state, and national databases of DNA profiles from convicted offenders, unsolved crime-scene evidence, and missing people. CODIS software has enabled local, state, and national crime laboratories to compare DNA profiles electronically. Thousands of matches have linked criminal perpetrators to DNA profiles in CODIS databases.

One unexpected dividend from DNA testing has been the reinvigoration of the investigation of "minor crimes." For decades, police have given the investigation of house burglary scenes and other property crimes low priority. Evidence now suggests that DNA evidence collected at property crime scenes may help law enforcement solve those crimes and identify perpetrators of more serious offenses. According to one state study, more than 50 percent of the DNA database hits against murder and sexual assault cases matched individuals who had prior convictions for burglary.

Apprehending perpetrators of property crimes can certainly discourage criminals from moving on to the commission of more serious violent crimes, and thus can have a dramatic long-term impact on decreasing the overall crime rate. In this respect, it is apparent that DNA collected at burglary scenes is a powerful investigative tool. In one major jurisdiction, DNA evidence from 201 burglaries yielded 86 DNA profiles for entry in CODIS. Most of the profiles resulted in links to multiple unsolved cases. One profile uncovered a five-burglary serial offender. A few were linked to more serious violent crimes such as sexual assault and robbery. Significantly, more than 30 of the burglaries were matched though CODIS to convicted offenders. In Florida jurisdictions, individuals associated with two hundred DNA samples collected from various burglary investigations were identified by CODIS. A more recent study showed that twice as many property crime suspects were identified and arrested when DNA evidence was collected than when crimes were investigated in a more traditional manner.

Unfortunately, in spite of the fact that crime laboratories are equipped with expensive and sophisticated instruments, often a forensic scientist cannot report to a police officer or a jury that a scientific examination of the evidence has itself solved a case. More often than not, a conclusive comparison of evidential and control material cannot exclude other possible sources. To further complicate matters, the statistical data available to support such conclusions are usually sketchy or nonexistent. In such situations, heavy reliance must necessarily be placed on the experience and opinion of the expert in interpreting the significance of the forensic examination.

Although class physical evidence for corroborating investigative findings is an important contribution to any criminal case, its nonexclusive character does not always motivate investigators to go all out in their search for class physical evidence. The items most sought at the crime site are those that possess potential individual characteristics—that is, DNA, fingerprints, firearms, bullets, tool marks, and track impressions—because these are more likely to have a greater impact on an investigation. Once these avenues have been exhausted, there seems to be little desire to progress further. Clearly, future research will have to concentrate on defining the value of class evidence so that these items can become statistically more meaningful and attractive to scientists and investigators alike. However, a salient point of this book is that all physical evidence, whether class or individual in nature, is critical to a properly conducted criminal investigation. Criminalists have become extremely proficient in conducting tests that will narrow the origin of class evidence to a limited number of possibilities. Yet some insist that if a scientist cannot define the significance of a comparison in statistical terms, the evidence should be excluded from consideration. To succumb to this reasoning is tantamount to eviscerating a core principle of criminalistics—the collection and presentation of impartial and objective information for evaluation by an adjudicator of fact. The criminalistic community must aggressively communicate its capabilities and objectives to both the police and legal communities.

A major thrust of forensic research must concentrate on defining the most distinctive properties of evidence and relating these properties to statistics that measure their frequency of occurrence. The creation of data banks to collect, store, and disseminate this kind of information will facilitate the task. Because the responsibility for providing forensic services is spread among more than 350 independent government laboratories in the United States, the task of accumulating meaningful statistical data applicable to the entire country or to large regions is exceedingly difficult. Future progress will depend on the willingness of all crime laboratories to enter into cooperative programs that will ensure uniform standards of analysis as well as providing for the collection and dissemination of analytical and statistical data.

Furthermore, the FBI has encouraged the formation of committees comprising forensic specialists in relevant forensic science disciplines to develop standardized analytical protocols in their field. These committees, known as SWGS (Scientific Working Groups), meet on a regular basis and are constantly fine tuning and updating developments in their respective fields. Their work products are disseminated to the entire forensic community to serve as an impetus for laboratory standardization of forensic technology.

The central role that forensic science has assumed in the criminal justice system led to the creation of a study by the National Academy of Science to assess the current and future roles of forensic science in the criminal justice system. The report was published in 2009 under the title *Strengthening Forensic Science in the United States: A Path Forward.* Some of the report's recommendations were controversial; however, few disagreed with the report's call for creating a culture in forensic science that is strongly rooted in science. The report correctly advocates support for research to address issues of accuracy, reliability, and validity in forensic science disciplines.

The FBI's Forensic Science Research and Training Center is a key ingredient in the development of criminalistics in the United States. The FBI has made a substantial commitment to the center in terms of personnel and equipment. This facility has established a research program concentrated in the areas of biochemistry, immunology, chemistry, and physics. The FBI's program is directed toward the development of new methods for forensic science. The research staff interacts with researchers from academia, industry, and other government and forensic science laboratories. The staff also participates in specialized scientific courses offered by the FBI to state and local crime laboratory personnel. These courses not only have improved the quality of forensic science practices in the United States but have encouraged standardization of many of the scientific procedures used by forensic laboratories throughout the United States.

A foundation of cooperation has been laid; much remains to be accomplished. How successful our profession will be in fulfilling its present and future obligations to justice depends on the skill, dedication, and ingenuity of its practitioners.

further references

Houck, M. M., "Statistics and Trace Evidence: The Tyranny of Numbers," *Forensic Science Communications* 1, no. 3 (1999), www.fbi.gov/programs/lab/fsc/current/backissu.htm

National Research Council, *Strengthening Forensic Science in the United States: A Path Forward,* Washington, D.C.: The National Academies Press, 2009, http://books.nap.edu/openbook.php?record_id=12589&page=R1

Roman, J. K., Reid, S., Reid, J., Chalfin, A. Adams, W., and Knight, C., *The DNA Field Experiment: Cost-Effectiveness Analysis of the Use of DNA in the Investigation of High-Volume Crimes,* www.ncjrs.gov/pdffiles1/nij/grants/222318.pdf

"Status and Needs of Forensic Science Service Providers: A Report to Congress," www.ncjrs.gov/pdffiles1/nij/213420.pdf

Appendixes

Appendix I Guides to the Collection of Physical Evidence—FBI

Appendix II Instructions for Collecting Gunshot Residue (GSR)

Appendix III Chemical Formulas for Latent Fingerprint Development

Appendix IV Chemical Formulas for Development of Footwear Impressions in Blood

Appendix I
Guides to the Collection of Physical Evidence— FBI

Amount Desired			
Specimen	**Standard**	**Evidence**	**Send By**
Abrasives	Not less than one ounce.	All	Registered mail or equivalent
Ammunition (Live Cartridges)			Live ammunition must be shipped via Federal Express. The following guidelines must be followed to comply with U.S. Department of Transportation regulations. Pack ammunition in a cardboard container. Label invoices FEDERAL EXPRESS. The shipper's certification for restricted articles must be included. The outside of the container must be labeled ORMD AIR, CARTRIDGES SMALL ARMS. The shipping papers must also include the weight in grams
Anonymous Extortion Letters and Bank Robbery Notes		Documentary evidence should be preserved in the condition in which it was found. It should not be folded, torn, marked, soiled, stamped, written on, or handled unnecessarily. Protect the evidence from inadvertent indented writing. Mark documents unobtrusively by writing the collector's initials, date, and other information with a pencil. Whenever possible, submit the original evidence to the Laboratory. The lack of detail in photocopies makes examinations difficult. Copies are sufficient for reference file searches.	Registered mail or equivalent
Bullets (projector without cartridge) (Live Cartridges)		All found.	Same as Ammunition
Cartridge Cases (shells only)		All	Same as Ammunition

Source: Courtesy of the Federal Bureau of Investigation, Washington, D.C.

Identification	Wrapping and Packing	Remarks
Outside container: type of material, date obtained, investigator's name or initials.	Submit abrasives in heat sealed or resealable plastic bags or paint cans. Avoid using paper or glass containers.	Abrasives settle in oil and fuel. Submit the oil and fuel from the engine sump and/or filters. Abrasives embed in bearings and other parts. Submit the bearings and other parts.
Same as above.	Ammunition components such as bullets, cartridge cases and shotshell casings can be sent via registered mail through the U.S. Postal Service. Evidence should be packaged separately and identified by date, time, location, collector's name, case number, and evidence number.	Unless specific examination of the cartridge is essential, do not submit.
Initial and date each document, if advisable.	Use proper enclosure. Place in envelope and seal with "Evidence" tape or transparent cellophane tape. Flap side of envelope should show: (1) wording "Enclosure(s) to FBI from (name of submitting office)," (2) title of case, (3) brief description of contents, (4) file number, if known. Staple to original letter of transmittal.	Do not handle with bare hands. Advise if evidence should be treated for latent fingerprints. Whenever possible, submit the original evidence to the laboratory. The lack of detail in photocopies makes examinations difficult. Copies are sufficient for reference file searches.
Do not mark bullets, cartridges and cartridge cases, and shotshells and shotshell casings. The date, time, location, collector's name, case number, and evidence number should be on the container.	Pack tightly in cotton or soft paper in pill, match, or powder box. Place in box. Label outside of box as to contents.	Unnecessary handling obliterates marks.
Same as above.	Same as above.	Spent cartridge cases.

Amount Desired			
Specimen	Standard	Evidence	Send By
Casts (Dental or Die Stone Casts of Tire Treads and Shoe Prints)	Send in suspect's shoes and tires. Photographs and sample impressions are usually not suitable for comparison.	All shoe prints and entire circumference of tires.	Registered mail or equivalent
Checks (fraudulent)		See Anonymous Letter (p. 508)	Registered mail or equivalent
Check Protector, Rubber Stamp, and/or Date Stamp Known Standards (if possible, send actual device)	Obtain several copies in full word-for-word order of each questioned check-writer impression. If unable to forward rubber stamps, prepare numerous samples with different degrees of pressure.		Registered mail or equivalent
Clothing		All	Registered mail or equivalent

DNA Examinations (see pp. 520–522)

Specimen	Standard	Evidence	Send By
Documents (charred or burned)		All	Registered mail or equivalent
Drugs:			
1. Liquids		All	Registered mail or equivalent
2. Powders, Pills, and Solids		All to 30 g.	Registered mail or equivalent

EXPLOSIVES: Detonators, Blasting Caps, Detonating Cord, Black Powder, Smokeless Powder, Explosives, and Accessories, call FBI Laboratory, for shipping instructions.

Specimen	Standard	Evidence	Send By
Fibers	Entire garment or other cloth item.	All	Registered mail or equivalent
Firearms (unloaded weapons)		Firearms must be packaged and shipped separately from live ammunition. All firearms must be unloaded.	Firearms and ammunition components such as bullets, cartridge cases, and shotshell casings can be sent via registered mail through the U.S. Postal Service. Evidence must be packaged separately and identified by date, time, location, collector's name, case number, and evidence number.

Identification	Wrapping and Packing	Remarks
On back of cast before it hardens, write location and date taken, and investigator's name or initials.	Wrap in paper and cover with suitable packing material to prevent breakage. Label "Fragile." Plaster of Paris is no longer recommended.	For shoeprint and tire tread file searches, submit quality photographs of the impressions. If photographs are not available, submit casts, lifts, or the original evidence. Detailed sketches or photocopies are acceptable.
See Anonymous Letters on p. 508.	See Anonymous Letters on p. 508.	Advise what parts are questioned or known. Furnish physical description of subject.
Place name or initials, date, name of make and model, etc., on sample impressions.	See Anonymous Letters on p. 508.	Do not disturb inking mechanisms on printing devices.
Mark directly on garment or use string tag indicating type of evidence, date obtained, investigator's name or initials.	Wrap each article individually. Place in strong container with identification written on outside of package.	Do not cut out stains; leave clothing whole. If wet, hang in room to dry before packing.
Outside container: indicate if fragile, date obtained, investigator's name or initials.	Pack in rigid container between layers of cotton.	If moisture is added use atomizer, otherwise, not recommended.
Affix label to bottle in which found, including date it was found and investigator's name or initials.	Make sure container does not leak. Seal with tape to prevent any loss.	Mark "Fragile." If possible, use heat-seal plastic bags.
Outside of pillbox: affix label with date found and investigator's name or initials.	Seal with tape to prevent any loss.	If powder, pills, or solids are found in paper bags, place them in plastic bags to prevent any loss. Do not submit used drug field test kits with evidence.
Outside container or on the object fibers are adhering, include date and investigator's name or initials.	Use folder paper or pillbox. Seal edges and openings with tape.	Do not place loose in an envelope.
Do not mark the firearm. Firearms should be identified with a tag containing the caliber, make, model, and serial number. The date, time, owner(s)' name(s), location, collector's name, case number, and evidence number should be on the container.	Wrap in paper and identify contents of packages. Place in cardboard box or wooden box.	The firearm should be handled minimally to avoid loss or destruction of evidence. Do not allow objects to enter or contact the firearm's barrel, chamber, or other operating surface.

	Amount Desired		
Specimen	Standard	Evidence	Send By
Flash Paper	One sheet	All to 5 sheets.	Call FBI Laboratory.
Gasoline	10 ml	All to 10 ml	Call Chemistry-Toxicology Unit for instructions.
General Unknown:			
1. Solids (nonhazardous)	10 gm	All to 10 gm	Registered mail or equivalent
2. Liquids (non-hazardous)	10 ml	All to 10 ml	Registered mail or equivalent
Glass Fractures		All	Registered mail or equivalent
Glass Particles	Submit the victim(s)'and suspect's air-dried clothing. Each item must be packaged separately in a paper bag. Search for particles in the victim(s)' and suspect(s)' hair, skin, and wounds. Submit particles in leakproof containers such as film canisters or plastic pill bottles. Do not use paper or glass containers. Search for particles in vehicles by vacuuming each section of the vehicle separately. Do not use tape for covering glass particles. Submit vacuum sweepings in leakproof containers. Do not use paper or glass containers.	All	Registered mail or equivalent

Identification	Wrapping and Packing	Remarks
Outside container: label indicating date and investigator's name or initials.	Flash paper is a hazardous material. Do not store flash paper near combustible materials. Seal flash paper in polyethylene envelopes and refrigerate.	
Outside container: label indicating type of material, date, and investigator's name or initials.	Use an all-metal container packed in wooden box.	An all-metal container should be used for its fireproof qualities.
Outside container: label indicating date and investigator's name or initials.	Same as Drugs (see p. 510).	Call Chemistry-Toxicology Unit for instructions.
Same as Liquid Drugs (see p. 510).	Same as Liquid Drugs (see p. 510).	Same as above.
Label the sides of the glass in the frame INSIDE and OUTSIDE. Label the glass where it was removed in the frame such as TOP, BOTTOM, LEFT, and RIGHT.	Wrap each piece separately in cotton. Pack in sturdy container to prevent shifting and breakage. Identify contents.	Submit all glass pieces so that the pieces can be fitted together to identify the radial cracks near and at the point(s) of impact and to increase the probability of matching edges. Pack all glass separately and securely to avoid shifting and breaking during transport.
Outside container: label indicating date and investigator's name or initials.	Place in film canister or plastic vial. Seal and protect against breakage.	Submit samples of glass from each broken window or source in leakproof containers such as film canisters or plastic pill bottles. Avoid using paper or glass containers.

| | Amount Desired | | |
Specimen	Standard	Evidence	Send By
Gunshot Residues The Laboratory provides gunshot residue examinations to assist FBI field office investigations only.		Usually gunshot residue examinations will only be performed when samples are collected from living person's hands. Gunshot residue evidence must be collected within five hours of exposure to the discharge of a firearm.	
On cloth only to determine weapon to target distance.		All	Clothing submitted for gunshot residue examination should be handled carefully, air dried, and wrapped separately in paper. Clothing with blood must be air dried and labeled BIOHAZARD on the inner and outer containers. The date, time, location, collector's name, case number, and evidence number should be on the container.
Hair	Twenty-five full-length hairs from different parts of head and/ or pubic region.	All	Registered mail or equivalent
Handwriting and Hand Printing Known Standards			Registered mail or equivalent
Insulation 1. Glass Wool	1" mass from each suspect area.	All	Registered mail or equivalent
2. Safe	Sample all damaged areas.	All	Registered mail or equivalent
Matches	One to two books of paper. One full box of wood.	All	Federal Express, UPS, or equivalent
Obliterated, Eradicated, or Indented Writing		Same as Anonymous Letters (see p. 508).	Registered mail or equivalent

Identification	Wrapping and Packing	Remarks
		Collecting gunshot residue samples requires five adhesive lifts suitable for scanning electron microscopic analysis. Dab the adhesive side of the stub against the surface (right palm, back of right hand, left palm, back of left hand). Use one stub per sampling surface. The remaining stub will be used as a control. Label each sampling surface stub (e.g., RIGHT PALM, BACK OF RIGHT HAND). Cap and seal the stubs in separate, resealable plastic bags.
Outside container: Indicate date, obtained from whom, description, name or initials.	Dry and package individually in **unused** brown wrapping paper or brown grocery bag.	The deposition of gunshot residue on evidence such as clothing varies with the distance from the muzzle of the firearm to the target. Patterns of gunshot residue can be duplicated using a questioned firearm and ammunition combination fired into test materials at known distances. These patterns serve as a basis for estimating muzzle-to-garment distances.
Outside container: Type of material, date, and investigator's name or initials.	Folded paper or pillbox. Seal edges and openings with tape.	Do not place loose in envelope.
Indicate from whom obtained, voluntary statement included in appropriate place, date obtained, and investigator's name or initials.	Same as Anonymous Letters (see p. 508).	Same as Anonymous Letters (see p. 508).
Outside container: type of material, date, name or initials.	Use pillbox or plastic vial. Seal to prevent any loss.	Submit known and questioned debris in leakproof containers such as film canisters or plastic pill bottles. Avoid using paper or glass containers. Pack to keep lumps intact.
Same as above.	Safe insulation can adhere to persons, clothing, tools, bags, and loot and can transfer to vehicles. If possible, submit the evidence to the Laboratory for examiners to remove the debris. Package each item of evidence in a separate paper bag. Do not process tools for latent prints.	
Outside container: label indicating type of material, date, and investigator's name or initials.	Pack in metal container and in larger package to prevent shifting. Pack matches in box or metal container to prevent friction between matches.	Keep and label: "Keep away from fire."
Same as Anonymous Letters (see p. 508).	Same as Anonymous Letters (see p. 508).	Advise whether bleaching or staining methods may be used. Avoid folding.

	Amount Desired		
Specimen	Standard	Evidence	Send By
Organs of the Body		200 g of each organ.	Call Chemistry-Toxicology Unit for instructions.
Paint:			
1. Liquid	Original unopened container up to 1/4 pint, if possible.	All to 1/4 pint.	Registered mail or equivalent
2. Solid (paint chips or scrapings)	At least 1/2 sq. in. of solid, with all layers represented.	Standard: Control paint chips must be collected from the suspected source of the evidentiary paint. Controls must be taken from an area close to, but not in, any damaged area. If no damage is obvious, controls should be taken from several areas of the suspect substrate. Each layer can be a point of comparison. Controls must have all of the layers of paint to the substrate.	Registered mail or equivalent
Rope, Twine, and Cordage	One yard or amount available.	Submit the entire rope or cord. If the rope or cord must be cut, specify which end was cut during evidence collection. Label the known and questioned samples. Handle the sections of rope or cord carefully to prevent loss of trace material or contamination.	Registered mail or equivalent
Saliva Samples	1.5" diameter stain in center of filter paper.	All	Registered mail or equivalent
Shoe Print Lifts (impressions on hard surfaces)	Photograph before making lift of dust impression.	For shoeprint and tire tread comparisons, submit original evidence whenever possible (shoes, tires, photographic negatives, casts, lifts).	Registered mail or equivalent

Identification	Wrapping and Packing	Remarks
Each biological specimen must be placed in a separate, labeled, sealed glass tube, plastic cup, or heat-sealed or resealable plastic bag. Affix BIOHAZARD labels to the inside and outside containers.	To avoid deterioration, biological specimens must be refrigerated or frozen during storage and shipping. Pack so that no breakage, leakage, or contamination occurs.	Submit a copy of the autopsy or incident report. Describe the symptoms of the suspect(s) or victim(s) at the time of the crime or prior to the death. List any known or questioned drugs consumed by or prescribed for the suspect(s) or victim(s). Describe any known or questioned environmental exposure to toxic substances by the suspect(s) or victim(s).
Outside container: Type of material, origin if known, date, investigator's name or initials.	Use friction-top paint can or large-mouth, screw-top jar. If glass, pack to prevent breakage. Use heavy corrugated paper or wooden box.	Protect spray can nozzles to keep them from going off. Avoid contact with adhesive materials. Wrap to protect paint smears. Do not use envelopes, paper/plastic bags, or glass vials.
Same as above.	Package paint specimens in leakproof containers such as vials or pillboxes. Do not stick paint particles on adhesive tape. Do not use plastic bags, cotton, or envelopes to package paint specimens.	Avoid contact with adhesive materials. Wrap so as to protect smear. If *small amount:* seal round pillbox, film cannister, or plastic vial to protect against leakage/breakage.
On tag or container: Type of material, date, investigator's name or initials.	Submit in heat-sealed or resealable plastic or paper bags.	
Outside envelope and on filter paper: Type of sample, name of donor, date of collection, and collector's initials or name.	Seal in envelope.	Stain should be circled in pencil for identification. Filter paper available from hospitals and drugstores. Allow to dry.
On lifting tape or paper attached to tape: date, investigator's name or initials.	Prints in dust are easily damaged. Fasten print or lift to bottom of box so that nothing will rub against it.	Always secure crime-scene area until shoe prints or tire treads are located and preserved.

	Amount Desired		
Specimen	Standard	Evidence	Send By
Soils and Minerals	Samples from areas near pertinent spot.	Collect soil samples from the immediate crime scene area and from the logical access and/or escape route(s). Collect soil samples at a depth that is consistent with the depth from which the questioned soil may have originated. If possile, collect soil samples from alibi areas such as the yard or work area of the suspect(s).	Registered mail
Tape (Adhesive Tape)	Recovered roll.	All	Registered mail or equivalent
Tools/Toolmarks	Send in the tool. If impractical, make several impressions on similar materials as evidence using entire marking area of tool.	If it is not possible to submit the tool-marked evidence, submit a cast of the toolmark.	Registered mail or equivalent
Typewriting, known standards	See Anonymous Letters (p. 508).		Registered mail or equivalent
Wire	3 ft. (Do not kink.)	All (Do not kink.)	Registered mail or equivalent
Wood	One foot or amount available.	All	Registered mail or equivalent

Identification	Wrapping and Packing	Remarks
Outside container: Type of material, date, investigator's name or initials.	Do not remove soil adhering to shoes, clothing, and tools. Do not process tools for latent prints. Air-dry the soil and the clothing and package separately in paper bags. Carefully remove soil adhering to vehicles. Air-dry the soil and package separately in paper bags.	Ship known and questioned debris separately to avoid contamination. Submit known and questioned soil in leakproof containers such as film canisters or plastic pill bottles. Do not use paper envelopes or glass containers. Pack to keep lumps intact.
Same as above.	Place on waxed paper, cellophane, or plastic.	Do not cut, wad, distort, or separate tapes that are stuck together.
On object or on tag attached to an opposite end from where toolmarks appear: date recovered and investigator's name or initials.	After marks have been protected with soft paper, wrap in strong wrapping paper, place in strong box, and pack to prevent shifting.	Photographs locate tool-marks but are of no value for identification purposes. Obtain samples of any material deposited on the tools. To avoid contamination, do not place the tool against the toolmarked evidence. Submit the tool rather than making test cuts or impressions. Mark the ends of the evidence and specify which end was cut during evidence collection.
On specimens: serial number, brand, model, etc., date recovered, and investigator's name or initials.	Same as Anonymous Letters (p. 508).	Examine ribbon for evidence of questioned message.
On label or tab: describe type of material, date, investigator's name or initials.	Wrap securely.	Do not kink wire.
Same as above.	Submit wood in heat-sealed or resealable plastic or paper bags.	

DNA Examinations

Deoxyribonucleic acid (DNA) is analyzed in body fluids, stains, and other biological tissues recovered from evidence. The results of DNA analysis of questioned biological samples are compared with the results of DNA analysis of known samples. This analysis can associate victim(s) and/or suspect(s) with each other or with a crime scene.

There are two sources of DNA used in forensic analyses. Nuclear DNA (nDNA) is typically analyzed in evidence containing blood, semen, saliva, body tissues, and hairs that have tissue at their root ends. Mithochondrial DNA (mtDNA) is typically analyzed in evidence containing naturally shed hairs, hair fragments, bones, and teeth.

If DNA evidence is not properly documented, collected, packaged, and preserved, it will not meet the legal and scientific requirements for admissibility in a court of law.

- If it is not properly documented, its origin can be questioned.
- If it is not properly collected, biological activity can be lost.
- If it is not properly packaged, contamination can occur.
- If it is not properly preserved, decomposition and deterioration can occur.

When DNA evidence is transferred by direct or secondary (indirect) means, it remains on surfaces by absorption or adherence. In general, liquid biological evidence is absorbed into surfaces, and solid biological evidence adheres to surfaces. Collecting, packaging, and preserving DNA evidence depends on the liquid or solid state and the condition of the evidence.

The more that evidence retains its original integrity until it reaches the Laboratory, the greater the possibility of conducting useful examinations. It may be necessary to use a variety of techniques to collect suspected body fluid evidence.

Blood Examinations

Examinations can determine the presence or absence of blood in stains. Examinations can also determine whether blood is human or not. Blood examinations cannot determine the age or the race of a person. Conventional serological techniques are not adequately informative to positively identify a person as the source of a stain.

Collecting Known Samples

BLOOD

- Only qualified medical personnel should collect blood samples from a person.
- Collect at least two 5-ml tubes of blood in purple-top tubes with EDTA as an anticoagulant for DNA analysis. Collect drug- or alcohol-testing samples in gray-top tubes with NaF (sodium fluoride).
- Identify each tube with the date, time, subject's name, location, collector's name, case number, and evidence number.
- Refrigerate, do not freeze blood samples. Use cold packs, not dry ice, during shipping.
- Pack liquid blood tubes individually in Styrofoam or cylindrical tubes with absorbent material surrounding the tubes.
- Label the outer container KEEP IN A COOL DRY PLACE, REFRIGERATE ON ARRIVAL, and BIOHAZARD.
- Submit to the Laboratory as soon as possible.

BLOOD ON A PERSON

- Absorb suspected **liquid blood** onto a clean cotton cloth or swab. Leave a portion of the cloth or swab unstained as a control. Air-dry the cloth or swab and pack in clean paper or an envelope with sealed corners. Do not use plastic containers.
- Absorb suspected **dried blood** onto a clean cotton cloth or swab moistened with distilled water. Leave a portion of the cloth or swab unstained as a control. Air-dry the cloth or swab and pack in clean paper or an envelope with sealed corners. Do not use plastic containers.

BLOOD ON SURFACES OR IN SNOW OR WATER

- Absorb suspected **liquid blood or blood clots** onto a clean cotton cloth or swab. Leave a portion of the cloth or swab unstained as a control. Air-dry the cloth or swab and pack in clean paper or an envelope with sealed corners. Do not use plastic containers.
- Collect suspected **blood in snow or water** immediately to avoid further dilution. Eliminate as much snow as possible. Place in a clean airtight container. Freeze the evidence and submit as soon as possible to the Laboratory.

BLOODSTAINS

- Air-dry **wet bloodstained garments.** Wrap **dried bloodstained garments** in clean paper. Do not place wet or dried garments in plastic or airtight containers. Place all debris or residue from the garments in clean paper or an envelope with sealed corners.
- Air-dry small suspected **wet bloodstained objects** and submit the objects to the Laboratory. Preserve bloodstain patterns. Avoid creating additional stain patterns during drying and packaging. Pack to prevent stain removal by abrasive action during shipping. Pack in clean paper. Do not use plastic containers.
- When possible, cut a large sample of suspected **bloodstains from immovable objects** with a clean, sharp instrument. Collect an unstained control sample. Pack to prevent stain removal by abrasive action during shipping. Pack in clean paper. Do not use plastic containers.
- Absorb suspected **dried bloodstains on immovable objects** onto a clean cotton cloth or swab moistened with distilled water. Leave a portion of the cloth or swab unstained as a control. Air-dry the cloth or swab and pack in clean paper or an envelope with sealed corners. Do not use plastic containers.

BLOOD EXAMINATION REQUEST LETTER

A blood examination request letter must contain the following information:

- A brief statement of facts relating to the case.
- Claims made by the suspect(s) regarding the source of the blood.
- Whether animal blood is present.
- Whether the stains were laundered or diluted with other body fluids.
- Information regarding the victim(s)' and suspect(s)' health such as AIDS, hepatitis, or tuberculosis.

SEMEN AND SEMEN STAINS

- Absorb suspected **liquid semen** onto a clean cotton cloth or swab. Leave a portion of the cloth or swab unstained as a control. Air-dry the cloth or swab and pack in clean paper or an envelope with sealed corners. Do not use plastic containers.
- Submit small suspected **dry semen-stained objects** to the Laboratory. Pack to prevent stain removal by abrasive action during shipping. Pack in clean paper. Do not use plastic containers.
- When possible, cut a large sample of suspected **seman stains from immovable objects** with a clean, sharp instrument. Collect an unstained control sample. Pack to prevent stain removal by abrasive action during shipping. Pack in clean paper. Do not use plastic containers.
- Absorb suspected **dried semen stains on immovable objects** onto a clean cotton cloth or swab moistened with distilled water. Leave a portion of the cloth or swab unstained as a control. Air-dry the swab or cloth and place in clean paper or an envelope with sealed corners. Do not use plastic containers.

SEMINAL EVIDENCE FROM SEXUAL ASSAULT VICTIM(S)

- Sexual assault victim(s) must be medically examined in a hospital or a physician's office using a standard sexual assault evidence kit to collect vaginal, oral, and anal evidence.
- Refrigerate and submit the evidence as soon as possible to the Laboratory.

BUCCAL (ORAL) SWABS
- Use clean cotton swabs to collect buccal (oral) samples. Rub the inside surfaces of the cheeks thoroughly.
- Air-dry the swabs and place in clean paper or an envelope with sealed corners. Do not use plastic containers.
- Identify each sample with the date, time subject's name, location, collector's name, case number, and evidence number.
- Buccal samples do not need to be refrigerated.

SALIVA AND URINE
- Absorb suspected **liquid saliva or urine** onto a clean cotton cloth or swab. Leave a portion of the cloth unstained as a control. Air-dry the cloth or swab and pack in clean paper or an envelope with sealed corners. Do not use plastic containers.
- Submit suspected small, **dry saliva- or urine-stained objects** to the Laboratory. Pack to prevent stain removal by abrasive action during shipping. Pack in clean paper or an envelope with sealed corners. Do not use plastic containers.
- When possible, cut a large sample of suspected **saliva or urine stains from immovable objects** with a clean, sharp instrument. Collect an unstained control sample. Pack to prevent stain removal by abrasive action during shipping. Pack in clean paper. Do not use plastic containers.
- Pick up **cigarette butts** with gloved hands or clean forceps. Do not submit ashes. Air-dry and place the cigarette butts from the same location (e.g., ashtray) in clean paper or an envelope with sealed corners. Do not submit the ashtray unless a latent print examination is requested. Package the ashtray separately. Do not use plastic containers.
- Pick up **chewing gum** with gloved hands or clean forceps. Air-dry and place in clean paper or an envelope with sealed corners. Do not use plastic containers.
- Pick up **envelops and stamps** with gloved hands or clean forceps and place in a clean envelope. Do not use plastic containers.

HAIR
- Pick up hair carefully with clean forceps to prevent damaging the root tissue.
- Air-dry hair mixed with suspected body fluids.
- Package each group of hair separately in clean paper or an envelope with sealed corners. Do not use plastic containers.
- Refrigerate and submit as soon as possible to the Laboratory.

TISSUES, BONES, AND TEETH
- Pick up suspected tissues, bones, and teeth with gloved hands or clean forceps.
- Collect 1–2 cubic inches of red skeletal muscle.
- Collect 3–5 inches of long bone such as the fibula or femur.
- Collect teeth in the following order:
    1. nonrestored molar.
    2. nonrestored premolar.
    3. nonrestored canine.
    4. nonrestored front tooth.
    5. restored molar.
    6. restored premolar.
    7. restored canine.
    8. restored front tooth.
- Place tissue samples in a clean, airtight plastic container without formalin or formaldehyde. Place teeth and bone samples in clean paper or an envelope with sealed corners.
- Freeze the evidence, place in Styrofoam containers, and ship overnight on dry ice.

Appendix II
Instructions for Collecting Gunshot Residue (GSR)

INSTRUCTIONS FOR COLLECTING GUNSHOT RESIDUE (GSR)
for Scanning Electron Microscopy and Atomic Absorption Analysis

---

NOTE

In control test firings, it has been shown that the concentration of gunshot residue significantly declines on living subjects after approximately 4 hours. In view of these findings, if more than 4 hours have passed since the shooting, it is recommended that you check with your crime laboratory before submitting samples for analysis.

S.E.M. COLLECTION PROCEDURE

(A) When the covering is removed from the metal stubs, the adhesive collecting surface is exposed and care must be used to not drop the stub or contaminate the collecting surface by allowing this exposed surface to come in contact with an object other than the area that is to be sampled. (See Figure 1.)

(B) *Do not* return paper stub cover to stubs after collection. (*Discard stub covers.*)

(C) Heavily soiled or bloody areas should be avoided if possible.

(D) When pressing the stubs on the questioned areas, use enough pressure to cause a mild indentation on the surface of the subject's hand.

STEP 1 Fill out all information requested on the enclosed Gunshot Residue Analysis Information Form.

STEP 2 Put on the disposable plastic gloves provided in this kit. *Do not substitute with other gloves!*

> NOTE: If there is blood on the subject's hands or clothing, the investigating officer should put on latex or other approved barrier gloves to protect him/her from bloodborne pathogens, then put on the plastic gloves provided in this kit.

STEP 3 **RIGHT BACK:**

(A) Carefully remove the cap from the vial labeled RIGHT BACK, then remove the paper covering from the metal sample stub.

(B) While holding the vial cap, press the collecting surface of the stub onto the back of the subject's right hand until the area shown below in Figure 2 has been covered.

(C) After sampling the back of the subject's right hand, return the cap, with metal stub, to the RIGHT BACK vial. *Do not return paper covering to metal stub!*

VIAL CAP
METAL STUB
COLLECTING SURFACE

Fig. 1

STEP 4 **RIGHT PALM:**

Repeat the procedure described in Step 3, using the metal stub in the vial marked RIGHT PALM. Make sure to sample the area shown below in Figure 3.

STEP 5 **LEFT BACK and LEFT PALM:**

For collection from the left hand, repeat Steps 3 and 4 using the vials labeled LEFT BACK and LEFT PALM.

STEP 6 After sampling all four areas, return capped vials to kit envelope.

Fig. 2 (BACK)

Fig. 3 (PALM)

Source: Tri-Tech, Inc., Southport, N.C., www.tritechusa.com

A.A. COLLECTION PROCEDURE

NOTE: (A) This second part of the GSR collection is *ONLY* to be performed *AFTER* sampling with the SEM stubs.

(B) If you feel that during the SEM collection procedure you have contaminated the gloves, discard contaminated gloves, then thoroughly wash your hands with soap and water and dry with a clean towel. At no time during the collection process should your hands (with or without gloves) come into contact with the cotton tip of the swab.

(C) When dispensing nitric acid, use 2 - 3 drops of 5% nitric acid solution to moisten each swab (do not over-moisten). In order to dispense an appropriate amount of the nitric acid solution, hold the acid dispenser in a horizontal position above and *almost* touching the top of the swab, and squeeze gently.

(D) To swab the subject's hands, the investigator should grasp the subject's arm above the wrist with one hand and swab with the other. The subject's hand should be in a "spread" position. Thorough swabbing of the hands is carried out by using moderate pressure while swabbing. The swab should be rotated during this procedure to insure that all of the surface of the cotton tip is utilized. At least 30 seconds per swab is required.

(E) When placing swabs in tubes, always place cotton tips *FACE DOWN*.

STEP 7 CONTROL SWABS: Remove *two* of the swabs from the unmarked ziplock bag. Moisten both swabs with 2 - 3 drops of the 5% nitric acid solution supplied in kit (do not substitute). Place both swabs in the tube labeled CONTROL. Then recap tube and set it aside.

STEP 8 RIGHT BACK:

(A) Moisten the tip of *ONE* swab with 2 - 3 drops of nitric acid solution, then thoroughly swab the back of the subject's right hand including the back of the fingers and all of the web area which would be exposed while holding a weapon. Fig. 4 illustrates the area of hand for swabbing. Place swab used in the tube labeled RIGHT BACK.

Fig. 4 (BACK)

(B) Repeat the above procedure using a *SECOND* swab. Place the second swab used in the RIGHT BACK tube, then recap tube and set it aside.

STEP 9 RIGHT PALM:

(A) Moisten the tip of *ONE* swab with 2 - 3 drops of nitric acid solution, then thoroughly swab the palm of the subject's right hand as shown in Fig. 5. Place swab used in the tube labeled RIGHT PALM.

(B) Repeat the above procedure using a *SECOND* swab. Place the second swab used in the RIGHT PALM tube, then recap tube and set it aside.

Fig. 5 (PALM)

STEP 10 LEFT BACK/LEFT PALM: Follow the same procedures described in Steps 8 and 9, but swabbing the subject's left hand.

STEP 11 CARTRIDGE CASE:

NOTE: For .22 cal and foreign manufactured ammunition, it is necessary that either Steps A and B described below be completed <u>OR</u> the casings be submitted to the laboratory. If latent prints are required on the expended casing(s), Steps A and B should be omitted and the casings should be submitted for latent print processing. If for any reason the CARTRIDGE CASE swabs are not used, mark the tube "*NOT USED*".

(A) Moisten the tip of *ONE* swab with 2 - 3 drops of nitric acid solution, then thoroughly swab the inside of the cartridge case. Place swab used in the tube labeled CARTRIDGE CASE.

(B) Repeat the above procedure using a *SECOND* swab. Place second swab used in the CARTRIDGE CASE tube, and then recap tube and set it aside.

FINAL INSTRUCTIONS

(A) Fill out all information requested on the front of the kit envelope.

(B) With the exception of the 5% nitric acid dispenser and the disposable gloves, return all other kit components, used or unused, to kit envelope.

(C) Moisten kit envelope flap, then seal envelope. Affix Police Evidence Seal where indicated, then initial seal.

(D) Mail or hand deliver sealed kit to the crime laboratory for analysis. (If mailed, package kit in a cardboard box to prevent damage in transit.)

Appendix III
Chemical Formulas for Latent Fingerprint Development

Iodine Spray Reagent

1. Prepare the following stock solutions:

Solution A
Dissolve gram of Iodine in 1 liter of Cyclohexane

Solution B
Dissolve 5 grams of a-Naphthoflavone in 40 ml of Methylene Chloride (Dichloramethane)

2. Add 2 ml of Solution B to 100 ml of Solution A. Using a magnetic stirrer, mix thoroughly for 5 minutes.
3. Filter the solution through a facial tissue, paper towel, filter paper, etc., into a beaker. The solution should be lightly sprayed on the specimen using an aerosol spray unit or a mini spray gun powered with compressed air.
4. Lightly spray the suspect area with several applications until latent prints sufficiently develop.

Remarks
- Solution A may be stored at room temperature. Shelf life is in excess of 30 days.
- Solution B must be refrigerated. Shelf life is in excess of 30 days.
- The combined working solution (A and B) should be used within 24 hours after mixing.
- The Iodine Spray solution is effective on most surfaces (porous and nonporous).
- A fine spray mist is the most effective form of application.
- The Cyanocrylate (Super Glue) process cannot be used prior to the Iodine Spray Reagent Process. Cyanoacrylate may be used, however, after the Iodine Spray Reagent.
- On porous surfaces, DFO and/or Ninhydrin may be used after the Iodine Spray.
- Propanol may be used to remove the staining of the Iodine Spray Reagent.
- 1,1,2 Trichlorotrifluoroethane may be substituted for Cyclohexane.

1,8-Diazafluoren-9-one (DFO)

Step 1: Stock solution: Dissolve 1 gram DFO in 200 ml Methanol, 200 ml Ethyl Acetate, and 40 ml Acetic Acid.
Step 2: Working solution (make as needed): Start with stock solution and dilute to 2 liters with Petroleum Ether (40° to 60° boiling point fraction). Pentane can also be used. Solution should be clear.

Dip the paper document into the working solution and allow to dry. Dip again and allow to dry. When completely dry, apply heat (200° for 10 to 20 minutes). An oven, hair dryer, or dry iron can be used.

Visualize with an alternate light source at 450, 485, 525, and 530 nm and observe through orange goggles. If the surface paper is yellow, such as legal paper, it may be necessary to visualize the paper at 570 nm and view it through red goggles.

Source: In part from *Processing Guide for Developing Latent Prints,* Revised 2000. Washington, D.C.: FBI http://njiai.org/fbi_2000_lp_guide.pdf

1,2-indanedione
2.0 g 1,2-indanedione
70 ml ethyl acetate
930 ml HFE 7100 (3M Company)

Ninhydrin

20 grams Ninhydrin
3,300 ml Acetone
Shelf life is approximately one month

or

5 grams Ninhydrin
30 ml Methanol
40 ml 2-Propanol
930 ml Petroleum Ether
Shelf life is approximately one year

Dip the paper document in the working solution and allow to dry. Dip again and allow to dry. When completely dry, heat may be applied. A steam iron should be used on the steam setting. Do not touch the iron directly to the paper. Rather, hold the iron above the paper and allow the steam to heat it.

Zinc Chloride Solution (Post-Ninhydrin Treatment)

5 grams of Zinc Chloride crystals
2 ml of Glacial Acetic Acid
100 ml of Methyl Alcohol
Add 400 ml of 1,1,2 Trichlorotrifluoroethane to the mixture and stir.
Add 2 ml of 5 percent Sodium Hypochlorite solution (commercially available liquid bleach such as Clorox, Purex, and others).

Lightly spray the paper with the Zinc solution. Repeat the spraying as needed. Do not overdo the spraying.

The ninhydrin-developed prints treated with this solution may fluoresce at room temperature with an alternate light source. For maximum fluorescence, place the paper in a bath of liquid nitrogen and examine again with an alternate light source.

Physical Developer

When mixing and using these solutions, make sure the glassware, processing trays, stirring rods, and stirring magnets are absolutely clean. Do not use metal trays or tweezer.

Stock Detergent Solution: 3 grams of *N*-Dodecylamine Acetate are combined with 4 grams of Synperonic-*N* mixed in 1 liter of distilled water.

Silver Nitrate Solution: 20 grams of Silver Nitrate crystals are mixed in 100 milliliters of distilled water.

Redox Solution: 60 grams of Ferric Nitrate are mixed in 1,800 milliliters of distilled water. After this solution is thoroughly mixed, add 160 grams of Ferrous Ammonium Sulfate, mix thoroughly and add 40 grams of Citric Acid, mix thoroughly.

Maleic Acid Solution: Put 50 grams of Maleic Acid into 2 liters of distilled water.

Physical Developer Working Solution: Begin with 2,125 milliliters of the Redox Solution and add 80 milliliters of the Stock Detergent Solution, mix well, then add 100 milliliters of the Silver

Nitrate Solution and mix well. Appropriate divisions can be used if smaller amounts of the working solution are desired.

Immerse specimen in Maleic Acid Solution for 10 minutes. Incubate item in physical developer (PD) working solution for 15–20 minutes. Thoroughly rinse specimen in tap water for 20 minutes Air-dry and photograph.

Cyanoacrylate Fluorescent Enhancement Reagents

Rhodamine 6G

Stock Solution
100 mg Rhodamine 6G
100 ml Methanol (Stir until thoroughly dissolved.)

Working Solution
3 ml Rhodamine 6G Stock Solution
15 ml Acetone
10 ml Acetonitrile
15 ml Methanol
32 ml 2-Propanol
925 ml Petroleum Ether (Combine in order listed.)

Ardrox

2 ml Ardrox P-133D
10 ml Acetone
25 ml Methanol
10 ml 2-Propanol
8 ml Acetonitrile
945 ml Petroleum Ether

MBD

7-(p-methoxybenzylaminol)-4-nitrobenz-2-oxa-1,3-diazole

Stock Solution
100 mg MBD
100 ml Acetone

Working Solution
10 ml MBD Stock Solution
30 ml Methanol
10 ml 2-Propanol
950 ml Petroleum Ether (Combine in order listed.)

Basic Yellow 40

2 grams Basic Yellow 40
1 liter Methanol

RAM Combination Enhancer*

3 ml Rhodamine 6G Stock Solution
2 ml Ardrox P-133D
7 ml MBD Stock Solution
20 ml Methanol
10 ml 2-Propanol
8 ml Acetonitrile
950 ml Petroleum Ether
(Combine in order listed.)

*Source: John H. Olenik, Freemont, Ohio.

RAY Combination Enhancer*

To 940 ml of either isopropyl alcohol or denatured ethyl alcohol add:

1.0 gram of Basic Yellow 40
0.1 gram of Rhodamine 6G
8 ml of Arodrox P-133D
50 ml of Acetonitrile (optional, but dye stain of prints will appear more brilliant)

MRM 10 Combination Enhancer

3 ml Rhodamine 6G Stock Solution
3 ml Basic Yellow 40 Stock Solution
7 ml MBD Stock Solution
20 ml Methanol
10 ml 2-Propanol
8 ml Acetonitrile
950 ml Petroleum Ether
(Combine in order listed.)

The above solutions are used on evidence that has been treated with cyanoacrylate (Super Glue) fumes. These solutions dye the cyanoacrylate residue adhering to the latent print residue. Wash the dye over the evidence. It may be necessary to rinse the surface with a solvent, such as Petroleum Ether, to remove the excess stain.

CAUTION: These solutions contain solvents that may be respiratory irritants, so they should be mixed and used in a fume hood or while wearing a full-face breathing apparatus. Also, these solvents may damage some plastics, cloth, wood, and painted surfaces.

Because of the respiratory irritation possible and the general inefficiency of spraying, it is *not* recommended to spray these solutions. To obtain the maximum benefit and coverage, it is recommended that evidence be soaked, submerged, or washed with these types of solutions.

Source: John H. Olenik, Freemont, Ohio.

Appendix IV
Chemical Formulas for Development of Footwear Impressions in Blood

Amido Black

Staining Solution:
0.2 g Napthalene 12B or Napthol Blue Black
10 ml Glacial Acetic Acid
90 ml Methanol

Rinsing Solution:
90 ml Methanol
10 ml Glacial Acetic Acid

Stain the impression by spraying or immersing the item in the staining solution for approximately one minute. Next, treat with the rinsing solution to remove stain from nonimpression area. Then rinse well with distilled water.

Coomassie Blue

Staining Solution (add in this order):
0.44 g Coomassie Brilliant Blue
200 ml Methanol
40 ml Glacial Acetic Acid
200 ml Distilled Water

Rinsing Solution:
40 ml Glacial Acetic Acid
200 ml Methanol
200 ml Distilled Water

Spray object with the staining solution, completely covering the area of interest. Then spray the object with rinsing solution, clearing the background. Then rinse with distilled water.

Crowle's Double Stain

Developer:
2.5 grams Crocein Scarlet 7B
150 mg Coomassie Brilliant Blue R
50 ml Glacial Acetic Acid
30 ml Trichloroacetic Acid

Combine the above ingredients, then dilute to one liter with distilled water. Place the solution on a stirring device until all the Crocein Scarlet 7B and Coomassie Brillant Blue R are dissolved.

Rinse:
30 ml Glacial Acetic Acid
970 ml Distilled Water

Apply the developer to the item(s) by dipping. Completely cover the target area, leaving the developer on for approximately 30 to 90 seconds, then rinse. Finally, rinse well with distilled water.

Diaminobenzidine (DAB)

Solution A (Fixer Solution):
20 g 5-Sulphosalicylic Acid
Dissolved in 1L Distilled Water

Solution B:
100 ml 1M Phosphate Buffer (pH 7.4)
800 ml Distilled Water

Solution C:
1 g Diaminobenzidine
Dissolved in 100 ml Distilled Water

Working Solution (Mix Just Prior to Use):
900 ml solution B
100 ml solution C
5 ml 30% Hydrogen Peroxide

Immerse impression area in fixer solution A for approximately 4 minutes. Remove and rinse in distilled water. Immerse impression area for approximately 4 minutes in the working solution or until print is fully developed. Remove and rinse in distilled water.

Fuchsin Acid

20 g Sulfosalicylic Acid
2 g Fuchsin Acid
Dissolved in 1L Distilled Water

Stain the impression by spraying or immersing the item in the dye solution for approximately one minute. Rinse well with distilled water.

Hungarian Red

This product is available from: www.forensicssource.com

Leucocrystal Violet

10 g 5-Sulfosalicylic Acid
500 ml 3% Hydrogen Peroxide
3.7 g Sodium Acetate
1 g Leucocrystal Violet

If Leucocrystal Violet crystals are yellow instead of white, do not use. This indicates crystals are old and solution will not work.

Spray the object until completely covered. Then allow object to air-dry. Development of impressions will occur within 30 seconds. Store the solution in amber glassware and refrigerate.

Leucocrystal Violet Field Kit*

When the reagents are separated in the listed manner below, a "field kit" can be prepared. The field kit separation will allow for an extended shelf life.

Bottle A:
10 grams 5-Sulfosalicylic Acid
500 ml Hydrogen Peroxide 3%

Bottle B:
1.1 grams Leucocrystal Violet
Weigh out reagent and place in an amber 60 ml (2 ounce) bottle.

Bottle C:
4.4 grams Sodium Acetate
Weigh out reagent and place in an amber 60 ml (2 ounce) bottle.

Add approximately 30 ml of Bottle A reagent to Bottle B. Secure cap and shake Bottle B for two (2) to three (3) minutes. Pour contents of Bottle B back into Bottle A.

Add approximately 30 ml of Bottle A reagent to Bottle C. Secure cap and shake Bottle C for approximately two (2) to three (3) minutes. Pour contents of Bottle C into Bottle A. Secure Bottle A's cap and shake thoroughly.

Spray the target area; development will occur within thirty (30) seconds. After spraying, blot the area with a tissue or paper towel. Then allow object to air-dry.

Patent Blue

20 g Sulfosalicylic Acid
2 g Patent Blue V (VF)
Dissolved in 1L Distilled Water

Stain object by spraying or immersing the item in the dye solution for approximately one minute. Rinse well with distilled water.

Tartrazine

20 g Sulfosalicylic Acid
2 g Tartrazine
Dissolved in 1L Distilled Water

Stain object by spraying or immersing the item in the dye solution for approximately one minute. Rinse well with distilled water.

*Source: John Fisher, Forensic Research & Supply Corp., Gotha, Fla.

answers
to review questions

Chapter 1
Odd-Numbered Review Questions

1. forensic science
3. Alphonse Bertillon
5. Leone Lattes
7. Albert Osborn
9. Edmond Locard
11. Los Angeles
13. regional
15. The Federal Bureau of Investigation; the Drug Enforcement Administration; the Bureau of Alcohol, Tobacco, Firearms and Explosives; the U.S. Postal Service
17. trace evidence
19. firearms
21. crime-scene investigation
23. *Daubert* v. *Merrell Dow Pharmaceuticals, Inc.*
25. *Coppolino* v. *State*
27. True
29. training

Application and Critical Thinking

1. There is a range of possible answers to this question. Under the British fee-for-service model, government budgets may limit the number and type of laboratory tests police and prosecutors may request. On the other hand, if they must pay fees for crime lab services, police and prosecutors may be more careful about the types of evidence they submit. The fact that the U.S. model allows investigators to submit a theoretically unlimited amount of evidence for examination means that it may encourage police to spend more time and resources than are necessary to investigate a case. Under a fee-for-service model, police must be more efficient in their investigations. However, this can be a drawback in cases in which initial tests prove inconclusive and more extensive methods of examination are needed.
2. The note would be examined by the document examination unit; the revolver would be examined by both the firearms unit and the latent fingerprint unit; the traces of skin and blood would be examined by the biology unit.
3. Again, this question could have several answers, which might include greater expertise in crime-scene investigation, using the skills of experts in several areas of criminalistics, and reducing the workload on patrol officers.
4. On appeal, the defense raised the question of whether a new test that has not been generally accepted by the scientific community is admissible as evidence in court. The court rejected the appeal, arguing that "general acceptance," as stated in *Frye* v. *United States*, is not an absolute prerequisite to the admissibility of scientific evidence.

Chapter 2
Odd-Numbered Review Questions

1. physical evidence
3. False
5. True
7. medical assistance
9. log
11. photography; sketching; notes
13. first responding officer
15. notes
17. unaltered
19. False
21. microchip
23. overview; medium-range; close-up
25. standard operating procedures
27. final sketch
29. rough
31. physical evidence
33. False
35. is not
37. False
39. air-dried
41. chain of custody
43. unwarranted

Application and Critical Thinking

1. While waiting for backup, you should summon medical assistance for the victim, take a statement from the victim, detain any suspects at the scene, establish the boundaries of the crime scene, and ensure that no unauthorized personnel enter the crime scene.
2. a. Grid or line search
   b. Quadrant (zone) search
   c. Spiral or line search
3. Officer Walter made a mistake by opening the window and airing out the house. He should have kept the window closed until an investigation team arrived. From the lack of blood or evidence of a struggle, he concluded that the murder occurred someplace else, and that the room containing the body was a secondary scene.
4. Officer Guajardo should not have removed the scrap of cloth until the photographer had arrived and taken a picture of the evidence. He also should have put on latex gloves or used a forceps or other tool to remove the scrap of cloth. Finally, he should have placed the cloth in a paper bag or other container where air could circulate, rather than in a sealed plastic bag where moisture could accumulate and cause mold to grow on the cloth.
5. Officer Gurney should have recorded his initials on the original seal and the date on which the evidence was sealed. The forensic scientist should have opened the package in a different place, not broken the old seal. The forensic scientist also should not have discarded the old seal.

6. The crime-scene sketch does not contain dimensions of walls and objects or reference measurements for labeled objects. The sketch does show some case information, but it should be condensed in a title block.

Case Analysis

1. The first challenge investigators faced was destruction of evidence. Mexican authorities autopsied the bodies twice before the corpses had been inspected, which likely destroyed potentially helpful evidence. Authorities also prevented forensic scientists from examining the corpses until the bodies had decomposed significantly. Mexican police removed all of the obvious evidence from the residence where the victims were held before allowing the FBI forensic team to enter the scene. Mexican authorities later seized a license plate found hidden at the scene and would not allow FBI agents to examine it or to conduct any further searches of the property. In addition, Mexican authorities destroyed much of the evidence that had been collected from the crime scene for "health reasons." The second main challenge was contamination of crime scenes linked to the murders. The location where the bodies were discovered was not sealed by police, thus allowing both police officers and onlookers to contaminate the scene. Also, the residence at 881 Lope De Vega—where the victims were believed to have been killed—was cleaned and painted before forensics experts had a chance to examine it. In addition, Mexican federal police officers had been living in the residence since shortly after the time of the murders, further contaminating the scene.

2. Investigators collected reference samples of carpeting from the victims' bodies as well as bits of the victims' clothing and the sheets in which the bodies were buried. The carpet samples matched samples taken from the residence at 881 Lope De Vega, where investigators suspected the victims were killed. The samples of burial sheet matched pillowcases found at the residence, and bits of clothing matching that worn by the victims were also found at the residence. In addition, hair and blood samples matching those of the victims were found in the residence at 881 Lope De Vega.

3. Investigators found that soil samples from the victims' bodies did not match the soil from the area where the bodies were found. They also found no significant bodily fluids in the area where the bodies were found. This evidence suggested that the bodies originally had been buried elsewhere and later transported to the location where they were found. Investigators later compared soil samples from the victims' bodies to samples taken from a park where the bodies of two Americans killed by drug traffickers had been discovered. Soil samples from the bodies of Camarena and Zavala exactly matched the soil found at the location where the Americans' bodies were found.

Chapter 3
Odd-Numbered Review Questions

1. identification	17. Forensic pathology
3. comparative	19. rigor mortis; livor mortis;
5. individual	algor mortis
7. True	21. forensic anthropology
9. weight	23. facial reconstruction
11. False	25. True
13. False	27. forensic entomology
15. livor mortis	29. temperature

Application and Critical Thinking

1. Determining whether an unknown substance contains heroin would require the least extensive testing because the investigator can select only procedures that are designed to identify the presence of heroin. Determining whether an unknown substance contains an illicit drug would require the next most extensive testing regime because the investigator must select as many procedures as necessary to test for all types of illicit drugs. Determining the composition of an unknown substance would likely require the most extensive testing because of the extremely large number of possible substances to test for.

2. From most common to least common, the order would be (a), (c), and (b).

3. a. Class characteristic
   b. Individual characteristic
   c. Individual characteristic
   d. Class characteristic
   e. Individual characteristic
   f. Class characteristic
   g. Individual characteristic
   h. Individual characteristic

4. PDQ and SICAR contain information that relates primarily to evidence exhibiting class characteristics. The paint finishes and sole prints in these databases can identify the manufacturer of a shoe or paint mixture, but cannot determine the exact source of evidence that matches the samples stored in the database. CODIS, IAFIS, and NIBIN, on the other hand, contain information that relates primarily to evidence exhibiting individual characteristics. The DNA profiles, fingerprints, and striation markings stored in these databases are unique and thus can be used to link specific individuals or weapons with a crime scene.

5. The low level or absence of rigor mortis would provide information about the relatively recent death. Algor mortis may or may not show a body temperature decrease of 1–1.5°F within the short time since death. Potassium levels in the vitreous humor would likely be of little assistance. Livor mortis begins immediately after death but could show only the position of the body in the given time interval. Stomach contents may help estimate

time since the decedent last ate but would provide no information about the postmortem interval.

6. Because of the presence of an unfused epiphyseal area on the clavicle, it can be estimated that the victim is less than 21 years old. The prominent cranial features suggest the victim is a male.

Case Analysis

1. The Williams case marked the first time that fiber evidence was used to tie a large number of murder victims to a single suspect. Also, fiber evidence is typically used to support other evidence and testimony in court. In the Williams trial, the fiber evidence was the centerpiece of the state's case, and other testimony was used to support the fiber evidence.

2. Investigators hoped to learn the source of the fibers. To do this, they studied the fibers under a microscope and photographed the fibers' cross-sectional shape. The investigators then showed the photographs to chemists and textiles experts to see if they could identify the likely source of the fibers. The investigators learned that the fiber was probably from a carpet but that its shape was unique. The fact that the fiber was relatively rare meant that it probably was not widely used. This significantly reduced the number of possible locations where the murders could have occurred, making it easier for investigators to focus their search for a suspect.

3. Information about the source of the fiber could help investigators determine where the crime might have occurred, which could lead them to a suspect. If investigators know who produced the item from which the fibers came, they can contact the manufacturer and get a list of local stores or individuals who purchased the item before the crime occurred. Interviews with the purchasers may provide investigators with leads to suspects or other information that can help them solve the case.

4. Investigators found that the company produced a carpet using the same rare type of fiber in the same color as that found on Cater's body and in Williams's home. This meant that there was at least a probable connection between Williams and Cater. Investigators also learned that the company used that type of fiber in its carpets for only one year. This significantly narrowed the number of places where such carpeting might be found. During the year the carpet was manufactured using the rare fiber, only a small amount was sold in the southeastern United States. This further narrowed the possible number of rooms in Georgia in which the carpet could have been installed. The extremely small number of possible locations where the carpet could be found in the Atlanta area meant that there could be very few likely suspects besides Williams.

5. The investigators used probability to connect the fibers found on Nathaniel Cater's body and Williams's home. By demonstrating an extremely low probability that the fibers came from anyplace but Williams's home, prosecutors were able to tie Williams to Cater's murder. Investigators also used probability to tie fibers and hairs found on other Atlanta-area murder victims to Williams. Prosecutors showed that each of the victims' bodies contained traces of fibers matching those found in Williams's home and cars, and/or hair belonging to Williams's dog. They pointed out that there was an extremely low probability of finding so many matching fibers and hairs on several different individuals. The only reasonable explanation, they argued, was that all the victims had contact with a common source of the fibers and hairs, namely, Williams.

Chapter 4
Odd-Numbered Review Questions

1. physical	21. True
3. metric	23. birefringence
5. 1/100	25. glass
7. 200	27. density; refractive index
9. True	29. Becke line
11. True	31. radial
13. 180	33. False
15. mass	35. will
17. density	37. minerals
19. refraction	39. 100

Application and Critical Thinking

1. Windows on U.S.-built cars use laminated glass in their windshields, and tempered glass for all other windows. Thus, from this evidence, the investigator knows that the other car involved in the accident has a broken side window, with its windshield intact.

2. Because the cracks from bullet holes A and C both terminate at the cracks from bullet hole B, bullet hole B was made first. Because the cracks from bullet hole C also terminate at the cracks from bullet hole A, bullet hole A was made second. Thus, bullet hole C was the last to be made.

3. If this is a radial fracture, the force was applied from the left side of the glass. If it is a concentric fracture, the force was applied from the right side of the glass. The 3R rule states that Radial cracks form a Right angle on the Reverse side of the force. The cracks in the picture form a right angle on the right side of the glass, so if it is a radial fracture, the force was applied to the reverse (left) side of the glass.

4. Jared made several mistakes. First, the samples he removed from the scene should have included only the top layer of soil. Second, he failed to collect soil samples from both alibi locations—the garden and the parking lot. Third, he should have packaged the shoes in paper, not plastic. Finally, he should have dried all of the soil samples under identical laboratory conditions before examining any of them.

Chapter 5
Odd-Numbered Review Questions

1. matter
3. 118
5. atom
7. molecule
9. has no
11. less
13. organic
15. qualitative; quantitative
17. chromatography
19. higher
21. gas chromatography
23. pyrolyzed
25. thin-layer chromatography
27. R_f
29. electrophoresis
31. wavelength
33. electromagnetic
35. laser
37. True
39. can
41. spectrophotometer
43. infrared
45. True

Application and Critical Thinking

1. Spectrophotometry requires that a material be in a relatively pure state, so it would not be a good choice in this case. Chromatography can be employed when spectrophotometry cannot be used to analyze physical evidence.
2. The best choice would be thin-layer chromatography because it is inexpensive and allows numerous samples to be analyzed simultaneously on one thin-layer plate.
3. a. phenobarbital
   b. butabarbital
   c. three minutes

Chapter 6
Odd-Numbered Review Questions

1. oxygen; silicon
3. trace
5. emission spectrum
7. line
9. False
11. carbon
13. does
15. proton; neutron; electron
17. positive
19. protons
21. True
23. light
25. isotopes
27. alpha particles; beta particles; gamma rays
29. gamma rays
31. neutron activation analysis
33. crystalline

Application and Critical Thinking

1. Disfigured bullets are often not suitable for traditional microscopic comparisons against an exemplar test-fired bullet. In this situation, ICP emission spectrophotometry should be used to obtain an elemental profile of the questioned bullet fragment for comparison against an unfired bullet generally found in the possession of the suspect. However, the analyst must keep in mind that comparisons of this type are class-defining in nature and do not provide a definite match.
2. A major weakness of neutron activation analysis is its expense and regulatory requirements. Also, sophisticated analyzers are needed to detect and discriminate gamma-ray emissions.
3. Because about 95 percent of all inorganic compounds are crystalline in nature, there is a good chance that the substance in question could be identifiable by X-ray diffraction analysis. However, it would not be suitable in this case for the detection of trace amounts of the substance because it often fails to detect the presence of substances constituting less than 5 percent of a mixture.

Chapter 7
Odd-Numbered Review Questions

1. lenses
3. compound
5. eyepiece or ocular lens
7. True
9. vertical or reflected
11. parfocal
13. magnifying power
15. numerical aperture
17. decreases
19. decreases
21. True
23. False
25. plane-polarized
27. polarizing
29. microspectrophotometer
31. X-rays

Application and Critical Thinking

1. The stereomicroscope should be used to view the outside of the leaf surface because the leaf is an opaque subject, which requires the use of vertical illumination. The transmitted light microscope should be used to view the leaf cells because they are translucent and light can be transmitted through them and to the analyst's eye using this instrument.
2. The crystals that show bright colors are polarizing crystals, and those that appear dark are nonpolarizing crystals. With this information it can be concluded that the white powder contains at least two different kinds of crystals and is, therefore, a mixture.
3. The analyst can use an infrared microspectrophotometer to identify the fiber's general class by its IR spectrum. The IR spectrum for the crime-scene samples can then be compared to those of the clothing fibers. Also, the analyst can identify the generic class of a fiber using a polarizing microscope for determining the fiber's parallel and perpendicular refractive indices.
4. They must first remove any possible gunshot particles remaining on the suspect's hands using adhesive tape. At the crime lab, the tape can then be examined under the scanning electron microscope. The X-rays produced by any particles on the tape are analyzed and displayed according to their energies. The examiner can then detect the presence of elements frequently found

in bullet primers and dispersed during the discharging of a firearm.

Case Analysis

1. The main aspects of the rail noted by Koehler were the presence of nail holes, the general condition of the wood, and the quality of the lumber used to make the rail. The nail holes were not made during the construction of the ladder, which indicated that the wood had been used for another purpose before being made into a ladder rail. The fact that the holes were clean and free of rust suggested that the wood was used inside and not exposed to the elements. The spacing of the nail holes suggested that the wood likely was used in a barn, garage, or attic. The wood itself was also in good shape and not weathered, further confirming that it was used inside. The lumber was of a poor quality, meaning it would have been used for rough construction (such as a floor or wall joist) and not finished work (such as a door frame or decorative trim).

2. Koehler found notches in surfaces and on the edges of the ladder rails that were caused by a defect in the cutting heads of the planer used to finish the wood. By measuring the distance between the notches, Koehler was able to calculate the speed at which the rails passed through the planer. His calculations showed that surfaces and edges of the wood moved through the planer at different speeds. This difference in speed told Koehler that the planer was belt-driven. Information about the speed and type of the planer helped narrow down the number of lumber mills that could possibly have produced the wood.

3. Koehler reasoned that because the wood was inexpensive, it would not be profitable to ship it very far from where it was milled. Because the ladder was found in New Jersey, Koehler believed it must have been milled somewhere in the Atlantic States region. This information helped narrow the number of possible mills to those along the Atlantic coast. When authorities contacted these mills they found only a handful that used planers of the type and speed used to mill the ladder rails. When the investigators asked for samples of wood from these mills, they found a sample that had the same notches as found on the ladder rails. This allowed the investigators to pinpoint the mill that produced the wood.

4. Koehler found marks on the wood that were made by a hand planer. He discovered that these marks were identical to those made by a hand planer found at Hauptmann's house. In addition, investigators found that a section of board had been sawed out of the floor joists in Hauptmann's attic. The nail holes in the ladder rail aligned perfectly with the nail holes in the floor joists. Also, the grain pattern of the wood used in the rail was an exact match with the grain pattern in the remaining portion of the floor joist that had been cut to make the ladder. These facts clearly connected Hauptmann with the ladder used in the kidnapping.

Chapter 8
Odd-Numbered Review Questions

1. True
3. physical
5. False
7. analgesics; depress
9. morphine
11. OxyContin
13. hallucinogens
15. tetrahydrocannabinol
17. liquid hashish
19. clandestine
21. Barbiturates
23. Methaqualone (Quaalude)
25. False
27. intravenous
29. Cocaine
31. False
33. Anabolic
35. five
37. IV
39. Marquis (THC)
41. marijuana
43. Microcrystalline
45. infrared
47. cystolithic

Application and Critical Thinking

1. The drug used by the individual was probably either amphetamine, cocaine, or phencyclidine. All of these drugs produce psychological dependence, which would explain the individual's behavior, but none are known to produce physical dependence that would cause sickness or physical discomfort.
2. a. Depressants; examples include alcohol, barbiturates, and tranquilizers
   b. Hallucinogens; examples include marijuana, LSD, PCP, and MDMA (Ecstasy)
   c. Stimulants; examples include amphetamines, methamphetamine, and cocaine
   d. Narcotics; examples include heroin, morphine, codeine, and synthetic opiates such as OxyContin and methadone
3. a. Schedule III
   b. Schedule V
   c. Schedule II
   d. Schedule I
4. A screening test you would perform for heroin would be the Marquis color test. If the powder tests positive for heroin, you would conduct confirmation tests, including mass spectrometry or IR spectrophotometry.

Chapter 9
Odd-Numbered Review Questions

1. ethyl alcohol
3. is
5. faster
7. watery
9. oxidized
11. breath
13. stomach; small intestine
15. pulmonary
17. 2,100
19. infrared
21. gas chromatography
23. False
25. alcohol-free
27. 0.08
29. morphine
31. acids; bases

33. acidic
35. immunoassay
37. carbon monoxide
39. False

41. poor
43. drug recognition
expert (DRE)

37. phenotype
39. will
41. AA; BB; AB

43. acid phosphatase
45. oligospermia
47. True

Application and Critical Thinking

1. a. Randy is four times as likely to have an accident as a sober person.
   b. Marissa's blood-alcohol concentration is approximately 0.13.
   c. Charles is more intoxicated; his blood-alcohol concentration is approximately 0.11.
   d. At the original NHTSA standard of 0.15, an individual is about 25 times as likely to have an accident as a sober person.
2. John, Gary, Frank, Stephen
3. Bill and Carrie are both legally drunk in Australia and Sweden. Sally is legally drunk in Sweden. Rich is legally drunk in all three countries.
4. Barbiturates are acidic drugs, which means they have a pH less than 7. You can use this knowledge to devise a simple test to determine which blood sample contains barbiturates. First, you would dissolve blood from each sample into separate containers of water. To each container you would add an acidic substance such as hydrochloric acid (to make the water more acidic). Then you would add an organic solvent such as chloroform to the water in each container. The blood sample containing barbiturates will be easily identified because acidic drugs are readily removed from an acidic solution with an organic solvent.
5. To determine whether the victim died before or as a result of the fire, you would measure the level of carbon monoxide in the victim's blood. High levels of carbon monoxide in the victim's blood would indicate that he or she breathed the combustion products of the fire and was therefore alive when the fire started. Low levels of carbon monoxide would indicate that the victim did not breathe the combustion products of the fire and was therefore dead before the fire started.

Chapter 10
Odd-Numbered Review Questions

1. type
3. Plasma
5. Red blood cells
7. A
9. A; B
11. antibodies
13. True
15. neither
17. serology
19. A

21. enzyme-multiplied immunoassay technique (EMIT)
23. 3
25. benzidine
27. precipitin
29. monoclonal
31. gene
33. 23
35. alleles

Application and Critical Thinking

1. Scott chose the acid phosphatase test because it is extremely useful in searching for semen on large areas of fabric, such as a blanket. He concluded that the blanket did not contain evidence of semen. First of all, he knew that certain fruit juices, including watermelon, can generate a positive reaction with acid phosphatase testing. However, these juices react much more slowly to the test than does semen. A reaction time of less than 30 seconds is considered a strong indication of semen. Because it took three minutes to obtain a positive reaction, Scott concluded that the positive reaction was caused by the watermelon.
2. Cathy made four mistakes in collecting evidence. First, she should have placed a paper sheet over the sheet on which the victim disrobed, in order to collect any loose material that might have fallen from the victim or the clothing. Second, she should have placed each item of clothing in a separate bag, instead of placing all of them in the same bag. Third, she should have taken two additional vaginal swabs, smearing them onto microscope slides. Finally, she failed to collect fingernail scrapings from the victim.

Chapter 11
Odd-Numbered Review Questions

1. gene
3. polymer
5. nucleotides
7. double helix
9. A–C–G–T
11. Proteins
13. True
15. False
17. True
19. False
21. True

23. tandem repeats
25. 18
27. multiplexing
29. male; female
31. mother
33. Two
35. 13
37. dry
39. EDTA (ethylenediamine tetraacetic acid)

Application and Critical Thinking

1. G–C–T–T–A–G–C–G–T–T–A–G–C–T–G–G–A–C
2. You would first collect any blood or skin scrapings under the victim's fingernails because these may contain DNA. You would then amplify the DNA in the sample using PCR and separate the fragments using electrophoresis. Finally, you would look for the bands of separated DNA that correspond to the amelogenin gene. If the sample contains two bands, the attacker is male; if the sample contains only one band, the attacker is female.
3. Investigators use mtDNA to determine whether the body is that of the victim of the unsolved murder. To do so, you would collect mtDNA from one of the victim's ma-

ternal relatives and compare it to the mtDNA recovered from the body. If the samples match, the body is that of the victim.

4. With an STR, you should expect to see a two-band pattern. The presence of more than two bands suggests a mixture of DNA from more than one source.

Chapter 12
Odd-Numbered Review Questions

1. Crime-scene reconstruction
3. bloodstain patterns
5. victims; suspects
7. increases
9. circular
11. impact spatter
13. low-velocity; medium-velocity; high-velocity
15. area of convergence
17. string
19. lightens
21. True
23. skeletonize
25. False
27. drip trail
29. void
31. grid method
33. True

Application and Critical Thinking

1. a. Drops 1, 5, and 8 struck the surface closest to a 90-degree angle because they are the most nearly circular in shape.
   b. Drops 3, 4, and 9 struck the surface farthest from a 90-degree angle because they have the most elongated shapes.
   c. Drop 2 was traveling right to left and drop 7 was traveling from bottom to top when they struck the surface. The tails of the drops point in the direction of travel.
2. Investigator Wright should conclude that the bullet did not exit the body.
3. The tiny droplets and linear pattern suggest that the weapon used in the assault was likely small and pointed, such as a knife.

Chapter 13
Odd-Numbered Review Questions

1. hair follicle
3. True
5. medulla
7. $\frac{1}{3}$; $\frac{1}{2}$
9. animal
11. cannot
13. Pubic
15. False
17. DNA
19. anagen-phase
21. 24
23. cotton
25. synthetic
27. Polymers
29. Proteins
31. visible
33. birefringence
35. class
37. layer structure
39. electrocoat primer
41. binder
43. True

Application and Critical Thinking

1. a. Telogen phase
   b. Anagen phase
   c. Anagen phase
   d. Catagen phase
2. Because hair grows at a rate of about 1 centimeter per month, the hair was dyed approximately six weeks earlier.
3. a. Caucasian
   b. Mongoloid
   c. Negroid
   d. Caucasian
4. Pete made several mistakes. First, all items of clothing containing fiber evidence should be packaged in paper, not plastic. Second, he placed fibers collected from two separate locations in the same bag, when each individual piece of fiber evidence should be placed in a separate container. Third, he should have carefully folded the sheet before packaging it, rather than simply balling it up. Fourth, he used his fingers, rather than a forceps, to collect fibers from the windowsill. Finally, the fibers from the windowsill should be folded inside a piece of paper and then placed in another container, not put into a regular envelope.
5. In a hit-and-run situation you would collect from each vehicle standard/reference samples that include all the paint layers down to the bare metal. This is best accomplished by removing a painted section with a clean scalpel or knife blade. Standard/reference samples should be collected from an undamaged area of each vehicle because other portions of the car may have faded or been repainted. To avoid cross-contamination of paints, carefully wipe the blade of any knife or scraping tool used before collecting each sample.

Chapter 14
Odd-Numbered Review Questions

1. False
3. False
5. chemical; mechanical
7. absorb; liberate
9. exothermic
11. endothermic
13. ignition
15. flash point
17. Glowing combustion
19. Spontaneous combustion
21. conduction
23. True
25. True
27. Airtight
29. pattern
31. True
33. mass spectrometer

Application and Critical Thinking

1. a. Radiation
   b. Conduction
   c. Convection
   d. Radiation
2. You should suspect arson. Although the conditions in which the oil was stored—high heat and lack of ventilation—may lead to spontaneous combustion with

some materials, spontaneous combustion does not occur with hydrocarbon lubricating oils such as motor oil. The owner is lying about the oil igniting spontaneously; he may have deliberately set the fire to collect on the increased insurance.

3. Mick made several mistakes. First, he should have used separate containers for each location where debris was collected. Debris should have come from the point of origin of the fire, not from the surrounding rooms. He should not have placed the timbers in plastic bags, which react with hydrocarbons and permit volatile hydrocarbon vapors to be depleted. Finally, Mick should have collected the suspect's clothes to undergo laboratory analysis for the presence of accelerant residues.

Chapter 15
Odd-Numbered Review Questions

1. oxygen
3. explosion
5. High
7. confined
9. primary; secondary
11. True
13. PETN or RDX
15. crater
17. ion mobility spectrometer
19. acetone
21. infrared spectroscopy
23. True

Application and Critical Thinking

1. a. High explosives. Lead azide is a common component of blasting caps, which are used to detonate high explosives.
   b. Low explosives. Nitrocellulose is an ingredient in smokeless powder, one of the most common low explosives.
   c. High explosives. Ammonium nitrate is the main ingredient in a number of high explosives that have replaced dynamite for industrial uses.
   d. High explosives. Primacord is used as a detonator to ignite several high-explosive charges simultaneously.
   e. Low explosives. Potassium chlorate mixed with sugar is a popular low explosive.
2. a. Alcoholic KOH. Tetryl is the only explosive that produces a red-violet color in response to this test.
   b. Alcoholic KOH. TNT produces a distinctive red color in response to the alcoholic KOH test.
   c. Diphenylamine produces a blue color. No color is produced in response to the Greiss test and to the alcoholic KOH test.
   d. Diphenylamine. Nitrocellulose produces a distinctive blue-black color in response to this test.
3. Matt made several mistakes. First, to avoid contaminating the scene, Matt should have put on disposable gloves, shoe covers, and overalls before beginning his search. Second, he should have used a wire mesh screen to sift through the debris instead of picking through it by hand. Third, all explosive evidence should be stored in airtight

metal containers, not plastic or paper bags. Fourth, Matt should have collected material from not only the immediate area of the blast, but also materials blown away from the blast's origin.

Chapter 16
Odd-Numbered Review Questions

1. Alphonse Bertillion
3. Sir Edward Richard Henry
5. is not
7. Fingerprints
9. dermal papillae
11. loops; whorls; arches
13. arch
15. type lines
17. one
19. plain whorl
21. do not have
23. 1/1
25. True
27. Plastic
29. powder
31. Iodine
33. Physical Developer
35. superglue fuming
37. alternate light sources
39. pixels

Application and Critical Thinking

1. a. Whorl
   b. Arch
   c. Loop
   d. Whorl
   e. Whorl
   f. Arch
2. The primary classification for this individual would be as follows:

$$\frac{0 + 8 + 4 + 0 + 1}{16 + 8 + 0 + 2 + 1}$$

Thus, the classification would be 13/27.
3. a. Chemicals
   b. Powder
   c. Powder
   d. Chemicals
   e. Chemicals
4. a. Scaling and resizing
   b. Spatial filtering
   c. Frequency analysis, or frequency Fourier transform (FFT)

Chapter 17
Odd-Numbered Review Questions

1. land
3. True
5. comparison microscope
7. False
9. gauge
11. True
13. True
15. 12; 18
17. yard
19. True
21. barium; antimony
23. scanning electron microscope
25. False

27. False
29. gunpowder residue
31. striations
33. electrostatic lifting device
35. individual

Application and Critical Thinking

1. a. 18–36 inches
   b. More than 36 inches
   c. 12–18 inches or less
   d. 1 inch or less
2. The correct answer is (a), 18 yards. A 12-gauge shotgun with no choke would be expected to produce a spread of about 1 inch for each yard from the shooter to the target. Thus, a spread of 12 inches would represent a distance of about 12 yards. A moderately high choke, however, would narrow the spread of the pattern somewhat. This means that at a distance of 12 yards, the spread would be less than 12 inches. At a distance of 6 yards, the spread would be much less than 12 inches. Answers (b) and (c), therefore, must be wrong. The distance in answer (d), 30 yards, is probably too far. Although the choke would narrow the spread of the pellets, it would probably not narrow it to such a great extent.
3. Ben made several errors. Before unloading the revolver, Ben should have indicated the chamber position in line with the barrel by scratching a mark on the cylinder. He then should have made a diagram of the gun, designating each chamber with a number. As he removed each cartridge, he should have marked it to correspond to the numbered chambers in the diagram. Ben also should have placed each cartridge in a separate envelope and he should have put the tag on the trigger guard, not the grip. Instead of using pliers to grab the bullet and pull it from the wall, Ben should have carefully broken away the surrounding wall material while avoiding direct contact with the bullet. Finally, he should have wrapped the bullet in tissue paper before placing it in an envelope.
4. a. Photograph the print.
   b. Photograph the tool mark, then make a cast of it.
   c. Photograph the tire marks, then make a cast of them.
   d. Photograph the shoe print, then bring the tile bearing the print to the laboratory.
   e. Photograph the print, then use an electrostatic lifting device to lift it off the surface.

Chapter 18
Odd-Numbered Review Questions

1. questioned document
3. known; questioned
5. False
7. *Gilbert* v. *California*
9. individual
11. infrared
13. Indented

Application and Critical Thinking

1. Julie made several mistakes. She should have given the suspect a pencil, not a pen, because the original notes were written in pencil. She also should have had the suspect prepare at least a full page of writing, and she should have had him write the material at least three times. Also, she should not have spelled any words for the suspect. Finally, Julie should have shown the original threatening notes to a document examiner before taking exemplars from the suspect, not afterward.
2. a. Photograph the document with infrared-sensitive film.
   b. Examine the document under infrared or ultraviolet light.
   c. Examine the document under ultraviolet light.
   d. Photograph the document with infrared-sensitive film, or reflect light off the paper's surface at different angles in order to contrast the writing against the charred background.
3. The aspects of the document you would examine to determine whether the document was authentic would be the paper and the ink. You would use thin-layer chromatography to characterize the dye used in the ink to determine whether that particular ink was in use when the original document was prepared.

Chapter 19
Odd-Numbered Review Questions

1. preserving; acquiring; extracting; analyzing; interpreting
3. Software
5. system unit
7. False
9. CPU
11. network interface card (NIC)
13. sectors; clusters; tracks; cylinders
15. byte
17. forensic image
19. swap
21. latent
23. RAM; file
25. unallocated space
27. True
29. cache
31. IP
33. log files; volatile memory; network traffic

Application and Critical Thinking

1. Because each sector is 512 bytes, a cluster consisting of six sectors would hold 3,072 bytes of data. Because each byte equals 8 bits, each cluster would hold 24,576 bits of data.
2. Tom made several mistakes. When he arrived, he should have sketched the overall layout as well as photographing it. He also should have photographed any running monitors. In addition to labeling the cord of each peripheral, Tom should have placed a corresponding label on the port to which each cord was connected. Before unplugging the computer, he should have checked to ensure that the computer was not

using encryption. Finally, he should have removed the plug from the back of the computer, not from the wall.

3. You probably would begin to search for latent data in the swap space on the hard disk drive. If the accountant was keeping fraudulent records, he may well have been transferring data from one accounting program to another. Data from those operations may well be left behind in the swap space, where it later can be retrieved.

4. On the first computer you probably would look first at the compound files created by Microsoft Outlook. On the second computer you probably would look first in the Internet cache.

Case Analysis 1

1. By examining Mr. Smith's computer, police hoped to prove that he had changed his wife's insurance policy shortly before the fire in which she died. They believed this would implicate him in his wife's murder because the increased insurance settlement Mr. Smith would receive upon his wife's death would serve as a strong motive for murdering her.

2. The documents titled *insurance1.doc* and *WRL1604.tmp* were important to tying Mr. Smith to his wife's death because they proved that he wrote the letter to his insurance company requesting an increase in his wife's life insurance.

Case Analysis 2

1. The physical evidence that most strongly implicated the driver of the van in a counterfeiting operation was the discovery of two $100 bills in his wallet. These suspicions were confirmed by the fact that the bills had identical serial numbers.

2. The documents titled *GapGiftCert1.jpg* and *GapGiftCert2.jpg* indicated that the suspects were producing more than counterfeit currency. From these files, the investigators concluded that the suspects were also producing counterfeit gift certificates to The Gap.

index

A

Abrasives, 508
Absorption, 134
Absorption and distribution, alcohol, 214–216, 219
Absorption spectrum, 134
Abstinence syndrome, 191
Accelerants, 361–362, 363
Acetone, 380–381
Acid, 230
Acid phosphatase test, 254
Admissibility of physical evidence, 15–16
AFIS (automated fingerprint identification system), 68, 396–399
Age, determining decedent's, 75
Agglutination, 243
Alcohol
   absorption and distribution, 214–216
   abuse of, 198
   blood alcohol concentration, 215, 218, 220, 222, 223, 225, 232, 236
   blood analysis, 224–225
   in the circulatory system, 216–219
   dependency and, 190–192
   as a depressant, 198
   drug recognition experts and, 234–236
   elimination and, 216
   legal issues, 225–227
   measuring intoxication, 214–215
   metabolism of, 196
   role of the toxicologist and, 227–234
   testing for intoxication, 219–224
Algor mortis, 72–73
Alleles, 252
Alpha particle, 155–156
Alterations, in documents, 459–460
Alternate light source system, 407
Alveoli, 216
Amelogenin gene, 275
American Medical Association, 225
Amido Black, 529
Amino acids, 267
Ammonium nitrate–based explosives, 376–377
Ammunition. *See* Firearms and ammunition
Amorphous solids, 100
Amphetamines, 199
Anabolic steroids, 201–202
Anagen hair growth phase, 324
Analgesics, 193
ANFO explosives, 376–377
Angle of impact, 300–301
Annealing, 107
Anthrax letters case, 15
Anthropologist, role of, 73–77
Anthropology, 4
Anthropometry, 6, 390

Antianxiety drugs, 198–199
Antibodies, 242–243
Anticoagulants, 224
Antifreeze (methyl ethylketone), 199
Antigens, 242–243
Antimony, 232, 432
Antipsychotics, 198–199
Antiserum, 243
Aqueous benzalkonium chloride (Zepiran), 224
Aqueous mercuric chloride, 224
Arches, in fingerprints, 394
Areas of convergence, 304
Areas of origin, 304
Arsenic, 144, 146, 152, 232
Arson
   analysis of flammable residues, 365–368
   chemistry of fire, 354–361
   collection and preservation of evidence, 364–365
   crime scene searches, 361–364
   Debora Green case, 352
Arterial spray spatter, 307
Arteries, 216
Aspermia, 255
ATF (Bureau of Alcohol, Tobacco, Firearms and Explosives), 11, 69, 426
Atomic absorption spectrophotometry, 152–153
Atomic mass, 155
Atomic number, 154
Atoms, 100, 120, 153–155
Audiotapes, 30
Automated fingerprint identification system (AFIS), 68, 396–399
Automobiles, 61, 343
Autopsies, 72

B

Backscattered electrons, 176
Back spatter, 301, 305, 306
Ballistic fingerprinting, 426
Barbiturates, 198
Bases (compounds), 230
Becke line, 103, 173, 338
Beer's Law, 135
Behavioral sciences, 4
Beltway sniper case, 416
Benedine color test, 247–248
Bertillon, Alphonse, 6, 390
Beta particle, 155
Binocular microscope, 169
Biology units, 4, 12
Birefringence, 100, 338
Bismuth, 148, 232
Bite mark analysis. *See* Odontology

Bits, 477
Bitter Harvest (Rule), 352
Black powder, 375
Blassie, Michael J., 281
Blitzer, Robert M., 381
Blood
   characterization of bloodstains, 247–251
   collection and preservation of, 43, 224–225
   discovery of grouping, 6, 242
   DNA and, 242 (*See also* DNA (deoxyribonucleic acid))
   as evidence, 60
   FBI Guides to Collection of Physical Evidence, 520–521
   heredity and, 251–253
   immunoassay techniques, 231, 245–247
   nature of, 242–245
Bloodstain pattern analysis
   arterial spray spatter, 307
   cast-off spatter, 306–307
   contact/transfer patterns, 309–310
   documenting, 313
   drip trail patterns, 311, 313
   expired blood patterns, 307
   flows, 310–311
   general features, 299–301
   gunshot spatter, 305–306
   impact spatter, 301–305
   pools, 311
   void patterns, 308–309
Blood typing, 243–245
Blow-back spatter, 301
Blowflies, 77–80
Bluestar, 249
Bomb investigation. *See* Explosions and explosives
Bones, 73–77, 522
Bookmarks (for websites), 487
Bores, gun barrel, 418
Borkenstein, R. F., 219
Borosilicates, 101
Brasscatcher (software), 425
Breathalyzers, 219
Breechblocks, 423–424
Broach cutters, 419
Browsers, 486
BTK killer, 470
Buccal cells, 287
Buccal swabs, 44, 522
Bulletproof (software), 425
Bullets and cartridges. *See* Firearms and ammunition
Bundy, Ted, 2
Bureau of Alcohol, Tobacco, Firearms and Explosives (ATF), 11, 69, 426

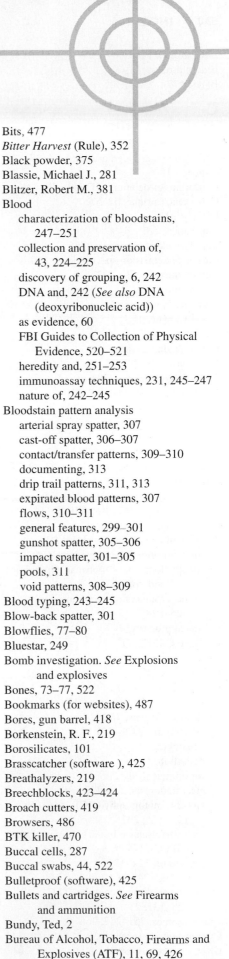

Butabarbital, 198
Button process, 419
Bytes, 477

C

Cabbane, R. A., 454
Cache, Internet, 486
CAD (computer-aided drafting), 34, 37
Caliber, 418
California Association of Criminalists, 9
Camarena, Enrique, 52–57
Cameras, 31
Capillaries, 216
Capillary electrophoresis, 275
Carbon arc emission spectrometry, 150–151
Carbon dioxide, 232–233
Carbon monoxide, 232–233
Carpenter's Forensic Science Resources
    website, 23
Carrier gas, 125
Carter, Nathaniel, 85–91
Cartridge cases, 423–424
Cast-off blood spatter, 306–307
Casts and casting, 441–442, 510
Catagen hair growth phase, 324
CDs (compact discs), 475, 480
Celsius scale, 96
Central processing units (CPUs), 474
Centre of Forensic Sciences (Toronto), 9, 345
Chain of custody, 43
Charred documents, 460
Chat technology, 487, 490–491
Checks (bank), 452, 510
The Chemical Detective website, 23
Chemical formulas
    for development of footwear impressions
        in blood, 529–531
    for development of latent fingerprints,
        525–528
Chemical property, 94
Chemistry, 4, 12, 505
China, 195
China White, 204
Chlorate mixtures, 375
Chlordiazepoxide (Librium), 198
Choke, in shotguns, 430
Chromatograms, 126–127
Chromatography
    definition, 123
    for drug analysis, 206
    electrophoresis, 131–132
    gas chromatography (GC),
        125–126, 231
    high performance liquid chromatography
        (HPLC), 127–128
    process of, 124–125
    theory of, 124
    thin-layer chromatography (TLC),
        128–131, 231
Chromosomes, 251–252, 266
Circumstantial evidence, 58
Class characteristics, 64

Classification systems
    blood, 242
    blood spatter, 301
    drugs, 202–203
    explosives, 375
    fingerprints, 395–396
    glass, 106–107
    ignitable liquids, 365
Clinton, William, 271
Clothing. See Fibers
Club drugs, 200–201
Clusters, 477
Cocaine, 199–200
Codeine, 194
CODIS (Combined DNA Index System),
    11, 69, 274–275, 278, 504
CODIS STRs, 274–275
Coherent light, 133
Collaborative Testing Services, 346
Collection and preservation of evidence.
        See also FBI Guides to the Collection
        of Physical Evidence
    arson, 364–365
    blood, 43, 224–225
    computers, 478–479
    for DNA analysis, 42–43, 281, 284–287
    drugs, 208, 229–230
    explosions and explosives, 380–384
    fibers, 342
    fingerprints, 409–410
    firearms and ammunition, 434–435
    glass, 110
    gunpowder residues, 523–524
    hair, 329–330
    handwriting and handprinting
        impressions, 438–443
    paint, 347–348
    of rape evidence, 256–260
    soils and minerals, 112–114
    tool marks, 436–437
    training in, 19–20
Color tests, 205–206, 247–248, 384
Combined DNA Index System (CODIS),
    11, 69, 274–275, 278, 504
Combustion, 356–359
Communications, Internet, 487, 489–492
Compact discs (CDs), 475, 480
Comparison analysis, 43–44, 61–62,
    419–420
Comparison microscopes, 6, 169–171, 421
Complementary base pairing, 266
Composition C–4, 379
Compound microscopes, 167–169
Compounds, 120
Computer-aided drafting (CAD), 34, 37
Computer forensics. See also Computer
        technology; Internet
    about, 21–22
    analysis of electronic data, 480–486
    BTK killer case, 470
    case readings, 495–498
    processing the crime scene, 478–480

Computer technology
    components, 472–476
    databases (See Databases)
    hardware and software, 472
    printers and, 458
    storing and retrieving data, 476–478
Concentric glass fractures, 107–108
Condensers, 169
Conduction, 360
Confirmation tests, 230–232, 384
Contact/transfer blood patterns,
    309–310
Continuous spectrum, 149–150
Controlled Substances Act, 202–204
Convection, 361
Cookies, Internet, 486–487
Coomassie Blue, 529
Coppolino case, 17–18
Cortex (hair), 322–323
Cosby, Ennis, 330
CPUs (central processing units), 474
Crack cocaine, 200
Crick, Francis, 266
Crime and Clues website, 23
Crime laboratories
    DNA (deoxyribonucleic acid) and,
        502–503
    drugs and, 10, 190, 502
    in Great Britain and Canada, 9
    growth of, 10, 502
    Locard and, 8
    mobile, 39
    organization and types of, 10–12
    services of, 12–15
    submitting evidence to, 44
    in the United States, 8–9
Crime Scene Investigator Network
        website, 23
Crime scenes. See also Collection
        and preservation of evidence;
        Murder scenes
    crime lab units for, 13
    ensuring crime-scene safety, 44–46
    legal considerations, 46–47
    reconstruction fundamentals, 298
    recording, 29–34 (See also Note-taking;
        Photography; Sketches)
    searching, 34–38, 46–47
    securing and isolating, 28–29
    submitting physical evidence to the
        lab, 44
Crime scene search vehicle, 39
Criminalistics, definition of, 4–5
Criminalists. See Forensic scientists
Cross-transfer, 41
Crowle's Double Stain, 529–530
Crystalline solids, 100. See also Soils
        and minerals
Crystal tests. See Microcrystalline tests
CSI effect, 5
Curley, Joann, 233
Cuticle, 322–323

Cyanoacrylate fluorescent enhancement reagents, 527–528
Cyclotrimethylenetrinitramine (RDX), 376, 379
Cytosine, 266

D

Databases
  animal hair, 324
  ballistics (NIBIN) (IBIS), 69–70, 425–426, 503
  DNA (CODIS), 11, 69, 274–275, 276, 278, 279, 504
  fiber, 339
  fingerprint (IAFIS), 68–69, 396, 425
  mtDNA database, 280–281
  National DNA Database (UK), 69
  paint (PDQ), 71, 346–347
  shoeprints (SICAR), 71, 443
  TTI fonts, 458
Daubert v. *Merrell Dow Pharmaceuticals, Inc.*, 16, 391
Deadman, Harold A., 85
Deflagration, 375
Defragmenting, 485
Density, 98–99, 102, 103
Dental evidence, 4, 21, 522
Deoxyribonucleic acid (DNA). *See* DNA (deoxyribonucleic acid)
Dependency, 190–192
Depressants, 198–199
Depth of focus, 169
Dermal papillae, 393
Dermis, 393
Detonation, 375
Detonators, 379
DFO (1,8-diazafluoren-9-one), 407, 525–526
Diaminobenzidine (DAB), 530
Diazepam (Valium), 198
Diffraction pattern, 158
Digital and multimedia sciences, 4–5, 30–33, 410–412, 462
Digital subscriber line (DSL), 486
Digital versatile discs (DVDs), 475, 480
Dille-Koppanyi screening test, 206
Dillinger, John, 394
Dillon, Marty, 308
Dispersion, 100
Distance determination, 427–430
DMNB (2,3-dimethyl-2,3-dinitrobutane), 385
DNA (deoxyribonucleic acid). *See also* Stain analysis
  Alec Jeffreys and
  CODIS (Combined DNA Index System), 11, 69, 274–275, 278, 504
  contamination of, 288
  crime labs and, 10–11, 502–503
  CSI effect, 5
  definition and description, 242, 266–268
  evidence collection and preservation, 42–43, 281, 284–287

FBI Guides to Collection of Physical Evidence, 520–522
  mitochondrial (mtDNA), 278–281
  O. J. Simpson murder case, 264
  polymerase chain reaction (PCR), 269–270
  typing, 270–278
  World Trade Center and, 293–295
DNA Thermal Cycler, 269
Documents
  alterations, erasures, and obliterations, 459–462
  document examination units, 12
  as evidence, 60
  FBI Guides to Collection of Physical Evidence, 510
  handwriting, 452–457
  indented writings, 462
  ink and paper comparisons, 463–464, 468
  Osborn and, 6
  Questioned-Document Examination website, 23
  role of document examiner, 452
  typescript, 457–459
  Unabomber case, 450
Double helix, 266
Doyle, Sir Arthur Conan, 5
Drawback effect, 306
DREs (drug recognition experts), 198, 234–236
Drip trail blood patterns, 311, 313
Drug analysis
  chromatography, 206–207
  color tests, 205–206
  EMIT (Enzyme-Multiplied Immunoassay Technique), 246–247
  mass spectrometry, 207–208
  microcrystalline tests, 206
  qualitative or quantitative determination, 205
  screening and confirmation, 204–205, 230–233
  spectrophotometry, 207
Drug Enforcement Administration (DEA), 11
DRUGFIRE, 425
Druggist fold, 41–42
Drug recognition experts (DREs), 198, 234–236
Drugs. *See also* Drug analysis; *specific drugs*
  classification of, 202–203
  collection and preservation of evidence, 208, 229–230
  crime labs and, 10, 190, 502
  defined, 190
  dependency, 190–191
  drug-control laws, 202–204
  as evidence, 60
  FBI Guides to Collection of Physical Evidence, 510
  identification, 204–206
  types, 192–202
Dry-cleaning solvent (trichloroethylene), 199
DSL (digital subscriber line), 486

Duquenois-Levine color test, 206, 208
DVDs (digital versatile discs), 475, 480
Dynamite, 376

E

Ecstasy (MDMA), 197, 200–201
EDTA (ethylenediamine tetraacetic acid), 287
Eggs (cells), 251–252
Ejectors, 423–424
Electromagnetic spectrum, 132
Electron orbitals, 154–155
Electrons, 153–158
Electropherogram, 275
Electrophoresis, 131–132, 250, 272
Electrostatic lifting technique, 439–440
Elements, 120–123, 154
E-mail, 490
Emission spectrograph, 150–151, 344
Emission spectroscopy, 149–150
EMIT (Enzyme-Multiplied Immunoassay Technique), 246–247
Empty magnification, 169
Emulsion explosives, 376–377
EnCase (software), 480–481
Endothermic reaction, 356
Energy, fire and, 355–356
Energy level, 154
Engineering, 4, 21
England, 69
Enrique Camarena case, 52–57
Entomology, 77–81
Enzyme-Multiplied Immunoassay Technique (EMIT), 246–247
Enzymes, 131
Epidermis, 393
Epithelial cells, 285
Equilibrium, 124
Erasures, in document examination, 459–460
Erythrocytes, 242
Escobar, Pablo, 188
Ethylenediamine tetraacetic acid (EDTA), 287
Evidence. *See* Collection and preservation of evidence; Crime scenes
Evidence technicians, trained, 19–20
Excited state, 154
Excretion, of alcohol, 216
Exemplars, handwriting, 455–456
Exothermic reaction, 356
Expert witnesses and testimony, 18–19, 503
Expirated blood patterns, 307
Explosions and explosives. *See also specific types*
  chemistry of explosions, 374–375
  collection and analysis of, 380–384
  as evidence, 60
  FBI Guides to Collection of Physical Evidence, 510
  triacetone triperoxide (TATP), 377–378, 380
  types of explosives, 375–380
Extractors, 423–424
Eyepiece lens, 166

F

Facial reconstruction, 77
Fahrenheit scale, 96
Familial DNA searching, 279
Farrar, Michael, 352
Fatal Vision (McGinniss), 296, 340
Fauld, Henry, 390
Fax machines, and document examination, 457–458
FBI (Federal Bureau of Investigation)
  crime laboratory, 11
  DRUGFIRE, 425
  Forensic Science Research and Training Center, 8–9
  General Rifling Characteristics File, 421
  Guides to Collection of Physical Evidence, 507–522
  Integrated Automated Fingerprint Identification System (IAFIS), 68–69, 396, 425
  National Integrated Ballistics Information Network (NIBIN), 69–70, 425–426, 503
Federal Rules of Evidence, 16
Fee-for-service concept, 9
FFT (Frequency Fourier Transform), 411
Fibers
  collection and preservation of, 342
  Ennis Cosby case, 330
  as evidence, 60
  FBI Guides to Collection of Physical Evidence, 510
  identification and comparison of, 335–339
  Jeffrey Macdonald case, 320, 340–341
  major generic fibers, 333–334
  manufactured, 331–332
  natural, 331
  polymers, 332, 335
  Wayne Williams case, 85–91, 335, 337
Field of view, 169
Field sobriety testing, 222–223
Fifth Amendment, 456
File allocation table (FAT), 477–478, 482, 485
File slack, 484–485
Fingerprints
  Automated Fingerprint Identification System (AFIS), 396–399
  classification of, 395–396
  digital imaging for enhancement of, 410–412
  as evidence, 60
  history of, 390–391
  Integrated Automated Fingerprint Identification System (IAFIS), 68–69, 396, 425
  Mayfield Affair, 400–401
  methods of detecting, 400–409
  Night Stalker case and, 399
  preservation of, 409–410
  principles of, 391–395

Finished sketches, 34
Firearms and ammunition
  Beltway Sniper case, 416
  bullet and cartridge comparisons, 418–424
  as evidence, 60
  evidence collection and preservation, 434–435
  FBI Guides to Collection of Physical Evidence, 510, 514
  gunpowder residues, 427–431
  primer residues, 431–434
  Sacco and Vanzetti case, 424
  search systems, 424–427
  serial number restoration, 434
  website for firearm identification, 22–23
Firearms units, 12
Fire investigation. *See* Arson
Firewalls, 491
Flammable range, 358
Flashover, 361
Flash point, 357–358
Float glass, 101
Floppy disks, 475
Flotation, 103
Flow blood patterns, 310–311
Fluorescence, 129, 406–407
Follicular tag, 324
Footprints. *See also* Impressions
Forensic Autopsy (Linux-based freeware), 480
Forensic science
  contributors to, 6–8
  definition and scope, 4–5
  development of crime laboratories, 8–9
  (*See also* Crime laboratories)
  history and development of, 5–6
Forensic Science Research and Training Center (FBI), 505
Forensic Toolkit (FTK), 490
Fourier transform infrared (FT-IR) spectrometer, 135
Fourth Amendment, 46
Frequency, 132
Frequency Fourier transform (FFT), 411
Freud, Sigmund, 199
Frye v. *United States,* 15–16
Fuchsin Acid, 530
Fuel cell detectors, 219–220

G

Gacy, John Wayne, 77
Galton, Francis Henry, 6, 390
Gamma hydroxybutyrate (GHB), 200–201
Gamma ray, 155
Gas-air explosives mixtures, 376
Gas chromatography (GC), 124–126, 207–208, 224, 365
Gas chromatography/mass spectrometry (GC/MS), 231, 367–368, 384
Gases (vapors), 120
Gasoline, 199, 354, 357–358, 361–362, 365–367, 512

Gatliff, Betty Pat, 77
Gauges, of shotguns, 421
GC (gas chromatography), 124–126, 125–126, 231, 384
GC/MS (gas chromatography)/mass spectrometry, 231, 367–368, 384
Gel diffusion, 250
Gender of decedent, 74
General Rifling Characteristics File, 421
Genes, 251–253, 266
Genotype, 253
Geology, 111
GHB (gamma hydroxybutyrate), 200–201
Gilbert v. *California,* 456
Glass
  classification of samples of, 106–107
  collection and preservation of evidence, 110
  comparing fragments of, 101–102
  composition of, 101
  density of, 103
  as evidence, 60
  FBI Guides to Collection of Physical Evidence, 512–514
  fractures, 107–110
  refractive index, 103–106
Glass Refractive Index Measurement (GRIM 3), 104–106
Global Positioning System (GPS), 74
Glowing combustion, 358–359
Goddard, Calvin, 6, 424
Goldman, Ronald, 264
GPS (Global Positioning System), 74
Graves, Tony, 70
Great Britain, 69
Green, Debora, 352
Green River killer, 240
Greiss test, 430–431
Grid method, 38, 313
GRIM 3 (Glass Refractive Index Measurement), 104–106
Grooves, gun barrel, 418
Gross, Hans, 8
Guanine, 266
Gun Control Act of 1968, 11
Gunpowder residues, 427–431, 435, 523–524
Gunshot residues, 514
Gunshot spatter, 305–306

H

Hacking, 491
Hair
  Central Park jogger case and, 328
  collection and preservation of, 329–330
  detecting drugs in, 232, 233
  as evidence, 60
  FBI Guides to Collection of Physical Evidence, 514, 522
  identification and comparison of, 324–329
  morphology of, 322–324
  as physical evidence, 327–329

Hallucinogens, 195–198
Hammer forging process, 419–420
Handwriting, 452–457, 514
Hard disk drive (HDD), 474–480
Hardware, computer, 472
Hashish, 195
Headspace technique, 365
Heat of combustion, 356
Heat transfer, 359–361
Heavy metals, 232
Hemoglobin, 248
Henry, Edward Richard, 390–391, 395
Henry, William, 124
Heredity, 251–253
Heroin, 193–195
Herschel, William, 390
Heterozygous, 252
High explosives, 376–379
High-performance liquid chromatography
        (HPLC), 127–128, 384
History, Internet, 487
Hitler diaries, 456–457
HLA (human leukocyte antigen) test, 253
Holmes, Sherlock, 5
Homozygous, 252
Hoover, J. Edgar, 8
Horizontal-gaze nystagmus field sobriety
        test, 222–223
Hot stage, 103
HPLC (high-performance liquid
        chromatography), 127–128, 384
Huffing, 199
Hughes, Howard, 454
Human antiserum, 250
Human genome, 268
Human leukocyte antigen (HLA) test, 253
Hungarian Red, 530
Hybridization, 270
Hybridoma cells, 247
Hydrocarbons, 365
Hypertext, 487

I

IAFIS (Integrated Automated Fingerprint
        Identification System), 68–69, 396, 425
IBIS (Integrated Ballistic Identification
        System), 425
Ice (meth), 199
Ignitable Liquids Reference Collection
        (ILRC), 367
Igniters, 364–365
Ignition temperature, 357
ILRC (Ignitable Liquids Reference
        Collection), 367
Immersion method, 103
Immunoassay testing, 231, 245–247
Impact spatter, 301–305
Implied-consent law, 227
Impressions
        casting, 441–442
        chemical formulas for footwear
                impressions in blood, 529–531

comparing, 443, 446
as evidence, 60
indented writings, 12, 60, 462
lifting, 439–440
O.J. Simpson trial and, 446
preserving, 438–439
IMS (ion mobility spectrometer,
        381–382, 383
Indented writings, 514–516
Inductively coupled plasma (ICP)
        discharge, 151
Inductively coupled plasma (ICP) emission
        spectrometry, 151–152
Infrared breath testers, 220, 221
Infrared luminescence, 460
Infrared microspectrophotometers,
        173–174, 339
Infrared spectrophotometry,
        207, 339, 344
Ink comparison, in document
        examination, 463
Inorganic analysis, 146–147
Inorganic vs. organic, 123
Input devices, 474
Insects, 77–80, 77–81
Institute of Legal Medicine and Police
        Science (Montreal), 9
Insulation, 514
Insulators, 360
Integrated Automated Fingerprint
        Identification System (IAFIS),
        68–69, 396, 425
Integrated Ballistic Identification System
        (IBIS), 425
Intensive property, 98
Interactive Investigator—Détective
        Interactif website, 23
International Association for
        Identification, 393
International Association for Identification
        Safety Committee, 44
International Civil Aviation
        Organization, 385
International Forensic Automotive Paint
        Data Query (PDQ), 71
Internet, 22–23, 486–487, 489–492
Internet protocol (IP), 489–490
Iodine fuming, 403
Iodine spray reagent, 525
Ion, 139
Ion mobility spectrometer (IMS),
        381–382, 383
Irving, Clifford, 454
Isotopes, 156

J

Jackson, Michael, 228
Jascalevich, Mario E., 247
Jeffreys, Sir Alec, 266
JonBenet Ramsey murder case, 282–285
Judges, 17
Jurisprudence, 4

K

Kaczynski, David, 450
Kaczynski, Ted, 450
Kastle-Meyer color test, 247–248
Kennedy, John F., assassination of, 147–149
Keratinization, 323
Ketamine, 201
King, Martin Luther, Jr., 388
Kirk, Paul, 9
Klann, Harry, 330
Koehler, Arthur, 183–187
Kumho Tire Co., Ltd. v. Carmichael, 17

L

Laminated glass, 101
Lands, gun barrel, 418
Landsteiner, Karl, 6
Langerman, Neal, 380–381
Lasers, 133
Latent data, 483–486
Latent fingerprint lab units, 13
Latent fingerprints, 393, 400, 525–528.
        See also Fingerprints
Lattes, Leone, 6
Legal issues, 46, 225–227
Leucocrystal Violet, 530–531
Lewinsky, Monica, 271
Librium (chlordiazepoxide), 198
Lie detectors, 15
Light, theory, 132–134
Lindbergh baby case, 164, 183–187
Line spectrum, 149–150
Liquid explosives, 380
Liquids, 120
Litvinenko, Alexander, 156 157
Livescan device, 398
Livor mortis, 72–73
Local crime labs, 11
Locard, Edmond, 8
Locard's exchange principle, 8
Locus (of genes), 252
London bombings (2005), 378
Loops, in fingerprints, 394
Los Angeles Police Department, 9
Low copy numbers, 284
Low explosives, 375–376
Low-velocity blood spatter, 301
LSD, 197
Luminescence, 249, 460
Luminol, 249, 289

M

MacDonald, Jeffrey, 296, 320
Macromolecules, 335
Magna Brushes, 403
Mailing lists (electronic), 23
Malvo, Lee Boyd, 416
Mandrel rifling, 419
Manufactured fibers, 331
Marijuana, 195–197, 208, 246
Markhasev, Mikail, 330

Marquis color test, 206
Martin Luther King, Jr. assassination, 388
Mass, 96–97
Mass spectrometry, 207–208
Matches (lighters), 514
Match point, 103
Matter, 120
Mayfield, Brandon, 400–401
McCrone, Walter C., 6–7
McVeigh, Timothy (Robert Kling), 372
MDMA (Ecstasy), 197, 200–201
Medical examiners, 72, 298
Medulla (hair), 322, 324
Meprobamat (Miltown), 198
Mercury, 96, 146, 149, 232, 354
Mescaline, 197
Message Digest 5 (MD5), 480
Message Digest 5 (MD5)/ Secure Hash
        Algorithm (SHA), 480
Metabolism, of alcohol, 227
Methadone, 194–195
Methamphetamine, 199
Methaqualone (Quaalude), 198
Methyl ethylketone (antifreeze), 199
Metric conversion, 95–96
Metropolitan Police Laboratory (London),
        9, 462
Michelson interferometer, 135
Michigan v. *Tyler,* 47
Microballoons, 377
Microcrystalline tests, 206, 249
Microgrooving, 421
Microscopy
    basics, 166
    comparison microscopes, 169–171
    compound microscopes, 167–169
    microspectrophotometers, 173–174
    polarizing microscopes, 172–173
    scanning electron microscopes (SEMs),
        175–178
    stereoscopic microscopes, 171–172
Microspheres, 377
Military high explosives, 379
Miltown (meprobamate), 198
Mincey v. *Arizona,* 47
Minerals, 111. *See also* Soils and minerals
MiniSTRs, 276
Minutiae, 391
Mitochondria, 279
Mitochondrial DNA (mtDNA), 278–281
Mobile crime laboratories, 39
Modus operandi, 354
Molecules, 335
Monochromatic light, 135
Monochromator, 135
Monoclonal antibodies, 247
Monomers, 335
Morphine, 193
Motherboards, computer, 473
MRM 10, 409
Muhammad, John Allen, 416
Multiplexing, 273–274
Murder scenes, 72–80

N

Napoleon I, 144
Narcotics, 192–195
National Automated Fingerprint
        Identification Systems, 425–426
National DNA Database (United
        Kingdom), 69
National Highway Traffic Safety
        Administration (NHTSA), 227
National Institute of Standards and
        Technology (NIST), 346
National Integrated Ballistics Information
        Network (NIBIN), 69–70,
        425–426, 503
National Safety Council, 225
Natural fibers, 331
Natural variations, in handwriting, 455–456
Necrophilious insects, 77–78
Ne'urim Declaration, 393
Neuron activation analysis, 149, 155–158, 344
Neutrons, 153, 155–158
NHTSA (National Highway Traffic Safety
        Administration), 227
NIBIN (National Integrated Ballistics Infor-
        mation Network), 69, 425–426, 503
Nichols, Terry, 372
Night Stalker case, 399
Ninhydrin, 404, 526
NIST (National Institute of Standards and
        Technology), 346
Nobel, Alfred, 376
Note-taking, 30–34
Nuclear DNA, 329
Nuclear forensics, 159–160
Nucleotides, 266
Nucleus, 153

O

O. J. Simpson murder case, 264
Objective lens, 166
Obliteration, in document examination, 460
Occupational Safety and Health
        Administration (OSHA), 44
Odontology, 4, 21, 522
Offender index. *See* Combined DNA Index
        System (CODIS)
Officer.com website, 22
O'Hara, Charles, 501
Oklahoma City bombing, 372
Oligospermia, 254, 255
1,2-indanedione, 407
One-leg stand field sobriety test, 222–223
Operating system (OS), 474
Opiates, 193
Orfila, Mathieu, 6
Organic analysis
    elements and compounds, 120–123
    mass spectrometry, 138–140
    spectrophotometry, 132–137
    techniques, 123–132
Organic *vs.* inorganic, 123
Organized Crime Control Act of 1970, 11

Organs and physiological fluids,
        60, 514–516
Osborn, Albert S., 6
OSHA (Occupational Safety and Health
        Administration), 44
OS (operating system), 476
Osterburg, James, 501
Oswald, Lee Harvey, 147
Output devices, 474
Oxidation, 216, 354
Oxidizing agents, 374
Oxley, Jimmie C., 381
OxyContin, 194

P

Paint
    collection and preservation of, 347–349
    composition of, 342–343
    FBI Guides to Collection of Physical
        Evidence, 516
    microscopic examination of, 343
    as physical evidence, 60
    significance of, 346
    techniques used in paint comparisons,
        343–346
Paint Data Query (PDQ), 346
Palmer method, 452
Palynology, 178–180
Paper comparison, in document
        examination, 463
Parfocal microscope, 169
Partitions (in HDDs), 476
Pat, Betty, 77
Patent Blue, 531
Paternity testing, 253
Pathologist, role of, 72–73
Pathology, 4
Patterns, bloodstain, 309–313
Payne, Jimmy, 85–91
PCP (Phencyclidine), 197
PCR (polymerase chain reaction), 268–269
PDQ (International Forensic Automotive
        Paint Data Query), 71, 346
Pentaerythritol tetranitrate (PETN), 376, 379
Pentobarbital, 198, 202
Perimeter method, of documenting blood
        stains, 313
Periodic table, 120, 122
Peroxide, 380–381
Personal identification. *See also* DNA
        (deoxyribonucleic acid); Fingerprints
Peterson, Scott and Laci, 58
PETN (pentaerythritol tetranitrate), 376, 379
Petroleum products, as physical evidence, 60
Phases, 123
Phenobarbital, 198
Phenotype, 253
Phosphates, 230
Photocopiers, and document examination, 457
Photography
    for bloodstain analysis, 313
    in crime lab units, 12
    at crime scene, 31–33

for the electronic crime scene, 478–479
for preserving impressions, 438
Photons, 134
pH scale, 230
Physical anthropology, 4
Physical dependence, 190–191
Physical Developer, 404, 526–527
Physical evidence. *See also* Collection and
preservation of evidence; FBI Guides
to Collection of Physical Evidence;
specific types
admissibility of, 15–16
analysis of, 15
assessment of, 64–67
collecting, 38–39
definition, 28
expert testimony, 18–19
identification and comparison, 61–64
judging, 16–17
training in collection of, 19–20
Physical properties, 94–100
Physical science units, 12
Physical state, 120
Physics, 4, 8, 12, 505
Picograms, 284
Pixels, 410, 462
Planck's constant, 134
Plane-polarized light, 172
Plasma, 242
Plastic, as physical evidence, 60
Plastic prints, 400
PMI (postmortem interval), 79
Poisons, 118, 144, 156–157, 232, 233.
See also Toxicology
Polarizers, 172
Polarizing microscopes, 172–173
Pollen and spores, 178–180
Polyclonal antibodies, 247
Polygraph lab units, 13
Polygraphs, 13, 15
Polymerase chain reaction (PCR), 268–269
Polymers, 60, 332, 335
Pooling, of blood, 311
Portrait parlé, 390
Postmortem interval (PMI), 79
Potassium levels, time of death and, 73
Povidone-iodine (Betadine), 224
Precipitin tests, 249–250
Precursors, 204
Preservatives, for blood, 224–225
Primacords, 379
Primary explosives, 376
Primer, 270
Primer residues, 431–434
Printers, 4, 58
Probability, 62
Product rule, 274
Product tampering, 118
Prostate specific antigen (PSA), 255–256
Proteins, 131, 267
Protons, 153–158
PSA (prostate specific antigen), 255–256
Psilocybin, 197

Psychiatry, 4, 21
Psychology, 4
Punnet square, 253
Pyrolysis, 126, 358
Pyrolysis gas chromatography, 126, 344

Q

Quaalude (methaqualone), 198
Qualitative or quantitative determination,
drug analysis, 205
Qualitative/quantitative analysis, 123
Questioned-Document Examination
website, 23
Questioned documents. *See* Documents
Questioned Documents (Osborn)

R

Race, of decedent, 75
Rader, Dennis, 470
Radial glass fractures, 107
Radiation, 360–361
Radioactivity, 155
Ramirez, Richard, 399
RAM (random access memory), 409, 474
Ramsey murder case, 26
RAM slack, 484
Random-access memory (RAM), 474
Rape evidence, 256–260
RAY, 409
Ray, James Earl, 388
RCMP (Royal Canadian Mounted Police),
9, 71, 346
RDX (cyclotrimethylenetrinitramine),
376, 379
Read-only memory (ROM)
Real image, 166
Recording, crime scenes, 29–34. *See also*
Note-taking; Photography; Sketches
Reddy's Forensic Home Page, 22
Redmond, Alice, 113
Reflected Ultraviolet Imaging System
(RUVIS), 401
Refraction, 99
Refractive index, 99–100, 102, 103–106
Regenerated fibers, 331
Reinsch test, 232
Replication, 269
Reserpine, 198
Residues
flammable, 365–368
gunpowder, 427–434, 514, 523–524
Reyes, Matias, 328
RFLP (restriction fragment length
polymorphisms), 271
Rh factor, 242, 243
Ridge characteristics (minutiae), 391
Ridgeway, Gary, 240
Rifling, 418–419
Rigor mortis, 72
Rocks, 111, 112. *See also* Soils and minerals
Roofies (Rohypnol), 200–201
Root (hair), 324

Rope, 516
Routers, 491
Royal Canadian Mounted Police (RCMP),
9, 71, 346
Rubber, as physical evidence, 60
Rule, Ann, 352
RUVIS (Reflected Ultraviolet Imaging
System), 401

S

Safety fuse, 375
Saliva, 60, 516, 522
Sam Sheppard case, 296
Satellite spatter, 299
Scanning electron microscopes (SEMs),
175–178, 432–434
Scher, Stephen, 308
Schmerber v. *California*, 227
Scientific method, 15
Scientific Working Groups (SWIGS), 505
Scott Peterson case, 58
Scott Test for drug screening, 206
Screening and confirmation, drug analysis,
204–205, 230–233
Secobarbital, 137, 198, 202, 207
Secondary explosives, 376
Sectors, 477
Self-incrimination, and alcohol breath tests,
225, 227
Semen, 60, 254–260, 521
SEMs (scanning electron microscopes),
175–178, 432–434
Sequencing, 280–281
Serial numbers, as physical evidence, 60
Serology, 243. *See also* Blood; Semen
Serum, 242
Severs, Roger, 92
Sex identification, 275–276
Sexual offenses. *See* Rape evidence
Sheppard, Sam, 296
Shoeprints, 516–518
Short tandem repeats (STRs), 271–273
Shotguns, 421, 429–430, 435
SICAR (Shoeprint Image Capture and
Retrieval), 71, 443
Simpson, Nicole Brown, 264
Simpson, O. J., 264
Sinsemilla, 195
Skeletal remains, 73–77
Skeletonization (bloodstains), 311
Sketches, finished and rough, 33–34
Slack space, 483–485
Slope detector, 220
SMART (Linux-based software), 480
Smart media cards, 475–476
Smith, Anna Nicole, 228–229
Smokeless powders (single-base and
double-base), 375
Smoldering, 359
Snow, Clyde, 77
Snow Impression Wax, 441
Software, computer, 472
Soils and minerals, 60, 110–114, 518

Solemate™, 443
Solids, 120
Spatial filtering, 410–411
Spatter, bloodstain, 301–308
Spectrophotometry
absorption of electromagnetic radiation, 134–135
atomic absorption, 152–153
definition, 123
drug analysis, 207
infrared (IR), 137
the spectrophotometer, 135–137
theory of light, 132–134
ultraviolet (UV), 137
visible, 137
Speed, 199
Spermatozoa, 251–252
Spontaneous combustion, 359
Stain analysis. *See* Blood; DNA (deoxyribonucleic acid)
Standard/reference samples, 43–44
State and regional crime labs, 11
State of Tennessee v. *Paul Ware,* 281
Stereoscopic microscopes, 171–172
Steroids, 201–202
Stimulants, 198–200
STR Blue Kit, 274
Strengthening Forensic Science in the United States: A Path Forward (National Academy of Science), 505
Stress marks, glass, 109
Striations, 419
String method of blood spatter analysis, 304–305
STRs (short tandem repeats), 271–278
A Study in Scarlet (Doyle), 5
Subatomic particles, 153–158
Sublimation, 122, 403
Substrate controls, 44, 287, 364
Superglue fuming, 404–405
Swabbing, 432
Swap files, 481–482
SWIGS (Scientific Working Groups), 505
Swipe blood patterns, 310
Sykes, Deborah, 279
Synthetic fibers, 331–332
Synthetic opiates, 194–195
System bus, 473

T

Taggants, 384–385
Takayama test, 249
Tandem repeats, 270–271
Tape-recording, 30–31
Tapes, as storage devices, 476
Tartrazine, 531
TATP (triacetone triperoxide), 377–378, 380
Technology, 10, 501, 503–505. *See also* Computer technology; Internet
Teeth, 4, 21, 522
Teichmann test, 249

Telogen hair growth phase, 324
Temperature, physical properties, 96
Tempered glass, 101
Temporary files, 482–483
Testimonial evidence, 23, 65, 66, 227
Tetryl (2,4,6-trinitrophenylmethyl-nitramine), 376
Thallium, 232, 233
THC, 196, 246
Thin-layer chromatography (TLC), 128–131, 231, 384
3R rule, 109
Thymine, 266
Tissue, 522
TLC (thin-layer chromatography), 128–131, 231, 384
TNT (trinitrotoluene), 376
Toluene, 199, 365
Tool marks, 61, 435–438, 518
Touch DNA, 285
Toxicologists, alcohol, 227–234
Toxicology, 4, 13, 234–236
Trace elements, 147
Trace evidence, 171, 174. *See also* Fibers; Glass; Hair; Paint; Soils and minerals
Trail patterns, blood, 311
Training, 19–20
Transmitted illumination, 167
Transmitting terminal identifier (TTI), 457
Triacetone triperoxide (TATP), 377–378, 380
Trial judges, 16–17, 18
Trichloroethylene (dry-cleaning solvent), 199
Trinitroluene (TNT), 376
Triplexing, 274
TTI (transmitting terminal identifier), 457
Tylenol product tampering case, 118
Typewriters, 518
Typewriters, document evidence and, 458–459

U

Ultraviolet (UV) spectrophotometry, 137
Unabomber case, 450
Unallocated space, 485–486
Uniform resource locator (URL), 487
United Kingdom, National DNA Database, 69
United States International Ink Library, 464
United States v. *Byron C. Mitchell,* 391
United States v. *Mara,* 456
Urine, 214, 216, 225, 227, 229, 231–232, 522
U.S. Constitution, Fifth and Fourth amendments, 46, 456
U.S. Postal Inspection Service, 11
USB thumb drives, 475–476, 487

V

Valium (diazepam), 198
Van Dam, Danielle, 80
Van Urk color test, 206
Vapor concentration, 365–367
Vegetative matter, as physical evidence, 61
Vehicle lights, as physical evidence, 61

Vehicles, automotive paint analysis, 343
Veins, 216
Vertical or reflected illumination, 167
Videotaping, 30–31
Virtual image, 166
Visible data, in computer forensics, 480–483
Visible light, 100, 132–133, 137, 174
Visible light microspectrophotometer, 463
Visible prints, 400
Visible spectrophotometry, 137
Voiceprint analyses lab units, 13
Void blood patterns, 308
Void patterns, blood, 308–309
Vollmer, August, 9
von Bayer, Adolf, 198
Vucetich, Juan, 390

W

Walk and turn field sobriety test, 222–223
Wallner lines, 108
War on terrorism, nuclear forensics and, 159–160
Warren Commission, 147
Water gels, 376–377
Watson, John, 266
Wavelengths, 132
Wayne Williams case, 85–91
Weapons. *See* Firearms and ammunition
Web sites, 22–23
Weight and mass, physical properties, 96–97
West, Will, 391
Westerfield, David, 80
Whorls, in fingerprints, 394
Williams, Wayne, 85–91
Wire, 518
Withdrawal sickness, 190, 191
Wood, 61, 358–359, 518
Working distance, 171
World Trade Center attack (2001), 287, 293–295
World Trade Center bombing (1993), 377
Wray, James Earl, 388

X

X chromosomes, 252
X-ray diffraction, 158–159, 344
X-rays, 133
X-ray spectroscopy, paint analysis, 344

Y

Y chromosomes, 252
Y-STR markers, 276

Z

Zaner-Bloser method, 452
Zeno's Forensic Site, 22
Zinc chloride solution, 526
Zygotes, 251–252

chapter opener
photo credits

Page 2: AP Wide World Photos

Page 26: AP Wide World Photos

Page 58: AP Wide World Photos

Page 92: John A. Rizzo, Getty Images, Inc.-Photodisc/Royalty Free

Page 118: CORBIS-NY

Page 144: Jacques-Louis David (French, 1748-1825) "Napoleon in His Study" 1812, oil on canvas, 2.039 × 1.251 (80 1/4 × 49 1/4); framed: 2.439 × 1.651 × .152 (96 × 65 × 6). National Gallery of Art, Washington. Samuel H. Kress Collection. © Board of Trustees, National Gallery of Art, Washington. Photo by: Lyle Peterzell

Page 164: © Griebel / CORBIS. All Rights Reserved

Page 188: Alain Masiero/SYGMA, CORBIS-NY

Page 212: PA/Topham, The Image Works

Page 240: AP Wide World Photos

Page 264: AP Wide World Photos

Page 296: CORBIS-NY

Page 320: AP Wide World Photos

Page 352: AP Wide World Photos

Page 372: © Reuters New Media Inc./CORBIS

Page 388: CORBIS-NY

Page 416: AP Wide World Photos

Page 450: AP Wide World Photos

Page 470: AP Wide World Photos

Page 500: Photodisc/Getty Images